T0392552

Introductory Psychology in Modules

Introductory Psychology in Modules: Understanding Our Heads, Hearts, and Hands is a unique and comprehensive introduction to psychology. It consists of 36 short modules that keep students engaged with humor, a narrative style, and hands-on activities that facilitate interactive learning and critical thinking.

Each stand-alone module focuses on a major topic in psychology, from the brain, sensation, memory, and cognition to human development, personality, social psychology, and clinical psychology. The modular format also allows a deep dive into important topics that have less coverage in other introductory psychology textbooks. This includes cross-cultural psychology, stereotypes and discrimination, evolutionary psychology, sex and gender, climate change, health psychology, and sport psychology. This truly modular format – ideal for both face to face and virtual learning – makes it easy for instructors to customize their readings and assign exactly what they wish to emphasize. The book also contains an abundance of pedagogical features, including numerous hands-on activities and/or group discussion activities, multiple-choice practice quizzes, and an instructor exam bank written by the authors.

By covering both classic and contemporary topics, this book will delight students and instructors alike. The modular format also makes this a useful supplementary text for classes in nursing, medicine, social work, policing, and sociology.

Brett W. Pelham is a UT Austin PhD. Brett has worked at UCLA, SUNY, Buffalo, St. Mary's College of Maryland, Swarthmore College, and Georgetown University. Brett studies the self, gender, stereotypes, health psychology, social judgment, and evolutionary psychology. He's the author of three other textbooks. Brett is currently at Montgomery College, Maryland – where he gets to teach students from 160 nations. For fun, Brett loves being with his dogs, wife, and kids, in exactly that order. He also enjoys art, astronomy, carpentry, cooking, juggling, metallurgy, music, and studying Spanish. Brett hopes this book will inspire a diverse group of future psychologists.

David Boninger began his academic career in 1991 as a professor of Psychology at UCLA, and later at the University of Haifa in Israel. He is currently a professor at Glendale Community College in Arizona. David earned a BA from Northwestern University and PhD from The Ohio State University and has conducted and published research in the areas of persuasion, stereotypes, counterfactual thinking, and consumer behavior. David's perfect day is one spent outside with his wife and two daughters. His outside antics include running, hiking, kayaking, and biking. David loves the oceans, the mountains, and the trees, especially Aspens.

Introductory Psychology in Modules
Understanding Our Heads, Hearts, and Hands

Brett W. Pelham
Montgomery College, Maryland
Georgetown University

David Boninger
Glendale Community College
Arizona

 Routledge
Taylor & Francis Group

NEW YORK AND LONDON

First published 2021
by Routledge
52 Vanderbilt Avenue, New York, NY 10017

and by Routledge
2 Park Square, Milton Park, Abingdon, Oxon, OX14 4RN

Routledge is an imprint of the Taylor & Francis Group, an informa business

© 2021 Taylor & Francis

The right of Brett W. Pelham and David Boninger to be identified as authors of this work has been asserted by them in accordance with sections 77 and 78 of the Copyright, Designs and Patents Act 1988.

All rights reserved. No part of this book may be reprinted or reproduced or utilised in any form or by any electronic, mechanical, or other means, now known or hereafter invented, including photocopying and recording, or in any information storage or retrieval system, without permission in writing from the publishers.

Trademark notice: Product or corporate names may be trademarks or registered trademarks, and are used only for identification and explanation without intent to infringe.

Library of Congress Cataloging-in-Publication Data
Names: Pelham, Brett W., 1961- author. | Boninger, David, author.
Title: Introductory psychology in modules : understanding our heads, hearts, and hands / Brett W Pelham, Montgomery College, Maryland, Georgetown University, David Boninger, Glendale Community College, Arizona.
Description: 1 Edition. | New York City : Routledge, 2020. | Includes bibliographical references and index. |
Identifiers: LCCN 2020022716 (print) | LCCN 2020022717 (ebook) |
ISBN 9780367418212 (hardback) | ISBN 9780367418274 (paperback) |
ISBN 9780367816360 (ebook)
Subjects: LCSH: Psychology–Textbooks.
Classification: LCC BF121 .P425 2020 (print) | LCC BF121 (ebook) |
DDC 150–dc23
LC record available at https://lccn.loc.gov/2020022716
LC ebook record available at https://lccn.loc.gov/2020022717

ISBN: 978-0-367-41821-2 (hbk)
ISBN: 978-0-367-41827-4 (pbk)
ISBN: 978-0-367-81636-0 (ebk)

Typeset in Times
by River Editorial Ltd, Devon, UK

Brett dedicates this book to his grandmother, Sybil Cooper Howard, who grew up as one of 17 children in a family of Alabama sharecroppers. She was a feisty and colorful storyteller whose devotion to her children, grand-children, great grandchildren, and great, great grandchildren knew no limits.

David dedicates this book to Talia, Alisa, and Faith – the joys of his life and three women who make the world a better place; and to Janine Carter Boninger, his mother and the foundation of it all; and to his brothers Ron and Mike who think that professors don't actually work. Newsflash: They do, but they have a lot of fun doing it.

Contents

About the Authors

Brett W. Pelham is the second of seven children and a first-generation high school graduate. He grew up in the buckle of the Bible belt, rural northwest Georgia, in a place where violence was commonplace and food was scarce. Brett's transformation from bumpkin to behavioral scientist is still underway. But it began in Louise Boyd's first grade classroom, where Brett learned to love learning. Flash forward 20 years, and Brett was learning social psychology from two prolific geniuses, Bill Swann and Dan Gilbert. Brett's first professorship was at UCLA, where one of his many wonderful colleagues was David Boninger – the second author of this textbook. In the years since Brett's decade at UCLA, he has had the pleasure of working in academic jobs at schools all over the nation – from SUNY, Buffalo to St. Mary's College of Maryland and Swarthmore College in Pennsylvania. Brett is also the author of about 60 empirical research papers and three textbooks other than this one.

In 2006, Brett moved to Maryland to be close to his toddler son (who is now a 6'1" tall teenager). After working a few applied jobs (mainly at Gallup and at the National Science Foundation), Brett eventually settled back into a teaching job at one of the most diverse colleges on earth, Montgomery College. Brett is honored to teach students who come from every corner of the planet. He is also delighted to be able to teach a class or two every year as an adjunct at Georgetown University.

When Brett is not teaching, writing, or doing research, he loves spending time with his family, including two of the most lovable and curious kids he has ever known (Brooklyn and Lincoln). They inspire him every day and keep him going when things get tough. When Brett's wife and kids are sleeping – which he himself rarely does – he enjoys carpentry, cooking, juggling, sculpting, creating cartoons, and almost all kinds of music. Brett aspires to becoming fluent in Spanish, although he is only about a third of the way there. As a highly unlikely psychological scientist, Brett hopes this book will contribute to the scientific education of many future psychological scientists – especially the unlikely ones.

David Boninger is the third of three sons and a child of immigrants. David's mom, Janine Carter Boninger, grew up in Bielsko, Poland and his dad, Walter Boninger, grew up in Hamburg, Germany. David grew up in Cleveland, Ohio which is just a hop, skip, and jump from Bielsko and Hamburg, and the flames of World War II – from which David's parents emerged. In contrast to his parents, David had an idyllic youth marred only by Cleveland's failure during those years to win a championship in any sport. Thankfully, that changed when the Cleveland Cavaliers and Lebron James finally brought a championship to Cleveland. That made David very happy. After leaving his beloved Cleveland, David earned a BA from Northwestern University and an MA and PhD in psychology from The Ohio State University.

David began his academic career in 1991 as a professor of psychology at UCLA, where he was fortunate to meet Brett W. Pelham, now a lifelong friend (and partner in crime on this book). After several years at UCLA, David and his wife Faith went on a six-year adventure to Israel where David was on faculty at the University of Haifa. David's distinct trajectory continued when he returned to the United States to become an entrepreneur. David was one of three partners in a business that developed leading edge technology to improve wheelchairs. While David loved his 14 years in business, he was thrilled when his company was acquired and he was able to return to academics. David is now a professor at Glendale Community College (Arizona), and an author of more than 20 published research papers. David's unusual path has given him a unique breadth and depth of experience that he brings into the classroom (and into this book).

David's perfect day is one spent outside with his wife and two daughters. His outside antics include running, hiking, kayaking, and biking. David has run seven marathons (slowly) and completed more than a dozen other endurance events (triathlons, trail runs, and half-marathons). He also hiked Mount Whitney – the highest peak in the lower 48. David loves the oceans, the mountains, and the trees (especially Aspens).

About this Book

This book is a playful introduction to psychological science. Yes, we mean playful. We hope you'll agree that one of the best features of this book is the humorous narrative style that we adopt. We also do our best to make each module read like a story rather than a disconnected set of facts. We hope that you will find our humor engaging and our storytelling compelling.

As suggested by the title, this book takes a scientific look at how people think, feel and behave. These three things – how we think, feel, and behave – cover a *lot* of ground. Psychologists study everything from how our brains help us regulate hunger and thirst to why we sometimes donate kidneys to strangers, pollute the planet that sustains us, and spread rumors about those we dislike. We explore the microchemical nature of genes and the social nature of memory and morality. We explain both our deep need to be connected to others and our fascination with being unique. We explore attraction and repulsion, and helping and hurting. And, if you read carefully, you might find that this book even offers a bit of practical advice about solving important social and personal problems.

One unusual feature of this book is the fact that we break psychology into 36 manageable modules rather than the typical 13 or 14 lengthy chapters. We strongly believe that shorter, more focused modules will facilitate engagement and improve learning. A closely-related feature of the book is the fact that we do not try to be as exhaustive and encyclopedic as most other introductory psychology textbooks. In about two thirds the space of the typical introductory psychology textbook, we still try to cover all of the classic theories and findings that every student of psychology should know about – along with a representative sample of modern, cutting-edge findings that either extend or challenge conventional psychological wisdom about human nature.

Another unusual feature of the book is our heavy use of anecdotes (many of them are our own personal stories) and hands-on activities to show how the principles of psychology apply to everyday life. In fact, each module in this text is followed by either a hands-on activity (that lets you experience psychological principles firsthand) or a group discussion activity (that lets you explain and discuss – perhaps even debate – your own personal take on each module). These unique features of the book are intended to help students become active, engaged learners as well as critical consumers of psychological science.

This book also includes self-testing questions at the end of each module – just after the hands-on or critical thinking sections. These self-testing questions should give you a sense of whether you are mastering a sample of the major ideas in each module. Research on *retrieval practice* (covered in detail in the module on memory) suggests that being tested on material one is trying to master is one of the best ways to retain and think deeply about the material.

One other feature of the book we hope you'll find helpful is our use of bold font (**like this**) that should draw your attention to the theories, ideas, and empirical studies that we feel are most crucial to mastering the basics of psychological science. Each term that is important enough to be included in bold in the text is included in a **glossary** – which is a list of definitions and explanations you'll find near the end of the book.

Students on whom we have pilot tested this book have almost uniformly told us that they really enjoyed reading the book – and that they especially enjoyed the humor, the enthusiasm, and the informal writing style. If you look forward to reading this book even half as much as we enjoyed writing it, you'll make us very happy. Of course, if you become an engaged reader of this book, we also hope that this book will enrich your own life, whether it is by helping you become a better scientist, a better person, or a better friend.

A Note to Instructors

This book has seven key features that – when taken together – make it unique. The first feature is that the book is truly modular. Rather than consisting of 13 or 14 lengthy chapters, it consists of 36 stand-alone modules. Further, each module is divided into a basic essay about a specific topic in psychology (e.g., sensation and perception, aggression) followed by a highly engaging hands-on activity or group discussion activity. These supplementary activities typically dig a little more deeply into the topics introduced in that module and give students a chance to learn more – by doing or by discussing. This modular format gives instructors a surgical form of precision in custom-building a course in introductory psychology. For example, some instructors may allow students to skip certain modules. Others may assign all 36 modules but use only a handful of the hands-on activities. In our own cases, we have allowed students themselves to choose and skip a few modules. For example, none of our students are allowed to skip the module on classical conditioning, but in the applied section of the text, we allow students to choose either sport psychology or climate change as an applied module. In fact, the first author once allowed his students to skip any one of the nine modules in each quarter of the course (1–9, 10–18, etc.). He did this by organizing the four main exams in the course into nine sections of 5-6 questions and allowing students to answer only eight of nine sections.

Speaking of exams, another key feature of this text is that your instructors wrote (and pilot tested) all of the multiple-choice questions that appear in the practice quizzes in the book itself as well as creating a set of 360 additional questions that are available only to instructors. So, unlike the test banks that come with most textbooks, our instructor-only test bank is especially useful because it is highly consistent with the style of questions students should get used to when they take the practice quizzes that appear at the end of every module. It is also written by instructors who collectively have more than 40 years of teaching experience.

The third and fourth key features of this book come as a package. More than any other introductory psychology book we know about, this book adopts a playful narrative style. It is full of real-life examples and personal stories that bring psychology to life. It also uses a lot of humor. And we mean a lot. The students on whom we have tested the book say that this is one of their favorite aspects of the book. It's fun to read.

Fifth, the book blends both classic and cutting-edge findings without trying to be encyclopedic. In our view, many introductory psychology textbooks simply try to cover too much. Our approach was to make sure that we cover the essential theories and findings that have stood the test of time (e.g., Skinner, Maslow, Piaget) but to update and balance these classic perspectives with plenty of discoveries from the past decade or so. By selecting slightly fewer topics than most other textbooks do, we allowed more room for a deep dive into some of the most important issues in psychology.

Sixth, because both of your authors have spent a lot of time living outside mainstream American culture (e.g., your second author lived in Israel for six years), and because we are both social psychologists who study topics such as culture, stereotypes, gender, and social cognition, we worked hard to emphasize how diverse human experience is. This is not mere handwaving. Although we do not always agree with the conclusions of cross-cultural psychologists, we integrate our knowledge of culture – and cultural evolution – into every module of this book. For example, one of our modules on research methods emphasizes the importance of understanding *populations* as one of the four key aspects of external validity.

Seventh, to a greater degree than most other books, our book challenges students to think critically and deeply about psychology. We frequently present research that reveals complexities and gray areas of cutting-edge research. We do not pretend that thoughtful researchers always agree with one another. We also encourage students to organize what they are learning into meaningful categories. For example, our first module on the brain introduces students to behavioral neuroscience by identifying six key features of the brain (which students can remember using a simple mnemonic). Along similar lines, in our second module on research methods, we explain that external validity always boils down to just one of four essential questions (operationalizations, occasions, populations, and situations). We summarize these four questions using the OOPS! heuristic. We hope that students and instructors alike will enjoy reading this thoughtful, student-friendly, and deeply conceptual approach to understanding psychology. We certainly enjoyed creating it!

Acknowledgments

Your first author is lucky to have taught psychology for about 10 years using the delightful and scholarly textbook written by three guys at Harvard who are all named Dan. He is not going to mention the last names of any of these Dans, or their textbook title, because he doesn't want you to compare this book with their extremely popular and ingenious intro psych book. Brett apologizes in advance for borrowing a few of their ingenious ideas about how to explain difficult things like how the hypothalamus helps us remember, and how consciousness works. Brett's work on this book was also directly inspired by the amazing writing of his textbook writing model, David Myers.

Long ago, at the University of Texas at Austin, your first author's two graduate mentors, Bill Swann and Dan Gilbert spent four long years with him, patiently teaching him to write. Shortly before that, Juanita Williams inspired Brett's longstanding interest in the psychology of gender. A bit before that, Brett's three undergraduate mentors, Dan McBrayer, David McKenzie, and E.J. Vatza, nurtured him and inspired him to blend his strong interests in philosophy and the physical sciences to become a psychological scientist. This is also the place to say that a few modules in this book (especially the modules on evolutionary psychology, helping, and aggression) are adapted from Brett's textbook on evolutionary psychology. The two modules on research methods are adapted from portions of Brett's book on research methods. That means that we thank Hart Blanton, Brett's ingenious co-author on that book.

Finally, without a doubt, the person who has taught your first author the most about psychology is the quirky, lovable, brilliant, curious, and deeply scientific Curtis Hardin.

Your second author, David, would like to first acknowledge ... drum roll please ... your first author, Brett. Without Brett, David would not have taken on this joyful endeavor. And joyful it has been. So thank you, Brett.

David would also like to thank some key influences along the way. First, Dorothy Herron, his high school British Literature teacher. Ms. Herron turned David on to the magic of words, the power of poetry, and the transformative nature of teaching. Fast forward to graduate school where Robert (Bud) MacCallum turned David on to the magic of numbers. David had low expectations. Who makes statistics and structural equation modelling interesting? Bud does (and he was a darn good basketball player too). Thank you, Bud. And a heartfelt thanks goes to Rich Petty and Jon Krosnick who were also important influences during David's graduate school years. Most of all, David would like to thank Tim Brock, his mentor and dissertation advisor. Tim embodied the wonderment that drives scientific discovery. Behind the sparkle in his eyes, brilliant ideas abounded, and David was fortunate enough to be able to explore some of those ideas. Tim made science fun. What could be better than that? Thank you, Tim.

And speaking of fun, David's graduate school years were exponentially more fun because of the other graduate students at Ohio State at the time – so thank you to all of you and especially to Sara, Alan, and Faith. Yes, that's the same Faith who later became, and still is, David's wife. And, boy, is David thankful for that!

I
History of, and Methods in, Psychology

Module 1
Psychology and the Four Ways of Knowing

The poet e. e. cummings argued that we human beings often lose sight of what many people call the secret of life. In cummings's opinion, by the way, one of the biggest secrets of life is staying in touch with the love, curiosity, and feelings of wonder we all had as children. It's hard to find an e. e. cummings poem that doesn't connect to this point in at least some way. This book is intended to introduce you to a few of the secrets of life – including a few that poets have overlooked. Of course, the specific secrets we will usually emphasize are those that have been uncovered by psychologists rather than poets. So, in this book, we will only rarely wax poetic. In fact, we hope this book will mainly serve as the opposite of a poem. We hope it will become a user's manual for better understanding yourself and other people. You could also consider it a journey. We're going to travel with you to *lots* of new places. We'll explore the depths of the human brain as well as the heights of the Earth's atmosphere – because psychology has a lot to say about things as diverse as why people get fevers and why some people are skeptical of global warming. Finally, you could think of this book as a series of 36 short stories. Each module of the book tells some kind of story, and sometimes there is even a final climax. One such story, for example, is that human intelligence ("IQ") does not work the way most people think it works. In this story you'll get to know people who have disabilities such as autism or blindness and yet are extreme geniuses when it comes to art, math, or music. Another story is that the brains of human beings are much more like the brains of mice and ants than you would ever imagine. So think of the 36 modules of this text as 36 stories that will help you learn as much as possible about the secrets of human experience.

This first module puts psychology in a very broad context by asking how people try to uncover the secrets of life. In other words, this module addresses how human beings know what we know. We'll summarize four different ways in which human beings develop beliefs about the world. These four "**ways of knowing**" (Pelham & Blanton, 2019) include **intuition** (trusting your guts), **authority** (trusting those high in status), **logic** (using reasoning), and **observation** (collecting evidence). As we define psychology and introduce you to the field, you will see that psychological scientists prefer ways of knowing that are often very different than those preferred by priests or poets. Accordingly, this module also examines the roles of the four ways of knowing as they have varied across human history and as they vary from person to person and field to field. The four ways of knowing can help us understand everything from dark matter to dark secrets, everything from gravity to levity (humor). Finally, this module briefly examines the pros and cons of each of the four ways of knowing.

Defining the Science of Psychology

The four ways of knowing are relevant to psychology because psychology is all about knowing! As we define it, **psychology** is the *scientific study of human thought, feelings, and behavior.* Let's pull this definition apart. This definition makes it clear that psychology is a science. Like physicists, chemists, and biologists, psychological scientists use the scientific method to explore their subject matter. Psychology is sometimes referred to as a "soft science" whereas physics, chemistry, and biology are usually referred to as "hard sciences." In our view, that perspective is just plain wrong. Psychology is just as rigorous as any other science. The only difference between psychology and the so called "hard sciences" is that the subject matter of psychology – the thoughts, feeling, and behaviors of human beings – presents a special set of measurement challenges. For example, copper plates don't ever try to make a good impression on engineers, and salt solutions don't dilute themselves because they know you are observing them. We'll learn more about the scientific method in Modules 3 and 4. But for now, consider this question: Given that psychology is a science, on which of the four ways of knowing do you think psychologists would be most likely to rely? If you answered "observation," you'd be correct. Thus, our definition of psychology already gives us a clue about *how* psychologists know what they know.

Our definition of psychology also specifies what psychologists study: human thoughts, feelings, and behaviors. That makes psychology a very broad field. There is virtually no aspect of human experience that escapes careful study by psychologists. If this sounds wrong, try a quick thought exercise: Try to think of anything you have ever experienced – from biting your lip to being stereotyped – that does *not* involve your thoughts, feelings, or behavior. Hard, isn't it? Psychologists study everything from the neural underpinnings of orgasms to the social underpinnings of organizations. One quick way to experience the wide variety of areas covered by psychology is to scan the table of contents of this book. You'll see modules on how the brain works, how our senses work, how we develop, how we form impressions of others, and how we remember. You'll also see modules on motivation, emotion, attraction, aggression, stereotypes, and psychological disorders – including their treatment by clinical psychologists. Psychology covers a *lot* of ground.

In fact, the same topic can often be understood from many different psychological perspectives. Consider reading. Yeah, that thing you're doing right now. Cognitive psychologists who study reading tell us that as you read this paragraph, your eyes will frequently and rapidly dart a few words ahead of where you are in a sentence. Doing this allows you to get the "lay of the land" as you decode a sentence. This is a much more efficient way of reading than merely decoding words one by one in the order in which they appear in a sentence (Cutter, Drieghe, & Liversedge, 2018). Developmental and educational psychologists also study reading. They are interested, for example, in which methods of teaching kids to read work best. Even evolutionary psychologists study reading. For example, they study why it is so much easier for kids to learn to talk than to learn to read. In contrast to all of these approaches, personality psychologists might seek to determine why some people love reading and others consider it a chore. Finally, social and health psychologists who study how people cope with emotional threats have shown that the topics we choose to read about vary with our psychological state. For example, a study of people in 16 nations all over the globe suggested that people become more interested than usual in reading about religious topics (on-line, at least) if they've recently been thinking about health concerns such as cancer or diabetes (Pelham et al., 2018).

This module is about the ways in which scientists – psychologists included – come to understand the world. But before we delve into the four ways of knowing as they apply to psychological scientists, let's see how they apply to you. We'll do so by examining your personal opinions about eight popular American aphorisms. An **aphorism** is a saying that expresses what is thought to be a general truth or piece of "folk wisdom." The aphorism "Don't bite the hand that feeds you" means you shouldn't harm those who take care of you. Aphorisms are popular the world over. For example, in much of the Spanish-speaking world a popular aphorism is "Cada oveja con su pareja" ("Every sheep with her partner"). This aphorism may sound vaguely familiar even if you don't speak any Spanish because it has a close English cousin: "Birds of a feather flock together." But aphorisms do vary across the globe. A popular Korean aphorism has it that "The bottom of the lamp is dark." If the meaning of this aphorism escapes you, that would be *apropos* because this Korean aphorism means that we often fail to see that which is right in front of us (because it is darkest under the base of the lamp). Now that you know what an aphorism is, we'd like you to evaluate some. Table 1.1 contains eight popular American aphorisms. Please take a moment to think about these *aphorisms*.

Now we'd like you to evaluate the *total set of aphorisms*. To simplify this complex job, let's boil things down to three options. Please answer the following question. "On the whole, this set of aphorisms is:

(a) more false than true, (b) neither true nor false, or (c) more true than false"

By far, the most common answer students offer to this question is that the aphorisms are *more true than false*. After all, aphorisms represent "folk wisdom" – not "folk wrongness." That certainly seems logical. But here's the rub. Occasionally, your first author has shown students a different set of aphorisms. The students who evaluated these aphorisms have consistently agreed that this other set of aphorisms is *also* more true than false. Table 1.2 contains this second set of aphorisms.

If you carefully compare the two sets of aphorisms, you'll see that the second set of aphorisms is the *opposite* of the first. If, "you can't teach an old dog new tricks," how can it be true that "it's never too late to learn"? If "birds of a feather flock together," how can "opposites attract"? This reveals one of the drawbacks of intuition. Our intuitions are not always logical. Can we use other ways of knowing to figure out which aphorism in each numbered pair is more correct? Sometimes. But whereas one *authority* figure might tell you that the "pen is mightier than the sword," another might tell you that "actions speak louder than words." You might also feel that you can logically defend one aphorism in a pair better than you can logically defend its rival. How could

Table 1.1 Eight American Aphorisms

1. The pen is mightier than the sword.
2. You can't teach an old dog new tricks.
3. The squeaky wheel gets the grease.
4. Absence makes the heart grow fonder.
5. Birds of a feather flock together.
6. Look before you leap.
7. Many hands make light work.
8. The early bird gets the worm.

Table 1.2 Eight Additional American Aphorisms

---

1.   Actions speak louder than words.
2.   It's never too late to learn.
3.   The nail that stands out gets pounded down.
4.   Out of sight, out of mind.
5.   Opposites attract.
6.   Strike while the iron is hot.
7.   Too many cooks spoil the broth.
8.   The second mouse gets the cheese.

---

anyone resolve all these possible contradictions? This is where the science of psychology comes in – to resolve questions that can't be resolved with intuition, authority, and logic. By carefully collecting data, psychological scientists hope to uncover the precise conditions under which these aphorisms may be true. But we're getting ahead of ourselves. Let's explore each of the four ways of knowing in some detail. As we do so, you'll see that although each way of knowing plays a role in almost all kinds of human belief systems, the relative emphasis placed on each varies dramatically from one belief system to the next.

Ways of Knowing

Authority

Authority refers to status or prestige, based on things like expertise, professional role, fame, or legitimately-acquired power. Authority figures include teachers, religious leaders, political leaders, experts in a given field, or famous people whose words may carry a lot of clout. We human beings appear to place a lot of emphasis on authority. In fact, the tendency to trust an authority is prevalent enough that it has been labeled the *expertise heuristic* by researchers who study persuasion (e.g., see Chaiken, Liberman, & Eagly, 1989; Hovland & Weiss, 1951; Petty & Cacioppo, 1986; Smith & Mackie, 2015). The **expertise heuristic** means that we often rely on a person's apparent level of expertise as a short-cut to deciding whether to believe the person. Whereas scientists and philosophers usually place limited stock in authority, followers of politicians or religious leaders often put their complete faith in it. If you trust your rabbi, minister, or imam, you are relying on authority to know what to do or believe. Likewise, if you consult with your parents, obey the police, or do as your prime minister asks you to do, you are relying (to at least some degree) on authority as a way of knowing.

Intuition

Governments and religions are also similar in that both systems consider intuition an important way of understanding the world. **Intuition** refers to people's automatic impulses or gut impressions, and intuitions are often based on casual (untutored, informal) rather than systematic observation. For instance, you may have an intuition that it's better not to tell your best friend that you saw her boyfriend flirting with another woman. Or you may have an intuition that it's best to run if you see a bear in the forest – even though experts say it's better to curl up on the ground and play dead. Intuitions can sometimes be helpful (they quickly tell you what to do). But they are not based on carefully collected evidence. In early human history, a great example of intuition was animism. **Animism** is the idea that natural phenomena or objects are alive – and thus have many of the same wishes and motives as people. Animism is alive and well today, but it is much more common in the thinking of small children than in the thinking of scientists (Arnett, 2012). If your three-year-old niece believes that her teddy bear loves her, she is engaging in animism. Ancient human beings engaged in animism when they concluded that the wind and ocean had wishes, or that gravity existed because objects wished to return to "Mother Earth." And whenever you become angry at your aging laptop – or annoyed at how thick-headed Siri can be – you are falling prey to a subtler version of animism. You are thinking with your guts or intuitions rather than your higher brain regions.

Logic

Speaking of higher brain regions, **logic** refers to the formal rules of correct reasoning. If you are taller than your brother, and your brother is taller than Steph Curry, then there can be no doubt that *you* are taller than Steph Curry. This is true according to the logic of **transitive inferences**. Likewise, if Alaska is larger than Rhode Island it follows, conversely, that Rhode Island is smaller than Alaska. Although scientists and philosophers both prefer logic to intuition or authority, scientists and philosophers differ in the relative emphasis they place on logic. To philosophers, logic typically trumps observation. Philosophers care deeply about the correct and incorrect rules of reasoning (Copi, 1978). They seem to believe that they cannot always trust their eyes (or even those of others). Philosophers have filled small libraries with books laying out the precise rules of correct and incorrect reasoning. They rely heavily on logic to answer basic questions about what is and is not real, what is and is not just, and what the human mind can and cannot do. Logic has at least some appeal to everyone, from farmers who grow cotton to framers who write Constitutions. But logic is particularly important to philosophers, who place a high premium on getting their reasoning exactly right.

Observation

To the typical scientist, logic is important, but it often takes a back seat to **observation** as the primary mode of figuring out the world. Observation is synonymous with **empiricism**, by the way. It refers to the practice of carefully collecting and analyzing data to decide whether something is true (Pelham & Blanton, 2019). Because scientists are empiricists, they prioritize experimentation over argumentation. They put more confidence in surveys than in syllogisms.

Truly relying on observation means a lot more than just counting or measuring. Scientists follow very strict rules when making observations – rules that laypeople are unlikely to know about. For example, scientists usually remain blind to the crucial conditions under which they make their observations. If Dr. Jay knows which participants received a drug and which participants did *not* receive a drug in his experiment, then his expectations may get the better of him. He may see what he hopes to see. The simplest solution to this problem is using **double-blind procedures**. Ideally, in an experiment, neither the participants themselves nor the experimenter knows what experimental treatment participants received. This might mean giving some participants a **placebo** – a pill with no active ingredients that looks just like the real pill. Using a placebo guarantees that any expectations participants have about what pills do is held constant in the experiment. If the experimental group and the control group behave differently even when the control group received a placebo, the observed difference between the two groups must be because of the power of the drug – not because of the power of expectations.

After running their experiments and collecting data, scientists usually conduct *statistical tests* to *see* just how much confidence they can place in their findings. In such tests, a finding based on a large sample is given much more weight than a finding based on a small sample. We'll delve a bit more deeply into research methods later in this text. For now, it's important to note that careful observation is a relative newcomer in the world of how people decide what they believe. The most brilliant philosophers of a few thousand years ago had only a vague appreciation of the value of observation. The kind of careful empirical observations that form the basis of most knowledge in psychology (e.g., true experiments) have only been around for about 140 years. Further, some of the most sophisticated forms of careful observation (e.g., high resolution brain imaging via fMRI) have only been around for a few decades.

Now that you're familiar with the four ways of knowing, let's apply them to a basic psychological question. How does human vision work? As you'll see in Module 9, we human beings are *extremely* visual creatures. Compared with many other animals, we rely heavily on vision. So, when you focus on an object, how good are you at seeing everything that is around that object? For example, if you stare at the center of your smartphone screen, does that make it hard to see what's on the edge of the screen? If you stare at a table, how well can you see the chair that's right next to it?

Because we are avid empiricists, let's be even more specific about what we're asking – and ask you to make a specific prediction. Take a look at Figure 1.1. It illustrates a careful observation we eventually (*not* yet!) want you to make. The observation requires you to pick up a small coin. Then you'll need to (a) shake the coin around while cupped in both hands, (b) take the coin into your right hand (*without* looking at it at all), and (c) grasp the coin between your thumb and first finger in your right hand – just like the model you see in panel 2 of Figure 1.1. Then, like the cartoon guy you see in panels 3–6 of Figure 1.1, you're going to (d) close your left eye completely (the cartoon guy's left eye is shut completely; we promise!) and (e) stare directly with

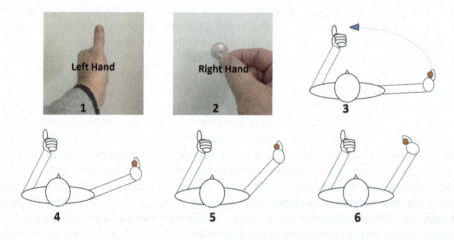

Figure 1.1 A careful observation that should reveal how your visual system works.

your right eye at your left thumbnail, which should be directly in front of you and facing you as if you were looking directly at your raised thumb (see panel 1). It's very important that you stare *directly* at your thumbnail, without ever cheating, while you do this exercise. As you grasp the coin in your right hand so that most of it is visible, you will *very slowly* move your right hand toward your left thumb – like the cartoon guy in panels 3–6. Now for the prediction: *Exactly how far away from your left thumbnail will the coin have to be before you can say for sure which side of the coin is facing you (heads or tails)?* Please write down an answer in inches or centimeters. "Pretty far away" and "pretty close" are *not* real predictions. By the way, be sure to start the exercise with your right arm stretched out to your right (as in image 3). For most people, this will put the coin well over a meter (100 cm) away from the left thumbnail.

Once you've written down your prediction – which you probably generated using your *intuitions* – do the careful observation. How does the value you got by making this careful observation compare with the value you got by using intuition? If you're anything like our past students, you predicted that you'd be able to see the coin pretty well when it was still far away from your thumbnail. When the first author of this book first made this observation – which he learned about from the cognitive neuroscientist Antonio Demásio (1994) – he predicted that he'd be able to see the details of a small object when it was two feet (about 60 cm) away from his thumbnail. The actual, empirically-based answer is more like two centimeters. The coin must almost be touching a person's thumbnail for the person to see which side is visible. And it must be right on top of a person's thumbnail before that person can read the writing on the coin. Thus, if you're like most other human beings, you can't read the writing on a coin without staring directly at it. But we hope you can read the writing on the wall: Careful observations reveal that our visual systems do not work the way we think they do!

Observations that are even more careful than the one you just made reveal why. We only have crisp, clear, full-color vision in one tiny area of the retina known as the *fovea*. In people, the fovea is about the size of the head of a pin. Once we leave the fovea, there are very few *cones* in the retina. Without a densely packed layer of these cones, all we can see is fuzzy – and it's also in black and white. This is because the other kind of photoreceptors, rods, do not offer our brains any information about color. We hope it's also *logical* that if the photoreceptors that give people detailed vison are densely concentrated in one part of the retina, forcing people to rely on the *other* parts of the retina (by requiring them to stare directly at their thumbnails) will seriously compromise their vision.

Putting it All Together

Fully modern human beings have been on Earth for about 200,000 years, and early human beings surely valued intuition over other ways of knowing (Pelham, 2019). But about 10,000 years ago, when people began to venerate official leaders and generate official scriptures, authority became a very important way of knowing. Human beings, like most other primates, evolved to pay keen attention to status. This means it would be awfully hard, if not impossible, to train people to ignore authority altogether. Having said this, authority may play a slightly less important role in human beliefs today than it did even a few hundred years ago. About 400 years ago, even the avid empiricist Galileo Galilei had to submit himself to the authority of the Catholic Church – to avoid being executed for heresy. Even today, though, those who personally consider it reasonable to drive

100 mph in a 50-mph speed zone must still defer to the authorities known as state troopers – if they wish to keep their driver's licenses. Thus, we suppose one could argue that modern thinkers still rely a lot on authority when it would be unwise or impractical to ignore it. Having said that, we hasten to add that one tricky aspect of authority as a "way of knowing" is that authority figures sometimes have their own agendas potentially compromising the integrity of the knowledge that they share.

The relative importance of authority, intuition, logic, and observation for religion, government, philosophy, and science is shown in Table 1.3. Although one could quibble with the exact rankings, this table should clarify an important distinction between scientific and nonscientific belief systems. Scientists and nonscientists prefer different ways of knowing about the world. Whereas scientists typically value observation (collecting data) over all other ways of knowing, most religious leaders would strongly disagree. In fact, the rankings for the four ways of knowing that appear in Table 1.3 are exact opposites for science and religion.

Three additional points about *ways of knowing* are in order. First, no one way of knowing is superior to others across all possible situations. Observation compelled scientists to invent complicated statistics. Intuition compels artists to create beautiful sculptures. If the U.S. Declaration of Independence had been written by political scientists rather than political activists, it surely would have been less awe-inspiring perhaps beginning with: "A meta-analysis of research in political science (Hummel, 1758) suggests a number of useful generalizations about self-governance...." Contrast that with the real deal. "We hold these truths to be self-evident ..."

The second point is that the far-right column of Table 1.3 describes the ways in which science is *supposed* to be carried out. Because scientists are fallible human beings, they sometimes fall back on ways of knowing that do not represent the ideals of science. For instance, scientists may rely more heavily on their intuitions than they would like to admit. Clinical psychologists once believed they could make solid inferences about a person's character or mental health by using the "Draw-A-Person" test. Patients who drew figures that had large eyes, psychologists assumed, were paranoid or delusional. As it turns out, this is not the case. When clinicians were unaware of a person's diagnostic status, research showed that they could not rely on a person's responses to the Draw-A-Person test to determine who did or did not suffer from schizophrenia. At times, scientists also rely more heavily on authority than they should. When ideas are proposed by well-known researchers or published in highly prestigious journals, they may be accepted more readily than they would be otherwise.

The third point about ways of knowing is that the different ways of knowing summarized here are not mutually exclusive. Just because you take one path toward knowing does not mean that you have to reject the other paths. In fact, true genius often

Table 1.3 Relative Importance of Different Ways of Knowing to Different Belief Systems

Religion	Government	Philosophy	Science
1. authority	1. authority	1. logic	1. observation
2. intuition	2. intuition	2. observation	2. logic
3. logic	3. logic	3. intuition	3. intuition
4. observation	4. observation	4. authority	4. authority

Note: Rank orderings are from (1) most to (4) least important.

consists of synthesizing different ways of knowing. Thomas Jefferson was a scientist as well as a politician, and his scientific side often influenced his political arguments. For example, Jefferson argued that systems of government, like scientific theories, should *change* based on new *evidence*. When asked, in 1816, whether the Virginia constitution should be revised, Jefferson argued that

> as new discoveries are made, new truths disclosed ... institutions must advance also, and keep pace with the times. We might as well require a man to wear still the coat which fitted him when a boy, as civilized society to remain ever under the regimen of their barbarous ancestors.
>
> (Letter to Samuel Kercheval, July 12, 1816)

Careful thinkers of any kind rarely limit themselves to a single way of understanding the world. When Galileo was conducting his empirical studies of gravity, he was plagued by the inaccuracies of the current technology of measurement. Instead of waiting a couple of hundred years for the invention of a good stopwatch, he slowed things down by studying the behavior of bodies *rolling down inclined planes* (Asimov, 1964; Harré, 1981). By doing so, Galileo was able to demonstrate that heavy and light objects "fell" at the same rate. In addition, he was able to show something subtler, and perhaps more important. Things don't simply fall at a constant rate: they constantly accelerate. Of course, accepting Galileo's conclusions requires us to make some logical inferences about the logical interchangeability of rolling and falling. But this is exactly the point. Galileo was not simply a good logician or a good observer. One of his unique talents was his ability to blend logic and observation into a seamless set of arguments that could knock someone's socks off – and predict how quickly they'd fall to the floor.

We hope we've made it clear that psychological scientists are strongly committed to the idea that the best way to know if something is true is **observation**. On the other hand, even avid scientists such as your authors recognize that all four "ways of knowing" reviewed here have a useful place in human knowledge systems. If you need to know very quickly if Garcia is a more common Latino surname than Carvallo – or if more Americans die every year of automobile accidents or hippopotamus attacks – you can probably get a correct answer by just consulting your intuitions. Likewise, if you are having trouble deciding whether you should marry Art or George, or whether you should become an artist or a geographer, you'd be better advised to consult your intuitions rather than collecting any empirical data. On the other hand, if you want to know the precise areas of the brain that register social pain – or exactly when and for whom "birds of a feather flock together," you'll be much better off collecting data (or reading the work of experts who have done so). The rest of this book focuses mostly on the empirical psychological literature as a way to understand the human experience. But we will not forsake logic, authority, or even intuition when they help us better understand psychology.

Questions for Critical Thinking and Group Discussion for Module 1

Although there appear to be four distinct ways in which people know about the world, the examples involving Thomas Jefferson and Galileo Galilei suggest that careful thinkers often blend or integrate different ways of knowing. Let's critically examine that concept in more depth.

1. Suppose you were to count the number of academic references in this chapter and compare it with the average number for all other chapters in this text. In which of the four ways of knowing would you be engaging?

2. Might it be a good idea to have more than one person count the number of references in any chapters you wished to analyze? Why or why not? What would a careful observer do if her two raters *disagreed* about exactly how many references were in a given chapter? Is that solution mostly logical, mostly intuitive, or equally both?

3. In what way does the idea that more judges is better show up in judgments of sports? How many referees are there in an NBA finals game? How about a typical junior high basketball game? How about a friendly pick-up game (a game played by those who happen to be on a public court at the same time)? How and why does the number of judges generally differ with the stakes of the event? Finally, why do you suppose Olympic figure skating usually has nine judges whereas Olympic long jumping traditionally had only two (one who watches for scratches at the jumping line and one who marks the length of the jump?).

4. Assume that you observed that this chapter had the fewest academic references of any chapter in this book. If this is true, what does it suggest about which way of knowing played a disproportionate role in the development of this chapter relative to all the others? Along these general lines, in what ways is providing a lot of references an example of using authority and in what way can it also be an example of observation?

5. Recall that one good way lab experimenters avoid bias in observation is to make judgments while remaining *blind* to a person's experimental condition – or to keep participants themselves blind to their conditions. When trying to translate this basic principle to many real-world judgments, this is impossible. NBA referees cannot remain blind to who is playing for the Warriors and who is playing for the Celtics. Olympic gymnastics judges cannot remain blind to the identity and the past success of the person whose routine they are judging. In such cases, the best one can do is to make sure judges avoid any kind of "conflict of interest." How might this play out in gymnastics and in basketball? If LeBron James's dad worked as an NBA ref, would he be allowed to referee a game in which LeBron played? Likewise, if a panel of Olympic judges in gymnastics included a judge from Portugal and a Portuguese gymnast were competing, how should this conflict of interest be handled?

6. In this text, we define psychology as *the scientific study of human thought, feelings, and behavior.* How did that simple definition work its ways into the title of this text?

Multiple-Choice Questions for Module 1

1. Arnelle conducts survey research on violence in close relationships. Is Arnelle likely to be a psychologist?

   A) probably not, because she does not conduct experiments
   B) maybe, her topic is mostly sociological, but her research methods are mostly psychological
   C) probably, because she uses empirical methods to study people's thoughts, feelings, and behavior

2. The logical analysis presented in Module 1 suggests that folk wisdom such as "Look before you leap" and "Opposites attract":

   A) is pretty accurate in the culture in which it evolved but does not apply well in other cultures.
   B) contains many logical contradictions
   C) has surprisingly high accuracy across cultures and time periods

3. What is an aphorism?

   A) a folk saying.
   B) a rule of inductive reasoning.
   C) a rule of deductive reasoning.
   D) a way of deciding the quality of empirical data

4. The four "ways of knowing" emphasized in this module include:

   A) authority, intuition, logic, and observation
   B) authority, intuition, knowledge, and wisdom
   C) perception, intuition, deduction, and application
   D) deduction, induction, perception, and sensation

5. Erin believes that homosexuality is wrong. One of her arguments in favor of her view is that "My preacher said they aint no homosexuality in the animal kingdom." (Empirically speaking, by the way, there is plenty of homosexuality in the animal kingdom.) In the language of your text, what appears to be the basis of Erin's belief?

   A) authority
   B) intuition
   C) perception
   D) induction

6. How would a physicist be likely to rank order the importance of the four "ways of knowing" emphasized in the text? (1= most, 4 = least important)

   A) 1. logic, 2. intuition, 3. observation, 4. authority
   B) 1. observation, 2. authority, 3. logic, 4. intuition
   C) 1. logic, 2. observation, 3. authority, 4. intuition
   D) 1. observation, 2. logic, 3. intuition, 4. authority

7. According to the text, which of the "ways of knowing" emphasized in the text would be ranked most highly (most favorably) by a politician or minister?

   A) logic   B) intuition
   C) authority   D) observation

8. Which of the four "ways of knowing" mentioned in the text is probably the basis of many commonly accepted stereotypes?

   A) authority   B) observation
   C) culture   D) intuition

9. The "Draw-A-Person Test" once used by clinical psychologists is an example of scientists relying on this "way of knowing":

   A) authority
   B) intuition
   C) logic
   D) observation

10. A way in which philosophers and psychologists disagree slightly about the ideal ways of knowing is that philosophers tend to value _____ a bit more than psychologists do.

   A) authority
   B) intuition
   C) logic
   D) parsimony

Answer Key: 1C 2B 3A 4A 5A 6D 7C 8D 9B 10C

References

Arnett, J.J. (2012). *Human development: A cultural approach.* New York, NY: Pearson.

Asimov, I. (1964). *Asimov's biographical encyclopedia of science and technology.* Garden City, NY: Doubleday.

Chaiken, S., Liberman, A., & Eagly, A. H. (1989). Heuristic and systematic information processing within and beyond the persuasion context. In J. S. Uleman & J. A. Bargh (Eds.), *Unintended thought* (pp. 212–252). New York: Guilford Press.

Copi, I. M. (1978). *Introduction to logic* (5th ed.). New York: Macmillan.

Cutter, M. G., Drieghe, D., & Liversedge, S. P. (2018). Reading sentences of uniform word length – II: Very rapid adaptation of the preferred saccade length. *Psychonomic Bulletin & Review, 25*(4), 1435–1440.

Demásio, A. (1994). *Descartes' error: Emotion, reason, and the human brain.* New York: Penguin Putnam.

Harré, R. (1981). *Great scientific experiments.* Oxford: Phaidon Press.

Hovland, C. I., & Weiss, W. (1951). The influence of source-credibility on communication effectiveness. *Public Opinion Quarterly, 15*, 635–650.

Pelham, B., & Blanton, H. (2019). *Conducting research in psychology: Measuring the weight of smoke* (5th ed.). Thousand Oaks, CA: SAGE Publications.

Pelham, B. W. (2019). *Evolutionary psychology: Genes, environments, and time.* London, UK: Red Globe Press.

Pelham, B. W., Shimizu, M., Carvallo, M. R., Arndt, J., Greenberg, J., & Solomon, S. (2018). Searching for God: Weekly search volume for major illnesses in Google predicts changes in Google search volume for religious content in 16 nations. *Personality and Social Psychology Bulletin, 44*, 290–303.

Petty, R. E., & Cacioppo, J. T. (1986). *Communication and persuasion: Central and peripheral routes to attitude change.* New York: Springer-Verlag.

Smith, E. R., Mackie, D. M., & Claypool, H. M. (2015). *Social psychology* (4th ed.). New York: Psychology Press.

"Well, first of all, Robert, I believe I speak for crows everywhere when
I say that by just coming here to meet with me today, you've already
answered one of our most important and long-standing questions."

Figure 1.2 According to this cartoon, which "way of knowing" do crows apparently prefer?

"I was hoping you could tell me something mildly
favorable—yet vague enough to be believable."

That "business trip" your wife took to Cleveland last
weekend was not really a business trip.

Figure 1.3 How do scientific and psychic or astrological predictions differ? How does the second
cartoon clarify that?

Module 2
Seven Windows on the History of Psychology

People have been keenly interested in the thoughts, feelings, and behavior of other people for as long as there have been people. Because we are a highly social species, we are always trying to understand each other. And as you learned in Module 1, we often come to conclusions about why other people do what they do by trusting our intuitions (our gut feelings). But intuitions about what makes other people tick are one thing, and psychological science is quite another. It took a long time for human beings to invent psychology. Consider Aristotle. Aristotle believed that the seat of our wishes, intelligence, and intentions was the heart. After all, the heart pumps blood throughout the body. And as Aristotle knew very well, someone who loses too much blood is a goner. Of course, Aristotle also knew we have brains. He reasoned that our humungous brains serve as radiators for the heart, cooling off the blood to keep us calm. Even a genius like Aristotle came to wrongheaded conclusions about the head. Today, we know that the brain, not the heart, is the primary seat of things like motivation, cognition, and emotion.

Despite Aristotle's mistaken theory of the brain, he knew that we are highly social creatures. In fact, if we were *not* social creatures, it's unlikely psychology would exist. If people were solitary, like bears and tigers, it is highly unlikely we would have evolved to use language (Pinker, 1994). Without language, there would be no agriculture, no science, no ice cream, and no Kendrick Lamar music. Nobody we know wants to live in that sad world.

But how did psychology become a science? The short answer is that a few thinkers in Germany in the late 1800s realized that one can blend (a) philosophical questions and (b) physiological research methods to study (c) human experience. If you want the history of psychology in three words and two symbols, it is this: **philosophy + physiology = psychology** (Schultz, 1981). And psychology can tell us many things that neither philosophy nor physiology alone could tell us. Let's begin this review of how psychology evolved to become what it is today by reviewing an early school of thought that paved the way for all the other schools of thought that came later. The first school of thought in psychology tried to blend ancient philosophical questions about human experience with research methods borrowed from the physical sciences, especially physiology.

Structuralism

In 1879, in Leipzig, Germany, Wilhelm Wundt came up with a new way to address what had previously been considered philosophical questions. Having had training in physiology, Wundt decided to collect data rather than relying exclusively on logic.

Wundt was interested in how we perceive and think about our world. He asked people to do things like press a telegraph key when they first heard a noise or first became aware of an image. Wundt was the father of **structuralism**, a school of psychological thought whose goal was to uncover the basic building blocks of human thought and perception. In Wundt's efforts to do so, he often asked people to engage in **introspection**. Introspection might involve looking at a familiar object and describing its essential perceptual features (e.g., red, round, smooth, delicious) *without* labeling the object. People had to be trained carefully to be able to do this. Further, precisely because structuralists were collecting data (they were empiricists), Wundt and his students eventually discovered two things. First, different observers often offered different reports about the same stimulus. Second, people who observed the same stimulus on more than one occasion sometimes offered different reports about it.

Another problem with structuralism is that Wundt's extreme fixation with perception caused him to underestimate what aspects of psychology can be studied scientifically. Wundt believed that only the simplest thoughts or percepts could be studied scientifically (Schultz, 1981). Wundt's extensive knowledge of chemistry probably contributed to this problem (Schmidgen, 2003). Inspired by the periodic table of the elements, Wundt thought he could break down human perception into its constituent parts – the way molecules can be broken down into atoms. Of course, it was Wundt's work in chemistry that made him appreciate the scientific method. So whereas chemistry helped Wundt invent psychology, it also seems to have gotten in his way. Needless to say, no one has ever developed anything like a periodic table of human thought or perception.

All of these problems meant that structuralism eventually faded from center stage in psychology. But like ancestors who are long-gone in a big family, structuralism never disappeared completely. Instead, it paved the way for the study of modern topics such as attention, sensation, and perception. Another legacy of structuralism is the use of response latencies ("reaction times") to understand human cognition. Many modern

Figure 2.1 To most of us, this is a ripe, freshly-picked apple. But structuralists like Wilhelm Wundt asked perceivers to engage in introspection – which meant putting aside labels and describing the essential physical features of things. This proved to be very hard to do. Because, you know, mmmm ... apples.

studies of memory, judgment, and decision-making rely heavily on response latencies (Neely, 1991). To close with the most important thing about structuralism, it was a structuralism that made psychology a *science*. Structuralists were avid empiricists.

Functionalism

Psychology may have been invented in Germany, but it very quickly spread to the U.S., where it really took off. This was true in large part because of Harvard psychologist William James. In fact, James taught the first course in psychology (at Harvard, in 1876; Asher, 2010). Further, in 1878, James became the first person to begin writing a psychology text-book. But James took 12 years to complete his text. By this time, several other psychology textbooks had been written. But perhaps James was wise to take this time. In his *Principles of Psychology* (1890), which still inspires research today, James made psychology more engaging, intuitive, and accessible than the structuralists had been able to do.

In James's *Principles*, he was willing to question almost anything people felt they knew about how we think, feel, and behave. If you noticed that James taught the first psychology course *before* Wundt opened the first lab in psychology, you might be wondering why James isn't considered the world's first psychologist. The main reason is that, unlike Wundt, James didn't begin his work in psychology by collecting data. Instead, James integrated and analyzed the findings of others. Thus, most psychologists say that Wundt founded psychology. But James did found *functionalism*, the second major school of thought in psychology. Further, functionalism still has a powerful impact on modern, cutting-edge psychological research whereas structuralism has all but disappeared. This fact might be easy to miss because modern psychologists don't refer to themselves as functionalists. Instead, they're more likely to call themselves evolutionary psychologists, and evolutionary psychology is a rapidly growing field. This is so true that evolutionary psychology gets its own module in this text.

Getting back to old school functionalism, the basic idea behind **functionalism** is that a lot of human experience is rooted in natural selection. This idea comes from Darwin's theory of evolution. James applied evolution to *psychology* by asking about the functions rather than the structure of human experience. By focusing on function, James was shining a spotlight on the various purposes of our thoughts, feelings, and behavior (how they help us survive and thrive). For example, James took inspiration from Darwin's analysis of emotions by assuming that the function of human emotions is to promote survival and reproduction. From this viewpoint, emotions should efficiently communicate information about our internal states to other people. And they should motivate us to (a) approach things that help us survive and (b) avoid things that can kill us.

James also assumed that the mind resides in the brain. And he poked a little fun at those who believed otherwise. We'll return to some of James's functionalist theories later in this text. For now, we merely note that James applied a functionalist approach to a wide range of psychological topics, from self-esteem to religion. In fact, James followed his *Principles* with a classic book about religion. James (2012/1902) concluded, for example, that one function of religion is to help us cope with our fear of death. A more pleasant function, he argued, is to make us kinder and more compassionate than we would be otherwise.

One way to think about functionalism is that it was a reaction to the problems and limitations of structuralism. In fact, one way to think about each of the schools of thought that followed structuralism and functionalism is that each was – at least in part – a reaction to all the schools of thought that came before it. But as we review

Figure 2.2 Pragmatic functionalists like William James would be the first to point out that apples are for eating. And they'd quickly add that both nutritious fruit and tough, smooth seeds evolved in apple trees because genes for both these traits promote apple tree reproduction.

the five schools of thought that followed structuralism and functionalism, we'd like you to think of each new school as a novel window on psychology – that is, a different way of viewing the many causes of human experience. So, don't feel you have to choose the one psychological school of thought that is correct. These schools of thought sometimes make competing predictions, but just as often they complement one another. To put this a little differently, we believe each school of psychological thought offers at least some truths offered by no other.

Psychoanalysis

More than 60 years before the invention of rock and roll, William James became a bit of a rock star by popularizing functionalism. He became world famous. But if James was a bit of a rock star, Sigmund Freud was more like the love-child of Elvis and Beyoncé. There is no psychologist who is more loved, more debated, or more hated than Sigmund Freud. Like James, Freud believed the mind is rooted in biology. Like James, Freud understood and believed in evolution. But unlike James, who had great respect for religion, Freud was an avid atheist. In Freud's view, God was a comforting illusion, a father figure taken to the extreme. Over the course of Freud's long career, he developed one of the most influential perspectives to ever exist in *any* discipline. One way of thinking about Freud's influence is to frame it within a modern expression: Freud went viral – without any help at all from the internet. Freud cleverly expressed and promoted his edgy ideas about sex and aggression (more on this to come) during a time in Europe (the Victorian Era) when conservative, "tight-laced" values normally squelched anything of this nature. Sex was a taboo topic for polite conversation. Then along came Freud.

Because Freud wrote about virtually everything, from potty training to mental illness, it's difficult to summarize his work. But we will try. Freud's **psychoanalysis** is a school of thought that emphasizes the role of unconscious desires and motives in human experience. It's safe to say that one of Freud's favorite unconscious drives was sex. But psychoanalysis is not *all* about sex. Psychoanalysis is also a deeply social and interpersonal theory (Hardin, 2018). Freud believed that our early relationships with our primary caregivers, including our deep desire to be adored by them, fuels a great deal of human behavior. This includes the desire to hurt others who may stand in the way of what we want.

It is not just Freud's focus on love, sex, and violence that has long been raising eyebrows. It's the fact that he questioned a deeply cherished canon of human beliefs. Freud viewed people *not* as rational and insightful but as rational*izing* and often self-deceiving. It's easy for us to deceive ourselves, Freud argued, because human mental activity is often *unconscious*. Freud believed that much of what we think, feel, and do is determined by invisible and largely inaccessible thoughts and desires. In fact, Freud's basic approach to psychotherapy was to help his patients become aware of unconscious forces that were fueling maladaptive behavior. Freud felt that it is only when we become aware of the roots of our problems that we can tackle them and make progress.

Freud recognized that people engage in conscious reasoning. But he proposed that the human mind is also a deep reservoir of many unconscious processes. Through **defense mechanisms** such as **repression**, Freud argued, people can banish uncomfortable thoughts to the unconscious. If Dave's jealousy makes him want to assault Uriah, and Dave's sexual urges make him want to sleep with Uriah's wife, Bathsheba, Dave may banish these inappropriate thoughts to the unconscious. In fact, together with his daughter Anna Freud (2018), Freud (1962/1894) argued that Dave might even replace his violent and sexual *un*conscious desires with conscious desires that are their opposites. Dave might praise Uriah – but insist that he finds Uriah's wife somewhat unattractive. Anna and Sigmund referred to this specific defense mechanism as **reaction formation**. Freud believed that what people consciously think they want is sometimes the opposite of what they really want.

Freud's view of the power of the unconscious shaped his view of the mind. According to Freud, the mind consists of three distinct structures. Freud's **id** is the selfish, greedy, oversexed, and aggressive part of the human psyche. The id wants what it wants, and it wants it now, dammit. Freud argued that the id obeys the **pleasure principle**. The id is like the metaphorical devil on your shoulder – who tells you to do whatever will make you feel good. At the other extreme, Freud's **superego** is like the metaphorical angel on your *other* shoulder. Unlike the id, which is almost completely unconscious, the superego operates both consciously and unconsciously. The superego is the result of years of socialization by authorities such as parents, teachers, and religious leaders. The superego is a strict moral compass always reminding you of what is right and wrong. The superego can certainly keep you out of trouble, but it never lets you have any fun. Freud argued that some of his clinical patients had *overdeveloped superegos*, which could lead, Freud felt, to the self-hatred that fosters clinical depression. But few people are slaves to the id, and few are ruled completely by their superegos. Freud argued that the ego negotiates between the two. The **ego** is the largely-conscious decision-maker that must weigh and balance the id and the superego. A healthy person presumably has an ego that can make peace between the childish, self-absorbed id and the prudish, strict superego.

Figure 2.3 Freud believed that we all cope with life's insults and challenges (ahem, insecurities) by using defense mechanisms, which largely operate at an unconscious level.

Modern critics of Freud argue that he overemphasized sex. Others argue that he was very sexist. Fans of Freud retort that Freud was less sexist than many of the other male thinkers of his day, psychological or otherwise. It is certainly possible to be a *modern* psychoanalyst while discarding the sexist baggage of Freud's historical era. Another common critique of Freud is that his ideas were based on unsound methods. The evidence that formed the basis for Freud's ideas came mainly from case studies of his own patients. Because these were patients that came to Freud for treatment, they all suffered from psychological disorders and would not have been representative of the general population. A final critique of Freud is that many of his ideas are both vague and extravagant. Here we agree partly with the extravagant part, but we would not characterize psychoanalysis as vague, especially in a historical light. There are good reasons why Freud has more citations than any other person in the history of psychology. He introduced a clever and novel point of view, and he ran with it. OK, maybe he ran *too* far with it. But there is virtually no aspect of human experience Freud did not address. Further, because of advances in modern research methods, it is now possible to put many of Freud's theories to some very rigorous empirical tests. Freud may have been wrong about many details of the mind, but he was almost certainly right about the power of the unconscious.

Behaviorism

Freud offended many people by arguing that the mind doesn't work the way people think it works. Advocates of another powerful school of thought in psychology offended people by suggesting that we should ignore the mind. **Behaviorism** is a school of thought that rejects the unobservable unconscious and emphasizes observable behaviors. Further, behaviorism takes the perspective that our behavior follows the rules of learning theory. For example, as you will see later in this text, one of the founders of behaviorism, E.L. Thorndike, proposed a law that vaguely resembles Freud's pleasure principle. The law of effect *sort of* states that we tend to do things that make us feel good. Specifically, it says that any behavior that is followed by good consequences becomes more likely in the future. Likewise, any behavior that is followed by bad consequences becomes *less* likely in the future. But whereas Freud just speculated about the pleasure principle, behaviorists have studied the law of effect in thousands of rigorous experiments. The experimental methods of behaviorists could hardly be further removed from the case study approach favored by Freud. Further, whereas Freud developed his theory mainly by interviewing patients with clinical disorders, behaviorists usually study animals, who are notoriously unresponsive in clinical interviews.

In short, pushing back against Freud, early behaviorists such as John Watson and B.F. Skinner argued that if psychology was to become a full-fledged science, we'd have to follow the same rules followed by physical scientists. One such rule is refraining from speculation about the unobservable. Show what can be shown with absolute certainty (Popper, 1974/1990). During the heyday of behaviorism (roughly 1935–1975), it was virtually impossible to know what was happening in a human brain. Thus, behaviorists such as Skinner said it was unscientific to speculate about minds. Instead, we should strive to understand the predictors of behavior, without regard for the unobservable **"black box"** of the brain (Watson, 1913). Skinner was fond of showing that if he set up the rules of reinforcement in just the right way, he could get a pigeon, rat, or person to do almost anything he wished. Skinner focused on *behavior*, not thoughts. Because of his focus on observable behavior, some have concluded that Skinner did not believe people think. A deeper reading of Skinner's work shows that he recognized that thoughts are real. He just felt they couldn't be studied scientifically.

Figure 2.4 To Skinner, a delicious apple was merely a positive reinforcer or, loosely speaking, a reward. Don't overthink it.

One thing Skinner shared with Freud was the willingness to question cherished beliefs. For example, Skinner argued that many human superstitions are grounded in the rules of reward (more technically, the rules of *reinforcement*) and punishment that take over when good or bad things happen to an animal completely at random. In his lab studies with pigeons, for example, Skinner showed that, much like people, pigeons placed in situations in which good or bad things happened at random intervals would often develop superstitious habits. And Skinner suggested that the development of many human superstitions – from wearing a lucky baseball cap to avoiding the number 13 – follow the same rules of reward or punishment that create superstitious behavior in pigeons. In his controversial book *Beyond Freedom and Dignity*, Skinner (1948) also questioned whether we have free will. If the invisible rules of learning theory determine what we do, why do we need to specu-late about things like "free choice"?

Psychoanalysis and behaviorism offer very different views of human experience. Con-sider marriage. In Freud's view, repressed experiences from your childhood might strongly influence your adult choice of a spouse. For example, you might marry someone very much like your mother. From Skinner's perspective, however, if you seem to have "mar-ried your mother," it would be because of the rewards and punishments you experienced in your mother's presence – not because of some unconscious sexual complex. Freud and Skinner also differed greatly in the importance they placed on early vs. recent experience. Freud believed that the first couple of years of life set the stage for much that comes later. Skinner believed that if the rules of punishment and reinforcement change in adult-hood, the person's behavior will quickly change to reflect these new rules. Freud empha-sized the invisible and poorly appreciated past. Skinner emphasized the observable and poorly appreciated present.

Humanism

If all these discussions of sex, violence, and odd attractions are starting to get you down, you'll be happy to learn that in the distant wake of Freud, and the immediate wake of behaviorism, a school of psychological thought emerged to give voice to those who believe in freedom, choice, growth, and love. That's right; psychology has its opti-mists. The school of thought known as **humanism** emphasizes self-determination, self-acceptance, human potential, and connectedness. In fact, humanists explicitly disagree with Freud by arguing that human beings are naturally good (rather than selfish). They explicitly disagree with Skinner – who believed we have about as much free will as a pigeon does – by arguing that we do have free will and personal choice – which is what makes us responsible for our own actions.

But like other psychologists, most humanists are empiricists. They form theories and collect data. But unlike behaviorists, humanists usually study people, not pigeons. And they place much more stock than Freud or Skinner would in people's conscious beliefs and self-reports. Although humanism does not quite have the stat-ure today that it did in its heyday (roughly 1955–1985), humanism has influenced many modern forms of psychotherapy. In fact, one of the founders of humanism was clinical psychologist Carl Rogers, who argued that one of the keys to human happiness is accepting and being accepted by others. Rogers argued that from a very young age, we all crave **unconditional positive regard** (acceptance independent of what we do) from our primary caregivers. Rogers added that, as adults, we continue to seek out unconditional positive regard in close friendships and/or romantic rela-tionships. This means that good therapists, while maintaining appropriate profes-sional boundaries, should offer their clients unconditional positive regard. It is only after establishing this foundation of trust and acceptance, humanists argue, that therapists can challenge their clients to heal and grow. If all this touchy-feely stuff sounds a little sappy to you, that's OK. We still accept you. In fact, we accept you unconditionally. Doesn't that feel good?

Humanists can be touchy-feely without being soft-headed. As you will learn later in this text, modern research on prosocial behavior and altruism supports the humanistic idea that we are capable of being both caring and unselfish. A great deal of modern research is also consistent with at least some of the other premises of humanistic psychology. For example, modern research in *positive psychology* reveals that being either thankful or thoughtful can increase people's well-being (Lyubomirsky, 2013). Likewise, recent research in health psychology strongly suggests that giving help and social support to *other people* is good for one's own physical health (Brown et al., 2003).

Another important contribution of humanism to modern psychology comes from Maslow's theory of human motivation. Maslow (1943) argued that human needs may be arranged in a hierarchy in which lower needs must be met before we can turn our attention to higher needs. Maslow's lower needs are familiar to almost everyone. Physiological needs come first. We must eat, poop, and breathe, for example. Once our physiological needs have been met, we'll try to meet our needs for safety and security. After this, all the other needs in Maslow's hierarchy reflect his humanistic viewpoint. After people feel safe and secure, they can begin to fill their need for love and belongingness. If all goes well in the love department, people can begin to fill the need for self-esteem, followed by need at the top of Maslow's pyramid – the need for self-actualization. Maslow (1943, p. 383) defines **self-actualization** as the desire "to become everything that one is capable of becoming." An empirical test of Maslow's theory in 123 nations (Tay & Diener, 2011) supported some of Maslow's most important assertions. On the other hand, Kenrick et al. (2010) argued that Maslow's hierarchy needs to be revamped in light of modern research. For example, rather than placing self-actualization at the top of their hierarchy, they argued that being a good parent is the pinnacle of human motivation – a point to which we will return in the module on motivation.

As we hope you can already see, psychology is a broad discipline that includes multiple perspectives, some of which are *somewhat* incompatible. However, as we noted earlier, there is no single school of thought in psychology that can ever give us all the answers. Because human behavior is complex and has many causes, it is best viewed through multiple windows. And we're not done yet; we still have two more schools of thought to consider.

Figure 2.5 To a humanist like Abe Maslow, an apple could fill a physiological need like hunger. But if you gave your last apple to a hungry friend, the apple could be a symbol of love, hope and connectedness.

Cognitive Psychology

A sixth psychological school of thought was also a reaction to behaviorism. In the early 1960s, many psychologists began to argue that we *can* study the mind scientifically. These psychologists founded cognitive psychology. **Cognitive psychology** is a school of psychological thought that examines human attention, consciousness, perception, memory, and judgment. Cognitive psychologists study everything from how you remember the name of your first-grade teacher (for one of your authors, this was Louise Boyd) to how best to teach first graders to read (Mrs. Boyd used phonics). To be fair to some old, dead guys, psychologists such as Hermann Ebbinghaus studied human memory as early as the 1880s. But there is pretty good consensus that the founder of modern cognitive psychology was George Sperling (1960), who was still alive and kicking at the time of this writing.

Sperling was interested in short-term memory, the kind of memory that fades away very quickly unless there is some way to commit to-be-remembered material to permanent storage. Sperling's (1960) **partial report technique** revealed that there is a very rapidly decaying form of short-term memory that we now call *iconic memory* (Neisser, 1967). Prior to Sperling's research, it looked like the short-term store for visual information couldn't hold more than three or four tiny pieces of information. Figure 2.6 provides examples of the kinds of arrays of letters one might use to study very-short-term visual memory.

H	X	S		B	W	P	J
G	M	N		L	M	S	R
E	T	D		K	O	G	C

Figure 2.6 Two examples of the kind of 3 x 3 or 3 x 4 arrays of letters used for Sperling's (1960) partial report technique.

When Sperling flashed these nine-letter and 12-letter arrays to participants for a mere twentieth of a second (50 ms), participants could only report a bit more than a third of the nine or 12 letters. Perhaps this rapidly decaying form of memory was wimpy. Perhaps not. Sperling thought people might be perceiving a lot more than they were able to report before the perception very rapidly decayed. **Iconic memory** (very short-term memory for visual information) might just be very, very short-lived. Sperling's partial report technique revealed that this is the case. In some conditions of his experiments, Sperling trained participants to listen for a high-pitched, a medium-pitched, or a low-pitched tone that he played just *after* each array of letters disappeared. The high-pitched tone meant participants would need to report all the letters in the top row. The medium-pitched tone meant participants would need to report all the letters in the middle row. And the low-pitched tone meant participants would need to report all the letters in the bottom row. High-top, medium-middle, low-bottom. That's simple enough. With a bit of practice, participants learned to use the tones to focus their attention on what they had *just seen* in a specific row of the array. It's important to note that the tones always chimed *after the arrays disappeared*. Participants could *not* use the tones to know where to focus their visual attention beforehand. They had to try to process the entire arrays. Sperling found that in the partial report conditions of his experiments, people could accurately report about 75% of the letters. In the 3 x 4 array, this meant participants could name three of the four letters from *any* of the three rows in the array (rather than about four letters, period). Notice that Sperling was following in the tradition of Wundt by testing the limits of people's perceptual systems. He was also redefining modern psychology. He did so by showing that clever experiments can reveal subtle details of the way the mind works that we could never appreciate by making more casual observations.

Cognitive psychology is flourishing. In fact, clever techniques for studying memory, attention, and judgment have now been adopted in every subdiscipline of psychology. For example, researchers in social, clinical, and developmental psychology routinely use looking times, response latencies, and indirect measures of memory to study thoughts and judgments as diverse as stereotypes, phobias, and infant's theories of how permanent objects are. Cognitive psychology is in no danger of going extinct any time soon. In fact, in the past few decades, as our ability to measure what is happening in the brains of living people has increased dramatically, the collaboration between cognitive psychology and the growing field of behavioral neuroscience has become very, well, fruitful. This takes us to our final school of psychological thought.

Behavioral Neuroscience

As you may recall from module 1, the microscopic structure of the back of your eyeball (your retina) determines what you can see well and what you can barely see at all. And as you will learn in Modules 5 and 6, your eyes are connected by millions of nerve fibers to many other parts of your brain. In fact, your sense of sight depends on complex interactions between many different areas of your brain. The incredibly complex three-pound object known as your brain is the seat of almost everything you experience. And behavioral neuroscientists argue that your brain is

Figure 2.7 To a cognitive psychologist, your repeated exposure to the concept of apples will influence the way in which you are most likely to complete the following word fragment:

FR _____

There are more than 3,000 English words that begin with "FR," but we're putting our money on "fruit." That's called priming.

the seat of many things – but not everything – you do. For example, you need the band of your outer brain known as the motor cortex to carry out conscious complex movements. But to pull your hand away from a hot stove, you do not need a functioning brain. This particular self-protective response – which we call the *hot stove reflex* – happens at the level of tiny bundles of nerve cells that are located in your spinal cord rather than your brain. We've known for well over a century that the hot stove reflex needs no brain because studies of animals whose brains have been removed show that they still show this reflex (until *rigor mortis* sets in). **Behavioral neuroscience**, then, is the modern school of thought in psychology that emphasizes the role of the nervous system (including the parts of your nervous system that exist outside your brain) in determining how we think, feel, and behave.

In the century or so since we began to understand the operation of the brain and spinal cord, our knowledge of the brain and nervous system has increased exponentially. In 1959, Hubel and Wiesel published a landmark study that showed that individual cells in the brains of cats responded to lines presented at different visual angles. This was the beginning of a long line of work that documented exactly how the brain creates a complex three-dimensional image of the world. Hubel and Wiesel won a Nobel Prize for this work in 1981. More than two decades later, Linda Buck won a Nobel prize for her behavioral neuroscientific work on how our brains process information about smell. More specifically, she and Richard Axel (Buck & Axel, 1991) documented that there are more than 1,000 unique odor receptors, each of which responds to a different molecule, and each of which sends a signal to a specific location in the brain. Buck and Axel also documented which genes code for many of these individual smell receptors. In much the same way that Hubel and Wiesel began to crack the complex neural code for vision, Buck and Axel began to crack the complex neural code for smell.

Figure 2.8 A behavioral neuroscientist might show people images of apples while they had their brains scanned in an fMRI. Whereas avid apple lovers might show activation in the brain's reward areas, people with apple phobias (assuming such people exist) would be more likely to show activation in the amygdala – an area of the brain that plays a major role in the experience of fear.

In the past 30 years, the growing popularity of high-tech brain imaging techniques such as fMRI (functional magnetic resonance imaging) has built on this earlier work by revolutionizing the way in which psychologists study the brain as it does its job. For example, we now have a very clear idea of exactly which areas of the brain become active when you experience pain or pleasure, and we know that the area of your brain that figures out what you are seeing (primary visual cortex) gets input not only from your eyes but also from an area deep in the brain known as the lateral geniculate nucleus. Using a different high-tech technique known as EEG (electroencephalography), neuroscientists measuring electrical activity in the brain can detect ERPs (event-related potentials). By measuring people's brain waves – millisecond by millisecond – psychologists can tell whether people find a specific stimulus surprising, for example.

Because of modern research on the brain, we have a better understanding than ever before of how your brain carries out routine functions such as breathing and face recognition. We also better understand what goes wrong in the brain when people suffer from major illnesses and diseases such as Alzheimer's, schizophrenia, or Parkinson's disease. In the interest of time and space, we will not belabor any more of the details of the brain. But the fact that we devote two separate modules to the brain and nervous system should tell you that the rapidly growing school of psychology known as behavioral neuroscience is enriching what we've learned from all the other schools. Wundt, James, Freud, and Maslow would all be proud of what we've learned about psychology by better understanding the brain. Sperling (the father of modern cognitive psychology) is surely elated. Skinner might still be on the fence, but we feel confident that behavioral neuroscientists would soon win him over. After all, modern behavioral neuroscience is now making the once invisible brain highly visible.

Wilhelm Wundt, 1902 (age 70)   William James, circa 1903 (age 61)   Sigmund Freud, 1921 (age 65)   B.F. Skinner, circa 1950 (age 46)

Abe Maslow circa 1970   George Sperling, date unknown   Torsten Wiesel 2011   Linda Buck 2015

Figure 2.9 Influential scientists who are strongly associated with the seven historical schools of thought summarized in this module. You will see that only the 2014 Nobel Prize winner Linda Buck is female. We are happy to say that in the past couple of decades psychologists are increasingly becoming female. As you can clearly see, psychologists have also gotten a lot happier over time.

In the remainder of this text we will explore research inspired by each of these seven basic windows on psychology. We hope you'll see that rather than always contradicting each other, each of these schools of thought is like an instrument that contributes to the symphony of modern psychological science. But before we begin to listen to any symphonies, let's learn a little about how to make music. The next two modules in this text will introduce you to modern psychological research methods.

Critical Thinking and Discussion Questions for Module 2

Missing Voices: The History of Social Inequality in Psychology

Take another look at Figure 2.9. Did you notice that all of the faces are White – and that all but one of them are male? As your great-great-great grandmother could tell you if she were still alive, the history of psychology is full of examples of ingenious female and ethnic minority psychologists who were overlooked and actively discriminated against. In the Europe of Wundt's heyday, there was no nation that recognized women's right to vote. In fact, the first European nation to respect women's right to vote was Finland, where women first voted in 1907. In Germany, women were not allowed to vote until 1918. In the U.S., the year was 1920. So for the first 30–40 years of psychology's 140-year existence, women throughout the most highly educated regions of the world were denied even the most basic civil rights. For this reason, you probably won't be surprised to learn that progressive thinkers who wished to change this state of affairs – psychologists included – faced a long, uphill battle. Here's how Myers (2015, p. 4) summarized the battle faced by **Mary Whiton Calkins**, the first female student of William James and the first female president of the American Psychological Association:

> In 1890, over the objections of Harvard's president, he [William James] admitted Mary Whiton Calkins into his graduate seminar (Scarborough & Furumoto, 1987). ... When Calkins joined, the other students (all men) dropped out. So James tutored her alone. Later, she finished all of Harvard's PhD requirements, outscoring all the male students on the qualifying exams. Alas, Harvard denied her the degree she had earned, offering her instead a degree from Radcliffe College, its undergraduate "sister" school for women.

As Myers goes on to note, Calkins refused the degree in protest. Her logic was that, by accepting the less honorific degree, she would be cooperating with a system that made women second-class citizens.

Despite the many barriers Calkins faced, she became successful. For example, she was one of the first psychologists to study the self-concept (Furumoto, 1979). She was far ahead of her time in this way, emphasizing the inherently social nature of the self. Her research on the interpretation of dreams also got Sigmund Freud's attention. In her original work at Harvard, Calkins also created the **paired-associate memory paradigm**, in which people are presented with many pairs of words (e.g., canoe-green, apple-dark), and then later asked to remember the second word in each pair – with the first word in the pair serving as a memory cue. This paradigm influenced a great deal of modern memory research.

There is a lot of debate about exactly how much progress psychology has made toward equality and fairness in the past 100 years or so. Some argue that women and people of color continue to face barriers to professional success, even in a field that makes it a point to study bias and social inequality. Others argue that psychology is pretty fair; it's society at large that denies large groups of people equal opportunities. Regardless of where one stands on this debate, the data show that things have changed since the 1880s. In fact, *women now outnumber men about 2:1 among clinical psychologists* (2005–13: Demographics of the U.S. Psychology Workforce, 2015). However, as more and more women have gravitated toward advanced degrees in clinical psychology, salaries in this area relative to other professions have decreased. Further, in academic rather than clinical circles, men still hold most of the top jobs. Men are much more highly represented than women among full professors, and men make up 82% of the editors – the scientific leaders, that is – at journals run by the American Psychological Association (Clay, 2017). A similar story applies to ethnic minority representation in psychology. As Robert Guthrie (2004) put it in his account of ethnic and racial bias in the history of psychology, "Even the rat was White." Today participation in psychological science among people of color is increasing. But people of color are not yet represented in psychology the way they are represented in the U.S. population.

1. What do you think about the fact that most clinical psychologists are now female? What do you think about the fact that about 80% of psychology's journal editors are still male? As you wrestle with this question, ask yourself whether a society that truly treated all people equally would see identical numbers of men and women in all occupations. Are men and women equally interested in being pre-school teachers? Should they be? If men are naturally more interested in the brain than women are, is it OK if men outnumber women in behavioral neuroscience?

2. Moving from social inequality back to psychological schools of thought, we'd like you to consider a few modern research findings. From the following list of research findings, explain which schools of thought are likely to have inspired his work.

    A. In their research on people who had undergone open-heart surgery, King and Reis (2012) found that marriage is good for you. Specifically, married people – including those who are not all that happy with their marriages – live longer than single or divorced people. Many other studies also support the idea that marriage has positive health consequences. Name two schools of thought that may have inspired this research. Be sure to explain and justify your selections.

    B. In a series of lab studies on stereotypes and split-second judgment, participants played a shooting game in which they had to evaluate photos of Black and White men very quickly. The men in the photos were very similar (e.g., same clothes, same age, same poses). Half the men were depicted holding cell phones, and half were depicted holding handguns. As the photos flashed up on a screen, participants tried to follow a simple rule: always shoot those people holding guns and never shoot those people holding cell phones. Correll (2002) measured both errors at this task and response latencies (how quickly people made their shooting decisions). Participants were more likely to shoot Black men holding cell phones than to shoot White men holding cell phones. Further, participants took longer to pull the trigger on White men holding guns than to pull the trigger on Black men holding guns. A follow-up study showed that working police officers were racially biased but *less so* than college students. Name at least two schools of thought that inspired this experimental research technique. What would you like to tell the public – and police officers across the nation – about these findings?

C. Fraley and Marks (2010) asked heterosexual participants to bring a photo of their opposite sex parents to the lab. Without telling participants they were doing so, the researchers quickly scanned the photos and secretly used them as experimental stimuli. Participants took part in a computerized task in which they rated 100 opposite-sex faces for how sexually attractive they were. Unbeknown to participants, Marks and Farley sometimes flashed up the photos of participants' opposite sex parents for a very brief period (so briefly that no one consciously perceived them) right before a photo of an opposite-sex stranger appeared. The photos of opposite sex strangers stayed up until participants made their sexual attractiveness ratings. Participants reported finding faces more sexually attractive than usual when the face of their opposite sex parent had flashed up right before the stranger's face appeared. Name at least three schools of thought that may have inspired this research.

D. People who suffer serious damage to a brain region known as the hippocampus forever lose the ability to form new memories. Thus, if you met such a person and interviewed her about her childhood, she'd be able to answer most of your questions. But if you left the room and came back in 20 minutes, she would have no memory whatsoever of having ever met you. Name at least three schools of thought that are relevant to this case study.

Multiple-Choice Questions for Module 2

1. According to the module on the history of psychology, philosophy + _____ = psychology.

   A) physiology
   B) biology
   C) science

2. About how old is psychology?

   A) 1,400 years old
   B) 140 years old
   C) 40 years old

3. Which psychological school of thought (promoted by William James) was heavily influenced by Darwin's theory of evolution?

   A) functionalism
   B) behaviorism
   C) pragmatism

4. The U.S. psychologist William James taught the first college course in psychology. Why didn't James become known as the world's first psychologist?

   A) James always self-identified as a philosopher
   B) Wilhelm Wundt opened the first psychological laboratory
   C) researchers in Germany were the first to hold a psychological research conference

5. What principle in learning theory shares at least some features of Freud's pleasure principle?

   A) the Law of Effect
   B) self-actualization
   C) the Law of Happiness

6. In Freud's structural hypothesis, what strives to balance the opposing desires of the id and the superego?

   A) the self
   B) the ego
   C) the judge

7. LaDonna makes many sacrifices for those she loves. Further, she works hard in school, hoping to become a civil rights attorney. LaDonna's unselfish attitude and her efforts to "be all that she can be" are highly consistent with the assumptions of a major school of psychological thought. Which one?

   A) humanism
   B) identity psychology
   C) utopianism

8. Jay Q studies how patterns of reinforcement in pigeons influences how quickly they acquire new responses. Jay Q probably identifies himself as what kind of psychologist?

   A) a psychoanalyst
   B) a behaviorist
   C) a cognitive psychologist

9. Mary Whiton Calkins was arguably the first female psychologist, but she was *not* the first woman to receive her PhD in psychology. This is because:

   A) Harvard University refused to award PhDs to women back in Calkins's day
   B) she dropped out of graduate school in protest over sexist treatment
   C) she was granted a PhD in philosophy rather than in psychology

10. In addition to conducting research on both dreams and the self, Mary Whiton Calkins became famous for developing the:

    A) partial report technique
    B) paired-associates learning paradigm
    C) first course in the psychology of gender

Answer Key: 1A 2B 3A 4B 5A 6B 7A 8B 9A 10B

References

2005–13: Demographics of the U.S. Psychology Workforce. (2015, July). APA Center for Workforce Studies. Retrieved February 11, 2019 from www.apa.org/workforce/publications/13-demographics/index

Asher, L. (2010, August 26). When William met Sigmund. The second compass. Retrieved February 9, 2019 from http://thesecondpass.com/?p=6447

Brown, S.L., Nesse, R.M., Vinokur, A.D., & Smith, D.M. (2003). Providing social support may be more beneficial than receiving it. Results from a prospective study of mortality. *Psychological Science, 14*, 320–327.

Buck, L., & Axel, R. (1991). A novel multigene family may encode odorant receptors: A molecular basis for odor recognition. *Cell, 65*, 175–187.

Clay, R. A. (2017, July/August). Women outnumber men in psychology, but not in the field's top echelons: A new APA report recommends ways to boost women's status and pay. Vol. 48, No. 7. Retrieved February 11, 2019 from www.apa.org/monitor/2017/07-08/women-psychology

Correl, J., Park, B., Judd, C. M., & Wittenbrink, B. (2002). The police officer's dilemma: Using ethnicity to disambiguate potentially threatening individuals. *Journal of Personality and Social Psychology, 83*, 1314–1329.

Fraley, R. C., & Marks, M. J. (2010). Westermarck, Freud, and the incest taboo: Does familial resemblance activate sexual attraction? *Personality and Social Psychology Bulletin, 36*(9), 1202–1212.

Freud, A. (2018). *The ego and the mechanisms of defence.* Routledge. Original German edition published 1936.

Freud, S. (1962/1894). The neuro-psychosis of defense. In J. Strachey (Ed.), *The standard edition of the complete psychological works of Sigmund Freud* (pp. 43–68). London: Hogarth.

Furumoto, L. (1979). Mary Whiton Calkins (1863-1930). Fourteenth President of the American Psychological Association. *Journal of the History of the Behavioral Sciences, 15*, 346–356.

Guthrie, R. V. (2004). *Even the rat was white: A historical view of psychology* (Allyn & Bacon Classics Edition). New York: Allyn & Bacon.

Hardin, C.D. (2018). Freud was a deeply social psychologist. Personal communication.

James, W. (1890). *The principles of psychology.* New York: Holt.

James, W. (2012). *The varieties of religious experience: A study in human nature.* Oxford, UK: Oxford World's Classics paperback. Original version published in 1902.

Kenrick, D. T., Griskevicius, V., Neuberg, S. L., & Schaller, M. (2010). Renovating the Pyramid of needs: Contemporary extensions built upon ancient foundations. *Perspectives on Psychological Science : A Journal of the Association for Psychological Science, 5*(3), 292–314. https://doi.org/10.1177/1745691610369469.

King, KB, & Reis, H.T. (2012). Marriage and long-term survival after coronary artery bypass grafting. *Health Psychol, 31*(1): 55–62. doi:10.1037/a0025061.

Lyubomirsky, S. (2013). The myths of happiness: What should make you happy, but doesn't, what shouldn't make you happy, but does. New York: Penguin Press.

Maslow, A. H. (1943). A theory of human motivation. *Psychological Review, 50*(4), 370–396.

Myers, D. (2015). *Psychology: Tenth edition in modules.* New York: Worth.

Neely, J. E. E. P. H. (1991). Semantic priming effects in visual word recognition: A selective review of current findings and theories. In D. Besner & G. W. Humphreys (Eds.), *Basic processes in reading: Visual word recognition* (pp. 264–336). Hillsdale, NJ: Lawrence Erlbaum Associates, Inc.

Neisser, U. (1967). *Cognitive psychology.* New York: Appleton-Century-Crofts.

Pinker, S. (1994). *The language instinct: How the mind creates language.* New York: Harper Collins.

Popper, K. (1974/1990). Unended quest: An intellectual autobiography. LaSalle, IL: Open Court.

Schmidgen, H. (2003). Wundt as chemist? A fresh look at his practice and theory of experimentation. *American Journal of Psychology, 116*(3), 469–476.

Schultz, D. (1981). *A history of modern psychology* (3rd ed.). New York: Academic Press.

Skinner, B. F. (1948). Superstition in the pigeon. *Journal of Experimental Psychology, 38*, 168–172.

Sperling, G. (1960). The information available in brief visual presentations. *Psychological Monographs, 74*(11), 1–29.

Tay, L., & Diener, E. (2011). Needs and subjective well-being around the world. *Journal of Personality and Social Psychology, 101*(2), 354–365.

Watson, J. B. (1913). Psychology as the behaviorist views it. *Psychological Review, 20*, 158–177.

Module 3
Doing Good Science
Internal Validity in Psychological Research

As you surely recall from Module 1 of this text, scientists make decisions about what is true very differently than non-scientists. Scientists place a lot of emphasis on observation and logic. They place only limited emphasis on authority and intuition. Psychological scientists also face ethical challenges that physical scientists such as chemists and astronomers rarely face. No one worries about whether it is ethical to figure out why iron oxidizes faster than copper. Likewise, no one needs to get **informed consent** from distant stars to track their movements. In contrast, psychologists who plan to publish their research usually need to get the permission of their research participants before studying their behavior. Likewise, no one who studies black holes, or the refraction of light, is required to get permission to do any of the observing necessary to answer these physical questions. But in psychology, **Institutional Review Boards (IRBs)** exist to make sure psychological scientists think carefully about participants' rights (and their own responsibilities) before conducting research on people. IRBs are committees of experts who evaluate whether a proposed study clears a series of ethical hurdles that must all be cleared before the researcher gets permission to carry out the study. Thus, before Jalen conducts his lab experiment on exposure to violent video games and aggression, he must run every detail of his experimental procedures before an IRB to be sure he is not putting his participants at any kind of undue psychological risk. If the experts who sit on an IRB are doing their job properly, they will make sure, for example, that Jalen protected his participants from any psychological harm. Further, because almost all research poses at least minor risks to research participants (e.g., embarrassment, boredom, paper cuts) ethical researchers must follow the **risk-benefit rule** when designing and carrying out research. The risk benefit rule states that if there are any meaningful risks at all to the participants who take part in research, there must be some potential benefits to society to offset those risks (e.g., a decrease in violence, an increase in healthy behavior).

A complete review of all the ethnical rules one must follow when conducting psychological research is beyond the scope of this text. If you wish to familiarize yourself with some of the details of ethnical rules for conducting psychological research, there are many good sources. The most recent version of the ethical principles of the American Psychological Association are available at www.apa.org/ethics/. The National Institutes of Health (NIH) also has a detailed set of ethical guidelines one must follow to receive NIH funding for proposed research. NIH also provides a useful tutorial on their ethics procedures, which you can find at http://www.nihtraining.com/ohsrsite/faq.html. Finally, the NIH also provides an excellent summary of the history behind the famous Belmont

Report, which led to the passage of the National Research Act in 1974. For a summary of this landmark report see http://ohsr.od.nih.gov/guidelines/belmont.html.

Assuming a researcher has cleared all the hurdles required to carry out ethical research on people, the researcher is left with a big challenge. Researchers almost always wish to uncover the true causes of human experience, and this is a trickier business than you might think. Likewise, they want their research to reveal truths – to tell us things that we didn't already know. In short, psychological scientists want their discoveries to be informative. As it turns out, there are just two basic ways in which research can be informative. Research can be informative because it maximizes **internal validity** (information about whether one variable is truly the cause of another) or because it maximizes **external validity** (information about how well a research finding applies to the real world). This module offers a set of basic insights about how to be sure research is high in internal validity. The module that follows (Module 4) tackles external validity. So let's dive right in. How can anyone show that one variable causes another?

Three Requirements for Establishing Causality

With very few exceptions, psychologists conduct research hoping to uncover the *causes* of human behavior. Another way to put this is that psychological scientists almost always test hypotheses – and the theories from which the hypotheses were generated. In psychology, **theories** are formal ideas about the causes of human experience. **Hypotheses** are specific predictions about observable events, and they are usually derived from one or more theories. For example, one theory of aggression posits that frustration causes anger, which then leads to aggression. One hypothesis that might be derived from this theory is that if children are forbidden from playing with a highly desirable toy (creating frustration and anger), they will become more likely to behave aggressively toward other children they encounter (e.g., by pushing and shoving them). The words "causes" and "leads to" in the theory and the "if-then" wording of the hypothesis indicate that both the theory and the hypothesis are all about understanding causes. So how, exactly, do scientists of any stripe or persuasion uncover causes? To answer this question, we need to go back to psychology's origins in philosophy.

Covariation

Most researchers who wish to understand causality rely heavily on the logical framework proposed by the British philosopher John Stuart Mill. If we may simplify Mill a bit, he proposed five methods that can be distilled down to three basic requirements for establishing that one thing causes another (Mill, 2002/1863, and see Copi, 1978, for a modern treatment of the five original methods). The first of Mill's requirements, **covariation**, is probably the easiest. For one variable to cause another, Mill argued, changes in one variable must correspond with changes in the other. As an example, many people strongly believe that the hormone testosterone causes aggression. However, a problem with this argument is that there is surprisingly little evidence that increasing a person's testosterone levels increases that person's tendency to behave aggressively. If testosterone levels don't covary with aggression, it's pretty hard to argue that testosterone levels cause aggression. By the way, for our purposes, covariation means exactly the same thing as *correlation* – which may be more familiar to you than covariation. Both terms have to do with whether two variables are systematically related. If the variables rise and fall together – or if one variable reliably increases as the other variable decreases, then they are correlated (they covary).

Getting back to our testosterone example, recent research suggests that even though testosterone may not automatically foster aggression, high levels of testosterone *are* associated with a desire for competition and social status. That argument seems much safer than the argument that testosterone directly leads to aggression (Boksem et al., 2013). Along similar lines, because there is a very clear correlation (because there is *covariation*) between biological sex and aggression, researchers spend a lot of time debating exactly which aspects of being male (e.g., hormonal aspects or cultural aspects) are responsible for the fact that men are about ten times more likely than women to commit highly aggressive acts such as murder. If there were no covariation between gender and aggression in the first place, no one would debate the exact sense in which being male causes people to be aggressive.

Consider the hypothetical examples of covariation (or the lack thereof) illustrated in Figure 3.1. The figure on the left shows that cigarette smokers die younger than non-smokers. To generate these hypothetical data, we used the best current medical projections of total lifespan for a 65-year-old married, well-educated Latina (left chart) and a 65-year old married, well-educated White man (right chart). Consistent with numerous past studies of longevity, assume that a large-scale study showed that Latina non-smokers who made it to the age of 65 lived much longer than Latina smokers who also made it to the age of 65. Smoking clearly covaries with (i.e., is correlated with) longevity. In contrast, a person's retirement status at age 65 has nothing whatsoever to do with longevity. Apparently, there is no net effect of retiring at roughly the age at which most Americans retire. Because there is covariation between smoking status and longevity, there is a real possibility that smoking reduces longevity (it kills you before your time). But because there is no covariation between retirement status at age 65 and longevity, it is hard to argue that retirement status at this particular age has an impact on longevity. To experiment with the real research tool that generated these hypothetical longevity findings, go to: https://www.blueprintincome.com/tools/life-expectancy-calculator-how-long-will-i-live/.

No one can easily make a claim about causation in the absence of covariation. Put simply, if one thing causes another, they must be correlated in some way. But covariation

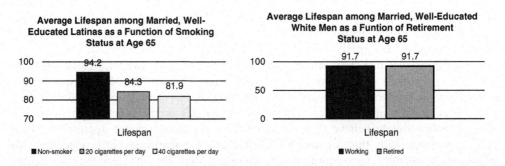

Figure 3.1 There is covariation between smoking status and lifespan but no covariation between retirement status and longevity.

by itself is not enough to establish causality. Consider divorce and distress. They certainly covary. And it might seem obvious that distress causes divorce. People get divorced because they are *unhappy*; don't they? Probably, but divorce itself can also cause distress (Ambert, 2009). Education and income covary, and education almost certainly increases income. But income surely facilitates education as well. A nice, well-educated guy like John Stuart Mill was probably financially comfortable and happily married, but he knew very well that covariation by itself is only one piece of the puzzle of understanding causality.

Temporal Sequence

Mill's second requirement for understanding what caused what is **temporal sequence**. To argue that changes in one variable cause changes in a second, one must be able to show that the changes in the first variable *preceded* the changes in the second. This is not always easy. For instance, researchers often measure a wide range of variables *at the same time* to see if different variables covary with one another. With this kind of **passive observational research design**, it's usually impossible to establish temporal sequence. We just can't tell what caused what. For this reason, researchers sometimes measure variables over time, that is, they use **prospective designs.** In prospective studies, *which measure all the variables of interest on at least two occasions*, researchers can see if changes in one variable truly precede changes in a second. Longitudinal studies qualify as prospective designs, for example. Unfortunately, prospective research is both expensive and time consuming. For this reason, very few studies in psychology are prospective. For every prospective study ever carried out there are surely dozens if not hundreds of **cross-sectional**, passive observational studies. The cross-sectional part means that everything was measured just once. The passive part means that there was *no experimental manipulation.* This leaves us unsure of temporal sequence, even when there is clear covariation. Thus, if we cannot be sure that A *preceded* B, we cannot be sure that A caused B.

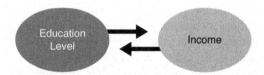

Figure 3.2 Even when two variables are highly correlated (when there's covariation), it can be hard to know which variable causes which. In the case of income and education, causality almost certainly runs in both directions. This is often called the problem of reverse causality. Maybe A causes B. Maybe B causes A. Or maybe both things happen.

Eliminating Confounds

Sometimes covariation and temporal sequence are *both* obvious, even in a passive observational design. For example, in their research on implicit egotism, Pelham and Carvallo (2015) showed that men disproportionately work in careers that match their surnames. To name just a few examples, Bakers, Carpenters, Masons, and Painters, and Porters do, in fact, gravitate toward the jobs that bear their names. Notice that there is covariation. Names and occupations go hand in hand at levels that exceed chance matching. There is also good knowledge of temporal sequence. No one decides to change his name to Carpenter after deciding to work as a carpenter. But even in this case, there's still a potential problem. Researchers can't be sure they've established causality unless they also fulfill John Stuart Mill's third requirement. This third requirement is eliminating **confounds**. This means we must systematically rule out all the *competing causes* of an outcome that happen to covary with the cause we *think* we've identified. Do men behave more aggressively than women (a) because of evolved, biological sex differences, or (b) because of socialization?

To better appreciate confounds, let's look at one that's easier to resolve. As national levels of ice cream sales increase, national homicide rates also increase. Do ice cream sales cause murders? Should we outlaw the production and distribution of ice cream? Surely not. It seems likely that both ice cream sales and homicide rates are influenced by a third variable, namely *seasonal temperature variation*. When it's hot out, people buy more ice cream. In addition, when it's hot out, people become more easily frustrated. Frustration is known to be a strong predictor of violence, including murder. The problem of confounds is also known as the **third-variable problem**, by the way. In this case the *third* variable – besides (1) ice cream sales and (2) murder rates – is (3) heat. Heat causes changes in both ice cream sales and murder rates, and so the two variables covary with one another – and give the *false appearance* of a causal relation. It's hard to overstate how big a problem the third variable problem is if you don't take careful steps to rule it out. The biggest part of this big problem is that the list of potential confounds in passive observational research is very long. For example, critics of field research on temperature and violence have argued that temperature may not truly influence homicide. During the warmer months of the year (when murder rates are higher) people may (1) drink more alcohol, (2) socialize more, or (3) get out of doors more often. All these third variables (or should we say fourth, fifth and sixth variables?) are likely to be **confounded** with temperature. Any of these **confounds** could be the real reason there is seasonal variation in homicides.

The only way to establish a clear causal connection between temperature and homicide would be to successfully eliminate these other confounds as possible explanations. Further, things are often even worse than this example suggests because environmental confounds such as how many people are out and about, or how many people are drinking alcohol at different times of the year are only one category of confound. In many studies, confounds often stem from **individual differences** between people. So, if Dr B. shows that introverts make more money than extroverts, we have to worry that some other individual difference (some other dimension on which people vary) may be the real reason why introverts earn more money than extroverts. Perhaps introverts are wealthier, harder working, more highly educated, or healthier than extroverts. Any of these individual differences (i.e., these confounds) might prove to be the real reason for the correlation between introversion and income. By the way, the list of individual differences is a very long one. People vary in stubbornness, body mass, height, weight, IQ, anxiety, optimism, pessimism, wealth, education level, self-confidence, fear of spiders, liking for ice cream, and interest in cage fighting. The list goes on and on. What's a researcher who is worried about confounds to do?

The Magic of Random Assignment

As it turns out, there's a very good way to eliminate all possible confounds involving individual differences between people. The solution is to create two identical groups of research participants and study them in a true experiment. A **true experiment** is a research design in which the researcher 1) randomly assigns participants to two or more conditions, 2) enacts a manipulation, and 3) assesses whether participants in the different conditions think, feel, or behave differently. The variable that is manipulated in an experiment is called the **independent variable**, and the variable that is measured (under the assumption that it is caused by the independent variable) is called the **dependent variable**. Thus, if you manipulate the temperature of a room in an experiment – expecting temperature to influence aggression – then temperature is your independent variable, and aggression is your dependent variable. Likewise, if you manipulate how symmetrical human faces are, expecting people to like the same faces more when you make them more symmetrical, then symmetry is your independent variable, and liking is your dependent variable. The key to eliminating all possible confounds in a true experiment is using *random assignment*. Random assignment is the methodological magic bullet that allows researchers to get rid of confounds based on individual differences.

In the modern research era, the person who did the most to popularize the use of random assignment in research was R. A. Fisher (1925, 1935). But what, exactly, is random assignment? Using **random assignment** means placing specific people in different conditions in an experiment based on nothing but chance. In psychology, it means that *every participant in an experiment has the same chance as every other participant of being assigned to any condition of the experiment* (Pelham & Blanton, 2019). Common ways of carrying out random assignment include flipping a fair coin or using a random number generator. If you do this for a large enough group, you're virtually guaranteed to create two nearly identical groups. The best thing about random assignment is that it equalizes two or more groups on *practically every dimension imaginable*. This is the magic methodological bullet John Stuart Mill didn't know about. Thus, if you create two groups of people – or frogs, or wart hogs – by using random assignment, you can rest assured that the two groups are identical in age, in sex, and in body mass. And if you happen to be studying people, you can rest assured that the two groups are identical on important psychological variables such as history of aggressive behavior, anxiety, educational background, wealth, or ice cream consumption. In short, Fisher essentially invented the experiment. In the footsteps of Fisher, experimental psychologists refined the experiment to make it a staple of basic psychological research (Aronson & Carlsmith, 1968).

It's worth adding that if you're studying people, rather than plants, there is one other very good way to eliminate individual differences as confounds in research. A second very good way to create two identical research groups is to make each person his or her own standard of comparison. **Within-subjects designs** expose the same group of people to different experimental conditions – to see if the same people think, feel, or behave differently in the two or more (within-subject) treatment conditions. If people behave differently in the different conditions – and if you control for important things such as the order in which people experienced the two different conditions – then you'll have fulfilled all three of John Stuart Mill's conditions for establishing causality. To be clear, all three of Mill's conditions must be met to demonstrate causality. Techniques such as random assignment and within-subjects designs allow researchers to meet these conditions by simply conducting experiments. But what do experiments look like in practice?

Experiments: Fulfilling Mill's Three Requirements

An **experiment** (aka **true experiment**) is a research design in which the researcher randomly assigns people to two or more conditions, treats them differently (i.e., exposes them to different levels of an independent variable), and then carefully measures a psychological consequence of interest (the dependent variable). To see why John Stuart Mill probably would have loved experiments, consider a clever lab experiment by New and German (2015). New and German were interested in whether people are predisposed to detect spiders. After reviewing evidence that venomous spiders used to be a very serious threat to human life and limb, New and German argued that if we're evolutionarily *predisposed* to stay away from spiders, spiders should be "detected, localized, and identified" more readily than other things, including other scary things that have not been around for very long in human evolutionary history. To test their idea, they gave people the task of staring at the center of a circle on a computer screen. People were told that a cross-hair (+) pattern would very briefly appear in the middle of the circle on each of eight trails. Participants had to press a button as quickly as possible to indicate that (a) the horizontal line was longer, (b) the vertical line was longer, or (c) the two lines were equal in length. This judgment task was more difficult than it might seem because a *mask* (a stimulus that competes with what came just before it, for short-term visual storage) replaced the crucial cross-hair image after the cross-hair had been on the screen for just 200 ms (that's 1/5 of a second; see the center column in Figure 3.3).

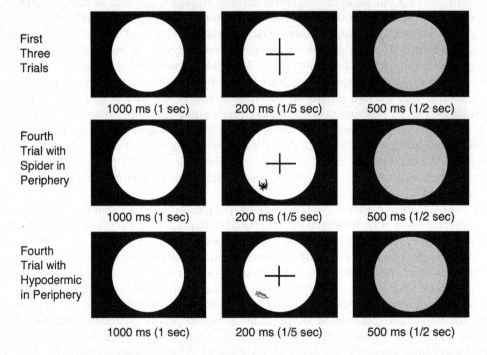

Figure 3.3 A close approximation of New and German's (2015) experimental stimuli. Note that the original unexpected stimuli were probably a little better drawn than these versions (drawn by one of your authors). Sometimes the unexpected stimuli were also presented closer to the center of the cross-hairs, but this distance variable was held constant across different types of stimuli.

After making this judgment for three trials, participants repeated the task for a fourth trial. On this crucial trial, though, they were exposed not just to the circle and cross-hairs but also to an unexpected stimulus – whose location in one of the four quadrants of the circle was determined at random. For *some* randomly-chosen participants the unexpected peripheral stimulus was a *spider* (see the middle row of Figure 3.3). For *other* randomly-chosen participants, the unexpected stimulus was a harmless housefly (not shown). For *still others* the unexpected stimulus was a scary but evolutionarily-irrelevant hypodermic needle (bottom row). Thus, the *independent variable* in this experiment was the type of unexpected peripheral stimulus to which participants were exposed in the fourth trial (spider or hypodermic needle).

Pretest participants reported that the hypodermic needle was just as scary as the spider. But the fear of needles is presumably a fear that's learned rather than hard-wired. (Ancient hominids didn't have controversial things like health care, and so they never got their inoculations.) As soon as participants made the line length judgments for the fourth trial, the experimenter interrupted them and asked them (a) whether they had seen anything at all, other than the expected cross-hairs, (b) in which of the four quadrants any unexpected stimulus had appeared and (c) what that unexpected stimulus might have been. Participants had to choose from eight different stimuli, only one of which was correct. The rate of correct responses to these questions served as the dependent variable in this experiment.

Averaging across two variations on this experiment, more than half (53%) of those who'd been exposed to the unexpected spider were able to detect it *and* locate *and* identify it. In contrast, only 11% of those exposed to an unexpected hypodermic needle were able to pass all three of the same attentional tests. Results for the natural but harmless housefly were much like those for the unnatural but scary hypodermic needle. Only 10% of participants were able to detect, locate, and identify it. Notice that we do not have to worry, for example, that 53% of the participants were able to pass all three visual tests for the spider because they were much more attentive, fearful, or thoughtful than the other participants. *Variables such as attentiveness (a potential confound) should have been identical in all of the randomly assigned experimental groups.* Further, imagine that people happen to see things better than usual when things appear in the upper righthand quadrant of their visual field. That's not a problem either because the experimenters randomly varied the location of all the stimuli. Spiders, houseflies, and hypodermic needles appeared *equally often* in all four quadrants. We hope you can see that experiments allow researchers a great deal of control over possible confounds. In fact, they're the only research design that controls completely for every conceivable confound involving individual differences.

Notice that in addition to eliminating all possible confounds, experiments also take care of both covariation and temporal sequence. If an experiment yields any results (e.g., 53% vs 11% detection rates) this constitutes a clear case of *covariation*. Likewise, in an experiment, researchers are able to control what happens *when*; temporal sequence is always known. But there is bad news as well as good news about experiments. One bit of bad news is that it's not always possible to conduct true experiments in psychology. It's easy to manipulate whether people are exposed to spiders or needles. It's also easy or to make a fake interaction partner smile or frown a lot. But you can't randomly assign people to be male vs. female, or to have had nurturing vs. critical parents. It would obviously be unethical to flip a coin to change someone's parents, to "assign" participants to experience a clinical disorder, or to deprive some children at birth of any exposure to spoken language. When researchers are interested in studying such variables, they must often make use of non-experimental techniques such as surveys, interviews, or other observational research techniques.

To summarize this module, one very important way in which psychological research can be informative is to be high in *internal validity*. When a study is high in internal validity, we can say with great confidence that levels of one variable (the independent variable) cause changes in the level of another variable (the dependent variable). Experiments are the best-known methodological tool for conducting research that is high in internal validity because they are best able to examine covariation, control temporal sequence, and eliminate confounds. But as you may recall, there is a second important way in which research may be informative. A second highly desirable feature of research is external validity. In Module 4, we'll examine the secrets to conducting research (much of it non-experimental research) that is as high as possible in *external* validity.

Questions for Critical Thinking or Group Discussion for Module 3

One of the most important critical thinking skills that separates scientists from non-scientists is the ability to spot **confounds** in empirical claims – including claims based on the results of poorly designed experiments. Another critical thinking skill has to do with thinking carefully about temporal sequence. Both getting rid of all possible confounds and getting temporal sequence right are very difficult – unless you conduct a true experiment. But people often make strong causal claims based on covariation alone – without going to the trouble of conducting a true experiment. This critical thinking will allow you to practice spotting both (a) confounds and (b) problems with temporal sequence in two different data-based claims.

See if you can debunk the claims made below by identifying as many confounds as possible – confounds that could easily be the real reasons for the *covariation* that is described. Then see if you can identify the subtle problems with temporal sequence that may also be at work. If you can do both, you'll surely make John Stuart Mill proud, and maybe increase your grade in your introductory psychology class. Ideally, you'll do this by working in small groups.

1. Long ago, when both of your authors lived in Southern California, a Los Angeles TV station reported the results of a surprising and alarming medical study. The author of the study argued that watching too much TV may be bad for children's hearts as well as their heads. More specifically, a study of TV viewing and blood cholesterol levels revealed that, relative to kids who watched very little TV, kids who watched a lot of TV have especially high cholesterol levels. The news reporter implied that TV watching *in and of itself* increases blood cholesterol levels. We are highly skeptical of this interpretation. Can you come up with some more reasonable explanations for the results of the study? Although confounds are the biggest threat to the interpretation offered by the reporter, don't limit yourself to confounds. Be sure to consider temporal sequence as well.

2. As undergraduates, each of us worked part-time jobs during the school year as well as full-time jobs in the summer. Sometimes we both wished we had more time to devote to our studies – or to having fun. However, a UPS ad that once appeared in student newspapers at more than one college suggests that students should all take on as many part-time jobs as possible. The ad depicts an attractive young woman who claims, "Last quarter, I earned $3,000 and a 3.5." [After adjusting for inflation, that'd be more like $7,000 today.] The ad implies that

being employed by UPS can *improve* one's GPA. Words like "improve" often imply causality, by the way. The ad concluded with: "Think of it – great pay, flexible hours, and maybe even better grades." Although UPS may run the tightest ship in the shipping business, it appears to run one of the loosest ships in the research methods business. What are some of the problems with the claim that working for UPS can improve student grades? By the way, you may assume that the ad's claim of covariation is true. That is, you may generously assume that students who work for UPS get better grades than students who do not work while going to school. This takes care of covariation. But what about confounds? What about temporal sequence?

Multiple-Choice Questions for Module 3

1. Arnelle conducted a large cross-sectional survey on violence in close relationships. Arnelle found that women who said they had grown up poor were much more likely than women who said they grew up wealthy to say that they had been the victims of sexual assault. Based on her research design and her findings, which of John Stuart Mill's three concerns about causality does Arnelle need to worry about?

   A) covariation and confounds
   B) confounds and temporal sequence
   C) covariation and temporal sequence

2. In her survey, Arnelle obtained a highly diverse sample. Further, Arnelle found that, regardless of age, education level, or ethnicity, the link between poverty and self-reported sexual victimization was very strong. For example, it held up separately for Blacks, Whites, Latinas, and Asian-Americans. What kind of validity can Arnelle safely boast about when she writes up her findings for publication?

   A) internal validity
   B) external validity
   C) construct validity

3. IRB stands for Institutional Review Board. What is the role of IRBs in research?

   A) they offer advice about the quality and importance of a research study
   B) they determine whether researchers get grant funding for their research
   C) they review the procedures of a study to be sure the study is ethical

4. Dr. Schooler studies success in first generation college students. Dr. Brand studies consumer blue jean preferences. They both propose studies that put their participants at risk for a small amount of embarrassment. Which ethical principle suggests that Dr. Schooler's proposed study is more ethical than Dr. Brand's?

   A) the risk-benefit rule
   B) informed consent
   C) the prime directive

5. A cosmologist, a historian, and a psychologist walk into a bar. Once they walk out of the bar and go back to work, who is most likely to conduct a true experiment?

   A) the cosmologist
   B) the historian
   C) the psychologist

6. From the perspective of John Stuart Mill's logical analysis of proving causality, what kind of research designs do a good job of establishing temporal sequence?

   A) prospective studies
   B) cross-sectional studies
   C) surveys and interviews

7. What is the technical term John Stuart Mill used to describe the "third variable problem"?

   A) autocorrelation
   B) covariation
   C) confound

8. Dr. J conducted a lab study in which she randomly assigned people to receive either (a) a dose of an over-the-counter pain reliever or (b) a placebo. Thirty minutes later, participants were all ostracized from ("iced out of") a group conversation. Dr. J found that those who had taken the pain reliever reported being less distressed by the negative treatment from the group. What was the design of Dr. J's study?

   A) it was a true experiment
   B) it was an unobtrusive observation
   C) it was a double-blind study
   D) it was a prospective study

9. In Dr. J's study, what was the independent variable?

   A) the delay period between taking the pill and getting rejected
   B) how distressed people reported feeling about being rejected
   C) whether people received a pain reliever or placebo

10. What kind of research design addresses all three of John Stuart Mill's concerns about establishing causality?

   A) a true experiment
   B) a longitudinal study
   C) an unobtrusive observation
   D) an open-ended interview

Answer Key: 1B, 2B, 3C, 4A, 5C, 6A, 7C, 8A, 9C, 10A

References

Ambert, A.-M. (2009). *Divorce: Facts, causes and consequences* (3rd ed.). Toronto, Canada: York University Press.

Aronson, E., & Carlsmith, J. M. (1968). Experimentation in social psychology. In G. Lindzey & E. Aronson (Eds.), *The handbook of social psychology* (pp. 1–78). Reading, MA: Addison-Wesley.

Boksem, M. A. S., Mehta, P. H., Van den Bergh, B., van Son, V., Trautmann, S. T., Roelofs, K., . . . Sanfey, A. G. (2013). Testosterone inhibits trust but promotes reciprocity. *Psychological Science, 24*, 2306–2314.

Copi, I. M. (1978). *Introduction to logic* (5th ed.). New York: McMillan.

Fisher, R. A. (1925). *Statistical methods for research workers.* Edinburgh: Oliver & Boyd.

Fisher, R. A. (1935). *The design of experiments.* Edinburgh: Oliver & Boyd.

Mill, J. S. (2002/1863). *A system of logic.* Honolulu, HI: University Press of the Pacific.

New, J. J., & German, T. C. (2015). Spiders at the cocktail party: An ancestral threat that surmounts inattentional blindness. *Evolution and Human Behavior, 36*, 165–173.

Pelham, B. W., & Blanton, H. (2019). *Conducting research in psychology: Measuring the weight of smoke* (5th ed.). SAGE Publishing.

Pelham, B. W., & Carvallo, M. R. (2015). When Tex and Tess Carpenter build houses in Texas: Moderators of implicit egotism. *Self and Identity, 14*, 692–723.

Module 4
Doing Relevant Science
External Validity and Archival Research

As we hope you recall, there's no better way to see if one psychological variable causes another variable than by conducting an experiment. This is true whether you're trying to figure out (a) if hot temperatures make people more aggressive or (b) if newborn babies prefer to look at "hot" (physically attractive) faces (they do). John Stuart Mill (2002/1863) would be happy to learn that lab experiments have become the gold standard for uncovering the causes of human behavior. Recall that lab experiments are usually high in *internal validity* – which means they're good at establishing covariation and temporal sequence while also eliminating all possible confounds. But a key strength of lab experiments can also be a weakness. Lab experiments are often artificial. They often have to be. Because people behave unnaturally when they know they're being watched, and because people are eager to please authority figures, lab experimenters must often do some highly unusual things to avoid error or bias. There are also ethical limits to what one can do in lab experiments. If Leon is conducting an experiment on the effects of temperature on aggression, he would only be allowed to study minor forms of aggression. Letting people truly harm each other simply is not ethical. Similar issues apply to experiments on interpersonal attraction, helping behavior, or workplace cooperation. Thus, lab experiments must often be artificial.

Limitations such as these mean that lab experiments, though usually high in internal validity, are often low in *external validity*. Recall that external validity refers to *generalizability* to the real world. Pelham (in press) argues that concerns about external validity boil down to four issues. A rule of thumb for remembering these four issues is the OOPS! heuristic. Each letter of the OOPS! heuristic represents a different concern. What are these concerns? After summarizing them, we'll suggest that one clever solution to the problem of external validity is to conduct archival research.

Operationalizations

We can only study things scientifically if we specify **operational definitions** (Pelham & Blanton, 2019). An operational definition takes a variable of interest (something abstract) and converts it to something concrete – in other words, something measurable. Variables are ideas. Operationalizations are measurable activities or physical procedures. A good operational definition of hunger is the number of hours since a person last ate. Another operational definition might be a person's numerical answer to a 7-point self-report scale ranging from 1 ("not at all hungry") to 7 ("extremely hungry"). There are many reasonable ways to operationalize most variables. Consider sexual arousal. In men, a useful operationalization is change in penis size, and it can be measured using a **penile plethysmograph** (a device that measures changes in the volume of the penis – yes, they exist; see Adams, Wright, & Lohr, 1996). But if we wish to study sexual arousal in the other 52% of the Earth's population, plethysmographs are useless. Researchers have thus developed a measure of sexual arousal that works for women as well as men. **Thermographic Stress Analysis (TSA)** involves assessing changes in genital temperature. A thermography camera can detect changes of about one fourteenth of a degree Celsius in a very brief period – in both women and men (Kukkonen, Binik, Amsel, & Carrier, 2010).

The key to operationalizations is this: *the external validity of a research finding grows stronger when the finding holds up well across a wide range of operational definitions.* Consider Pinker's (2010) claim that violence has declined over human history. Pinker's argument is convincing not just because his studies examine real indicators of violence (e.g., murder rates) but also because he gets the same results using *many* different operational definitions of violence, from killing or enslaving people to spanking children, or hurting animals in films. Across many, many operational definitions, violence has declined.

Occasions

"To everything there is a season." Human behavior varies greatly across the day, across seasons, and across millennia. Data collected by the Centers for Disease Control and Prevention (CDC) show that between 1999 and 2017, Americans were 22% more likely to commit suicide on a Monday than on a Saturday. The research tool Google Trends shows that the peak time of day at which Americans search Google for the phrase "happy hour" is 5 p.m. Furthermore, this effect is bigger on Fridays than on Sundays. College students report having sex much more often between 11 p.m. and 1 a.m. than at any other time of day (Refinetti, 2005). People's hormone levels also vary naturally over time. This variation matters. Welling and colleagues (2008) showed that men rated highly feminine female faces to be more attractive than usual on days when the men's testosterone levels were higher than usual.

Expanding the temporal window, both births and deaths vary seasonally. The archival data in Figure 4.1 show that Americans more often die in winter than in summer (despite higher accident rates in the summer; Rozar, 2012). The pattern is clearly *seasonal* rather than calendrical. The pattern disappears at the equator and is reversed in the Southern hemisphere. Marriage rates, too, vary over the course of the year. June is the most popular month for American weddings whereas January is, by far, the least popular month. Americans are less than half as likely to marry in January as in June. With all those funerals in January, who has time for a wedding?

Time also matters century by century. Two thousand years ago, Romans died more often in summer than in winter (because of summer diseases such as malaria; Scheidel, 2009). At that time, the entire population of the Earth was smaller than the current population of Indonesia. Turn the clock back to 10,000 years ago, and the Earth's human population was smaller than the current population of Chicago. Time matters. When evaluating any research finding, we must ask if that finding would hold true at other times. Time is particularly important in developmental and evolutionary psychology. What cognitive skills do most toddlers possess that most infants do not? How have hominids changed over the past million years? Such questions are inherently temporal. But even basic questions such as how often adults

Figure 4.1 Percentage of Yearly Deaths Occurring by Month in the U.S. vs. Australia and New Zealand, 1990–2010, Adjusted for the Number of Days in A Month.

Note. U.S. Data were harvested from the Social Security Death Index (SSDI). Australia and New Zealand data were harvested from the Australia and New Zealand "Find a Grave Index." Both archival data sources were accessed at ancestry.com.

stereotype others depend on time. "Night owls," for example, are more likely than usual to stereotype other people early in the morning (Bodenhausen, 1990). In a nutshell, then, *the external validity of a research finding grows stronger when the finding holds up well across a wide range of occasions – across, hours, days, weeks, seasons, decades, or millennia.*

Populations

Few research findings apply to every imaginable population. People have better color vision than dogs do; dogs can smell things people can barely imagine. European magpies recognize themselves in mirrors, but most other birds do not (Prior, Schwarz, & Gunturkun, 2008). Chimps are more sexually promiscuous than people or gorillas. Even if we limit ourselves to people, the validity of a specific research finding can vary dramatically with populations. Research findings may vary between athletes and non-athletes, between Democrats and Republicans, and between Chileans and Peruvians. For example, nuns and rednecks may differ radically in their attitudes about guns. And if you're offended by the first author's use of the term *redneck*, let him remind you that other populations would not be offended at all. This includes your first author, his six redneck siblings, and his 29 redneck cousins, some of whom have reclaimed the name. On further reflection, your first author suspects that his cousin Billie Sue (who is both beautiful and ingenious, by the way) might be offended to be called a redneck. Mea culpa, cousin. Moving to a less controversial example, the likelihood that people have perfect pitch varies based on whether they speak a tonal language (such as Chinese) or a non-tonal language (such as English; Monroe, 2004). Populations matter. *The external validity of a research finding grows stronger when the finding holds up well across a wide range of populations.*

Situations

Research takes place in a specific context, and context can influence what researchers observe. The way people think varies with the way in which an experimenter dresses. When experimenters dress casually, people seem to *think* casually (i.e., intuitively; see Simon et al., 1997). When experimenters dress more formally, participants are more likely to obey them (Bickman, 1974). It is a central tenet of social psychology that the specific situations in which people find themselves (e.g., a synagogue vs. a singles bar) have a huge impact on how people think, feel, and behave. To know how robust a research finding is, you need to know how well it holds up in a wide variety of situations. *The external validity of a research finding grows stronger when the finding holds up well across a wide range of situations.*

So, now you have each of the four key dimensions of external validity – operationalizations, occasions, populations, and situations – the OOPS! heuristic. Unfortunately, it's tough to conduct lab experiments that do well on all four of these dimensions. You can vary your operational definition of aggression, but you can't study real murders in the lab. You can vary the time of day when you run your experiments, but you can't see what you would have found 50 years ago. In principle, we could study very diverse populations in the lab, but the reality is that most lab experiments make use of **convenience samples** (samples of people who are handy, usually college students). Finally, there is only so much we can do to make people forget that they are in the lab. Laboratories are highly specific situations.

Archival Research and External Validity

What's a researcher to do? There are many solutions to the challenge of maximizing external validity, but perhaps one of the most underappreciated is conducting **archival research**. Archival research uses pre-existing records to test psychological theories. This includes a very wide range of records. To list only a few types, archival research includes research based on marriage or divorce records, crime records, incarceration rates, birth or death records, Google search volume records, recorded TV shows, secondary analyses of published psychological reports, and records of sporting events such as World Series baseball games. Speaking of baseball, baseball great Yogi Berra argued that, "You can observe a lot by just watching." Archival research, then, is research in which the keepers of public records have already done a lot of the watching for you. Through the lens of several examples, we will examine the methodological promises of archival research – in light of both (a) John Stuart Mill's rules for assessing internal validity (i.e., causality) and (b) the OOPS! heuristic for assessing external validity.

False Consensus

For more than 40 years, laboratory researchers have been studying the **false consensus effect** (Ross, Greene, & House, 1977). This is the tendency for people to overestimate the percentage of others who share their beliefs or behaviors. Many, many lab studies have replicated this bias – which has both motivational and cognitive origins. When we believe something, we are motivated to believe that others share our opinion because it validates us to think that others agree with us. From a cognitive perspective, this bias also exists because we tend to hang out with people similar to us. So we are frequently exposed to other people that think and act like we do. We seem to forget that those who are handy are not always like those who populate the rest of the Earth. Thus, for both motivational and cognitive reasons, we often fall prey to the aptly named "false consensus effect." We often believe that there is more consensus (agreement) for our beliefs and behavior than is really the case. Why else would Homer Simpson's neighbor Ned Flanders have opened his "Leftorium" – a store that only sells products designed for left-handed people?

Brian Mullen (1983) wanted to see if the false consensus effect would still appear when avoiding it could help people win thousands of dollars in cash and prizes. Mullen also suspected (correctly) that the false consensus effect is larger for people whose attitudes or behavior place them in the statistical minority rather than the majority. To study the false consensus effect, Mullen harvested data from a TV game show ("Play the Percentages"). The key data points provided by game show participants were their estimates of the percentage of studio audience members who would be able to answer specific trivia questions (e.g., "What state did Hubert Humphrey represent in Congress?") Back when people still remembered Hubert Humphrey, 72% of audience members were able to answer correctly that Humphrey represented Minnesota.

Mullen observed strong evidence of the false consensus effect. Participants overestimated the percentage of others who knew the answers to questions when they *themselves* had known the answers to the questions. Second, false consensus effects were larger than usual when people's own answers placed them in the statistical minority. The rare people who knew the answer to a difficult question were especially likely to overestimate the percentage of others who shared their unusual knowledge. This was all true even when people were trying very hard to guess correctly the percentage of audience members who did or did not know something. Offering incorrect estimates of what the studio audience members knew in this gameshow cost many of these contestants a lot of money.

Mullen documented a false consensus effect with a slightly different **operational definition** than the one usually used in the lab, with a novel **population**, and in a very different **situation** than the lab, satisfying three of the four OOPS! criteria. Further, it is hard to imagine any confounds could apply to Mullen's archival study that would not also apply to laboratory studies of this egocentric bias. For example, suppose more highly educated participants knew the answers to more of the trivia questions. If this were true, there is no reason to believe that being educated *in and of itself* would make people offer higher *consensus* estimates – or that this confound would happen in game shows but not in laboratories. Gender, too, seems like an unlikely confound. Even if the questions were biased to be easier for men than for women, for example, there is no reason to think that men generally overestimate the percentage of others who know a lot about trivia. In our view, Mullen's archival study of a gameshow is a big winner when it comes to both internal and external validity.

Counterfactual Thinking and Emotions

Another classic study using archival methods focused on competition among athletes rather than trivia lovers. Medvec, Madey, and Gilovich (1995) studied the consequences of **counterfactual thinking** in Olympians. A common example of counterfactual thinking is "if only …" statements in which an event happens and we then imagine how it could have happened differently (i.e., *counter* to *fact*). For instance, imagine that you try a different route to work in the morning and you get stuck in a terrible traffic jam. If you're like the rest of us, you'll think something like, "If only I had taken my regular route to work, I'd be enjoying a cup of coffee at my desk – instead of sitting in this horrible traffic." Prior to Medvec et al.'s archival study of counterfactual thinking, lab experiments on counterfactual thinking had already shown that when something good or bad happens, people often consider counterfactual alternatives. Further, research had already shown that considering counterfactuals sometimes creates counterintuitive emotions. For example, missing a flight by two hours usually produces regret. But missing a flight by two minutes usually produces a lot *more* regret (Roese, 1997). This is because it's so easy to imagine ways you could have made up those two minutes ("If only I hadn't gone back for my beloved psychology textbook, I'd have made my flight.").

When Medvec and colleagues conducted their archival studies of counterfactual thinking and emotions among Olympians, most lab experiments were using hypothetical scenarios ("How would you feel if ...?") rather than real outcomes. Medvec and colleagues put the factual into the study of counterfactuals. They did so by considering the emotional implications of earning a gold, silver, or bronze Olympic medal. Most Olympic gold medalists must be on top of the world. At a bare minimum they end up on top of the medal stand – and their gold medals often bring them fame and fortune. By contrast, many silver medalists may feel the pain of knowing how close they came to winning. For bronze medalists, however, *two* things would have to had gone differently for them to have won gold (e.g., Usain *and* Justin). The most salient counterfactual for bronze medalists is that they could have easily finished in fourth place, earning no Olympic medal at all. This logic suggests, counterintuitively enough, that athletes might be happier with an inferior outcome (a bronze medal) than with a superior one (a silver medal)!

To test this idea, Medvec et al. recorded NBC's televised coverage of the 1992 Olympics. They then extracted every scene that showed a bronze or silver medalist (in any sport NBC covered) the moment the athletes learned they had finished second or third. They did the same thing for the period when athletes stood on the medal stand. Finally, they showed all these video clips to raters who were kept blind not only to Medvec et al.'s predictions but also to athletes' order of finish. They also turned the volume down for all of the ratings so that raters wouldn't be biased by the comments of the NBC sports analysts, especially Bob Costas. Raters judged each athlete's expressed happiness on a 10-point scale.

Medvec and colleagues found that, despite finishing third rather than second, Olympic bronze medalists looked *happier* than their slightly faster, stronger, and more coordinated peers. This was true both immediately after their performances and as they stood on the Olympic medal stand – often many hours later. Of course, these results alone do not say whether *counterfactual thinking* was responsible for the observed emotions. To address this, Medvec et al. performed some additional archival analyses. This time they selected all of the available *interviews* with bronze and silver medalists and asked blind raters to judge the "extent to which the athletes seemed preoccupied with thoughts of how they did perform vs. how they almost performed." This follow up study suggested that bronze medalists were more focused on what they "at least" did whereas silver medalists were focused on what they "almost did." To be more confident of this interpretation, Medvec conducted a follow up study and replicated their findings among athletes taking part in the New York State Empire Games.

Medvec and colleagues were diligent about addressing confounds. For example, one confound is that in *some* Olympic events (e.g., wrestling, basketball), bronze medalists have just *won* a competition whereas silver medalists have just *lost* a competition. That's a potential problem (especially for the immediate reactions). But in a supplemental analysis, Medvec et al. focused solely on events (e.g., track and field, swimming) in which there was no such confound. The bronze medalists *still* looked happier than the silver medalists. In short, these researchers went to great pains to maximize internal validity. This archival research is also a standout when it comes to external validity. Consider the OOPS! heuristic. This work used novel operationalizations, it examined behavior that took place on different occasions, the participants came from all over the globe, and the situation in which people were studied was as real as it gets. We'd say the authors of this study struck methodological gold, which is apparently way, way better than methodological silver. This clever archival research suggests that counterfactual thinking matters in the real world.

Of course, the bad news is that all of these Olympic medalists are going to die, if they haven't already. Everybody dies. Because dying is so important, there are lots of archival death records. How's that for a smooth transition to the next example? Remember the archival study of seasonality in death rates? Archival studies of death are an important supplement to laboratory studies in health psychology because health psychologists have argued that people's personal beliefs influence their susceptibility to illness. Yet, for obvious reasons, one can't expose people to cancer or diabetes to see if positive attitudes help them pull through. But archival research can approximate this otherwise impossible study. Let's look at two telling examples of attitudes and longevity.

The Nuns Study

To see if viewing the world favorably helps people live longer Danner, Snowdon, and Friesen (2001) studied 180 nuns. Around 1930, when these women became nuns, they had to write a brief autobiography – which the Catholic Church dutifully retained. In the late 1990s, Danner and colleagues got permission to analyze these archival records. The research team blindly coded each young nun's life story for how many positive emotions it included. It's pretty easy to judge the frequency of positive emotion words in these essays. One sister wrote "With God's grace, I intend to do my best …" Another sister wrote "I look forward with eager joy to … a life of union with Love Divine."

Nuns in the top quartile (top 25%) for the use of positive emotion words in their life stories lived 9.4 years longer than those in the bottom quartile. This is clearly covariation. Further this "time machine" design addresses temporal sequence. First nuns wrote the essays, and then (much later) they died. Further, the research team was able to control for quite a few confounds. For example, they controlled for the age at which women wrote their essays and their eventual education levels. We also suspect that the lifestyle most nuns lead minimized a lot of other possible confounds. For example, we're guessing that few, if any, of the nuns died because of a lack of food or medical care. Because these were nuns, gender was also held constant.

The Baseball Players Study

Any nun with a decent sense of humor will tell you that she tries to fulfill her calling in life by saving souls and making sacrifices – all while having to wear a funny outfit.

Baseball players also care deeply about saving and sacrificing, and they, too, wear funny outfits. Like nuns, baseball players also appear to live longer when they express more positive emotions. Baseball players don't have to write autobiographies to play in the majors, but they do have to get their pictures taken. Abel and Kruger (2010) took advantage of this by conducting an archival study of professional baseball players whose photos appeared in the 1952 *Baseball Register*. They blindly rated all 230 of the official player photos for how happy the players looked. Photos in which the men were not smiling were given the lowest score, photos in which the men were smiling a polite but unnatural smile got a middle score, and those in which the men expressed a truly happy ("Duchenne") smile got the highest score.

Abel and Kruger reasoned that these photos would reflect a player's characteristic emotional state. Apparently, they did. When Abel and Kruger published their report in 2009, the vast majority of these men had died, and Abel and Kruger extracted these dates of death from archival sources. The men who showed a true smile lived seven years longer (mean age 79.9) than the men who did not smile at all (age 72.9). The men who smiled politely (mean age 75.0) also lived a bit longer than the non-smilers. These longevity differences held up even after controlling for a hefty list of competing predictors of longevity (e.g., body mass index, education, marital status, length of playing career).

The fact that Abel and Kruger used player photos from 1952 means that they came very close to controlling for ethnicity. In 1952, 94.4% of professional baseball players were White – with the remaining 5.6% being split evenly between Blacks and Latinos. On average, Blacks do not live as long as Whites do, but Latinos live a bit *longer* than Whites. For ethnicity to be a serious confound, then, almost all the Blacks would have to be looking solemn and almost all the Latinos would have to be happily smiling. It's thus unlikely that an ethnic confound could be responsible for their findings. Further, if a critic were still worried about this confound, it would be easy to code the 230 photos for ethnicity and add this variable to a statistical analysis. Finally, just as the nun study controlled for gender by studying only women, this study controlled for gender by studying only men. Taken together with the nun study, this archival study of real world behavior is clearly worth smiling about. And taken together with hundreds of other archival studies, on topics as diverse as birth, gender, marriage, divorce, altruism, and murder, we can say that archival research often represents a clever solution to the difficult problem of balancing internal and external validity.

Putting everything together, this module presents a methodological heuristic for evaluating the **external validity** of empirical research findings. The OOPS! heuristic involves four specific ways in which a set of research results might fail to generalize. The results might be different with different *operationalizations*, on different *occasions* (at different times), with different *populations*, and in different *situations* (e.g., formal vs. informal settings). Notice that after suggesting that **archival research** can allow researchers to maximize both internal and external validity, we analyzed three different archival studies that did just that.

Questions for Critical Thinking and Group Discussion for Module 4

Most methodologists argue that there is a trade-off between internal and external validity in psychological research. Along these lines, they argue that experiments tend to be very high in internal validity (information about causality) but are often low in external validity (generalizability to the real world). Conversely, archival studies and interviews often score well in external validity, but they may get much lower marks when it comes to internal validity (due to confounds or concerns about reverse causality). But some methodologists have argued that – if one is willing to put in some very hard work – there is no reason why experiments have to be low in external validity.

Part 1: A good example of a research program that supports this point is research on the **mere exposure effect** – the tendency to prefer things to which one has been frequently exposed (Zajonc, 1968, 2001). One of the first demonstrations of mere exposure (Zajonc, 1968) was the finding that the more often college students were exposed to fake Turkish adjectives (e.g., "zabulon") the more they later reported *liking* the fake adjectives. Consider the list of 12 empirical findings on the mere exposure effect listed as follows and place the letter from each finding into the category of OOPS! to which the specific finding is most relevant (the OOPS! concern that the finding best addresses). Notice that each aspect of OOPS! will be the answer three times.

Enhanced Preferences Based on Repeated Exposure Apply

A. to geometric shapes, fake Chinese ideograms, and foreign language words
B. to lab studies conducted across a period of more than five decades
C. in laboratory settings as well as in telephone interviews
D. to preferences assessed at home, at work, and in college psychology labs
E. when the study is conducted in a classroom as well as when it is conducted at an art museum
F. to Japanese quail, turkeys, and ravens
G. to guppies and other fish species
H. to liking for musical tones, yearbook photos, paintings, and colors
I. in archival studies of real-world choices that occurred over a range of more than 100 years
J. to macaque monkeys, rhesus monkeys, college students in France, and American senior citizens
K. to foods and drinks of many different kinds
L. to preferences assessed in the morning, around midday, and in the evening

Operationalizations	Occasions	Populations	Situations

Part 2: Find out what a *natural experiment* is and explain why this unusual research design could allow a researcher to conduct a study that is very high in both internal and external validity.

Multiple-Choice Questions for Module 4

1. Psychologists who submit their work for scientific publication describe exactly how they converted their theoretical variables (e.g., "anger," "attraction") into things that can be measured objectively. This conversion process is known as:

   A) operational definitions
   B) scientific validation
   C) conceptualization

2. The OOPS! heuristic is a set of dimensions on which one can evaluate whether a study or research program is high in:

   A) internal validity
   B) external validity
   C) experimental validity

3. Which of the following is a component of the OOPS! heuristic?

   A) seriation
   B) problem sets
   C) occasions

4. If Dr. Juniper routinely uses thermographic stress analysis (TSA) in her research, you can be pretty sure that Dr. Juniper studies:

   A) health psychology
   B) human sexuality
   C) security threats

5. By using TSA techniques on women as well as men (rather than using techniques that only work for men), Dr. Kukkonen has greatly increased what kind of validity in her research?

   A) internal validity
   B) external validity
   C) construct validity

6. Cross-cultural psychologists have argued that throughout much of the history of psychological research, researchers have focused too heavily on people in WEIRD cultures. WEIRD stands for Western, Educated, Industrialized, Rich, and Democratic cultures. About what aspect of the OOPS! heuristic are such cross-cultural researchers most likely to be concerned?

   A) operations
   B) sampling techniques
   C) populations

7. Jonah absolutely loves skiing. When asked to estimate the percentage of students at his school who have ever been snow skiing, Jonah guessed that the percentage is 80%. At Jonah's school, the actual percentage is closer to 30%. What judgmental error or bias does Jonah seem to have committed?

   A) the overconfidence bias
   B) counterfactual thinking
   C) the false consensus effect

8. Does the use of convenience samples pose a big threat to internal validity, external validity, or both?

   A) internal validity
   B) external validity
   C) both internal and external validity

9. Jon conducted a study of the effects of heat on aggression, but he ran his study at a Buddhist temple. This choice of a religious site made people highly reluctant to behave aggressively. Which aspect of the OOPS! heuristic may help explain why Jason is not seeing an association between heat and aggression?

   A) populations
   B) operationalizations
   C) situations

10. According to your text, the "Nuns study" conducted in Baltimore and Milwaukee did a good job of controlling for a lot of confounds because:

    A) Nuns generally have adequate nutrition and health care, and they typically live safe, predictable lives.
    B) Nuns worship routinely unless they are ill; thus, their total time spent worshipping was held constant.
    C) Nuns cannot marry, and thus all nuns had almost no chance of becoming pregnant or getting an STD.

Answer Key: 1A, 2B, 3C, 4B, 5B, 6C, 7C, 8B, 9C, 10A

References

Abel, E. L., & Kruger, M. L. (2010). Smile intensity in photographs predicts longevity. *Psychological Science, 21*, 542–544.

Adams, H. E., Wright, L. W., & Lohr, B. A. (1996). Is homophobia associated with homosexual arousal? *Journal of Abnormal Psychology, 105*, 440–445.

Bickman, I. (1974). The social power of a uniform. *Journal of Applied Social Psychology, 4*, 47–61.

Bodenhausen, G. Y. (1990). Stereotypes as judgmental heuristics: Evidence of circadian variations in discrimination. *Psychological Science, 1*, 319–322.

Danner, D. D., Snowdon, D. A., & Friesen, W. V. (2001). Positive emotions in early life and longevity: Findings from the nun study. *Journal of Personality and Social Psychology, 80*, 804–813.

Kukkonen, T., Binik, Y., Amsel, R., & Carrier, S. (2010). An evaluation of the validity of thermography as a physiological measure of sexual arousal in a nonuniversity adult sample. *Archives of Sexual Behavior, 39*, 861–873.

Medvec, V. H., Madey, S. F., & Gilovich, T. (1995). When less is more: Counterfactual thinking and satisfaction among Olympic medalists. *Journal of Personality and Social Psychology, 69*, 603–610.

Mill, J. S. (2002/1863). *A system of logic.* Honolulu, HI: University Press of the Pacific.

Monroe, D. (2004, November 9). Speaking tonal languages promotes perfect pitch. *Scientific American.* Retrieved December 22, 2018 from www.scientificamerican.com

Mullen, B. (1983). Egocentric bias in estimates of consensus. *The Journal of Social Psychology, 121*, 31–38.

Pelham, B.W. (in press). Data to die for: Archival research methods. Chapter to appear in H. Blanton (ed.) *Social Psychological Assessment.* Psychology Press.

Pelham, B. W., & Blanton, H. (2019). *Conducting research in psychology: Measuring the weight of smoke* (5th ed.). Thousand Oaks, CA: SAGE Publishing.

Pinker, S. (2010). *Better angels of our nature: Why violence has declined.* Penguin Books.

Prior, H., Schwarz, A., & Gunturkun, O. (2008). Mirror-induced behavior in the magpie (Pica pica): Evidence of self-recognition. *PLoS Biology, 6*, e202.

Refinetti, R. (2005). Time for sex: Nycthemeral distribution of human sexual behavior. *Journal of Circadian Rhythms, 3.* doi:10.1186/1740-3391-3-4

Roese, N. J. (1997). Counterfactual thinking. *Psychological Bulletin, 121*, 133–148.

Ross, L., Greene, D., & House, P. (1977). The false consensus effect: An egocentric bias in social perception and attribution processes. *Journal of Experimental Social Psychology, 13*, 279–301.

Rozar, T. L. (2012) Impact of seasonality on mortality. *Society of Actuaries Conference*, May 23, 2012. Retrieved from www.rgare.com/knowledgecenter/Pages/MortalitySeasonalityPresentation.aspx

Scheidel, W. (2009). Disease and death in the ancient city of Rome Version 2.0. Working Paper. Retrieved from www.princeton.edu/~pswpc/pdfs/scheidel/040901.pdf

Simon, L., Greenberg, J., Harmon-Jones, E., Solomon, S., Pyszczynski, T., Arndt, J., & Abend, T. (1997). Terror management and cognitive experiential self-theory: Evidence that terror management occurs in the experiential system. *Journal of Personality & Social Psychology, 72*, 1132–1146.

Welling, L. L. M., Jones, B. C., DeBruine, L. M., Smith, F. G., Feinberg, D. R., Little, A. C., & Al-Dujaili, E. A. S. (2008). Men report stronger attraction to femininity in women's faces when their testosterone levels are high. *Hormones and Behavior, 54*, 703–708.

Zajonc, R. B. (1968). Attitudinal effects of mere exposure. *Journal of Personality and Social Psychology, 9*,(Suppl. 2/2), 1–27.

II
The Brain

Module 5
Six Important Features of the Human Brain

Now that you've learned about the history of psychology – and learned a bit about how psychological science is done – you might expect that we'd jump right into some of the topics most people associate with psychology: How do we see, hear and taste? Why are some people more helpful than others? Why do some people develop clinical disorders such as schizophrenia or depression? We will address all of these questions – and then some – in this text. However, before we do so, we feel compelled to introduce you to the three-pound organ that is responsible for almost everything you do and experience. Of course, this organ is the brain. So, before we discuss vision, helpfulness, or schizophrenia, we'll share with you some of the key features of the brain. You could not see at all, for example, if many different areas of your brain did not communicate with one another and share information that your brain weaves into a compelling representation of the world. Likewise, some people have schizophrenia because their brains are different than the brains of people who do not have this clinical disorder. And, yes, research shows very clearly that the brains of extraordinary *altruists* (people who help others at great cost to the self) are measurably different from those of regular people (those who are not extraordinarily helpful).

To put all this a little differently, psychology is very firmly grounded in biology. Not that long ago, many psychological scientists wondered whether the brain and the mind were two separate things (Damasio, 1994; Dennett, 1991). But today the number of psychological scientists who believe there is any aspect of human experience that is not firmly grounded in biology is shrinking by the day (Lieberman, 2013). Every week, neuroscientists uncover the physiological basis of another aspect of human experience. If everything we do is grounded in our brains, then we had best possess at least a basic understanding of the nature and structure of the brain if we wish to appreciate why we do all the things we do. The health psychologist George Everly put this idea succinctly when he said, "To understand the stress response, we must possess a fundamental knowledge not only of psychology but of physiology as well." In this module and the next, we will explore the human brain. This module will focus on six key features of the human brain. The next module will explore the geography and function of most of the basic brain regions.

Your brain appears to be one of the most complex things in the universe. As recently as a few hundred years ago, scientists had virtually no idea how the brain works. Ancient scientists and philosophers debated whether nerves were filled with liquids, strings, or gases. Some otherwise thoughtful people argued that a little person known as a homunculus controlled the human body like a tiny puppeteer. But critics asked who controlled that puppeteer, or that puppeteer's puppeteer. Even today, there is active debate about the nature of the brain, and it remains one of the great frontiers of scientific research and discovery. This is all true precisely because brains are so complex. But due to modern marvels such as the microscope, DNA analysis, and brain imaging techniques such as **fMRI** (functional magnetic resonance imaging – which uses a powerful magnet to detect blood flow to different brain regions), we know quite a few things about the brain. In this module, we'll review just six key features of the brain. Understanding these six key features of the brain should lay a foundation for the deeper dive into the brain that we take in the next module.

Brains are Conservative

This does *not* mean that 63 million U.S. brains voted for Donald Trump, or that your brain is opposed to Obamacare. Instead, it has to do with the fact that brains evolved. Evolution is highly **conservative.** This means that when something works well, it often stays around in the gene pool for millions or even billions of years (Pelham, 2018). The noun form of conservative is *conservation*, and conservation happens outside the brain all the time. Economic and political systems are slow to change. Engineers who have happened upon an engine design that works well are very unlikely to reinvent it completely. Instead, they use variations on the same basic design. A Ford pick-up truck and a Porsche Boxster both rely on the same basic internal combustion engine. The aphorism "If it ain't broke, don't fix it," expresses the essence of conservation. The fact that brains are conservative means that the human brain is a lot more like a rat brain, an insect brain, or even a tiny, brain-like portion of the Venus flytrap than you might think. Venus fly traps are one of about 500 carnivorous plants on Earth, and as you may know, their clam-like traps move very quickly – which is how they catch unwary insects. Our brains also allow us to move very quickly when we need to, and like the very simple neural circuit that is the brain-like portion of the Venus flytrap, our brains rely on a chemical known as acetylcholine to allow us to move.

Focusing on the human brain, acetylcholine is one of about 70 neurotransmitters. **Neurotransmitters** are chemical communicators (chemical messengers) that allow the brain to do

Figure 5.1
The Venus flytrap is one of about 500 carnivorous plant species. The neurotransmitter that allows this flytrap to capture flies – acetylcholine – is the same chemical messenger that allows flies to move their wings – and allows people to swat flies away. Acetylcholine also allowed your authors to type this textbook, and it allows you to walk, talk, and do the dishes. Many other neurotransmitters play important roles in voluntary human movement. But evolution has stuck with this chemical workhorse for millions of years, and across millions of species, because it does its job so well.

everything that it does. Different neurotransmitters have different jobs in the brain, and **acetylcholine** has jobs that include the initiation of movement, attention, learning, and sleep. Focusing solely on the initiation of motor movement, you rely on acetylcholine to play hopscotch, use a fork to eat, sign your name, or walk to class. And you can be sure that a honeybee relies on acetylcholine to take flight or do a waggle dance. Acetylcholine does very much the same job in Venus flytraps, honeybees, ground sloths, and people. Brains (or the simple neural systems that vaguely resemble brains) are highly *conservative*.

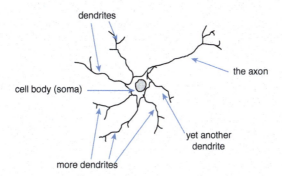

Figure 5.2 The basic structure of neurons is highly similar across all areas of the brain – and across all known animal species. There's always a cell body, one or more dendrites (usually many), and a single axon.

Figure Credit: Brett and Brooklyn Pelham.

Brains are also conservative at the level of the unusual cells that make them up. Like the brain of a finch or a fish, your brain is made up of millions of neurons (aka "nerve cells"). **Neurons** are cells that specialize in sending and receiving signals to one another, and the very large majority of neurons in your body are contained in your brain (though your eyes and your spinal column also contain neurons). Neurons are constantly – and we mean *constantly* – sending and receiving the signals that enable us to function. Figure 5.2 illustrates the fact that the basic structure of all **neurons** is highly conservative. Virtually all neurons in virtually all brains, regardless of species, have **three basic parts**: a **cell body** or *soma*, a single **axon** (an extension for "sending" signals) and one or more **dendrites** (one or more lines of "receiving" input to the neuron). The exact shape of neurons varies dramatically in different parts of the brain, but the three basic structures of the neuron are conserved across areas of the brain and across every species whose brain has ever been put under a microscope.

Brains are also conservative in their gross physical structure and general organization. In all mammals, for example, brains are bilateral (two-sided) and symmetrical, and the more recently evolved areas of the brain in people, monkeys, and mice are nearer the surface. You'll learn more about the basic structure of the brain in the next module. But for now, let us repeat that all vertebrates, from clownfish to circus clowns, have brains made up of two highly symmetrical ("mirror image") halves. This means these brains are all **bilaterally symmetrical** (they are made up of right and left sides that are mirror-images of one another). This highly conserved, two-sided organizational scheme has huge implications for things like handedness and consciousness (Gazzaniga, 2006). In fact, even many *invertebrate* brains (e.g., those of insects) are both bilaterally symmetrical and **lateralized** (specialized so that the different hemispheres of the brain are devoted to somewhat different activities; Frasnelli, 2013). The fact that our brains are divided neatly into two distinct hemispheres takes us to our second key feature of the brain.

Brains are Compartmentalized

Your brain is, by far, the most **compartmentalized** (i.e., segregated, ordered) organ in your body. This means that different parts of your brain usually do very different things. If you have a stroke that seriously damages **Wernicke's area**, you'll be able to speak smoothly and fluidly, but most of what comes out of your mouth will be ungrammatical gobbledygook. Your words will be jumbled, and you'll get them in the wrong order. But you'll say them smoothly, as if you are speaking correctly (e.g., "She were there, with the them over there, and … and the three saw not a speck … usually.") This is true, at least in part, because Wernicke's area is crucial to understanding the meaning of speech sounds. In contrast, if your stroke damages **Broca's area** instead (just a few cm forward on the left side of most right-handed people's brains; see Figure 5.3), you'll be able to understand language, but you'll no longer be able to speak. Unless the brain damage is minimal, no amount of re-training will ever get you back to the way you used to be. This is not an isolated example. If you have a motorcycle accident that damages your hippocampus in just the right way, you'll develop an incurable form of **anterograde amnesia**, and you'll live the rest of your life "forever in the present" (Tulving, 1993). You'll remember who you dated in high school, and you'll still know your grandmother's birthday, but *you'll never be able to form any new memories*. Experience damage to a different area of the brain, and you'll forever lose your ability to recognize human faces, to sense time, to smell, or to initiate voluntary motor movements. If you've heard of Phineas Gage, you know that serious damage to his *prefrontal cortex* (the large area of cortex roughly behind the forehead) left him forever unable to regulate his emotions and evaluate risks. As a final example, get some serious damage to the primitive area of your brain known as the *hindbrain*, and you'll lose the ability to breathe. That one *really* bites. Try to steer clear of that kind of major brain damage.

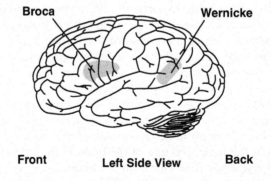

Figure 5.3 A left lateral (side) view of a typical right-handed brain. As you can see here, both Broca's area (crucial to speech production) and Wernicke's area (crucial to both understanding speech and producing grammatical, coherent speech) are in the cortex of the left hemisphere. They're only about two inches apart. They're both crucial speech areas, but they have different jobs.

Your prefrontal cortex can usually help with that. All of this underscores the important ways in which the brain is compartmentalized.

To be fair, we should mention that advocates of **brain plasticity** (the brain's flexibility to recover from injuries – or to adapt to radically new environments) might quibble with our position about just how specialized different brain regions are. For almost a century, we've known that stroke victims (both human and non-human) can sometimes recover from brain injuries (Lashley, 1930). The brain can *sometimes* repair and re-wire itself. In fact, Nudo (2013) argued that in the wake of major brain injuries, the same cascading events that are responsible for human development early in life kick in to help produce brain recovery. Nudo (2013, p. 887) further argued not only that brains are malleable but also that "the injured brain is *particularly* malleable" (emphasis added). Thus, despite the compartmentalized nature of our brains, they still have a surprising capacity for compensation and rewiring. Sometimes one area of the brain may be able to "pick up the slack" if another area of the brain is injured. Having offered this alternate view, we should add that even advocates of brain plasticity recognize that plasticity has its limits. Karl Lashley (1930), an early proponent of plasticity, proposed that the size of a brain injury determines the severity of impairment whereas the location of the injury determines the exact nature of the impairment (e.g., whether one loses vision or the ability to move a specific limb). The reason Phineas Gage did not ever recover from his injury to the prefrontal cortex is that his injury was big – and in just the right place to mess up his emotional regulation.

Brains are Computers

Your brain is not *literally* a computer, of course. But very much like a modern computer, brains have both limited short-term memory and enormous amounts of long-term memory. More important, like a laptop, your brain is a computing device. It constantly calculates. The job of most neurons is to sum up inputs from other neurons. Suppose you are a neuron. Now suppose three other neurons whose dendrites send you signals tell you to fire (to send an electrochemical signal along your axon). Unless a bunch of other *inhibitory* ("don't fire") neurons simultaneously tell you *not* to fire, you will fire. And neural firing is **"all or none,"** by the way. A neuron that receives two "fire" signals and one "don't fire" signal doesn't fire a wimpy, watered-down signal. It just fires at full force. Period. If you're a motor neuron that sends signals to a finger, this firing could help you type a research paper. In contrast, if you're a neuron in the neocortex, firing may help you stereotype someone – which could easily get you fired. To get back to the main point, your brain is a complex decision-making device. It's like the CEO of your body, and it's responsible for virtually everything you do, from loafing to loathing. By the way, most of the communications and calculations your brain engages in lead to activities that occur outside your conscious awareness. Just as we have no idea how our brains help keep our kidneys operating properly, we also have no idea how our brains nudge us into making thousands of everyday decisions. Only a sliver of what our brains do is available for conscious inspection and analysis (Nisbett & Wilson, 1977).

Brains are Communicators

The fact that brains are *compartmentalized computers* virtually guarantees that different brain regions must *communicate* with one another. If you live in one place, and your coworkers live elsewhere, you'll have to communicate with all of them to get anything done that you can't do alone. And your brain can't do much of *anything* alone. It can't even breathe or feed itself, for example. Likewise, if your eyes did not communicate with the areas of your brain that process visual information, your eyes would not allow you to see. Further, if the older and the newer parts of your brain that help you experience emotions did not "talk" to one another, you would not experience meaningful emotions – or be able to run away from danger. It's your brain that tells your legs to run, after all.

The scientists who first studied the brain with the help of things like powerful microscopes and electricity spent a lot of their time trying to figure out exactly how neurons communicate with one another. As researchers improved their techniques for making microscopic images of brain cells – and recording the electrical and chemical *activity* of brain cells – they eventually answered one of the questions that had stumped Cajal when he first took a close look at neighboring neurons. Cajal's careful microscopic observations revealed that neurons *never touch one another*. As shown in the upper-circle of Figure 5.4 (where it says "synapse"), there is always a *synaptic gap* between axons (sending devices) and the dendrites or cell bodies (receiving devices) to which the axons project. The **synaptic gap** is the tiny space between the very end of an axon (the **synaptic bouton**) and the part of a dendrite or cell body that receives messages from that axon. So Cajal knew two things. First, neural activity is at least somewhat electrical. Folks like Luigi Galvani had shown long before Cajal's time that nerves send signals electrically. But Cajal knew, based on his own careful microscopic observations, that nerve cells never quite touch one another. If an axon carries an electrical signal to a receiving cell but does not touch it, how does this electrical signal bridge the gap between the two nerve cells? Try severing the cord that charges your smartphone – even a teeny bit – and seeing how well the electrical charge makes it to the phone.

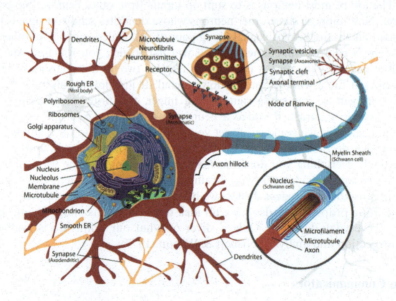

Figure 5.4 A much more detailed view of a neuron than you saw in Figure 5.2. Notice that it is "wired" for communication.

The answer to Cajal's puzzle proved to be neurotransmitters. As you probably recall, neurotransmitters are the brain's chemical messengers. Remember acetylcholine? We'll explore a few other neurotransmitters in more detail later in this module. But for now, the important point about how neurons communicate is that neurotransmitters quickly bridge the tiny synaptic gap between two neurons. This means that chemical messengers released from the axon of a *sending* neuron – into the synaptic gap of course – are quickly picked up and registered by the body or dendrite of a *receiving* neuron. The reason neurotransmitters spill out into the synaptic gap in the first place, by the way, is action potentials. An **action potential** is the all-or-nothing electrical signal that is carried quickly along an axon to produce the release of neurotransmitters at the ends of the axon. If we may be a bit redundant, recall that the basic job of any neuron is to keep tabs on all the chemical signals arriving from any incoming axons. If a certain threshold of excitatory input registers within a certain period, the receiving neuron will send an action potential of its own along its own axon, *communicating* with one or more of the neurons to which *it* sends signals. This chain of communication can get very complicated very quickly. But let us remind you of just one kind of complexity and one kind of simplicity. Recall that one kind of complexity is that neurons may send either *excitatory* or *inhibitory* signals to other neurons. And recall that – as we just noted – one kind of simplicity is that when a neuron does fire, it either fires at full force or does nothing at all. Action potential are always all or nothing. This means that all the subtle things your brain and body do are the result of dozens, hundreds, or even thousands of blended yes and no decisions, made by individual neurons.

So far, we've focused mainly on how one neuron communicates with another neuron. But as implied by the fact that the brain is compartmentalized, neurons are organized into many different functional regions of the brain and nervous system, from small clusters of neurons known as *ganglia* to much larger and more complex brain regions. Remember Broca's area? You may have also heard of the hypothalamus – which regulates things like hunger and thirst. We'll discuss it in some detail in the next module. If you know anyone who has Parkinson's disease, you've probably heard of the substantia nigra, which is a specific area of the brain that plays a crucial role in the initiation of motor movements. In the next module, you'll also learn a great deal about how the two hemispheres of the brain communicate with one another. We'll spare you the details of hemispheric communication for now. But suffice it to say that all the synapses that exist in your brain exist because each area of your brain has to communicate with many other areas of the brain. On top of that, we hope it makes sense that basic senses such as sight, hearing, and smell involve communication. Your optic nerves send visual information from the retina to the brain, and highly specialized receptors in your nasal cavities send olfactory (smell-based) information to different areas of your brain. Finally, you could not move your arms of chew your food if your brain did not communicate (by means of aptly named *motor neurons*) with every part of your body that you can move.

There is probably no single statement that describes brains better than to say that brains are communication machines. In fact, a large portion of the next module in this text describes (a) what happens when the two halves of the brain (the left and right hemispheres) cannot communicate with one another at all and (b) how information must often be relayed through many parts of the brain to produce important experiences such as vision or emotional reactions. In fact, to at least some degree, all the other sections of this module are about communication. For example, all the parts of the brain that are *conserved* – from neurons and neurotransmitters to regions and hemispheres – are involved in communication. Likewise, we hope you'll recall that brains are very much like computers. But computing things and then failing to communicate them to other parts of the brain – or to the body – just wouldn't be useful. Returning to the basic structure of the neuron, notice that the neuron has a cell body – whose main job is computing – and two other basic structures – each of which is a communication device. Dendrites bring information in to the neuron, and axons send information away from it. Brains are communication devices.

Brains Are Complex

All brains are complex, but human brains are *incredibly* complex. As you already know, the many areas of your brain are interconnected in various ways. Further, whereas a Venus flytrap can survive quite well using only the single neurotransmitter **acetylcholine**, your brain uses acetylcholine and about 70 other neurotransmitters. Dopamine and serotonin are two other heavy hitters in this long list of chemical messengers. **Dopamine** helps carry messages that create voluntary motor movements (we can't expect acetylcholine to do everything). Dopamine also helps create feelings of pleasure and sexual arousal. So, when your friend Ren compliments you on your new ride by saying it's "dope," he's saying that your new set of wheels is so awesome that it causes the release of dopamine in the areas of his brain that make him feel pleasure. If anyone you know well has ever suffered from clinical depression, you've probably heard of the neurotransmitter known as **serotonin**. This is because the category of new-generation anti-depressants known as **SSRIs** (selective serotonin reuptake inhibitors; Prozac^{TM} is an example) are serotonin agonists. **Agonists** are chemicals that strengthen or facilitate the activity of specific neurotransmitters. Thus, agonists of serotonin (such as SSRIs) crank up the usual effects of serotonin. Likewise, agonists of dopamine crank up the activity of dopamine. In fact, many of the modern chemical interventions for Parkinson's disease are dopamine agonists – meaning that they help dopamine initiate motor activities despite substantial damage to the substantia nigra.

The process by which many agonists work is also complex. Consider SSRIs. We used to think that SSRIs just make serotonin hang out in the gap between neurons longer than usual (so it has a better chance to do its job). Although that is true, the process by which SSRIs reduce symptoms of clinical depression is more complex than that. Even in the subset of people who benefit a lot from SSRIs, it usually takes about two weeks of continuous medication for SSRIs to begin to reduce the symptoms of depression. This suggests that SSRIs work mainly via a slower route than simply turning up the volume on serotonin. Experts now think that SSRIs reduce symptoms of depression by influencing processes such as **neurogenesis** ("nerve growth") and **long-term potentiation** (changes in how sensitive a neuron is to the signals it receives from another neuron; see Dale et al., 2016; O'Leary & Cryan, 2014). Neurogenesis and long-term potentiation are both more akin to what happens when you grow, learn, and develop than they are to what happens when you take ibuprofen to reduce a headache.

As another example of the complexity of the brain, consider the neurotransmitter **oxytocin** – the so-called "love hormone." This nickname will do in a pinch, but it is an oversimplification. Oxytocin *does* play a role in love. Thus, your levels of oxytocin should increase when your romantic partner hugs you – or looks you in the eyes. Moving on from romantic love to maternal love, oxytocin also plays a key role in labor, delivery, nursing, and mother-infant bonding. In fact, when a wayward mother ewe refuses to nurse her newborn lamb, farmers often give the mom an intranasal dose of oxytocin to get her to fall in love with (i.e., to care for) her new baby (Marsh, 2017). Nursing usually begins very quickly thereafter. In people, however, things are more complicated than these examples suggest. For example, oxytocin has different effects on our memories of our caregivers for people with different *attachment styles* (different beliefs and feelings about how much we can and should depend on, and get close to, others; see Bartz et al., 2010). Oxytocin can also increase fear reactions, even in mice (Guzmán et al., 2013). If you're wondering how the same neurotransmitter can have very different effects in different parts of the brain, welcome to the frustrating world of drug side effects. Very few, if any, neurotransmitters do one and only one job in one and only one area of the brain. This is why many drugs, whether prescribed or recreational, have serious side effects. *SSRIs* can reduce depression, but they also reduce sex drive. Many opiates reduce pain, but they also slow down digestion, which can lead to debilitating constipation. This is almost certainly why Elvis Presley (who was addicted to opiates) died straining on the toilet – rather than sitting comfortably in his lounge chair.

Speaking of opiates, your brain's natural pain killers are also neurotransmitters, and they are known as **endorphins.** As far as we know, these natural painkillers make you elated without ever making you constipated. If you have ever experienced a "runner's high" after a very long bike, swim, or run, you have endorphins to thank for that. If you have ever given birth naturally, you probably know that endorphins can help a lot with labor pains as well. If memorizing all these neurotransmitters feels like labor, by the way, we should tell you that endorphins are "endogenous opiates" (Pathan & Williams, 2012), and the "endogenous" part of that phrase means "coming from *within.*" The powerful painkiller morphine (which shares the "orphin" part of "endorphin") is an "exogenous opiate." It comes from *without,* meaning that Pfizer, Merck, or some other drug manufacturer has produced it. Your brain is also complex when it comes to the basic actions of different neurotransmitters. Whereas most neurotransmitters tell the neurons that receive them to fire, some specific neurotransmitters (e.g., gamma-aminobutyric acid, better known as **GABA**) are **inhibitory**; they tell other neurons *not* to fire. If you've ever heard of the drug Valium, you probably know it calms people down. It is often used to treat clinical levels of anxiety. Valium is a GABA agonist. It works by increasing the activity of GABA (Society for Neuroscience, 2012), which *reduces* the activity of neurons that fuel feelings of anxiety. If your head is spinning after learning about only six neurotransmitters, be thankful that we are skipping about 64 others. And recognize that the fact that there *are* about 64 others is a testament to the complexity of the human brain.

So far, we've argued that the brain is complex by arguing that it uses about 70 neurotransmitters – each of which plays a complex role in basic brain functions. But this is just one sense in which the brain is complex. Perhaps the most obvious way in which human brains are complex has to do with how many tiny parts make them up. Your brain may contain as many as 100 billion (yes billion, with a "b") neurons. It's very hard for our brains to appreciate how many neurons that is. If you increased the size of each neuron in your brain to the size of a grain of sand, it would take about 1.6 cement trucks to hold those 100 billion grains. We don't know about you, but we also have trouble picturing grains of sand. Let's blow up those 100 billion neurons even further – so that each is the size of a ping pong ball. According to our calculations, if you

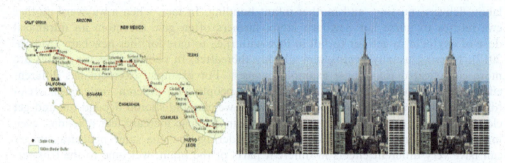

Figure 5.5 Two ways to appreciate how many neurons are in your brain. If you converted each neuron to a stone the size of a ping pong ball, you could fill a wall more than 3,000 km long, more than half a meter thick, and about 3.5 meters high. If you converted each neuron to a regular ping pong ball, you'd need three Empire State Buildings to hold them all.

poured 100 billion ping pong balls onto a standard (160 ft x 300 ft) U.S. football field, you'd have to build a wall a *mile high* to hold them all. If you converted these 100 billion ping pong balls to stone, you could build a wall 11 feet high by two feet thick that would stretch across the entire United States-Mexico border. That's the distance highlighted in the left half of Figure 5.5.

But suppose you have little interest in borders. Suppose you just needed storage space to hold about 100 billion ping pong balls. To do this, you'd need to rent out three Empire State Buildings worth of storage. But the numbers get even bigger. In addition to roughly 100 billion nerve cells, your brain also contains about 100 billion non-neuronal **glial cells** (helper cells that do everything from speeding up nerve transmission to cleaning up dead brain cells; Herculano-Houzel, 2009). If we count the helper cells, then, your brain may contain as many as 200 billion cells. Even more impressive, your brain may contain as many as 150 *trillion* synapses (points of communication between neurons).

Different parts of the brain also differ tremendously in the number of neurons and helper cells they contain. This is important. Many textbooks report that there are ten to 15 times as many helper cells in the brain as neurons. But this estimate of ten to 15 helper cells for every neuron was based on studies of the composition of the thalamus and the ventral palladium, which are deep in the brain. It is only in *these* brain regions that helper cells greatly outnumber neurons. In the parts of your brain that allow you to read this textbook – various parts of the cortex, that is – there are more neurons than helper cells. Averaging everything together, it looks like you have about one helper cell for every neuron. In the human brain, then, it is a lot harder to get good help than we used to think (Herculano-Houzel, 2009).

Brains are Conscious

We argued not long ago that much of the brain's work happens behind the scenes. However, we did *not* argue that *everything* happens behind the scenes. A highly unusual feature of the human brain is the fact that it can become *keenly aware of itself.* Many other animals experience forms of self-consciousness or self-awareness.

Chimps, dolphins, and even European magpies can recognize themselves in mirrors (Prior, Schwarz, & Gunturkun, 2008). But we human beings are *extremely* self-conscious. We even think about our own thought processes. It's called **meta-cognition** – which is thinking about thinking. Sometimes meta-cognition rescues us from blindly doing what others are doing – or doing what we've always done in the past. Identity, self-expression, and many complex forms of learning and problem-solving are all aspects of what most people call the conscious mind. And almost all modern neuroscientists agree that your conscious mind is the product of your complex human brain.

As a final example of both consciousness and meta-cognition, human beings appear to be the only species to use **mnemonics**. Mnemonics are mental tricks people use to help them memorize and learn things. A mnemonic for remembering the six aspects of the human brain emphasized in this essay is "Com Con 6." All six of the brain features emphasized here begin with COM or CON. If you'd like a more specific mnemonic, try "Conservative compartmentalized computers communicate complex cons." Perhaps this gives you hope that you'll be able to master the basics of the conservative, compartmentalized computer that communicates in complex ways and is the source of your consciousness. If so, you can be thankful that you possess a sophisticated brain that can help you (a) steer clear of tigers, (b) learn the Spanish word for tiger (*tigre*), and (c) decide to become a double major in Spanish and zoology. That's an amazing three-pound biological calculator, don't you think?

Hands-on Activity for Module 5

In 1850, 29 years before psychology was born, the 29-year-old Hermann von Helmholtz found a way to measure the speed of nerve transmission. His basic technique was to make a long portion of a freshly severed frog's leg *part of an electrical circuit* and measure how long it took an electric current that began at *one point* in the frog's leg to make it to a *different* point in the frog's leg. We will spare you the technical details of exactly how von Helmholtz did this (see Schmidgen, 2002, if you're an engineering major). But the crucial idea is that von Helmholtz found a way to see how long it took a neural signal to travel from a clear starting point on a nerve to other points along the nerve. Through some pretty simple math and logic ("It took the signal 1/1,000 of a second to go from point A to a spot 3.2 cm beyond point A."), von Helmholtz was able to estimate the speed of nerve transmission in a frog's leg – at least in the exact conditions under which von Helmholtz made his measurements.

Prior to the publication of von Helmholtz's study, most scientists assumed that nerve impulses traveled either *instantly* or much too fast for human measurement. But von Helmholtz's study showed that the speed of nerve transmission was roughly 32 meters per second. That's about three times faster than an Olympic sprinter can run the 100 meters, but it's *not* instantaneous. Your car goes faster than that on the open highway.

In the absence of a freshly severed human arm (and some fancy equipment), you might think it would be impossible to measure the speed of nerve transmission in the human nervous system. But it's not. If you can get your classmates to move around a bit and tap each other on the hand or shoulder, you can approximate von Helmholtz's experiment. Here's how to do so. Stand in a long line next to one another – like the people we've depicted in Figure 5.6. (Well, do so if it is safe to do so.)

Figure 5.6 The top row is the lineup for part 1 of this demonstration. The bottom row is the lineup for part 2.

First, line up exactly like the students in the top row – making sure that your left hand rests solidly on your neighbor's right shoulder. When all of you are ready, your instructor will say, "Ready, Set, Go!" The student at the beginning of the line (the one in the birthday party hat in Figure 5.6) will then *quickly* tap her neighbor on the shoulder while her hand rests there (*without* ever removing her hand from her neighbor's shoulder). Then her neighbor will quickly repeat the tap on *her* neighbor's shoulder. This race against the clock continues across the entire chain. Whoever is at the end of the chain will throw up a hand when she feels the final shoulder tap. Your instructor will time all this and record the time. You all then repeat the exact procedure while *holding hands* (and squeezing) rather than touching and tapping shoulders – as shown in the bottom row of Figure 5.6. To reduce practice effects, we recommend practicing each approach once and then using only the times (one per condition) that you get the second time around. We also recommend that all of the participants stare at the instructor during the activity, so that they cannot look around and see the subtle cues that mean that a tap or a squeeze is coming their way.

1. Compare the two times. Which is faster? Why? Is this what von Helmholtz would have predicted? If you want to be more rigorous, by the way, you should repeat the entire procedure several times, with the order of the conditions determined randomly. If you average the two or more times in the shoulder tapping condition and the two or more times in the hand-squeezing condition, this should help control for any practice effects. If you wanted to be even *more* rigorous, you could set up little stands around the room so that people could *tap the tops of the hands* of their neighbors rather than squeezing their hands. Why would this approach be slightly more rigorous?

By the way, this demonstration works best with a large number of people. In small groups of eight or ten, for example, a single distracted person who forgets to tap or squeeze when it is time to do so can throw things off a lot. In bigger groups, such distractions usually average out.

2. If you wanted to estimate the exact speed of nerve transmission in the human arm, what specific measurements would you need to make to do so? If you have time to do so in class, please take this next empirical step. Here's a clue: wingspan.

Multiple-Choice Questions for Module 5

1. Even insects have brains that are divided into two symmetrical hemispheres – just like those of people. This organizational principle of brain anatomy is a good example of which property of human brains?

   A) the fact that brains are efficient
   B) the fact that brains are conservative
   C) the fact that brains are compatible
   D) the fact that brains incorporate redundancy

2. Assume that a neuron gets input from only three other neurons and that all incoming signals have equal importance. If a neuron gets a signal to fire from two neurons and gets a signal not to fire from one neuron, what is the likely outcome?

   A) because of the "averaging rule," it will fire a weaker than average signal.
   B) because of the "all-or-none" rule, it will fire.
   C) because of the "veto rule," it will not fire.
   D) because of the "competition rule" it will fire a stronger than usual signal

3. About how many neurons are in the typical human brain?

   A) 10 million
   B) 100 million
   C) 10 billion
   D) 100 billion

4. What's the difference between a fiddle and a violin?

   A) about three hundred dollars ☺

5. Are there more neurons or more "helper cells" in a human brain?

   A) there are many more neurons
   B) there is a roughly equal number of neurons and helper cells
   C) there are many more helper cells

6. Which neurotransmitters play the role of the brain's natural painkillers?

   A) acetylcholine
   B) dopamine
   C) endorphins

7. If there is a very large amount of damage to the *substantia nigra* (a portion of the midbrain), a person will develop Parkinson's disease, which leaves people unable to initiate motor movements. No other brain region appears to be able to compensate for this damage and perform the functions of the *substantia nigra*. This finding is consistent with what basic feature of the human brain?

   A) compartmentalization
   B) conservation
   C) complexity

8. A neuron walks into a bar. The other patrons at the bar notice that the neuron has a cell body and several dendrites. Unless there is something badly wrong with the neuron, it is safe to assume that the neuron has at least one other basic structure shared by all neurons. What is it?

   A) microglia
   B) a Schwann cell
   C) an axon
   D) a synaptic fissure

9. Which of the five basic features of the brain discussed in your text is most consistent with the fact that all the neurons in the human brain share a very similar basic design?

   A) conservation
   B) intelligent design
   C) compartmentalization

10. As far as we know for sure, the human brain is the only object in the universe that studies its own function and microscopic structure. This is highly consistent with the idea that human brains possess what feature?

    A) they are complex
    B) they are insightful
    C) they are conscious

Answer Key: 1B, 2B, 3D, 4A, 5B, 6C, 7A, 8C, 9A, 10C

References

Bartz, J. A., Zaki, J., Ochsner, K. N., Bolger, N., Kolevzon, A., Ludwig, N., & Lydon, J. E. (2010). Effects of oxytocin on recollections of maternal care and closeness. *Proceedings of the National Academy of Sciences of the United States of America, 107*(50), 21371–21375. doi:10.1073/pnas.1012669107

Dale, E., Pehrson, A. L., Jeyarajah, T., Li, Y., Leiser, S. C., Smagin, G., ... Sanchez, C. (2016). Effects of serotonin in the hippocampus: How SSRIs and multimodal antidepressants might regulate pyramidal cell function. *CNS Spectrums, 21*(2), 143–161. doi:10.1017/S1092852915000425

Damasio, A. R. (1994). *Descartes' error.* New York: Avon Books.

Dennett, D. C. (1991). *Consciousness explained.* Boston: Little, Brown.

Frasnelli, E. (2013). Brain and behavioral lateralization in invertebrates. *Frontiers in Psychology, 4,* 939. doi:10.3389/fpsyg.2013.00939

Gazzaniga, M. S. (2006). Forty-five years of split-brain research and still going strong. *Nature Reviews Neuroscience, 6,* 653–659.

Guzmán, Y. F., Tronson, N. C., Jovasevic, V., Sato, K., Guedea, A. L., Mizukami, H., ... Radulovic, J. (2013). Fear-enhancing effects of septal oxytocin receptors. *Nature Neuroscience.* doi:10.1038/nn.3465

Herculano-Houzel, S. (2009). The human brain in numbers: A linearly scaled-up primate brain. *Frontiers in Human Neuroscience, 3,* 31. doi:10.3389/neuro.09.031.2009

Lashley, K. S. (1930). Basic neural mechanisms in behavior. *Physiological Review, 37,* 1–24.

Lieberman, M.D. (2013). *Social: Why our brains are wired to connect.* New York, NY: Broadway Books.

Marsh, A. (2017). *The fear factor: How one emotion connects altruists, psychopaths, & everyone in between.* New York: Basic Books.

Nisbett, R. E., & Wilson, T. D. (1977). Telling more than we can know: Verbal reports on mental processes. *Psychological Review, 84,* 231–259.

Nudo, R. J. (2013). Recovery after brain injury: Mechanisms and principles. *Frontiers in Human Neuroscience, 7,* 887. doi:10.3389/fnhum.2013.00887

O'Leary, O. F., & Cryan, J. F. (2014). A ventral view on antidepressant action: Roles for adult hippocampal neurogenesis along the dorsoventral axis. *Trends in Pharmacological Science, 35*(12), 675–687.

Pathan, H., & Williams, J. (2012). Basic opioid pharmacology: An update. *British Journal of Pain, 6* (1), 11–16. doi:10.1177/2049463712438493

Pelham, B. W. (2018). *Evolutionary psychology: Genes, environments, and time.* London, UK: Palgrave-MacMillan.

Prior, H., Schwarz, A., & Gunturkun, O. (2008). Mirror-induced behavior in the magpie (Pica pica): Evidence of self-recognition. *PLoS Biology, 6,* e202.

Schmidgen, H. (2002). Of frogs and men: The origins of psychophysiological time experiments, 1850–1865. *Endeavour, 26*(4), 142–148.

Society for Neuroscience. (2012). *Brain facts: A primer on the brain and nervous system* (7th ed.). Washington, DC: Author.

Tulving, E. (1993). Self-knowledge of an amnesic individual is represented abstractly. In T. K. Srull & R. S. Wyer, Jr. (Eds.), *The mental representation of trait and autobiographical knowledge about the self: Advances in social cognition* (Vol. 5, pp. 147–156). Hillsdale, NJ: Erlbaum.

Module 6
The Structure and Function of Key Brain Regions

Hemispheres: Your Two Brains

Let's begin with one of the most basic aspects of the structure of the human brain. It's the fact that, like all other vertebrates, people essentially possess not one but two separate brains. The typical, healthy human brain consists of two separate **hemispheres** – that is, two separated lateral halves. These two (left and right) halves of the brain are roughly mirror images of one another. Both of the images shown in Figure 6.1 reveal that the human brain has a left and a right hemisphere. Even the cerebellum that sits just behind the brainstem has a right and left hemisphere. Once we acknowledge that the brain is divided into two physically separate hemispheres, we must ask how the two halves of the brain communicate with one another. The answer is highlighted by the red portions of the center and right hand brain images in Figure 6.1 (especially the right-hand image). The two halves of the vertebrate brain are connected by the millions of nerve fibers that make up the **corpus callosum**. Without your corpus callosum, you really would have two separate brains that did not communicate with one another at all.

Before you can appreciate the implications of a brain composed of two separate hemispheres, you first need to know that the vertebrate brain – ours included – is wired to the body in an unexpected way. For both sensory systems and motor systems, the right half of your brain is connected to the left half of your body, and the left half of your brain is connected to the right half of your body. And yet most people can still do the Hokey Pokey. This strange "cross-over" neural wiring system is known as **decussation**, and it applies to all vertebrates from fish and reptiles to birds and mammals. It is crucial to know about decussation because it means that visual information that enters your right eye is projected to the left half of your brain. Likewise, poking your left foot with a needle activates sensory areas in your right hemisphere. This is why stroke victims who suffer brain damage to the left hemisphere may lose the ability to move a right arm or a right leg but never a left arm or left leg (Kinsbourne, 2013). Decussation is also very important because of lateralization. **Lateralization** refers to the fact that the different hemispheres of most people's brains are responsible for somewhat different functions. As you may recall from Module 5, for the very large majority of right-handed people – and for a smaller majority of left-handed people as well – the areas of the brain that are devoted to processing and producing speech (including Broca's area and Wernicke's area) are located in the left hemisphere. For example, a brain imaging study of more than 300 healthy adults showed that 94% of strongly right-handed people processed language mainly in the left hemisphere. Among strongly left-handed

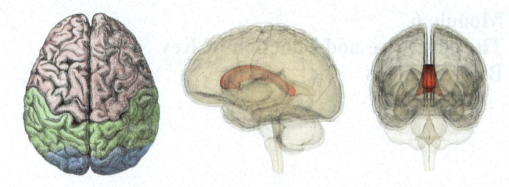

Figure 6.1 The human brain, like that of all other vertebrates, is made up of two separate hemi-spheres. They communicate by means of the millions of fibers that make up the corpus callosum (shown in red in the center and right hand image).

people, a much lower 73% of people (but still a clear majority) processed language mainly in the left hemisphere (Knecht et al., 2000).

Lateralization is real, and it has many behavioral and emotional implications. But most of these implications are subtler and more complex than many pop psychologists have led the public to believe. For example, it is incorrect to say that some people are "right-brain people." We are *all* both right- and left-brain people. Exactly what does lateralization mean, then? To begin to answer this question, consider Alan and Jake, depicted in Figure 6.2. Which of these two very similar guys looks happier? If you said it's Alan, there's a good chance your brain is lateralized in a pretty typical fashion. Because of lateralization, most of our brains process information about the facial expression of emotions mainly in the right hemisphere. Because of visual decussation (because your left eye sends a signal to your right hemisphere), this means that if you follow the typical lateralization pattern for emotion, the information coming in from your left eye will have emotional priority over the information coming in from your right eye. Notice that Alan is smiling from the part of his face that you'll mainly see with your left eye – which will send that information to your *right* (emotional) hemi-sphere. One way in which neuroscientists test for lateralization (in the absence of extremely expensive imaging equipment such as fMRI) is by giving research participants many mirror-images of faces like those of Alan and Jake on a computer and seeing how often (and how quickly) people judge faces like Alan's to look happier than faces like Jake's (Bourne, 2008). If your right hemisphere is more heavily loaded than your left with emotion-processing modules, this will have measurable consequences. Inciden-tally, faces such as those of Alan and Jake are known as **chimeric faces** (pronounced "Kim-Eric Fay-says") because they are a blend of each of two different half-faces. As you'll soon see, chimeric images are a very useful tool for studying brain lateralization.

Another consequence of laterality when it comes to emotions has to do with how we *express* rather than *decode* them. Check out the two happy men in the left half of Figure 6.3. Which man looks happier? Most people say the man on the left does. Now check out the two men in the right half of Figure 6.3. Who looks angrier? Most people say the man on the left does. Is the guy on the left just more emotionally expressive? Sort of. The man on the left is always a left-left composite of a single photo whereas

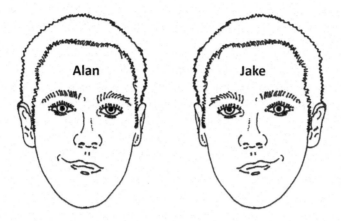

Figure 6.2 Which face looks happier? This may tell you something about which half of your brain
is more heavily devoted to processing emotional facial expressions. Sketch by B. Pelham,
adapted from Bourne (2008).

the man on the right is always a right-right composite of the *same* photo. So the left-
left composite face consists of the left half of the man's face (*his* left, that is) along with
a mirror image of that *same* left half. Research shows that most people express emotions more intensely with the side of the face that is wired to the more emotionally
astute (usually right) hemisphere. Because of decussation (again, cross-over wiring) this
means that most people are more emotionally expressive on the left half of their faces
(Okubo, Ishikawa, & Kobayashi, 2013).

We hasten to add that people differ both in the strength of lateralization and in the
specific side of the brain that is more heavily responsible for different functions. We
should further add that not everything about the brain is lateralized. Further, lateralization is rarely all or none. For example, the right amygdala plays a more important role
than the left amygdala in reactions to expressions of fear expressed by others. But
everyone does, in fact, possess both a right and a left amygdala. Likewise, if you are
right-handed, this does not mean you cannot use your left hand at all. It just means
you have more fine-motor control with your right hand than with your left. So, in most

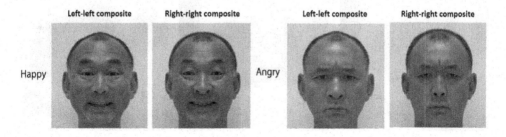

Figure 6.3 Who looks happier? Who looks angrier? These are left-left and right-right mirror image
composites of the two halves of the same person's face. But because of emotional lateralization, the two different composites do not usually express identical amounts of happiness or anger (Okubo et al., 2013).

people, lateralization is a subtle but important fact of neural wiring. Researchers once believed that only human beings possessed highly lateralized brains. But a review by Lindell (2013) revealed that, at least where emotions are concerned, brain lateralization exists in non-human primates such as macaque monkeys, baboons, and chimps. Lindell argued that lateralization is probably highly adaptive in that, like most other forms of specialization, it promotes survival. For example, baboons who are sizing up a potential opponent in a fight pay special attention to the expressions that emanate from the left of a rival's face (Lindell, 2013). Just as it may be useful to be right- or left-handed, it may be useful to be, let's say, right- or left- "emotioned."

An indirect argument for the idea that forms of neural specialization (such as lateralization of speech and emotions) are adaptive is that the form of specialization known as dominance is very pervasive. Handedness, as you now know, is only modestly associated with the lateralization of speech. But handedness is very common. Very few people are truly ambidextrous. In addition to differing in handedness, people also differ in footedness, eyed-ness and, yes, even eared-ness. We haven't yet looked into "nosed-ness" or "tongued-ness." If you want to identify your **dominant eye**, there's an easy test. Just make a "finger-scope" opening with one of your hands. Following the example in Figure 6.4, use this opening to spot a distant object such as a clock or a street sign. Use both eyes, and be sure to keep your "finger-scope" as far away from your face as possible. Now keep looking at your target through this opening but close your left eye. Did anything change? If it did *not*, you're probably right eye dominant. To be sure, look at your original target again with both eyes. Now close your *right* eye. If you have now lost the object, you're right-eye dominant. Reverse the outcomes, and you're left eye dominant. Most people also have a dominant ear, and this is not just a matter of having better hearing in one ear. If you want to assess the ear dominance of a friend, just face her head on – without moving your own head. Tell her you want to whisper something to her. She'll probably reveal an unconscious preference by presenting one ear to you, complete with a cupped hand behind it (Marzoli & Tommasi, 2009). The appropriate thing to whisper is something like: "*Thanks*! Now I know which of your ears is dominant."

Figure 6.4 To see which of your eyes is dominant, use both eyes (1) and spot a distant image through a "finger-scope." Without moving your hand, close only your left eye (2). Then close only your right eye (3). The eye that gives you the same vantage point as *both* eyes is your dominant eye. In this simulated case, the right eye was dominant.

Back to Lateralization and Hemisphericity

Getting back to the point that we all possess two physically separate brains, one way in which we know that the two different halves of the brain do different things is by studying the highly unusual people whose right and left cerebral hemispheres do not communicate with one another. These people are known as *split brain patients*. Decades ago, surgeons learned that they could sometimes stop dangerous epileptic seizures in patients by surgically severing the corpus callosum. Such **split-brain patients** possess two independently operating brains, each of which, as you know, is usually responsible for different jobs. Recall that in most right-handed people (split-brain patients included), the left hemisphere is mainly responsible for speech and language. In experiments with split-brain patients, one can send a picture directly to the nonverbal right hemisphere to get patients to do something. For example, a patient might be asked to point to or pick up any object of her choice while being shown a picture of an object that goes only to her nonverbal right hemisphere. (This is done by showing the crucial image only to the *left* eye.) When asked why she pointed to or picked up a shovel rather than a thimble, for example, the split-brain patient will rely on her verbal left hemisphere and confidently make up a fake reason – without knowing that the picture sent to her nonverbal right hemisphere is the real reason for her "decision" (Volz & Gazzaniga, 2017).

A classic study we'll call the **"eye-bee-rose" experiment** used chimeric familiar objects to show that the right and left hemispheres perform different jobs. Levy, Trevarthen, and Sperry (1972) exposed four split-brain participants to chimeric eye-bee-rose

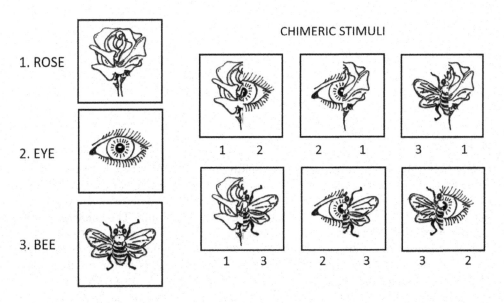

Figure 6.5 A close approximation of the familiar stimuli (left) and their chimeric composites (right) used by Levy et al. (1972) in their study of split-brain participants. When participants were asked what they saw, those who saw the image labeled "2 3" (eye-bee) usually reported "a bee" – because the half-bee went to the verbal left hemisphere. But when flashed the same chimeric image and asked to point to the object they saw with their left hand, split brain participants almost always pointed to the eye. This was true for all of the images. Drawings by B. Pelham.

combinations – to see how the patients described them verbally vs. what they pointed to with their left hands (the hand controlled by their nonverbal right hemispheres). By the way, in their daily lives, people with split brains can just move their eyes around to see both halves of any image they wish to examine. But in the lab, it's easy to control and keep track of exactly where people are looking. Under such conditions, Levy and colleagues flashed up centered chimeric images so briefly (a little less than 1/6 of a second) that they could be sure the different halves of the chimeric images went to the separate hemispheres. When asked to report what they had seen, participants usually reported the image that went to the verbal left hemisphere. But when asked to point with their left hands (controlled by the nonverbal right hemisphere) to what they had seen, participants almost always pointed to whatever had been seen by their nonverbal right hemispheres. In short, the brain's right and left hemispheres have somewhat different jobs, and careful experiments on people whose hemispheres can't talk to one another have revealed the somewhat different functions of our two separate brains.

From Hemispheres to Regions

In addition to being split laterally (left to right), the human brain is also divided in less obvious ways into three major regions – and the most complex of these three regions (the forebrain) includes the cortex which is itself divided into four lobes. Each lobe of the cortex is responsible for different functions, each of which we will get to pretty soon. For now, let's focus on the three main regions of the brain. The easiest way to think of the three regions is that we can divide up the brain using a rough, bottom to top approach. From this perspective, there is (a) a low and evolutionarily ancient hindbrain, (b) a small central midbrain that controls somewhat more complex functions, and (c) an evolutionarily newer forebrain that includes all the regions of the cortex responsible for things like language, planning, reasoning, and self-awareness. The forebrain is also responsible for higher-order calculations and decisions about sensory information such as visual, auditory, and tactile information. But let's begin our summary of the three regions with the oldest – the hindbrain.

The Hindbrain

It might help you to remember where the hindbrain is to remember that the hindbrain is both *beneath* and *behind* the part of your brain you probably picture when you think about a brain – just as your behind (i.e., your butt) is beneath and behind everything in your body but your legs. Figure 6.6 illustrates the hindbrain. The **hindbrain** is the ancient region of the brain that blends into the top of your spinal cord. In fact, as Schacter et al. (2011, p. 96) put it, it is "difficult to determine where your spinal cord ends and where your [hind]brain begins." One of the basic jobs of the hindbrain is to direct all the neurological traffic that is coming in and out of the spinal cord. An even more important job, one could argue, is to regulate breathing and cardiovascular activity (e.g., blood circulation). The part of the hindbrain known as the *reticular formation* is a major part of the biological thermostat that makes you go to sleep when you've been awake too long and wakes you up when you've been asleep too long. One of the ancient rules the reticular formation follows is that you should usually sleep when it is dark and be awake in the daytime. In fact, one of the worst things you can do to mess up your sleep patterns is to go to sleep having left the lights on (Albrecht, 1988).

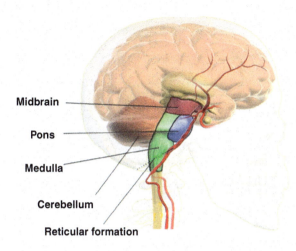

Midbrain

Pons

Medulla

Cerebellum

Reticular formation

Figure 6.6
Some of the key structures in the hind-brain and the midbrain. Taken together, the hindbrain and midbrain make up the *brain stem*. The evolutionarily-ancient human brainstem strongly resembles that of other mammals. It keeps us alive, but all by itself it doesn't make things very interesting. Image adapted from one by Bruce Blaus.

We should also note that the hindbrain includes the **cerebellum.** Fittingly, enough, this is Latin for "little brain." Despite being pretty small, the cerebellum contains roughly half of the neurons in your entire brain. It was once believed that the cerebellum was exclusively devoted to helping us smoothly carry out complex motor movements such as moving our limbs, grasping objects, bowling, riding a bike, or throwing rotten vegetables at a psychology professor. Although this is all true, recent research shows that the cerebellum is much more, well, *cerebral* than we once thought. At a minimum, the cerebellum plays an important role in certain aspects of language, emotion, and memory. In fact, the cerebellum shows the same kind of lateralization for language seen in the much larger cerebral cortex. It also seems to play an important role in attention (Buckner, 2013). This "little brain" plays a much bigger role in our mental and emotional life than we once believed (Schmahmann, 2019).

Moving on to the **midbrain**, this second major division of the brain is by far the smallest of the three divisions. As shown in Figure 6.6, the human midbrain is the tiny area in red. In reptiles, for example, the midbrain is a much larger portion of the total brain. In both people and reptiles, the midbrain is crucial to movement, arousal, and attention to abrupt changes in the environment. If someone startles you by popping a paper bag behind you, setting off firecrackers, or screaming and throwing rotten vegetables at you, you can thank (or blame) your midbrain for quickly turning and orienting your entire body to the source of the loud surprise. Taken together, the hindbrain and midbrain make up the *brain stem*. Although these regions help keep us alive, our experiences as humans would be a *lot* less interesting without the third division of the brain, the forebrain.

The Forebrain and Its Subcortical Structures

The forebrain is the largest and most complex of the three divisions of the human brain. It sits atop both the hindbrain and the midbrain, much like a *fore*st of tall trees sits atop the brush, grasses, and bushes that make up the forest floor. As you can see in Figure 6.7, the **forebrain** is what most people think about when they think about the human brain, and it fills the large majority of the skull. But the forebrain is typically divided into what's on the outside and what's on the inside. The left half of Figure 6.7 begins with the outside. Every-thing above the brainstem is the **cerebral cortex** whose many bumpy *gyri* ("hilltops" or

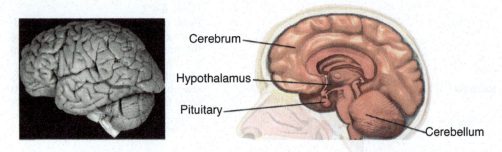

Figure 6.7 The two divisions of the forebrain. Left is the outer cerebral cortex, which is the home to a lot of "grey matter." Right is a small number of deeper subcortical ("beneath the cortex") structures.

"plateaus") and *sulci* ("canyons") set the human brain apart from simpler and smaller primate brains. We'll come back to the cerebral cortex soon. As shown in the right half of Figure 6.7, the other part of the forebrain is the complex collection of **subcortical structures** (structures "beneath the cortex") that play a crucial role in processes as diverse as "fight or flight," the formation of memories, the recognition of fear in the faces of others, and the regulation of sex and eating. For example, the **hypothalamus** is a subcortical structure deep in the brain that neuroscientists say is associated with "the four Fs" of basic biological regulation. The "four Fs of the hypothalamus" are feeding, fighting, fleeing, and mating. To focus on feeding, making lesions (i.e., causing damage) to one part of the hypothalamus in rats will cause them to stop eating altogether and starve. Create the lesions in a slightly different part of the hypothalamus, and rats become insatiable eating machines who, if food is freely available, will triple their normal body weight.

A quick consideration of two other subcortical structures should give you a sense of how important the deep, interior portions of the cerebral hemispheres are. Below the hypothalamus, deep in the center of the cerebrum, is a tiny, pea-sized structure known as the **pituitary gland**. Known as the "master gland," the pituitary gland works closely with the hypothalamus to control most of the hormone-producing systems in your body. Throughout your childhood, your pituitary gland also controlled the release of growth hormones that dictated whether you became 5'7" or 7'5". In fact, when a pituitary problem causes the pituitary gland to kick into overdrive in childhood, the result is *pathological giantism*. According to the Guinness Book of World Records, the tallest woman ever measured, Zeng Jinlian, suffered from such a form of giantism, and she grew to be 8'1" tall. Her parents and her brother were closer to 5'3" tall. Zeng Jinlian probably would have gotten taller than her final height of 8'1." But like many other extreme giants, she died very young – in her case, a few months short of her 18th birthday. In people *without* any pituitary gland malfunctions, the pituitary gland plays a crucial role in such regulatory activities as stress reactions, digestion, birth, nursing, and sexual behavior.

Another very important deep subcortical structure is the hippocampus. If you check out Figure 6.8, it should help you remember how the hippocampus got its name. Hippocampus is Latin for "seahorse." The **hippocampus** is crucial to the formation of new memories. For example, if your hippocampus were badly damaged, you would never be able to learn that hippocampus is the Latin word for *seahorse*. In fact, if a stroke or surgery destroys the hippocampus completely, the person without a hippocampus can

Figure 6.8 This side by side comparison of the human hippocampus and a seahorse should help you remember that *hippocampus* is the Latin word for seahorse. If you prefer to think of the hippocampus as an ugly letter C, that works, too. Either way, you'll need your hippocampus to commit such information to long-term conscious memory. Image courtesy of Laszlo Seress and Anthony Cole.

never commit new facts (semantic memories) or conscious experiences (episodic memories) to long-term memory. Patients with such hippocampal injuries live "forever in the present" (Thompson & Zola, 2003). Those without a hippocampus still have intact short-term memories. But the moment something slips out of short-term memory, it is gone forever. This means, for example, that a person without a hippocampus could meet Jimena, chat with her, learn that she grew up very near their own hometown, and briefly hold her name in short term memory. But if Jimena left the room and returned ten minutes later, the hippocampus-free person would believe he was meeting Jimena for the first time. And this could go on many times a day for years. Memories are stored in a complex, distributed fashion all over the brain. But *creating* long-term memories for new facts and experiences requires an intact hippocampus (Schacter, 1996).

The Cerebral Cortex

The outside of the cerebral cortex is the part you can easily see if you've ever been handed a human brain in a jar (as each of us has). This large, complex, wrinkly structure allows you to do all kinds of complicated things, from planning a wedding or learning a second language to identifying a common object by touch – or creating a three-dimensional visual map of a room using only a photo. In this short module, we'll only have time to delve very briefly into the four main **lobes** (four functionally separate divisions) of the cerebral cortex. To reduce the strain on your cortex a bit, you can relate the four lobes of the cortex in at least a rough way to the four directions on a map, remembering that in this particular map, the west is overrepresented a bit. (Blame the Californians if you like. Both your authors lived in California in the nervous '90s.) Figure 6.9 contains a pair of drawings of the four lobes of the cortex, one of which connects each lobe to one of the four geospatial directions – North, South, East, and West.

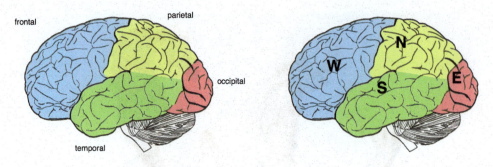

Figure 6.9 The four major lobes of the cerebral cortex.

The Interconnectedness of the Four Lobes

Dividing something as complex as the cerebral cortex into just four sections is an obvious oversimplification. These four lobes all blend neatly into one another, they communicate with one another continuously, and some important brain structures lie in the borders or grey zones between different lobes. For example, consider the two speech areas you may recall from Module 5. Broca's area is in a portion of the frontal (west) lobe that borders the temporal (south) lobe, and Wernicke's area is in the part of the temporal (south) lobe that borders the parietal (north) lobe. Further, notice that these two crucial speech areas are in different lobes even though you obviously need them both to be a fluent speaker. Further, each of these two speech areas is much more highly developed in whatever hemisphere is mainly responsible for language. OK; things are complicated. But having acknowledged this complexity, we can still explore the four lobes and highlight the different functions they serve.

The Parietal Lobes

Among other things, the **parietal** lobes are responsible for your sense of touch. In fact, the mostly-vertical (north-south) strip of the parietal lobe that borders the frontal lobes is known as the **somatosensory cortex** ("body-sensing cortex"), and it has a predictable layout and structure. First, your left parietal lobe processes all the tactile ("touch") information it gets from the skin, teeth, tongue, and throat on the *right* half of your body. More interestingly, the size of the different portions of the somatosensory cortex correspond very well to the level of tactile sensitivity of different parts of your body. The part of the somatosensory cortex that allows you to feel your lips is much larger than the part that allows you to feel your big toe, and the part that allows you to feel your feet (big toe included) is much larger than the part that allows you to feel your back. At the British Museum of Natural History there is a sculpture of the **somatosensory homunculus**. This sensory "little man," does a great job of representing how much of the somatosensory cortex is devoted to different parts of the body (see Figure 6.10). He tells you part of the reason why you'll almost always feel an insect that lands on your fingers or lips but might not notice it at all if the insect lands on your back or your calf. Presumably, mosquitos everywhere study up on the somatosensory homunculus in bite school.

Figure 6.10
This naked man may look like he wants a hand-out, but he's actually trying to give you a hand. This somatosensory homunculus was sculpted to help you understand part of the parietal lobe – by showing how much of your somatosensory cortex is devoted to your sense of touch in different parts of your body. Whereas your hands, lips, and tongue are very sensitive to touch, your back, butt, and ankles are not nearly so sensitive. This is partly due to how your parietal lobe is wired. Photo by Mpj29, based on a sculpture at the British Museum of Natural History.

The Temporal Lobes

Let's now move south to the temporal lobes, the lobes that sit roughly at the bottom center of each of the two hemispheres. The temporal lobes are mainly, but not exclusively, devoted to understanding sound, including everything from shrieks and gunshots and to music and human speech. For example, portions of the temporal lobes convert different frequencies of auditory information to the subjective thing we call pitch. Recall that Wernicke's area is the upper and posterior (rear) portion of the temporal lobe that borders the parietal lobe. But the temporal lobe is more than just an auditory processing center. Areas of the temporal lobe are also devoted to processing visual information – and helping us decide what that information means (Schacter et al., 2011). Thus, your temporal lobes help you recognize that some four-legged objects are things you often sit on (chairs) whereas other four-legged objects are things you often ask to sit (dogs). Good girl, Ginger.

The Occipital Lobes

Sticking with the map metaphor from Figure 6.9, the easternmost or posterior (back) portion of your cortex contains the occipital lobes. The occipital lobes are all about vision, and at the very rear of each occipital lobe is an area called primary visual cortex (aka V1). But the occipital lobe receives inputs from many different parts of the brain, not just the eyes. In fact, even the visual input that begins at the eyes makes a pit stop at the thalamus before being analyzed in the primary visual cortex. The primary visual cortex is not the only area of the occipital lobe that engages in visual processing. The two hemispheres of the occipital lobe work together to weave together a three-dimensional view of the world. The occipital lobe also allows you to make sense of the colors and edges of objects, and by working together with processing areas in other lobes, the occipital lobe helps create the very useful illusion of a mapped out and orderly world full of solid, colorful, meaningful objects.

The Frontal Lobes

The aptly named *frontal* lobes occupy much of the front of the brain (that's west on our metaphorical map). The **frontal lobes** seem to be the lobes that distinguish us most clearly from chimps or goldfish. They are crucially involved in many kinds of planning and self-regulation, and so they play a big role in decision-making, especially emotionally significant decision-making. The most frontal (most anterior) portion of the frontal lobes is known as the *prefrontal cortex*, and one of the oldest case studies in psychology reveals how important the prefrontal cortex is to emotional self-regulation. In the summer of 1848, a likable, energetic supervisor named Phineas Gage was laying down some railroad tracks in Vermont. A freak blasting accident meant that a metal rod about as long and thick as a broomstick blasted away a huge chunk of Gage's prefrontal cortex. Phineas survived the crazy accident. After a few months of recovery, Gage was able to speak normally, and he had the same good memory he had always had. However, as modern neuroscientists put it, "Gage was no longer Gage." (Damasio et al., 1994). The damage to Gage's prefrontal cortex turned this disciplined man into a social and emotional disaster. Both Gage's language and his behavior became abusive and irresponsible. He began cursing profusely, and he lost his ability to manage his money or his emotions. He lost his job as a railroad foreman, though he did eventually get a job as a stagecoach driver. Because Gage's skull remained in the hands of scientists after his death, Damasio et al. (1994) were able to use brain imaging techniques to pinpoint where Gage's brain damage was. Based not only on Gage's story but many modern stories of others who suffered major injuries to the prefrontal cortex, we know that we need our frontal lobes to make thoughtful decisions and to regulate our emotions. To round out this discussion of the frontal lobes, you may recall that the frontal lobes meet the parietal lobes. The two lobes meet at exactly the point at which somatosensory cortex in the *parietal* lobes processes sensory information from all over the body. Just to the front of this somatosensory cortex – but now in the frontal lobes – is the **motor cortex**. This is the main part of your brain responsible for carrying out voluntary motor movements. You probably won't be too surprised to learn that a homunculus that represents the details of the motor cortex would look very much like the somatosensory homunculus. Areas over which we have greater motor control require more of the frontal cortex.

A Memory Aid

If your frontal cortex is telling you that this highly technical module is going to make your life miserable for the next week or two, we might be able to take a little of the edge off that misery. If you revisit Figure 6.9, you may now have at least a vague sense of what each lobe does. If you can remember a way in which people often summarize the four directions on a map (*NSEW*) and if you can remember that *Parents Temporarily Occupy Frontiers*, perhaps you can more easily learn that the four lobes of the cerebral cortex (in the order NSEW) are the parietal, the temporal, the occipital, and the frontal. One of us used all four of his lobes (eight if you count both hemispheres) to create that suggestion.

There's a Lot We Skipped – For Now

Our goal in this module was not to convert you into a card-carrying behavioral neuroscientist overnight. In fact, neither of us is yet a card-carrying neuroscientist. But we both believe that many of the basic principles of psychology are hard to appreciate without appreciating the neural systems that make the principles possible. Thus, our main goal in this module was to offer you a few neurological facts and examples that reveal that the brain is a highly-organized computing machine. We both marvel at how a three-pound, bun-shaped biological object allows you to do everything you do – from sneezing when your nasal passages become irritated to becoming irritated at your friend Estornudo when she makes another joke about your nose. We will revisit the brain and the nervous system in many other modules in this text, especially when it comes to topics such as sensation, perception, human development, and health psychology. For now, we hope you've already gained a better appreciation than you had yesterday for how our brains make us everything that we are.

Critical Thinking Questions for Module 6: Gyri and Sulci

If you compared the surfaces of the brains of many mammals, you'd see that as mammals become more cognitively sophisticated, their brains usually have more gyri and sulci. As you can see in the left portion of Figure 6.11, a rat's cortex is very smooth. It has almost none of the gyri and sulci (hills and valleys) that are so prevalent in the human brain. Reptiles such as turtles and lizards have no gyri or sulci at all, by the way, because they have virtually no cerebral cortex. Thus, a good way to think about gyri and sulci is that they are evolution's way of packing as much grey matter (as many neuron *cell bodies*) as possible into the limited confines of the skull (Sun & Hevner, 2014).

If you look at the human brain shown in Figure 6.12, you can see that the grey matter that is so dense in neuron *cell bodies* exists mainly near the *surface* of the cortex. The white matter *beneath* that grey matter is white mainly because of the millions of myelinated *axons* that connect neocortical neurons to other parts of the brain. There's actually more cortical surface area in the human brain that one *cannot* see with the naked eye than cortical surface area that one *can* see. The hidden sulci ("canyons") have about 150% of the total surface area of the gyri ("hilltops"). Further, neuroscientists who are willing to break out their microscopes have shown that there is not a dramatic difference across mammalian species in the thickness of the grey layer. *Thus, the lion's share of the difference between the human brain and a lion's brain is found in the number and depth of the neocortical folds.* We do not wish to overstate this point. Relative to most other mammals, we human beings have (a) thick neocortical layers, (a) big brains for our body size, *and* (c) brains with lots of gyri and sulci (Kaas, 2013). But holding brain volume constant, more gyrification means more neocortex. And more neocortex – again, more grey matter – means many more neurons devoted to highly sophisticated forms of information-processing.

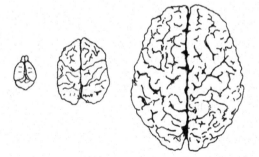

Figure 6.11 Sketches (bird's-eye view) of a rat brain (left), a macaque monkey brain (center), and a human brain (right). The images are only roughly to scale. The rat and macaque brains have been enlarged relative to the human brain. Human brains are much higher in gyrification than the brains of most other mammals.

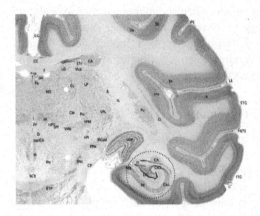

Figure 6.12
A cross-section of the cerebral cortex reveals that almost all the grey matter in the cortex sits near the *surface* of the gyri and sulci. More surface area, then, means more grey matter – thus, more neurons. (The white matter is mainly the axons of these neurons.) This section is from a macaque monkey rather than a person.

Questions

Imagine that you needed to fit a big sheet of gift-wrapping paper (with images on just one side) into a shoebox box *without* simply cutting up the wrapping paper. Ideally, you'd want to be sure that none of the colorful part of the wrapping paper was touched by any other part of the paper that contains the colorful images. Notice that if there were an image on the external surface of the brain depicted in Figure 6.12, very little of that image would touch other images.

1. How might you solve this problem – using only the sheet of wrapping paper and 20 or 30 ping pong balls? Did you solve the problem the way evolution solved it? Does your solution resemble the surface of the cerebral cortex?
2. There are plenty of problems in physics, engineering, and even agriculture that resemble this neuroscientific and evolutionary problem – to at least some degree. Analyze each state of affairs or question that follows – pointing out exactly how it is like and exactly how it is unlike the problem of maximizing the surface area of the cerebral cortex within the constraints of a finite skull. The images that follow these questions may help you visualize the questions more clearly.

    A. Why are both planets and soap bubbles perfectly spherical – with no gyri or sulci? FYI, if you think the hills, mountains, and valleys of the Earth are like gyri and sulci, allow us to remind you that the world tallest mountain is about 6 miles high. The diameter of the Earth is about 8,000 miles. Proportionately speaking, the Earth is much smoother than a rats' brain.
    B. Why do many motorcycle engines have metal fins – which make for a huge amount of "gyrification?"
    C. Why do automobile radiators send "to-be-cooled" fluids through many different small coils rather than pushing the fluid into or through a single flat, smooth tank?
    D. In what sense are paper books solutions to the problem of fitting a lot of crucial stuff (in this case, a lot of words rather than a lot of neurons) into a very small space? In what sense is a map an even better metaphor than a book?

E. What is terrace farming, and how does it maximize usable surface area for farmers who live in mountainous regions?
F. Why do bath towels have a very different kind of surface than bed sheets?
G. Finally, if more cortical neurons are better (for people, at least), will evolutionary forces just keep making the human skull bigger and bigger? Or more and more gyrified? Why or why not?

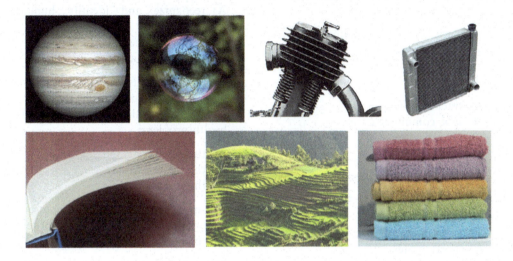

Figure 6.13

Multiple-Choice Questions for Module 6

1. What is the name of the band of millions of nerve fibers that connect the right and left halves of the brain?

   A) the trans-hemispheric bundle
   B) the lateral neural pipeline
   C) the corpus callosum

2. Chimeric faces and chimeric drawings of everyday objects have been used to study what aspect of brain structure?

   A) tract myelination
   B) lobe communication
   C) lateralization

3. Decussation refers to a peculiarity of the neural wiring system of what kinds of animals?

   A) arthropods
   B) vertebrates
   C) invertebrates

4. Evolutionarily speaking, what's the oldest region of the human brain?

   A) the hindbrain
   B) the pseudo-brain
   C) the midbrain

5. Evolutionarily speaking, what's the newest and most complex region of the human brain?

   A) the cerebellum
   B) the higher brain
   C) the forebrain

6. What brain structure is crucial to the formation of long-term memories for facts and experiences?

   A) the hypothalamus
   B) the hippocampus
   C) the parietal ganglia

7. As suggested by the case study of Phineas Gage (the railroad construction foreman), the prefrontal cortex plays a crucial role in allowing people to do what?

   A) recognize and identify human faces
   B) perceive three-dimensional space
   C) regulate emotions

8. Disorders of this pea-sized structure in the brain can lead people to become so tall that they have serious health problems.

   A) the pituitary gland
   B) the hypothalamus
   C) the growth nodule

9. The motor cortex and the somatosensory cortex are located at the borders of which two lobes of the brain?

   A) frontal and parietal
   B) motoric and somatic
   C) temporal and occipital

10. In the memory cue, "Parents Temporarily Occupy Frontiers," what does the word "Parents" stand for?

    A) the rule-making functions of the brain
    B) the parasympathetic nervous system
    C) the parietal lobe

11. In most people, which part of the brain specializes in the comprehension and production of speech and language?

    A) the linguistic lobe
    B) the left hemisphere
    C) the verbal neocortex

Answer Key: 1C, 2C, 3B, 4A, 5C, 6B, 7C, 8A, 9A, 10C, 11B

References

Albrecht, D. (1988). *Personal communication about the reticular activating system.*

Bourne, V. J. (2008). Chimeric faces, visual field bias, and reaction time bias: Have we been missing a trick? *Laterality, 13*(1), 92–103.

Buckner, R. L. (2013). The cerebellum and cognitive function: 25 Years of insight from anatomy and neuroimaging. *Neuron, 80*(3), 807–815. doi:10.1016/j.neuron.2013.10.044

Damasio, H., Grabowski, T., Frank, R., Galaburda, A. M., & Damasio, A. R. (1994). The return of Phineas Gage: The skull of a famous patient yields clues about the brain. *Science, 264*, 1102–1105.

Kaas, J. H. (2013). The evolution of brains from early mammals to humans. *Wiley Interdisciplinary Reviews in Cognitive Science, 4*, 33–45.

Kinsbourne, M. (2013). Somatic twist: A model for the evolution of decussation. *Neuropsychology, 27*(5), 511–515.

Knecht, S., Dräger, B., Deppe, M., Bobe, L., Lohmann, H., Flöel, A., ... Henningsen, H. (2000). Handedness and hemispheric language dominance in healthy humans. *Brain, 123*(12), 2512–2518. doi:10.1093/brain/123.12.2512

Levy, J., Trevarthen, C., & Sperry, R. W. (1972). Perception of bilateral chimeric figures following hemispheric deconnexion. *Brain: A Journal of Neurology, 95*, 61–78.

Lindell, A. K. (2013). Continuities in emotion lateralization in human and non-human primates. *Frontiers in Human Neuroscience, 7*, 464. doi:10.3389/fnhum.2013.00464

Marzoli, D., & Tommasi, L. (2009). Side biases in humans (homo sapiens): Three ecological studies on hemispheric asymmetries. *Naturwissenschaften, 96*(9), 1099–1106. doi:10.1007/s00114-009-0571-4

Okubo, M., Ishikawa, K., & Kobayashi, A. (2013). No trust on the left side: Hemifacial asymmetries for trust-worthiness and emotional expressions. *Brain & Cognition, 82*, 181–186.

Schacter, D. L. (1996). *Searching for memory: The brain, the mind, and the past.* New York: Basic Books.

Schacter, D. L., Gilbert, D. T., & Wegner, D. M. (2011). *Psychology* (2nd ed.). New York: Worth Publishers.

Schmahmann, J. D. (2019). The cerebellum and cognition. *Neuroscience Letters, 688*(1), 62–75.

Sun, T., & Hevner, R. F. (2014). Growth and folding of the mammalian cerebral cortex: From molecules to malformations. *Nature Reviews. Neuroscience, 15*(4), 217–232. doi:10.1038/nrn3707

Thompson, R. F., & Zola, S. M. (2003). Biological psychology. In D. K. Freedheim & I. B. Weiner (Eds.), *Handbook of psychogy: Volume 1, history of psychology* (pp. 47–66). Hoboken, NJ: John Wiley & Sons.

Volz, L.J., & Gazzaniga, M.S. (2017). Interaction in isolation: 50 years of insights from split-brain research, *Brain, 140*(7), 2051–2060. https://doi.org/10.1093/brain/awx139

III
Genetics and Evolution

Module 7
Genetics

Our Biological Origins

In the previous two modules, we argued that virtually everything you think, feel, and do is grounded in your brain and your nervous system. In this module, we'll argue that you possess the kind of brain and nervous system you possess – in large part – because of your genes. Before we delve into the history of **genetics** (the study of the biological transmission of physical and psychological traits), we'd like to note that we are *not* arguing that genes are destiny. If destiny exists at all, it is very complicated. As you will learn later in this module, genes and environments clearly interact to make us who we are. In fact, some genes program us to be certain kinds of people (big risk-takers, for example) only if we grow up in certain kinds of environments. So in our view, most important human traits – traits such as happiness, health, and humility, for example – are determined partly by genes and partly by environments. Other important human traits and tendencies – such as our huge brains, our very long lifespans, our highly social nature, our ability to walk upright, and our ability to use language – are grounded in **fixed genes**. Fixed genes are genes that are shared by virtually all members of a species. People the world over use complex language, for example, because we are all genetically programmed to do so (because of fixed genes). Foxes the world over, in contrast, use their excellent sense of smell to track down prey precisely because they are programmed by a different set of genes. But we're getting ahead of ourselves. Let's get a few genetic basics under our belts, and then we'll explore how genes and environments interact to make us all exactly who we are.

In the 1850s, more than two decades before the birth of psychology, an Austrian monk named Gregor Mendel was working diligently on his genetic studies of 29,000 pea plants. Mendel began his work in 1856 and did not complete data collection until 1863. Mendel wanted to understand *inheritance*. Why do two tall parents usually – but not always – have tall children? Why do two blue-eyed parents almost always have blue-eyed children? Stranger yet, how can two brown-eyed parents sometimes have a blue-eyed child? In Mendel's day, biologists couldn't answer such questions because they knew almost nothing about genetics. **Genetics** is the study of the **heritability** (biological transmission) of physical and psychological traits and tendencies, including how environments interact with genes to influence development. Mendel's painstaking genetic studies of pea plants paved the way for biological and psychological revolutions Mendel could scarcely have anticipated. In fact, Mendel himself did not use words like "gene" or "genetics." These terms would not be coined until the early 1900s, after Mendel's work finally got the attention it deserved. A **gene**, by the way, is one of the fundamental units of inheritance. Genes code for proteins; they are bits of the biological instructions for building your entire body. According to the National Human Genome Research Institute (2018), people have about 20,500 genes. As we have long known, all of our genes are found on 23 pairs of chromosomes (See Figure 7.1).

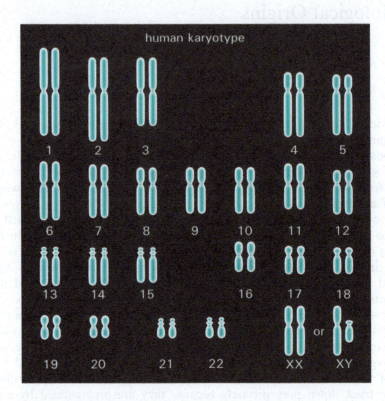

Figure 7.1 Your roughly 20,000 genes are divided into 23 pairs of chromosomes. If you are genetic-
          ally female, you have two X chromosomes (XX) rather than the male (XY) chromosome
          shown here.

One of Mendel's main discoveries led to the distinction between genotype and phenotype. An organism's **genotype** is its exact genetic make-up. In contrast, an organism's **phenotype** is its physical properties if it's a plant, or it's physical and psychological properties if it's an animal (which includes human beings, of course). Interestingly, an organism's phenotype may not be what one would expect from either its genotype or the phenotype of its parents (Roll-Hansen, 1979). Because Mendel studied traits for which **dominant-recessive inheritance** is at work (e.g., seed color, plant height), he found that some genetically-determined traits were **dominant** over others. To define dominant-recessive inheritance, we must first explain alleles. **Alleles** refer to the paired sets of genes we get from each of our parents. Sticking to Mendel's pea plants, a given plant might get an allele that says "be tall" from one parent and an identical allele – that also says "be tall" – from the other parent. It shouldn't take either a rocket scientist or a geneticist to figure out that this **homozygous** plant – this plant that got the same ("matching") allele from each parent – is genetically-programmed to be tall. But what happens when a pea plant gets the tall version of the plant height gene from one parent and the short version of the plant height gene from the other parent? You might expect that plant to split the difference and grow to a medium height. But under normal growing conditions, that never happens. Instead, because the tall version of the pea plant height gene is **dominant** over the short version, a plan that is **heterozygous** for the pea plant height gene (a plant that got a different version of the gene from each parents) will grow to be *just as tall* as it would have if it had been "tall-tall" homozygous. So dominant-recessive inheritance is the kind of inheritance in which one version of a gene (one allele) only gets expressed physically (and/or psychologically, if we're talking about people) if the organism ends up with matching (homozygous) alleles for that gene. The version of a gene that only gets expressed in an organism when the organism is homozygous for that variation on the gene is known as the **recessive** version.

With this idea in mind, consider what happened when Mendel crossed two *heterozygous* yellow-seeded pea plants. This means he was working with two pea plant parents – each of which possessed one "be yellow" allele and one "be green" allele. Because the yellow version of the pea color gene is *dominant* over the *recessive* green version, Mendel observed a 3:1 ratio of yellow-seeded to green-seeded offspring (well, he did after doing this breeding study many, many times). Mendel went into studies like this one having little idea what to expect, but based on his observed 3:1 ratio he correctly concluded that as far as pea plants go, the allele for being yellow-seeded is *dominant* over the allele for being green-seeded. Again, a dominant allele that came from one parent is always expressed over a recessive allele that came from the other parent. In contrast, a recessive allele is only expressed when an organism gets the recessive alleles from both parents.

At the risk of being highly redundant, let us remind you that *phenotype* (an organism's actual physical traits and tendencies) does not always match its *genotype* (the specific genetic makeup of an organism). Notice that a plant could be tall and yellow *phenotypically* even though it carried a recessive allele for both shortness and green-seededness. The recessive genes a plant or person carries have no impact at all on that organism's phenotype. But a moment's reflection should clarify that it is easy to pass recessive traits onto one's children or grandchildren. In fact, part of the genetic and evolutionary staying power of recessive genes is the fact that they normally remain hidden in organisms whose descendants will often express them. The popular phrase, "Some things skip a generation." is a bit of folk wisdom that appears to be firmly grounded in dominant-recessive inheritance. The things that may skip a generation, then, are recessive traits that do not show up in your kids but may show up when your kids or grandkids have kids.

The left half of Figure 7.2 illustrates this genetic dominant-recessive inheritance process for human eye color. If mom and dad both carry a dominant allele for brown (B) eyes as well as a recessive allele for blue (b) eyes (they're both Bb), this means they are both heterozygous for eye color. This means there's a 25% chance that any one of their kids will have blue eyes. If, on the other hand, mom is **homozygous** for brown eyes (BB) and dad is homozygous for blue eyes (bb), *all* their kids (100% of them) will have brown eyes (as in the righthand example in Figure 7.2). To make this second example concrete, your first author's mom almost certainly had two dominant alleles for brown eyes. We say this because his dad had blue eyes (meaning he had two recessive blue-eyed alleles). Nonetheless, all six of his mom's children (himself included) have brown eyes. His parents have plenty of blue-eyed as well as brown-eyed *grandchildren*, however, because most of their brown-eyed children mated with blue-eyed partners. If your brown-eyed first author weren't carrying a recessive blue-eyed allele from his dad, he couldn't have produced a blue-eyed daughter – even with a blue-eyed mate.

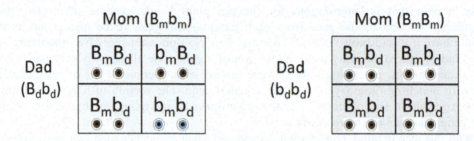

Figure 7.2 Two examples of dominant-recessive inheritance using Punnett squares. The simplest Punnett squares are 2 x 2 grids that allow users to plot out all the possible combinations of the paired alleles that come from each parent. The prior examples simplify things to assume (a) that eye color is determined by one gene (it's more complex than that) and (b) that brown eyes are dominant. B represents an allele for brown eyes whereas b represents an allele for blue eyes. Subscripts indicate from which parent (mom or dad) the alleles come.

In the example on the left, each parent is heterozygous for brown eyes. Across many pairings, we should observe the 3:1 ratio of brown to blue eyes Mendel observed for tall vs. short pea plants (tallness being dominant). In the righthand example, mom is homozygous for brown eyes (with matching dominant alleles) whereas dad is homozygous for blue eyes (with matching recessive alleles). All the offspring of these parents should have brown eyes. There is sometimes a big difference between genotype and phenotype.

Do dominant alleles "dominate" numerically? Many students who first learn about dominant-recessive inheritance assume that dominant traits "take over" in **natural selection**, the process by which genes that promote successful reproduction become more likely to be passed on to offspring. After all, just as dominant people often take over conversations, dominant soccer players often take over soccer games. People may also feel that recessive genes get "weeded out of the gene pool" because some well-known genetic diseases (e.g., Tay-Sachs, sickle cell anemia) occur only when people receive recessive alleles from both parents. But in genetics, dominant traits are simply those that get expressed phenotypically when a dominant allele co-occurs with a recessive allele. Dominant traits do *not* dominate natural selection. Whether alleles are dominant, recessive, or neither, they only increase in frequency in a population when they promote **selective fitness** (e.g., by helping an organism attract a mate, produce hardier offspring, or avoid predation; Dawkins, 1976).

If this doesn't make sense, consider that some recessive traits are common and that some dominant traits are rare (in some populations). For our purposes, blue eyes are recessive. But most Norwegians and Estonians have blue eyes. Having a second toe that's longer than one's "big toe" (aka *Morton's toe*; see Figure 7.3) is *probably* dominant. But it's also rare. An even more dramatic example is **polydactyly** (having more than five fingers or toes). This trait is dominant, but we can count on one finger the number of people either of us has ever known who had an extra digit (the first author's uncle Gary). If this still doesn't feel right, consider some logic. The righthand half of Figure 7.3 shows what would be expected if a small population of four people (one of whom was heterozygous for Morton's toe and three of whom were homozygous for "normal" toes) paired up in two couples – and produced four children each. Like the parents, 25% of the children would have Morton's toe. Of course, this is just one example. But if you run through every logical possibility, you'll see that dominant alleles *don't* become any more common than recessive alleles – at least not because of their dominance. As a final way to illustrate this point, let's return to eye color. Your first author's mom and dad possessed a grand total of two brown-eyed and two blue-eyed alleles. Their kids possess a grand total of six brown-eyed and six blue-eyed alleles. The 1:1 *genotype* ratios didn't change. Those recessive genes hung around – and eventually found their way into the phenotypes of multiple grandchildren.

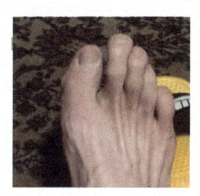

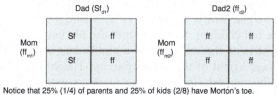

S = allele for second toe longest (Morton's toe).
f = allele for first toe longest (normal).

Here's a population of 4 adults: Sf_{d1}, ff_{m1}, ff_{d2}, and ff_{m2}

Sf_{d1} mates with ff_{m1} and has four kids. And ff_{d2} and ff_{m2} mate, too.

Dad (Sf_{d1})			Dad2 (ff_{d2})	
Mom (ff_{m1})	Sf	ff	Mom (ff_{m2})	ff	ff
	Sf	ff		ff	ff

Notice that 25% (1/4) of parents and 25% of kids (2/8) have Morton's toe.

Figure 7.3 Dominant genes do *not* necessarily become more common over generations. Foot selfie by Barry Pelham.

Post-Mendelian genetics. One of the many things we've learned since Mendel is that people are not pea plants. If Mendel had studied people, he might have discovered **incomplete dominance** or **codominance**. Incomplete dominance happens when the alleles we get from different parents average out somehow. Thus, if you were to cross a homozygous white flower (WW) with a homozygous red flower (RR), the offspring would be pink. This is roughly what happens when a tall parent and a short parent produce offspring of medium height. One big complication is that height, like many other human traits, is determined by more than one gene. In fact, as many as 700 genes appear to play at least a tiny role in height (Marouli et al., 2017).

Genetic inheritance can also happen by means of codominance. **Codominance** happens when two or more alleles express themselves to some degree. If codominance were at work in the simple case of flower color, red (RR) and white (WW) parent flowers might produce offspring with a mixture of red and white patches. A good example of codominance in people is blood type. The first author doesn't know the blood types of his parents, and he cannot ask them because they are both deceased. However, his blood type is AB, and it is likely that one of his parents gave him the A allele whereas the other gave him the B allele. In a sense both alleles here were dominant – as the term *co*dominance suggests.

Quantitative genetics and heritability. Pea plants were a great place to begin studying genetics because the rules of inheritance in pea plants are very simple. But once we move from peas to people, a lot of genetics proves to be quantitative genetics. Unlike dominant-recessive genetics, **quantitative genetics** involve traits that vary along a continuum (e.g., height in cm, foot size, visual acuity, density of taste buds on the tongue, physical strength). As it turns out, the large majority of human traits exist along some kind of *continuum*. And the large majority of such continuous traits are influenced not by a single gene but by multiple genes. Recall that as many as 700 genes seem to influence height. A person's risk for schizophrenia and autism both seem to be influenced by multiple genes (Gejman, Sanders, & Duan, 2010). Most personality traits also appear to be influenced by quantitative genetics. A good understanding of quantitative genetics requires some statistics. For example, quantitative geneticists describe the **heritability** of different traits (the degree to which the phenotype in question is influenced by genes rather than by environments) using a statistic called **h^2**, the **heritability coefficient**. For a given trait, h^2 presumably tells you how much genes matters (rather than environment) in the expression of that trait.

The word *presumably* is important because, as we'll argue later, we may not always be able to accept h^2 at face value. The observed value of h^2 can also drop in highly unfavorable environments (Turkheimer, Haley, Waldron, D'Onofrio, & Gottesman, 2003). But sticking with the traditional interpretations for now, h^2 has a maximum value of 1.0 (meaning genes are *all* that matter) and a minimum value of 0.0 (meaning genes don't matter at all). The left-hand portion of Figure 7.4 provides a hypothetical example of h^2 for height, which is known to be strongly genetic (h^2 = .81 here). Tall parents usually have tall children. Short parents usually have short children. You can account for about 4/5 (.81) of the variation in a child's height (within gender, of course) by knowing the average height of the child's parents. Height is *highly heritable*. Unless a kid is reared in highly unusual circumstances (such as extreme food scarcity) you can predict a kid's adult height very well by knowing the heights of the kid's biological parents.

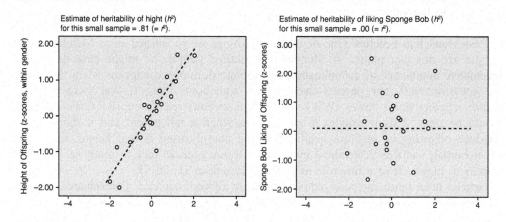

Figure 7.4 Hypothetical Heritability Estimates for (a) Physical Height and for (b) Liking *Sponge-Bob SquarePants* Cartoons in a Small Sample.

The right-hand portion of Figure 7.4 provides a second example of how h^2 works. If these hypothetical data were real, they'd suggest that liking for *SpongeBob SquarePants* cartoons has no genetic component whatsoever (h^2 = .00). We chose attitudes about SpongeBob, by the way, to illustrate that if you can get the data, you can estimate the heritability of almost anything. In people, there are lots of continuous traits whose heritability has been measured. A recent **meta-analysis** (a study of multiple studies) of hundreds of twin studies showed that heritability varies widely across traits (Polderman et al., 2015). Whereas h^2 is very high for height ($h^2 = .82$), it is extremely low for "gene expression" ($h^2 = .06$).

Quantitative genetics also explains why so many of the traits psychologists study turn out to be **normally distributed** (following a bell-shaped curve). If a trait is influenced by multiple genes, rather than just one, there are many, many genetic routes by which an organism can prove to be average, but very few routes by which the organism can prove to be extremely high or extremely low on the trait. Even if only five genes influence a trait, it will be the rare organism who happens to get only the five alleles that determine very high (or very low) levels of the trait in question (see Yule, 1902). This logic about quantitative genetics did not apply to Mendel's work. He always focused on dichotomous ("either-or") traits that were determined by a single gene.

Mendel could have scarcely anticipated how far modern scientists would extend his basic genetic findings. For example, scientists have now decoded the human *genome*. In contrast to genes and genotypes, genomes are much broader. The **genome** for any given species refers to all the possible sets of genetic instructions that exist for making all possible specific members of that species. This includes every possible allele that exists for every specific gene, as well as all the billions of possible nucleotides (the tiny bits of genetic information that make up genes) and their locations (e.g., within a specific codon, within a specific gene, within a specific chromosome).

The automotive analogy of genetics. If we may introduce an analogy, the *genome* for a species is like the specific instructions for assembling every possible variation on a specific make and model of a car. For example, Toyota made 2014 RAV-4s in a wide variety of possible colors and trim packages. This means that 2014 RAV-4s came with or without sunroofs and with or without mag wheels. In contrast, the size of the steering wheel might have been fixed for the 2014 RAV-4 while its color may have varied. The equivalent of the genome for this particular "species" of car would specify some unique potential combinations that don't exist in any actual cars. If we continue with this automotive analogy, notice that **genotype** would be the equivalent of the manufacturing instructions for creating one specific, concrete 2014 RAV-4. The **phenotype** would be the way that a specific 2014 RAV-4 existed not only as it rolled off the assembly line but years later, after the battery and tires had been replaced, and after years of city driving had left dings on the body. The phenotype would also include some invisible aspects of this 2014 RAV-4 (such as how much engine wear it has experienced). We all have both highly visible (e.g., height) and less visible (lactose intolerance, preference for sweets) phenotypes. In this same analogy, the **gene** would be a small set of instructions for making one specific part of the car, perhaps something as small as a nut or bolt, perhaps something as large as the engine block. One informative area where the automotive analogy breaks down is that each part of a car itself does *not* contain the entire set of genetic instructions for making that entire car. In contrast, every cell (except sex cells) in your body does contain all 46 of your chromosomes, and thus every bit of your unique genotype.

Genotype-Environment Interactions: The PEA Model

The PEA model. Genes and genotypes do not exist in isolation. We are social creatures and our development unfolds in complex social *environments*. One cannot fully appreciate genetics without appreciating this fact. Geneticists have argued that there are typically positive genotype-environment correlations – because of three different ways in which genes create environments that tend to support their biological effects (Kendler & Baker, 2007; Scarr & McCartney, 1983). In honor of Mendel (and as a memory aid), we refer to this model of

genotype-environment effects as the **PEA model**. Each letter of "PEA" reflects a different way (passive, evocative, and active) in which genes can shape environments.

Perhaps the simplest way in which genes can produce environments that reinforce them is through **passive** genotype-environment effects. Children are typically reared by close biological relatives, who share many of their genes. On average, both our parents and siblings will share half their genes with us. Biological aunts, uncles, and grandparents share a quarter. Because most of us grow up surrounded by others who share genes with us, we tend to live in worlds that foster the effects of most of our genes. You probably know a family in which everyone loves sports. Most geneticists would say that Jason didn't just become athletic because he was born with a lot of athletic talent. He also grew up surrounded by jocks. Any genes he got that predisposed him to be athletic were reinforced by the fact that he lived in a world full of jerseys, cleats, and helmets, usually filled with sweaty people. This extends well beyond athletics. Your first author's mom was deeply religious and highly empathic. She often read Bible stories to her children. But she didn't choose the story of David slicing off Goliath's head or God smiting the toddlers of Gomorrah. Instead she selected stories such as Jesus healing the sick and the blind, or the Good Samaritan rescuing a stranger in distress. These are called *passive* genotype-environment effects because the developing person doesn't do anything to be exposed to the environment. It comes from others, who share the developing person's genes. The developing person passively absorbs it.

But people, children included, are not always passive. **Evocative genotype-environment effects** exist because people possess inherited traits and preferences that habitually *evoke* responses from others. An artistically gifted child may catch the eye of her art teacher. A child who can sing well may become the teacher's pet in music class. Conversely, a child like your authors – who were naturally gifted at sinking and flailing in the water – was unlikely to be approached by any swim coaches. Evocative effects often extend beyond the family. When your first author was a child, he hated hunting, and he was not good at it. You could even say he was a liability, if not a danger, on a two-person hunting team. The last time he remembers going hunting, his dad sent him with his friend James, who was an excellent hunter. When he asked his dad why he'd paired him up with the best hunter, his dad replied, in James's presence. "Well, James aint kin to us. And besides, he's the only one who's got life insurance." This comment *evoked* quite a bit of laughter, which is another example of evocative genotype-environment effects. Your first author's dad wouldn't have kept making such jokes if his friends and relatives didn't encourage him.

Moving beyond evocative effects, people actively choose some of their environments. **Active genotype-environment effects** exist because people with specific inherited inclinations choose specific situations. All three of your first author's brothers gravitated toward sports whereas most of his sisters gravitated toward art. He once had to choose between staying on the high school wrestling team and maintaining a high GPA. (The wrestling coach gave everyone a low A in the class one had to take to remain on the team, which brought down his GPA.) He was a mediocre wrestler, but a very good student. Despite pressure from his dad to stay on the team, he chose wrestling with ideas over wrestling with people. He also actively sought out a sport, track and field, in which he could participate without reducing his GPA. Genes and environments often support one another.

A problem with the PEA model. As clever as the PEA model is, we have a criticism of it. We think it's precisely because of the *evocative* component of the PEA model that twin studies overestimate the heritability of many traits – by overlooking powerful environmental effects on human development. Consider the fact that twin studies suggest that IQ is highly heritable. Studies of **monozygotic** (identical) vs. **dizygotic** (fraternal) twins show that

(a) monozygotic twins tend to have very similar IQs (the twin-pair correlations for IQ are very high) whereas (b) dizygotic twins have only *somewhat* similar IQs (the twin-pair correlations are more modest). The logic of twin studies seems airtight. We know that monozygotic twins share virtually all their genes. Dizygotic twins share only half of their genes. Thus, if identical twins behave in a more similar fashion than do fraternal twins, this would seem to be due to the extra genes shared by identical twins. A few methodologically rigorous twin studies even focus on twins who were *separated at birth.* Such twins grow up in different places, with different parents. Studies of twins separated at birth are very clever.

But there's a problem with twin studies, including studies of twins separated at birth. The problem is that identical twins *look* almost exactly alike. In fact, a close look at the heritability of the long list of traits assessed by geneticists such as Polderman et al. (2015) shows that many observable physical traits, such as height, "structure of the mouth," and "weight maintenance functions" have very h^2 values (high heritability coefficients). This means that if Leslie is tall, thin, and beautiful, with olive skin and curly hair, you can be very confident that her identical twin sister had all these same physical traits. You can thus be pretty sure that even if Leslie grew up in Sarasota while her twin grew up in Minnesota, the physical appearance of Leslie and her twin would evoke very similar responses among teachers, coaches, romantic suitors, police officers, and adoptive parents.

Figure 7.5 Three sets of identical twins. Even if we were to separate these twins at birth, research shows that, for all their lives, the individual members of each twin pair would be treated in very similar ways by others – which means that the identical twins were not truly "separated" after all.

If people accurately judge other people's IQ and personality from their height, weight, and level of physical attractiveness, these might be mere examples of evocative genotype-environment correlations. The problem, though, is that people strongly assume that many physical traits are associated with psychological traits (IQ, sociability, leadership, etc.) that have little to do with them. For example, research shows that we judge physically attractive people to be more sociable, honest, and competent than physically unattractive people (Eagly, Ashmore, Makhijani, & Longo, 1991). All the twins you see in Figure 7.5 are attractive. But if they were all unattractive, their physical appearance would consistently evoke lukewarm – if not negative – reactions from strangers the world over. And recall that identical twins don't just share the same faces; they also share the same heights, body types, hair colors, skin tones, and often the same shoe sizes, not to mention the same biological sex.

To see how powerful stereotypes about physical appearance can be, consider Jennifer Eberhardt's studies of "Afrocentrism" – the degree to which people (including those *within* a specific ethnic group) have physical features stereotypically associated with African Americans. These include dark skin, large lips, and broad noses. In a group of Black men who had been convicted of killing White victims, Eberhardt and colleagues (2006) found that the more "Afrocentric" facial features Black men possessed the more likely they were to receive the death penalty. This was true after controlling for a long list of known predictors of who receives the death penalty (e.g., aggravating circumstances, severity of the murder, and even the defendant's level of physical attractiveness). Even after controlling for these important confounds, Black men with a more stereotypically Black appearance were twice as likely as Black men with a less stereotypically Black appearance to be given a death sentence. Notice that these men all self-identified as Black. Thus, this is not a simple matter of "racism" as it's usually defined. Further, we hope it's clear that if any of these men had identical twins, these men and their twins would receive almost identical Afrocentrism scores.

Physical appearance is among the most heritable of all traits. Furthermore, physical appearance plays a huge role in social perception – and often in ways that it logically shouldn't. In fact, research shows that people strongly rely on facial features to judge a person's competence, dominance, extraversion, and trustworthiness (Olivola & Todorov, 2010; Todorov et al., 2015). People who live in the same culture appear to share many of the same largely inaccurate stereotypes about physical traits and personality. There is probably no trait for which this is truer than height. Taller people are much more likely than shorter people to be elected to leadership positions, and taller people earn more money than shorter people (Rietveld, Hessels, & van der Zwan, 2015). The average height of male U.S. senators is about 6'2". In short, the fact that we're quick to judge a book by its cover suggests that twin studies may greatly overestimate the power of genes to determine important traits such as aggression and IQ. Of course, none of these findings mean that genes do not matter at all. Instead, they suggest that the aspect of the environment known as stereotypes sometimes masquerades as a simple effect of genes. Just how often and how strongly this is the case is a good question for future research on genotype-environment interactions.

Where does this leave us? In our opinion, it leaves us in the quirky position of arguing that some of the most powerful effects of genes may be grounded in the ways in which genes make people look. Having said that, it seems highly likely that – consistent with the PEA model – there are plenty of genes that make people interested in and well-suited to certain kinds of activities. Further, as we suggested at the beginning of this module, there can be no doubt that genetic differences between human beings and other species (fixed aspects of genomes, that is) play a huge role in shaping human experience. We were able to write this module, in large part, because we were genetically programmed to use language. It is also possible that your second author, who is much more practical and organized than your first author, is the kind of person he is not only because he grew up in a family of practical and organized people but also because he inherited plenty of genes that nudged him in that direction.

"That's right. Your DNA test very clearly shows that you are *not* the only one."

Figure 7.6

Hands-on Activities for Module 7: Punnett Squares and Hidden Genes

In this hands-on activity you will calculate the likelihood that a couple with different known genotypes produces offspring with different genotypes – and then determine offspring phenotype from offspring genotype. We begin with an example involving eye color. Assume that B represents a dominant allele for brown eyes and that b means that a parent has a recessive allele for blue eyes. As we hope you can see, mom has two recessive alleles for blue eyes. So she has blue eyes. Dad has brown eyes, but he carries both a dominant brown eyed allele and a recessive blue-eyed allele.

1. If this couple were to have 100 kids (yes, we realize that's a lot, but they both came from very big families), how many of their kids would you expect to be blue-eyed? How many would you expect to be brown-eyed? If mom gave birth to just ten kids and all ten of them had blue eyes, should dad be worried that there is another man in the picture? Why or why not?

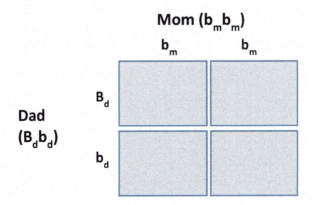

Figure 7.7

2. Our friend K.W. had a friend who got married and had a kid. This friend, whom we'll call Jenna, thought of herself as White, and she certainly looked White. Jenna's husband, whom we'll call Isaac, also identified as White, and he, too, looked White. But when Jenna gave birth to her first child, the child was *obviously* African-American, (though a bit fairer-skinned than the average African-American). Isaac was hurt and angry. He had never suspected his wife of having an affair. At first, Isaac planned to divorce Jenna. But Jenna insisted earnestly that she had not had any kind of affair. Eventually Isaac made peace with this situation and decided that his wife must have had some kind of "nervous breakdown" or temporary lapse in judgment. Isaac eventually decided to put this aberration behind him and forgive his wife. Two years later, Jenna and Isaac had another child. This child was *also* African-American. Isaac immediately filed for divorce. Before he could complete the paperwork, though, Jenna's mom pulled her aside and told Jenna something she should have told Jenna when Jenna was a child: Jenna's dad was African-American. To protect Jenna from racism, her mother decided not to tell her anything about her ancestry. If you think this situation is impossible, check out this National Geographic story on the myth of race – and how human skin tone is determined by multiple genes, rather than just one: www.nationalgeographic.com/magazine/2018/04/race-twins-black-white-biggs/ Discuss what you learned about genetics, racism, and the myth of race.

Multiple-Choice Questions for Module 7

1. The study of how physical and psychological traits are passed down from parents to children is known as:

   A) genotypes
   B) genomics
   C) genetics

2. Traits such as height and physical appearance (e.g., nose shape, skin tone, eye color) have a large genetic component – which is to say that the h^2 statistic is very high. The term for the precise degree to which a specific trait is influenced by genes is:

   A) heritability
   B) genomic fit
   C) determinism

3. The type of inheritance studied most by Mendel (in pea plants) is one reason why phenotype does not always match genotype. What type of inheritance is this?

   A) dominant-recessive inheritance
   B) stochastic inheritance
   C) quantitative inheritance
   D) dizygotic inheritance

4. A man who had brown eyes fathered nine children with a woman who had blue eyes. All nine of their children had brown eyes. This means that there is an extremely high chance that the father of these nine children was _____ for brown eyes.

   A) homozygous
   B) heterozygous
   C) determinant
   D) robust

5. The ability to taste PTC (phenylthiocarbamide – which is very bitter to those who can taste it) appears to be dominant over the inability to taste it. A mother was heterozygous for the single gene thought to be responsible for this perceptual trait. Her husband, who fathered 16 children with her, was also heterozygous for this same gene. What is your best guess about how many of their 16 children can taste PTC?

   A) 4
   B) 8
   C) 12
   D) 16

6. In people, most traits are influenced by more than one gene, sometimes dozens of them. This explains why most inheritance in people is best described by what term for genetic inheritance?

   A) quantitative genetics
   B) incomplete dominance
   C) mixed inheritance

7. In the automotive analogy for understanding genetics, what genetic term is analogous to all the possible ways to produce a specific make and model of car (e.g., all the possible ways to make a 1966 Volvo 122 series)?

   A) genetics
   B) genome
   C) phenotype
   D) genotype

8. Jenna's parents both love art, and they have always encouraged Jenna to enjoy and produce art. As a result, Jenna is majoring in art in college, and she hopes to work as a professional artist someday. A fan of the PEA model of genotype-environment interactions would say that Jenna's keen interest in art was fostered by:

   A) active genotype-environment interactions
   B) passive genotype-environment interactions
   C) the "copycat" effect of nuclear families

9. NBA All-Star Kawhi Leonard's huge hands are hard to miss. When Kawhi shakes hands with another person, his hand swallows up the other person's hand. Assume that Kawhi's basketball coaches noticed this when he was young – and thus encouraged him to devote himself to basketball. What aspect of the PEA model does this example support?

   A) active genotype-environment effects
   B) proactive genotype-environment effects
   C) evocative genotype-environment effects

10. If two twins are not the same biological sex, you can be guaranteed that they are fraternal twins. What's the technical term for this type of twin?

    A) semizygotic
    B) bizygotic
    C) dizygotic

Answer Key: 1C, 2A, 3A, 4A, 5C, 6A, 7B, 8B, 9C, 10C

References

Dawkins, R. (1976). *The selfish gene.* Oxford: Oxford University Press.

Eagly, A. H., Ashmore, R. D., Makhijani, M. G., & Longo, L. C. (1991). What is beautiful is good, but: A meta-analytic review of research on the physical attractiveness stereotype. *Psychological Bulletin, 110*, 109–128.

Eberhardt, J. L., Davies, P. G., Purdie-Vaughns, V. J., & Johnson, S. J. (2006). Looking deathworthy: Perceived stereotypicality of Black defendants predicts capital-sentencing outcomes. *Psychological Science, 17*, 383–386.

Gejman, P. V., Sanders, A. R., & Duan, J. (2010). The role of genetics in the etiology of schizophrenia. *Psychiatric Clinics of North America, 33*, 35–66. doi:10.1016/j.psc.2009.12.003

Kendler, K. S., & Baker, J. H. (2007). Genetic influences on measures of the environment: A systematic review. *Psychological Medicine, 37*, 615–626.

Marouli, E., Graff, M., Medina-Gomez, C., Sin Lo, K., Wood, A.R., Kjaer, T.R., Fine, R.S., Lu, Y., Schurmann, C., Highland, H.M., Rüeger, S., Thorleifsson, G., Justice, A.E., Lamparter, D., Stirrups, K.E., Turcot, V., Young, K.L., Winkler, T.W., Esko, T. . . . & Lettre, G. (2017, February 9). Rare and low-frequency coding variants alter human adult height. *Nature, 542*, 186–190. doi:10.1038/nature21039

National Human Genome Research Institute. (2018) An overview of the human genome project: What was the human genome project? Retrieved on December 20, 2018 from www.genome.gov/12011238/an-overview-of-the-human-genome-project/

Olivola, C. Y., & Todorov, A. (2010). Fooled by first impressions? Reexamining the diagnostic value of appearance- based inferences. *Journal of Experimental Social Psychology, 46*, 315–324.

Polderman, T. J. C., Benyamin, B., de Leeuw, C. A., Sullivan, P. F., van Bochoven, A., Visscher, P. M., & Posthuma, D. (2015). Meta-analysis of the heritability of human traits based on fifty years of twin studies. *Nature Genetics, 47*, 702–712.

Rietveld, C. A., Hessels, J., & van der Zwan, P. (2015). The stature of the self-employed and its relation with earnings and satisfaction. *Economics and Human Biology, 17*, 59–74.

Roll-Hansen, N. (1979). The genotype theory of Wilhelm Johannsen and its relation to plant breeding and the study of evolution. *Centaurus, 22*(3), 201–235.

Scarr, S., & McCartney, K. (1983). How people make their own environments: A theory of genotype greater than environment effects. *Child Development, 54*, 424–435.

Todorov, A., Olivola, C.Y., Dotsch, R., & Mende-Siedlecki, P. (2015). Social attributions from faces: Determinants, consequences, accuracy, and functional significance. *Annual Review of Psychology, 66*, 519–545.

Turkheimer, E., Haley, A., Waldron, M., D'Onofrio, B., & Gottesman, I. I. (2003). Socioeconomic status modifies heritability of IQ in young children. *Psychological Science, 14*, 623–628.

Yule, G. U. (1902). Mendel's laws and their probable relation to intra-racial heredity. *New Phytology, 1*, 222–238.

Module 8
Evolutionary Psychology
How the Past Informs the Present

About 66 million years ago, we're pretty sure it was on a Tuesday, something truly terrible happened in modern-day Mexico. A meteorite 10 km wide smashed into our planet at a very high speed. Striking in what is now the Yucatan Peninsula, the meteorite created a blast some *30 billion* times more powerful than the sum of the atomic bombs that destroyed Hiroshima and Nagasaki in World War II. In an instant, a tropical paradise became a smoldering crater 20 km deep and 160 km wide. Massive tsunamis, earthquakes, and volcanoes were triggered worldwide. Climate change, forest fires, and acid rain occurred on an unimaginable scale. For the first time in millions of years, it became a very bad time to be a dinosaur. As thick clouds of dust choked the planet, even the cleverest and most resourceful dinosaurs proved to be unprepared to survive on a burning-then-freezing planet practically devoid of plant life (Brusatte et al., 2014).

This epic tragedy for dinosaurs proved to be a wonderful opportunity for mammals like you and your cousin Isabella. Actually, the mammals who survived in the wake of this catastrophe resembled Alvin and Theodore (of chipmunk movie fame) much more than they resembled anyone you know. Beginning with descendants of the chipmunkish morganucodon, many ancient mammals survived the cosmic disaster and then evolved to become the incredibly diverse family of fuzzy, warm-blooded creatures that zookeepers and preschoolers know and love. Post-asteroid, most of Morgie's mammalian descendants had some huge advantages over most dinosaurs. For starters, having fur and being good at staying warm probably helped small mammals survive the harsh nuclear winter that extinguished all the big dinosaurs. It was probably an even bigger advantage for small mammals that they could live in small *places*, away from the fire, snow, and acid rain. Morgie, for example, was only about 10 cm long, roughly as big as you see her in Figure 8.1. Some small bird-like dinosaurs *also* survived this mass extinction, by the way. The reason why is that it's a lot easier to survive a lengthy global famine when you eat like a bird than when your idea of dinner is half a ton of fresh grass – or filet of triceratops.

In the millions of years since the Yucatan meteor strike, the Earth's inhabitants have dramatically diversified. About 15 or 20 million years after the strike, some of Morgie's descendants gradually returned to the oceans, evolving into whales and dolphins. Incidentally, one reason we know that whales and dolphins evolved from land mammals is that their skeletons strongly resemble those of other mammals. Dolphins have forelimb ("flipper") bones that strongly resemble the front appendages of virtually all mammals (see Figure 8.2.). Some whales and dolphins have tiny rear leg bones that never emerge from their bodies. In addition to breathing air, nursing their young, and having special mammalian ear bones, dolphins and whales also share a much greater percentage of their genes with you than they do with the sharks or other large fish that they more closely resemble.

Figure 8.1 Say hello to your great, great, great, great ... great grandma. This is "Morgie," one of
the first known proto-mammals. Morgie's fur, special jaws, and mammalian inner ear
bones set her apart from dinosaurs or reptiles.

Sketch courtesy of B. Pelham.

It would be another 20 million years after some mammals returned to the oceans
(25–30 million years ago) before the common ancestors of monkeys and apes split into
these two different groups. The apes, by the way, are the ones without tails. One particular
species of *great* ape, *Homo sapiens*, emerged only about 200,000 years ago (Ermini, Der
Sarkissian, Willerslev, & Orlando, 2015). So our species has only been around for about
a fifth of a million years. In fact, it was roughly 11,000 years ago that we *Homo sapiens*
made the agricultural – and then cultural – leaps that have made us the most successful
and destructive animals on the planet (Diamond, 1997). But it seems safe to say that no
human leaps of any kind would have ever happened if the dinosaurs still ruled.

If you're wondering what this paleontology lesson has to do with *psychology*, the beginning of the answer is that you and your loved ones are all mammals. Mammals and
proto-mammals lived alongside dinosaurs for more than 100 million years without
becoming a very diverse family. Seventy million years ago there were no bats, whales, gir-
affes, or gorillas. They didn't exist because tens of millions of years *before* mammals hit
the scene, dinosaurs had cornered the market on the ecological niches needed to support
such highly unusual modern-day mammals. Morgie and most of her ancient mammalian
cousins filled a unique environmental niche by eating bugs and being agile enough to
stay out of the way of T-Rex and other predators. Although there were some notable
exceptions to this rule of tiny rat-likeness among ancient mammals, mammals never
became very diverse and populous until the dinosaurs became extinct (Meng, Wang, &
Li, 2011; O'Leary et al., 2013). Thus, in the absence of that deadly meteorite strike, the
chances are virtually zero that any species of *dinosaur* would have ever evolved into
a quirky, brainy, highly social creature that reads and writes textbooks. Only the unique
mammals known as people have ever done that. Because we are still mammals, however,
we have a lot more in common with our mammalian relatives than most people appreciate (de Waal, 1996; Diamond, 1992).

We're not *that* special. You may have heard that we share more than 98% of our
genome with chimpanzees. Perhaps that's not so shocking. Consider this thought

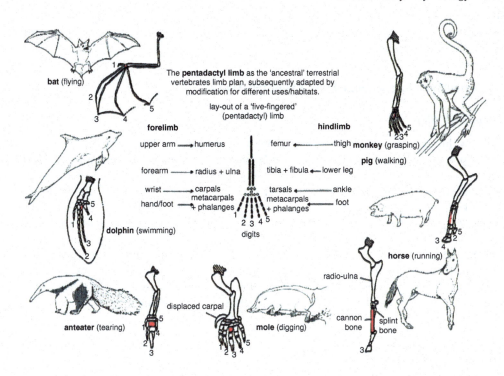

Figure 8.2 This image illustrates homology, the idea that related species often share common physical traits – because they share genes derived from a common ancestor. Despite their extreme diversity, the mammals you see here have amazingly similar forelimb and hindlimb bones. In the case of the forelimb, notice that there's always one humerus (in you, it's under your biceps) as well as exactly two forearm bones (the radius and the ulna) and usually five phalanges ("finger" bones). This is true even for dolphins, who look totally ridiculous in gloves.

Image by Jerry Crimson Mann.

experiment, adapted from Jared Diamond (1992): Take a male chimpanzee, and sedate him (so he doesn't rip anyone's arms off). Now shave his entire body, put a Boston Red Sox cap on him, and drop him onto a New York City subway seat – making sure the train is headed to the Bronx. On second thought, replace the BoSox cap with a Yankees cap – so no one rips the poor *chimp's* arms off. More than 98% of subway passengers will see a very ugly old man who should be arrested for indecent exposure. Chimps are a *lot* like human beings. This is why chimpanzees make tools, deceive each other, organize themselves into social groups, inspect the genitals of newborns to assess their sex, and have sex face to face – very much like we do. Jared Diamond even refers to people, half-seriously, as the "third [kind of] chimpanzee."

Speaking of chimps, both people and chimps also have something in common with bananas. What percentage of our genome, if any, do you think we share with bananas? Bananas are in a whole different kingdom than animals, but they are life forms, after all. The answer is 50%. Yes, we share about half of our genome with bananas. These shared genes go back to a time about 1.6 billion years ago when plant and animal life seem to have diverged from a common, very primitive ancestor (Meyerowitz, 2002).

Our surprising similarity to chimps and bananas, including the very ancient point in our planet's history when plants and animals diverged, suggests at least five important things about evolution.

Five Important Facts about How Evolution Works

Evolution is Slow

First, evolution typically operates on a *very* long time-scale. Both people and banana plants possess successful genes that have been in the global gene pool for 1.6 *billion* years. The Earth has existed for about 4.5 billion years. So, remembering that our species has existed for about 200,000 years, this means that we've been on Earth for less than one twenty thousandth (1/22,500, to be more exact) of the time the Earth has existed. If you compacted the Earth's entire history into a single day, we human beings would have existed for about 3.8 seconds of that day. It took a very long time to get to us. And we are not any kind of inevitable evolutionary destination. We are just one of many millions of species that have ever existed on Earth. Many times, laypeople who question whether something as complex as flight, eyes, or nursing could have evolved have difficulty because they are thinking in terms of decades or centuries rather than millions of years.

Evolution is Conservative

Second, when something works (like a gene that contributes to basic cell metabolism) nature rarely abandons it. Nature, it turns out, is highly conservative. You may recall from Module 5 that our brains show lots of evidence of conservation. So sometimes, great minds really do think alike. As an example of conservation in evolution, consider that the single gene *BOULE* is necessary for sperm production in males of virtually all species (Shah et al., 2010). It seems to have first appeared about 600 million years ago. Without this gene, no male mountain goat, mountain lion, or mountain gorilla will ever produce even a mole hill of sperm. As another example of conservation, consider how eyes are positioned. The same PAX6 gene determines eye location in a very wide range of animals, from octopuses to ocelots (Glaser, Walton, & Maas, 1992). On the other hand, eyes themselves evolved independently in vertebrates (like ocelots) and invertebrates (like octopi). Homology (having similarities as a result of shared ancestry) suggests this because virtually all vertebrates share one kind of eye structure whereas virtually all invertebrates share another.

Evolution Comes with Baggage

A third important fact about evolution is that organisms possess millions of years of evolutionary heritage, and all the baggage that comes with it. For example, most people, like most other primates, are born adoring sugar. The strong human preference for sweets was surely adaptive in an ancient world where sugary foods like honey or ripe bananas were precious commodities. Ripe fruit is usually more nutritious than sour fruit. But in a modern world where most people are constantly surrounded by sugary foods, this natural craving for sweets contributes to obesity epidemics. And if sugar doesn't get you, fatty or salty foods may get you for evolutionarily similar reasons.

Along the same lines, we also inherited several kinds of **preparedness** from our mammalian ancestors. Preparedness is a readiness or predisposition to learn some things very easily. It's *much* easier to teach people to fear spiders or snakes than to teach them to fear guns or motorcycles. We hope it's clear, though, that guns and motorcycles are much more dangerous (see Figure 8.3). But we're stuck with the stone-age brains that helped us navigate a very different world. As the sociobiologist E.O. Wilson noted (1978), evolutionary pressures have guaranteed that we are *not* the "tabula rasa" (*blank slate*) that the philosopher John Locke once suggested.

Figure 8.3 Be very afraid of motorcycles. But don't worry about the coastal garter snake – unless you're a mole.

Motorcycle photo by Dennis Mojado. Snake photo by Steve Jurvetson.

Evolution Implies Continuity

A fourth important fact about evolution is that it implies continuity across species, especially species that are closely related. For this reason, evolutionary psychologists tend to emphasize traits and adaptations we share with other animals. For example, Frans de Waal (1996) argued that we are not as cognitively or morally superior to other animals as we like to assume. In fact, many of the cognitive and social skills that we once thought were uniquely human are not quite as special as we once thought. Naked mole rats use tools – which help keep them from choking – when they dig elaborate underground burrows with their front teeth (Shuster & Sherman, 1998). Chimps and ravens not only use but also *make* tools (see also Mann & Patterson, 2013). Both dogs and parrots have problem-solving skills that rival or exceed those of human toddlers, in at least some specific areas. Likewise, chimps and dolphins can readily do what we once thought only people could do – by recognizing themselves in mirrors or in photos. You will also learn in the module on language and human reasoning that many great apes (and a very smart border collie named Chaser) can use language to at least a limited degree. Chaser, for example, has a well-documented vocabulary of more than 1,000 words (Pilley & Reid, 2011). Chaser can also solve logical problems – such as concluding that if you ask her to retrieve something she has never heard of before ("Chaser, get *Darwin*.") the unfamiliar word in that command probably refers to the only unfamiliar object in a large collection.

Evolution is (Pretty) Efficient

A fifth important fact about how evolution works has to do with how individual organisms develop over time, and it, too, suggests a way in which we are very much like both chimps and bananas. It is this: There are many useful and important adaptations that do not exist at all at the beginning of an organism's life. Organisms develop, and development is almost never willy-nilly. Instead, things that are metabolically costly or biologically complex rarely develop until – and if – they are needed. Banana trees do not – and cannot – produce fruit until they have produced trunks and then fronds (leaves). Moving closer to people, imagine how inefficient things would be if mammals were born sexually mature, with long horns, or with a full set of adult teeth. Things that are *needed* first *develop* first, and things that aren't needed until later in a particular species almost always wait. Think about it! That is a very efficient developmental pattern. It occurs because what develops quickly in a species and what waits depends heavily on evolutionary forces. For example, gazelles can run within hours of birth because if they could not do so they would quickly become a meal for large predators. In contrast, lion cubs are born blind and helpless because few predators wish to deal with a protective mother lioness, to obtain an otherwise easy meal.

It's precisely because of the importance of principles such as baggage, continuity, and efficiency that evolutionary psychology has done so much to enrich modern psychology. But what is evolutionary psychology? To paraphrase Buss and colleagues (1998) **evolutionary psychology** is an interdisciplinary science that combines insights from evolutionary biology and psychology. It's the scientific study of how our thoughts, feelings, and behavior (psychology) are influenced by forces such as **adaptation** and **natural selection** (evolution). Let's take a quick peek at each of these crucial evolutionary concepts.

Adaptation and Natural Selection

Adaptation refers to the ways in which species change over long periods to cope with the basic problems of survival and reproduction in specific environments. It's the way a specific gene, or set of genes, ends up sticking around inside one or more species. A close cousin of adaptation – and a driving force behind it – is **natural selection**, which is the process by which genes that promote successful reproduction become more likely to be passed on to offspring – compared with genes that confer no such advantage. A turtle's bony shell is a specific adaptation to the problem of predators who like to make quick meals of slow-moving targets. A snake's venom is another reptilian adaptation. This adaptation solves two problems – by serving both as a defense against predators and an efficient method of killing one's own prey. It's probably no evolutionary accident, then, that no known snake venom is a stomach poison. If it were, how would highly venomous snakes stomach a meal into which they had just squirted a bunch of it? Snake venom is only deadly when it gets into your bloodstream, which is why venomous snakes have special venom-injecting adaptations known as fangs. So adaptation is a specific consequence of natural selection, and natural selection is the engine that drives all of evolution.

We would also like to emphasize that natural selection is driven mainly by successful *reproduction* (i.e., passing on specific genes to future generations) rather than survival. Of course, it's hard to reproduce if you don't survive long enough to mate. But once some animals have mated successfully they seem quite content to die. Consider salmon who tirelessly swim a marathon upstream – to the place where they themselves were spawned. After reaching their destinations, they "mate" in the peculiar way Bill Clinton says he did – without actually having sexual relations – and then they die.

Male honeybees actually die in the process of having sex. When male honeybees have successfully delivered their sperm to a queen bee, their genitals literally explode with a pop and are ripped away from their bodies (Judson, 2002). If you're wondering how this could ever be a good reproductive strategy, let me remind you (a) that the genitals explode *after* the delivery of sperm and (b) that queen bees are very promiscuous. Even more important, (c) the exploded bee penises stay inside the queen and act as partial chastity belts, making it harder for *other* male honeybees to get their sperm past the carnage! This means that the gene or genes that created exploding genitals right after successful mating became common in male honeybees. If this still sounds crazy, you should know that the percentage of male honeybees who ever get to mate *at all* is ridiculously low (less than 1%). So, in short, male honeybees make their only shot count (a clear precursor to the lesson in the Broadway smash *Hamilton*, "I am not throwing away my shot!"). Thus, natural selection promotes successful reproduction – not the survival of specific organisms.

Love, *Prey*, Eat. So natural selection promotes reproduction even at the expense of an organism's survival! Another example of this comes from Australia's highly venomous **redback spider** (see Figure 8.4.). These deadly predators are responsible for many painful bites to Australia's human population. In the days before hospitals got the right anti-venom, the bites of redbacks occasionally killed people. Like many other arachnids (and most insects) female redbacks are much bigger than males. And here's where it gets really weird. When a scrawny male redback mates with a big, strapping female, which only a lucky 20% of males ever get to do, he almost invariably somersaults right into her fangs after copulation. Of course, this puts him in a very vulnerable position, and about 65% of the time the female redback rewards this acrobatic feat by consuming the male just as eagerly as she consummated with him.

Figure 8.4 The female redback spider depicted here has taken out a small lizard. There's a good chance that she will also take out and consume any male redback spider who mates with her. What's more, this process seems to be highly adaptive, even for the males who get eaten.

Photo by Calistemon.

Why would male redbacks do this?! It sounds downright crazy. But studies show that male redbacks who are eaten produce more offspring than do male redbacks who escape being eaten (Andrade, 1996, 2002). One reason for this extra success is simple. When male redbacks are in the jaws of the females, they're not praying for mercy. They are busily depositing extra sperm they would not otherwise have been able to deposit. Evolutionarily speaking, then, sex is just the way successful genes make their way into future bodies. A gene that promotes self-sacrifice will be passed on precisely to the extent that the self-sacrifice promotes *reproductive* selfishness (e.g., lots of offspring). And this will happen even at the cost of the body of the unfortunate animal that happens to carry the gene for self-sacrifice. Evolution follows some fascinating rules. And many of these rules apply to people as well as to spiders.

Evolution and Human Behavior

OK, so we evolved. And the principles of evolution apply to people as well as to spiders. But what, exactly, can evolution tell us about human behavior that common sense or behaviorism cannot. In the interest of time, we will provide only a couple of examples. Two of the most important topics studied by evolutionary psychologists are mating and child rearing. Let's take a brief look at just one thing evolution tells us about each topic. First, evolution suggests that, on average, men and women should have different attitudes about mating. We'll delve into this topic much more deeply in the module on sex and sexuality, but for the present purposes, consider the evolutionary implications of being male or female. The average healthy woman can expect to produce at most 400–500 eggs in her lifetime (before menopause begins), and some of these eggs will not be viable. In contrast, most healthy men produce about 1,500–2,500 sperm per second, yes, per *second*. Sperm are also teeny compared with eggs, and this means there isn't much of a biological cost to making them. Notice that, right off the bat, women put more biological effort into producing kids than men do. Sperm also leaves the bodies of men during sexual intercourse, and eggs never do so. They stay housed safely inside women, and if an egg is fertilized this automatically begins a very costly nine-month pregnancy. A developing fetus gets every speck of its nutrition from its mother, for example. Finally, once a child is born, chances are it will receive a lot more care and attention from its mother than from its father. Unlike most other mammal dads, human dads do often provide care for their children, by the way. But men cannot nurse their children, for example, and thus throughout human history women usually did most of the caretaking. That means that for many, many millennia – going back to our earliest mammalian ancestors – mothers made much greater investments in their offspring than fathers did.

With all this in mind, Trivers (1972) developed parental investment theory. **Parental investment theory** suggests that when one sex puts more effort into sexual reproduction and/or offspring care than the other, the sex that makes the bigger investment (behaviorally or biologically) will be a pickier mater. In keeping with this prediction, studies of people across the globe show that men report being less picky – and more sexually promiscuous – than women (Schmitt, 2005). This prediction has also held up in a wide range of animal species in which female members of the species make bigger investments than the male members of the species. In fact, it even holds up in species in which the dads put more effort into offspring care than the moms do. In seahorses, as you may already know, dads take all the eggs into their bodies shortly after they are fertilized. And seahorse dads feed and protect the developing eggs until it is time to give birth (well, to pop out the baby seahorses once they're ready, whatever that's called). In keeping with parental investment theory, it's the heavily invested male seahorses that are pickier maters – and the female seahorses that are less picky and more promiscuous. The same thing holds for a few bird species (such as the red necked phalarope) in which the males do all the incubating and provide all the care for the hatchlings. It's the male birds who are the picky maters.

Getting back to people, another evolutionary prediction about childcare is that people are more likely to care for others – especially kids – when they share more genes with these others. This is a variation on **kin selection** – the hypothesis that it is much more adaptive to help those with whom you share genes than to help those who are genetically unrelated to you. There can be no doubt that most people help genetic relatives more than they help strangers – or even close friends. But kin selection theory makes some subtler predictions that go beyond what one would expect from cultural norms about helping. For example, Nancy Segal and colleagues (2019) found that aunts and uncles reported feeling closer to their nieces and nephews – and offering them more care – when these aunts and uncles were the *identical twins* rather than the *fraternal twins* of a child's parents. Socially and legally, an aunt or uncle who is a blood relative is a sibling of one of your parents, period. But if your aunt Sonja is the identical twin rather than the fraternal twin of your mom, then aunt Sonja will share just as many of her genes with you (half of them on average) as she would with her own biological children. More shared genes with a young relative translates into greater feelings of closeness and greater care, even when the legal and social relationship is the same.

These are but two of hundreds of examples of how the rules and principles of evolution shed insight on human thought, feeling, and behavior. From who we help or hurt to how the evolutionarily significant risks present in our physical environments shape culture, evolutionary psychology offers many interesting insights into how we live our lives that are not readily generated from any other perspective. Likewise, when we discuss language and reasoning later in this text, we hope you'll see that how well we reason about complex problems depends, in large part, on whether the problems are framed in ways we were very likely to encounter in our ancestral environments. For example, if you frame a logical problem as a "cheater detection task" rather than an abstract (logically identical) task, people are much more likely to be able to solve the problem. From offering insights about how we select mates or how we rear children to identifying hidden advantages and disadvantages of living in social groups, evolutionary psychology provides a unique and often surprising vantage point on human experience.

Questions for Critical Thinking and Group Discussion for Module 8

Evolutionary psychologists often distinguish the typical world in which genetically modern human beings evolved (the **environment of evolutionary adaptiveness** or **EEA**) and the worlds in which many people live today. They also argue that the evolutionary baggage you just learned about often exists because of big differences in these two worlds. Many millennia separate these two worlds. In this critical thinking activity, we encourage you to consider the implications of this principle for three questions about how evolution may have shaped modern life.

1. In the EEA food was scarce, and people were born ready to store fat during times of plenty – so that they did not starve during times of scarcity. This ability to store fat was surely adaptive in the EEA, but how adaptive is it now? What are some drawbacks of this ability in cultures where food is usually plentiful? How might food producers and marketers take advantage of our innate preference for sugar and fat in the ways in which they create and market modern foods?

2. Human beings evolved in small, tightly-knit social groups (e.g., family units, tribes). Thus, in the EEA people knew very well those with whom they usually interacted (e.g., Who's dishonest? Who's helpful?). It may also have been very adaptive to be wary of (if not downright aggressive toward) strangers. What are the implications of the EEA for (a) how well different social groups get along and (b) how people survive today in cities where they have brief contact with dozens of strangers in a given day?

3. In the EEA if you saw something, it was real, and it existed locally. There were no photos or news stories, for example. But today we see lot of images of things that occur thousands of miles away (e.g., violent TV dramas, school shootings) and some of which occurred either months or years ago. How might modern technology operate on our EEA-evolved brains to bias our view of how dangerous the world is?

Principles such as natural selection and selective fitness often suggest some harsh predictions about human nature. Although there is little doubt that people can be downright generous under the right circumstances, there is also evidence for what Richard Dawkins called the "**selfish gene**." Genes will be passed on to one's offspring to precisely the degree that such genes promote successful reproduction and/or survival. With this in mind, consider the following question.

4. It is a core premise of evolutionary thinking that people are nicer to those with whom they share genes. All else being equal, you should be more likely to help your sister than your cousin, and more likely to help your cousin than to help a stranger. As you probably call, the theory that makes this prediction is known as **kin selection** theory. The distressing flip side of kin selection is that we should be much more likely to *harm* those with whom we do *not* share any genes? What distressing prediction would this concept suggest about whether stepparents (who share no genes with their stepchildren) or biological parents (who share half their genes with their children) are more likely to abuse the children for whom we might otherwise expect them to care?

Multiple-Choice Questions for Module 8

1. Housecats *love* catnip. Big cats such as lions show the same favorable response to catnip – whereas very few other animals do so. This reaction among different species of cat is probably grounded in genes that all cats share with a common ancestor. This is thus a behavioral example of:

   A) homology
   B) convergent evolution
   C) neurology

2. Morganucadon (aka "Morgie") was:

   A) an apparent common ancestor of all modern mammals
   B) a small warm-blooded dinosaur that appears to have evolved into modern birds
   C) one of the last known surviving dinosaurs

3. What aspect of dolphin locomotion illustrates homology with locomotion in other mammals?

   A) their up and down rather than side to side swimming movements
   B) tiny movements in their vestigial rear legs that occur as they swim
   C) the use of the same regions of the cerebellum that prompt movement in four legged mammals

4. Several birds and mammals not only use but also make tools, just as we do. This fact is highly consistent with the idea that:

   A) if an ability is useful enough, it can evolve very quickly
   B) evolution implies continuity
   C) warm-blooded animals are more highly evolved than cold blooded animals

5. As suggested by redback spiders, most animals seem to be programmed above all else to maximize:

   A) survival
   B) reproduction
   C) success against rivals

6. No mammals begin life with their adult teeth. Likewise, no horned animals begin life with very long horns, and no birds (not even the toucan) begin life with very long beaks or bills. This is all consistent with the idea that:

   A) evolution is efficient
   B) evolution often solves the same problem in many ways

7. Why do male redback spiders who get eaten by females usually produce more offspring?

   A) because they only engage in self-sacrifice when they have found a highly fertile female
   B) because the extra time they spend in the jaws of the female allow them to fertilize more eggs
   C) because the nutrition they provide the female helps her produce very healthy eggs

8. The idea that human evolution "often comes with baggage" could easily be true because:

   A) the environments in which we evolved were very different than the environments in which we live today
   B) there is no easy way to remove a specific gene from the gene pool once it becomes highly common
   C) the costs a gene that creates "baggage" must greatly outweigh its benefits before natural selection kicks in

9. The idea that evolution comes with baggage appears to play a big role in:

   A) the difficulty human beings have learning to cooperate rather than to compete
   B) high murder rates in places that are very crowded (e.g., big cities)
   C) high rates of obesity in many wealthy nations

10. It is much easier to teach people to associate the faces of unattractive people with unpleasant words than to teach people to associate the faces of highly attractive people with unpleasant words. This finding supports the learning principle known as (this is the time for leaping – my students like this question):

   A) associative learning
   B) face learning
   C) preparedness
   D) evolution is driven by intelligent design.

Answer Key: 1A, 2A, 3A, 4B, 5B, 6A, 7B, 8A, 9C, 10C

References

Andrade, M.C.B. (1996). Sexual selection for male sacrifice in the Australian redback spider. *Science, 271*, 70–72.

Andrade, M.C.B. (2002). Risky mate search and male self-sacrifice in redback spiders. *Behavioral Ecology, 14*, 531–538.

Brusatte, S. L., Butler, R. J., Barrett, P. M., Carrano, M. T., Evans, D. C., Lloyd, G. T., ... Williamson, T. E. (2014). The extinction of the dinosaurs. *Biological Reviews.*

Buss, D. M., Haselton, M. G., Shackelford, T. K., Bleske, A. L., & Wakefield, J. C. (1998). Adaptations, exaptations, and spandrels. *American Psychologist, 53*, 533–548.

de Waal, F. B. M. (1996). *Good natured: The origins of right and wrong in humans and other animals.* Cambridge, MA: Harvard University Press.

Diamond, J. (1992). *The third chimpanzee: The evolution and future of the human animal.* New York: Harper Collins.

Diamond, J. (1997). *Guns, germs, and steel: The fates of human societies.* New York: W.W. Norton & Company.

Ermini, L., Der Sarkissian, C., Willerslev, E., & Orlando, L. (2015). Major transitions in human evolution revisited: A tribute to ancient DNA. *Journal of Human Evolution, 79*, 4–20.

Glaser, T., Walton, D. S., & Maas, R. L. (1992). Genomic structure, evolutionary conservation and aniridia mutations in the human PAX6 gene. *Nature Genetics, 2*, 232–239.

Judson, O. (2002). *Dr. Tatiana's sex advice to all creation.* New York: Metropolitan Books.

Mann, J., & Patterson, E. M. (2013). Tool use by aquatic animals. *Philosophical Transactions of the Royal Society, 368*, 20120424.

Meng, J., Wang, Y., & Li, C. (2011). Transitional mammalian middle ear from a new Cretaceous *Jehol eutriconodontan. Nature, 472*, 181–185.

Meyerowitz, E. M. (2002). Plants compared to animals: The broadest comparative study of development. *Science, 295*, 1482–1485.

O'Leary, M. A., Bloch, J. I., Flynn, J. J., Gaudin, T.J., Giallombardo, A., Giannini, N.P., Goldberg, S.L., Kraatz, B.P., Luo, Z.-X., Meng, J., Ni, X., Novacek, M.J., Perini, F.A., Randall, Z.S., Rougier, G.W., Sargis, E.J., Silcox, M.T., Simmons, N.B., Spaulding, M., Velazco, P.M., Weksler, M., Wible, J.R., & Cirranello, A.L. (2013). The placental mammal ancestor and the post-K-Pg radiation of placentals. *Science, 339*, 662–667.

Pilley, J. W., & Reid, A. K. (2011). Border collie comprehends object names as verbal referents. *Behavioural Processes, 86*(2), 184–195.

Schmitt, D. P. (2005). Sociosexuality from Argentina to Zimbabwe: A 48-nation study of sex, culture, and strategies of human mating. *Behavioral and Brain Sciences, 28*, 247–311.

Segal, N., Naji, D. A., Preston, K. S., & Marelich, W. D. (2019, May 30). *Social closeness revisited in MZ and DZ twin families: Aunt/uncle-niece/nephews relations.* Presented at the 2019 Human Behavior and Evolution Society Conference, Boston, MA.

Shah, C., VanGompel, M. J. W., Naeem, V., Chen, Y., Lee, T., Angeloni, N., Wang, Y., & Xu, E.Y. (2010). Widespread presence of BOULE homologs among animals and conservation of their ancient reproductive function. *PLOS, Genetics*, July 15.

Shuster, G., & Sherman, P. W. (1998). Tool use by naked mole-rats. *Animal Cognition, 1*, 71–74.

Trivers, R.L. (1972). Parental investment and sexual selection. In *Sexual selection and the descent of man.* (B. Campbell, Ed.) Chicago, IL: Aldine.

Wilson, E. O. (1978). *On human nature.* Cambridge, MA: Harvard University Press.

IV
Sensation and Perception

Sensation and Perception

Module 9
How the World Gets Inside You

Sensation and Perception

One of the most fundamental questions in psychology has to do with how the external world becomes a part of our internal world. For example, how do the physical characteristics of things (e.g., the temperature of a stone, the amplitude of a sound wave) get translated into our *experience* of these things (e.g., "That's hot!", "That's quiet."). Psychologists call the physical things in the world **stimuli** (plural of *stimulus*). Stimuli can be described objectively (e.g., the frequency of the sound was 250 Hertz, the ball weighed 250 grams). In contrast, **sensations** (the activity triggered in our brain by stimuli) and **perceptions** (our interpretation of that activity) exist inside us. We must usually report them verbally (e.g., "That's a C-sharp." "That's Beethoven"). No complex animal could survive if it couldn't reliably convert at least *some* stimuli into perceptions.

Consider the survival consequences of visual impairments. Compared with sighted people, visually impaired people have much greater difficulty getting around. People with visual disabilities are also at elevated risk for injury (Legood, Scuffham, & Cryer, 2002; Manduchi & Kurniawan, 2011). For good reason, then, many people say that going blind would be worse than going deaf, losing one's memory, or losing a limb (Scott, Bressler, Folkes, Wittenborn, & Jorkasky, 2016). Like other primates, people are *extremely* visual creatures. In fact, our preference for visual information is so powerful that visual cues often trump other sensory cues. Consider the **McGurk effect**. To document this powerful effect, researchers ask a speaker to say "ba ba ba." This "ba ba ba" sound is then carefully edited into a *video* of the same speaker saying, "fa fa fa." Figure 9.1 fleshes this out a bit. The image on the left reveals a girl who's about to say "fa." The image on the right reveals a girl who's about to say "ba." Those who see a doctored video with the "ba ba ba" *sound* and the "fa fa fa" *lip movements* clearly hear "fa fa fa." To see this powerful illusion yourself, go to www.youtube.com/watch?v=G-lN8vWm3m0. The McGurk effect still happens even when you know all about it, by the way. This suggests that our preference for visual information over other kinds of

Figure 9.1 The eyes have it. When your eyes suggest that someone is saying "fa, fa, fa" (like the kid on the left), but the person is really saying "ba, ba, ba" (like the kid on the right), you will quite convincingly hear "fa, fa, fa." That's the McGurk effect.

information is pretty irresistible. Your eyes sometimes trump your ears even when your conscious mind knows that you should disregard what you see.

Getting back to how our senses are adaptive, hearing problems, like visual disabilities, can pose a risk to our safety. A large study of children admitted to emergency rooms in South Carolina suggested that children with hearing impairments face about twice the risk of personal injury faced by other children (Mann, Zhou, McKee, & McDermott, 2007). Your first author has conducted informal surveys about sensation on people of all ages. Most people report that the sense they would *least* be willing to lose is vision, followed by hearing. Things are less predictable for other senses. Some people say they absolutely could not do without a sense of smell, taste, or touch. Others report that it wouldn't be a big deal to give up one of these less celebrated senses. When your first author asked his teenage son how much money it would take to convince him to give up his sense of taste for the rest of his life, this teenager's price was five million dollars. When your first author asked his middle-aged wife the same question, her response was that if this magical procedure would stop her from craving ice cream, she would expect no payment. In fact, she would gladly pay to receive it.

So from an evolutionary perspective, at least, our senses exist because they help us survive and successfully navigate our worlds. Both hearing and vision let us know that something is out there when we haven't even touched it yet. Likewise, smell can tell us that something invisible recently happened. This could be as mundane as the gastric aftermath of a bean burrito or as important as a gas leak. Likewise, taste can tell us that eating something now would make us very sick tomorrow. Sensation is a miraculous thing.

Consider a less obvious example of the survival value of sensation. Imagine you could go through the rest of your life without ever experiencing any physical pain. That means no migraines, back aches, or ear aches, and no pain when you burn, scrape, or cut yourself. Although this may sound like a dream come true, studies of those who never experience pain suggest that having no sense of pain is more nightmarish than dreamy. Acute pain is a mechanism for letting us know that our bodies are in trouble (Inoue, 2018). Without this important warning system, we'd get into very serious trouble. The rare disease known as **congenital insensitivity to pain with anhidrosis (CIPA)** robs its victims of the ability to feel any physical pain whatsoever. The result is that CIPA patients become horribly injured. We will spare you some of the gory details, but those with this disorder often grab red hot objects or break bones without knowing they have done so. In June of 2018, the Associated Press reported the heartbreaking story of a teenage girl who had no teeth because her insensitivity to pain had caused her to break them all off (Huppert, 2018). Patients who suffer from CIPA never suffer from headaches, but they suffer plenty of heartaches. Sensation matters.

Our Senses Determine What We Can and Cannot Do

Across the animal kingdom, there is tremendous variation in what animals can perceive. Bees see in ultra-violet. Pit vipers can detect the infrared. Thus, even in the dark, pit vipers can see the heat that emanates from your body. Homing pigeons can sense the Earth's magnetic field (Wiltschko & Wiltschko, 2008). Sticking with birds, most birds of prey can see much better than people can, especially at great distances. The bald eagle has three foveae (three spots in the retina where photoreceptors are densely concentrated). People have only one fovea. Further, our one fovea is much less densely packed with photoreceptors than any of the foveae of the eagle. Figure 9.2 should reinforce the point that eagles have amazing eyesight.

Figure 9.2 As suggested by this bald eagle skull, eagles have eyes that are proportionately much
larger than human eyes. In fact, an eagle's eyes weigh as much as its brain. Eagles also
have three fovea – compared with one for people. Furthermore, each of the eagle's
foveae is five to six times as densely packed with photoreceptors as is ours. Saying someone has an "eagle eye" is thus a very big compliment.

Cross-species differences in sensory capabilities have a clear basis in biology. Consider
the eagle. Their two eyeballs weigh as much as their brains. Or consider the lovable dog.
Dogs have *10,000–100,000 times* the olfactory sensitivity of people (Walker et al., 2006).
One reason why dogs have such an amazing sense of smell is that they have
200–300 million scent-detecting cells in their noses. In comparison, we have about
5 million. Dogs also have **olfactory bulbs** (brain regions devoted to processing smells) that
are proportionately *much* bigger than ours. The olfactory abilities of dogs explain why
there are bomb-sniffing dogs at airports but no bomb-sniffing turtles or owls. If you're wondering why there are no bomb-sniffing *cats* at airports, it's not because cats have a poor
sense of smell. It's because cats could care less if we all get blown to bits.

"Hey, isn't that ole' Rex Conley over there? Why I haven't
smelled him in years!"

Figure 9.2b

But we don't have to make cross-species comparisons to see that perception dictates behavior. People can't respond to what they can't detect, and there are **absolute
thresholds** for our senses. This means that stimuli of extremely low intensities are
not registered at all by the human senses. This is probably why, in 1608, Hans Lip-
pershey invented the "Dutch perspective glass," better known as the telescope
(O'Callaghan, 2018). The absolute thresholds for five well-studied senses appear in
Table 9.1. Many people are surprised to see that some extremely faint stimuli can
be detected at above chance levels. Remember, however, that absolute thresholds

Table 9.1 Absolute thresholds for five senses

Sense	Absolute Threshold for Typical Human Perceiver
Vision	a medium candle flame from 30 miles away on a clear, moonless night
Hearing	a clock ticking 20 feet away in an otherwise quiet room
Taste	half a teaspoon of sugar in a gallon of otherwise pure water
Touch	the wing of a fly being dropped on one's cheek from a height of 1 cm
Smell	one puff of perfume in a six-room house

(adapted from Schacter et al., 2011)

Note. These thresholds are not *truly* "absolute." They vary with motivational states and with alertness, for example. Thresholds also vary within a sensory dimension. For example, 3,000 Hertz tones have a much lower absolute threshold than much higher or much lower pitched tones.

represent the minimal point at which most people can *guess*, at levels slightly higher than chance, whether they were exposed to a stimulus. If we wanted people to be *sure* they'd seen, heard, or tasted something, we'd have to crank up these signals quite a bit.

People also differ from one another in their sensory acuity, and this is especially true for taste (Bartoshuk, Duffy, & Miller, 1994; Hayes & Keast, 2011). As shown in Figure 9.3, about half of all people (40–50%) are simply **tasters**. They have a roughly average number of **fungiform papillae** on their tongues. These little structures are homes to your taste buds. Another 25–30% of people are **hypo-tasters**. They have very few fungiform papillae on their tongues, and thus the electrochemical signals sent by their tongues to register tastes such as "bitter" or "sour" are not very rich. At the other gustatory extreme, **supertasters** (also 25–30% of the population) have tongues that boast numerous fungiform papillae. This means many more taste buds than average – to send detailed taste signals to the brain. In fact, supertasters have about ten times the taste sensitivity hypo-tasters have. If this kind of individual difference existed for vision, "super-seers" could see as well at 200 feet as "hypo-seers" could see at 20 feet.

Differences in taste sensitivity have consequences. Relative to hypo-tasters, supertasters are at reduced risk of becoming alcoholics – and for good reason. If you ever tried to toss back a shot of 100 proof tequila, you know that alcohol tastes downright unpleasant. To a supertaster, a glass of cabernet might taste as harsh as a shot of vodka does to a hypo-taster. The same logic explains why supertasters often dislike spicy foods – and why super-tasters are less likely than hypo-tasters to become obese. Extremely sweet or fatty foods do not taste good to a supertaster; they taste overwhelming. But there are also costs of being a supertaster. Because healthy-but-bitter vegetables such as broccoli taste *extremely* bitter to supertasters, more supertasters than hypo-tasters steer clear of healthy green vegetables. This appears to put supertasters at elevated risk for colon cancer.

Transduction

Transduction, transduction, transduction. The point of much of this chapter is that our senses exist to help us know what is out there in the world. But how do our senses work? That is, how do heat, light waves, or a sip of Coca-Cola become sensations? The short answer is transduction. **Transduction** is the physiological process by which physical stimuli

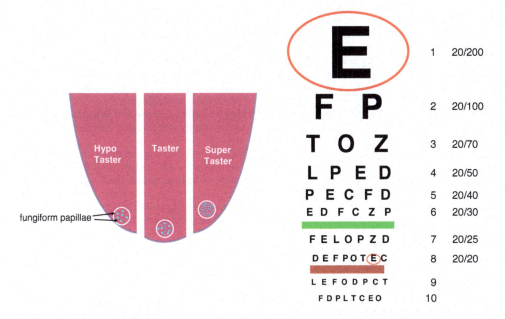

Figure 9.3 The left image is a comparison of the tongues of non-tasters (aka "hypo-tasters"), tasters, and supertasters. The right image illustrates, by analogy with vision, just how much more sensitive to bitterness supertasters are compared with hypo-tasters. Super-tasters have about ten times the sensitivity to taste hypo-tasters have. If you can barely read the 20/20 line of this eye chart from two feet away, step 20 feet away. It should be about equally difficult now to read the *top* line. That's a visual factor of 10.

become electrochemical signals that are sent to the brain for interpretation. Recall that **sensory neurons** (aka, **receptor neurons**) are one of the three kinds of neurons. Their job is transduction. Near the surface of your skin, receptors convert touch or warmth to neural signals. Deep in your inner ear, the **basilar membrane** converts sound waves to neural signals. In your eye, the retina converts the visible portion of electromagnetic radiation into signals about the color, brightness, and location of physical objects. In the interest of space, we will only delve deeply into transduction as applied to vision. However, Table 9.2 summarizes how transduction works for each of six human senses.

Transduction begins with the work of two well-known **photoreceptors.** The **cones** allow you to experience detailed color vision, and they are heavily concentrated in the **fovea**. Without your fovea, you'd barely see in color at all. Further, though you'd be able to see the gist of your surroundings, you'd be legally blind (everything would be blurry). As shown in Figure 9.5, which reveals the microstructure of the retina, **rods** are the other type of photoreceptor. Rods are much more evenly distributed across the retina than cones, but their spatial concentration also varies. Rods are most highly concentrated in a donut-shaped ring of the retina that sits a bit outside – and is concentric to – the fovea. Rods are responsible for black and white, low-light vision. Interestingly, there are *no* rods in the cone-rich fovea. You may also recall that there are neither rods nor cones in the aptly named **blind spot**, which is the area where the optic nerve leaves the eye to deliver visual information to the brain. Remember the disappearing moon illusion? This illusion exists, in part, because of our blind spots.

Table 9.2 Transduction and related processes for six human senses

Vision: Cells in the retina convert visible electromagnetic radiation (light) to neural signals about the brightness, color, and location of physical objects.

Hearing: Tiny, hair-like cilia in the basilar membrane convert soundwaves to information about the frequency of the sound sources. By comparing the timing of signals from each ear, the brain also makes inferences about the likely location of sound sources. A sound coming from the right arrives at your right ear about 2/3 of a millisecond before it arrives at your left ear.

Taste: Your taste buds fire in response to molecules that we perceive along five well-accepted dimensions: sweet, sour, bitter, salty, and umami (savory). Other candidates for basic tastes include fattiness, spiciness, and coolness (Hadhazy, 2011).

Smell: Specialized olfactory ("smell") cells in the lining of your nose convert molecules of specific shapes to neural signals for specific smells. Olfactory cells share some features with the photoreceptors known as rods and some with the tiny cilia that allow us to hear. Smell, then, works a bit like seeing and a bit like hearing.

Touch: Unlike your eyes or ears, your skin (the main organ that lets you experience touch) covers your entire body. Specialized receptor cells in your skin allow you to detect pain, heat, cold, or simple contact with an object.

Proprioception (bodily position): Even in total darkness, you can detect the position of your body, your limbs, and even your fingers. You can also detect how forcefully your muscles contract. This is possible because muscles and tendons contain receptors that report how much tension or pressure is placed upon them.

Visual Transduction. When a source of light enters the lens of your eye and passes through the clear liquid inside your eyeball, it strikes the **retina**, the layer of photoreceptors (sensory neurons) and helper cells that line much of the inside of your eyeball. The basic structures of the human eye appear in Figure 9.4. Here you can see, for example, where light enters the eye (through the lens) and where the optic nerve leaves the eye, carrying signals to the brain. The retina, which is where transduction happens, is shown in yellow.

If you take a careful look at Figure 9.5, you'll notice something surprising about the microscopic structure of the retina. The rods and cones that convert light into neural impulses are buried several layers deep. Light must pass through the retina's ganglion cells and bipolar cells (both of which are full-fledged neurons) – not to mention a forest of optic nerve axons – before it ever reaches the place where transduction begins. This may seem downright backwards, but it works. Transduction in the eye begins when the light waves striking a rod or cone trigger that photoreceptor to produce an action potential that eventually sends a signal to the brain. The word "eventually" in the previous sentence is a sneaky way to skip over many of the complexities of visual transduction. However, even in this introductory text, we feel compelled to note that unlike your other sensory organs, your eye is really a part of your brain. One sense in which this is true is that complex neural processing happens *in the eye itself*. This includes the synapses, action potentials, and complex neural communication patterns that happen as rods and cones communicate with bipolar and ganglion cells. As Purves et al. (2001) put it, the retina is "a full-fledged part of the central nervous system" because it "comprises complex neural circuitry that converts the graded electrical activity of photoreceptors into action potentials that travel to the brain via axons in the optic nerve." Your eye is a "tiny bit of brain that exists outside of your brain case" (Albrecht, 1988). Figure 9.6 should help you appreciate visual transduction a bit more – by giving you a close look at the structure of the two basic types of photoreceptors in the human eye (rods and cones). If nothing else, Figure 9.6 should help you better appreciate the retina's extreme complexity.

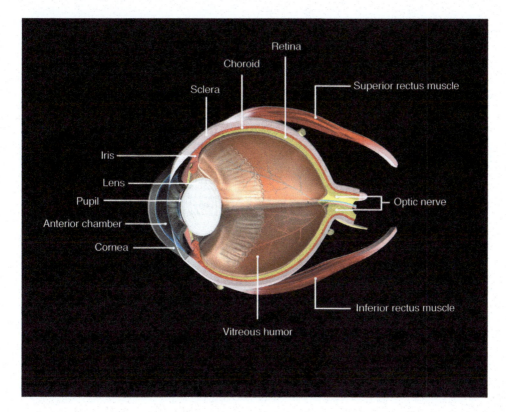

Figure 9.4 The gross structures of the human eye, as seen from above. The retina, where transduction takes place, includes the sensitive area known as the macula and the tiny, even more sensitive area known as the fovea. The fovea is about the size of the head of a pin, but it's where almost all your clear, full-color vision originates. The optic disk is otherwise known as the blind spot. In vertebrates, there are no photoreceptors at all in the spot where the optic nerve leaves the retina for the brain.

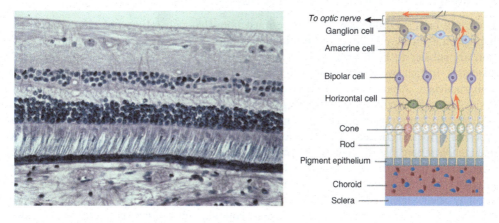

Figure 9.5 A micrographic (left) and a stylized (right) look at the microstructure of the retina. Both images reflect the fact that light must pass through several layers of the retina before reaching the rods and cones that are directly responsible for converting light into neural signals.

Stylized microstucture image credit: Alila Medical Media/Shutterstock.com

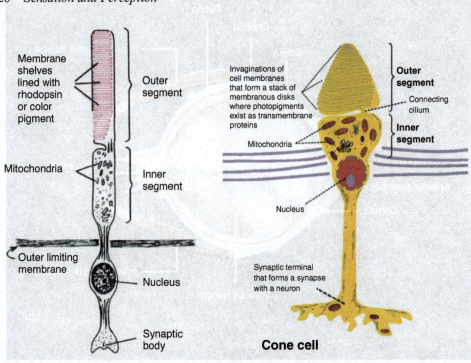

Membrane shelves lined with rhodopsin or color pigment

Outer segment

Mitochondria

Inner segment

Outer limiting membrane

Nucleus

Synaptic body

Invaginations of cell membranes that form a stack of membranous disks where photopigments exist as transmembrane proteins

Mitochondria

Nucleus

Synaptic terminal that forms a synapse with a neuron

Outer segment

Connecting cilium

Inner segment

Cone cell

Figure 9.6 The image on the left is a rod (responsible for black and white vision). The one on the right is a cone (responsible for color vision). A typical rod is about 100 microns (1/254th of an inch) long, and the "outer segment" alone contains about 1,000 of the "membrane disks" (shown in pink) that represent the first step in converting light into an electro-chemical signal headed to the brain. Note that the phrase "color pigment" in the description of the rod does *not* mean that rods allow for color vision.

Sensation and Perception are Two-way Streets

Even in a brief module such as this, we must note that perception and sensation do not happen in a social, cognitive, or emotional vacuum. Even processes as basic as transduc-tion are subject to both bottom-up ("stimulus driven") and top-down ("theory-driven") processes. In fact, we devote a good portion of Module 10 to the perceptual principle of constructivism. Among other things, **constructivism** means that our desires and expect-ations have a powerful impact on perception. A *lot* of perception is constructed, meaning it is subject to top-down processes driven, for instance, by our preconceived notions, stereo-types, or prior experiences. To cite a few examples, fearful people who are atop a hill on a skateboard perceive the hill as physically steeper than those that do not feel fearful (Ste-fanucci, Proffitt, Clore, & Parekh, 2008). As a very different example, consider taste. In an interview with *Slate* (Shwedel, 2015), food psychologist Charles Spence noted that color strongly affects taste. For example, artificially coloring a candy red makes it taste sweeter than making it any other color. This is one reason why red candies sell better than candies of other colors, and why many products flavored with real strawberries are artificially col-ored red or pink. Desirable labels also have a big impact on taste. Coke lovers who mislabel Coke and Pepsi in a blind taste test report liking what they wrongly *believe* to be Coke (but which is really Pepsi) much more than Coke itself (Pelham, 2017). Of course, Pepsi lovers show the opposite bias, saying they really liked Coke when they wrongly believed it to be Pepsi. A big part of marketing is selecting the right name for your product, and this is true whether you are selling deodorant or anti-depressants.

Miguel Brendl and colleagues (2005) showed that one of the nicest ways you can label a fake Japanese tea is by using people's own first names. They did so by taking the first part of a person's first name and adding "-ioke" to it – to create what tea consumers thought was a real Japanese tea. As a concrete example, whereas Daniels and Danielles preferred Danioke tea over Brenioke tea Brendas and Brendans showed the opposite preference. (Luckily, the experimenter in this study reports that he did not encounter any participants named Kari.) We suspect that it is because of the power of labeling effects that in the summer of 2014, the U.S. division of the Coca-Cola Company rolled out "one of the most successful marketing campaigns in the company's history" (Tarver, 2019). Coke began selling 20-ounce bottles of Coke whose labels featured 250 of the most popular first names in the United States. Your first author himself has often have selected Cokes labeled *Jason*, *Kelli*, and *David* from the cooler because he has friends and family members with these nice names. To be clear, however, he refused to share these Cokes with the specific people after whom they were named. That stuff is just too delicious to share.

Cyborgs, Bionics, and the Future of Human Perception

One of the most interesting aspects of human perception is the fact that we are developing technology that can alter or improve our sensory abilities. Ideas that once seemed like science fiction are now becoming a reality. Consider **cochlear implants**. Many people who would have been completely deaf not very long ago can now hear because of cochlear implants. Unlike hearing aids, which merely amplify sounds to make them easier to hear, cochlear implants convert sounds to electrical signals that are then sent to the brain for auditory processing (as if they had been generated by a heathy inner ear). Scientists have also made recent advances in the development of **bionic eyes** (artificial vision systems). Currently, bionic eyes are a far cry from natural vision, and they are only helpful to people who once had normal vision and lost it. Further, patients who have bionic eyes describe the experience as being more like a series of chaotic white flashes than a continuous stream of visual information (Petoe, Ayton, & Shivdasani, 2017). But as advances in computing and nanotechnology continue, experts are hopeful that bionic eyes may bring a reasonable semblance of natural vision to those who would otherwise live in complete darkness.

Recent developments in sensory technology already allow people who are born color-blind to perceive color. The artist Neil Harbisson has benefited greatly from such technology. In a TED talk you can see at www.ted.com/talks/neil_harbisson_i_listen_to_color?language=en, Harbisson describes himself as a **cyborg** (part biological being and part machine). Born completely color-blind, Harbisson lived the first 21 years of his life seeing only shades of grey. In 2003, Harbisson began working with scientists to develop a device that converts color to sound. Because both color and sound are determined by the frequency of the waves that create them, Harbisson's visual assistance system merely converts reflected light of different frequencies to *sounds* of different frequencies. Like most other people, Harbisson perceives variations in sound frequency as pitch. Thus, Harbisson *hears* color – via a device that sends signals directly to his brain. In fact, once Harbisson had mastered the process of matching auditory frequencies to colors, he began to "see color" in sounds. A phone might ring "purple." A musical note or a person's voice might register as vivid green. In fact, after Harbisson mastered the full range of visible colors, he got an upgrade that allowed him to perceive both infrared and ultraviolet light. As a result, Harbisson can look out on a warm spring day and decide whether he should apply sunscreen before talking a long walk. As our understanding of sensation and perception increases, and as we develop devices that can mimic the functions of our eyes, ears, and other sensory organs, sensory disabilities may largely become a thing of the past, at least for those lucky enough to afford high-tech interventions. In fact, cyborgs such as Harbisson may someday make the rest of us wish that we, too, could see the ultraviolet or hear the ultrasonic.

Figure 9.7

Hands-on Activities for Module 9

Part 1: All vertebrates, yourself included, have a blind spot in each eye – where the optic nerve leaves the eye for the brain. Normally you do not suffer any negative effects of having a blind spot because of your **binocular vision**. Your brain integrates the separate images it gets from each eye to create a coherent whole that has no blind spot. Binocular vision also makes you very good at depth perception, by the way. As you'll see soon, it even gives you a quirky ability to see through things that would otherwise obstruct your view of what is ahead of you. Getting back to your blind spot, if you limit yourself to using just one eye, you should be able to see that you do, in fact, have a blind spot.

Figure 9.8

Close your left eye and stare at the red dot in the center of the Earth. Now, slowly and carefully, move your face closer to the screen. When you get about 8–10 inches from the screen (or the page) the moon should completely disappear, and you should see only the Earth and the darkness of space. In addition to showing that you have a blind spot, this demonstration also illustrates a basic higher-order principle of perception. Do you recall the name of it?

Part 2: OK. You have blind spots. We all do. But you *also* have x-ray vision, sort of. *Close your left eye* and put your thumb in front of the man in the center of Figure 9.9 – until you can't see him at all. If you wish, move your thumb closer to your face until you have *completely* blocked out the center man entirely. Now open your right eye. Once you get to take advantage of your binocular vision, there should be no part of the man in the center you cannot see. If there *is* any part of him you can't see, just move your thumb closer to your face and you'll see the entire photo.

Figure 9.9

Multiple-Choice Questions for Module 9

1. Stimuli are converted to sensations and perceptions by means of which physical and biochemical conversion process?

   A) capitulation
   B) conversion
   C) transduction

2. What snail-shaped part of the inner ear is the main organ responsible for converting sounds waves into neural activity that is then sent to the brain to be processed as sound?

   A) the eardrum
   B) the vestibular canals
   C) the basilar membrane

3. The brains of dogs contain _____ that have about 50 times as many cells as our brains do.

   A) olfactory bulbs
   B) gustatory centers
   C) fungiform papillae

4. It is only because we have two eyes that are pointed in slightly different directions that our _____ do not create serious visual "dead spots" in small portions of our visual fields.

   A) cones
   B) blind spots
   C) foveas

5. Relative to the rest of the retina, the fovea contains a very dense concentration of:

   A) rods
   B) cones
   C) myelination

6. People who possess a much greater than average number of fungiform papillae are known as:

   A) supertasters
   B) taste experts
   C) olfactory prodigies
   D) acoustic aficionados

7. The rare genetic condition known as CIPA involves a congenital insensitivity to pain. What often happens to people with CIPA?

   A) they often become very seriously disfigured and/or disabled
   B) they use their others sense (e.g., vision) to compensate for a lost sensitivity to pain.
   C) they often become extremely successful endurance athletes (e.g., bikers, marathoners)

8. What's the technical term for the physical things outside the person that lead to sensations and perceptions?

   A) matter
   B) stimuli
   C) energy
   D) transducers

9. Your chapter on sensation and perception emphasized the fact that, above all else, sensation and perception promote our:

   A) survival
   B) felt safety
   C) well-being
   D) understanding

10. Joan applies for a job as a taste tester for Paul Mondavi winery. The staff at Mondavi give Joan a test that shows that she is a hypo-taster. What is the most likely consequence of Joan's tasting status?

    A) it will take Joan longer than usual to become a wine tasting expert
    B) it will not take Joan very long at all to become a wine-tasting expert
    C) she is probably a poor fit for a job as a taste tester
    D) she is probably a great fit for a job as a taste tester

Answer Key: 1C, 2C, 3A, 4B, 5B, 6A, 7A, 8B, 9A, 10C

References

Albrecht, D. (1988). Personal communication (in a lecture on the brain and visual perception).

Bartoshuk, L. M., Duffy, V. B., & Miller, I. J. (1994). PTC/PROP tasting: Anatomy, psychophysics, and sex effects. *Physiology and Behavior, 56*(6), 1165–1171.

Brendl, C.M., Chattopadhyay, A., Pelham, B.W., & Carvallo, M.R. (2005). Name letter branding in consumer choice: Attribute specific valence transfer. *Journal of Consumer Research, 32*, 405–415.

Hadhazy, A. (2011, December 30). Tip of the tongue: Humans may taste at least 6 flavors. *Live Science*. Retrieved on December 2018 from www.livescience.com/17684-sixth-basic-taste.html

Hayes, J. E., & Keast, R. S. (2011). Two decades of supertasting: Where do we stand? *Physiology and Behavior, 104*(5), 1072–1074.

Huppert, B. (2018, June 2). Minnesota girl who can't feel pain battles insurance company. Associated Press. Retrieved on December 18, 2018 from www.apnews.com/

Inoue, K. (2018). A state-of-the-art perspective on microgliopathic pain. *Open Biology, 8*(11), 180154. doi:10.1098/rsob.180154

Legood, R., Scuffham, P., & Cryer, C. (2002). Are we blind to injuries in the visually impaired? A review of the literature. *Injury Prevention: Journal of the International Society for Child and Adolescent Injury Prevention, 8*(2), 155–160.

Manduchi, R., & Kurniawan, S. (2011). Mobility-related accidents experienced by people with visual impairment. *Insight: Research and Practice in Visual Impairment and Blindness, 4*(2). Retrieved from http://users.soe.ucsc.edu/~manduchi/papers/MobilityAccidents.pdf

Mann, J. R., Zhou, L., McKee, M., & McDermott, S. (2007). Children with hearing loss and increased risk of injury. *Annals of Family Medicine, 5*(6), 528–533.

O'Callaghan, J. (2018, June 17). Did Galileo invent the telescope? *Space Answers*. Retrieved from www.spaceanswers.com/astronomy/did-galileo-invent-the-telescope/

Pelham, B. W. (2017). Unpublished data from dozens of blind cola taste tests.

Petoe, M., Ayton, L., & Shivdasani, M. (2017, August 16). Artificial vision: What people with bionic eyes see. *The Conversation*. Retrieved on December 2018 from https://theconversation.com/artificial-vision-what-people-with-bionic-eyes-see-79758

Purves, D., Augustine, G. J., Fitzpatrick, D., Katz, L.C., LaMantia, A.-S., McNamara, J.O., & Williams, S.M. (2001). *Neuroscience* (2nd ed.). Sunderland, MA: Sinauer Associates. Retrieved *NCBI Bookshelf* on December 17, 2018 from www.ncbi.nlm.nih.gov/books/NBK10885/

Schacter, D.L., Gilbert, D.T., & Wegner, D.M. (2011) *Psychology* (2nd Ed). New York: Worth.

Scott, A. W., Bressler, N. M., Folkes, S., Wittenborn, J. S., & Jorkasky, J. (2016). Public attitudes about eye and vision health. *JAMA Ophthalmology, 134*(10), 1111–1118. doi:10.1001/jamaophthalmol.2016.2627

Shwedel, H. (2015. Everyone likes red and pink candies best. *Slate*. Retrieved June 27, 2019 from https://slate.com/human-interest/2015/07/red-is-the-best-flavor-popsicle-red-classics-starburst-favereds-and-the-science-of-how-candy-color-affects-taste.html

Stefanucci, J. K., Proffitt, D. R., Clore, G. L., & Parekh, N. (2008). Skating down a steeper slope: Fear influences the perception of geographical slant. *Perception, 37*(2), 321–323.

Tarver, E. (2019). Why the 'Share a Coke' campaign is so successful. *Investopedia*. Retrieved March 9, 2019 from https://www.investopedia.com/articles/markets/100715/what-makes-share-coke-campaign-so-successful.asp

Walker, D. B., Walker, J. C., Cavnar, P. J., Taylor, J. L., Pickel, D. H., Hall, S. B., & Suarez, J. C. (2006). Naturalistic quantification of canine olfactory sensitivity. *Applied Animal Behavior Science, 97*, 241–254.

Wiltschko, W., & Wiltschko, R. (2008). Magnetic orientation and magnetoreception in birds and other animals. *Journal of Comparative Physiology A, 191*, 675–693. doi:10.1007/s00359-005-0627-7

Module 10
Four Windows on Human Perception

As you learned in Module 9, the things we sense and perceive usually begin on the outside of our bodies. A sound wave hits your eardrum. A cactus needle pokes your skin. Salt hits your taste buds. After transduction, all this raw sensory material is converted to subjective sensations such as loud, painful, or salty. If the sensations you learned about in Module 9 are like paints, bricks, and lumber, perceptions are more like doors and walls. **Perceptions** are complex experiences that often combine multiple sensations – either within or across sensory categories. We *sense* things like the pitch of a sound or how loud it is. In contrast, we *perceive* things like words and sentences. Likewise, we *sense* musical tones, but we *perceive* musical tunes. Whereas sensation relies heavily on transduction, perception relies more heavily on things like induction. Basic sensory material must usually be converted by the brain into complex perceptions such as "tall," "funny," or "scary." This module focuses mainly on perception, with occasional references to the sensations that are the building blocks of perception. More specifically, this module provides you with four windows on perception that apply to almost anything you can perceive, from handsomeness to life satisfaction. These four windows on perception include psychophysics, constructivism, the Gestalt perspective, and the dueling principles known as contrast and assimilation. We begin with psychophysics.

Psychophysics

More than 250 years ago, Daniel Bernoulli (1738; cited in Stevens, 1975) became one of the first human beings to suggest that there is a systematic, mathematically specifiable connection between what is out there in the physical world and what we perceive. It is fitting that Bernoulli was a physicist because he was laying the foundation for an area of psychology that eventually became known as psychophysics. It is also fitting that Bernoulli was a mathematician because psychophysics is very mathematical. **Psychophysics** is the study of the precise rules by which stimuli become sensations and perceptions. A **stimulus** is usually either a physical object or an energy pattern (e.g., a 500 Hertz tone, a 5 cm black circle). In contrast, both sensations and perceptions refer to our **responses** to stimuli. To paraphrase Gilbert and Malone (1995), stimuli exist outside our skin, in the physical world. Responses exist inside our skin, mainly in our brains. Bernoulli discovered that an experienced sensation is directly proportional to the logarithm of the physical stimulus that gives rise to such sensation. With the benefit of more than 250 years of research, we tend to think that Bernoulli would have been better to refer to perception rather than sensation because he was mainly interested in higher order concepts such as happiness. In case you're no fan of logarithms, we can make Bernoulli's mathematical statement more accessible by saying what early psychophysicists said. Weber and Fechner developed the **Weber-Fechner law**. It is the idea that perception is *proportional* rather than absolute. For a person to be able to detect a change in a given stimulus, you'll need to increase or decrease the stimulus by a predictable *percentage* of the original stimulus. This means that we can often detect even very small changes in small or less intense stimuli. However, when it comes to larger or more intense stimuli, we will be unable to detect exactly the same absolute amount of change.

It is easiest to understand this principle by example or experimentation. Many people are surprised to learn that they can tell the difference between the weight of (a) a nickel and (b) a nickel with a penny glued to the top of it. For the record, a new U.S. nickel weighs 5.0 grams and a new U.S penny weighs 2.5 grams. When we have asked volunteers to close their eyes and try to say which is heavier (see Figure 10.1), most volunteers can reliably detect the extra 2.5 grams added to one nickel. By "reliably" we mean over and over. Notice that getting this question correct just once tells us very little. This could happen easily based on guessing. So, we're saying most judges can *reliably* tell which finger holds the heavier object – meaning they can tell us well over half the time in repeated testing. OK, so people can detect the 2.5-gram weight of a U.S. penny. Or can they? When we've asked the same judges to detect the weight of a penny just moments later, they've proven wholly incapable of doing so. The reason is that perception is proportional. On the second testing, we ask judges to tell us (blindly) which of two two-pound cans of tomato sauce is 2.5 grams heavier. Two pounds converts to a little more than 907 grams. No human judge we've encountered has been able to tell the difference between 907 grams and 909.5 grams – not reliably.

If you'll forgive us for being a bit technical, the psychophysicist Smitty Stevens (1957, 1961, 1964, 1975) showed about 60 years ago that Bernoulli's logarithmic rule is more precise, flexible, and empirically correct than the Weber-Fechner law. Stevens referred to his more precise psychophysical rule as the *power law*, and for the rest of this module, this is the term we'll most often use to make the point that perception is often proportional. So how did Stevens state his law? For our purposes, his **power law** says that for

Figure 10.1 While blindfolded, most people can reliably tell the difference between a 7.5-gram weight (a nickel with a penny glued atop it) and a 5.0-gram weight (a nickel). But no one can reliably tell the difference between a 909.5-gram weight and a 907-gram weight.

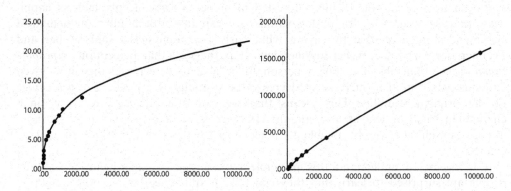

Figure 10.2 The concave downward power law as it applies to perceived brightness (left) and the rapid estimation of frequency (right). For mathematically-inclined readers, the exponent used for brightness was .333. For frequency the exponent used was .80. For psychophysicists, yes, log transforming these judgments would yield straight lines rather than curves – and the slope of each straight line would be equal to the value of the exponent (Stevens, 1961).

most dimensions of perception and judgment, the relation between (a) objective stimulus magnitude (how much of something there is) and (b) how intensely we perceive something is curvilinear and concave downward. Figure 10.2 (adapted from Stevens, 1975) shows what this means. For many judgments, perceived intensity rises very quickly at lower levels of stimulus intensity but rises much more slowly at higher levels of stimulus intensity. *People are more sensitive to changes in small stimuli than they are to changes in large stimuli.* Notice that this is *very* similar to the Weber-Fechner law. People can easily tell the difference between weights of 10 and 20 grams, but people *cannot* easily tell the difference between weights of 1,010 and 1,020 grams. Stevens also refined the Weber-Fechner law by showing that the precise shape of his curved power law differs greatly across sensory dimension or judgmental domain. For example, if we wish to double the perceived brightness of a light, we will have to increase its objective intensity (light energy in lumens) by a factor of about eight. But when it comes to the subjective perception of frequency (e.g., Are there really 80 jellybeans in that pile, or is it more like 50?) we can usually double perceived frequency by increasing actual frequency by a factor of about 2.5 rather than 8.0.

As these examples both suggest, an important judgmental consequence of the power law is that people often underestimate things that are big, bright, or numerous. Candle B *seemed* twice as bright as candle A. But, in reality, it was eight times as bright. Furthermore, this bias toward underestimation will usually get stronger as absolute magnitudes (the amount or intensity of stimuli) get bigger. This means you'll be especially likely to underestimate the true brightness of a light when we make it much, much brighter than a comparison standard. In addition to lots of evidence supporting the power law for basic sensory judgments, studies of "**social psychophysics**" show that many social perceptions obey the power law. Stimuli as varied as statements about religion (judged for favorability), wristwatches (judged for desirability), and the severity of thefts (as a function of amount of money stolen) all follow Stevens's power law (Gescheider, 1988, 1997; Stevens, 1975). Most people consider the theft of a $2,000 laptop to be somewhat more serious than the theft of a $1,000 laptop – but not *twice* as serious. So, if you ever plan to become a bank robber, psychophysics suggests you should try to steal a *lot* of money. Even conformity seems to obey the power law (Asch, 1956; Knowles, 1983; Latané, 1981). People are more likely to conform to a behavior (by copying it) if two people engage in the behavior than if just one person does. But two people do not quite have twice the impact of a single person. Further, six people have more influence on conformity than do five people, but only a little bit more.

As a final example of the power law, consider the **association between income and happiness** with one's life (aka, life satisfaction or overall well-being). Most people firmly believe that rich people are happier than poor people. But in ways that are highly consistent with the power law, this presumed truism is only partly true. Among very poor people, even small increases in income are associated with large bumps upward in happiness or well-being. But at middle and upper-income levels, especially in nations *without* strong social safety nets, the association between income and life satisfaction typically becomes much flatter (Biswas-Diener & Diener, 2001; Der, 2001; Diener & Biswas-Diener, 2002; Sengupta et al., 2012).

In the United States, you could pretty safely bet that a person who earned $20,000 per year would be happier than a person who earned only $10,000 per year. Compare that pretty safe bet with the much riskier bet that a person earning $220,000 per year would be happier than a person earning $210,000 per year. The association between income and life satisfaction is curvilinear. People are very sensitive to modest increases in income when they are very poor, moderately sensitive to such increases when they are middle class, and barely sensitive at all to such increases when they are rich. To be fair, the power law is *not* the only explanation for the non-linear association between income and happiness. But it is probably the simplest. This psychophysical analysis is not merely an intellectual exercise. If the U.S. political leaders who gave huge tax breaks to wealthy Americans in 2017 had truly appreciated the non-linear connection between income and well-being, we hope they would have changed tax laws in a very different way than they did. As a team of Bloomberg analysts summarized it, the 2017 changes to U.S. tax laws added $37 billion dollars in 2018 net income to Americans who made a million dollars or more in 2018 (Steverman, Merrill, & Lin, 2018). If Congress had given the money from this upper-class tax break to the roughly 900,000 Americans who work full-time in minimum wage jobs, the pre-tax annual incomes of these struggling workers would have more than tripled. You can bet that this would have powerfully influenced their well-being. In fact, an economic analysis by Gertner, Rotter, and Shafer (2019) suggested that one of the most cost-effective ways in which Americans could reduce suicide rates would be to increase the minimum wage. In our view, psychophysics can and should inform public policy. This analysis applies at the cross-national level very much the way it does at the level of the individual personal level. Moving from a very poor nation to a poor nation, we see a large increase in average life satisfaction. But moving from a rich nation to a very rich nation, we see very little average increase (see Deaton (2008). So cry a lot for Venezuela, and cry a little for Argentina, but don't cry at all for Belgium or Norway. They're doing fine.

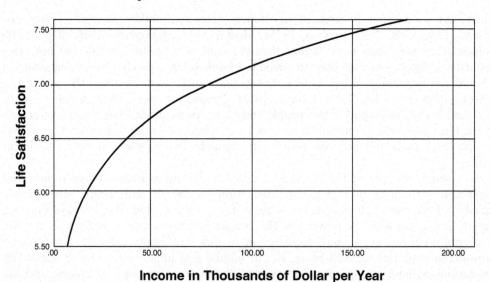

Figure 10.3 At low levels of income, small increases in income are associated with big increases in life satisfaction and emotional well-being. But at higher levels of income, the same absolute increases in income have very little apparent impact. Figure is based on data presented in Kahneman and Deaton (2010).

Constructivism

Many years ago, your first author (Brett) was playing a game of pick-up basketball with some friends when a huge argument broke out. This happened when a group of former professional basketball players kicked Brett and his friends off the court on which they were playing on the UCLA campus. This kicking off process was completely unnecessary, by the way, because two other empty courts were available in the same large gym. But the professional players, led by Magic Johnson (we're not making this up), didn't just want Brett and his friends to leave "their court." They told them to leave the gym. Because Brett knew that Magic did not have the court reserved, he refused to leave the court. It got ugly. But nothing ugly happened to anyone in the group but Brett (he was the one involved in the argument). And Brett obviously had no beef with any of his friends. Your second author, who was also a professor at UCLA at the time and played basketball, was conveniently away on sabbatical – in Israel.

Half an hour later, after the assaults and arguments were all done, Brett was in the locker room getting dressed when his friend (and teammate that day) Josh walked by. "I'm sorry," Josh offered somewhat sheepishly. "It's not your fault." Brett answered. Brett thought little of the brief conversation. But later that day Josh politely asked Brett if he was still mad at him. Confused, Brett asked Josh what he was talking about. "Well, when I said I was sorry, you mumbled something and then said, 'F*ck off!' Are you still mad?" Brett quickly reassured Josh that Josh had misheard him. Why did Josh hear a harsh insult when Brett had offered mild reassurance? Our best guess is that Josh entered the locker room with a mind full of aggressive words and images. When Brett made a short statement – part of which did vaguely resemble what Josh thought he heard – Josh heard an insult. This awkward story is a fitting example of our second basic window on human perception. Of course, this second window is constructivism. **Constructivism** is the idea that a great deal of human perception is actively created by the perceiver rather than passively processed. This means that things like wishes, fears, and expectations powerfully shape what we perceive. Module 9 included a couple of examples of constructivism. You may recall that people's perceptions of the steepness of a hill, like the flavors of Coke, Pepsi, or fancy Japanese teas are partly constructions. Let's explore constructivism in greater detail.

Let's begin with research on wishful thinking. Can hoping to see something make us see it? To find out, Balcetis and Dunning (2006) conducted an experiment in which they made people want to see either a number or a letter. To create these hopes, they claimed to be conducting market research. In this fake marketing study, participants learned they would be taste-testing just one of the two drinks shown in Figure 10.4. The two drinks were (a) some delicious, fresh-squeezed orange juice and (b) a disgusting organic veggie smoothie. As Balcetis and Dunning put it in their report, the dreaded smoothie "consisted of assorted vegetables like creamed corn & other ingredients to add chunkiness … It was green. It was foul smelling. It had pink flecks." Which beverage participants would drink – they all learned – would depend on a game of chance played on the computer. If the last image that appeared in the game was a letter, half the participants learned, they would get to drink the OJ. If the last image was a number, they'd have to drink the horse puke, er, umm, the veggie smoothie. By the way, for the sake of experimental control, the researchers switched things up for half the participants. For these participants, a number rather than a letter meant that they'd get to drink the OJ.

The image that appeared on the last trial of the game was identical for everyone. It was always the ambiguous image in the left-hand half of Figure 10.5. As the axiom of constructivism would dictate, many people saw what they hoped to see (so they could drink the delicious OJ). Those hoping to see a *number* usually saw a 13. Those hoping to see a *letter* usually saw a B. In a follow-up study, Balcetis and Dunning made people hope for either a farm animal or a sea animal. In this study, everyone saw the ambiguous image in

Figure 10.4
A re-creation of Balcetis and Dunning's (2007) experiment on the effects of wishful thinking on perception. As we hope you can see, the look on his face says, "Wait. I may have to drink WHAT?" Photo courtesy of Brooklyn Pelham.

Figure 10.5
The number B or the letter 13? Your wishes and desires can influence your answer. Balcetis and Dunning (2007) showed that people hoping to see a *letter* usually saw the letter B in an image much like the one on the left. But people hoping to see a *number* usually saw the number 13. Based on their findings, imagine you were really hoping to see either a mammal or a bird – and you saw the image to the right of the B/13. What mammal might you see? What bird? Images courtesy of Brett Pelham – based on concepts in Balcetis and Dunning (2007).

the right half of Figure 10.5. Those hoping to see a farm animal usually saw a horse or mule. Those hoping for a sea animal usually saw a seal. Follow-up studies suggested people were reporting their true perceptions rather than lying to get out of a heinous chore.

Many other studies reveal that beliefs and wishes influence perception. For example, we have long known that stereotypes and mindsets can alter what people perceive. In a classic study on exactly this topic, Allport and Postman (1947) showed White participants a line drawing of a Black man and a White man on a subway. The White man was holding a knife. The original observer of this drawing described it to a stranger who had not seen the drawing. This second person then described the drawing to a third. This game of "telephone" continued until a sixth person heard and had to describe the image. Half of the time in this game of telephone, the knife had switched hands by the final telling – so that the Black man was holding the knife. Of course, this form of constructivism may have more to do with the fallibility of the human tongue rather than the human ear. But we hope you can see that constructivism is everywhere.

There is also direct evidence that people often hear what they expect to hear. Warren and Sherman (see Warren & Warren, 1970) documented constructivism in speech perception in a surprising way. In their work on the **phoneme restoration effect**, Warren and Sherman asked participants to listen to sentences in which a small part of a word was deleted and replaced by a very short cough. But instead of saying they heard things like "orange – eel," for example, participants reported having heard things like "orange peel." Further, even when told truthfully that a cough had covered up one phoneme in a word (roughly speaking, one letter sound), almost no participants could report which exact phoneme had been missing. That is, people did not know which piece of a damaged word they had unconsciously repaired. Remarkably, this form of linguistic constructivism occurred even when a crucial word that clarified meaning – allowing listeners to repair a damaged word – occurred *after* the damaged word. People don't just construct. Sometimes they *re*-construct. Consider four of the crucial ("to-be-repaired") sentences reported in Warren and Warren (1970):

It was found that the – eel was on the axle.
It was found that the – eel was on the orange.

It was found that the – eel was on the shoe.
It was found that the – eel was on the table.

Notice that the "– eel" could have been a wheel, a peel, a heel, or a meal, in any of these sentences. There is no way to know which kind of "–eel" one is hearing about *until one hears the last word in each sentence.* And yet people restored the missing phoneme, after the fact.

So human perception is a two-way street, influenced not only by the stimuli that are out there but also by the theories, fears, and wishes that exist inside the perceiver. As neuroscientist Abigail Marsh (2017, p. 209) argued, the world we perceive is "more illusion than reality." She adds that

> The world as it really exists is a colorless, swirling soup of atomic particles made up of nearly empty space. The rich, textured colors and shapes and feelings that we experience – like solid and white and rough and sharp – *feel* real, but they are not. They are a product of the interpretive machinery inside our brain. Eighty percent of the fibers entering the visual processing areas of the brain emanate from the rest of the brain, not from our eyes.

In other words, score a physiological point for constructivism.

Gestalt Principles of Perception

A third important window on human perception comes from a school of thought known as Gestalt psychology. The gist of the **Gestalt perspective** on human perception is that we are constantly seeking out form, structure, organization, and meaning in what we perceive. In fact, in keeping with the German roots of Gestalt psychology, the German word *Gestalt* translates to the English word *form* or *shape*. Historians of psychology often summarize Gestalt psychology by noting that Gestalt psychologists believe that "the whole is more than the sum of its parts." (Schultz, 1981). Whereas this is true, this simple statement cannot do complete justice to the Gestalt tradition, which includes dozens of irresistible perceptual rules we all use to make sense of the world. Like the power law, Gestalt psychology is best understood by means of concrete examples or direct experiences. Let's explore a few.

Perhaps the best known of all Gestalt principles of perception is the **figure-ground distinction**. When trying to make sense of almost any scene, we often try to identify what is **figure** (what we should focus on) and what is **ground** (what is background). But sometimes scenes are ambiguous. Sometimes, we can easily flip back and forth between two competing ways to view a scene. The left half of Figure 10.6 contains a simple version of the famous **face versus vase** figure-ground image. The image in the right half of Figure 10.6 contains a much more intricate modern reimagination of the same Gestalt demonstration. In this modern version of the figure-ground demonstration, you can perceive four realistic silhouettes or five complex spindles. Which you see depends on what you consider figure and what you consider ground.

Many artists exploit principles of Gestalt perception. In the case of Figure 10.6, the artists wanted to bring the concept of figure and ground to your conscious attention. More often, however, artists capitalize on Gestalt principles to influence perception with the

Figure 10.6 An important Gestalt principle of perception is the figure-ground distinction.

expectation that viewers will *not* be aware of what is happening. In Figure 10.7, you can see a common photographic technique involving "depth of field." This technique can be used to make an object the focus of attention (the figure) and to make less important elements fade from awareness (to make them the ground). In the case of the daffodils on the left the ground is *literally* the ground.

Another well-documented Gestalt principle is **closure**. This Gestalt principle states that we often interpret partial, imperfect, or corrupted versions of a complete object as the complete ("closed") thing. Taken to the extreme, closure can mean we create a shape or other perception where it does not exist at all. Figure 10.8 offers three examples of closure. In the photo of former President Barack Obama, you most certainly do not see a photo of a man who is missing his hands. Instead, your mind wisely gets closure on the image by making the reasonable assumption that Obama's hands are in his pockets. The principle of closure also explains why you see a circle in the middle portion of Figure 10.8 rather than a series of unrelated arcs. Finally, the principle of closure is sufficiently powerful that you surely see a square in the right-hand

Figure 10.7 In the image on the left, the daffodils are the only thing in focus. That makes them the figure.

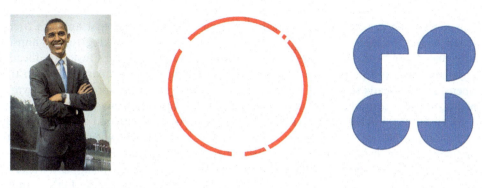

Figure 10.8 Three examples of the Gestalt principle of closure. From left to right: President Barack Obama: you most certainly do not see a photo of a man who is missing his left hand. That's probably a circle. And that sure looks like a square, but it's not.

Barack Obama image credit: Three Sixty Images/Shutterstock.com

Figure 10.9 A big square (left), two columns (center), and three small squares (right). At least that's what the Gestalt principles of proximity and similarity should be telling you.

portion of Figure 10.8, even though no such square exists. That's constructivism, of course, but it's also Gestalt psychology.

Yet another important Gestalt principle is **proximity**. We perceived objects that are physically near one another as related. Adding labels to grouped objects strengthens this impression. This is true, moreover, even when labels have little meaning. Figure 10.9 provides some examples of proximity. Most people see the left image as a large square made up of many smaller squares. But if we remove some squares from the center, people now perceive two columns. Proximity is not the only Gestalt principle we use to decide what things go together. **Similarity** is another Gestalt principle. It means we assume that like goes with like. So, making shapes the same color also causes us to assume the shapes belong together. In the image on the far right in Figure 10.9, virtually everyone will see three squares. The pieces that make up each square are very near one another (proximity), they are the same color (similarity), and they even have handy, if arbitrary, labels.

Contrast and Assimilation

The two opposing principles we'll explore last in this module are based on the idea that when people perceive things and make judgments, they rarely do so in a vacuum. So, when Julio says that Consuela is "very tall," he does not mean that she is taller than a skyscraper. Nor does he mean that she is taller than a pill bug. What he probably means is that she is taller than most other women. Likewise, your first author's friend and fellow Berry College track team member Scott Jones was making fun of himself (and redheads the world over) when he said that he was "the world's fastest redhead." Many judgments and perceptions involve an explicit or implicit comparison. When this happens, it often leads to one of two processes. The first perceptual process is known as contrast, and the second is known as assimilation. **Contrast** happens when an object is judged to be (a) smaller or less intense than usual when compared with something bigger or more intense or (b) bigger or more intense than usual when compared with something smaller or less intense. In other words, two objects are perceived to be *more different* than they really are. **Assimilation** is exactly the opposite. It happens when an object is perceived to be *more similar* than it really is to something else. Let's examine each of these robust perceptual phenomena.

One of the first discoveries of judgmental contrast (aka "contrast effects") was made by the German psychologist Hermann Ebbinghaus. Ebbinghaus discovered the aptly named **Ebbinghaus illusion**, which is illustrated in the left half of Figure 10.10. This visual illusion refers to the fact that a circle that is surrounded by much larger circles looks smaller than an identical circle that is surrounded by much smaller circles. Things next to big things often look smaller by comparison. Things next to small things often look bigger. That's how contrast works. Contrast applies to color perception as well as to size. The green centers of the two squares in the right-hand half of Figure 10.10 illustrate this. The center square with the yellow background probably looks greener.

Contrast effects apply to a wide range of judgments. As a social example of contrast effects, check out the vintage photo of the small man on the right in Figure 10.11. This small man was Harold Wadlow. But Harold wasn't really small at all. In that photo, Harold is depicted with his son – Robert Pershing Wadlow. Robert P. Wadlow is the tallest man whose height has ever been medically documented, and he was still growing when he died at the tender age of 22. Robert was just over 8'11" tall. His wingspan was an even greater 9'5". He wore specially made size 37 shoes, and he made some very tall people feel very short by comparison. If you want to see an example of this, Google, "Shaq and world's tallest man." You should be able to find a photo of Shaquille O'Neal posing next to a realistic life-sized *sculpture* of Robert P. Wadlow. Our guess is that this is one of the few times in Shaq's life that Shaq felt short by comparison.

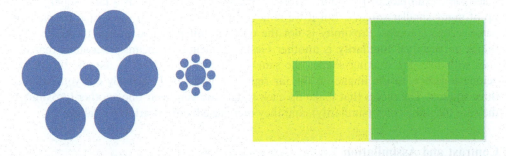

Figure 10.10 Two classic examples of contrast effects. The center blue dot on the far left looks smaller than the center blue dot to the right of it. This is a size contrast. The center green square with the yellow background may also look greener than the identical green square with a darker green background. This is color contrast.

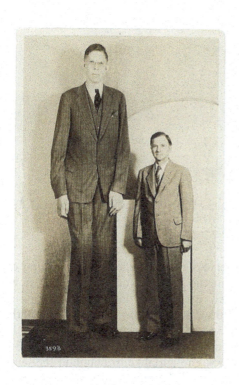

Figure 10.11
The guy on the right is Harold Wadlow. Harold was *not* objectively short. But he sure looks short in this photo. And he probably felt short himself during this photo shoot. This is because Harold is depicted standing next to next to his very tall son, Robert P Wadlow. At 8'11.1", Robert was the tallest man to ever be measured by a doctor. Robert's dad looks very short here because of a social form of contrast effects known as social comparison.

Sadly, the tallest man to ever live had terrible trouble with his legs and feet (nerves can only grow so long, you know). In fact, this is what killed him at age 22 – when he got an infection caused by blisters from an ankle brace. We feel very lucky by comparison. Don't you?

Contrast effects that involve comparing our own traits and abilities with others are so common and powerful that they have been given their own name. Festinger's (1954) **social comparison theory** states that when we wish to know where we stand on any evaluative or attitudinal dimension, we compare ourselves with others. If we fall short compared with even one salient other, we can feel like a failure by comparison. Conversely, if we score higher, run faster, or interview better than just one salient other, this can change our self-views for the better (Morse & Gergen, 1970). There are few theories in social psychology that have been investigated more thoroughly than social comparison theory. Social comparison is particularly powerful when you are competing with someone for a prized resource such as a job or a grade. Along these lines, you may recall a time when you received what seemed like a high or low score on an important exam. Your score of 58 may have been devastating, for example, until you learned that only one person in your class scored higher. We hate that guy.

But as commonplace and intuitive as contrast effects are, they do not always rule the perceptual day. Very often, people judge two different objects to be more *similar* than they really are. Recall that this is known as assimilation. An intriguing pair of visual illusions based on the **Koffka ring** capitalizes on both contrast and assimilation. First, consider the ring in the left-hand portion of Figure 10.12. There's nothing special about it. It's basically a grey donut. But as you can see in the center of Figure 10.12, if we

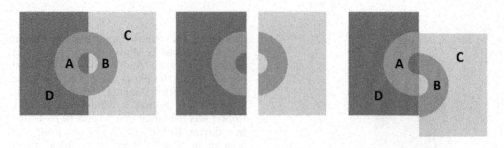

Koffka rings drawn by B. Pelham

Figure 10.12 Our subtle variation on the Koffka ring, which illustrates both a contrast effect
(center images) and an assimilation effect (right-hand image.)

pull the two halves of the image apart, we observe a contrast effect. The half-ring on
the right in this center image looks darker than the half-ring on the left. But if we
move the two halves of this image a different way, as shown in the far-right portion of
Figure 10.13, you should now experience perceptual assimilation. Remember that the
portions of the ring labeled A and C are very different shades of grey – as are the
shapes labeled B and D. Look back at the image on the far left to reconfirm this. But
now, sections A and C, like sections B and D look enough alike to maintain the sense
that two rounded curls are snugly interlocking. One of the broad rules of assimilation
is that people often assimilate things that seem to belong to the same *category* (or that
are part of the same physical object). It is only when things are not a part of a physical
or conceptual whole that they are likely to be contrasted.

Perceptual assimilation is everywhere. It shows up in all kinds of human and animal
perceptions and judgments. In fact, as you will learn later in this text, the developmental psychologist Jean Piaget used exactly this term – *assimilation* – to refer to the lifelong human tendency to assume that a new experience is usually very much the same
as a lot of older experiences. When two-year old Mia sees a horse for the first time and
exclaims, "Doggie!" she is engaging in assimilation. She is focusing on the hair, legs,
and tail of this newly encountered creature and placing it in a familiar hairy, four-
legged, one-tailed category. People often assimilate other people that they place in the
same category. An old joke about medical school makes this point very well. "What do
you call a guy who graduated last in his medical school class?" The answer? "A doctor,
of course." As a final example of assimilation based on categories, Krueger and Clement (1994) asked Brown University students to try to estimate the average daily temperatures for many different days of the year in Providence, Rhode Island. They found
that during the transitional windows of spring and fall, students overestimated how
similar average temperatures were *within* a transitional month (assimilation) and overestimated how different average temperatures were in the days that were on the borders
of transitional months (contrast). For example, judges overestimated how much warmer
April 2nd would be than March 31. They also underestimated how much the weather
would warm up between early and late April. Focusing on the part of their findings
that indicated assimilation, participants assimilated days within a given month. Months
are very familiar categories. Decades of research on contrast and assimilation have

revealed not only that both of these judgmental tendencies are pervasive but also that each tendency exists for multiple reasons, from the physiological to the cognitive. Although this has led to some spirited debates about the exact nature of contrast and assimilation, there can be little doubt that these two dueling judgmental rules are at work in thousands of everyday judgments and perceptions.

Hands-on Activity for Module 10

Light adaptation: One of the ways in which the human perceptual system maintains a stable and coherent sense of the world is via sensory *adaptation*. A small dot of light that you would never see in the bright daylight easily catches your attention in a very dark room. As a very different example, before moving to Georgia – and drinking tea that is "Georgia sweet" for two years – you thought that McDonald's sweet tea was much too sweet. Now, chances are, the same McDonald's sweet tea seems a little weak to you. Adaptation happens at many levels, from the retina or the tongue to higher cortical areas such as primary visual cortex. One quick (though perhaps slightly uncomfortable) way to see how rapidly your visual system adapts to different levels of illumination requires you to use the small, bright light that comes with most smartphones.

In a room that is well-lit enough for you to read comfortably, turn on the light to your smartphone. *While keeping your left eye firmly closed*, flip your phone around and – if you can bear to do so – stare directly at your phone's light from about a foot (30 cm) away. Count slowly to 30 (one, one thousand, two, one thousand, etc.) while you keep staring at the light – but only with your right eye. Hold your phone still so that the bright light does not move around too much on your retina. After you've done this for 30 seconds, take note of how bright the light appears. To see how bright the light appeared about 30 seconds ago – prior to adaptation – quickly close your right eye and look briefly at the light with your *left eye only*. Your closed or well-covered left eye did not adapt to bring the light, and so the light should now look much brighter to your left eye than to your right. To appreciate the difference fully, you may wish to alternate looking at the light (the quicker the better) with your left eye only and with your right eye only. Just don't wink one eye and then the other in a crowded bar. There may be unintended consequences.

By the way, a similar form of adaption happens when you enter a very dark place – or when it gets dark outside and you use no artificial lights. Faint lights that you could not initially see become visible. This is why, when stargazing, you should ideally get away from all kinds of artificial lights and give your eyes at least 10 minutes to adjust to conditions of very low light. Now – especially if you are in a very rural area where there is limited *light pollution* – you'll be able to see the Milky Way as it was meant to be seen.

The perception of sweetness. To explore the perception of levels of sweetness, your instructor may arrange a blind taste test involving several different teas. We won't spoil the test by telling you exactly what to expect, but we will say that blind taste tests can often separate things like expectations about a stimulus from actual changes in the nature of the stimulus. And they can be a great source of psychophysical exploration. For example, based on what you know about the power law, do you think it'd be easier for you to tell if someone added 15 grams of sugar to unsweetened tea – or if they added the same 15 grams of sugar to a tea that already contained a lot of sugar?

Multiple-Choice Questions for Module 10

1. Dr. Percy studies the connection between the physical size of a stimulus and how much people like it. As it turns out, most people like big circles more than small circles, for example. Dr. Percy probably thinks of herself as what kind of psychologist?

   A) a psychobiologist
   B) a psychophysicist
   C) a psychochemist

2. What perceptual rule, promoted by S.S. Stevens, replaced the original Weber-Fechner Law of "proportional perception"?

   A) the power law
   B) the percentage law
   C) the quadratic law

3. What is the best way to summarize the association between (a) wealth or income and (b) happiness or life satisfaction?

   A) bumps up in income make you happier when you're very poor but have little or no effect when you're wealthy
   B) the more money you make the happier you tend to be, but different things make rich and poor people happy
   C) there is surprisingly little evidence that richer people are happier than poor people

4. "A white five-cm diameter circle presented in the center of a computer screen that was kept exactly 30 cm from participants' eyes – and was surrounded by a red background." This is an example of what?

   A) a stimulus
   B) a percept
   C) a perception
   D) a stimulus-response set

5. Balcetis and Dunning (2006) asked people to report whether they saw a letter or a number (or a farm animal versus a sea animal). They were studying the perceptual principle known as:

   A) hope
   B) subjectivism
   C) constructivism

6. The "phoneme restoration effect" is a great example of which broad window on human perception?

   A) contrast effects
   B) Gestalt perception
   C) constructivism

7. Proximity and similarity are basic principles of:

   A) Gestalt psychology
   B) perceptions of causality
   C) perceptual assimilation

8. Which of the following visual illusions seems to be an example of a contrast effect?

   A) the hard-soft (stone-pillow) illusion
   B) the Ebbinghaus (dots) illusion
   C) the Franz Kafka (happy-sad) illusion

9. A Gestalt psychologist would say that the object on which you focus when making a judgment is the what?

   A) focal point
   B) center of attention
   C) figure

10. Feeling short when you stand next to an NBA center and feeling tall when you stand next to a professional jockey are examples of what?

   A) social comparison processes
   B) perceptual relativity
   C) automatic evaluation

Answer Key: 1B 2A 3A 4A 5C 6C 7A 8B 9C 10A

References

Allport, G. W., & Postman, L. (1947).*The psychology of rumor.* New York: Henry Holt & Co.

Asch, S. (1956). Studies of independence and conformity: A minority of one against a unanimous majority. *Psychological Monographs, 70*, 416.

Balcetis, E., & Dunning, D. (2006). See what you want to see: Motivational influences on visual perception. *Journal of Personality and Social Psychology, 91*(4), 612–625. https://doi.org/10.1037/0022-3514.91.4.612

Biswas-Diener, R., & Diener, E. (2001). Making the best of a bad situation: Satisfaction in the slums of Calcutta. *Social Indicators Research, 55*, 329–352.

Deaton, A. (2008). Income, health, and well-being around the world: Evidence from the Gallup World Poll. *Journal of Economic Perspectives, 22*(2), 53–72.

Der, G. (2001). Commentary: Income and health: Why are curves so appealing? *International Journal of Epidemiology, 30*(60), 1405–1406.

Diener, E., & Biswas-Diener, R. (2002). Will money increase subjective well-being? *Social Indicators Research, 57*, 119–169.

Festinnerger, L. (1954). A theory of social comparison processes. *Human Relations, 7*, 117–140.

Gertner, A. K., Rotter, J. S., & Shafer, P. R. (2019). Association Between State Minimum Wages and Suicide Rates in the U.S. *American journal of preventive medicine, 56*(5), 648–654. https://doi.org/10.1016/j.amepre.2018.12.008

Gescheider, G. A. (1988). Psychophysical scaling. *Annual Review of Psychology, 39*, 169–200.

Gescheider, G. A. (1997). *Psychophysics: The fundamentals* (3rd ed.). Mahwah, NJ: Erlbaum.

Gilbert, D. T., & Malone, P. S. (1995). The correspondence bias. *Psychological Bulletin, 117*, 21–38.

Kahneman, D., & Deaton, A. (2010). High income improves evaluation of life but not emotional well-being. *PNAS, 107*(38), 16489–16493. doi:10.1073/pnas.1011492107

Knowles, E. (1983). Social physics and the effects of others: Tests of the effects of audience size and social distance on social judgments and behavior. *Journal of Personality and Social Psychology, 45*, 1263–1279.

Krueger, J., & Clement, R. W. (1994). Memory-based judgments about multiple categories: A revision and extension of Tajfel's accentuation theory. *Journal of Personality and Social Psychology, 67*, 35–47.

Latané, B. (1981). The psychology of social impact. *American Psychologist, 36*, 343–356.

Marsh, A. (2017). *The fear factor: How one emotion connects altruists, psychopaths, & everyone in between.* New York: Basic Books.

Morse, S., & Gergen, K. J. (1970). Social comparison, self-consistency, and the concept of self. *Journal of Personality and Social Psychology, 16*, 148–156.

Schultz, D. (1981). *A history of modern psychology* (3rd ed.) New York: Academic Press.

Sengupta, N. K., Osborne, D., Houkamau, C. A., Hoverd, W. J., Wilson, M. S., Halliday, L. M., … Sibley, C. G. (2012). How much happiness does money buy? Income and subjective well-being in New Zealand. *New Zealand Journal of Psychology, 41*(2), 21–34.

Stevens, S. S. (1957). On the psychophysical law. *Psychological Review, 64*, 153–181.

Stevens, S. S. (1961). To honor Fechner and repeal his law. *Science, 133*, 80–86.

Stevens, S. S. (1964). Concerning the psychophysical power law. *Quarterly Journal of Experimental Psychology, 16*, 383–385.

Stevens, S. S. (1975). *Psychophysics: Introduction to its perceptual, neural, and social prospects.* New York, NY: Wiley.

Steverman, B., Merrill, D., & Lin, J.C.F. (2018, December 18). A year after the middle class tax cut, the rich are winning. Bloomberg. Retrieved July 18, 2020 from https://www.bloomberg.com/graphics/2018-tax-plan-consequences/

Warren, R. M., & Warren, R. P. (1970). Auditory illusions and confusions. *Scientific American, 223*(6), 30–36. https://doi.org/10.1038/scientificamerican1270-30

V
Learning

Module 11
Classical Conditioning
Learning by Association

In the 1880s, while William James was toiling away on his *Principles of Psychology*, a Russian physiologist named Ivan Pavlov became very interested in digestion. By 1904, Pavlov had won a Nobel prize in medicine and physiology – his reward for nearly two decades of painstaking work on the previously undiscovered world of the stomach. However, it was not this Nobel prize that made Pavlov one of the most famous psychologists ever. Instead, it was his work on what he called "psychic secretion." In his years of working with hungry dogs, Pavlov had noticed that dogs originally salivated when they saw that a researcher had just brought them some meat powder. This natural tendency to salivate – especially when presented with very dry food – was evolution's way of helping dogs swallow and digest the ancient Russian version of Purina or Alpo. Pavlov (1927) noticed that, eventually, the mere appearance of the researcher before the food was delivered, or even the sound of the researchers' approaching footsteps, would usually trigger some serious drooling. Although Pavlov never anticipated making this discovery, he realized that this learned response – and the "psychic" rules that governed how it came about – were worthy of very serious study.

Figure 11.1 This is Bella, a well-trained dog who absolutely *loves* salami. Bella is patiently waiting for a piece of salami until her owner gives her the signal that it is OK to take it. Your first author made poor Bella sit for almost a minute before giving her the signal. But Bella knew that food was coming. If you look very carefully inside the blue circle, you'll see that Bella has drooled on the floor. No one had to teach Bella to drool to help her wolf down a tasty treat. Ivan Pavlov studied this natural response in some very hungry dogs. He called this tendency to salivate in response to food an unconditional response (UCR for short). And then he started ringing some buzzers just before he delivered the food. The rest is history.

Until Pavlov died in 1936, he remained keenly interested in what is now called classical conditioning. According to Mackintosh (1974), **classical conditioning** occurs when an organism forms a stable association between one event and another event that follows it. Pavlov studied classical conditioning by examining experimental situations in which he arranged a contingency "between a stimulus and an outcome." If you sound a previously-neutral buzzer just before delivering meat powder to a hungry dog, nothing special will happen at first. The dog will merely drool in the presence of the meat powder. This natural tendency – Pavlov's "reflex" – does not have to be taught. Pavlov dubbed stimuli that naturally produce specific responses (e.g., drooling, wincing in pain) **unconditional stimuli** (here abbreviated as **UCS**). Likewise, he dubbed the dog's natural reaction to the stimulus the **unconditional response** (or **UCR**). More generally, desirable food will typically be an unconditional stimulus, and salivation (in both dogs and humans) will be the unconditional response. The world is full of both unconditional stimuli and the unconditional responses they produce. For instance, intense electric shock is an unconditional stimulus. A dog's fear and yelping in response to the shock are unconditional responses. These are all associations that do not have to be taught. They are built in (aka "unconditional"). In people, by the way, many unconditional stimuli are social. Angry faces, hugs, and compliments delivered with a beaming smile may be considered unconditional stimuli. And the fear, joy, and feelings of competence and acceptance that follow each of these respective social stimuli could easily be considered unconditional responses.

Pavlov's ingenious insight was that if you reliably sound a buzzer shortly before you deliver the meat powder, dogs will form an association between the *buzzer* and the delivery of the meat powder. Under ideal conditions, dogs can form such a conditioned association in only a handful of conditioning trials. Once learning has happened, the previously-neutral stimulus now becomes the **conditional stimulus** or **CS** (often mistranslated as "condition*ed* stimulus," by the way; Kimmel, 1984; Mackintosh, 1974). Of course, the learned response (drooling to the buzzer, alone, even before the meat arrives) becomes the **conditional response** (**CR**). To summarize then, classical conditioning is a form of learning in which an originally neutral stimulus becomes a conditioned (CS) after it is repeatedly paired with a stimulus (UCS) that produces a natural response (UCR). Conditioning has happened when the CS produces a conditioned response (CR) that strongly resembles the UCR. Figure 11.2 reveals how this typically works best (for *delay conditioning*).

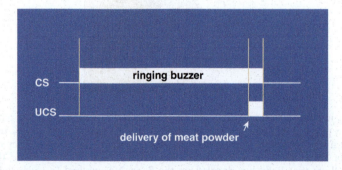

Figure 11.2 A typical time sequence for delay classical conditioning. An unfamiliar buzzer goes off, and a second or two later, the hungry dog gets some food. Repeat as necessary.

Table 11.1 summarizes the four key terms (two stimuli and two responses) that are the cornerstones of classical conditioning. Let's apply these four key terms to some stimuli and responses with which you are highly familiar. Is a $100 bill an *unconditional* or a *conditional* stimulus? That's right, it's a conditional stimulus; it had to be learned. If it were an *un*conditional stimulus (UCS), newborn babies would like $100 bills as much as you do. And we already know how Pavlov's dogs treated food in his original research. So this next one should be easy. Is salivating – or feeling happy – when you've seen a bowl of Kellogg's Froot Loops a UCR or a CR? That's right; it's a UCR because no one had to teach you to drool in the presence of dry but delicious food. (We said dry but delicious – *not* healthy.) Toucan Sam, on the other hand, is a CS. That's because kids only like Toucan Sam (and maybe even drool in his presence) because his appearance so often predicts the delivery of Froot Loops. And what about the single "ding" of your cell phone? Is that UCS or a CS? Right again; it's a CS that we've learned to associate with valued communication (it might be a text from Bradley Cooper inviting you to the Oscars!). So most of us check our phones (the CR) immediately after hearing this ding.

Because we all love cash, let's return to that $100 bill. Consider this: Cash has been associated with so many good things for most people that some people refer to liking money as an example of **second-order conditioning**. Second-order conditioning can only happen after regular (first-order) conditioning has already been established, and it involves three stimuli rather than two. Here's how it worked in Pavlov's lab. After conditioning hungry dogs to know that a buzzer predicts the delivery of meat powder, Pavlov could complicate things. Now he might light up a small light, then sound the same buzzer (which is now a CS, of course), and then deliver the meat powder. You're right. If he repeated this procedure long enough, his dogs would begin to drool merely in the presence of the light. Some people refer to money as a second order CS – like Pavlov's light in the given example. But in our experience, money is more like a regular CS. We associate it directly with many good things. To paraphrase Jackson Brown, money can buy a person everything from clothes and cars to presidencies. So what's not to like about it – even if it is usually a regular – not a second-order – CS.

One of the most famous studies of how classical conditioning works in *people* was conducted about 100 years ago by Watson and Rayner (1920). They studied a healthy nine-month-old infant they referred to as Little Albert. Little Albert was initially exposed to a few furry objects. He typically found them either neutral or mildly interesting. He would often reach out and touch them. The novel stimuli included a white rat, which Albert seemed to like pretty well. But after being exposed to the rat on the first baseline trial, Watson presented Albert with the white rat again and struck a four-foot-long metal bar with a metal hammer. The bar was positioned behind

Table 11.1 Four Key Terms that are Crucial to Classical (Pavlovian) Conditioning.

1. **unconditional stimulus** (UCS): Something that produces a natural reflex or reaction (e.g., meat powder, electric shock)
2. **unconditional response** (UCR): The natural reaction (e.g., salivation, happiness, wincing in pain)
3. **conditional stimulus** (CS): A once-neutral stimulus (e.g., a buzzer) that now produces a response much like the UCR
4. **conditional response** (CR): The post-conditioning response that follows the CS and resembles the UCR (e.g., *drooling* in response to a buzzer).

Little Albert, which meant he never saw the loud noise coming. Watson only had to do this a couple of times, always in the presence of the white rat, to get Little Albert to cry. And pretty soon, just like Pavlov's puppies, who came to drool in response to buzzers that predicted the delivery of food, Albert began to cry in the presence of the white rat that predicted the delivery of the loud and scary noise. We hasten to add that the famous Little Albert study was not quite as rigidly controlled as Pavlov's studies with dogs. For example, whereas Pavlov had an objective physical measure of exactly how much dogs drooled under differing experimental conditions, the signs of interest or fear that Little Albert expressed were subject to some degree of interpretation.

Having said that, a century of follow-up studies on classical conditioning in people shows that we are, in fact, a lot like Pavlov's puppies. It is possible to make people like or dislike things, for example, by merely pairing those things in the right way with things that people strongly like or dislike. For example, Staats and Staats (1958) paired national group names (*Dutch* or *Swedish*) with either positive or negative words (e.g., *gift, happy, sacred, bitter, ugly, failure*). Students for whom the word *Dutch* had always been paired with pleasant words later reported liking the word *Dutch* more than the word *Swedish*. Students for whom the word *Swedish* had been paired with the positive words showed the reverse pattern. Your second author has four important things to say about that: (1) Brett: Bitter, (2) David: Happy, (3) Brett: Failure, (4) David: Sacred. It's OK; David won the coin toss fair and square. And we have another thing to say about this classic study. Staats and Staats (1958) showed that this classical conditioning procedure worked just as well for highly familiar male first names (*Bill* and *Tom*) as it did for less familiar nationalities. We can be classically conditioned to like or dislike things to which we may have already had some pretty strong associations. We are a lot like Pavlov's puppies.

Subtleties of Classical Conditioning

Pavlov discovered many subtleties of classical conditioning. For example, he discovered that it is easiest to condition dogs when they have no previous experience with the neutral stimulus that one hopes to convert to a CS. In fact, when Pavlov presented his dogs with a potential CS several times in the absence of any meat powder, this greatly disrupted the potential for this stimulus to become a CS (Pavlov, 1927, p. 302). This is known as *latent inhibition* (Mackintosh, 1974). Pavlov also found that conditioning only occurs reliably when things happen in a certain order. That ideal order is delay conditioning, which you see in Figure 11.2 and (for comparison) again in Figure 11.3. Pavlov found no support at all for **backward conditioning**. A backward conditioning procedure means that the experimenter delivers the meat powder and *then* presents the potential CS just after the meat powder is consumed (or taken away). Along similar lines, both Pavlov's original work and that of many who have followed in his footsteps show that conditioning works best when there is a brief delay between the presentation of the CS and the presentation of the UCS – but while the CS is still present (e.g., still buzzing). If you make the delay either too long or too short, if you present the CS and allow it to stop for a while before presenting the UCS (called *trace conditioning*), or if you present two potential conditioning stimuli at the same time, you're likely to see little conditioning (Mackintosh, 1974). Figure 11.3 illustrates some of these subtleties. Things need to be just right to facilitate classical conditioning.

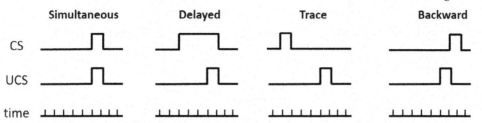

Figure 11.3 The exact order of presentation of the CS and the UCS matters a great deal in classical conditioning. We believe John Stuart Mill would tell us that the temporal pattern known as delayed conditioning is the one that most strongly implies that the CS *causes* the appearance of the UCS. Image recreated from Mackintosh (1974, p. 57).

If you're beginning to think classical conditioning is a bit finicky, think again. Is it finicky that a billiard ball only moves immediately after – and never *before* – it is struck by another billiard ball? A great way to summarize the research on classical conditioning is that animals who are being classically conditioned behave as if they have carefully read and digested John Stuart Mill. Animals evolved in worlds full of causes, and they are excellent contingency detectors. It is largely for this reason that Rescorla and Wagner (1972) proposed their "**predictiveness hypothesis**" to unify and organize a lot of research on classical conditioning. According to this hypothesis, animals do not merely associate two things because they occurred at *roughly* the same time. If a stimulus is to become a CS, it must predict the appearance of a UCS in a way that would make sense in the animal's natural environment. This means that (a) the CS must not be accompanied by any likely confounds (any other competing causes) and (b) the CS must appear shortly before the UCS.

In fact, a serious violation of the usual rules of classical conditioning is highly consistent with the idea that organisms evolved to learn some kinds of associations very readily – while not learning others very easily at all. If you recall the idea of *preparedness* from Module 8, you know that both people and animals learn some things much more easily than others. It's much easier to teach people to fear spiders or snakes, for example, than to teach them to fear guns or motorcycles. Remember the New and German study of spider detection? Spiders jump out at us (both literally and figuratively) in ways that hypodermic needles do not. The most extreme version of preparedness is probably **one-trial learning**. Allow a rat to taste a novel and distinctive food or drink (e.g., licorice or saccharine-flavored water). Then give the rat a dose of radiation that will make the rat very sick a few hours later. The likely result is that the rat will steer the heck away from the novel food or drink for the rest of its life (Garcia, Ervin, & Koelling, 1966). One-trial learning originally puzzled learning researchers, but it is now well accepted by most that there is an evolved readiness for animals to learn to avoid foods that are followed by experiences strongly resembling poisoning. Research on one-trial learning explains, for example, why your second author does not like rum. In his younger years he had an unfortunate encounter with rum and grape juice that made him very sick. Decades later, he has not been able to undo that powerful association (see Figure 11.4).

Animals, people included, also live in worlds in which the rules can change. And sometimes both people and animals can kind of undo *some* associations. Not all learning is cast in stone. Consistent with this idea, Pavlov found that if he continued to present a CS for food for a while – and stopped following the CS with the UCS – his dogs

Figure 11.4 Garcia et al. (1966) showed that rats learn to avoid a novel food that appeared to make them very sick after only a single exposure to the food. This is one-trial learning.

would eventually stop drooling in the presence of the CS. This is known as **extinction** – the disappearance or reduction of a previously conditioned response to a CS when it is no longer followed by the UCS. An example of extinction in people happened to your first author in college when he originally responded very negatively (via classical conditioning, we assume) to a woman who physically resembled a woman who had broken his heart in high school. When the woman he met in college did not reject him – or break any commitments she made to him over the course of many months – he learned that he could trust her. The learned negative response had been extinguished.

Pavlov discovered many other subtleties of classical conditioning. For example, he noticed that, unlike the biological extinction of a species, *psychological* extinction is not *quite* forever. After complete extinction seemed to have occurred, Pavlov found that dogs who had not heard a CS in a while often showed what we call a "just in case" response. They occasionally showed **spontaneous recovery** of a previously extinguished response. Imagine that your dog has learned that the crinkly noise she hears when you're at your fridge means that you are taking out a piece of salami. It won't take too many trips to the fridge until your dog begins to drool whenever she hears that crinkly noise. That's classical conditioning. The crinkly sound of the plastic package is like Pavlov's buzzer. It becomes a CS. But imagine that your vet tells you how horrible salami is for dogs. (It's still OK for people, right?) Your vet insists that you stop giving your dog salami, and you follow her advice. After a while your dog should stop salivating when she hears you open the salami – because she will have learned that the old rules no longer apply. That's extinction. Finally, suppose you go on a work trip for ten days. On your first day back, if you go to the fridge and take out a piece of salami for yourself – and if your dog hears that crinkly noise – don't be surprised if she drools. That's spontaneous recovery. And we won't be surprised if you cave – like we usually do – and toss her a sliver of salami. That's guilt, or maybe permissive dog care. Either way your dog will love you for it.

Another form of flexibility Pavlov observed has to do with the precise properties of the CS itself, and things that resemble it. Suppose your dog drools when she hears you open the salami. At your first author's house, he's also been known to eat a slice of bologna right from the package. When his dog Bella hears that similar-but-not identical crinkly noise, she's likely to drool. In fact, on more than one occasion he has opened a toy, lock, or small electronic device from a crinkly plastic package. This, too, led Bella to drool. This is known as generalization. **Generalization** happens when an organism responds to a stimulus that resembles a CS as if it *were* the CS. You won't be too surprised to learn that generalization is most likely when the new stimulus in question strongly resembles the original CS. You could think of Brett's negative response to his female college friend as an example of generalization. She was *not* his high school crush, but she resembled her. So he generalized. Con artists, marketers, and counterfeiters often rely on generalization to get you to like something. Figure 11.5 illustrates this principle of generalization with batteries.

Suppose you purchased some of these fake Duracells for your favorite toddler's toy cell phone. And imagine that these fake Duracell batteries stayed fresh about as long as a toddler's diaper. This might lead you to engage in **discrimination**. As applied to classical conditioning, **discrimination learning** happens when an organism learns *not* to treat a stimulus that resembles the CS as if it were the CS. This will only happen, by the way, if the stimulus that resembles the CS is never (or rarely) followed by the UCS that led to the original conditioning (while the original stimulus keeps predicting the delivery of the UCS). A *lot* of learning involves discrimination. A toddler who calls all four-legged animals "doggy" will soon learn to discriminate among the various four-legged beasts. Likewise, a person who accepts a counterfeit $100 bill will quickly learn to pay careful attention to subtle differences between the real thing and the imposter. As these examples suggest, discrimination learning can be painful. Many years ago, the brilliant and lovable psychologist Bob Josephs borrowed some money from your first author when Bob didn't have his wallet on him. The next day, Bob wrote Brett a check to pay him back. But Bob's check bounced. That's what the red "NSF" stamp ("Not Sufficient Funds") means in the lower right-hand corner of Figure 11.6. We should be clear that Bob's check bounced not because he was trying to scam anyone, but because Bob is very absentminded. Bob eventually made good on this loan, but after he bounced a second check to Brett a month later, Brett began insisting that Bob pay with cash. That's discrimination learning. Just because it looks like a check doesn't mean it always cashes like a check. The same thing goes for walking ducks, or so we've heard. At any rate, that's discrimination learning. As you will soon see, discrimination learning, like several other principles of classical conditioning, also applies to operant conditioning.

If you are wondering if these examples involving fake Duracell batteries and bounced checks happen to anyone other than your quirky first author, you should have lunch with an intellectual property attorney. Consider McDonalds and their famed golden arches – or Nike and their unmistakable swoosh symbol. Suppose you wanted to open

Figure 11.5 If you couldn't read, you might have the same positive conditioned associations to the package of batteries on the left that most of us have to genuine Duracell batteries. If you were a terrible speller, you might be fooled by the package in the middle. Should you insist on the genuine DURACELL seal you see on the battery in the right-hand image? Definitely *not*. Genuine DURACELL batteries (the real product) have *no such seal*.

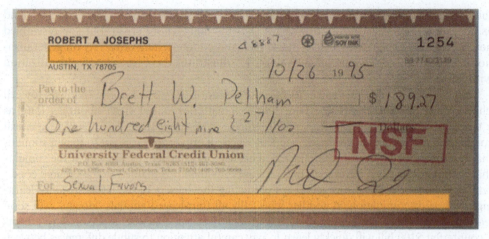

Figure 11.6 You can always trust Bob Josephs to give you good personal or scientific advice, and he is a great guy. But one of us no longer accepts personal checks from him. That's called discrimination learning.

a new fast food chain, and you decided to use a pair of yellow double arches (ahem, the *McDonald's* logo) as part of your restaurant name. Or suppose you created a new brand of athletic shoes, and you wanted to put a Nike swoosh on your shoe – perhaps with a tiny modification or two. What do you think McDonalds and Nike would do in response? If you said, "Sue my butt off!" you'd surely be correct. In fact, there are whole branches of law built around these kinds of lawsuits. Both intellectual property law and trademark law deal directly with whether new products and product symbols are likely to lead to stimulus generalization or discrimination. If using a familiar symbol or copying a design is likely to lead to generalization – and it thus makes people want to purchase your "new" product or service – then this is usually considered stealing a brand's value (one that another company probably built up over many years). It's thus illegal. When new trademarks are reviewed for approval, one of the main jobs of the United States Patent and Trademark Office (USPTO for short) is to make judgments about stimulus generalization and discrimination. One of the many interesting distinctions legal experts have to make is whether a new product is merely pretending to be the original (and hoping to capitalize on generalization) or whether the new product is spoofing the original (and thus relying on the fact that people *will* notice the differences between the two symbols or products). For example, your second author once purchased a spoof of a North Face[TM] shirt that was called "South Butt." When North Face sued the high school entrepreneur who started this parody of the North Face brand, the high schooler's defense was, "How hard is it to tell a face from a butt … ?"

Matching Activity for Module 11

Match the letter of each concept on the list that follows to one of the numbered phenomena that follows the list. Use each letter (A–M) exactly once. Notice that the last match (14) has already been made for you.

A. classical conditioning
B. unconditional stimulus (UCS)
C. unconditional response (UCR)
D. conditional stimulus (CS)
E. conditional response (CR)
F. delay conditioning
G. backward conditioning
H. predictiveness hypothesis
I. one-trial learning
J. second-order conditioning
K. generalization
L. discrimination learning
M. extinction
N. spontaneous recovery

____ 01. Shaun had a spider phobia. Even a picture of a spider made him feel very anxious. After a month of psychotherapy, Shaun was no longer afraid of spiders because he saw that they didn't hurt him.

____ 02. After seemingly being cured of his spider phobia, Shaun had not seen a spider in many months. But on a trip to Peru, Shaun came across a tarantula, and he was suddenly overcome with fear.

____ 03. I (your first author) am a fan of NFL running back Marshawn Lynch (ML). This is weird because I don't follow NFL football very much, and I'm not a fan of the teams for which ML played. However, I do live on Lynch street, and my birthday number is 24, which is ML's jersey number. Why do I like ML?

____ 04. When Lamar was a kid he really *loved* Kellogg's Frosted Flakes. Even as an adult, Lamar really likes Tony the Tiger, who is the cartoon mascot you can see on any box of Frosted Flakes. What is Tony to Lamar?

____ 05. What are Frosted Flakes cereal to Lamar?

____ 06. What is the feeling of happiness Lamar feels when eating Frosted Flakes?

____ 07. What is the feeling of happiness Lamar feels when he sees Tony the Tiger?

____ 08. Which finding or idea from research on classical conditioning suggests that animals are very good at detecting when one stimulus *causes* the appearance of another stimulus?

____ 09. This is the specific kind of conditioning that most reliably (most consistently) leads puppies to salivate in the presence of a previously-unfamiliar light or tone (which predicts the delivery of meat powder).

____ 10. Erin is a toddler who recognized her name pretty well. In fact, she could find her locker in her preschool classroom on the second day of class – by finding her name atop the locker. However, when a new student named Ernie joined the class a week late, Erin insisted that his locker was also hers. Why?

____ 11. After a few weeks of class, Erin learned that Ernie's name had a small "e" that her name did not have. And she stopped responding to his locker as if it were hers.

____ 12. Some people say we like money because of second-order conditioning. However, one could also argue that money merely predicts the delivery of a variety of very pleasant things (e.g., food, shelter, attention). By this simpler account, we like money merely because of:

___ 13. At the age of nine, Giana rode a roller coaster and got very sick after she got off. At the age of 35, Giana still has no interest in riding roller coasters, even though she is generally a thrill-seeker.

_G_ 14. After I give my dog a treat that I take right from the fridge, I always close the fridge door. Nonetheless, my dog does *not* drool when she sees me close the fridge door. This is because _____ doesn't work.

Note. A way to do this as a class exercise is to work on this activity for a few minutes individually – and then break into small groups who compare notes about the answers. Instructors could move around the room and offer corrections, suggestions, or feedback to the groups. In the end, groups should have a set of answers that everyone in the group agrees upon, and which an instructor validates as correct. If this is too easy for some students, they can generate their own examples of each concept – and have an instructor check them.

Multiple-Choice Questions for Module 11

1. People like their names so much that one can use a person's name to get people to like anything that is associated with their names (Jones et al., 2004). For example, if you present a person's photo repeatedly and then quickly present the name "John Jones," someone named John Jones will begin to like the person depicted in the photo. This is almost certainly due to:

   A) the rule of paired associates
   B) the reflexive rule of liking
   C) classical conditioning

2. After a while, dogs in Pavlov's early studies of digestion began to salivate at the sound of the footsteps of a researcher who always gave the hungry dogs meat powder. In the language of classical conditioning, the sound of the researchers' footsteps approaching the lab would be:

   A) the unconditional stimulus (UCS)
   B) the conditional stimulus (CS)
   C) the training stimulus

3. When your optometrist gives you the glaucoma test that delivers a strong puff of air to your eyeball, you blink. This is a natural reflex that protects your eyes from injury. In the language of classical conditioning, the puff of air is the:

   A) the unconditional stimulus (UCS)
   B) the conditional stimulus (CS)
   C) the training stimulus

4. In the prior example, your natural tendency to blink when you feel something touching your eye is:

   A) the conditional response (CR)
   B) the conditional stimulus (CS)
   C) the unconditional response (UCR)
   D) the unconditional stimulus (UCS)

5. A dog is trained to salivate in response to a bright circle that reliably predicts the delivery of meat powder. When the dog is exposed to a bright *oval*, she salivates almost as much as she did to the bright circle. In the language of classical conditioning, this is an example of:

   A) assimilation

   B) generalization
   C) stimulus insensitivity

6. A stimulus that reliably precedes another stimulus that reliably predicts the appearance of something inherently wonderful (e.g., pasta, meat powder, a hug) will eventually lead to what kind of conditioning?

   A) second-order conditioning
   B) indirect learning
   C) three-stage learning
   D) latent learning

7. The philosopher John Stuart Mill would probably be very impressed to learn that _____ conditioning simply does not work. Dogs who are exposed to a stimulus that reliably appears *after* the delivery of a dry food reinforcer do *not* salivate when you present the stimulus.

   A) reversed
   B) delay
   C) backward

8. What rule or school of thinking in psychology suggests that one-trial learning makes a great deal of sense?

   A) the law of effect
   B) evolutionary psychology
   C) structuralism

9. The _____ strongly suggests that anything that suggests that a novel stimulus does not cause the appearance of the naturally reinforcing stimulus will not reliably produce conditioning to the novel stimulus.

   A) associative rule
   B) predictiveness hypothesis
   C) covariation principle

10. Jobi learned that a bad generic cola whose can vaguely resembles a Pepsi can does *not* taste as good as Pepsi, and she stopped buying this generic cola. In what aspect of classical conditioning has Jobi engaged?

    A) discrimination learning
    B) refinement
    C) distinction learning

Answer Key: 1C, 2B, 3A, 4C, 5B, 6A, 7C, 8B, 9B, 10A

References

Garcia, J., Ervin, F. R., & Koelling, R. A. (1966). Learning with prolonged delay of reinforcement. *Psychonomic Science, 5,* 121–122.

Jones, J. K., Pelham, B. W., Carvallo, M. C., & Mirenberg, M. C. (2004). How do I love thee? Let me count the Js: Implicit egotism and interpersonal attraction. *Journal of Personality and Social Psychology, 87,* 665–683.

Kimmel, H. (1984, September). Personal communication.

Mackintosh, N. J. (1974). *The psychology of animal learning.* New York, NY: Academic Press.

Pavlov, I. P. (1927). *Conditioned reflexes.* Oxford: Oxford University Press.

Rescorla, R. A., & Wagner, A. R. (1972). A theory of Pavlovian conditioning: Variations in the effectiveness of reinforcement and nonreinforcement. In A. H. Black & W. F. Prokasy (Eds.), *Classical conditioning II: Current research and theory* (pp. 64–99). New York, NY: Appleton-Century-Crofts.

Staats, A. W., & Staats, C. K. (1958). Attitudes established by classical conditioning. *The Journal of Abnormal and Social Psychology, 57*(1), 37–40. https://doi.org/10.1037/h0042782

Watson, J. B., & Rayner, R. (1920). Conditioned emotional responses. *Journal of Experimental Psychology, 3,* 1–14.

Module 12
Operant Conditioning
Learning the Consequences of Our Behavior

If you read Module 11, we hope you know that Pavlov was clearly on to something. In fact, his work on classical conditioning had a huge impact on behaviorists such as John B. Watson, who replicated many of Pavlov' findings on people. But Watson knew all too well that classical conditioning is but one important category of conditioning. Watson was also heavily influenced by the learning theorist E.L. Thorndike. Thorndike greatly expanded the scope of learning theories by studying what some experts consider a fundamentally different kind of learning, operant or instrumental learning. Procedurally, at least, operant conditioning differs in a basic way from classical conditioning. In the case of **operant conditioning**, the organism must *do something* to ensure the delivery of a reinforcer (or to avoid a punishment). As Mackintosh (1974, p. 4) explained it,

> Experiments on classical conditioning may be defined as those in which a contingency is arranged between a stimulus and an outcome; experiments in instrumental learning may be defined as those in which a contingency is arranged between a response and an outcome.

Operant learning requires the organism to do something (to operate on the environment) to bring about a consequence; classical conditioning does not. The key difference between these two kinds of learning centers around the association that is learned: classical conditioning involves stimulus-stimulus learning (when stimulus 1 comes, stimulus 2 will usually follow) whereas operant conditioning involves stimulus-response learning (when an organism makes a certain response a stimulus will usually follow).

If you want another way to keep classical and operant conditioning straight, you might do well to remember that whereas Pavlov was clearly a dog person, Thorndike was a cat person. Thorndike's most famous experiments involved placing hungry cats in puzzle boxes like the ones you see in Figure 12.1. He specifically designed the boxes so that cats had to make an arbitrary response – such as stepping on a lever or pulling a string – before they could free themselves. When cats did free themselves, by the way, Thorndike usually rewarded them with food (as if freedom from imprisonment wasn't reward enough in and of itself; we *told* you he was a cat person).

These and many other experiments with animals led Thorndike to propose his famous Law of Effect. To paraphrase Thorndike, his **Law of Effect** states that behaviors followed by a pleasant state (e.g., food) become more likely. It adds that, in contrast, behaviors followed by an unpleasant state (e.g., pain) become less likely. From the perspective of Thorndike's trapped cats, the accidental response of stepping on a lever might open the puzzle box. This pleasant state known as freedom would make any

Figure 12.1 Some of Thorndike's "puzzle boxes." Thorndike found that when cats were placed in one of these puzzle boxes for the first time, the cats often took a great deal of time before stumbling on the "escape route." However, when the cats were put back in the same boxes multiple times, they eventually learned – via trial and error – how to get out of the boxes immediately. These boxes also illustrate very well why Thorndike chose to go into psychology rather than carpentry.

trapped cat happy and thus serve as a reinforcer. With each successive entrapment, the liberating response would become more and more likely until the cat had learned to escape. As an avid learning theorist, Thorndike did not make the assumptions that cats had gained any insights from their time in the slammer. Instead, they had just become conditioned (in this case, via operant conditioning), based on his fundamental law of reward and punishment. In fact, Thorndike often poked fun at researchers who assumed that animal learning involved complex processes such as insight or perspective-taking. To Thorndike, operant learning was about strengthening associations between responses and outcomes rather than forming insights. In his influential book on animal intelligence, Thorndike (1911, p. 22) lamented the fact that most psychologists spent more time praising animals than trying to understand their behavior. He added that previous studies of animal behavior "have all been about animal intelligence, never about animal stupidity." Yeah, Thorndike was definitely a cat person.

Thorndike was also a dedicated experimenter. His basic approach to research was putting animals in highly controlled situations, manipulating features of these highly controlled situations, and carefully measuring how long it took the animals to make easily measured responses. This approach, together with Pavlov's very similar experimental approach, was surely much of the inspiration for the work of the most influential learning theorist of all time. This was B.F. Skinner. Skinner came of age in the 1930s and 1940s, when psychology had truly become an empirical science. Even more than the behaviorists who came before him, Skinner was heavily influenced by the philosophical school of scientific thought known as *logical positivism*. Logical positivists believe that we should only study and make claims about that which we can *observe* with absolute certainty. They eschewed any manner of spiritual or metaphysical explanation. And they delighted in **falsification**, which is trying to see if and when a theory or idea is wrong, rather than whether there is any support for it (Popper, 1974/1990). A pigeon either pecked at a light in a Skinner box, or she did not. A cat either got out of Thorndike's puzzle box or she remained trapped there. Thus, things like time and frequency counts became the easy-to-document variables of operant conditioning (and behaviorism in general).

Skinner took the precision, skepticism, and pragmatism of behaviorism to a whole new level. Instead of merely trying to see if the Law of Effect was correct, for example, Skinner carefully documented how different rules for delivering reinforcement lead to different patterns of conditioned behavior. Specifically, his work on **reinforcement schedules** revealed that the precise way in which organisms get rewarded for engaging in an operant response determines exactly when and how often they are likely to emit the reinforced response. Before we delve too deeply into Skinner's work, we want to emphasize that whereas research on operant conditioning started primarily with animals, operant conditioning happens all the time in our own daily lives. Parents reward and punish their children, teachers (try to) reinforce good behavior in their students, employers give bonuses (rewards) and demotions (punishments) to their employees. Kids even reward and punish their fellow kids (e.g., when one teenager breaks an unwritten rule about how to dress, when one toddler grabs a toy from another and the victim fights back). As you consider how operant conditioning applies to animals, please don't jump to the conclusion that operant conditioning applies *only* to animals. As far as anyone has been able to tell, all the rules of operant conditioning apply to people. But let's begin with rats and pigeons, and we'll make sure to circle back to people on occasion.

Much of Skinner's work on operant conditioning boiled down to an analysis of two crucial questions. The first question has to do with time vs. frequency counts. Are rewards delivered contingent on whether an organism has produced any critical responses in a certain *time*? Or are rewards delivered contingent on whether an organism has produced a certain *number* of critical responses (since the time of the last reinforcement, regardless of time). Skinner identified both **interval** and **ratio** schedules of reinforcement. An **interval schedule** means that the organism gets a reinforcement so long as it made at least one appropriate response after a predetermined temporal window. A **ratio schedule** means that the organism gets reinforcement so long as it made a certain number of responses (sometimes only one response) regardless of the temporal window in which the response or responses happened. Completely independent of the question of time vs. frequency is the question of whether reinforcements are delivered in a *fixed* or *variable* fashion. A **fixed schedule** of reinforcement means that the reinforcers *always* comes after a certain number of responses (which again, might be just one response). A **variable schedule** means that there is some random variation in the delivery of the reinforcers. For example, a rat might get a food pellet for pressing a bar five times – on average. But in some instances, she would get the food pellet after only two bar presses. In others, she might need to press the bar nine times to get the food pellet. On average, five presses would be required for a pellet, but there would be lots of variation. So time vs. frequency is one dimension of reinforcement. Predictability of reinforcement is the other. A fixed schedule is predictable whereas a variable schedule is not. Because these two facets of reinforcement schedules are independent, this leads to four unique kinds of reinforcement schedules. These four schedules are summarized in Table 12.1.

Table 12.1 Skinner's Basic Reinforcement Schedules of Operant Conditioning.

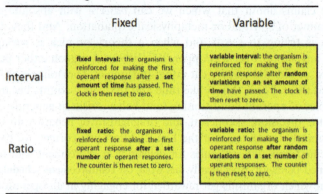

	Fixed	Variable
Interval	**fixed interval:** the organism is reinforced for making the first operant response after a **set amount of time** has passed. The clock is then reset to zero.	**variable interval:** the organism is reinforced for making the first operant response after **random variations on an set amount of time** have passed. The clock is then reset to zero.
Ratio	**fixed ratio:** the organism is reinforced for making the first operant response **after a set number** of operant responses. The counter is then reset to zero.	**variable ratio:** the organism is reinforced for making the first operant response **after random variations on a set number** of operant responses. The counter is then reset to zero.

Consequences of Reinforcement Schedules

These differing schedules lead to very different rates of performance of a conditioned operant behavior. Once an organism becomes well-trained, the variable ratio and fixed ratio schedules produce the highest average rates of responding. In the world of Skinner's pigeon, this means that a pigeon will consistently peck at a light, for example, when every twentieth – or about every twentieth – response is reinforced. Response rates are lower but steady under a *variable interval* schedule. But the most interesting schedule is the fixed interval schedule. It produces moderate levels of responding that follow a highly predictable pattern. Put yourself in the shoes – well, the feet – of a rat or pigeon that gets reinforced on a fixed interval schedule. No amount of responding really matters until you've reached a certain point on the clock. Then even a single correct response gets reinforced. As you can see in the left half of Figure 12.2, animals placed on a fixed interval schedule show very low rates of responding immediately after being reinforced. Then as the fixed time approaching possible reinforcement approaches, rates of responding increase greatly. They shoot up even higher just before the exact time that reinforcement is available, and they drop to nearly zero immediately after the delivery of a reinforcer.

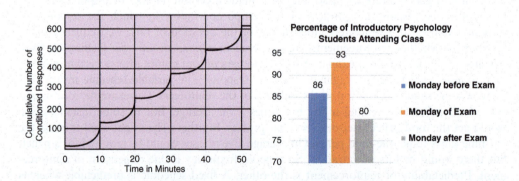

Figure 12.2 The left panel shows idealized data from pigeons who have learned very well under an FI 10m (fixed interval, ten minutes) reinforcement schedule (adapted from Mackintosh, 1974; Skinner, 1961). The right panel shows attendance data for 83 students who took exams in an introductory psychology class in the fall of 2018.

The right portion of Figure 12.2 shows attendance data from all three of your first author's fall 2018 sections of introductory psychology. As you can see, the operant response of attending class was a bit higher than average exactly a week prior to the exam, was extremely high the day of the exam, and dropped off notably the week immediately after the exam (when the next exam was still three weeks away). In the past, when (a) attendance was not taken daily and rewarded and (b) students were not allowed to drop any exams scores, attendance patterns even more strongly followed what Skinner would predict. As you well know, exam dates are usually fixed. Class attendance generally shoots up as exams approach, is highest on the days of the exams themselves, and then drops off immediately after exams. Skinner was delighted to see that regardless of what species he studied, his reinforcement schedules did a great job of predicting behavior.

If you think about the variety of ways in which people get paid for working, you can probably guess that reinforcement schedules apply to employment as well as education. If a person gets paid a certain amount of money for completing a specific job (or gets paid a certain amount per small task completed), this would be an example of a fixed ratio schedule. But if a person gets paid by the hour or by the week, this would be a fixed interval schedule. Notice that the person only gets paid if he or she performs some minimal amount of work in a specified window. As a kid, your first author and his older brother used to take turns cutting their neighbor's yard. Mrs. McCraw insisted on paying by the hour. Knowing about this rule, one of the brothers (we won't say who) used to take his time and stretch out the job to take about 2 hours. The less patient brother consistently did the same job in an hour and a half and got paid 75% of what the more patient brother got. Eventually, the speedier brother convinced his neighbor to pay him by the job rather than by the hour. But he only got paid, by the way, if his work passed Mrs. McCraw's high standards of quality. Because some employers know about Skinner's schedules of reinforcement, they vary the way they pay different workers. Security guards almost always get paid by the hour, for example. Again, that's a fixed interval schedule. If guards got paid by the crime prevented, this would not provide them with a very reliable source of income. In contrast, some manufacturers pay line workers who sew or create many copies of the same product using a fixed ratio schedule – by paying them by the piece.

Extinction and the Partial Reinforcement Effect

Like Pavlov had done well before him, Skinner also studied extinction. Skinner documented that extinction applied to operant as well as classical conditioning. However, he went way beyond this by showing that the way in which a response had been rewarded during the acquisition (learning) phase of operant learning had a huge impact on how extinction worked. When Skinner consistently rewarded a response (continuous reinforcement) and then suddenly stopped doing so, the behaviors he had established in his rats and pigeons quickly evaporated. However, when he had rewarded behaviors only intermittently (partial reinforcement), he found that his subjects would often persist in their learned responses for a very long time before their learned behavior extinguished. This is the **partial reinforcement effect:** rewarding an organism only some of the time (rather than all the time) during training makes the response less susceptible to extinction. From the perspective of at least some theories of learning this was paradoxical. If rewards "stamped in" learning, for example, as early learning theorists believed, how could rewarding an organism less in the past make learning more "durable"? One highly intuitive explanation that doesn't require too many assumptions is that when an organism has not always been reinforced in the past for doing something, they have already continued to make a response "in a situation similar to that encountered in extinction" (Mackintosh, 1974). Put simply, the organism is used to responding without always getting reinforced. Thus, extinction takes longer when the organism has more often responded in the past without getting an immediate reinforcement.

Incidentally, Skinner insisted that he discovered the partial reinforcement effect by accident – when he ran low on food pellets while running a simple conditioning experiment and decided to make do by rewarding only some responses (Schultz, 1981). Doing so led to learning that was highly resistant to extinction. Do Skinner's reinforcement schedules apply to anything other than work or school? Do people ever experience *variable* or *partial* reinforcement schedules? Notice that the examples we've offered so far (e.g., the exam example, the employment examples) all involved fixed and more or less continuous schedules. Can you think of situations in which people are rewarded for their behavior in inconsistent ways? Parents, professors, and pit bosses could surely offer a few examples. Some parents reward their children only *some of the time* when the kids clean their rooms, earn good grades, or proof read a module about operant conditioning. Some professors only take attendance some of the time – or offer bonus activities on random, unannounced days. Students who want to do well in such situations have to attend practically every class to ensure they'll be rewarded. But the reward is contingent on attending just some of the days when class is held. Finally, if you have ever been to a casino, you've surely seen people lined up in front of slot machines repeatedly pulling the arms of the "one-armed bandits" more politely known as slot machines. In casino games, then, is reinforcement continuous or partial? Do gamblers tend to persist in their behavior? Or do they give up and turn their attention to golfing or knitting the first time they pull a lever and get no reinforcement?

Generalization, Discrimination, and Shaping

Like Pavlov, Skinner remained an active researcher all his adult life (both men died at age 86). Further, like Pavlov, Skinner and other behaviorists discovered that **generalization** and **discrimination** were just as applicable to operant as to classical conditioning. In fact, one could say they are even more applicable. Because operant conditioning requires an organism to do something, this leaves room for both **stimulus generalization** (e.g., responding to a stimulus that resembles but is not identical to the one on which you were trained) and **response generalization** (producing a response that resembles but is not identical to the originally reinforced response). If you have ever come close to brushing your teeth with hemorrhoid medication, you were engaging in stimulus generalization. You treated a decidedly un-minty cream that came in a tube as if it were tooth paste. On the other hand, if you have ever tried to use your house or apartment key to open an office door at work, you were engaging in response generalization. In our experience our house-keys have yet to open our office doors. Worse yet, and we are not making this up, when we have each pulled out our car keys, pointed them at our office doors, and pressed the unlock button, our office doors have never once popped open.

Skinner was keenly aware that when an animal is first being trained to make an operant response, the animal will often behave somewhat cluelessly. Rather than concluding, as Thorndike did, that animals are just dumb, Skinner decided to offer them a little help. Skinner's research on **shaping** showed that one can dramatically speed up the operant learning process by initially rewarding even very rough approximations of a desired behavior (Peterson, 2004). Over time, the experimenter gradually becomes increasingly picky about what behavior yields a reinforcer. In addition to using shaping to speed up simple learning, experimenters, coaches, and teachers can use shaping to produce some highly complex behaviors. For example, mice can be shaped to play a rodent version of basketball against other mice. A multi-step shaping process begins, for example, by reinforcing the mouse for simply walking near a very small wooden ball. After a while, the mouse only receives a reinforcement for touching the ball. Next, the mouse must pick the ball up to earn a reinforcer. By the end of the week, the mouse will have learned to play basketball – and put the ball only though her own hoop. Today, an entire field (applied behavior analysis) is dedicated to using shaping and other basic principles of operant conditioning to help people change behavior they have found difficult to change any other way, from quitting smoking to overcoming specific phobias (see Gullapalli, 1997).

Reinforcement vs. Punishment

Skinner believed that reinforcing desired behaviors is usually a much better way to produce learning than punishing undesirable behaviors. This view was more controversial in Skinner's day of punitive parenting practices than it is today. This idea might be of great interest to parents who would like to teach their kids to keep their rooms clean, go to worship services, or stop assaulting those with whom they disagree. Advocates of the parental use of reward rather than punishment to shape their children's behavior argue, for example, that punishment sometimes models exactly the behavior it was intended to prevent. Hitting a kid for hitting others, for example, seems likely to send a mixed message about violence (Straus, Sugarman, & Giles-Sims, 1997). Further, from a purely logical perspective, whether you are dealing with a toddler or a pigeon, it makes sense that rewarding a specific behavior would increase the likelihood of that specific behavior. Punishment may surely decrease the likelihood of the specific punished behavior, but in and of itself it does not tell the organism what to do next time (Schacter et al., 2011).

Speaking of **punishment** vs. **reinforcement**, it is important to discriminate punishment from a Skinnerian concept that sounds a lot like punishment. Punishment is *not* the

Figure 12.3 Experts in learning theory can use *shaping* to teach a mouse to play basketball: A 3-minute video is available at www.youtube.com/watch?v=8nuI2RrJTfA. And the mouse is cuter than this one. We promise.

same as **negative reinforcement**. Remember the Law of Effect. It states that punishment *reduces* the likelihood of a response that preceded it whereas reinforcement *increases* the likelihood of a response that preceded it. The other thing to remember to avoid confusion about punishment and reinforcement is that Skinner used the terms **positive** and **negative** *not* to indicate if something was good or bad but to indicate if something was *introduced or added* (positive) or *removed or subtracted* (negative). Thus, as you can see in Table 12.2, there are both positive and negative forms of both reinforcement and punishment.

Let's summarize where we are and provide a few examples. First, getting punishment (positive or negative) makes it less likely you'll do the punished deed in the future. In contrast, getting reinforcement (positive or negative) increases the likelihood that you'll do the reinforced deed in the future. Taking a pain reliever to relieve a bad headache is a great example of *negative reinforcement* because doing this makes your headache go away. If the pain reliever does its job, that is, it removes something aversive. Giving your kids candy to get them to stop crying is also, from the parent's perspective, an example of negative reinforcement. This is because something aversive (the loud crying) is removed contingent on a response. Of course, from the kid's perspective, getting candy when they cry is positive reinforcement making them more likely to cry the next time they want candy. That's how spoiled kids get spoiled in the first place! If, instead, when a child cries, the parent takes away the child's favorite toy, this would be negative punishment at work. As the child gets older, crying might be replaced with whining and a confiscated toy may become a confiscated cell phone. Yes, having your car "booted" qualifies, too.

Social Learning

We cannot close this module on operant conditioning without noting that, in highly social creatures (people included), a very important subcategory of operant conditioning is social learning (also referred to as observational learning). The basic idea behind social learning is that rather than always learning by our own trial and error, we often learn from the mistakes or successes of others. Psychologists once thought that only human beings engaged in **social learning**. E.L. Thorndike (1911) looked for evidence of social learning (aka **modeling**) in cebus monkeys. He concluded that "Nothing in my experience with these animals … favors the hypothesis that they have any general ability to learn to do things by seeing

Table 12.2 Two Kinds of Reinforcement and Two Kinds of Punishment.

	Reinforcement	Punishment
Positive	Positive reinforcement: after engaging in an operant behavior, the organism receives something desirable. Example: A child rakes leaves and gets a special dessert.	Positive punishment: after engaging in an operant behavior, the organism experiences something undesirable. Example: A boy pulls a dog's tail, and the dog nips his hand.
Negative	Negative reinforcement: after engaging in an operant behavior, the organism stops experiencing something undesirable. Example: A person removes a splinter from her finger and then feels better.	Negative punishment: after engaging in an operant behavior, the organism stops experiencing something desirable. Example: A girl strikes her little brother, and her mom takes away her dessert.

others do them." To his credit, Thorndike was quick to add that this question was not settled by a mere handful of studies. But others latched boldly onto his cautious conclusion that human beings may be special in this way. It wasn't until Thorndike was long dead and gone that some clever experimenters showed that rhesus monkeys could learn just by watching. Darby and Riopelle (1959) set up pairs of rhesus monkeys so that one monkey could always watch another monkey try to get food – by choosing one of two arbitrarily marked food cup covers. After the chance to observe just one trial of this monkey game show, observer monkeys who watched the other contestant succeed usually tried a similarly-marked cup in their own separate cages. This worked just as well, by the way, when the clueless other monkey made the *incorrect* choice. That is, a monkey who watched another monkey screw up by picking the wrong cup usually tried the *unselected* cup. Fast forward another five decades or so, and now we know that a hungry octopus can do something equally impressive. She can watch another octopus unlock the lid on a clear acrylic container to retrieve a delicious crab and immediately copy this novel and highly unusual behavior. "Octopus see. Octopus do." As you will see in the modules on human aggression and prosocial behavior, the octopus is not alone. A great deal of human behavior is powerfully influenced by social learning.

Let's examine two examples of social learning in people. In a classic study of social learning and aggression, Bandura and his colleagues (Bandura, Ross, & Ross, 1961) placed preschool kids in one corner of a room in which they played with various arts and crafts. In one condition, an adult model in another part of the room began playing aggressively with an inflatable Bobo doll (the kind that bounces back up after you punch it down – there is a picture of a Bobo doll near the end of the module on aggression). In this "violent model" condition, the model who gave poor Bobo a smackdown punched him in the face and pounded him with a toy hammer. While doing so, the model yelled things like "Sock him in the nose!" In another condition, the kids observed an adult model play peacefully with other toys and ignore the Bobo doll. The kids who watched the aggressive model were much more likely than the kids who watched the non-aggressive model to behave aggressively – both by copying some of the exact behaviors in which the model had engaged and engaging in novel acts of aggression. For example, one boy put a toy gun to Bobo's nose and threatened him – something the model herself had *not* done. Incidentally, people model nice as well as nasty behavior. Furthermore, our ability to model begins very early in life. Schuhmacher and colleagues (2018) showed that even toddlers engage in social learning. A large group of toddlers observed an experimenter who needed help reaching some cups. Half of the toddlers saw that another adult helped the needy woman, and the other half saw that the other adult failed to do so. After being exposed to the helpful or unhelpful model, all the toddlers saw that the woman needed help again – with the other adult now out of the picture. Almost none of the toddlers who saw the unhelpful model helped the experimenter out. Among the toddlers who had just observed a helpful adult model, almost half gave her help (by giving her the cups she could not reach).

Exceptions to Basic Principles of Learning

Learning follows some very predictable rules. But these rules are not without some apparent exceptions. In fact, some have argued that *social learning* violates the Law of Effect. Sometimes, you can learn to do things *not* by being rewarded or punished but by watching *others* get rewarded or punished. You may also recall that *one-trial learning* flies in the face of Pavlov's classic work on classical conditioning. Normally it takes *multiple* exposures to a CS – which appears *immediately* before the UCS – for an organism to learn to love or hate the CS. But when we eat unfamiliar foods that make us sick many hours later, we often develop a strong aversion to such foods. There are other things people seem to be predisposed to learn very easily. For example, human toddlers engage in **fast mapping**. They often learn the meaning of a new word – and begin to use it to get what they want – after being exposed to the new word just once or twice. This natural penchant for language, like our natural aversion to spiders and snakes, seems to be hardwired.

There also appear to be other exceptions to Thorndike's Law of Effect. If you recall the *mere exposure effect*, you know that people come to like things to which they are repeatedly exposed – *even in the absence of reward*. Finally, research on **latent learning** shows that both people and animals can learn complicated things in the absence of rewards. Even in the heyday of behaviorism, Tolman & Honzik(1930) showed that rats learn using what he cautiously labeled "insight." For example, if you place hungry rats in a complex maze where there are no reinforcements (e.g., no food), they will wander around the maze aimlessly. Now put another group of rats in the maze and consistently put a reinforcement at the end of the maze. By the end of ten days, the second group of rats will race to the end of the maze to get the food, with very few errors. So far this is exactly what the Law of Effect dictates. But now suppose you change things up for the first group of initially unrewarded rats. If you now begin to put food at the end of the maze for this first group, they will very quickly learn to go right to this location. In short, the rats who just meandered around in the maze were learning something in the absence of any obvious rewards. In fact, by day 11 or 12, this first group of rats will navigate the maze just as well as the group of rats who were rewarded consistently for 12 straight days. That's latent (hidden) learning, and as you can see from Figure 12.4, latent learning can involve some complex behavior.

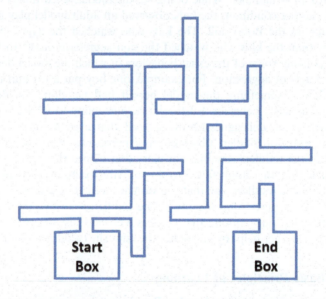

Figure 12.4 A maze Tolman and Honzik (1930) used to study *latent learning*. The maze was more challenging than it looks here because all the choice points contained doors or curtains that prevented the rats from seeing what lay ahead. The maze was also covered. Thus, rats cold not stand up and get their bearings. Rats who explored the maze aimlessly when there was no reinforcement in the end box learned to get to the end box very quickly once Tolman and Honzik began placing food there. The rats had apparently learned something without being reinforced.

Modern Research on Learning

If you noticed that this module is heavy on classic findings, please do not jump to the conclusion that learning theory is a thing of the past. In fact, principles of learning often work their way into a great deal of modern research. For example, building on Staats and Staats's (1958) classic research on the classical conditioning of attitudes, Jones, Pelham, Carvallo, and Mirenberg (2004) used classical conditioning to get people to like a stranger more than they would otherwise. Further, modern learning theorists are using cutting-edge neuroimaging techniques such as fMRI to get a handle on which exact areas of the brain are responsible for different kinds of learning (see Koelsch & Skouras, 2014; Pessiglione et al., 2008). This means, for example, that I hope you are using your striatum a lot as you read and digest this chapter on learning. The more we learn about the biological basis of learning, the better prepared we should be in the future to help people learn as well as possible. Treatments for phobias, post-traumatic stress disorder (PTSD), and common learning disorders benefit greatly from both our classic understanding of learning and our expanding knowledge of the biological basis of learning (Sherin & Nemeroff, 2011). As you'll see in our module on the treatment of psychological disorders, many clinical interventions are based on basic principles of learning. For example, when people suffer from specific phobias, they often receive **exposure therapy.** This means patients are exposed to a mild version of what they fear (e.g., pictures of a spider rather than a live spider) and taught to relax in the presence of the feared object. Once that step is done, the next step might be exposure to a realistic looking plastic spider – along with some help reaching a state of relaxation. The exposure therapy continues until the patient is comfortable being in the presence of the object that once was the basis of his or her phobia. In other words, therapists walk people through a step by step *extinction* process. The same principles of classical and operant conditioning that explain why rats and pigeons peck or press buttons in the lab can be turned on their heads to help people cope with at least some clinical disorders.

"So always remember: If you *peck* and nothing happens, you don't give up. You just peck again."

Figure 12.5

Review Sheet or Group Activity for Classical and Operant Conditioning

Explain exactly how each cartoon illustrates each concept summarized on this page. Some cartoons are open to many interpretations, by the way. So you may have to create a *story* that shows that you understand the concept in question). An example would be to explain why the man next to the law of effect is bowing. Is he an actor?

classical conditioning: a form of learning in which a neutral stimulus (a CS) is paired with a stimulus (a UCS) that produces a natural response (UCR). Conditioning has occurred when the CS produces a conditioned response (CR) that strongly resembles the original UCR. Example: Pavlov presents hungry dogs with: (1) ringing buzzer, (2) then meat powder, and (3) gets salivation. If you do this 6–8 times under ideal conditions, dogs will now salivate to the *buzzer*.

Pavlovian (Classical) Conditioning Involves Four Things

1. **unconditional stimulus** (UCS): something that produces a natural reflex or reaction (e.g., meat powder, electric shock)
2. **unconditional response** (UCR): the natural reaction (e.g., salivation, happiness, wincing in pain)
3. **conditional stimulus** (CS): a once-neutral stimulus that (e.g., a buzzer) that now produces a response much like the UCR
4. **conditional response** (CR): the post-conditioning response that follows the CS and resembles the UCR (e.g., *drooling* in response to a buzzer).

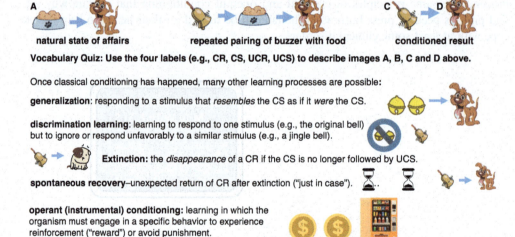

A   natural state of affairs   repeated pairing of buzzer with food   C   D   conditioned result

Vocabulary Quiz: Use the four labels (e.g., CR, CS, UCR, UCS) to describe images A, B, C and D above.

Once classical conditioning has happened, many other learning processes are possible:

generalization: responding to a stimulus that *resembles* the CS as if it *were* the CS.

discrimination learning: learning to respond to one stimulus (e.g., the original bell) but to ignore or respond unfavorably to a similar stimulus (e.g., a jingle bell).

Extinction: the *disappearance* of a CR if the CS is no longer followed by UCS.

spontaneous recovery–unexpected return of CR after extinction ("just in case").

operant (instrumental) conditioning: learning in which the organism must engage in a specific behavior to experience reinforcement ("reward") or avoid punishment.

law of effect: behaviors followed by happy states (e.g., warmth, food) become more likely. Behaviors followed by unhappy states (e.g., injury, shame) become less likely.

shaping: a form of operant conditioning in which the organism first gets rewarded for rough approximations of a desired behavior and eventually gets rewarded only for a complex behavior

observational learning: social learning, modeling. Learning by watching another organism do something that gets rewarded or punished.

preparedness: an evolved tendency to learn some things much more easily than others; explains **one-trial learning**.

Multiple-Choice Questions for Module 12

1. The idea behind giving people tickets for speeding is that having to pay a big fine for going too fast will reduce the likelihood that a person speeds in the future. Assuming this works, it is a good example of Thorndike's:

   A) Law of Effect
   B) principle of trial-and-error learning
   C) drive reduction rule

2. Being punched by a drunken stranger when you insult her is an example of:

   A) negative punishment
   B) positive punishment
   C) negative reinforcement
   D) positive reinforcement

3. Being banned from a fun bar because you always insult the patrons and cause barfights is an example of:

   A) negative punishment
   B) positive punishment
   C) negative reinforcement
   D) positive reinforcement

4. Attending a review session and then doing exceptionally well on an exam is an example of:

   A) negative punishment
   B) positive punishment
   C) negative reinforcement
   D) positive reinforcement

5. Limping to avoid putting too much pressure on an injured knee is a good example of:

   A) negative punishment
   B) positive punishment
   C) negative reinforcement
   D) positive reinforcement

6. Working in a factory where you get paid by the hour – as long as you engage in some minimal amount of work every hour – is an example of what specific way of being reinforced?

   A) fixed interval schedule
   B) fixed ratio schedule
   C) steady state reward

7. Erin sews socks for Nike. She receives fifty cents in pay for each individual sock she sews properly, regardless of how long it takes her to sew a sock. What's the term for this specific way of being reinforced?

   A) fixed interval schedule
   B) fixed ratio schedule
   C) steady state reward

8. In many games of chance, it is not exactly clear when a reward will come following an operant behavior. For example, if you play slot machines it could be three pulls until you win some money, or it could be 300 pulls. What is Skinner's term for this specific way of being reinforced?

   A) fixed interval schedule
   B) fixed ratio schedule
   C) variable interval schedule
   D) variable ratio schedule

9. The kind of bit-by-bit operant conditioning that allows cats to learn how to escape from a puzzle box is known as:

   A) insight learning
   B) vicarious learning
   C) incremental learning
   D) trial-and-error learning

10. A week before Christmas, a three-year-old child sees a chubby white-haired man with a beard at the airport. The man also happens to be wearing a red shirt. The moment the child sees the man she happily yells, "Santa!" This is an example of:

    A) generalization
    B) stimulus substitution
    C) discrimination learning

Answer Key: 1A, 2B, 3A, 4D, 5C, 6A, 7B, 8D, 9D, 10A

References

Bandura, A., Ross, D., & Ross, S. A. (1961). Transmission of aggression through imitation of aggressive models. *Journal of Abnormal and Social Psychology, 63*, 575–582.

Darby, C. L., & Riopelle, A. J. (1959). Observational learning in the rhesus monkey. *Journal of Comparative and Physiological Psychology, 52*, 94–98.

Gullapalli, V. (1997). Chapter 16 - Reinforcement learning of complex behavior through shaping. In J. W. Donahoe & V. P. Dorsel (Eds.), *Advances in psychology, North-Holland* (Vol. 121, pp. 302–314). doi: 10.1016/S0166-4115(97)80102-1

Jones, J. K., Pelham, B. W., Carvallo, M. C., & Mirenberg, M. C. (2004). How do I love thee? Let me count the Js: Implicit egotism and interpersonal attraction. *Journal of Personality and Social Psychology, 87*, 665–683.

Koelsch, S., & Skouras, S. (2014). Functional centrality of amygdala, striatum and hypothalamus in a "small-world" network underlying joy: An fMRI study with music. *Human Brain Mapping, 35* (7), Epub 2013 Nov 25, 3485–3498.

Mackintosh, N. J. (1974). *The psychology of animal learning.* New York: Academic Press.

Pessiglione, M., Petrovic, P., Daunizeau, J., Palminteri, S., Dolan, R. J., & Frith, C. D. (2008). Subliminal instrumental conditioning demonstrated in the human brain. *Neuron, 59*(4), 561–567.

Peterson, G. B. (2004). A day of great illumination: B. F. Skinner's discovery of shaping. *Journal of the Experimental Analysis of Behavior, 82*(3), 317–328.

Popper, K. (1974/1990). *Unended quest: An intellectual autobiography.* LaSalle, IL: Open Court.

Schuhmacher, N., Köster, M., & Kärtner, J. (2018). Modeling prosocial behavior increases helping in 16-month-olds. *Child Development.* doi:10.1111/cdev.13054

Schultz, D. (1981). *A history of modern psychology (3rd ed.)* New York: Academic Press.

Sherin, J. E., & Nemeroff, C. B. (2011). Post-traumatic stress disorder: The neurobiological impact of psychological trauma. *Dialogues in Clinical Neuroscience, 13*(3), 263–278.

Skinner, B. F. (1961, November). Teaching machines. *Scientific American*, 91–102.

Staats, A. W., & Staats, C. K. (1958). Attitudes established by classical conditioning. *Journal of Abnormal Psychology, 57*, 37–40.

Straus, M. A., Sugarman, D. B., & Giles-Sims, J. (1997). Spanking by parents and subsequent antisocial behavior of children. *Archives of Pediatric Adolescent Medicine, 151*(8), 761–767. doi:10.1001/archpedi.1997.02170450011002

Thorndike, E. L. (1911). *Animal intelligence: Experimental studies.* New York: MacMillan.

Tolman, E. C., & Honzik, C. H. (1930). Degrees of hunger, reward and non-reward, and maze learning in rats. *University of California Publications in Psychology, 4*(16), 241–256.

VI
Motivation, Emotion, and More

Module 13
Motivation

The Psychology of Wants and Needs

What do you want most in life? Fame? Love? Wealth? Or just an ice cream sandwich? Research on human motivation suggests that these are all good answers. **Motivation** refers to the desires and drives that fuel what we think, feel, and do (Buck, 1985). Curiosity, aspirations, lust, thirst, hopes, fears, goals, wishes, and needs: these are but a few of the many words that describe the nuances of human motivation. In fact, one of the difficulties in making sense of human motivation is that none of us want just one thing. Further, in keeping with the idea that we should all "be careful what we wish for," we don't always know what we really want. Finally, different motivations often compete with one another. Your lowly desire to eat ice cream is no friend to your lofty desire to be lean and healthy. As a nobler example, our desire to help others in distress can sometimes overpower our concerns for our own safety (Marsh, 2017).

Studying Motivation Is Tricky

Psychologists have long been interested in motivation. In the world's first psychology textbook, James (1890) wrote about motivation in great length. James believed that a lot of human behavior is driven by instincts – which are biologically hardwired and presumably adaptive responses to important situations. On the heels of James's speculations, William McDougall (1909) and others promoted the **instinct theory of motivation**. This is the idea that a great deal of human behavior is driven by specific tendencies to engage in certain activities. If you've heard of reflexes, and you think that instincts are like reflexes, you're not completely wrong. **Reflexes** are extremely specific, hardwired, and automatic responses to specific stimuli. Shivering in the cold, sneezing to expel irritants, and blinking to protect one's eyes from blowing sand are all reflexes. But instincts were never as well-specified as reflexes, and early psychologists applied the concept of instincts to some complex and highly modifiable behaviors. James argued that we have

Figure 13.1 People are motivated to achieve and experience many things.

an instinctive fear of any large biological creature that is moving toward us. But research with children suggests that this is not a reliable response. Some kids are afraid of incoming dogs while others can't wait to pet them. But all kids blink when dogs kick sand in their faces. This is a reflex. After thirty years of psychological speculation about instincts, Faris (1921, p. 184) summarized the state of the field by noting that "Nothing is commoner than the belief that we are endowed with instincts inherited from the lower creatures. Whole systems of psychology have been founded on this assumption."

But the instinct theory of human motivation ran into some trouble. Before we examine the trouble with instincts, however, let's examine their appeal. In the heyday of instinct theory, instincts were used to explain almost everything. Why do people fear death? Freud identified **Eros** as the "life instinct" – a built-in will to live. But if Eros is so powerful, why do some people kill themselves? Freud had that one covered, too. It's because of **Thanatos**, the "death instinct." So we've covered life and death. By the mid-1920s, instinct theorists had covered life, death, and just about everything in between. In 1924, a critical Luther Bernard tallied more than 5,500 presumed instincts. Why do people play baseball? There must be a "playing instinct." Why do kids catch and kill bugs? There must be a "hunting instinct." The problem with these explanations is that they are tautological. A **tautology** is a circular argument. It's the logical mistake of substituting description for explanation. It is giving something a label (the "hunting instinct") and then assuming that the label is an explanation. It is like saying that this textbook is great because it's a great textbook. In a scathing critique of instinct theory, Faris (1921) asserted that we can't understand human motivation by just labeling it.

So instead of speculating about human motivation, maybe we should just ask people why they do what they do. Unfortunately, people often fail to realize why they do things. In their famous **panty hose study**, Nisbett and Wilson (1977) asked female shoppers to evaluate four pairs of panty hose. To make the test blind, they arbitrarily labeled the four pairs of hose A-D. Shoppers showed a strong preference for the fourth pair. When asked to explain *why* they had chosen their preferred pair, some shoppers said they preferred the shading of their chosen pair. Others said their preferred pair felt smoother or more durable. None of these shoppers had any trouble answering this motivational question. But none of them answered it correctly. We know this because the four pairs of panty hose were identical. The strong preference shoppers showed for pair D was a "shopping around effect" (an order effect). Nisbett and Wilson (1977) argued that when people explain why they've made decisions, they often fall back on their intuitions about human preferences – because they often have little or no knowledge of what motivated their decisions. We often know *what* we want without knowing *why* we want it. Many studies have confirmed this result (e.g., see Johansson, Hall, Sikström, & Olsson, 2005).

This does *not* mean it's impossible to study motivation. It just means we must be very careful about it. Ironically, one of the reasons why we fail to appreciate how motivation works has to do with the nature of motivation itself. Motivation has been characterized as existing along a *"hot-cold" dimension*, meaning that motivational high and lows vary dramatically with time and context. Studies of **hot vs. cold motivational states** show that hungry grocery shoppers buy more food than they had planned (Nisbett & Kanouse, 1969). Further, those who are not currently dehydrated fail to appreciate the importance of having ready access to drinking water. As Nordgren, van der

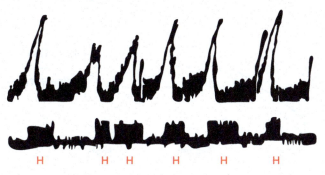

Intensity of Washburn's Stomach Contractions

H   H H   H   H   H

Washburn's Subjective Reports of Hunger (H)

Figure 13.2 The top panel shows the strength of the contractions of Washburn's stomach in a ten-minute period. The bottom panel represents Washburn's self-reported hunger pangs (yes or no) during the same period. Adapted from Cannon and Washburn (1912).

Pligt, and Harreveld (2006, p. 635) put it, people in cold states "underestimate the influence of a future hot state." We have all, at one point or another, sworn off chocolate chip cookies – until we smelled them baking. Motivation waxes and wanes. In fact, sometimes it just waxes and waxes. This means we often fail to appreciate the power of important motivational states such as hunger or sexual arousal unless we are currently experiencing them.

Those who study animal learning have long appreciated the dynamic nature of motivation. This is why they make sure the animals they study are *extremely* hungry – and thus highly motivated (Mackintosh, 1974). Such complications notwithstanding, there are many clever ways to study motivation. While others were speculating about instincts in the early 1900s, A.L. Washburn managed to swallow a very durable balloon. Washburn and his collaborator, Walter Cannon, then inflated the balloon, so it would fill Washburn's stomach. The balloon was connected (via a tube coming out of Washburn's throat) to a recording device that monitored Washburn's stomach contractions. Without seeing the device's readout, Washburn pressed a key every time he felt hungry. As you can see in Figure 13.2. Washburn's feelings of hunger coincided well with his stomach contractions (Cannon & Washburn, 1912). This **stomach contraction study** took psychology a long way toward being an empirical (data-driven) rather than a spiritual or philosophical enterprise.

Drive Theory, Yerkes-Dodson, and Social Facilitation

Rather than trying to identify thousands of specific instincts, learning theorists in the early to middle part of the 20th century took it for granted that there are a few basic reinforcers such as food, sex, and water. Learning theorists spent decades painstakingly studying the effects of **drive** (excitement or arousal due to the strength of an unfulfilled need; Seward, 1956) on (a) the rate at which an animal learned something and (b) the likelihood that an animal was able to perform something already learned (Mackintosh, 1974). Consistent with the **Yerkes-Dodson Law** (see Figure 13.3), there appears to be an

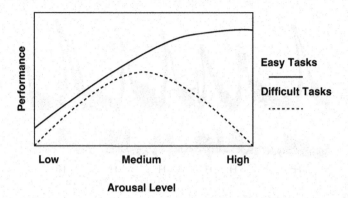

Figure 13.3 The Yerkes-Dodson Law of arousal and performance. For difficult or poorly-learned
tasks, a moderate amount of arousal leads to ideal performance – whereas very high or
very low arousal leads to poor performance. But for simple tasks, performance
increases with increasing arousal and then plateaus at high arousal levels.

optimal level of drive that maximizes performance on all but the simplest tasks. If you
want a rat to learn a maze quickly, make her hungry but not *too* hungry. If you want
a decent free-throw shooter to be make a free-throw, put some pressure on her – but
not too much pressure. Extreme levels of pressure may lead to "choking under pressure" (Baumeister, 1984).

In social psychology, a closely related finding comes from **social facilitation theory**,
which predicts that knowing you're being evaluated facilitates performance for highly
skilled performers but disrupts performance for the less skilled. This is because
arousal increases dominant (i.e., highly accessible) responses on a given task. For the
highly skilled free-throw shooter, the dominant response is success (making the free-
throw) whereas for the less skilled free-throw shooter, the dominant response is failure
(not making the free-throw). Consider some examples. In a field study of recreational
pool players, Michaels, Blommel, Brocato, Linkous, and Rowe (1982) secretly
observed pool players to identify good and weak players – based on the percentage of
shots they made when they didn't know anyone was watching. Then the members of
the research team let players know there was an audience by moving nearer to the
table and paying attention to them. Weaker players made 12% fewer of their shots
when they knew someone was watching. Stronger players made 12% *more* of their
shots when they knew someone was watching. In a context that's more like the classroom than the pool room, Bartis, Szymanski and Harkins (1988) convinced some
people that their work would be individually evaluated by an experimenter. They convinced others that no individual evaluations were possible. Some of these performers
did something easy – they listed as many uses for a knife as they possibly could.
Other performers did something more demanding – they listed as many *highly creative*
uses for a knife as possible. Those given the easy task performed better under the
pressure of evaluation. Those given the difficult task performed worse (see also
Pelham & Neter, 1995). Even cockroaches seem to be susceptible to an insect version
of social facilitation. Zajonc (2001) found that when cockroaches were put in a very

simple maze (a single straightaway with no turns), they ran faster in the presence of another cockroach than they did when running alone. But when Zajonc complicated the mazes by introducing a single turn (the cockroach version of matrix algebra, we presume), the presence of another roach now disrupted performance. Higher levels of drive push us forward when things are easy but throw us for a loop when things are hard (Carson & Collins, 2016).

From Instincts to Needs

Before we move on to describing some basic human needs, we want to note that modern researchers have not completely abandoned the idea of instincts. For example, Pinker (1994) argued that there's a uniquely human **language instinct**. By that, he meant that there is a very powerful evolved tendency for people to use language. Of course, the details of language are learned based on one's culture, but there are no known human cultures that fail to use spoken language. Further, Pinker notes that children learn language effortlessly and that kids can quickly create languages from scratch when it suits their purpose. Further, he notes that all world languages have a lot more in common than most people realize. We're willing to concede that language is certainly instinct-*like*. Having noted this, we'd like to focus mainly on basic human needs rather than instincts. There is plenty of evidence that human beings do have basic needs. Needs are much broader than instincts, and we share some basic biological needs with most animals.

To paraphrase the drive theorist Clark Hull (1943), **needs** are states that drive us to achieve certain goals. But unlike instincts, needs are usually tied in obvious ways to survival. Further, needs can often be filled in a wide range of specific ways. Finally, needs obey the principle of **homoeostasis**. Homeostasis is the tendency for a system to remain within a set of optimal parameters. Loosely speaking, homeostasis is balance. When a system is out of balance, there is a motivation (drive) to return the system to a balanced state. Hunger and thirst both obey the rules of homeostasis. If you just ate an enormous meal, this should make food unappealing to you for a while. Likewise, if you just drank a liter of water, the likely homeostatic consequence is that you'll temporarily lose interest in water. Conversely, if a 50-km bike ride has made you extremely thirsty, a bottle of water that had little value to you two hours ago, suddenly becomes very valuable. That's homeostasis. But human needs do not end with physiological needs like thirst or sexual desire. People also have higher-order needs.

Maslow's Hierarchy of Needs

Abe Maslow would certainly agree that people possess both physiological and psychological needs. Maslow (1943) proposed a hierarchy of human needs – which can be summarized using a five-level pyramid. Maslow argued that we share physiological needs with most other animals – while also possessing other needs that no other animals possess. Maslow also offered clear definitions of his needs. His belief (a) that his five needs were universal human needs and (b) that they exist in a hierarchy also means it's possible to put his theory to some basic tests.

Maslow's hierarchical theory is summarized in Figure 13.4. The base of Maslow's pyramid represents the physiological needs we share with other animals, from alligators

Figure 13.4 Maslow's hierarchy of needs. Maslow argued that we cannot easily fill any upper need in the pyramid until we've filled all the needs that sit below it. Just as you could not build the fourth (green) level of a real pyramid until you had built all three of the lower levels (in order), Maslow argued that you won't focus much attention on filling your esteem needs until you've filled all the lower needs.

to zebras. Maslow believed that these physiological needs usually need to be satisfied first. If we are to survive and reproduce, we must eat, breathe, stay hydrated, and relieve our bodies of waste. Maslow's theory predicts that people whose physiological needs are currently unfilled will be highly fixated on them.

Once you've filled your basic physiological needs, you can try to fill the need for safety and security. If you had just washed ashore on a desert island, your first order of business would probably be to find food and water. Once you had done so, you'd want to start building a hut. It's going to be dark soon. Because you're probably not living on a deserted island, we suspect that you spend more time each day thinking about belongingness – or self-evaluation – than you do thinking about getting safe drinking water. Maslow conceded that the rules of his hierarchy are not absolute. In fact, you began filling your need for love and belongingness as an infant, and this was probably true even if you were often hungry (Erikson, 1980). Along similar lines, having just one loving friend or family member might fill your need for belongingness well enough to allow you to pursue activities that could give you a basic sense of self-esteem. Once you sorted out self-esteem, you'd presumably begin to try to fill the need at the top of Maslow's pyramid. Maslow (1943, p. 383) defined **self-actualization** as "the desire for self-fulfillment ... the desire ... to become everything that one is capable of becoming." Of course, the details of self-actualization will vary greatly from person to person – because everyone has unique interests. Maslow also emphasized that self-actualized people have self-insight. A self-actualized person might be stingy, but she is likely to recognize and acknowledge this weakness. In fact, she's likely to be comfortable poking fun of herself in this area.

Maslow's theory jibes with most people's experience. All of us have interrupted a deep conversation – or stopped working on a highly engaging textbook module – because we really, really had to go to the bathroom. It is perhaps for this reason that

Maslow's theory was rarely put to any comprehensive empirical tests in the first 70 years after he proposed it. But that changed when Tay and Diener (2011) conducted a massive cross-cultural study putting Maslow's theory to the test in 123 (yes, 123) nations. They zeroed in mainly on the prediction that our **well-being** (e.g., how favorably we evaluate our lives) is influenced by how well we've been able to fill the needs in Maslow's hierarchy. Their global study was complex. Furthermore, because they capitalized on a survey that was not specifically designed with Maslow's theory in mind, they sometimes had to accept approximations of how well people had filled each of Maslow's five needs. But in our view, the further down in Maslow's pyramid one goes, the better Tay and Diener were able to assess whether people had filled that need. For example, two questions that assessed physiological needs had to do with whether people said they had gone hungry – or had found it hard to pay for food – in the past year. Two questions about safety and security needs had to do with whether people reported feeling safe when walking alone or had been assaulted in the past year. Tay and Diener (2011) argued that their findings generally supported Maslow's model. For example, they report (p. 363) that "as hypothesized by Maslow (1943), people tend to achieve basic and safety needs before other needs." But they also argued that each of Maslow's needs plays a separate and independent role in promoting overall well-being. In other words, even though people tend to fill basic needs first, "a person can gain well-being by meeting psychosocial needs regardless of whether his or her basic needs are fully met." Their basic results were consistent across world regions. Finally, they observed something a humanist like Maslow probably would have loved – even though his theory doesn't predict it. An important source of well-being for people across the globe was being lucky enough to live in a culture where the basic needs of most *other* people were routinely filled. Apparently, we are happiest when our own basic needs have been met and when the basic needs of our neighbors and fellow country members have *also* been met.

Figure 13.5
In Maslow's famous hierarchy of needs, he proposes that we must all take care of our basic physiological needs first before we can begin to focus on social or psychological needs (such as the need for self-esteem or self-actualization). Thus, *base* physiological needs – such as the one illustrated here – are at the *base* (bottom) of Maslow's pyramid.

Criticisms and Extensions of Maslow's Model

Not everyone considers Maslow's pyramid the final word on how basic human needs play themselves out. For example, in their critical analysis of basic human motivations. Kenrick and colleagues (2010) begin by praising Maslow for thinking deeply about how biological and psychological needs exist in a hierarchy. However, they also argue that whereas "the basic foundational structure of the pyramid is worth preserving ... it should be buttressed with a few architectural extensions." In their view, the most important extensions are grounded in evolutionary psychology, which did not exist in any coherent form in Maslow's day. Kenrick and colleagues (2010) make two main points. First, human needs may not be quite as hierarchical as Maslow believed. Filling a basic need does not mean it falls off the radar completely. Further, people may sometimes overlook their own physical needs – at least for a while – in the service of higher needs. For example, devoted parents may go long periods without food – or put their own safety and security at risk – so that they can feed their hungry children. Fair enough. This is somewhat similar to Tay and Diener's (2011) point that Maslow's hierarchy is not truly absolute. Second, Kenrick and colleagues (2010) also argue that an evolutionarily enlightened pyramid of human needs would be topped not by self-actualization but by attracting mates, followed by keeping mates, followed by being a good parent (at the very top of the pyramid). In fact, they view what may look like self-actualization (e.g., becoming the best pianist or photographer you can possibly be) as a by-product of mating and parenting efforts. Many people desire to become great at things precisely because doing so often helps people attract mates and care for children.

As a final example, in the provocative book *Social*, Lieberman (2013) argues that there is a problem with Maslow's hierarchy. Specifically, he argues that the need for love and belongingness often trumps even the basic physiological needs. Lieberman reviews a wide range of findings on the strength of our need to care for and be connected to others. For example, he reviews cutting-edge research in neuroscience showing that the areas of the brain known to indicate reward are activated not only when something good happens to *us* but also when we make something good happen to *others*. Along similar lines, Marsh (2017) argues that **empathic concern** (feeling distress when we see others who are in distress) can motivate us to help others even when it is very costly for us to do so – and even when the others are complete strangers. Finally, in their classic paper on the potency of social motives, Baumeister and Leary (1995, p. 497) argue that "the need to belong is a powerful, fundamental, and extremely pervasive motivation." In support of this idea, they review work from many areas of psychology suggesting that the **need to belong** – that is, the need to interact with and feel connected to others – is so powerful that it sometimes trumps other needs. We suspect that you can recall examples of people in your life who sacrificed their own basic needs either to care for loved ones or to pursue needs of their own that are higher up in Maslow's pyramid.

Baumeister and Leary (1995) argue that the need to belong has nine basic properties that make it very much like other widely accepted needs. For example, they argue that the need to belong is universal; it exists in every known culture on Earth. They also argue that, like other needs, the need to belong is crucial to human survival and well-being. People become psychologically disturbed, and even physically ill, when this basic need goes unmet. The need to belong also fuels "goal-relevant behavior" that is specifically designed to satisfy it. In keeping with the principle of *satiation* (i.e., homeostasis) the need to belong also becomes stronger when it has been thwarted. And it also becomes lessened when it has recently been filled, much like hunger or thirst. Speaking of hunger and thirst, perhaps the strongest evidence for the potency of the need to belong comes from Harlow's (1958) classic work with one of our primate cousins.

Harlow (1958) conducted a series of innovative studies that revealed the depth of our need for contact with others. Harlow separated infant rhesus monkeys from their biological mothers and reared them artificially. In one of his most telling studies, Harlow offered these infants a choice between two very different **surrogate mothers**. A surrogate is a substitute or replacement. Thus, Harlow's infant monkeys had to choose between two substitute moms – which were equally available to the infants, but which were always separated by a partition. On one side, a wire mom with a bottle near its face provided these monkeys with their only source of nutrition. On the other side, a terrycloth mom provided no nutrition at all but was soft and huggable. Harlow's juvenile monkeys spent almost all their time with the terrycloth mom. Further, when they were experimentally scared by a sinister mechanical monster, they ran immediately to the terrycloth mom – the one that offered an opportunity for comforting contact but with no source of nutrition.

The gist of Harlow's surrogate mother studies is that infant bonding has more to do with the motivation to hold and be held than it does with the basic biological need to be fed – at least when you are a baby. Before Harlow came along, psychologists had virtually ignored the strong bonds we forge at birth with our caregivers. Those who did address topics such as love, bonding, and attachment assumed that these processes were

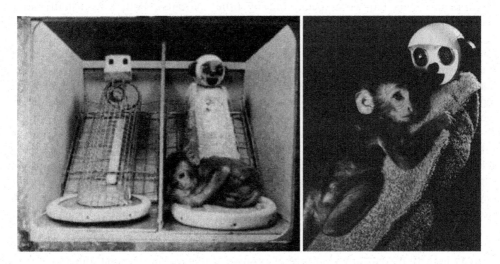

Figure 13.6 Harlow's two surrogate moms – a wire vs. a terrycloth mom. On the right, you can see which one a typical infant rhesus monkey chose to be with 20 times more often than the other. Infants showed this strong preference for the cuddly mom even when the wire mom provided nutrition and the cuddly mom did not.

the results of simple conditioning. I associate mom with *food* – and maybe *safety* – and so I love her. Harlow felt there was much more to love and attachment than milk. As he put it in a classic paper (1958, p. 573), "The little we know about love does not transcend simple observation, and the little we write about it has been written better by poets and novelists." Harlow's brilliant work quickly eliminated this blind spot. There can be little doubt that, as one of the most social creatures on the planet, we have a deep and abiding need to be connected to others.

Intrinsic vs. Extrinsic Motivation

Modern theories of motivation sometimes make counterintuitive predictions. Consider research on intrinsic vs. extrinsic motivation. Lepper, Greene, and Nisbett (1973) gave some children a promised reward for engaging in a behavior the children had originally loved (coloring with magic markers). Other children also colored with the markers but received no reward. The children were later given the chance to play with the magic markers during some free time. Those who had been rewarded were about half as likely to play with the markers as were those who had not been rewarded. Notice that *rewarding* kids for doing something that was inherently enjoyable *reduced* their interest in it. That's counterintuitive. This study suggests that even small children have a sense of the difference between intrinsic and extrinsic motivation. **Intrinsic motivation** refers to a desire to do an activity *for its own sake* – because you find the activity inherently challenging or joyful (Lepper, Corpus, & Iyengar, 2005). In contrast, **extrinsic motivation** refers to the desire to do something for reasons that are *not* connected to the activity itself (e.g., because you were paid to do something). Kids usually love to draw because drawing is fun. They don't need to be paid to draw. In contrast, it seems safe to say that very few kids consider cleaning their rooms fun. But kids do *sometimes* clean their rooms (so we've been told by other parents). And kids usually do it because their parents provide them with an external justification for doing so (e.g., an allowance, a special dessert). The reduced interest people show in an activity after they have been rewarded for doing it is known as the **overjustification effect**. It's the finding that you can reduce intrinsic motivation to engage in an activity by making people think perhaps they engaged in the activity because of an extrinsic motivation. By the way, if paying people to do something can make them like it *less* than usual, you may wonder what would happen if people had to work very hard to do or attain something. In animals as diverse as ants and people, those who have to suffer or work hard to achieve something value it more highly than those who achieve the same outcome at a lower cost. People often come to love groups for which they have suffered, for example (Aronson & Mills, 1959). Likewise, ants who have to climb a vertical wall to obtain food later prefer that food over an equally sweet and nutritious food that they obtained by merely walking across flat ground (Czaczkes, Brandstetter, Di Stefano, & Heinze, 2018).

As Di Domenico and Ryan (2017) noted, a person's level of intrinsic motivation to perform an activity predicts a wide range of positive academic and personal outcomes, from good grades to creativity. Most educators are deeply interested in both intrinsic and extrinsic motivation because each is connected to classroom success. Lepper and colleagues (2005) assessed both intrinsic and extrinsic academic motivation in a large study of kids in grades 3–8. An item that assessed the level of intrinsic motivation was "I work on problems

Figure 13.7 Dad: "Want to color?" Kids: "It depends. How much are you paying?" This is the *over-justification effect*: the tendency for external rewards to undermine intrinsic motivation.

to learn how to solve them." An item that assessed extrinsic motivation was "I work on problems because I am supposed to." Kids who scored higher than average in intrinsic motivation got higher grades and higher standardized test scores. In contrast, kids who scored higher than average in extrinsic motivation got *lower* grades and *lower* standardized tests scores. The study also showed that, on average, intrinsic motivation decreased with age (see also Harter, 1981). Taken together with research on the over-justification effect, this suggests some important practical applications. For example, in 2008 and 2009, educators in Washington, DC tried to improve student academic performance by paying them to get good grades. As far as we can tell, there were no solid data attesting to the effectiveness of this program. We hope you can see that experts on intrinsic motivation would have suggested a very different intervention – especially if we're concerned about long-term rather than short-term benefits. In fact, the same DC school systems that claimed to be making great academic progress not long after this and other programs were begun around 2008 later became the target of an FBI investigation – because of allegations of widespread fraud in grade reports (Jamison & Nirappil, 2018).

Just the Tip of the Iceberg

Researchers who study motivation are a highly motivated lot. In addition to studying the topics summarized here, they also study many other motivational topics, from how to stick to a diet to how men and women differ in their perspectives on work, mastery, and competitiveness (Spence & Helmreich, 1983). Likewise, experts in human motivation have long studied how we are motivated to behave in ways that are consistent with our core attitudes – and how we try to restore the balance (or homeostasis, if we may stretch the definition a bit) between our attitudes and our behavior when the two are inconsistent (Festinger, 1957). There is also work suggesting that who we are and how we define ourselves has a great deal to do with motivation. In his analysis of self-esteem, William James (1890) argued our basic sense of self-worth has as much to do with what we *aspire* to do as it does with how we evaluate ourselves. Specifically, James (1890, p. 310) argued that:

> I, who for the time have staked my all on being a psychologist, am mortified if others know much more psychology than I. But I am contented to wallow in the grossest ignorance of Greek. My deficiencies there give me no sense of personal humiliation at all. Had I 'pretensions' to be a linguist, it would have been just the reverse. So we have the paradox of a man shamed to death because he is only the second pugilist or the second oarsman in the world. That he is able to beat the whole population of the globe minus one is nothing; he has 'pitted' himself to beat that one; and as long as he doesn't do that nothing else counts.

James went on to offer a simple formula for self-esteem: **"Self-esteem = Success/Pretension."** Success, of course, is all about whether one feels one has achieved one's goals. Pretension, the way James used the term, is all about which specific goals one chooses in the first place. Empirical research on self-esteem and well-being has provided strong support for James's assertions (Higgins, 1987; Pelham & Swann, 1989). People derive self-worth, in great part, by deciding that they are good at the specific things that really matter to them. We feel good about ourselves when we feel we have achieved what really counts (to us, at least). Motivation allows us to survive. It should not be surprising that it also helps define who we are.

Critical Thinking: How to Get What You Want

One tricky aspect of motivation is that we are motivated to do many different things. And many of the things we want get in the way of other things we want. Eating lots of ice cream fills a basic physiological need to consume delicious food. But it does little to promote a healthy body weight. Further, even when we know we want something, self-doubt and self-sabotage sometimes seem to get the better of us. Legendary rock singer Jackson Browne put it all very cynically when he said, "And while the future's there for anyone to change, still you know it seems, it would be easier sometimes to change the past." Can motivational psychologists offer us any good advice about how to make the future better – and get what we want?

We think Tim Wilson can. In his 2011 book *Redirect*, he argues that there are some simple steps most people can take to get what they want and avoid what some see as self-sabotage. Wilson offers many tips for getting what you want out of life. We'll just summarize a couple. First, a thread that runs throughout Wilson's book is the idea that the *stories we tell ourselves* are important. And unfortunately, these stories can often be self-defeating. For example, many college students seem to believe that anyone who ever struggles academically – or feels out of place in college – may not belong in college. In a 1982 study, Wilson and colleagues identified a group of struggling college freshmen. These were students that, as Wilson (2011) put it "were at risk of blaming themselves and thinking they weren't 'college material.'" Half the students were just followed over time – as a control group. The other half got a simple experimental treatment. They simply learned that a lot of students struggle in their first year of college. They further learned that struggling students merely need to adjust to college and improve their study skills. The experimenters reinforced this message with videos of real college students who reported having had exactly this experience. This simple manipulation had a lasting effect, increasing the future GPAs of the students who were invited to "edit their stories."

There are many other ways to help people edit their (unhelpful) stories. For example, giving students a chance to write about a painful or traumatic experience over a period of several weeks helps them tell a new story about the painful event. And according to work by Jamie Pennebaker and colleagues (see Smyth & Pennebaker, 2008), this simple writing manipulation has beneficial health effects. Finally, simply getting people to begin doing something they wish to do regularly or getting people to do things that will make them feel valued (as Wilson puts it, "do good, be good") can help people rewrite their personal stories. ("If no one needs me, then why are the men at the homeless shelter so appreciative when they see me every Wednesday?") There is probably no magic bullet for making constructive changes to our lives, but Wilson's research – and his careful look at the research of many others – offers us reason to believe that getting what we want may be within our grasp after all.

1. McGuire's research on *attitude inoculation* and smoking gives some seventh graders practice (via role-playing) resisting social pressure to try cigarettes. Other kids get no such intervention. Kids who get the practice resisting social pressure (the inoculation) are much less likely to become smokers over the course of the next few years. In what ways is this work like the work of Wilson and colleagues? In what ways is it different?
2. Instead of waiting to identify a group of students who are struggling, as Wilson and colleagues did, might it not be better to familiarize college students *prior* to the first week of college with the idea that they may face difficult challenges in college? Are there any reasons to expect at-risk students (such as first-generation college students) to benefit more from such as forward-looking intervention than would students whose backgrounds do not put them at extra risk for academic problems?

Multiple-Choice Questions for Module 13

1. The movie *Rabbit Proof Fence* is a dramatization of a true story about three aboriginal girls who walked 2,400 km across Australia in 1931 – in hopes of reuniting with their families after the government sent the girls far away from their homes. This amazing trek puts the girls in constant physical danger. Which theory of human motivation is most consistent with the idea that these girls would risk life and limb to be with those they loved?

   A) Maslow's hierarchy
   B) the homing instinct
   C) the need to belong

2. Once professional athletes receive contracts that pay them millions of dollars per year to play a sport they have long adored, they sometimes report getting a lot less joy from playing the sport than they did when they were amateurs. This observation is consistent with research on:

   A) the Law of Effect
   B) social facilitation
   C) the overjustification effect
   D) the Yerkes-Dodson Law

3. R.D. Kotzker (2007) asked ten "expert" and ten "non-expert" basketball players to shoot 50 free throws. They all took 25 shots while alone and 25 shots while in front of an audience. The non-expert players made more free throws when shooting alone than when shooting in front of an audience. The experts showed the reverse pattern, doing better when there was an audience. These findings support:

   A) Maslow's hierarchy of needs
   B) social facilitation theory
   C) regression toward the mean
   D) extrinsic motivation

4. A classic study by Cannon and Washburn involved balloon-swallowing. The study was designed to see if:

   A) artificially filling someone's stomach would reduce feelings of hunger
   B) hunger is increased when a person is presented with highly desirable foods
   C) felt hunger is caused by stomach contractions

5. Social facilitation theory is a very close cousin of what other motivational theory?

   A) social comparison theory
   B) drive-reduction theory
   C) the Law of Effect
   D) the Yerkes-Dodson Law

6. What famous study cited in the module on motivation suggested that we *cannot* always know why people do things by just asking them to tell us about their reasons?

   A) the stomach-contraction study
   B) the panty hose study
   C) the magic marker study

7. The findings of Harry Harlow's classic studies of young rhesus monkeys who had surrogate mothers are highly consistent with research on:

   A) the need to belong
   B) hot-cold state studies
   C) the maternal instinct

8. What psychological needs are just above physiological needs in Maslow's hierarchy of needs?

   A) esteem needs
   B) social needs
   C) safety needs

9. What psychological needs are just below self-actualization in Maslow's hierarchy?

   A) esteem needs
   B) social needs
   C) safety needs

10. Janelle attended medical school not because she truly loves medicine but because her parents strongly pressured her to do so. It sounds like Janelle's went to medical school because of _____ motivation.

    A) familial
    B) extraneous
    C) extrinsic

Answer Key: 1C, 2C 3B, 4C, 5D, 6B, 7A, 8C, 9A, 10C

References

Aronson, E., & Mills, J. (1959). The effect of severity of initiation on liking for a group. *Journal of Abnormal and Social Psychology, 59*, 177–181.

Bartis, S., Szymanski, K., & Harkins, S. G. (1988). Evaluation and performance: A two-edged knife. *Personality and Social Psychology Bulletin, 14*(2), 242–251. https://doi.org/10.1177/0146167288142003

Baumeister, R. F. (1984). Choking under pressure: Self-consciousness and paradoxical effects of incentives on skillful performance. *Journal of Personality and Social Psychology, 46*(3), 610–620.

Baumeister, R. F., & Leary, M. (1995). The need to belong: Desire for interpersonal attachments as a fundamental human motivation. *Psychological Bulletin, 117*, 497–529. doi:10.1037/0033-2909.117.3.497

Bernard, L. L. (1924). *Instinct: A study in social psychology.* New York, NY: Holt.

Buck, R. (1985). Prime theory: An integrated view of motivation and emotion. *Psychological Review, 92*, 389–413.

Cannon, W. B., & Washburn, A. L. (1912). An explanation of hunger. *American Journal of Physiology, 29*, 441–454.

Carson, H. J., & Collins, D. (2016). The fourth dimension: A motoric perspective on the anxiety–performance relationship. *International Review of Sport and Exercise Psychology, 9*(1), 1–21. https://doi.org/10.1080/1750984X.2015.1072231

Czaczkes, T. J., Brandstetter, B., di Stefano, I., & Heinze, J. (2018). Greater effort increases perceived value in an invertebrate. *Journal of Comparative Psychology, 132*(2), 2000–2009.

Di Domenico, S. I., & Ryan, R.M. (2017). The emerging neuroscience of intrinsic motivation: A new frontier in self-determination research, Frontiers in Human Neuroscience, 11, 1–14.

Erikson, E. H. (1980). *Identity and the life cycle.* New York, NY: W. W. Norton & Co.

Faris, E. (1921). Are instincts data or hypotheses? *American Journal of Sociology, 27*(2), 184–196.

Festinger, L. (1957). *A theory of cognitive dissonance.* Stanford, CA: Stanford University Press.

Harlow, H. F. (1958). The nature of love. *American Psychologist, 13*, 573–586.

Harter, S. (1981). A new self-report scale of intrinsic versus extrinsic orientation in the classroom: Motivational and informational components. *Developmental Psychology, 17*, 300–312.

Higgins, E. T. (1987). Self-discrepancy: A theory relating self and affect. *Psychological Review, 94*(3), 319–340.

Hull, C. (1943). *Principles of behavior.* New York, NY: Appleton-Century-Crofts.

James, W. (1890). *The principles of psychology.* New York, NY: H. Holt and Company.

Jamison, P., & Nirappil, F. (2018, February 2). Once a national model, now D.C. public schools target of FBI investigation. Washington Post. Retrieved January 24, 2019 from www.washingtonpost.com

Johansson, P., Hall, L., Sikström, S., & Olsson, A. (2005). Failure to detect mismatches between intention and outcome in a simple decision task. *Science, 310*(5745), 116–119. doi:10.1126/science.1111709

Kenrick, D. T., Griskevicius, V., Neuberg, S. L., & Schaller, M. (2010). Renovating the pyramid of needs: Contemporary extensions built upon ancient foundations. *Perspectives on Psychological Science, 5*(3), 292–314. https://doi.org/10.1177/1745691610369469

Lepper, M. R., Corpus, J. H., & Iyengar, S. S. (2005). Intrinsic and extrinsic motivational orientations in the classroom: Age differences and academic correlates. *Journal of Educational Psychology, 97*(2), 184–196.

Lepper, M. R., Greene, D., & Nisbett, R. E. (1973). Undermining children's intrinsic interest with extrinsic reward: A test of the "overjustification" hypothesis. *Journal of Personality and Social Psychology, 28*(1), 129–137.

Lieberman, M. D. (2013). *Social: Why our brains are wired to connect.* New York, NY: Broadway Books.

Mackintosh, N. J. (1974). *The psychology of animal learning.* New York, NY: Academic Press.

Marsh, A. (2017). *The fear factor: How one emotion connects altruists, psychopaths, and everyone in between.* New York, NY: Basic Books.

Maslow, A. H. (1943). A theory of human motivation. *Psychological Review, 50*(4), 370–396. doi:10.1037/h0054346

Michaels, J.W., Blommel, J.M., Brocato, R.M., Linkous, R.A., & Rowe, J.S. (1982). Social facilitation and inhibition in a natural setting. *Replications in Social Psychology, 2,* 21–24.

McDougal, W. (1909). *An introduction to social psychology* (2nd ed.). London: Methuen & Co.

Nisbett, R. E., & Kanouse, D. E. (1969). Obesity, food deprivation, and supermarket shopping behavior. *Journal of Personality and Social Psychology, 12*(4), 289–294.

Nisbett, R. E., & Wilson, T. D. (1977). Telling more than we can know: Verbal reports on mental processes. *Psychological Review, 84,* 231–259.

Nordgren, L., Van der Pligt, J., & Van Harreveld, F. (2006). Visceral drives in retrospect: Explanations about the inaccessible past. *Psychological Science, 17*(7), 635–640.

Pelham, B. W., & Blanton, H. (2018). *Conducting research in psychology: Measuring the weight of smoke* (5th ed.). Thousand Oaks, CA: SAGE publishing.

Pelham, B. W., & Neter, E. (1995). The effect of motivation on judgment depends on the difficulty of the judgment. *Journal of Personality and Social Psychology, 68,* 581–594.

Pelham, B. W., & Swann, W. B., Jr. (1989). From self-conceptions to self-worth: On the sources and structure of global self-esteem. *Journal of Personality and Social Psychology, 57,* 672–680.

Pinker, S. (1994). *The language instinct: How the mind creates language.* New York, NY: Harper Collins.

Seward, J. P. (1956). Drive, incentive, and reinforcement. *Psychological Review, 63*(3), 195–203. https://doi.org/10.1037/h0048229

Smyth, J. M., & Pennebaker, J. W. (2008). Exploring the boundary conditions of expressive writing: In search of the right recipe. *British Journal of Health Psychology, 13*(1), 1–7.

Spence, J. T., & Helmreich, R. L. (1983). Achievement-related motives and behaviors. In J. T. Spence (Ed.), *Achievement and achievement motives : Psychological and sociological approaches.* (pp 10–74). San Francisco, CA: W. H. Freeman.

Tay, L., & Diener, E. (2011). Needs and subjective well-being around the world. *Journal of Personality and Social Psychology, 101*(2), 354–365.

Wilson, T. D. (2011). *Redirect: The surprising new science of psychological change.* New York, NY: Back Bay Books.

Zajonc, R.B. (2001). Mere exposure: A gateway to the subliminal. *Current Directions in Psychological Science, 10,* 224–228.

Module 14
Emotions

Are You Feeling It?

In late November of 2018, your first author Brett was basking in the warm glow of the feeling that his life had finally begun to settle down a bit. He had just published two books, and he had enjoyed a relaxing Thanksgiving. Both his favorite dog and his favorite nephew had survived their recent surgeries. Christmas was in the air. His daughter Brooklyn even volunteered to help him put up outdoor Christmas lights. Then he got the following text from his sister Rhonda:

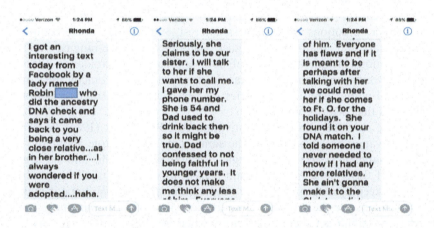

Figure 14.1 A text message from a sister your first author grew up with – about a sister he would soon meet for the first time. It began a cascade of many emotions.

Brett's first response was a blend of amazement and disbelief. He had always believed he was one of six kids. Was he really one of seven? Was this "Robin" a con artist? Maybe. But he remembered all too well that when he was a child, his dad would often disappear for days at a time. If Robin proved to be his real sister, would she prove to be the first of several siblings he never knew growing up? Robin did prove to be Brett's real sister. As soon as it dawned on him to check his ancestry.com mailbox, he saw that he had long ago received an official message telling him about the DNA match (he had not used his ancestry account in many months). The DNA test in question showed that Brett and Robin shared 1,834 centimorgans of DNA. The likelihood that they were close genetic relatives was 100%.

Brett has experienced many emotions in the weeks since learning that he has another sibling. One early emotion was anger. He was angry that his dad had betrayed his mom. And he was confused by his own anger. Both his parents had been dead for well over a decade when he got this news. Why was he angry at a dead person – in the defense of another dead person? He was also very surprised. No one expects to pick up a sibling in middle age. And he was very curious. Would Robin look like his dad? Did Brett have any new nieces or nephews? Was Robin rich enough to take care of him in his old age? As Brett learned about his new sister's childhood, he also came to feel great sadness. He was sad for her that she never got to meet her biological father. He was sadder that she spent much of her childhood wondering why she didn't look like any of the three sisters with whom she grew up (none of whom had the same father she had). In the end, especially after getting to meet Robin in person, Brett felt very happy. He felt connected in an important way to someone new. A bit of his dad was living on in a way he never would have expected.

This story illustrates that familiar roller coaster psychologists call emotions. **Emotions** are affective states (feelings) we have in reaction to the good and bad events of everyday life. We might be reacting to seeing a cockroach, hearing a weird noise, getting rejected by a potential date, seeing our favorite sports team win a championship, being insulted by a rival, losing a loved one, getting an A on a test, or discovering a new sibling. Emotions are closely tied to motivations to approach or avoid something. Some common *approach* emotions are happiness, interest, and surprise. Some common *avoidance* emotions are fear, shame, and disgust. Emotions are wide-ranging and complex, and many emotions include a mixture of both approach and avoidance. Emotions are also highly subjective and complex in that no two emotions are exactly the same. There are also a lot of unique emotion categories. In fact, the English language contains more than 200 words that describe emotions.

Emotions are so closely linked to motivation that Ross Buck (1985) described emotions and motivation as "two sides of the same coin." Buck wrote about the "**primary emotional/motivational system**" as a single psychological system, and he argued that a major goal of this system is to maintain *homeostasis*. In a nutshell, the main goal of emotions is to keep us alive and kicking (and comfortably so). We hope it makes sense, then, that emotions are the flip side of motivation. If we didn't *want* things, we'd never be sad when we didn't get them – or happy when we did. If we weren't motivated to stay safe, we wouldn't feel afraid when facing apparent dangers. Winning can make you feel ecstatic. But it feels particularly good to win something you care about. We'd much rather win a Nobel prize than a lottery. Likewise, we'd be much happier to bump into a loved one than to bump into a friend from the gym. Motivation and emotion are inseparable (Arkes, 1982.

To put this in much simpler terms, emotions make life worth living. Your first author has often asked his students if they would accept a tax-free check for a billion dollars to lose forever their ability to experience *any* kind of emotion. When students are given a little time to think about it, almost none of them say they'd accept this deal. That's because it's a raw deal. If you completely lost your ability to experience any emotions, you wouldn't get a speck of enjoyment from being a billionaire. And you'd probably die very young. Why bother to get out of the way of an oncoming car that doesn't scare you? Why bother to eat or drink if you'll get no pleasure from either? What good would a billion dollars do you if your life became a series of hollow, empty experiences?

An Evolutionary Perspective on Emotions

Charles Darwin was fascinated with emotions because he realized they have tremendous survival value, especially in social creatures like us. In fact, there is good evidence that we come into the world ready to express and to decode emotions – or at least ready to learn to do so. People who are blind from birth (and thus have never observed a smile) still smile *themselves* when something very good happens to them (Matsumoto & Willingham, 2009). Johnson, Dziurawiec, Ellis, and Morton (1991) found that babies less than one-hour old tracked a moving image longer than usual when the image resembled a human face. This was not a mere preference for more complex stimuli. Infants followed the stimulus that looked more like a face (left side of Figure 14.2) even longer than an equally complex stimulus in which the pieces of the face were scrambled (middle of Figure 14.2).

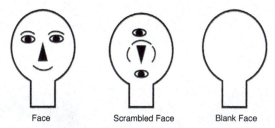

Face   Scrambled Face   Blank Face

Figure 14.2 Infants less than one-hour old worked harder to look at a face like the one on the left than they did to look at either of the other two non-face stimuli. Images are very similar to stimuli used by Johnson et al. (1991).

People of all ages seem to be drawn to human faces. And people are very good at reading faces – to figure out the likely emotions occurring in the brains connected to the faces. Ekman (1970, 1992) showed that hunter-gatherers from Papua New Guinea – who had no exposure at all to Western culture – were very good at reading basic emotions on the faces on Westerner strangers. Westerners were also very good at detecting basic emotions on the

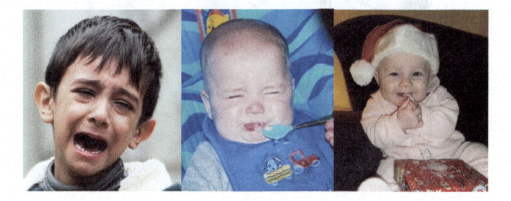

Figure 14.3 People anywhere on Earth would quickly recognize the basic emotions expressed by these three youngsters. Just as there is little doubt that the Iranian boy on the left is sad, there is little doubt that these two American infants are experiencing the basic emotions known as disgust (center) and happiness (right). Infant photos by Brett Pelham. Iranian boy image credit: arfa adam/Shutterstock.com

faces of Papua New Guinean strangers. People are very good at detecting emotions, *especially* basic emotions. Ekman's research underscores the nearly universal nature of the facial expression and identification of basic emotions. By the way, there is a bit of debate about exactly which emotions are **basic emotions.** But Ekman identified *happiness, sadness, fear, anger, disgust and surprise* as the six basic emotions. Ekman refers to these six emotions as basic because they seem to be cross-culturally pervasive, because people express them spontaneously beginning in infancy, and because these emotions have obvious implications for survival.

An evolutionary perspective on emotions suggests that we should be especially quick to detect emotions that communicate threat or danger. Research on the **face-in-the-crowd effect** is consistent with this idea. The face-in-the-crowd effect refers to the finding that people are quicker to recognize that a sea of otherwise similar faces contains an "oddball face" (a face expressing an emotion different than the emotion expressed in all the other faces) when the mismatching face expresses anger than when the mismatching face expresses non-threatening emotions such as happiness (Pinkham et al., 2010). See Figure 14.4 for an approximation of one of the many arrays of faces used in this experiment.

Figure 14.4 Does the *angry* face in this set of nine young, attractive faces jump out at you? Pinkham and colleagues (2010) used many 3 x 3 arrays of faces to show that "oddball faces" (those expressing an emotion different than any of the others) are detected more quickly when the oddball faces express *anger* than when they express other emotions.

Although there are good non-evolutionary explanations for the face in the crowd effect, this finding certainly suggests that, as Vaish, Grossman and Woodward (2008) put it, "not all emotions are created equal." Vaish et al. note that an important way in which emotions vary has to do with valence (i.e., positivity or negativity). Consistent with the idea that "bad is stronger than good" (Baumeister, Bratslavsky, Finkenauer, and Vohs, (2001), there are more negative than positive emotions words. Consider the six basic emotions: happiness is highly favorable, and surprise is mildly so. The other four basic emotions are all negative. Vaish et al. argue that the **negativity bias** for emotions is innate and highly adaptive. After all, negative experiences require us to do something specific to remedy things. Positive experiences signal that business as usual is OK (see also Haselton & Funder, 2006).

In case the angry faces in Figure 14.4 didn't jump out at you, consider a very different way of appreciating the evolutionary significance of emotions – this one suggested by Haidt (2001):

> Julie and Mark are brother and sister. They're traveling together in France on summer vacation from college. One night they are staying alone in a cabin near the beach. They decide that it would be interesting and fun if they tried making love. At the very least, it would be a new experience… Julie was already taking birth control pills, but Mark uses a condom too, just to be safe. They both enjoy making love, but they decide never to do it again. They keep that night as a special secret, which makes them feel even closer to each other. What do you think about that? Was it ok for them to make love?

Almost everyone who hears this story agrees that there is something deeply yucky about sex between siblings, even when there is no chance at all it could lead to any offspring, even when it is not illegal, and even when it seems to have brought these two siblings closer together. Why? Evolutionary models suggest that certain things are inherently disgusting because they were usually a terrible idea in human evolutionary history. There's no logic to this kind of gut emotional reaction. It comes from millions of years of natural selection. Genes that make incest feel gross are very likely to remain in the gene pool. This is because mating with a close genetic relative often has devastating consequences for the fitness of one's offspring.

Emotions Often Override Reason

Speaking of disgust, some of the clearest examples of the power of emotions come from studies of culinary disgust. Emotions are powerful and immediate. Careful reasoning, as you know, takes a lot of time and energy. And even when reasoning is fast and easy, it doesn't often compel you to action – the way emotions do. It is thus our view that when push comes to shove, emotions often trump cognition, even when cognition points to a very simple conclusion. As the American poet e. e. cummings put it, "feeling is first." By this, we assume, cummings meant that emotions are more powerful than thoughts. At least that's roughly how Bob Zajonc (1980) interpreted this poem. He argued that emotions didn't always require any thinking (at least not any *conscious* thinking).

Paul Rozin would surely agree. Rozin and colleagues (1986) suggest that emotional beliefs in things like "contagion" and "bad magic" often override thoughtful reasoning. In one study, Rozin and colleagues (1986) showed this by opening a new, perfectly-clean flyswatter, and using it to stir a pitcher of lemonade. To most people the lemonade suddenly became a *lot* less desirable. No one thought the flyswatter carried any diseases; they just associated the flyswatter with flies, which *do* sometimes carry diseases. Rozin called this powerful aversion to things that resemble or touch disgusting things the **principle of contagion**. The principle seems to be even stronger for poo than for flyswatters. Making otherwise delicious chocolate candies shaped like dog poo makes them a lot less desirable. These irrational feelings matter. They're a strong reason why most people are disgusted by the thought of "recycled water." For some people, no amount of evidence documenting the extreme purity and safety of water that was recently *sewage* makes them willing to drink it. In arid countries like Australia, the public seems more interested in paying handsomely for desalination plants – that remove salt from seawater – than in setting up plants to make recycled water from sewage. Apparently, people would rather drink water that was recently peed out by fish than water that was recently peed out by their fellow human beings.

Your first author Brett has often carried out a colorful class demonstration of this emotional contagion principle. Several times every year he brings a small carton of milk to his general psychology class and asks the students if anyone is willing to open it and have a sip. Many hands go up. Then he takes out a sealed condom, opens it, and assures everyone that there's nothing in the condom that has any flavor, or could possibly make anyone sick. Next, he pours a bit of milk into the condom and dangles it around. Finally, he offers $5 to anyone who is willing to drink the milk directly from the condom. Sometimes he ups the offer to $10 or even $20. Brett has done this demonstration with many groups of students. So far, only two brave students have ever taken him up on the offer to drink milk from a condom. They each earned some quick cash. On the many occasions when no one has drunk the milk from the condom, Brett had to drink the condom-encased milk himself. There is usually wailing and gnashing of teeth in the classroom. And, your second author, David, is also thoroughly disgusted just reading this story. Can't we go back to flyswatters? Getting back to the milk in a condom, Brett always ignores the pleas of the students who ask him not to drink the milk. Brett believes that people need to learn that emotions override cognitions.

"So, after much debate, and by a narrow vote of 4-3, we've agreed to call it *not* 'Cheez Pee,' *not* 'Cheez Urine,' and *definitely not* 'Cheese Piss' but rather 'Cheez Whiz.'"

Figure 14.5

The Physiology of Emotions

One of the first psychologists to adopt an evolutionary perspective on emotions was William James, who also developed one of the first theories of the physiological basis of emotions. James (1890) wanted to know exactly how emotions work. For example, do we feel afraid because we detect our racing hearts, elevated blood pressure, sweating palms, and dry mouth? Or do our feelings of fear create these physiological symptoms? Both William James (1890) and Carl Lange believed that our physiological reactions to a stimulus precede and produce our subjective feelings. As James (1890, p. 503) put it, "Every emotion has its 'expression,' of quick breathing, palpitating heart, flushed face, or the like. The expression gives rise to bodily feelings; and the emotion is thus necessarily and invariably accompanied by these bodily feelings." Notice that James said the physiological stuff "gives rise to" the feelings and emotions. On the other hand, in this same passage, James noted that emotions are so tightly bundled with their physiological precursors that it is virtually impossible to separate felt emotions and their physiological basis (at least this was true in 1890). At any rate, the theory of emotions that James and Lange independently proposed has become known as the **James-Lange theory**. We've represented this theory of the physiology of emotions in the top portion of Figure 14.6 (as one might apply it to fear). James's view of emotions makes at least some evolutionary sense. He assumed that emotions serve as a quick readout of our body's immediate physical responses to the good or bad things that could help us out – or do us in.

But not everyone bought the James-Lange theory. The same William Cannon who convinced A.L. Ashburn to swallow a sturdy balloon – so that they could study hunger empirically (see Module 13) – had a very different theory of the physiology of emotions. Cannon and Phillip Bard independently concluded that our body's physiological and psychological reactions to emotion-inducing stimuli occur simultaneously and independently. Their two closely related views of emotions have come to be known as the **Cannon-Bard theory**, which is summarized in the bottom half of Figure 14.6. Thus, the James-Lange theory and the Cannon-Bard theory are competing theories.

Interestingly, James argued that one could put his "physiology first" theory of emotions to a critical test. Unaware that Cannon and Bard would someday propose a competing physiological explanation for emotions, James (1890, p. 503) argued that others could prove him wrong by discovering a "pathological case of an individual who shall have emotions in a body in which either complete paralysis will have prevented their [physiological] expression, or complete anesthesia will have made the latter unfelt." This is a clever argument. James assumed that emotions exist mainly in the brain and that bodily reactions exist, well, in the body. His theory of emotions – unlike the thoughtful competing theory of Cannon-Bard – predicts that emotions will be reduced in intensity, if not eliminated completely, in people suffering from total paralysis. This should be true because the brain of a person whose spine is severed at the neck never gets any physiological feedback from the body. If the physiological response is presumed to produce the emotional response, then it stands to reason that if there's no physiological response, then there's no emotional response.

About 30 years after William James died, World War II began. It produced many survivors of serious spinal cord injuries. This made it possible to carry out James's proposed natural experiment. Hohmann (1966) identified soldiers who had both higher and lower

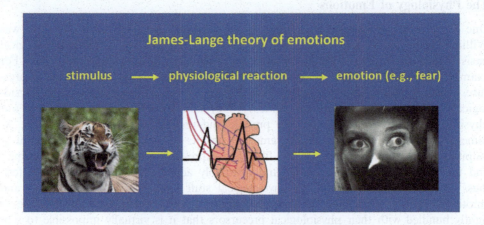

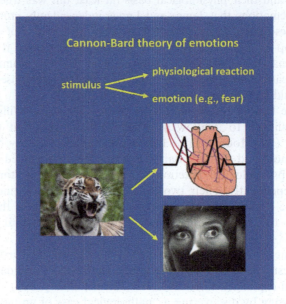

Figure 14.6 The James-Lange (top) vs. Cannon-Bard (bottom) theories of emotion. ANS = autonomic nervous system.

spinal cord injuries. The veterans with lower spinal cord injuries still had feeling in their bodies, but they had lost the use of their legs. In contrast, the veterans with higher spinal cord injuries had total paralysis and little if any feeling from the neck down. So the brains of *some* of these unfortunate vets no longer received any signals from their bodies. The men with higher spinal cord injuries – but not those with lower spinal cord injuries – reported big changes in how they experienced emotions. Arousal-related emotions such as anger became much less intense. Further, emotional experiences that seem to be physiologically-centered *above* the neck – such as crying and getting a lump in one's throat when sad – became *more* intense. The results of this natural experiment seem much more consistent with the James-Lange theory than with the Cannon-Bard theory. But don't count out the Cannon-Bard theory completely. Some specific emotions seem to work in ways more consistent with the Cannon-Bard theory than with the James-Lange theory. Blushing when embarrassed is a good example. People feel embarrassed almost immediately after doing something humiliating (Schacter, Gilbert, & Wegner, 2011). But the blushing that is associated with embarrassment seems to *follow* the subjective emotional experience of embarrassment (Leary, Britt, Cutlip, & Templeton, 1992). That's not at all what James would have expected and is more consistent with the Cannon-Bard model.

Constructivist Theories of Emotion

In contrast to both evolutionary perspectives and physiological models of emotion, both of which assume that people are great at perceiving their own emotions, many social cognitive models of emotions emphasize the flexible, socially-constructed nature of emotions. From the perspective of **two-factor theories of emotions**, emotions are often the combination of diffuse (vague, non-specific) physiological arousal (factor one) plus cognitive labeling (factor two). Cognitive labelling refers to "giving a name" to the arousal that one is experiencing. This means, for example, that if a person becomes physiologically aroused, a clever experimenter or interaction partner might be able to convince the highly aroused person that his or her arousal signals any of several emotions, from fear to happiness.

In keeping with this idea, research on **excitation transfer theory** shows that the judgments we make about the source of elevated physiological arousal often influence our emotional experience. For example, in the case of anger. Zillman and colleagues have found that people who are physiologically aroused in ways that having nothing to do with the obnoxious behavior of a stranger get angrier than usual at the stranger (Zillman & Cantor, 1975; Zillman, Johnson, & Day, 1974; Zillman, Katcher, & Milavsky, 1972). In a typical study of excitation transfer processes, some people engage in taxing aerobic exercise whereas others do not. When both groups of people are subsequently exposed to an obnoxious confederate, those who have recently exercised behave more aggressively to the confederate than do those who've not exercised. Presumably, this occurs because freshly-insulted people who've recently engaged in aerobic exercise falsely interpret their high level of arousal as an indication that they are strongly angered by the insult.

But people are not quite as easy to dupe about their emotions as this finding might make it seem. Excitation transfer seems to occur only under conditions that minimize people's awareness of the extraneous source of their extra arousal. This means the length of the delay after exercise is important. People apparently experience excitation transfer only when they are physiologically aroused *but have had time to forget about* the extraneous arousal when provoked by a stranger. When people are insulted immediately after stepping off an exercise bike, the high level of arousal they experience does *not* usually get converted into heightened anger or aggression. Presumably, this is because people who are keenly aware of the source of the arousal carefully dissect their feelings of rage into the portion that is attributable to a bothersome confederate and the portion that is attributable to a burdensome bike ride. On the other hand, there are other tests of two-factor theories that suggest that people are even easier to fool than Zillman's studies suggest.

One of these tests of two-factor theories is the classic **Dutton and Aron bridges study**. Dutton and Aron (1974) showed that it may be possible to engineer the emotion of romantic attraction. They did so by exposing men at a park in Vancouver, British Columbia (Canada) to a friendly and attractive experimenter. The experimenter always approached the men in the study after they had just crossed a bridge. One bridge was the Capilano

Figure 14.7 Notice that the suspension bridge in this park in British Columbia is scary. The hand rails are low, and the bridge sways some 230 ft (70 m) above a very shallow river bed. Just try crossing the bridge without experiencing an increase in heart rate and general arousal.

Suspension Bridge – a scary (i.e., highly arousing) swinging suspension bridge that hung 230 feet over a gorge (see Figure 14.7). The other bridge was a solid wooden bridge that spanned a small creek. It wasn't scary at all.

Regardless of which bridge the men crossed, the experimenter asked them to fill out a short survey. Most of the men agreed. When the men were done with the short survey, the attractive experimenter "tore the corner off a sheet of paper, wrote down her [or his] name and phone number, and invited each subject to call, if he wanted to talk further." There were thus two manipulations in this study. First, there was the gender of the attractive experimenter (male or female). Second, there was the level of arousal the men were experiencing when the experimenter thanked them and offered them a phone number. (This boiled down to which bridge the men had just crossed.) The main dependent variable in this study was the percentage of men who later called the experimenter back. The results are shown in Figure 14.8. As you can see in the left-hand portion of Figure 14.8, when the experimenter was male, almost no one called him back, period. This merely suggests that most of these men were heterosexual. Thus, few of them were romantically interested in a handsome man, even when they were physiologically aroused when they met him. But when the attractive experimenter happened to be female, whether the men called her back depended greatly on which bridge they had just crossed.

Exactly half the men (9 out of 18) who crossed the scary bridge called the female experimenter back. In contrast just 12.5% of the men (2 out of 16) who crossed the safe bridge called the female experimenter back. Consistent with two-factor theories of emotions, this study – and two replication studies – suggested that it's possible for people to interpret (label) their physiological arousal as a marker of strong romantic attraction to an attractive stranger – even if the real source of the arousal is fear.

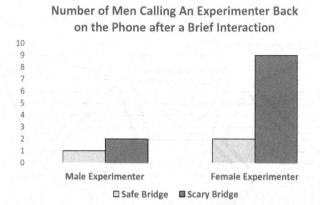

Figure 14.8 Men who crossed a scary (physiologically-arousing) bridge and then met an attractive female experimenter were much more likely to call the experimenter on the phone compared with men in any other condition of this experiment. This "arousal plus labelling" effect is consistent with two-factor theories of emotions. Figure adapted from Dutton and Aron, Study 1 (1974).

So who's right? Are our emotions reliable readouts of our predictable reactions to the world? Or is it easy to nudge people into experiencing whatever emotions one wishes to push upon them? Both views are right to some degree. Emotions are *somewhat* malleable, especially in unfamiliar or highly ambiguous situations. But you will recall, for example, that the same manipulation of arousal that increased men's romantic attraction to an attractive female stranger had no such effect on their attraction to an equally attractive male stranger. Likewise, Dutton and Aron's tricky manipulation could make some men more attracted than usual to a female stranger. But it seems unlikely that arousal could crank up feelings of sadness, disgust, or boredom, which are emotions that do not naturally involve elevated arousal. One thing is for sure, though. Wherever emotions come from and whatever their exact physiological basis, emotions are more than just the spice of life; they are the very essence of life. We don't know about you, but we wouldn't sell ours for a billion dollars.

Activities for Critical Thinking and Group Discussion for Module 14

Robert Plutchik (2002) argued that there are eight (rather than six) basic human emotions. Plutchik developed a nice way to represent different emotions, and to grade them for intensity. Emotions become more intense as we work our way toward the center of Plutchik's emotion circle. So, ecstasy is a more intense version of joy while serenity is a milder version of joy. Plutchik also argues that each of his eight basic emotions (six of which we've circled in this image) has an opposite emotion that is physically opposite of it in his model. Joy and sadness are thus opposites – as are anger and fear. Plutchik also argues that complex emotions such as contempt are *blends* of adjacent emotions.

A. A topic for group discussion is whether Plutchik's opposites all feel like opposites to you.
B. Does Plutchik overlook any of Ekman's six basic emotions? Recall that Ekman's six basic emotions are anger, disgust, fear, happiness, sadness, and surprise.
C. Do you accept Plutchik's "trust" and "anticipation" as basic human emotions?

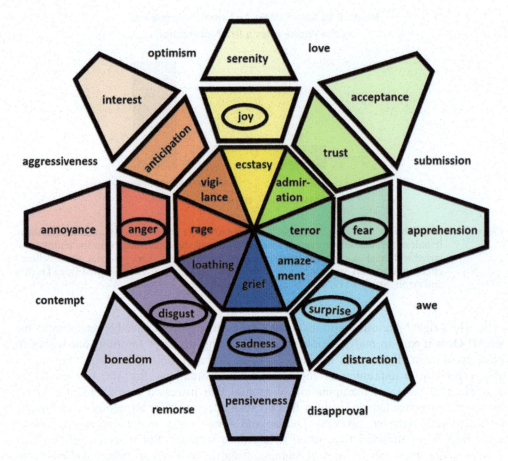

Figure 14.9 Image by B. Pelham, adapted from Plutchik (2002)

Multiple-Choice Questions for Module 14

1. A study of World War II veterans who were paralyzed from the neck down showed that after their injuries, these veterans experienced emotions such as anger with greatly reduced intensity. Which theory of the nature of emotions does this finding support?

   A) the James-Lange theory
   B) the Cannon-Bard theory
   C) the theory of homeostasis
   D) excitation-transfer theory

2. People who embarrass themselves usually *feel* the emotion of embarrassment way before they experience blushing (which happens when blood rushes to your face). This finding is problematic for a classic theory of the physiological basis of emotion. Which theory?

   A) the James-Lange theory
   B) the Cannon-Bard theory
   C) the theory of homeostasis
   D) excitation-transfer theory

3. Some researchers – who are probably big fans of constructivism – argue that emotions are highly malleable and flexible rather than serving as perfectly reliable readouts of how a person ought to be feeling in a specific situation. What theory or theories of emotions would these researchers probably find most agreeable?

   A) emotional ambiguity theory
   B) homeostatic theories
   C) two-factor theories

4. In the animated movie *Inside Out*, five of the main characters run the brain and emotions of an 11-year-old girl named Riley. These five characters represent happiness, fear, disgust, anger and sadness. Which of Paul Ekman's six basic emotions is **missing** from this list of five emotions?

   A) anticipation
   B) surprise
   C) trust

5. Many researchers assume that we are predisposed to notice anger in others because doing so in our evolutionary history would have led to big survival advantages. What research finding is highly consistent with this evolutionary assumption?

   A) social regulation
   B) the face-in-the-crowd effect

   C) the facial primacy bias
   D) the danger detection effect

6. Which theory of emotions is a very close cousin of two-factor theories of emotion?

   A) the James-Lange theory
   B) the Cannon-Bard theory
   C) the theory of homeostasis
   D) excitation-transfer theory

7. Negative emotions seem to have precedence over positive emotions, perhaps because they require action whereas positive emotions do not. In addition to the idea that "bad is stronger than good," what is another name for the human tendency to attend to and care more about negative rather than positive emotions?

   A) the survival bias
   B) the emotional pessimism effect
   C) the negativity bas

8. Paul Rozin's research on disgust (e.g., the "flyswatter study") identified a principle that explains why people don't like to wear a t-shirt that was worn by a serial killer? What principle?

   A) assimilation
   B) impurity
   C) contagion

9. Based on findings such as those of the "flyswatter study" and the study of chocolate candies shaped like dog poo, your textbook argues that when push comes to shove, emotions almost always:

   A) follow the law of learned aversion
   B) override cognitions
   C) follow the rule of primary superstitions

10. Bea has had a crush on Jake for almost two years. Jake is nice to Bea, but he has never expressed any romantic interest in her. Bea convinces Jake to take her on a "real date" for her birthday. This may be her only chance to get Jake to fall in love with her. She asks you to recommend a place for the date. Based on two-factor theories of emotion, what place do you recommend?

    A) a trip to an amusement park famous for its scary roller coasters
    B) a trip to a museum famous for its beautiful landscapes
    C) a visit to a documentary film festival focusing in Elizabethan politics

Answer Key: 1A, 2A, 3C, 4B, 5B, 6D, 7C, 8C, 9B, 10A

References

Baumeister, R. F., Bratslavsky, E., Finkenauer, C., & Vohs, K. D. (2001). Bad is stronger than good. *Review of General Psychology, 5*(4), 323–370.

Buck, R. (1985). Prime theory: An integrated view of motivation and emotion. *Psychological Review, 92*, 389–413.

Dutton, D., & Aron, A. (1974). Some evidence for heightened sexual attraction under conditions of high anxiety. *Journal of Personality and Social Psychology, 30*, 510–517.

Ekman, P. (1970). Universal facial expressions of emotion. *California Mental Health Research Digest, 8*(4), 151–158.

Ekman, P. (1992). Are there basic emotions? *Psychological Review, 99*(3), 550–553.

Haidt, J. (2001). The emotional dog and its rational tail: A social intuitionist approach to moral judgment. *Psychological Review, 108*, 814–834.

Haselton, M. G., & Funder, D. (2006). The evolution of accuracy and bias in social judgment. In M. Schaller, D. T. Kenrick, & J. A. Simpson (Eds.), *Evolution and social psychology* (pp. 15–37). New York, NY: Psychology Press.

Hohmann, G. W. (1966). Some effects of spinal cord lesions on experienced emotional feelings. *Psychophysiology, 3*(2), 143–156.

James, W. (1890). *The principles of psychology.* New York: Holt.

Johnson, M. H., Dziurawiec, S., Ellis, H., & Morton, J. (1991). Newborns' preferential tracking of face-like stimuli and its subsequent decline. *Cognition, 40*(1-2), 1–19.

Leary, M. R., Britt, T. W., Cutlip, W. D., & Templeton, J. L. (1992). Social blushing. *Psychological Bulletin, 112*(3), 446–460.

Matsumoto, D., & Willingham, B. (2009). Spontaneous facial expressions of emotion of congenitally and noncongenitally blind individuals. *Journal of Personality and Social Psychology, 96*(1), 1–10.

Pinkham, A.E., Griffin, M., Baron, R., Sasson, N.J., & Gu, r R.C. (2010). The face in the crowd effect: anger superiority when using real faces and multiple identities. *Emotion, 10*(1):141–146.

Plutchik, R. (2002). *Emotions and Life: Perspectives from psychology, biology, and evolution.* Washington, DC: American Psychological Association.

Rozin, P., Millman. L., & Nemeroff, C. (1986). Operation of the laws of sympathetic magic in disgust and other domains. *Journal of Personality and Social Psychology, 50*, 703–712.

Schacter, D.L., Gilbert, D.T., & Wegner, D.M. (2011). *Psychology (2nd Edition).* New York: Worth.

Vaish, A., Grossmann, T., & Woodward, A. (2008). Not all emotions are created equal: The negativity bias in social- emotional development. *Psychological Bulletin, 134*(3), 383–403.

Zajonc, R. B. (1980). Feeling and thinking: Preferences need no inferences. *American Psychologist, 35*(2), 151–175.

Zillman, D., & Cantor, J. R. (1975). Effect of timing of information about mitigating circumstances on emotional responses to provocation and retaliatory behavior. *Journal of Experimental Social Psychology, 12*, 38–55.

Zillman, D., Johnson, R. C., & Day, K. D. (1974). Attribution of apparent arousal and proficiency of recovery from sympathetic activation affecting excitation transfer to aggressive behavior. *Journal of Experimental Social Psychology, 10*, 503–515.

Zillman, D., Katcher, A. H., & Milavsky, B. (1972). Excitation transfer from physical exercise to subsequent aggressive behavior. *Journal of Experimental Social Psychology, 8*, 247–259.

Module 15
Sex, Gender, and Sexuality

Why Is There Sex?

About 1.4 billion years ago, the first sexually reproducing creatures on Earth evolved. Since that time, millions of species have stuck with **sexual reproduction** (reproduction that requires two parents, who both pass on genetic information to offspring) rather than **asexual reproduction** (reproduction that involves making exact copies of oneself). To be sure, some animals, especially very simple ones such as the amoeba, reproduce without sex. In fact, there are a few complex animals, such as the clownfish, that can change their sex in adulthood – based on environmental conditions. Further, some complex animals (e.g., copperhead snakes) sometimes reproduce by means of *parthenogenesis* ("virgin birth"). In such cases, females produce the functional equivalent of self-fertilized eggs (Switek, 2012).

But why has sexual reproduction become, by far, the most common way for organisms to reproduce? You probably recall that evolution favors genes that promote their own survival. But from at least one evolutionary perspective, the tremendous popularity of sexual reproduction is puzzling. As John Maynard Smith (1978) argued, sexual reproduction entails a two-fold cost. To put this cost bluntly, males seem like a waste of evolutionary energy. After all, males are offspring who cannot themselves produce offspring. That seems like an evolutionary dead-end.

A thought experiment should illustrate Smith's **two-fold cost of sexual reproduction**. Imagine that a group of 100 sexually-reproducing organisms continued to reproduce sexually. In contrast, a different group all reproduced *asexually* – making exact copies of themselves. In generation 2, the sexually reproducing creatures would have produced only 50 offspring. But the asexually reproducing (self-cloning) creatures would have produced 100 offspring. In each successive generation, the sexually reproducing creatures would fall further behind. To make matters worse, parents who reproduce sexually produce offspring that carry only half their genetic information (Dawkins, 1976). Parents who produce exact genetic copies of themselves obviously produce offspring who share 100% of their genes. From the purely selfish perspective of natural selection, wouldn't the genes that make organisms reproduce *asexually* win out?

It might in some worlds. But in ours, there are major advantages of sexual reproduction. Such advantages seem to compensate for the high costs of mating. *One advantage of sexual reproduction is genetic diversity.* When a male and female produce offspring, their genes become intermixed via meiosis. When an environment changes, as environments invariably do, genetic variation allows any offspring that happen to do well in the new conditions to survive. Producing exact copies of yourself yields no such benefit.

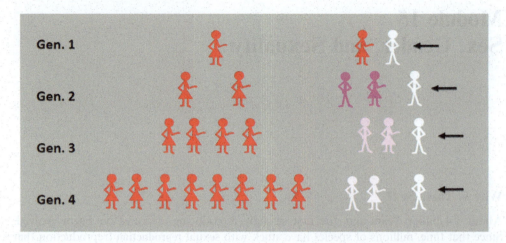

Figure 15.1 John Maynard Smith's two-fold cost of sexual reproduction. All else being equal, the woman who can make exact copies of herself (left panel) gets *way* more copies of her genes into the future gene pool than the woman who must mate sexually. Notice that the sexually reproducing woman on the right not only produces fewer daughters but also produces offspring who share only half her DNA. Thus, all else must *not* be equal. Sex must promote survival.

It also looks like sexual reproduction has advantages over asexual reproduction because *harmful genetic mutations build up more quickly in asexual than in sexually-reproducing organisms* (Barton & Charlesworth, 1998; Hollister et al., 2014). For these and other reasons, the very large majority of the Earth's animals reproduce sexually.

Sex *Differences* in Sexual Interest

In sexually-reproducing animals, people included, male and female organisms face different consequences of having sex. As you may recall from the module on evolutionary psychology, **parental investment theory** focuses on the sexual and parental consequences of this fact (Trivers, 1972). As applied to people, parental investment theory suggests that women's much greater biological investment in their offspring usually makes them pickier in choosing mates than men are. A close cousin of this idea is that, on average, men are more sexually promiscuous than women are (Symons, 1979). This elegant theory does not suggest that male members of a species are always less picky and more promiscuous than females. It depends critically on which sex puts more time and energy into producing and caring for offspring. In people, this sex is women. Let's look at this idea in some detail.

Like most other sexually mature female primates, women typically produce only one egg per month. In contrast, the average man produces about a *million* sperm every six minutes. Young men produce mature sperm at about *three billion times* the rate at which young women release mature eggs. Most men also have a lot of choice about when and where they release their sperm. In contrast, women's eggs almost always stay inside their bodies. Further, assuming a woman's one mature egg is healthy, it's only available for fertilization for about three days. This means that about 90% of the time, most young, healthy women are effectively *in*fertile. Biological "scarcity" alone suggests that women should be choosier maters than men.

There are other factors that make this biological imbalance even more lopsided. For example, unlike any other female primates, women experience **menopause**. This is the time, at about age 50, when most women stop producing eggs. This means that adult women are only highly fertile for a couple of decades of their lives. In contrast, men continue to produce millions of sperm hourly until they die. Would you be more careful with a possession if your mother gave it to you at birth, and if you only had access to it once monthly, or if you were constantly making millions of others very much like it (see Figure 15.2)?

The investment women and men must make in their offspring post-fertilization is also lopsided. If a woman becomes pregnant, and all goes well, she faces a taxing pregnancy, childbirth, breastfeeding, and many years of keeping children out of harm's way. Throughout human history, then, mothers who ignored their children lost their children. If children represent a huge investment to women, then the average woman might be wise to invest in a healthy and trustworthy mate. But from a selfish evolutionary perspective, men could often afford to invest less in their children, and they did not need to be so picky when selecting mates. Importantly, a common mistake people make when they first learn about parental investment theory is to assume that this theory justifies sexually exploitative behavior. It does not. This flawed way of thinking is called the **naturalistic fallacy**. Evolutionary psychologists have long recognized that the existence of a tendency in nature does *not* mean that the tendency is morally acceptable. As Olivia Judson (2002) put it, "Evolution does not obey human notions of morality, nor is human morality a reflection of some natural law." She adds, "Understanding human evolution and genetics may one day tell us why we are the way we are. But it can tell us nothing about what we would like to become."

But is parental investment theory correct? On average *are* women pickier (i.e., less promiscuous) maters than men are? This is no easy question, especially if one wishes to argue that this difference between the sexes is biological rather than cultural. Although we're a firm believer that culture can trump biology, we believe the bulk of the evidence suggests that women are pickier maters than men.

One of the most ambitious tests of parental investment theory was a cross-national survey that asked women and men about their interest in casual sex. In 48 countries, Schmitt (2005) asked people whether they agreed with statements such as "Sex without love is OK." and "I can imagine myself being comfortable and enjoying 'casual' sex with different partners." In all 48 nations, from Argentina to Zimbabwe, men were more likely than women to agree with such statements. But do men and women really possess different attitudes about sex? Or is it simply more acceptable for men than for

Figure 15.2 On the left, see a large diamond ring. On the right, see a pile of cheap glass beads. With which would *you* be more careful?

women to admit that they'd like to get it on with a stranger? To address this critique, it would be nice to know whether men are more likely than women to act on – or try to act on – their sexually lax attitudes.

Two classic **field studies by Clark and Hatfield (1989, 2003)** took exactly this approach. Clark and Hatfield trained average-looking, young male and female confederates to approach attractive, opposite-sex strangers on the Florida State University campus. In one condition of these studies, confederates made a very forward pass: "I have been noticing you around campus and I find you to be very attractive. Would you go to bed with me tonight?" Now that you've picked your jaw up off the floor, let me add that this jaw-dropping line may have been a *little* less jaw-dropping when the studies were run (1978 and 1982) than it would be today. Further, remember that this was a college campus, not a meeting to elect a new Pope.

Averaging across the two studies, more than 70% of men accepted the confederate's offer. Furthermore, many of the men who *refused* the offer explained that they would have accepted it – except for the fact that they were currently in a monogamous relationship. Almost all men seem to have felt the woman had made them an offer no single man could refuse. Maybe no single man could. But plenty of single women could. And they did. In both studies, not a single woman agreed to have sex with the male stranger. That's right; zero percent. The college-aged men in this study were much, much more likely than the college-aged women to agree to have casual sex with a stranger. To be sure, this is not the whole story. When Clark and Hatfield replaced their jaw-dropping request with a more socially acceptable request ("Would you go out with me tonight?") the huge gender differences they observed disappeared. Now 53% of men and 50% of women accepted the offer. In light of these and many other studies (e.g., studies of rates of masturbation, viewing pornography, and sexual promiscuity in gay men vs. lesbians; Pelham, 2019) it appears that – on average – men are less picky maters than women are. Let us also add that, in species in which the male members of the species make greater investments in their offspring, it is the males who are pickier maters. In seahorses, for example, the males carry around and nourish their offspring until they give birth to them. Male seahorses are the picky ones when it comes to mate choice. Likewise, in a species of water bird known as red-necked phalaropes, it is the males who incubate the eggs and care for the hatchlings. It is also the males who are much pickier and less sexually promiscuous (Trivers, 1972)

Sexual Orientation and the Reproduction Puzzle?

If sex exists mainly to foster reproduction, this suggests another puzzle about sex. Why are there plenty of people who have no interest in having heterosexual sex? Let us preface this discussion by noting that we are going to focus mainly on that subset of **gender-nonconforming** people who identify as gay or lesbian, and whose sexual preferences and behavior are inconsistent with the cultural expectation that people are attracted to members of the opposite sex. But to be clear, there are many ways to be gender nonconforming. **Gender-nonconforming** people are those who violate the written and unwritten stereotypical rules for how men and women ought to look and behave. Thus, a heterosexual man who is much more interested in flowers than in football is gender-nonconforming in his personal interests. A growing number of people in most wealthy nations also view gender as a non-binary trait. Although these are all interesting topics, this module will focus mainly on the puzzle of why some people engage in exclusively homosexual rather than heterosexual behavior. Let's begin with a thought experiment. What would happen

"Yes, Brian, I know I'm your soul mate.
The problem is you're not *my* soul mate."

Figure 15.3 Parental investment theory predicts that, because women must make greater biological and behavioral investments in their offspring, women will (on average) be pickier maters than men. If this is a robust finding, it should hold true across cultures, across time, across contexts and across different measures of "pickiness." That appears to be the case.

to the human species if *everyone* were exclusively gay? The answer, of course, is that barring medical interventions, we would go extinct. So, from an evolutionary standpoint, how can we understand the puzzle of homosexuality?

One intriguing answer to this question comes from Bem's (1996) **exotic becomes erotic (EBE)** theory. Bem's EBE theory poses that there are no genes that, in and of themselves, make people sexually attracted to members of the same sex. Instead, all children have genes that predispose them to ways of being that may be male-typical (such as "rough and tumble") or female-typical (such as "delicate and dainty"). These ways of being influence how children interact and play with one another. These play preferences lead to self-segregation into sex-typed play groups. Regardless of biological sex, then, those who enjoy rough and tumble play (boys or "tomboys") will tend to play together. Conversely, those who enjoy smoother and less tumultuous play (girls or effeminate boys) will *also* tend to play together. Bem's theory goes beyond such well-established observations to add that most boys and girls experience discomfort or arousal in the presence of the other sex. Many boys think "girls have cooties." Many girls think "boys are gross." At a minimum, even the most tolerant gender-traditional boys and girls often feel that members of the other sex are strange or – in Bem's terms – exotic. Now consider girls who grew up as tomboys and boys who grew up being effeminate. For both groups, the group that would have seemed different from them (exotic in Bem's terms) would have been their same-sex but more gender-conforming peers. Finally, the EBE theory adds that when puberty kicks in and hormones sexually transform the bodies and brains of both boys and girls, that which was *exotic* in childhood becomes *erotic* in adolescence and adulthood. This may be thought of as a *critical period* when most people form an enduring sexual interest in certain kinds of partners. This should result in a relatively stable sexual preference. So, a broad way to view EBE theory is that it argues we are sexually attracted as adults to that group of people we found unfamiliar, interesting, and maybe even gross, as children.

An important strength of EBE theory is the fact that it is an effort to explain *heterosexuality* as well as homosexuality. Whereas many existing theories of sexual orientation take heterosexuality as a given, Bem argued that this view is **heterosexist** (i.e., that it accepts heterosexuality as a default that requires no explanation). Another strength of the EBE theory is that it tries to explain both gay and lesbian sexual preferences. EBE is highly comprehensive. To be sure, there have been criticisms of the EBE theory. For example, some have argued that the EBE account applies better to gay men than to lesbians (Peplau et al., 1998). Critics have also argued that there have been no strict and comprehensive tests of the truly novel predictions of the theory. These are thoughtful concerns and they provide important directions for future research rather than a reason to reject EBE theory altogether.

Another way to resolve the evolutionary puzzle of same-sex attraction is to recognize that evolution does not have goals. It simply predisposes people to do things that generally promote survival and reproduction. As Abramson and Pinkerton (2007) argued, the immediate reason why both people and animals have sex is that sex feels good! No one has trouble accepting that logic when it comes to eating. We do not eat because we want to get our genes into the gene pool! Instead, we eat to enjoy things that taste delicious. If food weren't delicious, no one would have invented bacon or chocolate. That is, there wouldn't be so much diversity in what people eat. Likewise, if sex weren't so pleasurable, there would probably be a lot less diversity in the number of ways in which, and in the kind of partners with whom, people like to have sex. This doesn't resolve all the evolutionary paradoxes posed by homosexuality. But if organisms like to have sex *mainly* because it feels good, this does suggest a lot of room for nontraditional, non-reproductive ways of feeling good. Because there is no evolved desire to get one's genes into the gene pool – but only an evolved desire to do what is pleasurable – there is a lot of room for different kinds of sexual preferences. Notice that this broad, pleasure-based view of human sexuality also explains, for example, why people masturbate, why women have sex well after menopause (after they no longer produce eggs), and why some children engage in sex play. Sex feels good (Abramson et al., 2007).

Finally, even most critics of Bem's EBE theory agree with him that if we better understood sexual orientation, we could reduce a great deal of unnecessary human suffering. Many studies have shown that LGBTQ (lesbian, gay, bisexual, transgender, and queer) people are at increased risk for bullying, hate crimes, and mental as well as physical illness (Remafedi, French, Story, Resnick, & Blum, 1998; Toomey & Russell, 2013). Among adolescents and young adults, many of these negative outcomes are particularly strong when people report coming from homes in which their parents did not accept their sexual identities (Ryan, Russell, Huebner, Diaz, & Sanchez, 2010). Despite recent reductions in the number of laws and practices that blatantly discriminate against LGBTQ people, we still have a long way to go before all people feel fully accepted by society regardless of their gender identity or sexual orientation.

The Power of Sex, Gender, and Gender Stereotypes

It's hard to overstate the importance of sex, gender, and gender stereotypes in daily life. But before we dive into research in this area, let's define some key terms. **Sex** is a classification of someone as male or female based on biological characteristics (such as having two X chromosomes). In contrast, **gender** refers to both how a person identifies (e.g., thinking of oneself as male) and how most people in a culture expect people to behave based on their apparent sex. In short, sex is a biological classification and gender is a cultural prescription. To better understand what we mean by a cultural prescription, consider gender roles. **Gender roles** are culturally dictated rules and norms about what kind of behavior is appropriate for each gender. Gender roles prescribe how to be feminine or masculine, who should do what, and in what context (e.g., work vs. home). Close cousins of gender roles are gender stereotypes. **Gender stereotypes** are thoughts and beliefs about others based solely on their male or female group membership. As we will soon see, both gender roles and gender stereotypes influence how we perceive and remember gender-relevant events and information. This is especially true when the event or information is *inconsistent* with our beliefs about gender roles or our gender stereotypes.

Consider how gender roles and gender stereotypes play themselves out in daily life. In today's world, women are playing a bigger role than ever before in politics, business, sports, and in many other walks of life. On the other hand, the way in which women are perceived in these roles remains dramatically colored by gender related biases and stereotypes. For example, research by **Hess, Adams and Kleck (2004)** shows that when men and women pose the same facial expression known to indicate anger, women are perceived as angrier than men. This seems to happen because women who look angry are perceived to be more strongly in violation of gender norms. This "shifting standard" based on gender is so well learned that people are typically unaware that they judge men and women using different yardsticks. The result is that men are given much more social permission than women to engage in certain masculine activities, and this includes the expression of anger (Lewis, 2000). Consider a physical rather than emotional example. Melissa is exactly 6′ tall. Almost everyone would agree that Melissa is very tall. But if Melissa's cousin Sam is also exactly 6′ tall, most people would describe him as average in height, or perhaps slightly tall. We apply these "shifting standards" to men and women all the time, usually without realizing we are doing so (Biernat, 2012). Are there consequences to these shifting standards? Just ask Ann Hopkins.

Ann Hopkins was the plaintiff in a famous gender discrimination lawsuit that went all the way to the United States Supreme Court (Fiske, Bersoff, Borgida, Deaux, & Heilm, 1991). The case ultimately became known as Price Waterhouse v. Ann Hopkins, and it began in 1982 – when Ann Hopkins was being considered for partnership with Price Waterhouse, a very large accounting firm. Hopkins had better numbers than anyone else coming up for partnership that same year. In fact, in the year before she came up for promotion, she brought in $25 million worth of business to the firm. She also happened to be the only woman in a group of 88 people who were up for partnership that year, Further, when Hopkins was up for promotion, only seven of the 662 partners at Price Waterhouse were female. Despite Ms. Hopkins's stellar performance, she was denied partnership merely because – it eventually became clear – she wasn't feminine enough. Those who reviewed her case argued that she needed a "course at charm school," and that she needed to be "more feminine." As Fiske and colleagues (1991, p. 1050) noted, Hopkins was told by one of her biggest *supporters* that she would have a better chance of being promoted if she were to "walk more femininely, talk more femininely, dress more femininely, wear make-up, have her hair styled, and wear jewelry."

Consider what it must have taken in the early 1980s for Ms. Hopkins to have gotten her company $25 million worth of business. Did she do so by being passive and soft-spoken, or did she often need to be aggressive to win over new clients? Didn't the men against whom she was competing also have to be aggressive? So, what happened? Ann Hopkins was punished for doing the same thing that brought rewards to the men. The only differ-ence is that she was apparently doing a better job than any of the 87 men who were also up for partner. In short, Hopkins was being punished for being "too masculine" in her job! She was violating a gender role (women are not supposed to be aggressive) that would have never led a man to be punished. The Supreme Court ruled in favor of Ms. Hopkins because they noted that the norms and the gender roles and gender stereotypes she was expected to follow placed her in a "no-win" situation: If she behaved aggressively to succeed in her job, she would be punished for being too masculine; if she behaved in a passive, more "feminine" way, she would not bring in enough business. In either case, the outcome would be the same. She would be denied partnership.

Because gender bias in how we judge people begins so early in life (Rubin, Provenzano & Luria, 1974) and is so pervasive, we all see others through gendered lenses, whether we want to or not. Consider a few other examples of the power and pervasiveness of gender. Consider play. A great deal of gender socialization happens by means of segregated play. In an impressive study of gender segregation in 12 nations, Whiting and Edwards (1988) found that kids as young as two and three played in same-sex groups about 35% of the time. By the age of 11, rates of gender-segregation during play had increased to a whopping 94%. To paraphrase Martin and Ruble (2010), sex segregation becomes so powerful by middle childhood, that boys and girls practically grow up in different worlds.

Whether for physical reasons, cultural reasons, or both, men and women even walk differently. If you show judges "point-light displays" (videos of just a few dots of lights that appear on people walking in an otherwise dark room), almost all judges can reliably tell the difference between male and female walkers. If you don't believe us, check out the static images you see in Figure 15.4. The leftmost image has some labels to help you get your bearings. Now that you know what all the dots represent, can you tell which of the two remaining walkers is female? If you have any doubts, go to www.biomotionlab.ca/Demos/BMLwalker. html. At this interactive web site, you can manipulate the gendered cues of walkers yourself to see how differently men and women walk – and to see the power of the normally invisible rules of gender. As another example of the power and importance of gender, consider how curious – or even uncomfortable – most people become when they interact with others whose gender they cannot determine. This is so true that in the 1990s, there was a long-running Saturday Night Live skit about a gender-ambiguous character named "Pat."

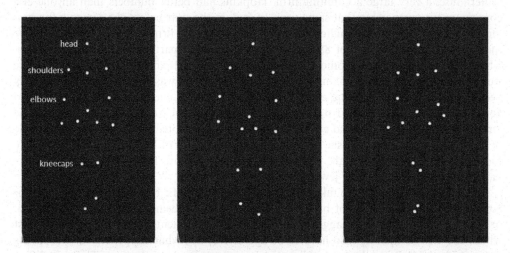

Figure 15.4 Static images of a gender-neutral walker, and two "gendered" walkers. Even if you can't tell the gender of the two unlabeled walkers from these static images, you'll be able to do so easily when you see them move. To try this yourself, go to the Web site linked in the text.

Everyone was positively dying to know if Pat was male or female. If Pat had been ethnically ambiguous or ambiguous in age, people would not have been nearly so curious.

But gender does not just shape social perception. It also shapes what we do. For example, once kids reach the age of five or six, they begin to engage in **self-socialization**, which means they act like the "gender police" and enforce the rules of socially-acceptable behavior for boys and girls. Thus, if a girl behaves too much like a "tomboy" or if a boy behaves like a "sissy," other kids will quickly let the gender-nonconforming kid know that he or she is breaking a set of important norms and rules. Anything from polite reminders to ostracism or abuse may follow if the gender-nonconforming kid does not begin to play by the gender rule book. Self-socialization is but one of numerous examples of the invisible but powerful effects of gender and gender stereotypes on daily behavior. Let's consider two more examples. First, men and women seem to internalize very strongly the unwritten social rules dictating that the work of men is more valuable than the work of women. Research shows that if you ask men and women to perform a task, and then ask them how much they should be paid for their work, women ask for less pay than men. This is true even when an objective analysis of the work done shows that women perform as well as or better than men (Jost, 1997; Major, 1994; Pelham & Hetts, 2001). Gender stereotypes and norms for gendered behavior are so powerful that we all seem to buy into them – often without knowing that we are doing so.

Yet another example of the power of gender comes from research on what happens when you nudge people into violating the usual norms and rules of gendered behavior. Getting people to do something *gender-incongruous* (i.e., something inconsistent with gender-stereotypes) can make people keenly aware of the gender-based rules they have just broken. Consider research on **precarious manhood** (Bosson & Vandello, 2011). The key idea behind precarious manhood is that, to a much greater degree than woman-hood, manhood is easily threatened (thus the term "precarious") and must constantly be defended. Thus, if men are nudged into engaging in behaviors that threaten their sense of masculinity, they will quickly do their best to *restore* their sense of masculinity. To test this idea, Bosson et al. (2009) asked some men to braid rope in the lab. They asked other men to do a much more stereotypically-feminine task – to braid a doll's hair. After all this work was done, the men who had done the stereotypically feminine task showed an exaggerated preference for hitting a punching bag rather than solving a logical puzzle. In a follow-up study, both the men in the rope-braiding condition and the men in the hair-braiding condition got the chance to hit a punching bag. Compared with the men whose masculinity had not been threatened, the men whose masculinity had just been threatened hit the punching bag harder. Pelham and Hardin (2017) showed that precarious manhood seems to be alive and well outside the lab. Using data from the entire 1940 U.S. Census, they found that relative to women, men showed a mild aversion toward living on streets whose names included the decidedly feminine words "Princess" or "Queen." Further, this symbolic way of avoiding precarious manhood was more pronounced than usual for men who were employed in stereotypically feminine occupations (cook, nurse, or teacher). A field study of more than 75,000 Florida school children yielded conceptually-similar findings. Figlio (2005) found that beginning in middle-school, boys with names that were much more common among girls than among boys (e.g., Ashley, Kelly, Shannon) began to get into serious trouble at school – as marked by a much higher than usual rate of school disciplinary violations. As country singer Johnny Cash argued long ago, it's tough to be "A Boy Named Sue."

Unplanned Pregnancies and Sexually Transmitted Diseases

A simple explanation for why rules and norms about sex and gender are so powerful is that sex and gender – including sexual acts – are so important. Even in the high-tech world of modern reproduction, sexual activity is almost always the route through which people come to exist. Further, sex is a very powerful physical and psychological drive. Even in cultures in which people know they can be disfigured or imprisoned for engaging in forbidden sexual acts, such forbidden sexual acts still happen. Further, people often engage in unsafe sexual behaviors that can lead to unwanted pregnancies or give people **sexually transmitted diseases** (STDs). In 2016, slightly more than one in 50 adolescent American girls (aged 15–19) gave birth in the United States. It seems safe to assume that many of these girls and women had *unintended* pregnancies. According to the United States Department of Health and Human Services (2018), these adolescent birth rates are a dramatic improvement over the peak U.S. adolescent birth rate observed in 1991 – when it was three times as high as in 2016. On a less positive note, the United States has a long history of having the highest teenage pregnancy rate of any highly developed nation in the world. Teenage pregnancy rates are especially high among poor Americans, and among Blacks and Latinas as compared with Whites. In fact, in a study of more than 140 nations, Pelham (2019) found that teenage pregnancy rates are elevated in nations where living conditions are more difficult (e.g., where there is more disease). This is strongly true even after controlling for national wealth. Many people who live in difficult environments appear to respond to their difficulties by having children when they are very young (which is part of a "fast life history strategy"). Your first author is very familiar with this strategy. He grew up in extreme poverty, and his mother gave birth to her fourth of six children when she was still 21 (without any twins in the mix). A similar story applies to his aunt Patsy – except that she had 12 children.

But poverty or hardship alone are not the only drivers of unwanted pregnancies and risky sexual behavior. Another reason why rates of teenage pregnancy are so high in the United States appears to be cultural. Sexually speaking, the United States is a **semi-restrictive** nation. The fact that we are not **sexually permissive**, like many Western European nations, means that U.S. parents often fail to talk to their teenage children about the details of sex and the importance of using protection when having intercourse. Your first author has a friend in the Netherlands who takes it for granted that his teenage daughter has sex with her boyfriend. But accordingly, he makes sure that she always has plenty of condoms and is knowledgeable about both pregnancy and STDs. Incidentally, there is a third sexual cultural category. In **sexually restrictive** nations such as much of Asia and the Middle East, premarital sex is so taboo that teenage pregnancy rates are low. The United States is in the risky middle ground when it comes to the culture of sexual permissiveness.

The U.S. is also doing poorly relative to other wealthy nations where **sexually-transmitted diseases** (STDs) are concerned. STDs range from relatively harmless infections that are easily cured to **Acquired Immune Deficiency Syndrome** (AIDS). By the year 2016, AIDS had taken the lives of more than 39 million people worldwide (and about 675,000 people in the U.S. alone). In the past two decades the development and refinement of retroviral drugs (often referred to as the AIDS "cocktail") has made it possible for many people to live in relative health even if they are infected with the **human immunodeficiency virus** (HIV; the virus that causes AIDS). Nonetheless, poor people the world over, especially poor people in the world's poorest nations often have little access to such life-saving HIV drugs. The AIDS crisis is still a serious public health problem. And it is increasingly becoming a problem of social justice. For some suggestions about how to address this public health problem in a biologically and psychologically informed way, see Randolph, Pinkerton, Bogart, Cecil, and Abramson (2007).

"You had me at 'billionaire'."

Figure 15.5

Hands-On Activities for Module 15: Is Gender Everywhere?

There are probably no biological or social forces that have as much impact on our lives as do sex and gender. These brief hands-on activities are designed to increase your awareness of the roles of sex and gender in daily life. We'll begin with a couple of subtle demonstrations and then move on to the obvious.

1. Imagine that on Planet Numero, girls and boys are given first *numbers* rather than first names, and that boys and girls rarely play with one another after the age of five. Figure 15.6 shows two six-year old (gender-segregated) play groups. Which consists of girls and which consists of boys? Trust your intuitions and make a quick guess.

Figure 15.6

2. On Planet Geo, all the inhabitants are *geometric figures*. Here, the rules about gender-segregated play are very strict. Boys and girls *never* play together. Which group contains the boys? Which the girls?

Figure 15.7

3. On Planet Earth, people associate boys and men with some activities and associate girls and women with others. Next to each role, job, trait, thing, or activity, enter an "M" if you think *most people* consider it a male thing, and enter an "F" if you think most people consider it a female thing. If you're able to do this in groups, we hope you can have a respectful conversation about how many of these gendered things (from none to all) really *ought* to be gendered.

____ 1. truck driver	____ 6. cleaning	____ 11. likes pink	____ 16. superhero
____ 2. stinky	____ 7. childcare	____ 12. motorcycles	____ 17. crying
____ 3. likes the opera	____ 8. farts	____ 13. glitter	____ 18. nurse
____ 4. diet cola	____ 9. make-up	____ 14. beer	____ 19. cooking
____ 5. dancer	___ 10. prostitute	____ 15. carpenter	____ 20. giving birth

Reading that May Promote Group Discussion

Wilkie, J.E., & Bodenhausen, G.V. (2012). Are numbers gendered? *Journal of Experimental Psychology, General, 141(2)*, 206–210.

Multiple-Choice Questions for Module 15

1. If you could just make exact copies of yourself rather than engaging in sexual reproduction, your offspring would all share virtually 100% of your genes rather than 50%. Further, all of your off-spring would be able to produce EXACT copies of themselves (which would also be copies if you). This suggests some major drawbacks of sexual reproduction. John Maynard Smith called these drawbacks the:

   A) sexuality enigma
   B) cost model of two-gamete parenting
   C) two-fold cost of sexual reproduction

2. Female human beings experience an extremely rare phenomenon known as _____, which has long puzzled both evolutionary biologists and evolutionary psychologists.

   A) estrus
   B) menopause
   C) infertility

3. Kato justifies his extremely selfish behavior by arguing that evolution programs all living thing to be selfish. This is an example of the:

   A) naturalistic fallacy
   B) base-rate fallacy
   C) egocentrism fallacy

4. Unlike female human beings, many female insects can produce millions of eggs in a very brief window. Sure enough, such female insects are usually very promiscuous, which is highly consistent with:

   A) the promiscuity principle
   B) natural selection
   C) parental investment theory

5. There are some species of fish and bird in which the male members of the species spend more energy producing or caring for young than the female members of the species. Seahorses are a good example. In keeping with parental investment theory, the males of these unusual species are:

   A) highly monogamous
   B) very picky maters
   C) much longer-lived than the females

6. In two field studies by Clark and Hat-field, an opposite-sex stranger asked men and women on a college campus if they would be interested in having sex that night. About 70% of the men said yes. What percentage of the women said yes?

   A) 0
   B) 25
   C) 50

7. Psychologists refer to men and women who do not obey the usual rule and norms regarding sexual interests, sexual roles, or sex-typed behavior as gender-_____.

   A) atypical
   B) neutral
   C) nonconforming
   D) deviant

8. When Lisa tells her parents that she is sexually-attracted to other women, her parents ask her if there is something terrible they have done to make her attracted to people of the same sex. Experts in human sexuality would say that Lisa's parents are expressing _____ attitudes.

   A) heterosexist
   B) sexually normative
   C) conservative

9. The T in LGBTQ stands for:

   A) transsexual
   B) transgender
   C) transitional

10. Which theory of human sexual preference seeks to explain both heterosexuality and homosexuality?

    A) exotic becomes erotic
    B) erogenous preferences theory
    C) the genetic drift model
    D) bifurcation theory

Answer Key: 1C, 2B 3A, 4C, 5B, 6A, 7C, 8A, 9B, 10A

References

Barton, N. H., & Charlesworth, B. (1998). Why sex and recombination? *Science, 281*, 1986–1990.

Bem, D. J. (1996). Exotic becomes erotic: A developmental theory of sexual orientation. *Psychological Review, 103*, 320–335.

Biernat, M. (2012). Stereotypes and shifting standards: Forming, communicating and translating person impressions. In P. G. Devine & E. A. Plant (Eds.), *Advances in Experimental Social Psychology, Vol. 45* (pp. 1–59). New York: Elsevier.

Bosson, J. K., & Vandello, J. A. (2011). Precarious manhood and its links to action and aggression. *Current Directions in Psychological Science, 20*, 82–86.

Bosson, J. K., Vandello, J. A., Burnaford, R. M., Weaver, J. R., & Wasti, S. A. (2009). Precarious manhood and displays of physical aggression. *Personality and Social Psychology Bulletin, 35*(5), 623–634.

Clark, R. D., & Hatfield, E. (1989). Gender differences in receptivity to sexual offers. *Journal of Psychology and Human Sexuality, 2*, 39–55.

Clark, R. D., & Hatfield, E. (2003). Love in the afternoon. *Psychological Inquiry, 14*, 227–231.

Dawkins, R. (1976). *The selfish gene*. Oxford: Oxford University Press.

Figlio, D.N. (2005) Boys named Sue: Disruptive children and their peers. *Education Finance and Policy, 2*(4), doi: 10.1162/edfp.2007.2.4.376

Figlio, D. (2007). Boys named Sue: Disruptive children and their peers. *Education Finance and Policy, 2*, 376–394.

Fiske, S. T., Bersoff, D. N., Borgida, E., Deaux, K., & Heilm, M. E. (1991). Social science research on trial: Use of Sex stereotyping research in Price Waterhouse v. Hopkins. *American Psychologist, 46*, 10, 1049–1060.

Jost, J. T. (1997). An experimental replication of the depressed-entitlement effect among women. *Psychology of Women Quarterly, 21*, 387–393.

Judson, O. (2002). *Dr. Tatiana's sex advice to all creation*. New York: Metropolitan Books.

Hess, U., Adams, R. B., Jr., & Kleck, R. E. (2004). Facial appearance, gender, and emotion expression. *Emotion, 4*(4), 378–388.

HHS.gov. Trends in teen pregnancy and childbirth: Teen births. Retrieved December 24, 2018 from: www.hhs.gov/ash/oah/adolescent-development/reproductive-health-and-teen-pregnancy/teen-pregnancy-and-childbearing/trends/index.html

Hollister, J. D., Greiner, S., Wang, W., Wang, J., Zhang, Y., Wong, G. K., . . . Johnson, M. T. (2014). Recurrent loss of sex is associated with accumulation of deleterious mutations in Oenothera. 896–905. doi: 10.1093/molbev/msu345.

Lewis, K. M. (2000). When leaders display emotion: How followers respond to negative emotional expression of male and female leaders. *Journal of Organizational Behavior, 21*, 221–234.

Major, B. (1994). From social inequality to personal entitlement: The role of social comparisons, legitimacy appraisals, and group memberships. *Advances in Experimental Social Psychology, 26*, 293–355.

Martin, C. L., & Ruble, D. N. (2010). Patterns of gender development. *Annual Review of Psychology, 61*, 353–381. doi:10.1146/annurev.psych.093008.100511

Maynard Smith, J. (1978). *The evolution of sex*. Cambridge, U.K.: Cambridge University Press.

Pelham, B. W. (2019). *Evolutionary psychology: Genes, environments, and time*. London, UK: Palgrave MacMillan Publishing.

Pelham, B. (2019). Life history and the cultural evolution of parenting: Pathogens, mortality, and birth across the globe. *Evolutionary Behavioral Sciences*. Advance online publication.

Pelham, B.W., & Hardin, C.D. (2017). Real men don't live on Princess Street: Preacarious manhood and street name selection. Under revision.

Peplau, L. A., Garnets, L. D., Spalding, L. R., Conley, T. D., & Veniegas, R. C. (1998). A critique of Bem's "Exotic Becomes Erotic" theory of sexual orientation. *Psychological Review, 105(2)*, 387–394.

Randolph, M. E., Pinkerton, S. D., Bogart, L. M., Cecil, H., & Abramson, P. R. (2007). Sexual pleasure and condom use. *Archives of Sexual Behavior, 36*(6), 844–848.

Remafedi, G., French, S., Story, M., Resnick, M. D., & Blum, R. (1998). The relationship between suicide risk and sexual orientation: Results of a population-based study. *American Journal of Public Health, 88*(1), 57–60.

Rubin, J. Z., Provenzano, F. J., & Luria, Z. (1974). The eye of the beholder: Parents' views on sex of newborns. *American Journal of Orthopsychiatry, 44(4)*, 512–519.

Ryan, C., Russell, S. T., Huebner, D., Diaz, R., & Sanchez, J. (2010). Family acceptance in adolescence and the health of LGBT young adults. *Journal of Child and Adolescent Psychiatric Nursing.* https://doi.org/10.1111/j.1744-6171.2010.00246.x

Schmitt, D. P. (2005). Sociosexuality from Argentina to Zimbabwe: A 48-nation study of sex, culture, and strategies of human mating. *Behavioral and Brain Sciences, 28*, 247–311.

Switek, B. (2012). Virgin births seen in wild vipers. *Nature News.* Retrieved June, 2019 from https://www.nature.com/news/virgin-births-seen-in-wild-vipers-1.11397

Symons, D. (1979). *The evolution of human sexuality.* New York: Oxford University Press.

Toomey, R. B., & Russell, S. T. (2013). The role of sexual orientation in school-based victimization: A meta-analysis. *Youth & Society.* https://doi.org/10.1177/0044118X13483778

Trivers, R.L. (1972). Parental investment and sexual selection. In *Sexual selection and the descent of man.* (B. Campbell, Ed.) Chicago, IL: Aldine.

Whiting, B. B., & Edwards, C. P. (1988). *Children of different worlds: The formation of social behavior.* Cambridge, MA: Harvard University Press.

VII
Memory and Cognition

Module 16
Memory
Making the Past the Present

If you remember the first day of kindergarten, or what you had for breakfast this morning, you possess an amazing skill. You can mentally reconstruct experiences that no longer exist – and use these reconstructions to guide your current behavior. Those breakfast burritos are gone, all three of them. But if you remember you had them, you can more easily say no to the donut Raj just offered you. Likewise, because you remember the sacrifices your mom made for you when you were young, you'd do almost anything for her today. Because you remember where the brake pedal is in your car, you've been able to keep your driver's license. Memory is a life-saver. But what is memory? **Memory** is a mental record of an event, procedure, or fact. McLeod (2013) says it's "the structures and processes involved in the storage and subsequent retrieval of information." As it turns out, there are four kinds of memory, and memory consists of at least three stages.

The Things We Store: Four Kinds of Memory

Tulving (1972) argued long ago that there are at least two kinds of memory. **Episodic memory** is memory for a past event or experience. If you remember the first time you rode a roller coaster, or the last time you threw up, you're using episodic memory. Episodic memory is so basic that many nonhuman animals seem to have it (Templer & Hampton, 2013). Not surprisingly, episodic memories are laden with sensory information ("We were laughing hysterically," "She was wearing a green cape."). By contrast, **semantic memory** is memory for facts, concepts, and definitions. Semantic memory is abstract, which means it depends heavily on language. Knowing the capital of Kazakhstan, knowing the name of the goalie for the Washington Capitals, and knowing the difference between "capital" and "capitol" all require semantic memory. These facts or ideas exist independent of your personal experience. Somewhere between episodic and semantic memory lies procedural memory. **Procedural memory** is memory for how to perform something; it's action memory for the rules of doing. Juggling, sailing, playing the guitar, and making biscuits all require procedural memory. Procedural memory is like episodic memory in that it involves doing and feeling (knead the dough for at least five minutes; it should feel stretchy). It's like semantic memory in that it involves facts and rules (if you don't use self-rising flour, add 10 ml baking powder).

Most modern memory researchers recognize **priming** as a fourth kind of memory (Tulving & Schacter, 1990). Priming refers to being influenced by your previous exposure to information – usually without being aware of this influence. Because priming is less intuitive than the three forms of memory we have just defined, let's consider two examples.

First, research has demonstrated that when people are exposed to a category, that exposure influences how people later respond to things that are part of that category. If your visit to the hospital yesterday makes you recognize the word "nurse" more quickly than usual today, this is because of priming. Notice that something that happened to you *yesterday* has an effect on your judgment today. That requires memory. As a more intriguing example, consider a classic priming study by Bargh, Chen, and Burrows (1996). They found that priming people with sentences related to old age (e.g., "She collected social security.") caused participants to *walk* more slowly than usual to the elevator when they thought the experiment was over. Thus, priming can influence goals and physical behavior as well as word recognition. This happens even when people are completely unaware of the influence of the priming material. Although there has been some debate in the past two decades about how robust behavioral priming is, an analysis of 133 studies of behavioral priming showed that this priming effect is modest but robust (Weingarten et al., 2016).

Keep, and Get Again: Three Stages of Memory

The first stage of developing a memory is encoding. **Encoding** is the stage in which information enters the memory system – and when the person who will remember the information *forms a mental record* of it. Encoding is going from "What was your name again?" to "Sup, Jackson?" As a very different example, if you can ride a bike, it's because you have *encoded* information about how to steer, brake, and keep your balance on a crazy vehicle that can't even stand up by itself. As you can see from these two examples, many things happen during encoding, and encoding takes many forms.

Episodic Memory (Experiential)

"I rode this roller coaster in Melbourne."
"We had just eaten ice cream sundaes."
"My brother almost threw up on me."

Procedural Memory ("How To")

Before boarding *this* roller coaster, you must remove any hats, glasses, loose jewelry, or loose footwear.

Semantic Memory (Factual)

Melbourne is Australia's capital.

The population of Melbourne is 5 million people.

In Australia, there are more kangaroos than people.

Koalas eat eucalyptus leaves.

Priming (Incidental Memory)

Try to unscramble the following mixed up words:

paltsupty   manergoob

If you were recently thinking about Australia, rare words like "platypus" will come to mind more easily than usual.

Figure 16.1 Four Kinds of Memory: Episodic (event memory), procedural memory (memory for how to do something), semantic memory (factual knowledge) and priming (subtle effects of past experience on present experience).

Encoding Beyoncé's last name is very different than encoding how to juggle, or where you parked your car on Tuesday. Encoding can happen effortlessly (when a two-year-old picks up a first language), or it can be very hard work (when a 42-year-old picks up a second language). Because encoding is complex, and because we can take some control over it, we'll revisit encoding later in this chapter – when we discuss tips for improving your memory.

One way in which encoding happens is **long-term potentiation.** This refers to tiny but important changes in the wiring of the brain (mainly in synaptic gaps – the tiny spaces between neurons where an axon from one neuron approaches the cell body or dendrite of a different neuron). Encoding can also involve the growth of new dendrites. As neuroscientists often put it, "neurons that fire together wire together." When neurotransmitters spill into the synaptic gap between a dendrite and an axon, this chemical process has self-reinforcing properties that strengthen this neural connection (Cooke & Bliss, 2006). Just as using a muscle can strengthen that muscle, using a neural pathway can strengthen that pathway. When psychology was still in its infancy, Semon (1921) began searching for the physiological basis of memory, which he referred to as the **engram**. Lacking modern techniques to study the brain, Semon was a little fuzzy on the exact physical nature of engrams (Tonegawa, Liu, Ramirez, & Redondo, 2016). Today, we know that most specific memories don't have a single location. As Eichenbaum (2016, p. 209) noted, "the engram is widely distributed both within and across brain areas." A memory is more like a play or a dance than a painting, even if it's a memory of a painting. Neuroscientists are now unraveling the physical and chemical basis of memory, including the elusive engram, but the answers are proving to be complex.

Once a memory has a stable physical and chemical basis, we've moved to stage two of memory. This is **storage** – which refers to holding on to or maintaining long-term memories. Memory is surprisingly durable, but memory storage is not like locking something safely in a vault. Things are easier to recall, for example, if you call them up from memory frequently. It's probably easier for you to find your favorite coffee mug than it is for you to find the smoked paprika. Of course, if you're a Hungarian chef who cares little for coffee, the details would flip, but the principle is the same.

The third stage of memory is **retrieval**. Retrieval refers to calling up stored information, usually for immediate use. Memory researchers have long been fascinated with exactly how we pull things up from memory. But in the past couple of decades retrieval has gotten even more attention than it did previously. One practical reason for this is that, as we'll see later, practicing retrieval is one of the best ways to commit new information to memory.

It's important to note that this three-step memory process depends on many other processes. Before encoding (step 1) can begin, things like attention, perception, and interpretation must have already happened. The ultraviolet light that hits your retina can't become a visual memory because the human visual system only converts limited frequencies of electromagnetic radiation to perceived color or brightness. If you recall the term *transduction* – the conversion of a physical stimulus into sensory activity – then you should realize that encoding can't happen without transduction. There's also little or no encoding without attention. We can only focus on a limited portion of all the incoming stimuli we're capable of registering. If beautiful music is playing, but you're wholly unaware of it, it won't get encoded or stored. Memory is amazing, but it has its limits.

Remembering: Both Easy and Hard

Speaking of limits, all things are not encoded equally. Novel smells, for example, are usually more memorable than novel shapes. Smells are very memorable. This is probably because the olfactory bulb is strongly connected to two brain areas that are crucial to memory: The *amygdala* and the *hypothalamus* (Herz, Eliassen, Beland, & Souza, 2004). Likewise, scary events, such as seeing a terrible car crash, become memories more easily than mundane events, such as reading a terrible memory chapter. Vivid and long-lasting memories of dramatic events are called **flashbulb memories** (recall that most cameras once had "flashbulbs"). There is some debate about the details of flashbulb memories. They were once thought to be especially accurate, but there is reason to doubt this. On the other hand, they are formed very quickly, and they do seem to be highly enduring (Neisser & Harsch, 1992). You may be thankful for some flashbulb memories (e.g., vivid memories of dancing at your sister's wedding) while wishing you could forget others (even more vivid memories of having a groomsman throw up on you). Memories of national tragedies – such as the assassination of President John F. Kennedy in 1963 or the terrorist attacks of 9/11 – are examples of flashbulb memories. People who observed these events report that they know "exactly where they were when they heard the news." The events that become flashbulb memories are not always remembered exactly as they really happened, but they do seem to have a quick and easy route to storage.

Another sense in which all things are not remembered equally can be found in research on learning. As we hope you remember, *preparedness* means that people, like many other animals, are born ready to learn and remember some things much more readily than others. Because of our long and unhappy evolutionary history with venomous creatures, for example, we learn to fear spiders or snakes much more readily than we learn to fear guns or motorcycles. Research on *one-trial learning* also shows that rats usually learn to avoid a novel food that nearly killed them after eating the food *just once* (Garcia & Koelling, 1966). We also learn some things during certain periods of life more easily than at other periods. Toddlers soak up a first language like sponges whereas adults have great difficulty learning a new language even when they already have one language under their belts. Some things seem to take a very direct shortcut to long-term storage.

But as any squirrel could tell you, storage doesn't always guarantee retrieval. Recall that retrieval happens when you pull something from long-term memory into consciousness. Who was the third U.S President? What's the third element in the periodic table? What's the name of that cute kid you liked in third grade? If those were easy, try naming the navigational device seafarers once used to sail the oceans? It takes measurements from stars. If you're having trouble with retrieval, then you're probably having a **tip-of-the-tongue** experience (Brown & McNeill, 1966). It's the frustrating feeling of *almost* being able to retrieve something that you know you know. The tip of the tongue phenomenon reveals important facts about retrieval. For example, when a word is on the tip of people's tongues, they can often report what letter it starts with, and even how many syllables it has. These turn out to be some of the cues people use for successful retrieval. To some degree, then, your mind may be like a dictionary; it organizes words by their initial sounds.

To summarize much of this module thus far, memory is a many-splendored thing that involves encoding, storage, and retrieval. If you find these three terms unfamiliar and frustrating, consider a metaphor that may help you remember them.

The Museum Metaphor of Memory

Imagine you're the curator of a museum. Because of your limited budget, you rarely display original objects. Instead you create *representations* of them (e.g., photographs, audio recordings). From the perspective of this metaphor, we assume you've already created your own personal representation of something suitable for display. Now let's look at the three stages of memory:

Encoding is like putting the representation in the museum's *archives* (permanent storage) where the representation may be retrieved and brought forth for display or examination when needed.

Storage is like keeping things safe in your archives. This may seem very passive, but like a museum's curator, your memory system goes to great lengths to store things well. Printing things on acid free paper, keeping them warm and dry, and maintaining an organizational system are all analogous to effective memory storage.

Retrieval is like going to the exact location in the archives where an item of interest is being kept in long-term storage – and bringing it out for display when needed.

In museums, there's a limited amount of space for public display but virtually unlimited space in the archives (in storage). Imagine that there's a special spot in your museum's display rooms where you show off artifacts you've never seen before (e.g., a new dinosaur bone). Because you can't usually purchase such artifacts; you put them on temporary display in this special display room. This special room is like **short-term memory**, and if it were like human short-term memory, it would only hold about six or seven objects (Miller, 1956). As already noted, there's no capacity limit for permanent archives. They're like **long-term memory**.

How do short-term and long-term memory differ? **Short-term memory** is characterized by limited capacity. Only a certain amount of information can be held in short-term memory at one time. Short-term memory is also characterized by limited duration. Short-term memory fades quickly. But don't let all these limits deceive you. Short term memory is absolutely critical for our survival. Without it, we'd be unable to carry on conversations, go shopping, or recall the directions somebody just gave us. By the way our survival also depends on a very rapidly decaying category of short-term memory called sensory memory.

Figure 16.2 From seven dwarfs and seven-digit phone numbers to the seven notes of the Western musical scale, many things seem to come in sevens. George Miller (1956) argued that there's a good reason for this. Seven is about the maximum number of items most people can hold in short-term memory. If you noticed that a dwarf is missing, blame Doc or COVID-19. But remember, as well, that it's seven *plus or minus two.*

Sensory memory includes both iconic (visual) memory (covered in Module 2) and echoic memory (very short-term auditory memory – to be covered in Module 17). In the case of both iconic and echoic memory, we must filter vast amounts of visual and auditory stimuli that we hold in memory for just a split-second (automatically and below our awareness). Unless that information is flagged as relevant and brought into awareness, it fades *very* quickly. A great example of this is when we hear our name called out in a loud and crowded room (in Module 17 we will learn that this is called the "cocktail party effect").

Holding things in short-term memory is mentally taxing (just as renting a temporary exhibit may be expensive). But if it's important to us to remember something new, and if we can't record it or photograph it, we'll often rehearse it. **Rehearsal** refers to mentally repeating material held in short-term memory. An example is repeating a phone number to yourself until you can add it to your smartphone contacts. By the way, simple rehearsal is a good way to keep things in short-term memory but a poor way to memorize them. If you've memorized something, you've put it in long-term memory. In contrast to short-term memory, **long-term memory** is characterized by unlimited capacity and, in some cases, unlimited duration (many long-term memories can last a lifetime). But some stable things are more stable than others. As noted earlier, memories that have been retrieved recently are retrieved more easily than memories that have not. This is the principle of **accessibility**. It's one reason skilled musicians, speakers, and athletes still practice and "warm up" even when they know things well.

The museum metaphor also reveals why memory can be so frustrating. Remember the "the tip of the tongue" phenomenon? Many of the problems we have with memory happen precisely because we know so much. There are many, many places and ways we could have stored things. I know I have a T-rex femur some place, and I want to examine it. But did I shelve it under *dinosaurs*, *femurs*, or *big stuff*? According to Bob Bjork (1998), we're great at both encoding and storage, but not so good at retrieval. This implies that a good way to memorize things is to *practice retrieving them*. This has proven to be true. A good way to memorize things is to test yourself on them – to *practice retrieving* them. Thus, **retrieval practice** refers to strengthening memories by seeing if you can recall them. After you read the aforementioned definition twice, can you repeat it? Can you wait 15 seconds and *still* repeat it? Can you repeat it in 20 minutes? What about tomorrow? A great way to retain information is to test yourself on it. This is why we include multiple-choice questions at the end of every module in this text.

This museum metaphor implies that memories exist not just for you but also for your museum's audience (your social world). There are many ways in which memory is a social process (Hardin & Higgins, 1996). One way in which we all remember much more than we otherwise could is by remembering who in our lives knows what. If I have questions about the NBA, I'll ask Curtis. If I have questions about getting an MBA, I'll ask Kari. If my friends fail me, I'll ask Google (Sparrow, Liu, & Wegner, 2011; Wegner, Erber, & Raymond, 1991).

Measures of Memory

The fact that the final stage of memory is retrieval suggests that the exact way in which we assess memory will have a big effect on how good people's memories appear to be. Anything someone does to facilitate retrieval will increase the likelihood that a person remembers something. The most obvious distinction along these lines is the one between **recall** and **recognition** memory. **Recall memory** refers to unaided, open-ended memory. If we ask you what the capital of the U.S. state of Georgia is, we are asking you to *recall* a semantic memory, and we are not giving you any retrieval cues. On the other hand, if you're not sure what the capital of Georgia is, we could ask you to choose from one of the following cities: Athens, Atlanta, Augusta, Birmingham, Columbus, Paris, Rome, Savannah, Sevilla.

Thus, even if you could not recall the capital of Georgia, there is a good chance you'd be able to *recognize* it on a list. **Recognition memory** refers to our ability to identify an answer to a question from a list of plausible candidates (some of which may serve as retrieval cues) for the correct answer. The point behind this memory exercise is that *how good memory appears to be has a lot to do with how you measure it.* The undisputed father of memory research began his work on memory when psychology was barely born. Hermann Ebbinghaus (1885) found, for example, that measures of recognition memory often show that people have some memory of things they cannot recall at all. And even when measures of recognition memory seem to show that a person remembers little or nothing, measures of savings often show that measures of recognition memory just weren't sensitive enough. **Savings** refers to the advantages people have in learning material that they once knew but seem to have forgotten. If you once knew all 66 books of the Protestant Bible, but you think you've forgotten them completely, we'll put our money on you any day to learn the 66 books much more quickly than an equally bright, equally motivated person who never studied the Bible until today. Because we are great at storage but mediocre to poor at retrieval, anything someone else does to help us with retrieval will often reveal that we remembered a lot more than we thought we did.

Eight Tips for Improving Your Memory

These points about measuring memory notwithstanding, memorizing new things is rarely easy. If you'd like to improve your ability to remember new material (like most of the material in this course, we're guessing), you should take some advice from memory experts. Memory researchers don't just develop theories of memory; they also develop ways of improving memory. Let's examine eight well-documented ways to improve your memory. As we summarize these eight memory tips, we'll reinforce some important principles of memory:

Retrieval Practice

You're right. We've already defined this one. Can you retrieve the definition?

Spacing (Distributed Learning)

As we noted, the father of memory research was Hermann Ebbinghaus, who began his work in Germany in 1879, when psychology had just begun to exist. A typical Ebbinghaus memory study was no fun for his participants. It involved learning long lists of **trigrams** or **nonsense syllables** (e.g., CAF, VED, KIF). One of the first things Ebbinghaus learned using this technique was the **spacing effect:** People learn things much better if they distribute their studying over time. This means you'll usually do better on your biology exam by studying the topic for an hour a day for ten days rather than cramming ten hours of study into a single day. So consider this a new reason for making procrastination your enemy. Slow and steady wins the memory race.

Meaning (Semantic Encoding)

Ebbinghaus studied nonsense syllables precisely because he knew that meaning has a humungous impact on memory. Ebbinghaus was trying to sidestep the effects of meaning by creating stimuli that were meaningless. But inadvertently, Ebbinghaus also taught us that the best way to memorize something is to make it meaningful. Consider how hard it would be to learn the following 13-word list *in order*: "him was blame for little the her took scared she how brother understanding." Now compare memorizing that word list with memorizing a different word list, also in order: "Understanding how scared her little brother was, she took the blame for him." That's the same list, of course, but now it has *meaning*. Anything you can do to make material meaningful will help you memorize it more quickly – and retain it longer. When you're trying to learn new material, this often boils down to relating unfamiliar (not so meaningful) material to meaningful material that you already know very well. Introducing you to the museum metaphor of memory was our attempt to connect memory terms to your existing semantic knowledge of museums.

The Self-referent Memory Effect

One of the best ways you can learn anything is to relate it to *yourself* (Klein et al., 1999). Your first author Brett observed this long ago when he was running a memory experiment in which participants had to learn a long list of words presented in a random order. Although Brett emphasized that participants were *not to speak* while the words appeared, one participant couldn't contain himself. He narrated my entire word list. It went something like this: OREGANO "Oh good, I love Italian food. So oregano." SHEPHERD "Shepherd, that's my dog, a German Shepherd." TULIP "I'll get mom tulips for Mother's Day!" This guy wasn't any good at following instructions, but he was very good at memorizing – by making a long list of words highly relevant to *himself*. If you're thinking that this tip about memory overlaps a lot with the previous tip about *meaning*, you're correct. The self is inherently meaningful.

The Forgetting Curve

Ebbinghaus also discovered the **forgetting curve**. As shown in Figure 16.3, this curve reveals that after you're exposed to new information, forgetting happens quickly at first, then tapers off. This means that if you don't understand something in a course lecture, you're better off asking about it right away rather than at the end of the lecture. And you're way better off asking your question at the end of lecture rather than waiting a week to ask. Because memory decays very quickly at first, you're better off asking your question while the new ideas that prompted it are still fresh in your mind. (See the forgetting curve in Figure 16.3.)

Overlearning

Another way to maximize long-term memorization (e.g., exam performance) is to keep studying material (and testing yourself on it) well *after* you think you've learned it. This may sound like a waste of time. But if you recall how accessibility and spacing work, we bet you can see how studying and retrieving material you remembered well yesterday can make it likely you'll be able to remember the material even in a context (the classroom) that may be different than the context in which your learned it (your

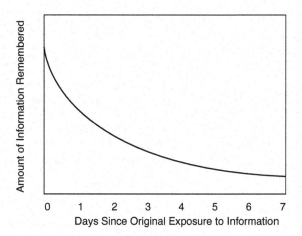

Figure 16.3 A typical forgetting curve. It shows that forgetting happens very quickly at first and then levels out.

kitchen table). As Turner (2017) put it. "your brain may have a shortcut that helps you lock in learning. Instead of practicing until you're decent at something and then taking a siesta, practicing just a little longer could be the fast track to solidifying a skill."

Sleep

Speaking of siestas, another tip for improving memory is sleeping. First, failing to get enough sleep (8–9 hours per night for most young adults) is one of the biggest known barriers to learning and intellectual performance. If you're routinely failing to get enough sleep, you're taxing your brain. Second, going to sleep right after you have studied facilitates **memory consolidation**, which is the active transfer and organization of information from short-term into long-term storage (Rasch & Born, 2013). If you're lucky enough to be able to take a real siesta in the afternoon, it'd be ideal to study for an hour before doing so. If you're like the rest of – and a siesta is just a pleasant fantasy – then you can still maximize learning by studying before you go to sleep. While you're sleeping, the things you rehearsed ("More than 99% of the normal matter in the universe is either hydrogen or helium.") will become more consolidated in long-term memory.

Organization

If your memory were wholly and completely disorganized, retrieval would be a random mental walk that would almost always lead to frustration. Think of a middle schooler's room. But luckily memory is highly organized. Think of an accountant's room. Almost anything you can do to organize material *as you study it* promotes memory. Memory researchers use the term **organizational encoding** to refer to thoughtful things you can do when studying that will facilitate memory. Can you organize eight key terms into a story? Can you rank seven events based on which happens first? Can you use a mnemonic trick such as an acronym?

Long, long ago, when Pluto was still a planet, we memorized the planets in order of distance from the sun. we *organized* them using the mnemonic "My Very Educated Mother

Just Served Us Nine Pickles." Today you could replace "Nine Pickles" with "Nutmeg." Or you could say mom served us "Nine Dill Pickles." Now you'll remember that, after Neptune, there are *dwarf planets*. **Mnemonic devices** (memory tricks) such as this allow us to capitalize on the alphabetical organization of our mental dictionaries. They also allow us to capitalize on our knowledge of grammar. Of course, organization imparts meaning as well as structure. If you were to argue that part of the secret of organizational encoding is adding meaning, we'd have to agree. But not all organizational techniques impart meaning. **Chunking** a 15-digit number into three five-digit numbers (which makes the big number much easier to remember) is a good example of an organizational technique that does *not* impart a lot of meaning. It just helps us cope with the limits of short-term memory. If you'd like to improve your own memory, a good start might be using organizational encoding to memorize this list of eight memory tips.

There are two themes that can help us tie together all eight of these memory tips. The first theme is something memory researchers call depth of processing. When we create meaning, organize to-be-learned material, and capitalize on the self-referent memory effect – by thinking about how things relate to the self – we are processing the information at hand more *deeply* than we would otherwise. Think of depth of processing as a general tip that summarizes three of the more specific tips described. When we process things more deeply, we remember them better! Along very different lines, another theme is using time to your advantage when trying to learn new material. First, because of the forgetting curve, don't wait until something has faded from memory before you ask about it. Second, space out your learning over a long period. That's the spacing effect. Third, along somewhat similar lines, study right before you go to sleep – and get plenty of sleep. Fourth, keep studying past the point at which you seem to have learned everything. That's overlearning. Fifth, test yourself both along the way, and when you are pretty sure you know everything. That's retrieval practice. Did you notice that we just boiled these eight principles of memory down to two broader principles? Think deeply and use time wisely. If you can do both of these broad things in the particular ways that work best for you, you'll be well on your way to improving your memory.

Hands-On Activity for Module 16: Memory Problems

In the past few decades, legal experts have taken a great interest in memory. After all, the form of human memory known as eyewitness testimony often puts people in prison. With that in mind, let's do a fun and quick memory activity. To begin the activity, turn this page upside down so that you can read the 15 words that follow. Just read the list of words once and then turn your book right side up again. It's OK to read them aloud.

sour, candy, sugar, bitter, good, taste, tooth, nice, honey, soda, chocolate, heart, cake, tart, pie

Now please spend about 30 seconds thinking about the 15 words *without looking at the list*.
Now check out the five words that follow and – *without consulting the list* – circle (or write down on a separate page) any of the five words that you vividly remember from the list. Please don't circle or write down a word unless you *vividly* remember it. Don't trust something if it is merely a guess:

   halo   sugar   table   tattoo   sweet

Most people have little trouble eliminating the words "halo," "table," and "tattoo." That's probably because none of these three words appeared on the list. Further, if you said you vividly remember the words "sugar" and "sweet," you're in good company. About 80% of the people who read the list you read say they vividly remember the words "sugar" and "sweet" (e.g., see Roediger & McDermott, 1995; Schacter, 1996). But there's a problem: the word "sweet" is *not* on the list. Go ahead and check out the list. Most people think they read the word "sweet" because it is strongly associated with the 15 words on the list. It's difficult to read those words without activating the word "sweet" in memory. We human beings are not as good as we might hope at knowing the difference between *thinking* something and *experiencing* that something. That turns out to be a very important point in legal circles because most jurors fail to appreciate the extreme malleability of human memory.

So can we trust eyewitness testimony? Whereas memory experts have maintained for decades that human memory is biased and imperfect, our legal system (often reliant on eyewitnesses) and many psychotherapists (often reliant on childhood memories) have historically put extreme faith in the accuracy of human memory (Loftus, 1993). Thus, when adults claimed to have unearthed repressed memories from their early childhoods (sometimes of relatives committing heinous crimes), jurors and psychotherapists often took these reports at face value. In the 1970s and 1980s, many people were convicted of crimes based solely on what are now considered highly questionable "recovered" memories. Today, most legal experts and psychotherapists are trained to recognize – and avoid – interview procedures and eyewitness memory tests that can bias people's memories. For example, imagine that some witnesses reported that a Latino man committed a bank robbery. Now imagine that a single eyewitness is asked to pick out the perpetrator from a five-person "line-up." Witnesses will be much more likely to say Carlos was the perpetrator if Carlos is put in a line-up with four White men than if he is put in a line-up with four other Latino men. If Carlos is unlucky enough to be roughly the same height and build as the actual perpetrator, and if he happens to be sporting the same kind of goatee, he is in even more trouble. We hope it's also obvious that if you can form a false memory of something that just happened a minute ago, you can surely form one of something that happened three months ago. Memory experts often become consultants in criminal legal cases and have also played an expert advisory role in the development of new laws and procedures designed to minimize bias and error in the courtroom (Schacter, 1996).

Multiple Choice Questions for Module 16

1. Why did Herman Ebbinghaus use three-letter "trigrams" in his classic studies of memory?

   A) because he was studying children, who have great difficulty with lengthy words
   B) because he realized that meaning has a large effect on memory and he wanted to control for this
   C) because he wanted to see how people learn languages to which they've never been exposed

2. Keeping information in short-term memory by mentally repeating it is called:

   A) rehearsal
   B) echoic repetition
   C) memorization

3. A quickly-decaying (2 second) store for visual information is known as the:

   A) iconic store
   B) perceptual store
   C) Apple store

4. A quickly-decaying (5 second) memory store for auditory information is known as the:

   A) audible store
   B) phonetic store
   C) echoic store

5. What kind of memory seems to have a capacity limit of about seven items?

   A) pre-attentive memory
   B) short-term memory
   C) object memory

6. Semantic and episodic memory are considered forms of what kind of memory?

   A) cognitive
   B) explicit
   C) implicit

7. Maricela is taking French 101 and is studying the simple present tense. She is having an easier time learning the first-person form (e.g., *je suis = I am*) than the third-person form (e.g., *elles sont = they are*) of many verbs. This memory bias may be due to the phenomenon known as what?

   A) egocentric encoding
   B) personal elaboration
   C) the self-referent memory effect

8. A very effective way to learn things well (and retain them for a long time) is to use:

   A) retrieval practice
   B) displacement
   C) repetition

9. Lorenzo learned to speak Hebrew when he was a child living in Israel. His family moved to France when he was 12, and he never spoke Hebrew for 10 years. After graduating from college, he took a trip to Israel – thinking that he remembered "no Hebrew at all." However, within a few weeks of his long trip to Israel, Lorenzo was speaking enough Hebrew to communicate OK with Israelis who spoke no French. Lorenzo's ability to learn Hebrew very quickly the second time around is a good example of what principle of memory?

   A) the power of meaning
   B) savings
   C) the forgetting curve

10. Long-term potentiation plays a role in memory formation. Long-term potentiation takes place in:

    A) the amygdala
    B) the semantic cortex
    C) synaptic gaps between neurons

Answer Key: 1B, 2A, 3A, 4C, 5B, 6B, 7C, 8A, 9B, 10C

References

Bargh, J. A., Chen, M., & Burrows, L. (1996). Automaticity of social behavior: Direct effects of trait construct and stereotype activation on action. *Journal of Personality and Social Psychology*, *71*, 230–244.

Bjork, R. (1998). Personal communication.

Brown, R., & McNeill, D. (1966). The "tip of the tongue" phenomenon. *Journal of Verbal Learning and Verbal Behavior*, *5*, 325–337.

Cooke, S. F., & Bliss, T. V. (2006, July). Plasticity in the human central nervous system. *Brain*, *129* (Pt. 7), 1659–1673. Epub May 3, 2006.

Ebbinghaus, H. (1885). *Memory: A contribution to experimental psychology*. New York, NY: Dover.

Eichenbaum, H. (2016). Still searching for the engram. *Learning & Behavior*, *44*(3), 209–222.

Garcia, J., & Koelling, R. A. (1966). Relation of cue to consequence in avoidance learning. *Psychonomic Science*, *4*, 123–124.

Hardin, C. D., & Higgins, E. T. (1996). Shared reality: How social verification makes the subjective objective. In R. M. Sorrentino & E. T. Higgins (Eds.), *Handbook of motivation and cognition: The interpersonal context* (Vol. 3, pp. 28–84). New York, NY: Guilford.

Herz, R. S., Eliassen, J., Beland, S., & Souza, T. (2004). Neuroimaging evidence for the emotional potency of odor- evoked memory. *Neuropsychologia*, *42*(3), 371–378. doi:https://doi.org/10.1016/j.neuropsychologia.2003.08.009

Klein, S. B., Loftus, J., & Burton, H. A. (1989). Two self-reference effects: The importance of distinguishing between self-descriptiveness judgments and autobiographical retrieval in self-referent encoding. *Journal of Personality and Social Psychology*, *56*(6), 853–865.

Loftus, E. F. (1993). The reality of repressed memories. *American Psychologist*, *48*(5), 518–537.

McLeod, S. (2013). Simply psychology. *Memory*. Retrieved from www.simplypsychology.org/memory.html

Miller, G. (1956). The magical number seven, plus or minus two: Some limits on our capacity for processing information. *Psychological Review*, *63*, 81–97.

Neisser, U., & Harsch, N. (1992). Phantom flashbulbs: False recollections of hearing the news about Challenger. In E. Winograd & U. Neisser (Eds.), *Emory symposia in cognition, 4. Affect and accuracy in recall: Studies of "flashbulb" memories* (pp. 9–31). New York, NY: Cambridge University Press.

Rasch, B., & Born, J. (2013). About sleep's role in memory. *Physiological Review*, *93*, 681–766.

Roediger, H. L., III, & McDermott, K. B. (1995). Creating false memories: Remembering words not presented in lists. *Journal of Experimental Psychology: Learning, Memory, & Cognition*, *21*, 803–814.

Schacter, D. L. (1996). *Searching for memory: The brain, the mind, and the past*. New York: Basic Books.

Semon, R. W. (1921). *The mneme*. London, The MacMillan Company.G. Allen & Unwin Limited.

Sparrow, B., Liu, J., & Wegner, D. M. (2011). Google effects on memory: Cognitive consequences of having information at our fingertips. *Science*, *333*, 776–778. doi:10.1126/science.1207745

Templer, V. L., & Hampton, R. R. (2013). Episodic memory in nonhuman animals. *Current Biology: CB*, *23*(17), R801–6.

Tonegawa, S., Liu, X., Ramirez, S., & Redondo, R. (2016). Memory engram cells have come of age. *Neuron*, *87*, 918–931.

Tulving, E. (1972). Episodic and semantic memory. In E. Tulving & W. Donaldson (Eds.), *Organization of memory* (pp. 381–403). New York, NY: Academic Press, Inc.

Tulving, E., & Schacter, D. L. (1990, Jan. 19). Priming and human memory systems. *Science*, *247* (4940), 301–306. doi: 10.1126/science.2296719.

Turner, V. S. (2017, Feb. 28). The power of overlearning: It can help to work on something you already know how to do. *Scientific American*. Retrieved from www.scientificamerican.com

Wegner, D. M., Erber, R., & Raymond, P. (1991). Transactive memory in close relationships. *Journal of Personality and Social Psychology*, *61*, 923–929.

Weingarten, E., Chen, Q., McAdams, M., Yi, J., Hepler, J., & Albarracín, D. (2016). From primed concepts to action: A meta-analysis of the behavioral effects of incidentally presented words. *Psychological Bulletin*, *142*(5), 472–497.

Module 17
Consciousness (or the Lack Thereof)

You may recall that psychology came to be in 1879, when Wilhelm Wundt began doing experiments on *introspection* – a technique for reporting one's personal sensations and experiences. You may also recall that introspection had some problems. For example, even after carefully training observers to do introspection, Wundt found that their reports were not very reliable. Research now suggests that one reason why this was the case is that conscious experience is not always a good indicator of what's happening in the human mind. In fact, many modern cognitive and social psychologists study the disconnect between what is happening in people's minds and what people *think* is happening in their minds. Most of these researchers would tell you they study **consciousness** – which is our subjective personal experience of the world, including both everything outside us and all of our own thoughts and feelings. Consciousness is closely associated with awareness. But many researchers who study consciousness emphasize the relative power of the *unconscious* mind – and the many limitations of the conscious mind. We don't always know what we want, or why we did something. So we sometimes do things because of forces we could never put our fingers on. This module examines the mysteries of consciousness – with an emphasis on what Kihlstrom (1987) called the **cognitive unconscious**. The cognitive unconscious refers to the idea that a great deal of what we feel and do is determined by mental processes of which we are unaware. Let's begin our analysis of the cognitive unconscious with a brief look at automatic vs. controlled information processing. Then we'll move on to a classic study that raises serious questions about the power of the conscious mind – and the validity of everyday introspection.

Automatic and Controlled Processes

Research in social and cognitive psychology reveals sharp limitations on how much conscious access people have to their own thoughts (Banaji & Hardin, 1996; Kahneman, 2011; Zajonc, 2001). For decades, researchers have distinguished between two very different kinds of thinking. As Shiffrin and Schneider (1977) noted, **controlled processes** are slow, conscious, optional, and cognitively taxing. But after people have practiced a judgment or skill for a very long time, thought processes that were once controlled become **automatic processes** – meaning they are now fast, unconscious, mandatory, and efficient (effortless). A *lot* of routine mental processes are automatic. Further, because we are constantly bombarded by huge amounts of information, there is no way we can be consciously aware of everything that is happening to us at once. Consider everything that's happening as you drive a friend to lunch. There's a conversation with the friend, as well as information about the physical features of the friend. There's the way your hands press against the steering wheel, the feel of the accelerator and the brake. Moving outside the car, there are numerous road signs, traffic signals, pedestrian foot traffic, the rain, the sun, billboards, and plenty of other cars switching lanes. Some of what you are encountering must be carefully processed because it is critical for safe driving (cars changing lanes) and some of what you are encountering is not critical (the clothing of the pedestrians on the sidewalk), which means it can be quickly discarded. Automatically shifting your attention to what is crucial is a way of coping with what would otherwise overload your conscious mind. In a moment, we'll describe the "cocktail party effect" and you'll see how we know that some information is privileged over others when it comes to the battle to make it to consciousness. But before we do so, let's explore the basic concept of automatic processing.

The main theme of a lot of research in social cognition is that many human decisions, judgments, and preferences are grounded heavily in automatic processes (Chartrand & Bargh, 1999; Gilbert, 1989). To the degree that any judgment has automatic components, people are likely to have little or no access to the thoughts that led to the judgment. Further, automatic processes are notoriously difficult to control. Let's return to driving as an example: If you have ever driven your car for a while on a familiar path – and then realized that you took the path that leads you to school or work – rather than taking the path you *meant* to take when you first got in the car, you've been the victim of automatic processing. And unless you're a truly exceptional person, you're about to become the victim of automatic processing again. Here's how. Figure 17.1 contains 20 common words. Your job is to ignore those common words and rattle off in numerical order all the *ink colors* (or screen colors) that *print* these 20 common words (e.g., "1 green, 2 blue, 3 brown," etc.). Go ahead and do it – as quickly as possible. The five colors, by the way, are blue, brown, green, purple, and red.

So far, so good. Now that you've had a little practice, we'd like you to try the same thing using the 20 words from Figure 17.2. We used the same five ink colors (or virtual ink colors), and your job is to *ignore* the words themselves and rattle off the 20 colors that print the words in numbered order (e.g., "1 red, 2 blue," etc.).

1. BIG	9. CAST	17. CAT
2. READY	10. TIME	18. PRINT
3. GATE	11. GLUE	19. APPLE
4. BOWL	12. HELP	20. WHEEL
5. SNAKE	13. MOUSE	
6. TRUE	14. LAKE	
7. WHAT	15. TOWN	
8. HERS	16. SHADOW	

Figure 17.1 Twenty words whose five ink colors you can probably name very quickly.

1. RED	9. PURPLE	17. GREEN
2. PURPLE	10. RED	18. PURPLE
3. GREEN	11. PURPLE	19. BLUE
4. BLUE	12. BLUE	20. BROWN
5. BROWN	13. RED	
6. GREEN	14. BROWN	
7. RED	15. GREEN	
8. BLUE	16. BROWN	

Figure 17.2 Twenty words whose five ink colors you'll probably find it very hard to name quickly.

You have just experienced the **Stroop interference effect**. This refers to the difficulty people have naming letter colors when the letter colors spell color words that are different than the letter colors. This effect was discovered long ago by J. Ridley Stroop (1935). Since Stroop's original discovery, researchers have used variations on this task to study everything from reading problems in kids to clinical phobias in adults. For our purposes, the most important aspect of the Stroop interference task is the finding that this interference effect occurs because reading is automatic. In fact, if you knew your colors well but you showed no evidence of a Stroop effect, we'd be very worried that you are not a fluent reader. The Stroop task gives most people trouble because reading is *automatic*. Among other things, it happens quickly, and it is largely mandatory. Thus, the automatic comprehension of the words in Figure 17.2 interferes with identifying the letter colors – which is a more controlled process. In the case of the Stroop interference effect, dual, competing processes are at work – a highly automatic reading process and a more controlled color-naming process. In other words, the mental processes in which you engage when you read are so well-learned that the processes occur unconsciously. If you must stop and think consciously about the sound that "G" makes when you see the word "GREEN," you're not a fluent reader. And because many of the mental processes in which you engage in a typical day are automatic, it can sometimes be very hard to answer questions about what you were just thinking. Let's take a close look at this surprising idea.

Consciousness: What We Notice and What We Don't

As you may recall from the module on motivation, Nisbett and Wilson (1977) asked a group of female shoppers to evaluate four pairs of panty hose. To make the test blind (e.g., to avoid name-brand biases), Nisbett and Wilson arbitrarily labeled the four pairs of panty hose A, B, C or D. Their findings were clear. Four times as many shoppers preferred the fourth pair of panty hose as the first pair. When asked to explain their preferences, the shoppers offered many reasons. Some said they preferred the subtle shading of their favorite pair; others said their favorite pair felt smoother or seemed more durable. None of these shoppers had any difficulty answering this question about reasons. But none of them answered it correctly. This is because the four pairs of panty hose were identical. The 4:1 preference for pair D over pair A was a *"shopping around effect"* (an order effect). Nisbett and Wilson (1977) refer to this failure of introspection as "telling more than we can know." They argue that when people explain why they've made decisions, they often fall back on lay theories about human preferences – because they often have little direct access to their own thought processes. Failures of introspection have been documented for a very wide range of decisions (Millar & Tesser, 1986; Sabini & Silver, 1981). For example, people who've just been tricked into thinking they said one unfamiliar human face was more attractive than another have no difficulty explaining why they thought the face they had just rated as *less* attractive was more attractive. That's right. If you just said that you think Alicia is more attractive than Janelle, you'll have no trouble at all explaining a few seconds later why you think Janelle is more attractive than Alicia (Johansson, Hall, Sikström, & Olsson, 2006).

In the wake of Nisbett and Wilson's clever research, numerous studies in cognitive and social psychology began to illustrate the limitations of consciousness. Or maybe it would be better to say many studies underscored the power of *un*consciousness – the power of mental processes to which we have little or no access to shape what we feel and do. An example of the cognitive unconscious appears in Figure 17.3. Did you notice anything funny about the cartoon? It is funny in at least seven ways. First, it's

"Yes, Helen, get me the %&$#! employment agency again."   "I'd like to remind those jerks that I asked for ELVES, tiny little ELVES!"

Figure 17.3 Check out this cartoon. Do you think it's funny? Is there anything funny *about* it?

funny to see Santa curse about his employment agency, even if it's G-rated cursing. More important, six other funny things happened in this cartoon. You probably didn't notice any of them. First, in the second version of the cartoon, the mouse hole disappeared. Maybe it's the power of elves. Second, in cartoon 2, the leftmost Elvis got shorter. Maybe he's hoping to pass as an elf now that he knows he can't get a job as Elvis. Third, the wall lights are now upside down. Fourth, Santa's "help wanted" sign is now a "hello Wanda" sign. Fifth, the microphone cord for the second Elvis has gotten shorter. Finally, Santa and Rudolph have changed places in the background portrait.

If you're thinking this only happened because this was a cartoon, think again. People who interact directly with other real people often fall prey to change blindness. Simons and Levin (1997) had a confederate ask for directions on the Harvard campus. The confederate held up a map and asked unsuspecting strangers for directions. Not long after helpful others began pointing and offering directions, two men carrying a large door (held horizontally) interrupted things, by cutting between the confederate and the directions-giver. During this sneaky, two-second interruption, the confederate *changed into another person* (by grabbing the back of the door and having the *original* door holder take his place behind the moving door). The new person was using the same map the confederate had used, and this person picked up right where the original confederate had left off with his questions. Half the helpful strangers failed to notice that the man had turned into someone else! Both this dramatic example, and the subtler example involving the Santa cartoon are examples of change blindness. **Change blindness** is the finding that – after a brief interruption – it's often possible to change an aspect of a person's immediate environment without the person detecting the change. Change blindness has been documented dozens of ways, often by asking people to watch video clips of impossible events. But many studies have now shown that change blindness is real outside the lab. You can see a reenactment of the Simons and Levin "door study" at www.youtube.com/watch?v=vBPG_OBgTWg. We like this version a lot because, in one case, the original White male confederate becomes an *Asian woman* – and the helpful but unsuspecting pedestrian doesn't seem to notice. In another case, the White confederate magically becomes a Black man! Many people fail to notice this change. If this sounds impossible to you, check out the video we just mentioned – and for which you have a link.

Change blindness reveals that we are *not* consciously aware of nearly as much as we think we are. Another problem with consciousness is that sometimes we have limited control over what enters our consciousness and what gets ignored. For instance, it is often hard to focus our conscious attention on any one thing for an extended period. Suppose we asked you to think of absolutely nothing but your favorite singer for a full minute, and to press a button any time another thought intruded into consciousness – briefly eclipsing Beyoncé, Kendrick Lamar, or Billie Holiday. After a while, you'd almost certainly find that other thoughts intruded into consciousness. And trying *not* to think about something is even more difficult than trying to focus on something. This is true, at least in part, because your very efforts to monitor your success at thought suppression will usually act as an intrusion. An example might be, "Wait, why am I thinking about lasagna? Oh yeah, I'm trying NOT to think about polar bears. Dang it!" Further, once you have spent a while trying very hard not to think about something, you will often find that thoughts of that thing become almost irresistible once you have been given permission to think about anything you want (Wegner, Schneider, Carter, & White, 1987). Just ask Adam and Eve about how hard it was to stop thinking about that forbidden fruit. If all this wasn't bad enough, research also suggests that certain things force their way into consciousness – even when you are trying very hard to ignore them.

Cherry (1953) showed this in her classic studies using a **dichotic listening task**. When taking part in this task, a participant dons a pair of stereo headphones that play a *different* message in each ear. The participant is specifically instructed to ignore the message in one ear and focus on the message in the other. To be sure participants are really attending to just one ear, they're instructed to **shadow** what is being said in the attended ear (to repeat it, word for word). After a brief adjustment period, most people report that what is coming in to the unattended ear fades away. In fact, Cherry found that most people failed to notice it when the person speaking in the unattended ear switched to speaking German after beginning in English. That's pretty good control over consciousness! But pretty good is not perfect. Cherry also observed the **cocktail party effect**. The same highly focused listeners who failed to notice that a speaker had begun speaking German almost always noticed it when the speaker casually spoke the listener's first name. Our names almost always grab our attention. Have you ever been at a loud party, sporting event, or billiards game when you were listening intently to your conversation partner? Have you ever noticed someone

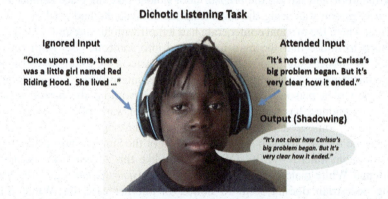

Figure 17.4 In a dichotic listening task, people focus on the message played in one ear while ignoring the message played in the other. People are usually asked to shadow (repeat) the message to which they are attending. People are so good at ignoring the unattended ear that they usually do not notice it when the speaker switches from English to German. But these same listeners *do* usually notice it when the speaker says their own first name. This is the *cocktail party effect* (Cherry, 1953).

else calling out your own name even in this noisy environment? Most of the time the stranger was calling out the name of a different Joshua or Jessica. But your attentional system sets the threshold for name-detection very low, just in case it is you.

The Influence of Unconscious Processes

Of course, showing that we don't have perfect control over consciousness is not the same as showing that the unconscious mind often runs the show. If the unconscious is invisible, how can we observe its influence? One answer is that we can manipulate or measure things over which the person is unaware, and then see if these forces (of which researchers are aware) influence people's behavior. Consider a classic study of **behavioral priming**. In a study you may recall from the module on memory, Bargh, Chen, and Burrows (1996) argued that a great deal of goal-directed behavior is influenced by unconscious priming. Specifically, they showed that activating social concepts such as personality traits (e.g., "politeness") and stereotypes (e.g., "Old people are slow.") can influence people's goal-directed behavior. In one study, students unscrambled a list of sentences. In one condition of one pair of these experiments (2a and 2b), most of the sentences referred to old people (e.g., "He collected social security." "She forgot her reading glasses."). In the other condition, none of the sentences made any mention of old people. After thinking they'd been dismissed from the experiment, participants headed for the elevator. Unbeknown to participants, a research assistant kept blind to conditions unobtrusively timed exactly how long it took participants to walk to the elevator. Averaging across two studies, it took participants about 16% longer than usual to walk to the elevator when they had recently been thinking about old people. This classic study was first met by excitement, then by skepticism, and finally by a careful meta-analysis (an analysis that combines the findings of multiple studies) that showed that the effect is modest but very real. It is important to note that in studies of behavioral priming, participants are almost never aware of the influence of primes on their behavior.

There are still plenty of critics of the idea that unconscious processes drive a lot of human behavior. A common criticism is that the unconscious preferences documented in the lab are likely to disappear when people are making important decisions. Liking a pair of panty hose more than usual – and not knowing why – is not the same as marrying someone or choosing a career (and not knowing why). Do unconscious forces influence major life decisions? Or are they interesting but wimpy effects that disappear outside the lab? The research that your first author and his students have conducted over nearly two decades suggests that unconscious influences are alive and well in the real world. This research has examined **implicit egotism**, which is an unconscious preference for people, places and things that resemble the self (Pelham & Carvallo, 2015; Pelham, Mirenberg, & Jones, 2002). Because most people have positive unconscious associations about the self (e.g., one's name, one's birthday number) people should gravitate toward things that resemble the self (usually without realizing why). For example, Pelham et al. (2002) found that people gravitate toward states and cities whose names resemble their own first or last names (e.g., Cal moves to California, Virginia to Virginia). Likewise, Jones and colleagues (2004) showed that people are much more likely than one would expect by chance to marry others whose surnames match or resemble their own. Moving to the lab, Jones et al. (2004) showed that people liked an attractive woman more than usual when her jersey number had been repeatedly paired (without their awareness) with their own full names.

Some of the early field studies of implicit egotism are open to the criticism that people gravitate not toward people who resemble the self but toward members of their own ethnic groups. Does Smith marry Smith because of implicit egotism or because almost everyone named Smith is White (and as we well know, people tend to marry within their own ethnic groups). To address this critique, Pelham and Carvallo (2015) looked at both birthday-number matching and birth-month matching in two large sets of state-wide marriage records. Although African-Americans are named Johnson more often than White Americans are, it is unlikely that more African-Americans than White Americans are born in September. Likewise, it is unlikely that more African Americans are born on the 24th of the month rather than the 11th. So the ethnic confounds that apply to at least some last names should not apply to birthday months or birthday numbers. But most people like their birthday numbers just as much as they like their names (Kitayama & Karasawa, 1997). Pelham and Carvallo (2015) documented reliable birthday number – and birth month – matching effects in all the marriage records they could locate that allowed them to assess implicit egotism in marriage. Figure 17.5 shows the findings for birthday number matching in a large set of Ohio marriage records.

There was a modest but reliable 6.5% bias for people to marry others who shared their birthday numbers. Further, this 6.5% bias became a nearly 40% bias in the subset of people who liked their birthday numbers enough to have gotten married on them. This is no small bias. The same patterns shown in Figure 17.5 held for month rather than day of birth (e.g., people born in October "over-married" other people born in October). This includes the fact that month-matching effects in marriage were stronger than usual for people who got married in their birth months. All these effects replicated in a very large set of Minnesota marriage records.

Implicit egotism appears to be robust outside the lab. Pelham and Carvallo also provided data on implicit egotism and career choice. They were able to do so because, in April, 2013, the 1940 U.S. Census data were released to the public. Before analyzing these records, Pelham and Carvallo (2015) identified all 11 of the common male career names (e.g., baker, carpenter) that doubled as exact surnames. This eliminated the need for judgment calls about sampling specific names or careers. Findings from this study appear in Figure 17.6. For each of these 11 stereotypically-male careers, men were at least modestly overrepresented in a career when the career name happened to match their surname. When we used population base-rates rather than using this specific set of careers as the comparison standard, these effects of surname on career choice only grew larger. In other words, these effects held up no matter how we coded and compared our data.

Using these same census data, Pelham and Carvallo showed that these career-surname matches did not occur because of any obvious ethnic or educational confounds. For example, these career-name matching effects held up focusing only on Black men (or only on White men) who all had exactly the same levels of education. Finally, lab studies of implicit egotism show that implicit egotism is, in fact, implicit (e.g., see Jones et al., 2004). Virtually none of the participants in any lab experiments on implicit egotism were able to report the true reasons for their preferences for stimuli that resembled the self.

Research on many other unconscious biases and preferences strongly suggests that unconscious forces influence a great number of daily judgments and decisions. Let's consider a few examples. In their research on **transference**, Andersen and Berk (1998) have shown that we often like strangers who resemble other people in our lives that we

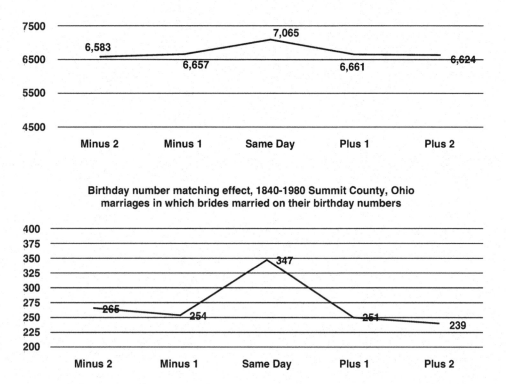

Figure 17.5 Implicit Egotism in Marriage Decisions. People with the same birthday number are disproportionately likely to marry. This effect was much stronger than usual for brides and grooms who got married on their birthday numbers (suggesting that they really liked them).

already like. It's called transference, by the way, because we unconsciously transfer the feelings we have about others we have long known to strangers who vaguely remind us of those we have long known. Along similar lines, research on the **chameleon effect** shows that when a person subtly mimics our own nonverbal behavior – in ways that we do not consciously recognize – we come to like such "chameleons" more than we otherwise would (e.g., see Chartrand & Bargh, 1999). The *mere exposure* effect you learned about earlier in this text – that is, the preference we have for things to which we have frequently been exposed – usually seems to fly under the radar of the conscious mind.

Some of the most compelling examples of the power of the unconscious also suggest that the conscious brain is highly adept at generating false, after-the-fact explanations for things that are determined unconsciously. The conscious mind may be better at making stuff up than at calling stuff forth. You may recall research cited in Module 6 that focused on "split brain" patients. Recall that in most people, the *corpus callosum* allows continuous communication between the right and left hemispheres of the brain. But a few decades ago, surgeons learned that they could sometimes stop life-threatening seizures in epileptic patients by

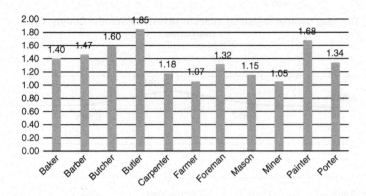

Figure 17.6 Implicit egotism and career choice. Ratio of Observed to Expected Surname-Occupation Matches for Men with Common Surnames that Also Serve as Male Occupation Names. Source: 1940 U.S. Census. Values greater than 1.0 indicate a tendency to work in careers that match one's last name. The score of 1.34 for "Porter" means that people with the last name Porter were 34% more likely to work as porters than we would expect based on chance name-career pairing.

severing the corpus callosum. Doing so created "**split-brain**" **patients** who possess two independently operating brains, each of which typically directs different cognitive functions. As you may recall, in most right-handed people (split-brain patients included), speech production resides in the left hemisphere. In experiments with split-brain patients, one can send a pictorial signal directly to the *nonverbal* right hemisphere to get patients to engage in a behavior (e.g., picking up an object or pointing to an image). When asked *why* they engaged in the pictorially-dictated behavior, such patients unknowingly generated false, after-the-fact justifications (Volz & Gazzaniga, 2017).

Critics of these studies argue that split brains patients are highly unusual people. Perhaps their behavior reveals no information about normal people. We beg to differ. Plenty of errors of awareness exist even for people with wholly intact brains. In a study of the timing of motor control, Libet (1985) asked participants to move their fingers at will. While participants were doing this, Libet measured the brain activity as well as the muscle activity that produced the finger movements. Further, Libet used an ingenious "clock" (a dot of light that moved at a quick and steady pace around a circle) to allow people to report exactly when they decided to move their fingers. Not surprisingly, brain activity always preceded muscle activation – and thus finger movement. A little more than half a second after the initiation of brain activity, people first moved their muscles. No one would expect otherwise. However, Libet also found that people's self-reports of the exact moment they decided to move their fingers took place only about 200 milliseconds (1/5 sec) before they moved their fingers. This is about 300 milliseconds *after* their brains had already begun the neural activity responsible for producing finger movements! People are very poor observers of many aspects of their inner mental states. And as we hope you now know, Libet's findings are just one of dozens of findings in social and cognitive psychology that suggest that the unconscious mind works in ways of which we are not always aware – including exerting invisible influences on some very important decisions.

Altered States of Consciousness: Sleep and Drugs

In people, consciousness takes many forms. As you may recall, for example, we engage in *meta-cognition*. This is thinking about thinking. We also use written language to help us manage our conscious thoughts. Try to solve a complex geometry problem in your head. But there's more to consciousness than meta-cognition or geometry. In fact, we frequently drift in and out of *altered* states of consciousness such as sleep and dreaming. And *unlike* almost any other animal on Earth, we consume **psychoactive substances**. These are substances – such as alcohol and drugs – that change our states of consciousness. Alcohol relaxes people. But if you consume too much of it, you cannot drive safely. Consume even more, and you'll go to sleep and never wake up. Let's take a brief look at altered states of consciousness.

Let's begin with sleep. It's that stuff that you probably don't get enough of. In fact, having good **sleep hygiene** – getting adequate amounts of sleep on a regular basis – is essential to everything from learning to maintaining a healthy immune system. The average 18-year-old needs 8 to ten solid hours of sleep per night. If you don't regularly get that much – ideally at the same time every night – it will be hard for you to think clearly (Dinges, et al., 1997; Jewett, Dijk, Kronauer & Dinges, 1999). Every spring, Americans lose about an hour of sleep on the Sunday (at 2 a.m.) when daylight savings time begins. The result is an increase in major traffic accidents on the Monday that follows the change to Daylight Savings Time (Coren, 1996). And the more sleep you lose, the worse things get. Just missing an hour or two of sleep for a few days reduces people's ability to think deeply and clearly. Modestly sleep deprived people also become susceptible to nodding off into microsleep – which is a short period of sleep that happens without the person wanting it to happen. We've all seen students microsleep in microeconomics class – especially during parts of the term when most students are more sleep-deprived than usual. In extreme cases of sleep deprivation, people may even begin to hallucinate and fall apart psychologically. In the 1960s, New Yorker Peter Tripp tried to go 200-hours (more than eight days) without sleeping. After about four days of sleep deprivation, Tripp started having intense hallucinations. He began seeing and hearing things that did not exist. Shoes grew cobwebs, clocks grew human faces, clothing turned into worms, or flames. After about 170 hours of wakefulness, Tripp was barely able to maintain contact with reality. Eventually, Tripp had to be restrained by the scientists who were monitoring his personal experiment (Suter & Lindgren, 1989).

In short, we need sleep – and there is no easy way around this. In human evolutionary history (when there were no flashlights or street lights) sleep kept us from stumbling around in the dark and breaking a knee cap. But sleep also serves psychological purposes, helping us do things like consolidate learning. This is one reason why infants and toddlers need a lot more sleep than adults. They have a *lot* to learn. Even if you have good sleep hygiene, you've almost certainly experienced some odd things when sleeping. One of the weirdest is dreaming. **Dreaming** is having a story-like experience that usually feels real to you while you are otherwise unconscious (i.e., asleep). If, in your waking life, you talked to cartoon characters, flew, or thought you were being chased by a Beyoncé zombie, you'd be referred to a psychotherapist. But when you're dreaming, nothing is off limits. During dreams, your coauthors have flown helicopters, arm-wrestled superheroes (OK, the Hulk won, but it was close), and talked to deceased loved ones. Each of us has also experienced that unusual kind of dreaming known as **lucid dreaming** – which is dreaming while knowing you're dreaming. In fact, almost everyone has had at least one lucid dream in his or her life, and about a quarter of people say they engage in lucid dreaming on a regular basis (Bourke & Shaw 2014). The nice thing about lucid dreaming is that it can allow you to get some control over a bad dream. Your first author has escaped the clutches of many evil doers via lucid dreaming. Once, your second author even escaped the clutches of your first author via lucid dreaming.

We're also happy to say that neither of us is a regular sleepwalker. In fact, **sleep walking** – walking around or doing other mundane activities while asleep – is sort of the opposite of lucid dreaming. It is as if the person has become so deeply embedded in a dream that he or she begins to act it out. By the way, this is typically done with eyes wide open – which is not the way you see it in Phineas and Ferb cartoons. As long as we're on this topic, allow us to say that the best thing you can do if you know someone is sleepwalking is to wake the person up – as gently as possible (Schacter et al., 2011). A small minority of people become aggressive after being awakened from a sleepwalking event, but there are no other known dangers to waking a sleepwalker. And there are *many* dangers to allowing the person to move about the house or yard while asleep. Some adult sleep walkers have even driven cars while sleepwalking – probably to get away from a Beyoncé zombie.

Figure 17.7 Contrary to what you've seen in hundreds of cartoons, sleepwalkers do *not* usually walk with their eyes closed – or their arms stretched out. But they *can* easily hurt themselves. So go ahead and wake them up.

Drugs and Altered States of Consciousness

Like people, some animals sleepwalk. Remember the YouTube video of the sleep walking dog who ran into a wall? But almost no animals use psychoactive drugs. This is a people thing. All over the Earth, people use a lot of psychoactive chemicals – from caffeine and nicotine to mushrooms, and heroin. We won't review the long list of popular psychoactive drugs that people use. But we can say that there are at least two reasons why people use drugs. First, many psychoactive drugs make people feel good. They alter our states of consciousness in pleasant or interesting ways. At least some people smoke pot and drink cabernet for the same reason people eat ice cream. The difference is that ice cream only tastes good while you are eating it. Some drugs make people feel good for hours. The problem of course, is that using drugs can become unhealthy or addictive. But in addition to this obvious reason why people use drugs that change their states of consciousness, it looks like plenty of people use drugs to self-medicate. **Self-medication** refers to using nonprescribed drugs to reduce unpleasant states – from physical and psychological pain to the risk of disease or infection. Anthropologists have shown, for example, that across the globe, people who smoke tobacco or cannabis seem to reduce their risk of infection from worms (Roulette, Kazanji, Breurec, & Hagen, 2015). Connecting this work to consciousness in an indirect way, anthropologists who look at drug use as a form of self-medication argue that people who naturally self-medicate are *not* usually consciously aware that they are self-medicating. They just drift toward behaviors that reduce short-term suffering. Remember operant conditioning?

Questions for Group Discussion

1. Public opinion polls show that more Americans than ever before believe that marijuana should be legalized. In 1969, a Gallup poll revealed that only 12% of Americans said they believed "marijuana should be made legal." By late 2018, that figure had increased to an all-time high of 66% (McCarthy, 2018). In your view, what cultural, legal, or religious factors have led to this dramatic change in public opinion about this psychoactive drug? If the recreational use of marijuana becomes legal all over the U.S. – as it already has in Canada – does this mean people who are currently serving long prison terms for selling or possessing marijuana should be released? Why or why not?
2. Do you believe you're an exception to the rule that most adults need at least eight or nine hours of sleep per night? If you get less sleep than this, and you think you can get by just fine on five or six hours of sleep per night, there is an easy way to see if you're correct. What happens to you when you sit through a long, dry lecture at 2 p.m. – or try to take a nine-hour car drive *without* using any caffeine to stay awake artificially? If the answer is that you tend to nod off, you are sleep deprived. People who are getting plenty of sleep do not fall asleep when faced with a boring lecture or a long drive. Instead, they feel awake but – you guessed it – bored. So, do you *still* think it's OK to live your life on five or six hours of sleep per night?
3. Bourke's (2014) research on lucid dreaming shows that, on average, lucid dreamers are more creative and have more control over their own minds when *awake*. For example, on average, frequent lucid dreamers make fewer errors on the Stroop interference task (the whacky color naming task) than do less frequent lucid dreamers. Does this mean that teaching yourself to become a lucid dreamer would help you become more creative or gain better control your own thoughts in daily life? Why or why not? Be sure to give some thought to the "third variable problem" as you consider your answer to this question.
4. As you now know, consciousness varies on a continuum. A person may be fully awake and highly self-aware or deeply asleep and essentially "dead to the world." But a lack of consciousness can go even further than deep sleep. Sometimes a person who is very ill can go into a life-threatening coma. Fischer and colleagues (2008) studied 50 severely comatose patients by hooking them up to a machine that could read their brain waves. Fischer and colleagues already knew that in healthy, alert people, the brain responds to surprises with a so-called "novelty response." Thus, hearing "sandwich, lunch, drink,

dinosaur" should lead to a measurable novelty response – at precisely the time when the oddball word "dinosaur" is played. In contrast, hearing "sandwich, lunch, drink, meal" should *not* lead to a novelty response. Fischer et al. (2008) found that the sound of people's own names (in the oddball spot) yielded more robust novelty responses than comparable but self-unrelated words (also in the oddball spot). So "sandwich, lunch, drink, Jason" leads to an even bigger surprise response in healthy, conscious people (well, people named Jason) than does the "dinosaur" or "Kenneth" version of the same activity. Fischer and colleagues found that, in these comatose patients, the best predictor of whether the patients ever awoke from their comas (the best predictor of whether they were "brain dead") was whether the patients showed a robust novelty response when their own first name was the oddball term in a list. What does this finding tell us about the power of the unconscious to grab our attention? In what way is this demonstration like the "cocktail party" phenomenon? What does it tell us about how understanding consciousness can help families make painful life-or-death medical decisions?

Multiple Choice Questions for Module 17

1. In the context of the Nisbett and Wilson (1977) panty hose study, what does "telling more than we can know" mean?

   A) we exaggerate how good a product is if we like it
   B) we often have little or no idea why we like something
   C) we think we know how others think and feel but base this solely on how we think and feel

2. In what way does research on split brain patients support the idea of the cognitive unconscious?

   A) it shows that unconscious processing is controlled mainly by the left brain
   B) it shows that Freud's id, ego, and super-ego have a clear basis in brain physiology
   C) it shows that people often generate false explanations for things when they don't know why they did them

3. Sometimes drivers who get into accidents report that "the other car just appeared out of nowhere." In some of these cases, traffic patterns shifted because of a new traffic light or stop sign, but drivers familiar with a specific path failed to notice this. Such drivers may have had accidents because they fell prey to what phenomenon?

   A) sensory overload
   B) controlled disruption
   C) change blindness

4. Why is the cocktail party effect named so?

   A) because it explains why people might hear their names – but little else – during a noisy party
   B) because it involves people forgetting the names of people they just met minutes ago
   C) because it shows that the mental overload of a busy, noisy environment creates change blindness

5. What is a dichotic listening task?

   A) a task in which people use headphones to focus on one message while ignoring another
   B) a task in which people use echoic memory to remember how many long and short clicks are in a recording
   C) a task that requires bilingual people to listen to a message and quickly translate it into a second language

6. Is it possible that part of the reason for implicit egotism is the mere exposure effect?

   A) yes, because both effects make the prediction that people like their names and birthday numbers
   B) no, because implicit egotism is an unconscious bias whereas the mere exposure effect is a conscious bias
   C) yes, because both processes seem to be firmly rooted in classical conditioning

7. Right before the start of a 100m race, Justin asks Bo, his competitor, how his grandparents are doing. While Bo answers the question in great detail, Justin smiles and blocks him out – while focusing on the typical properties of Olympic sprinters. What psychological phenomenon is Justin trying to use to gain an advantage over Bo?

   A) change blindness
   B) behavioral priming
   C) mere exposure

8. What happens when a person has been forbidden from thinking about something for a while?

   A) they think about it a lot more than usual once told that they're allowed to do so
   B) they find indirect ways to think about it without thinking about it consciously
   C) they get good at blocking it out – and are able to suppress it well in the future

9. Josey is a four-year-old who knows her colors very well, but she can barely read at all (because she's four). Is Josey likely to show much evidence of interference in a typical Stroop task?

   A) no; because the Stroop effect happens only when reading is automatic
   B) yes; the Stroop effect is automatic for anyone who knows his or her colors
   C) maybe; the effect depends a lot on one's motivation to please the experimenter

10. What do transference, implicit egotism, and the chameleon effect have in common?

    A) they all represent failures of introspection that have been observed both in the lab and in daily life
    B) they all require people to focus intently on what they are doing, which is very difficult
    C) they all operate unconsciously – so they're part of the cognitive unconscious

Answer Key: 1B, 2C, 3C, 4A, 5A, 6A, 7B, 8A, 9A, 10C

References

Andersen, S. M., & Berk, M. S. (1998). The social-cognitive model of transference: Experiencing past relationships in the present. *Current Directions in Psychological Science, 7*(4), 109–115.

Banaji, M. R., & Hardin, C. D. (1996). Automatic stereotyping. *Psychological Science, 7*, 136–141.

Bargh, J. A., Chen, M., & Burrows, L. (1996). Automaticity of social behavior: Direct effects of trait construct and stereotype activation on action. *Journal of Personality and Social Psychology, 71*, 230–244.

Bourke, P., & Shaw, H. (2014). Spontaneous lucid dreaming frequency and waking insight. *Dreaming, 24*(2), 152–159. doi:10.1037/a0036908

Chartrand, T. L., & Bargh, J. A. (1999). The chameleon effect: The perception–behavior link and social interaction. *Journal of Personality and Social Psychology, 76*(6), 893–910.

Cherry, E.C. (1953). Some experiments on the recognition of speech, with one and with two ears. *Journal of the Acoustical Society of America, 25*(5), 975–979.

Coren, S. (1996). *Sleep thieves: An eye-opening exploration into the science and mysteries of sleep.* New York: Free Press.

Dinges, D. F., Pack, F., Williams, K., Gillen, K. A., Powell, J. W., Ott, G. E., ... Pack, A. I. (1997). Cumulative sleepiness, mood disturbance and psychomotor vigilance performance decrements during a week of sleep restricted to 4-5 hours per night. *Sleep: Journal of Sleep Research & Sleep Medicine, 20*, 267–277.

Fischer, C., Dailler, F., & Morlet, D. (2008). Novelty P3 elicited by the subject's own name in comatose patients. *Clinical Neurophysiology, 119*, 2224–2230.

Gilbert, D. T. (1989). Thinking lightly about others: Automatic components of the social inference process. In J. S. Uleman & J. A. Bargh (Eds.), *Unintended thought* (pp. 189–211). New York: Guilford Press.

Jewett, M. E., Dijk, D.-J., Kronauer, R. E., & Dinges, D. F. (1999). Dose-response relationship between sleep duration and human psychomotor vigilance and subjective alertness. *Sleep: Journal of Sleep Research & Sleep Medicine, 22*(2), 171–179.

Johansson, P., Hall, L., Sikström, S., Tärning, B., & Lind, A. (2006). How something can be said about telling more than we can know: On choice blindness and introspection. *Consciousness and Cognition: An International Journal, 15*(4), 673–692.

Jones, J. K., Pelham, B. W., Carvallo, M. C., & Mirenberg, M. C. (2004). How do I love thee? Let me count the Js: Implicit egotism and interpersonal attraction. *Journal of Personality and Social Psychology, 87*, 665–683.

Kahneman, D. (2011). *Thinking, fast and slow.* New York, NY: Farrar, Straus, & Giroux.

Kihlstrom, J. F. (1987, Sep. 18). The cognitive unconscious. *Science, 237*(4821), 1445–1452.

Kitayama, S., & Karasawa, M. (1997). Implicit self-esteem in Japan: Name letters and birthday numbers. *Personality and Social Psychology Bulletin, 23*(7), 736–742.

Libet, B. (1985). Unconscious cerebral initiative and the role of conscious will in voluntary action. *Behavior and Brain Sciences, 8*, 529–566.

McCarthy, J. (2018). *Two in three Americans now support legalizing Marijuana.* Retrieved June 28, 2019 from Gallup.com. https://news.gallup.com/poll/243908/two-three-americans-support-legalizing-marijuana.aspx

Millar, M. G., & Tesser, A. (1986). Effects of affective and cognitive focus on the attitude-behavior relationship. *Journal of Personality and Social Psychology, 51*, 270–276.

Nisbett, R. E., & Wilson, T. D. (1977). Telling more than we can know: Verbal reports on mental processes. *Psychological Review, 84*, 231–259.

Pelham, B. W., & Carvallo, M. R. (2015). When tex and tess carpenter build houses in Texas: Moderators of implicit egotism. *Self and Identity, 14*, 692–723.

Pelham, B. W., Mirenberg, M. C., & Jones, J. K. (2002). Why Susie sells seashells by the seashore: Implicit egotism and major life decisions. *Journal of Personality and Social Psychology, 82*, 469–487.

Roulette, C. J., Kazanji, M., Breurec, S., & Hagen, E. H. (2015). High prevalence of cannabis use among Aka foragers of the Congo Basin and its possible relationship to helminthiasis. *American Journal of Human Biology.* May. doi: 10.1002/ajhb.22740.

Sabini, J., & Silver, M. (1981). Introspection and causal accounts. *Journal of Personality and Social Psychology, 40*(1), 171–179.

Schacter, D.L., Gilbert, D.T., & Wegner, D. M. (2011). *Psychology* (2nd Edition). New York: Worth.

Shiffrin, R. M., & Schneider, W. (1977). Controlled and automatic human information processing: II. Perceptual learning, automatic attending, and general theory. *Psychological Review, 84,* 127–190.

Simons, D. J., & Levin, D. T. (1997). Change blindness. *Trends in Cognitive Sciences, 1*(7), 261–267.

Stroop, J. R. (1935). Studies of interference in serial verbal reactions. *Journal of Experimental Psychology, 18,* 643–662.

Suter, W. N., & Lindgren, H. C. (1989). *Experimentation in Psychology: A guided tour.* Boston: Allyn & Bacon.

Volz, L.J., & Gazzaniga, M.S. (2017). Interaction in isolation: 50 years of insights from split-brain research. *Brain, 140* (7), 2051–2060.

Wegner, D. M., Schneider, D. J., Carter, S. R., III, & White, T. L. (1987). Paradoxical effects of thought suppression. *Journal of Personality and Social Psychology, 53,* 5–13.

Zajonc, R. B. (2001). Mere exposure: A gateway to the subliminal. *Current Directions in Psychological Science, 10,* 224–228.

Module 18
Exploring the "Snap" in Snap Judgment
Judgment and Decision Making

"We hold these truths to be self-evident ..." This telling phrase begins the second paragraph of the U.S. Declaration of Independence. This opener is followed by a long list of reasons why a group of colonists feel compelled to dissolve their union with the British government. Like philosophers and spiritual leaders, political leaders have long put great faith in human reasoning. This remains true today. After all it was a person – not an aardvark – who painted the Sistine Chapel. We're the species that created written language, went to the moon, and invented smart phones. We all know that if Barry is taller than Jason, and Jason is taller than Stacy, Barry is taller than Stacy. That's called transitive inferences. Try explaining it to an aardvark. Likewise, your parents would be quick to tell you that one reason you should finish college is to become a thoughtful and critical thinker. But how thoughtful is the typical human being? Can we always trust our own judgment?

In 1968, Peter Wason put human reasoning to a simple test. Wason (1968) showed college students four cards, asking them to "reason about a rule." **Wason's card task** appears in Figure 18.1. Why not test the rule yourself? All four cards in Figure 18.1 have a number on one side and a letter on the other. That's a given. The rule to be tested is this: "*If a card has a vowel on one side, then it must have an even number on the other side.*" You'd like to know for sure if this rule is true or false in these four cards. Let me also tell you that you need to turn over exactly two of the cards to test the hypothesis properly. Which two cards would you flip over?

Most people say they'd turn over cards A and 4. That was the response of both of your authors when we first saw the problem. But we were wrong. We *should* have turned over the A and the 7. Why ignore the 4? The rule didn't say consonants can't have an even number. It said that vowels *must* have one. To test the rule, one must turn over the A and the 7. If the 7 has a vowel on the other side, then the rule is false. But most judges make the same mistake we made. They seek evidence that would *support* the hypothesis – and neglect evidence that would disprove it. This is known as the **positive test bias**, and it's just one of a large family of hypothesis-confirming biases (Klayman & Ha, 1987). For example, stereotypes and self-fulfilling prophecies (e.g., losing because you think you are jinxed) are also examples of confirming what you suspected rather than trying to prove it wrong.

If we're good at reasoning, we shouldn't fail so badly on the Wason card task. On the other hand, Atran (2001) argues that the Wason task may be unfair (see also Sugiyama, Tooby, & Cosmides, 2002). In case that's true, let's try another reasoning task, one that has only one interpretation, and one for which we'll accept any decent approximation of the right answer. Let's move on from cards you've never seen before to a familiar sheet of paper and look at numerical estimation.

Figure 18.1 Each card has a letter on one side and a number on the other. Here's a rule: "If a card has a vowel on one side, then it must have an even number on the other side." Which two cards should you turn over to test the rule?

Anchoring and the Paper-Folding Problem

Imagine that you folded an ordinary sheet of copy paper in half 100 times, doubling its thickness over and over. This is not physically possible, by the way, but please use your imagination. Assume that the sheet of paper was 0.1 mm thick. After the first fold, it'd be 0.2 mm thick. After the second fold, it'd be 0.4 mm. After the third fold, it'd be 0.8 mm. How thick would it be after the 100th fold? Please *don't* read on until you've written down a specific thickness estimate.

We have some bad news. Your guess is too low. Please make your guess *much* larger. Are you done? Let's see. Nope, it's *still* too low. In fact, it's still *much* too low. Try making a guess that is much, much larger than your second. Hmmm. We're sorry to say that your third guess is still much too low. You must be wondering how we can possibly know that. Here's how. The correct answer to this question is 850 trillion astronomical units. That's 2^{100} (2 to the 100th power) x 0.1 mm. This turns out to be

1,267,650,600,228,229,401,496,703,205,376 x 0.1 mm.

In scientific notation, it's 1.2677×10^{29} mm or 1.2677×10^{23} km. That's nearly 850 trillion times the distance between the Earth and the sun. It's almost as wide as the known universe. Now that's *thick*! We felt very thick ourselves the first time we learned this. Plous (1993) created the paper-folding problem to illustrate the tendency for judges to stick too close to an initial starting point (an "anchor") when revising a judgment. This is known as **anchoring and adjustment**, with the important warning that after we anchor at a certain value, our adjustment is often insufficient. Clearly, we are not human calculators; we don't always do the math. Instead we rely on our intuitions (what would a piece of paper look like when folded over on itself 100 times) to get us close to the correct answer. Yet, our best guesses can sometimes be way off-base. In fact, sometimes they are way off-galaxy.

Judgmental Heuristics: Flying on Autopilot

The literature in human reasoning, judgment, and decision-making is full of examples like these. Thus, Daniel Kahneman (2011) argues that we typically get through life not by making careful calculations but by using **judgmental heuristics** – shortcuts or rules of thumb for making rapid judgments – including estimating the frequency, magnitude, or likelihood of events. One such heuristic is the **representativeness heuristic** (Kahneman & Tversky, 1972). We often judge the likelihood of events based on how much they *resemble* (represent) another event. Consider Tversky and Kahneman's (1974, p. 1125) hospital problem:

A certain town is served by two hospitals. In the larger hospital, about 45 babies are born each day, and in the smaller hospital, about 15 babies are born each day. As you know, about 50% of all babies are boys. However, the exact percentage varies from day to day. Sometimes it may be higher than 50%, sometimes lower.

For a period of one year, each hospital recorded the number of days on which more than 60% of the babies born were boys. Which hospital do you think recorded more such days?

(Circle one letter)

a.   the larger hospital
b.   the smaller hospital
c.   about the same (that is, within 5% of each other)

If you're like most other people, you chose answer C. Yet, consider this: results that vary from a population (60% boys instead of 50% boys) are much more likely in a small sample than in a big sample. Instead of applying this statistical rule, most people use the representativeness heuristic. They reason that 60% of 15 is a lot like 60% of 45. That is, the two hospitals seem to be similar – to *represent* one another. If you don't see why the unusual result (60% or more male births) is more likely in the smaller hospital, consider some coin flips. Is it easier to flip 100% heads when flipping two coins (2/2), or 45 coins (45/45)? With this in mind, Pelham and Neter (1995) changed the hospital problem to be more extreme (making the math a lot easier) to see if people would answer the problem correctly. They asked people to consider the number of days in a year in which not 60% but *all* (100%) of the babies born would be boys. Further, they made the small hospital tiny. It had only 2 (not 15) births per day. We hope you can see that in the tiny hospital, 100% of the babies (both of them) would be boys 25% of the time ($0.5 \times 0.5 = 0.25$). In the big hospital, 100% of the babies (45/45) would be boys about 0 times per millennium. So, if you make the math very easy and set up a problem in a highly user-friendly way, people can sometimes steer clear of heuristics. But real life is not always so user-friendly.

Speaking of how life can be unfriendly, let's consider how the representativeness heuristic might affect your judgment and behavior in a real-life setting. Imagine you live in a big city and that you are walking back to your apartment late at night. You see another person coming toward you on the sidewalk. As you watch the person approach, you consider moving to the other side of the street – because you're concerned about violent crime in your neighborhood. What you decide to do here (whether you move to the other side of the street) will depend greatly on whether the person coming toward you looks like your stereotypical image of a mugger. If the approaching person is, for you, highly *representative* of a mugger, you will very likely walk to the other side of the street – despite the fact that the actual odds that this person intends to harm you is very low.

Consider another judgmental heuristic. If you ask people how frequently something happens, they will often consider how easily that thing comes to mind. Using that shortcut means using the **availability heuristic**. As a result of using this heuristic, many people think U.S. murder rates are higher than U.S. suicide rates. They're not. Suicides slightly outnumber homicides. But murders are more *memorable* than suicides because they get more media attention and are more frequently the subject of crime shows. If we can *remember* more murders, surely there must *be* more of them. In the rush of daily life, we use shortcuts (like considering how easily something comes to mind) rather than researching the answer to the question or consulting a public health expert. The availability heuristic is also a big reason why most Americans overestimate their chances of dying in a plane crash or being attacked by a shark. Such dramatic events get lots of media attention, and they are highly memorable. But they are very rare. Our reliance on the availability heuristic to estimate frequency or probability means that we overestimate the risk of highly memorable events.

Research on judgmental heuristics has its fair share of critics. For example, Gigerenzer (2008) argues that we can reduce or erase many judgmental biases if we merely ask people about concrete *frequencies* rather than abstract probabilities. Gigerenzer argues that we deal better with frequencies than with probabilities because we have millions of years of evolutionary history dealing with counting – but very little evolutionarily history dealing with probabilities. The evolutionary psychologist in us agrees. But in our view, this doesn't render research on judgmental heuristics misleading. Not every real-world problem naturally presents itself in terms of counting frequencies. We suppose researchers could make sure to present problems in the language of frequencies. But in our view, this just means that if you set up questions in a very user-friendly way, people become pretty good judges. In our view, this implicitly concedes that human beings are not very good at abstract thinking. A general-purpose reasoning machine would deal with probabilities just as comfortably as with frequencies. But that's not how our brains work.

Do Basic Counting Skills Always Help Us Avoid Bias?

If we're predisposed to prefer frequency information, this, too, can get us into trouble. As Pelham, Sumarta, and Myaskovsky (1994) argued, people often treat frequency as if it were a perfect indicator of amount or magnitude. Pelham and colleagues found that when the same stimulus is divided into multiple pieces, people tend to overestimate its total magnitude. This tendency to rely too much on counting is called the **numerosity heuristic**. Denes-Raj and Epstein (1994) independently documented a very similar bias.

Figure 18.2 On the left (to the lower right of the U.S. penny) is a lethal dose of the drug fentanyl. On the right is a crude depiction of a murder scene. Suicides, especially quiet ones, get little media attention. Murders get a *lot*. Because of the availability heuristic, most people overestimate murder rates relative to suicide rates. Many public overreactions to small but memorable risks are grounded in the availability heuristic.

This is the preference for gambles with a greater number of winning possibilities – even when such gambles offer no true advantage. In a study we'll refer to as the **jelly bean lottery**, participants needed to select a red jelly bean at random to win a lottery. Participants got to choose between two lotteries. In the first lottery, there was one red (winning) jelly bean and nine white (losing) jelly beans. In the second lottery, there were ten red (winning) jelly beans but 90 white (losing) ones. The odds were identical in the two lotteries, and everyone knew this. But most people preferred having "ten chances to win." This is why Kellogg's cereal company brags that their Raisin Bran contains not one but "two scoops of raisins," hoping we'll forget that a scoop, like a bag, or a hammer, is a tool rather than a unit of measurement.

If you've ever seen the classic mockumentary film *This is Spinal Tap*, you may recall Nigel, the lovable but dimwitted guitarist of the heavy metal band that was the subject of the film. Nigel, was obsessed with cranking up the band's music as loudly as possible to take things "to the next level" during concerts. In one interview, the audience learns that Nigel's prized possession is an old-school analogue amplifier (the kind with volume knobs you physically turn). However, unlike the other amplifiers, this "very special" amplifier had knobs that could be cranked up not to ten, but to *11*. When the interviewer skeptically asks Nigel if this amplifier is really any *louder* than the others, Nigel confidently replies: "Well, it's *one* louder now, isn't it?" Nigel is not alone in his thinking. People who claim that Michael Phelps is the "greatest Olympian of all-time" are surely falling prey to the numerosity heuristic – because they are not adjusting for the fact that swimming has five or six races for every race that exists in track and field. (see Pelham, 2019, for more details). Our evolved tendency to count is *not* a judgmental panacea (it does not fix or cure all judgmental biases).

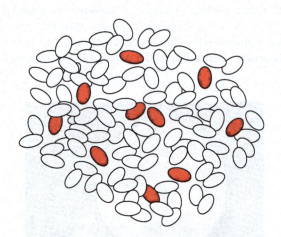

Lottery 1:1 red jelly bean, 9 white
(10% chance of winning)

Lottery 2:10 red jelly beans, 90 white
(10% chance of winning)

Figure 18.3 The jelly bean lottery. Most people preferred a lottery in which they had ten chances in 100 to win rather than one chance in ten to win. In fact, even when players saw the odds printed out and knew that one or two of the red jelly beans in the 100-bean lottery would be removed, they still preferred "more chances to win." Image by Brett Pelham. Study by Denes-Raj and Epstein (1994).

Allow us to note another way in which thinking in frequencies doesn't rescue us from error. Most athletic actions are easy to count. Birdies in golf, completed passes in football, and service faults in tennis are expressed as frequencies. Further, when sports statistics are stated as probabilities, they're usually very easy to understand. When we last checked, Steph Curry's career NBA three-point shooting percentage was 44%. His career free-throw shooting percentage was 90%. Further, when we last watched Curry play, he made five consecutive three-point shots in the second half of a game. No one has difficulty understanding this. Nonetheless, when Curry makes five straight three-point shots (which happens pretty often), sports fans have a ready explanation: Curry has the **hot hand**." Many basketball experts believe strongly in the hot hand. But your first author has won friendly bets against such experts much more often than he has lost them by betting *against* a player with the "hot hand" on a given shot. Gilovich and colleagues (1985) would be happy to know they've helped him win these bets (four in a row, as a matter of fact). This is because they've carefully documented that there is *no such thing* as the hot hand in basketball. If Curry just made a clutch three-point shot, he is no more likely to make his *next* three-point shot than he would be if he had just missed. The best predictor of whether Curry will make any specific three-point shot is his *season three-point shooting percentage*. Likewise, asking players if they feel they have the hot hand right before they take a shot does *not* predict how likely they are to make that shot.

Another way to put this is that a lot of apparent clumping in event sequences (e.g., winning four bets in a row) is randomness – not hotness. Gilovich et al. argue that people believe in the hot hand because they apply the representativeness heuristic to very short event sequences. The shooting sequences are *representative* of what good shooting looks like for them. Whatever explanation one prefers for the **hot hand bias**, it's a bias involving frequencies, not abstract probabilities. People who think Steph has the hot hand believe he is much more likely than usual to make his next shot. And they fully realize that Steph has made his last four shots in a row. Thinking in frequencies does nothing to protect human judges from the hot hand bias. Our obsession with frequencies may even predispose us toward it. But researchers who have carefully crunched the probabilities know that the hot hand is more myth than reality.

Bias Matters

Studies show that heuristics and judgmental biases are highly seductive. And errors fueled by heuristics can often be costly. Medical professionals sometimes overlook symptoms of heart attacks in women because heart attacks are perceived as more representative of men (i.e., more stereotypical of men) than of women. Things as subtle as the color of a team jersey can influence important social judgments – by means of judgment by representativeness. Frank and Gilovich (1988) found that U.S. professional football and hockey teams whose jerseys were black got called for more penalties than teams with any other color jersey. This is because referees associated the color black with aggression. That's judgment by representativeness. Finally, in keeping with the availability heuristic, Pelham (2018) found that across the 50 U.S. states, and across the globe, people living in colder places were more skeptical of the reality of global warming. There was also seasonal variation in this belief. People are more skeptical of global warming in winter than in summer. Heuristics can contribute to our destruction of the only planet we've ever lived on (more on that in Module 36).

Why are Judgmental Heuristics so Seductive?

So why not just think everything through – and avoid heuristics altogether? There are many answers to this question, but the answer we like most is that heuristics are seductive because they are highly overlearned and thus *automatic*. As you should recall from the module on consciousness, decades of research on human thinking suggests that human thinking comes in two basic forms (Shiffrin & Schneider, 1977). When you first begin thinking about something, thinking is usually a *controlled* process. But after a great deal of practice, controlled processes eventually become *automatic* processing. And as you know, one of the properties of automatic processes is that they operate unconsciously. Further, they are fast, sometimes mandatory, and highly efficient – meaning they don't tax your cognitive resources. If you guessed that judgmental heuristics are usually automatic, you guessed correctly. In keeping with this idea, Pelham and colleagues (1994) showed that people are more likely than usual to use judgmental heuristics when they must make a judgment quickly, and when they must perform a taxing secondary task while they are rendering a judgment. Bodenhausen (1990) also found that people are more likely than usual to use judgmental heuristics if you catch them at a time of day when they are tired (e.g., late in the afternoon if a judge is an "early bird," and early in the morning if a judge is a "night owl"). One of the big reasons why judgmental heuristics are so powerful and pervasive is that they are automatic. In the demands and distractions of daily life, automaticity makes using mental shortcuts such as availability or numerosity highly alluring.

Why Can Judgmental Heuristics be Dangerous?

One reason why heuristics and biases can be dangerous has to do with another basic property of human judgment. But before we explore this property of human judgment, please answer a trivia question. Because the question is pretty obscure, we'd like you to offer not a single answer but an answer *range* – similar to when weather forecasters say things like "Typical high temperatures in Miami in January range between 69 degrees and 78 degrees Fahrenheit." They mean that a January high temperature in Miami is rarely below 69 and rarely above 78. OK, so please guess *the average gestation period (length of pregnancy) of Asian elephants in days.* More specifically, provide a *low* and a *high* estimate so that you are *95% sure that your answer range includes the correct answer.* What's your low estimate? OK, now what's your high estimate? Please write both these values down.

Now, *we're* going to make a prediction. You were probably overconfident. By that, we mean that you gave a range that you were 95% sure included the correct answer. In reality, there is a much greater than 5% chance that your answer range *failed* to include the correct answer. The answer is 645 days. Apparently, it takes a very long time to make such a big baby. If you are already complaining that this is an unfairly tough question, don't be such as big baby yourself. Admit that you were wrong. But at least you're in good company. Most people are **overconfident**. Overconfidence is the tendency to be more confident than correct. One way to be overconfident is to provide overly narrow confidence intervals when asked to guess the answers to questions such as this one (Soll & Klayman, 2004). People are often overconfident. Simply ask most college students if they are above average or below average drivers, and 75–90% of them will usually report that they are above average. Statistically speaking, of course, only half of all people can truly be above average. In fact, most people think they're above average at a great number of things, from driving ability to being unlikely to get cancer (Weinstein, 1980). Blanton and colleagues (2001) showed that even after controlling for how correct we really are, we often overestimate our performance on more important tasks. While we're not claiming that we're overconfident *all* the time, we are frequently overconfident – even in some situations in which we *ought* to be very cautious. So, getting back to our question: Why is it that judgmental heuristics can be dangerous? It's because it's one thing to be wrong. It's another to be wrong and to be sure you are correct.

Are We Really so Incompetent?

Critics of research on error and bias in human judgment are quick to note that we are not grossly incompetent. Some of us invented writing. Two of us (Newton and Leibniz) invented calculus. This is a good point. In fact, some clinical exceptions notwithstanding, controlled processing typically becomes automatic processing (the kind of processing that causes us to use judgmental heuristics) only when a response is usually adaptive. It's an automatic response for you to steer your car *away* from danger rather than toward it. If reading weren't a handy way to communicate rapidly and accurately, few people would practice it until it became automatic. Most experts thus argue that we rely on judgmental heuristics precisely because they *usually* work. If heuristics *didn't* usually work, we'd find a different way to breeze (automatically) through life. Consider your ability to estimate the popularity of different names. Which is a more popular first name in the United States, Jelinda or Jennifer? Which is a more popular last name, Garcia or Guardado? Without doing any research, you instantly knew the answers to these questions. Likewise, you know that five apples *usually* make more apple sauce than three. We use judgmental heuristics because they are useful. Finally, we know that some biases in human judgment are highly adaptive because sometimes it's safer to be wrong in one direction than the other (Haselton & Buss, 2000). For instance, weighting negative events more heavily than positive events is usually adaptive. Negative events can kill us. As far as we know, positive events can't bring us back to life. So please avoid poison and pythons even more than you approach fame and fortune. We want you to live long enough to tell other people to read this amazing book.

Questions for Critical Thinking and Discussion for Module 18

We spend much of our daily lives making judgments and decisions, often without realizing what fuels the decisions. Should we try this detergent on this wine stain? Should we deter Tyler from marrying Deborah? For this reason, many other modules in this text have something to do with judgment and decision making. With this in mind, let's examine a couple of topics we've already covered, and one we'll be covering soon, to explore the implications of what you just learned about judgment and decision-making.

1. One of the first modules in this text examined the four "ways of knowing." Recall that they include intuition, authority, logic, and observation. First, which of the four ways of knowing most closely resembles using a judgmental heuristic to answer a question? Second, which way of knowing do people most often ignore or violate when using heuristics? Third, if Joel accepts something as true merely because a famous or attractive person said it (without providing any good evidence in favor of the position), is it

appropriate to say that Joel has used a heuristic? Finally, recall that the module on ways of knowing provided you with a list of opposing aphorisms. What judgmental concept covered in the present module on human judgment can explain why people can agree in one moment that "You can't teach an old dog new tricks" while agreeing a few days later that "It's never too late to learn?"

2. Another module in this text has direct implications for whether people are truly general-purpose reasoning machines. This is part of the module on emotions suggesting that "emotions override cognitions." Give an example of how a person might spend the time to engage in a careful, rational analysis but end up making an error or failing to do what is logical because of emotional influences. Choose an example that has to do with (a) choosing a marriage partner, (b) succumbing to peer pressure to smoke, or (c) developing a phobia (e.g., a debilitating fear of heights, spiders, or dogs). Do such emotional examples support or fly in the face of the idea that people are usually rational decision makers?

3. Throughout this text, we will discuss findings that – while they do not formally fit the definition of any of the heuristics covered here – have many of the properties of a heuristic. Let's consider two findings we've already covered. First, consider research on *implicit egotism*. People named Carpenter gravitate toward careers in carpentry. And people are more likely to marry another person who shares their birthday number. Could you restate implicit egotism in the form of a heuristic? Even if it is not a heuristic per se, what features does implicit egotism have in common with judgmental heuristics such as availability? Now do the same thing for the *mere exposure effect*. Again, the mere exposure effect is *not* technically a heuristic. But what cognitive properties does this judgmental rule have in common with heuristics?

4. When people are making big decisions (e.g., marriage or career decisions) they often engage in behaviors that should reduce the likelihood that they will make a poor decision. Name (a) at least one cognitive strategy people often adopt and (b) one social strategy people often adopt when making a really important decision. When and how will such strategies reduce error and bias? Are there any times when such strategies might backfire – and make people more confident of poor decisions? Be specific.

Multiple-Choice Questions for Module 18

For each judgment, choose the judgmental heuristic or bias that's most likely to be the basis of the judgment.

1. **Assuming you'll *definitely* die young because your mom did.**   availab. repres. numer. overconf. anchor

2. Assuming that a batter who hit 40 home runs for Colorado* is a better hitter than a batter who hit 38 home runs for San Francisco.   availab. repres. numer. overconf. anchor

3. **Thinking a lot of people die every year from shark attacks.**   availab. repres. numer. overconf. anchor

4. Red cars get more speeding tickets than white cars.   availab. repres. numer. overconf. anchor

5. **Trusting the advice of a TV doctor (in a commercial).**   availab. repres. numer. overconf. anchor

6. Thinking 3 tacos for $3 is a great deal – until you see how tiny they are.   availab. repres. numer. overconf. anchor

7. **Offering someone $3,000 for a car that you know is worth $5,000.**   availab. repres. numer. overconf. anchor

8. Buying a pair of KD (Keven Durant) basketball shoes & thinking they'll really improve your game.   availab. repres. numer. overconf. anchor

9. **Assuming you'll be able to babysit your sister all weekend AND also study well for Monday's big English exam.**   availab. repres. numer. overconf. anchor

10. Preferring a lottery ticket that offers "40 chances to win" (vs. one).   availab. repres. numer. overconf. anchor

11. **Leon sets an 11 p.m. curfew for his 17-year old son because this time used to be Leon's curfew time when he was a teenager.**   availab. repres. numer. overconf. anchor

12. Theo says he "is a great ice hockey player." Then Audrey reminds Theo that he doesn't even know how to ice skate.   availab. repres. numer. overconf. anchor

13. **JD believes that "Junior" is a common male first name because three men or boys in JD's extended family are named "Junior."**   availab. repres. numer. overconf. anchor

14. When Marie Antoinette was told "the peasants have no bread to eat," she presumably said, "Let them eat cake."   availab. repres. numer. overconf. Anchor

15. **In the movie *the Great and Powerful Oz* the Wizard says to his assistant "How hard can it be to kill a wicked witch?"**   availab. repres. numer. overconf. anchor

16. Without knowing this is why, Janine agrees to go to the prom with John – because he looks like Johnny Depp.   availab. repres. numer. overconf. anchor

*It is easier to hit home runs in Colorado than in San Francisco because Colorado is at a high altitude.

Note. So that this can be used as a group activity, we provide no key for the activity here. However, here are some clues. First, the frequencies for each answer option are as follows: availab. = 3, repres. = 5, numer. = 3, overconf. = 3, anchor = 2. Second, overconf. is the answer to questions whose question numbers add up to 36. Finally, repres. is only the answer to one question whose number is a two-digit number. Do you see how useful careful reasoning can be?

References

Atran, S. (2001). A cheater–detection module? Dubious interpretations of the Wason selection task and logic. *Evolution and Cognition, 7*, 1–7.

Blanton, H., Pelham, B. W., DeHart, T., & Carvallo, M. (2001). Overconfidence as dissonance reduction. *Journal of Experimental Social Psychology, 37*, 373–385.

Bodenhausen, G. V. (1990). Stereotypes as judgmental heuristics: Evidence of circadian variations in discrimination. *Psychological Science, 1*(5), 319–322.

Denes-Raj, V., & Epstein, S. J. (1994). Conflict between intuitive and rational processing: When people behave against their better judgment. *Journal of Personality and Social Psychology, 66*, 819–829.

Frank, M. C., & Gilovich, T. (1988). The dark side of self- and social perception: Black uniforms and aggression in professional sports. *Journal of Personality and Social Psychology, 54*, 74–85.

Gigerenzer, G. (2008). Why heuristics work. *Perspectives on Psychological Science, 3*, 20–29.

Gilovich, T., Vallone, R., & Tversky, A. (1985). The hot hand in basketball: On the misperception of random sequences. *Cognitive Psychology, 17*, 295–314.

Haselton, M. G., & Buss, D. M. B. (2000). Error management theory: A new perspective on biases in cross- sex mind reading. *Journal of Personality and Social Psychology, 78*, 81–91.

Kahneman, D. (2011). *Thinking, fast and slow*. New York, NY: Farrar, Straus, & Giroux.

Kahneman, D., & Tversky, A. (1972). Subjective probability: A judgment of representativeness. *Cognitive Psychology, 3*, 430–454.

Klayman, J., & Ha, Y.-W. (1987). Confirmation, disconfirmation, and information in hypothesis testing. *Psychological Review, 94*, 211–228.

Pelham, B. W., & Neter, E. (1995). The effect of motivation on judgment depends on the difficulty of the judgment. *Journal of Personality and Social Psychology, 68*, 581–594.

Pelham, B. W., Sumarta, T. T., & Myaskovsky, L. (1994). The easy path from many to much: The numerosity heuristic. *Cognitive Psychology, 26*, 103–133.

Plous, S. (1993). *The psychology of judgment and decision making*. New York: McGraw-Hill.

Shiffrin, R. M., & Schneider, W. (1977). Controlled and automatic human information processing: II. Perceptual learning, automatic attending and a general theory. *Psychological Review, 84*(2), 127–190.

Soll, J. B., & Klayman, J. (2004). Overconfidence in Interval Estimates. *Journal of Experimental Psychology: Learning, Memory, and Cognition, 30*(2), 299–314.

Sugiyama, L., Tooby, J. & Cosmides, L. (2002). Cross-cultural evidence of cognitive adaptations for social exchange among the Shiwiar of Ecuadorian Amazonia. *Proceedings of the National Academy of Sciences, 99*, 11537–11542.

Tversky, A., & Kahneman, D. (1974). Judgment under uncertainty: Heuristics and biases. *Science, 185*(4157), 1124–1131.

Wason, P. (1968). Reasoning about a rule. *Quarterly Journal of Experimental Psychology, 20*, 273–281.

Weinstein, N. D. (1980). Unrealistic optimism about future life events. *Journal of Personality and Social Psychology, 39*, 806–820.

Module 19
Look Who's Talking
Language and Reasoning

Cognitive psychologists study more than memory, consciousness, and heuristic judgments. Some of the most hotly-debated topics in cognitive psychology have to do with language, and the many things we can do with it. **Language** refers to the use of abstract symbols – most often spoken or written words – to communicate with others. You may recall from the module on motivation that we seem to have evolved a unique talent for using spoken language. Kids pick up spoken language effortlessly – and without even knowing they are doing it. Experts on language love to use their words to debate exactly why this is the case.

Some non-human animals appear to be able to use language. But none of them can keep up with people. Consider chimps, who can develop vocabularies as large as 600 words. Chimps can also be taught to use sign language to some degree (Gardner & Gardner, 1969), and they can even create phrases and simple sentences they've never before heard. But compare a chimp's vocabulary with that of the typical college student, who can understand about 200,000 words. The fact that we learn language effortlessly (as children, at least) also stands in contrast to the fact that animals must work their butts off to master even the simplest linguistic tasks. It's also clear that human kids think deeply about language. Kids develop **grammar**, which is an appreciation of the deep *rules* of language. This includes how to express future tense, how to convert singulars to plurals, and how to switch words around to change meaning. There's a big difference between "Flo bit Amy" and "Amy bit Flo." There's an even bigger difference between "a *brief case* of diarrhea" and "a *briefcase* of diarrhea." Kids learn grammar even when they're not explicitly taught it – and without knowing they know it.

Language Acquisition

We first learned that kids understand grammar because of the "**wug test**." Brown and Berko (1960) showed kids of different ages some drawings and asked the kids to fill in a missing word. Figure 19.1 shows our version of one of Berko's questions (her hand-drawn wugs were cuter). As you can see, only kids who understand the rule for making plurals can correctly answer the wug question. If you pose this question to two-year-olds, they'll say "There are two wug." But by the age of five or six, virtually all kids will tack on the obligatory "s." Another question from the test was: "This wug knows how to fripple. Right now, he is frippling. He did the same thing yesterday. Yesterday he _____." Most kindergartners know that he "frippled."

Another entertaining line of evidence that young children understand grammar comes from the cute mistakes they make. When your first author's daughter Brooklyn

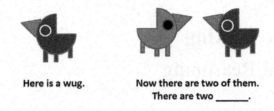

Here is a wug.   Now there are two of them.
                      There are two _____.

Figure 19.1 How many wugs does it take to show that kids understand grammar? Just two.

was five, she would often say things such as "We went yesterday, and Uncle Barry goed with us." or "She already eated her candy." These are examples of **overregularization**, which is the tendency to apply the rules of grammar *too* stringently. In this case, Brooklyn conjugated an irregular ("oddball") verb as if it were a regular verb. If she had said, "Let's go feed the gooses," this, too, would qualify as overregularization. She would have turned an irregular plural into a regular plural. Such mistakes are telling because it's obvious children never hear adults say such things. Instead, kids seem to have learned the deep rules of grammar, having completely *forgetted* that the rules have some exceptions. As another example of how easily kids learn language, you may recall that toddlers and preschoolers possess a remarkable ability known as **fast mapping**. This refers to learning the meaning of a word you've heard just once – often without having been given any definition of the word.

Along similar lines, how well people learn to speak a second language depends heavily on when they first begin learning it. If kids are consistently exposed to a second language beginning in infancy or toddlerhood, they become fluent in that second language with great ease. As adults, they'll usually speak the second language with little or no accent. But almost everyone who picks up a second language in adulthood will have to work tirelessly to learn it, and they'll usually speak it with an accent. Your second author David's family is a living example of this. David's family lived in Israel in the 1990s and David's two daughters were born there and learned Hebrew and English from infancy. In contrast, David and his wife Faith learned Hebrew as adults. David and Faith had to work a *lot* harder than their daughters did to learn Hebrew, and they speak it with obvious accents. In contrast, David's two daughters learned Hebrew easily. David's oldest daughter (who got heavy exposure to fluent Hebrew speakers until about the age of five) speaks Hebrew with virtually no accent – despite having forgotten much of her Hebrew vocabulary.

Such findings suggest there may be an evolved, uniquely-human talent for language. Chomsky (1986) believed so. He said we possess an evolved ability to soak up language (any language) very easily. Along similar lines, Hockett (1958, 1960) argued that all languages share a basic set of evolved features and that human language serves the same basic functions we see in animal **communication**. The line between language and communication is a bit fuzzy. But two of the main differences are that communication is much simpler and requires no grammar. A mating call is communication. A love letter is language. But like language, communication involves using arbitrary sounds or symbols to signal a state of affairs to others. When we use language, the sounds we emit are usually words, and the symbols we write represent those words. But there are exceptions. Sign language, for example, uses neither words nor written symbols. It's probably safer to say that ants communicate than to say they use language, but their means of communication is chemical rather than vocal. Ants release about 20 different chemical signals to communicate things as varied as distress and the location of food. But like the words used by people, these distinct chemical signals are largely arbitrary. Almost all complex animals communicate in some way. Mammals are particularly good at it. Dogs bark differently to warn about an approaching stranger than they do to express a desire to play (Hare & Woods, 2013). Likewise, vervet monkeys emit one call to advertise that they've spotted a leopard but emit a different call to warn others about an eagle, and yet another call to warn others about a snake (Diamond, 1992). Human language surely evolved from less complex forms of primate communication.

Universal Features of Language

But do all human languages really share certain basic features? Do all of the roughly 7,000 human languages that exist today follow many of the same basic rules? Hockett argued that one of the basic features of human language is **arbitrariness** – which means that sounds have no obvious connection to their meaning. There is nothing inherently carrot-like about the word "carrot" in English. Thus, the word "zanahoria" in Spanish and the word "wortel" in Dutch do exactly the same trick. The feature of arbitrariness also means that two words that sound very much alike often have very different meanings. Consider "elves" vs. "Elvis" or "face" vs. "phase." Conversely, two words that mean the same thing can sound nothing alike. We know that sounds both peculiar and bizarre, but it's true as well as factual. According to Hockett, another universal aspect of human language is **displacement**. All languages allow us to describe things that are not in front of us right now. This allows us to talk about the past or the future. It also allows us to talk about hypothetical or abstract things that do not exist at all. At least that's what the leprechauns tell us. Along similar lines, Hockett argued that all languages can be used to engage in **prevarication** (lying) and other intentional misrepresentations. Getting back to a comparison between language and communication, we hope you can see that arbitrariness describes communication as well as language. In contrast, both displacement and prevarication are unique to language.

Prior to Hockett's theory of universalism, a more popular position on language was the **Sapir-Whorf linguistic relativity hypothesis**. This hypothesis states that human thought depends heavily on language, and it implies a great deal of cross-cultural variability in how people think (Sapir, 1929; Whorf, 1956). The argument was that people who speak very different languages must, by necessity, *think* very differently. An anecdote often cited in favor of this idea is that the Inuit language has a hundred words for snow. The idea is that this rich meteorological vocabulary allows the Inuit to make and remember very fine distinctions between different kinds of snow – distinctions the rest of us couldn't make. This anecdote has been the source of great debate, including debates about whether the Inuit really even *have* numerous words for snow. By one reasonable accounting system, *English* has just as many words for snow as does the Inuit language. We'll come back to the Sapir-Whorf relativity hypothesis later in this module. For now, let us say that *critics* of this idea that language shapes thought argue that the support for it is pretty sparse (e.g., see Au, 1983; Brown, 1986).

© BWP
& BEP

"Well, we only have **one** word for 'snow.' But we do have about 100 words for 'freezing your ass off.'"

Figure 19.2

In contrast, until very recently, things went much better for Hockett's argument that language has many universal properties. For example, evidence that people across the globe speak in ways that suggest a deep universal grammar has usually been taken to show that certain features of language are hardwired. But then, in 2004, all heck began to break loose. First, Gordon (2004) published a paper arguing that a group of Brazilian hunter-gatherers (the Pirahã) spoke a language that simply had no words for number. As a result, the Pirahã performed abysmally at even the simplest numerical tasks. Show Pirahã tribesmen three batteries and ask them a minute later how many objects they saw, and they will be clueless – even if you present the answer options as pictures. It might seem obvious that people who don't have a word for algebra would have difficulty with equations, but the Pirahã's numerical deficits seem to run very deep. Is numerical thinking really *so* constrained by language?

Gordon argued that the answer is yes. Furthermore, shortly after Gordon published his paper, Everett (2005) argued that the Pirahã language violates many of the other presumed universal properties of language. For example, Everett spent months trying to teach the Pirahã to count to ten or perform very simple addition problems (such as 2 + 1). He had no success. This happened despite the extreme eagerness of the Pirahã to learn to count – and their extreme ingenuity about complex matters better suited to expression in their language. Let's assume that some aspects of Pirahã thought and language raise doubts about Hockett's list of linguistic universals. If so, what's so terrible about *nearly* universal? In the case of the Pirahã, it looks like no one ever invented specific number words because the Pirahã are so incredibly interconnected with one another that they never *needed* them. In fact, it is only when the Pirahã trade with dodgy outsiders that their lack of number words gets them into trouble.

It is possible that language does possess some universal or near-universal features, but that the specific language a person speaks still has an impact on memory or judgment. In further support of universalism, Regier, Kay, and Cook (2005) conducted an impressive cross-cultural study of color words in cultures that used 110 different languages. Their cross-cultural samples spanned most of the globe. They showed people the color grid reproduced in Figure 19.3 and asked people to use the color words from their native languages to name the different squares. They also asked people to identify

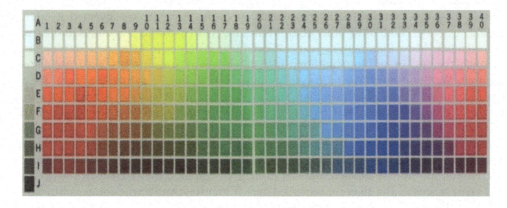

Figure 19.3 A color grid used by Regier et al. (2005) to see if people who spoke 110 different languages referred to color words in common ways. People did. Copyright (2005) National Academy of Sciences, U.S.A

the particular spots on the giant color grid that best represented all the common color words that were in use in their native languages. This meant, for example, that Spanish speakers had to say which spot was the best example of "rojo" (red) and which was the best example of "azul" (blue).

Regier et al. (2005) observed a lot of similarity across the globe in the way people used color labels to refer to different parts of the color grid. Color words that correspond to the English color words *red, yellow, green,* and *blue* showed up consistently in many languages – and the labels for these four basic colors in languages across the globe consistently referred to very similar portions of this 40 x 8 grid. Color words are *not* arbitrary.

On the other hand, Regier and colleagues (2010) also argued that the specific language we speak does, in fact, have an impact on how we think. In addition to the early studies of the Pirahã (which Regier et al. acknowledge), other studies suggest that the particular words that exist in a language can impede or facilitate thought (Kay & Kempton, 1984). How do we put all this together? In our view, it is clear that some of Hockett's universals are not *absolutely* universal. Further, the evidence is growing that language can sometimes affect thought. But neither of these states of affairs requires us to discard completely Hockett's universalist theory. In fact, the Pirahã language that has posed so many challenges for fans of universalism is a great opportunity to understand the origins of language. It stands to reason that the languages human beings spoke 100,000 years ago bore a much stronger resemblance to the Pirahã language than they do to modern Portuguese. It seems highly unlikely that the first human protolanguage included subtleties such as the past perfect. Language is constantly evolving. The number of words in the English language has doubled in the last century alone. It's hard to imagine that *all* of Hockett's universal rules applied to the very *first* spoken human language. Studying the Pirahã – or the other indigenous groups – may offer us insights into ancient spoken languages that cannot be gained any other way.

Finally, it's worth noting that spoken and written language appear to be very different beasts. In contrast to how easily children learn *spoken* language, many children have great difficulty learning *written* language. Spoken language surely paved the way for written language, but written language did *not* evolve. Instead, we invented it, about 10,000 years ago. Like most other cool inventions, written language requires an instruction manual. Most kids require years of careful instruction to learn written language. Between the two of us, your authors have taught many preschoolers and reared four children. We thus know how hard it is for most kids to master *written* language. Here's our favorite story that illustrates that point.

One of the first things Jennifer Howell noticed when she became an elementary school principal was that children were constantly tattling to her about the misdeeds of their classmates. One warm spring day in South Georgia, first grader Ray Ann approached Ms. Howell on the playground and said, "Missiz Howell, CH called me the B-word." Ms. Howell was at first stunned that CH (a mere first grader) may have used such coarse and sexist language. But then she reminded herself that Ray Ann might not mean the same thing by "the B-word" that an adult might. She was rooting for "butt-head" or "booger." Thus, Ms. Howell reluctantly asked: "Ray Ann, I know that's a bad word, but can you tell me exactly *what* B-word it was, so that I can talk to CH about it?" Ray Ann replied "Yeah, but I have to whisper it …. It was … *asshole*." Learning to speak is as easy as falling off a log. Learning to read and write is more like carrying a log around with you.

Are We Uniquely Good at Reasoning?

It is mainly because of our extreme facility with language that we're able to do many things other animals cannot do. From completing moon missions to doing the moon walk, our species has engaged in some very sophisticated forms of thinking, reasoning, and communication. We don't want to be *too* critical of our critical thinking skills. But we'll argue here that there's often a big gap between how we *can think*, with a great deal of time, training, and concentration, and how we typically *do* think, as we muddle through life. In short, we'll argue that we are *not* general-purpose reasoning machines. Instead, we possess many specific reasoning skills that seem to exist in isolation. You may also recall that we often rely on quick but imperfect *heuristics* when making many routine judgments. There are limits and constraints on our logical reasoning skills. In the rest of this module, we'll summarize some additional ways in which we fall short of being uniquely good at reasoning. First, many forms of reasoning we once thought were uniquely human appear to exist in non-human animals. Second, we often fall short of purely rational judgments. Finally, whether we prove to be ingenious or clueless depends heavily on things like how we tackle a problem and how others frame it.

Animal Intelligence

Even during the heyday of behaviorism, some researchers argued that animals might be capable of reasoning. Edward Tolman and colleagues argued that, much like people, rats develop "cognitive maps" of their environments. Further, he cautiously used terms such as "insight" to refer to the fact that rats were good at selecting novel shortcuts that more efficiently took them to a location where they had previously found food in a complex maze (Tolman, Ritchie, & Kalish, 1946). Many years later, Gallup (1970) showed that, even more like people, chimpanzees who have never been exposed to a mirror quickly learn to recognize that the chimp they see in a mirror is their own reflection. To put chimp **mirror self-recognition** to a stringent test, Gallup (1970) left a full-length mirror in the living quarters of four chimps who had never before seen a mirror. By the third day of exposure to the mirror, the chimps began to behave as if they recognized themselves in the mirror. To be sure this was truly self-recognition, Gallup put the chimps to sleep (with anesthesia) and painted two obvious red marks on them – one mark above one of their eyebrows and the other mark on the opposite ear. By the time the chimps woke up, the odorless red marks were completely dry. Thus, the chimps could neither see nor feel them. When the chimps were reintroduced to the mirror for the first time after awakening, they quickly began to touch the spots where the red marks had been placed. Two other chimps who had never been exposed to the mirror before showed no such tendency to touch the red spots. This ability to recognize oneself in a mirror suggests **self-awareness** – an appreciation of the fact that you exist as a physical entity with a body of your own. Of course, self-recognition is not the same as a conscious search for identity or self-esteem. But before Gallup's groundbreaking work, many researchers would have been highly skeptical of the idea that any non-human animals possessed *any* kind of self-awareness.

It is now widely recognized that chimps and people are not the only animals that possess self-awareness. Both dolphins and orangutans, for example, show clear evidence of self-recognition using variations on Gallup's mirror test. In fact, European magpies (a large-brained bird in the crow family) readily pass the bird version of Gallup's mirror test (Prior et al., 2008). Sophisticated forms of thinking and reasoning in non-human animals go well beyond self-recognition. Naked mole rats use tools – which help keep them from choking – when they dig elaborate underground burrows with their front teeth (Shuster & Sherman, 1998). Moving from the terrestrial back to the celestial, crows and magpies can identify

Figure 19.4 Almost all experts who study animal cognition agree that chimps possess a basic sense of self-awareness. In fact, Prior and colleagues (2008) showed that at least one non-mammal, the European magpie, shows clear evidence of self-recognition in a mirror. They pass Gallup's mirror test. In images A and B, the magpie is clearly trying to scratch off the mark that has been placed just beneath its beak (while it was anesthetized). Images C and D show self-directed behavior that would *not* be taken as evidence for self-recognition. Images from Prior et al. (2008).

and remember individual human faces – especially the faces of those who have previously trapped them (later to release them, of course). This holds true even when the researchers have dramatically changed their hats and clothing.

Like chimps, ravens also **make and use tools**. Aquatic animals are missing the fingers or beaks needed to make tools, but quite a few aquatic animals certainly use them. This includes fish that spray jets of water as tools, crabs that carry stinging anemones for protection, and octopi that strategically carry broken coconut shells for the same reason (Mann & Patterson, 2013). Further, quite a few animals seem to engage in *teaching*. For example, mother cheetahs scaffold their older cubs by bringing back live prey to their dens. They then release the living but injured prey, so the cubs can do the killing. Scholars disagree about whether ants ever truly teach, but as you already know, ants engage in communication (Franks & Richardson, 2006; Leadbeater, Raine, & Chittka, 2006). Both dogs and parrots have problem-solving skills that rival or exceed those of human toddlers, in at least some domains. Some octopi also seem to be able to learn the solution to a complex, unfamiliar problem in a matter of moments – by watching another octopus solve the problem. A couple of animals even seem to rival some aspects of our facility with language. Chaser the border collie has a vocabulary that exceeds 1,000 object names (Pilley & Reid, 2011). Like human toddlers, Chaser even seems to engage in *fast mapping* (learning the meaning of a word after being exposed to it only once or twice).

The most obvious barrier researchers face when studying animal cognition is the fact that animals can't talk. But there is a delightful exception to this barrier. African gray parrots can produce almost any speech sound that is produced by people. For about 30 years, psychologist Irene Pepperberg took advantage of the vocal abilities of a parrot named Alex to see just what Alex could do. In some of her earliest experiments, Pepperberg (1987) showed that **Alex could engage in categorization**. He could reliably make same versus different judgments involving the shape, color, or physical composition of novel objects. Thus, if one novel object was made of wood and the other was made of wool, Alex could reliably report that they were "different." If both objects were made of the *same* material, whether rock, wood, or wool, Alex could report that, too.

Alex died in 2009, but toward the end of his career, Alex learned some basic math. For example, when Pepperberg and Carey (2012) showed him three separate arrays of jelly beans and nuts of different sizes, he could usually add up the total number of objects in all three sets (presented separately) and answer the question, "How many, total?" But Alex's most impressive – and most endearing – ability seems to be the fact that he would sometimes direct *questions* at Pepperberg and his other trainers. To date, no other animal, including chimps, seems to have demonstrated this ability.

The Limitations of Human Reasoning

Animals are surely smarter than we once thought. But are people also dumber than we once thought? Of course, this is an obnoxious way to put it, but it does seem that we fall a bit short of the ideal of the general-purpose reasoning machine. Consider **Gick and Holyoak's analogical reasoning study**. Gick and Holyoak (1983) asked participants to read a story about a military commander who wanted to attack a fortress. But the fortress was well-defended against an attack by a large army all coming from the same place. The commander solved the problem by breaking his army into small units that all converged on the fortress at the same time – from many different directions. Those who designed the fortress hadn't thought of this strategy. After reading this story of creative problem solving, people had a chance to solve a problem of their own. This one involved medicine. A patient had an inoperable tumor. Doctors had developed a beam of radiation that would kill tumors at high levels of intensity. But this high-intensity radiation also killed *healthy* tissue. A low intensity version of the radiation wouldn't harm any healthy tissue, but it wouldn't kill the tumor either. How could doctors safely destroy the tumor? Only 30% of Gick and Holyoak's participants solved the tumor problem. Are you in that 30%? Give yourself a little time if you like, but don't read ahead until you have either solved the problem or given up on it. Are you ready? The solution is to point several low intensity beams at the tumor from different locations and have them all converge on the tumor. Even though people had just read about a problem that was logically identical to the tumor problem, only 30% solved it. When people were specifically *instructed* to use the military solution as a guide to solve the medical problem, nearly everyone was able to do so. After leading a horse to water, then, you may need to remind the horse that water is for drinking. Gick and Holyoak refer to this as an example of the limits of **analogical reasoning**. When analogical reasoning goes *well*, it means using what you know about one problem to solve a conceptually similar problem. In general, we may not be that great at transferring our knowledge across different problems, or different skill sets.

Mental Modularity

Because Jerry Fodor had observed that human thinking seems to be highly insulated, Fodor (1983) argued that the human problem-solver possesses a large collection of **mental modules**. These are distinct mental systems, each of which is geared toward solving a different problem. Some of Fodor's favorite examples of mental modularity were visual illusions. As you may recall from the module on constructivism, knowing that a visual illusion is at work does little or nothing to make the illusion go away. The cognitive systems that help you appreciate the explanation for illusions have nothing to do with the separate cognitive systems that create the illusions. Consider Edelson's famous checkerboard-shadow illusion, shown in Figure 19.6. Many people who've never before seen the illusion find it hard to believe that squares A and B are exactly the same shade of gray. More important, even after confirming that the two squares are, in fact, the same shade, people continue to experience the visual illusion.

"Well *of course* I've heard that story, Chromis. *Everyone's* heard that story. But as you'd know if you had looked more carefully, this one is not a horse at all. It's a donkey."

Figure 19.5

Figure 19.6 Edelson's checkerboard shadow illusion.

These and many other **dissociations** (observed disconnections between things that one might logically expect to be related) led Fodor to his hypothesis about mental modularity. Fodor thought that, rather than being a general-purpose problem-solver, the human mind is a loose confederacy of many separate problem-solving units (specific, highly insulated information-processing tools). Fodor reasoned that if experiencing a visual illusion is divorced from your knowledge that the illusion is not to be believed, different parts of your mind must be going about their business in a highly insulated fashion. Fans of mental modularity argue that just as your car's brakes are separate from the ignition system, your brain consists of many separate systems that each do their own thing, often in complete physical and psychological isolation from other systems.

Reasoning about Rules

Modularity has its pros and cons. Consider two variations on a logical problem you may recall from the module on judgmental heuristics. People often show evidence of the *positive test bias*. In case you did not read the module on heuristics, or in case you wish to refresh your memory, check out the cards that appear in Figure 19.7. In the famous **Wason card task**, Wason (1968) asked people to find out if a specific rule is true or false in a set of four 2-sided cards like these – all of which have a *number* on one side and a *letter* on the other side. The rule he asked people to test was this: "If a card has a *vowel* on one side, then it must have an *even number* on the other side." Which two cards should you flip over to test the rule?

Figure 19.7 Which two cards should you turn over to test the rule?

In Wason's studies and many others since, most people who turn over two cards choose cards A and 4. But this is problematic because there is no need to turn over the 4. The rule didn't say that only vowels can have even numbers on the other side; it said that vowels *must* have an even number on the other side. This means that the correct approach to this problem is to turn over the A and the 7. If we're competent general-purpose reasoning machines, we shouldn't be prone to problems such as the positive test bias.

Furthermore, if we're general-purpose reasoning machines that suck at reasoning, we should be consistently sucky at it. Unless you change the logical structure of a problem, it shouldn't matter exactly how you label the four cards. In other words, there should be no problem content effects. **Problem content effects** refer to differences in how well we reason that depend on the specific way in which we label the parts of a problem.

But according to Cosmides and Tooby, it matters a great deal how you label some problems. They argue that this is the case because human beings have evolved to be great at social exchange. In fact, they argue that there is an evolved human **cheater-detection module**. This module presumably makes us very good at figuring out whether someone has screwed someone else over. Let's see right now if anyone cheated. Your goal is to see if a specific rule is true or false in the set of four 2-sided cards that appear in Figure 19.8 One side of each card tells you whether a person used a friend's car. The other side tells you whether that same person filled the car's gas tank. Here's the rule: "If a person *borrows the car*, then the person must *fill the car's gas tank*." To see if anyone cheated, which two cards should you turn over?

When faced with this "cheater detection" version of the card task, most people do very well. The very large majority of people correctly state that you should turn over the "used the car" card and the *"didn't* fill the tank" card. This does not seem to be a simple question of problem familiarity. The "cheater detection" boost in reasoning occurs even for novel social exchanges. Sugiyama, Tooby, and Cosmides (2002) showed that the residents of a remote tribe in the Amazon, who could neither read nor write, performed very well on a variation of this task. There has been some debate about whether the card task is ideal for testing evolutionary hypotheses (because good or bad performance on the task may be open to so many interpretations, e.g., see Atran, 2001, but compare Fiddick, Cosmides, & Tooby, 2000). However, virtually everyone who studies logical reasoning acknowledges that the specific content of many reasoning problems can have a big impact on how well people are able to reason about the problems.

Problem content effects do not prove that people are poor reasoners, but they do suggest that we are imperfect reasoners. Problem content effects also suggest that how good we are

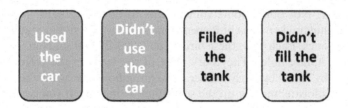

Figure 19.8 Which two cards would let you test the social exchange rule?

at reasoning depends on exactly which mental module gets activated when we tackle a problem. Remember the Linda problem and the conjunction fallacy? Tversky and Kahneman (1983) found that even professional statisticians made the logical mistake of thinking that a liberal-sounding woman named Linda was more likely to be a feminist *and* a bank teller than she was to be a bank teller. But these statisticians presumably made this mistake because they answered the Linda question as if it were a social question – involving stereotypes – rather than a math question. Whether we reason well or flounder depends on many factors, only one of which is which module gets activated. For example, research on automatic and controlled information processing shows that we reason more carefully than usual when we have plenty of time, motivation, and cognitive resources (e.g., Basel & Brühl, 2013; Petty & Cacioppo, 1986). Simon (1956) foreshadowed such modern findings long ago when he argued that human judges are best characterized not as deeply flawed goofballs or as infallible geniuses but rather as **satisficers**. Simon's satisficers are pragmatic realists who balance the need for accuracy against the need to get quick answers whose quality rises above a minimal threshold. To some, this idea of constantly making cognitive compromises may be highly dissatisfying. But Simon would be OK with this. After all, life cannot always be fully satisfying. But Simon argued it can be full of satisfi*c*ing. Linguistic universalists like Hockett would be proud to know that you can make this important linguistic distinction.

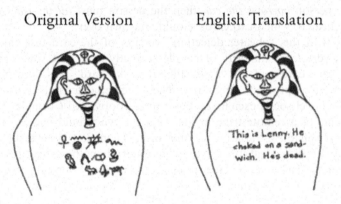

Figure 19.9

Critical Thinking and Discussion Questions for Module 19

In this module, you learned a bit about the amazing cognitive abilities of animals. But if there were a cross-species thinking and reasoning Olympics, people would still win all the gold medals, right? Not quite. Some animals can do things virtually no person can do. Consider Clark's nutcracker. This bird spends most of the late summer and fall extracting seeds from pine cones. Each year, these birds hide 5,000–20,000 seeds in locations all over an area of a few square miles. They bury most of the seeds in the ground – where they become covered by snow by early winter. All throughout the winter and well into the spring, these birds locate and dig up the seeds they've hidden. It's not exactly clear what cues the birds use to locate the seeds, but however they do it, they are remembering thousands of specific burial spots – all without a map or a GPS.

Another amazing example of animal cognition involves short-term memory for written numbers. Inoue and Matsuzawa (2007) pitted chimps against people in a highly demanding test of short-term memory for the exact positions of numbers. Both people and chimps saw a display screen that contained numbers between 1 and 9, each placed randomly in one of 48 spots. On the most demanding trials of one memory test, any five of the numbers 1–9 flashed up on the screen for only 1/5 of a second. Participants (chimps) then had to touch the squares where those five numbers had appeared – in numerical order. The adult chimps tested on this task performed slightly worse than people. But the juvenile chimps performed much better than people. In short, juvenile chimps seem to have a form of short-term photographic memory. To see a video of the chimps performing this task, go to: https://www.cell.com/current-biology/fulltext/S0960-9822(07)02088-X and check out the last couple of videos posted at the end of this *Current Biology* article.

Finally, the gorilla Koko (who died in June of 2018) had a sign language vocabulary of 1,000 (yes, 1,000) words. According to researchers who knew Koko well, she understood death. For example, Koko long mourned a pet cat she had lost when it was young. When Koko saw a picture of a cat that looked like her long-dead pet cat, she pointed at the picture and signed "Sad. Cry." (Morin, 2015). Likewise, when a caregiver spontaneously asked Koko where animals go when they die, Koko signed, "A comfortable hole," and then she gestured a goodbye kiss. Unlike most other gorillas, Koko also seems to have recognized herself in a mirror, and there is at least some evidence that she used language to tell fibs and jokes.

1. As we learn more and more about the amazing intellectual abilities of animals, what kinds of questions does this raise about how we treat them? For example, it has not been very long since people routinely killed chimps and gorillas and sold their body parts as souvenirs. Despite the best efforts of wildlife activists, there is still a lively demand for ivory taken from elephant tusks. But if elephants can recognize themselves in mirrors – and perhaps show evidence of mourning their dead – what does this mean for how we treat them? Should an animal's ability to reason have any bearing at all on how we treat them? Or should all animals, regardless of reasoning capabilities, be treated humanely?
2. If any advanced alien civilizations ever make their way to Earth, do we have any reason to expect them to treat us any better than we treat other animal members of our own planet?

Multiple Choice Questions for Module 19

1. Many animals use mating calls to attract a mate. Some animals also use alarm calls to alert other members of their species to the fact that a predator is near. What's the technical term for these two specific ways to transmit information?

   A) communication
   B) transference
   C) language

2. Much like measures of overregularization, performance on Berko and Brown's wug test is taken as an indicator of what?

   A) people's knowledge of the rules of grammar
   B) people's reasoning and logical thinking skills
   C) people's episodic memory skills

3. The deep rules of language (e.g., how to make plurals, how to make future tense) are known as:

   A) linguistics
   B) proscriptions
   C) grammar

4. According to Hockett, quantification, arbitrariness, and prevarication are all what?

   A) culturally universal aspects of language
   B) three aspects of language that vary widely across cultures
   C) higher-order linguistic rules

5. What is the basic idea behind the Sapir-Whorf linguistic relativity hypothesis?

   A) that different modern language families reflect the roots of the original languages from which they evolved
   B) that the complexity of human language has increased dramatically in the past century or so
   C) that the specific language one speaks has a big effect on how one thinks, reasons, and remembers

6. In the Regier et al. (2005) color perception study, the researchers used a giant grid of 320 colors to see:

   A) why there is cross-cultural variation in how many color words exist in different languages
   B) if kids and adults differ in the sophistication of their color words
   C) if there is cross-cultural agreement in the way people use words to refer to different colors

7. What does it mean to say that human judges and thinkers are *satisficers*?

   A) we're often satisfied that we've solved a problem when we really have not
   B) we're not usually satisfied with an answer to a question until we feel we have solid proof
   C) we try to balance getting quick and easy answers against being as accurate as possible most of the time

8. What animals appear to be able to recognize themselves in a mirror?

   A) none, only people can do this
   B) chimps, dolphins, and European magpies
   C) people and chimps but apparently no other animals

9. In a study of analogical reasoning, Gick and Holyoak had people read about a study of soldiers attacking a fortress from different directions to see if it helped them solve a problem involving what?

   A) an inoperable tumor
   B) a child trapped in a well
   C) a cook who needed to infuse flavors into a cake

10. A dissociation is a disconnect between performance on two things that people would expect to be very related (but which prove *not* to be related). This is often taken as evidence for what?

    A) being a satisficer
    B) mental modularity
    C) a lack of categorization skills

Answer Key: 1A, 2A, 3C, 4A, 5C, 6C, 7C, 8B, 9A, 10B

References

Atran, S. (2001). A cheater–detection module? Dubious interpretations of the Wason selection task and logic. *Evolution and Cognition, 7*, 1–7.

Au, T. K.-F. (1983). Chinese and English counterfactuals: The Sapir-Whorf hypothesis revisited. *Cognition, 15*, 155–187.

Basel, J. S., & Brühl, R. (2013). Rationality and dual process models of reasoning in managerial cognition and decision making. *European Management Journal, 31*(6), 745–754.

Brown, R. (1986). Linguistic relativity. In S. H. Hulse (Ed.), *One hundred years of psychological research in America: G. Stanley Hall and the Johns Hopkins tradition* (pp. 241–276). Baltimore: The Johns Hopkins University Press.

Brown, R., & Berko, J. (1960). Word association and the acquisition of grammar. *Child Development, 31*, 1–14.

Chomsky, N. (1986). *Knowledge of language: Its nature, origin, and use.* New York: Praeger.

Diamond, J. (1992). *The third chimpanzee: The evolution and future of the human animal.* New York: Harper Collins.

Everett, D. L. (2005). Cultural constraints on grammar and cognition in Pirahã: Another look at the design features of human language. *Current Anthropology, 46*, 621–634.

Fiddick, L., Cosmides, L., & Tooby, J. (2000). No interpretation without representation: The role of domain-specific representations and inferences in the Wason selection task. *Cognition, 77*, 1–79.

Fodor, J. A. (1983). *Modularity of mind: An essay on faculty psychology.* Cambridge, MA: MIT Press.

Franks, N. R., & Richardson, T. (2006). Teaching in tandem-running ants. *Nature, 43*, 153.

Gallup, G. G., Jr. (1970). Chimpanzees: Self-recognition. *Science, 167*(3914), 86–87.

Gardner, R. A., & Gardner, B. T. (1969). Teaching sign language to a chimpanzee. *Science, 165*, 664–672.

Gick, M. L., & Holyoak, K. J. (1983). Schema induction and analogical transfer. *Cognitive Psychology, 15*, 1–38.

Gordon, P. (2004). Numerical cognition without words: Evidence from Amazonia. *Science, 306*, 496–499.

Hare, B., & Woods, V. (2013). *The genius of dogs: How dogs are smarter than you think.* New York, NY: The Penguin Group.

Hockett, C. F. (1958). *A course in general linguistics.* New York: Macmillan.

Hockett, C. F. (1960). The origin of speech. *Scientific American, 203*, 88–96.

Inoue, S. & Matsuzawa, T. (2007). Working memory of numerals in chimpanzees. *Current Biology, 17*(23), PR1004–R1005.

Kay, P., & Kempton, W. (1984). What is the Sapir-Whorf hypothesis? *American Anthropologist, 86*, 65–79.

Leadbeater, E., Raine, N. E., & Chittka, L. (2006). Social learning: Ants and the meaning of teaching. *Current Biology, 16*(9), R323–R325.

Mann, J., & Patterson, E. M. (2013). Tool use by aquatic animals. *Philosophical Transactions of the Royal Society, 368*, 20120424.

Morin, R. (2015, August 28). A conversation with Koko the gorilla. *The Atlantic.* Retrieved June 2019 from Whorfhttps://www.theatlantic.com/technology/archive/2015/08/koko-the-talking-gorilla-sign-language-francine-patterson/402307/

Pepperberg, I. M., & Carey, S. (2012). Grey parrot number acquisition: The inference of cardinal value from ordinal position on the numeral list. *Cognition, 125*(2), 219–232.

Pepperberg, I. W. (1987). Acquisition of the same/different concept by an African Grey parrot (Psittacus erithacus): Learning with respect to categories of color, shape, and material. *Animal Learning & Behavior, 15*(4), 423–432.

Petty, R. E., & Cacioppo, J. T. (1986). *Communication and persuasion: Central and peripheral routes to attitude change.* New York: Springer-Verlag.

Petty, R. E., & Cacioppo, J. T. (1986). The elaboration likelihood model of persuasion. In L. Berkowitz (Ed.), *Advances in experimental social psychology* (Vol. *19*, pp. 123–205). New York: Academic Press.

Pilley, J. W., & Reid, A. K. (2011). Border collie comprehends object names as verbal referents. *Behavioural Processes, 86*(2), 184–195.

Prior, H., Schwarz, A., & Gunturkun, O. (2008). Mirror-induced behavior in the magpie (Pica pica): Evidence of self-recognition. *PLoS Biology, 6*, e202.

Regier, T., Kay, P., & Cook, R. S. (2005). Focal colors are universal after all. *PNAS, 102*, 8386–8391.

Regier, T., Kay, P., Gilbert, A., & Ivry, R. (2010). Language and thought: Which side are you on, anyway? In B. Malt & P. Wolff (Eds.), *Words and the mind: How words capture human experience* (pp. 165–182). New York: Oxford University Press.

Sapir, E. (1929). The status of linguistics as a science. *Language, 5*, 207–214.

Shuster, G., & Sherman, P. W. (1998). Tool use by naked mole-rats. *Animal Cognition, 1*, 71–74.

Simon, H. A. (1956). Rational choice and the structure of the environment. *Psychological Review, 63*(2), 129–138. https://doi.org/10.1037/h0042769

Sugiyama, L., Tooby, J. & Cosmides, L. (2002). Cross-cultural evidence of cognitive adaptations for social exchange among the Shiwiar of Ecuadorian Amazonia. *Proceedings of the National Academy of Sciences, 99*, 11537–11542.

Tolman, E. C., Ritchie, B. F., & Kalish, D. (1946). Studies in spatial learning. I. Orientation and the short-cut. *Journal of Experimental Psychology, 36*(1), 13–24.

Tversky, A., & Kahneman, D. (1983). Extensional versus intuitive reasoning: The conjunction fallacy in probability judgment. *Psychological Review, 90*, 293–315.

Wason, P. (1968). Reasoning about a rule. *Quarterly Journal of Experimental Psychology, 20*, 273–281.

Whorf, B. L. (1956). The relation of habitual thought and behavior to language. In J. B. Carroll (Ed.), *Language, thought and reality* (pp. 134–159). Cambridge, MA: MIT Press.

Module 20
Intelligence and the Insularity of Genius

Overview: In contrast to the popular idea that genius is innate, this module suggests that genius and expert skill in a specific area develop only when people engage in a great deal of **deliberate practice** in a particular activity. A close corollary of this argument is the idea that when a person is a genius in a particular area, this says virtually nothing about the person's level of physical or intellectual performance in *other* areas. We refer to this as the **insularity of genius**, and we apply it to intelligence, to elite *athletic performance*, to *human* development, and to **savants** and **prodigies**. This module also touches on some modern views of intelligence (e.g., the idea of multiple intelligences) that further suggest that there are many different kinds of intelligence – and thus that there is probably no such thing as general intelligence.

The Intelligence Quotient and Measuring Intelligence

In 1905, the French government passed a law separating church and state (Guerlac, 1908). This meant that the education of French children was now in governmental rather than religious hands. It is no coincidence that in that same year (1905), Alfred Binet introduced the concept of the **intelligence quotient** (**IQ**) – along with a test designed to measure it. Binet and his collaborator, Theodore Simon, wanted to measure the basic intellectual capabilities of French schoolchildren. They assessed abilities such as memory, attention span, judgment, reasoning, and problem solving – with the idea that knowing a child's intelligence would help teachers reach each child at his or her own level. After getting data from many children of all ages, Binet and Simon defined IQ *in children* as a ratio – which they appropriately dubbed **ratio IQ**. It was simply a child's *mental age* divided by the child's *chronological age*. So, the ratio IQ score of a child who had just turned ten – but could answer as many IQ questions correctly as the typical 12.5-year-old – would be 12.5/10. To keep people from having to think about decimals, Binet and Simon multiplied this ratio score by 100. Thus, a ten-year-old who's as smart as the average 12.5-year-old would receive a ratio IQ score of 125. There have been many improvements and refinements in IQ scores over the decades. Because of the work of a research team at Stanford University, Simon and Binet's test quickly evolved into the Stanford-Binet IQ test – which has been revised many times. In fact, it is still in common use today. Another modern measure of IQ is the WAIS-IV (Wechsler Adult Intelligence Scale – Version 4), which is often favored by clinical psychologists.

But what about IQ in adults? In adults, the ratio of mental age to chronological age no longer works. I know a couple of 60-year-olds who think (and act) like 15-year-olds, but they don't have IQs of 25 (15/60 * 100 = 25). In adults, IQ scores are defined using the familiar bell curve (i.e., the normal distribution). Adult IQ scores still have a mean score of 100 because a score at exactly the population average is set at 100. On the WAIS-IV, for example, every standard deviation a person scores above or below this average score of 100 adds or subtracts 15 points from his or her score. As you can see in Figure 20.1, the unusual young adult who scores exactly two standard deviations above the mean on a modern IQ test would receive an IQ score of 130 [100 + (2 x 15)]. This more sophisticated way of calculating an IQ score is known as a **deviation IQ score** (i.e., how much the score varies from the mean), and it has the advantage of working for kids as well as adults.

All IQ tests (for kids and adults) consist of a great number of questions, judgments, and problems. How do you convert all those individual responses to a single score – for comparison with other people? In the early 1900s, the statistician Charles Spearman proposed the existence of "**g**" or **general intelligence**. The gist of this idea is that, like general strength, general honesty, or general outgoingness, IQ has a stable component that will show up across the board (for many different tasks). Spearman assumed that a child who is above average at math is a very good bet to be above average at spelling and logical reasoning. It is only because researchers accepted Spearman's view of IQ that it became popular to average together all the individual responses to an IQ test and thus give people a single IQ score. To be clear, tests such as the WAIS also offer sub-scores on different mental abilities (e.g., working memory capacity vs. processing speed). However, in common practice, IQ is often treated as if it were one single thing. To make matters worse for those who score poorly on IQ tests, some educators and psychologists have concluded that IQ has a very large genetic component – meaning that many believe that our intellectual capacities are largely set from birth. You may recall that we called that statement into question in our discussion of genetics in Module 7. The environment in which we develop may interact powerfully with our genetics in determining characteristics such as intelligence. Further, the power of stereotypes may make it seem like IQ has a much bigger genetic component than it really does.

Modern research is increasingly showing not only that IQ is not destiny but also that different kinds of intelligence (e.g., spelling vs. math, musical vs. artistic ability) are not very highly correlated. This means, for example, that if you correlate the different items in a traditional IQ test, you'll see that the individual items are not *nearly* as highly correlated with one another as Spearman's g concept suggests. If

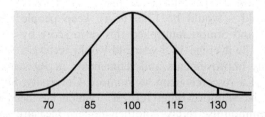

Figure 20.1 Deviation IQ scores. A person who scored exactly one standard deviation below the population mean on an IQ test would receive an IQ score of 85. Compare this with scoring exactly two standard deviations *above* the mean. Because IQ scores are based on the normal curve, only about 2.5% of people score 130 or higher in IQ.

verbal reasoning, geometric pattern matching, and mathematical calculations all measure the basic trait known as intelligence (Spearman's g), they should be highly correlated with one another. They typically aren't. Even if we examine individual subtests of the most recent version of the WAIS (a modern IQ test), we see that different indicators of the *same subtest* are often poorly correlated with one another. In a highly sophisticated analysis of the entire updated WAIS-IV, McFarland (2013, p. 7) concluded that WAIS "subtest performance is determined by multiple orthogonal factors" This is a polite statistician's way of saying that the different parts of the WAIS are measuring *very different things*. Just a bit later, McFarland (2013) adds that, "The assertion that a single g factor accounts for most of the variance in cognitive test performance [4] may be based on the application of an overly simplistic model." An example of an *overly simplistic model* that has been frequently applied is Spearman's g. In our view, at least, the evidence does not support the premise that there is a single, general kind of intelligence.

The Insularity of Genius

Many experts on *expertise* seem to share our skepticism for Spearman's general intelligence. For example, K. Anders Ericsson is an ingenious cognitive psychologist who has long been fighting an uphill battle against centuries of Western folk wisdom suggesting that genius (or IQ, if you will) is something you're born with. As an anonymous social critic once put it, "Life's hard. It's harder when you're stupid." Some experts on IQ still accept this general viewpoint. Some unfortunate people were born dumb. Many were born average. A lucky few were born brilliant. We call the lucky people geniuses because they seem to learn things effortlessly that the rest of us struggle to comprehend. But Ericsson would beg to differ (Ericsson & Pool, 2016). Ericsson argues that genius has less to do with predetermination and more to do with determination. Ericsson's view is that genius is *not* a general property of the person (a rejection of Spearman's g). Instead, genius is domain-specific and is not predetermined by our genes. Ericsson's contrarian view seems to have been inspired, at least in part, by Chase and Simon's (1973) classic studies of chess masters. Then, as now, the chess master was the poster child of genius.

Chase and Simon presented chess masters and college students with images of an in-progress chess game, giving both groups a mere five seconds to study the boards before trying to recall them. If you're like us and you have trouble telling a castle from a pony, you'll be impressed to learn that college students were able to remember the *exact* locations of about 7 chess pieces (out of 32). The average chess master, though, remembered 28 pieces. Maybe you think that's obvious. Chess masters are geniuses, right? Not if you mix things up a little. Consider what happened when the experimenters changed the task slightly by placing the chess pieces on the board *at random* rather than the way they'd appear in a real game. This hardly mattered at all for the college students. Their memory dropped slightly, to six pieces. But the memories of the chess masters plummeted. Just like the college students, the chess masters now remembered an average of six pieces. So these experts were no better than the rest of us when the rules were changed. Examples of the **insularity of genius** are widespread. Despite the popular notion that human beings are reasoning machines, we argued in module 19 that the human mind is *not* a good or bad general-purpose thinker. Instead, we learn to solve specific problems and rarely generalize to even closely related problems. Let's begin with an example from the world of sports.

Ted Williams, arguably the greatest baseball hitter ever, once agreed to bat against an elite, female, fast-pitch softball pitcher, Joan Joyce. He did so to raise money for charity. The two athletes raised quite a bit of money, but only at Williams's emotional expense (Scheiber, 2011). Williams struck out repeatedly – and eventually threw down his bat in frustration – when the best he could do during a long bout at the plate was to foul away three balls. That's right. He *never* got a hit. In fairness to Williams, we suspect that with some amount of work, Williams could have *eventually* become a very good fast-pitch softball hitter. But the general point remains. Athletic genius is highly specific. If you don't believe us, ask Michael Jordan, one of the greatest basketball players ever, why he failed at minor league baseball. Getting back to baseball, modern professional baseball hitters have no luck getting hits off top-ranked Wiffle Ball pitchers. Of course, Wiffle ball players never play in major league baseball either. These are very different skill sets.

Moving from physical athletes to memory athletes, mnemonic geniuses who train themselves to remember novel 100-digit numbers after hearing them just once or twice perform no better than you or me when asked to remember *letters* rather than numbers (Schacter, 1996). You may have heard of memory athletes who compete in a variety of grueling multi-day memory feats – from pairing hundreds of unfamiliar names and faces to memorizing the exact order of a well-shuffled deck of 52 cards (in 20–30 seconds). Your second author once ate at a restaurant with a large group of about 20 diners. The waiter took everyone's order without writing down a single word. And the waiter served them all exactly what they ordered. These memory athletes become extremely good at *several different* memory feats. But, just like the rest of us, they'll tell you they sometimes misplace their car keys – or come home from the grocery store having forgotten the Lysol (Shapiro, 2017).

Insularity even applies to being a psychologist. Psychotherapists who are good at helping patients save marriages are probably a little *worse* than the rest of us when it comes to saving their *own* (McCoy & Aamodt, 2010), especially when you consider that highly educated people usually have low divorce rates. This idea is beautifully illustrated in the comedy *Arrested Development*. Lindsay asks her husband, Tobias, the psychotherapist, if it might strengthen their marriage if they were to experiment by having an open marriage (an arrangement in which both partners may openly seek sex with other people). Tobias quickly retorts that, in his experience with patients who've tried open marriage, it's a *terrible* idea. Specifically, Tobias argues, "It never works ...these people somehow *delude* themselves into thinking it might [work]." Then, after a very pensive moment, Tobias adds, slowly, "But it *might* work *for us.*"

The insularity of skills (the genius we acquire through learning and hard work) applies to the reasoning and capabilities of kids as well as adults. Karen Adolph studies infant and toddler cognition. Adolph (2000) found that infants who are getting the hang of crawling eventually learn *not* to crawl over a glass "visual cliff." However, when the same babies begin to *walk* a few months later, they walk right off the same cliff just as foolishly as a coyote in an old Warner Brothers cartoon. Infants didn't learn a lesson about general principles of locomotion; they learned a specific lesson about *crawling*.

We have specific forms of genius in addition to specific forms of reasoning. Consider savants. **Savants** are people who suffer from serious mental disabilities – such as learning disorders or severe autism. Across the globe there are about 100 known **"prodigious savants."** These are people with major disabilities who possess incredible intellectual, mathematical, calendrical, memorial, or artistic talents. Consider the American sculptor Alonzo Clemons, whose work is depicted in Figure 20.2. Clemons

Figure 20.2 Alonzo Clemons and a sample of his work. Used with kind permission of Alonzo Clemo

can spend a few moments looking at a photo of an animal and then sculpt a highly realistic version of the animal in motion – from memory, without ever looking at the photo again (www.alonzoclemons.com/). Because of his disability, Clemons has some difficulty communicating with other people. If not for his affable and friendly demeanor, and the support of devoted caregivers, he might spend a lot of time alone. But he certainly is not alone as a savant. There are savants who can perform all kinds of other amazing feats. The late artist Richard Wawro spent decades doing with crayons and paper what Clemons has long been doing with clay. Wawro could carefully observe a landscape photo and render a vibrant, full-color crayon drawing of the scene years later (see www.wawro.net for some examples). The blind and autistic pianist Derek Paravicini can listen to any musical piece only once and then play it back beautifully, note for note. Derek also has absolute pitch, can improvise, and can compose novel pieces of music on the spot.

Culture, Genius, and Hard Work

Culture also influences genius. Worldwide, boys are more likely than girls to score in the "genius" range on standardized math tests. However, gender differences in math disappear *or reverse* in cultures where stereotypes about gender and math are weaker than usual (Nosek et al., 2009). Malcolm Gladwell (2008) argued that something as seemingly arbitrary as whether people live in a culture where farmers historically grew a lot of rice (which is extremely labor intensive) or wheat (which is much less so) is a strong predictor of that culture's work ethic and level of conscientiousness. Pelham (2013) confirmed this prediction across the globe by strongly predicting national scores on a standardized math achievement test (the PISA) from national per capita rice production. Even within a large group of *Asian* nations, for example, students performed much better in math in nations where more people grow rice. Why? As Gladwell proposed, perhaps it was because they worked harder.

As Ericsson and Pool (2016) note, even a talent as rare as absolute pitch is influenced heavily by culture and experience. **Absolute pitch** (informally known as *perfect pitch*) refers to the ability to hear a single musical note out of context and reliably identify it. In the United States, only about one person in 10,000 has absolute pitch. This percentage is much higher among highly trained U.S. musicians, but absolute pitch is rare even in this elite group (perhaps one elite musician in seven). But in China, where most people speak the tonal language known as Mandarin, more than half of all highly trained musicians seem to have absolute pitch (Deutsch, 2013). Early critics of research on absolute pitch suggested that this ability probably has a big genetic component. After all, the gene pool in China is presumably different than the gene pool in the United States. Further, in both nations, people whose genes give them a good ear for music may gravitate toward musical careers. Maybe. But a study by Sakakibara (2014) very strongly suggests that 12–18 months of focused daily training can give almost anyone absolute pitch. Sakakibara got a group of 24 kids aged two to six and had them spend a few minutes a day trying to identify one of 14 target chords. Two kids who were doing just fine dropped out of the program for reasons having nothing to do with their performance. After 12–18 months of daily training, every remaining kid in this program (that's right; 22/22 kids) passed a test for absolute pitch. So much for the idea that this rare ability is mainly genetic. A lot of hard work produced the same rare talent.

Ericsson and others have now conducted many, many studies that suggest both the flexibility and the insularity of human genius. Ericsson has spent decades, that is, confirming Thomas Edison's insight that "genius is 1% inspiration and 99% perspiration." However, Ericsson has gone well beyond Edison to show exactly *what kind* of perspiration creates a genius. **Prodigies** (average people who have a specific area of genius) require thousands of hours of intensely-focused practice at a specific activity to become true geniuses in that area. This is true for intellectual activities such as chess, music, or spelling, for physical skills such as juggling or swimming, and for more familiar activities such as carpentry, cooking, or typing (Ericsson & Pool, 2016). It's important to add that there is practice, and there is practice. To become a true expert at anything complicated, people have to engage in **deliberate practice**. Unlike casual practice, **deliberate practice** involves the constant effort to look for new and better ways to do things. It thus means making a lot of mistakes. If you're trying to improve your juggling and you aren't frequently dropping things, you're *not* engaging in deliberate practice. Likewise, if you hit every note you ever try to sing or never branch out beyond drawing clowns, you are not engaging in deliberate practice.

Another secret to becoming a true expert (i.e., a genius) in most areas is having a very good coach or mentor. In most PhD and MD programs, for example, students don't just hit the books; they work closely with experts who offer them practical advice and extreme challenges. The same principle applies to sports and music. Professional athletes cannot run physical drills 40 hours per week, but they spend lots of time every week with coaches and fellow players reviewing film and analyzing good and bad ways to carry out their athletic jobs. Unlike casual pianists, concert pianists constantly work with other musical geniuses to try new musical pieces and learn new techniques. And they do this tirelessly (hopefully because they love doing so) for many thousands of hours before they become true experts. In an interview with *Golf Digest* (Yocom, 2010) Hall of Fame golfer Sam Snead put it well,

People always said I had a natural swing. They thought I wasn't a hard worker. But when I was young, I'd play and practice all day, then practice more at night by my car's headlights. My hands bled. Nobody worked harder at golf than I did.

So the next time you feel a little jealous of the late Steven Hawking, Venus Williams, or your cousin, the math whiz, you should take some solace in the fact that we all have our potential pockets of brilliance – if we're willing to put in enough deliberate practice. And you should feel bad for K. Anders Ericsson. After all, a lot of his own incredibly ingenious research shows that he is *not* a born genius. Apparently, he's just engaged in a *lot* of deliberate practice thinking about the amazing but highly specific effects of deliberate practice.

Multiple Intelligences

You may have noticed that a lot of the evidence we cite against Spearman's "g" is indirect and comes from research on toddler cognition, case studies of athletes and savants, and studies of extreme expertise. Even expertise is somewhat different than intelligence *per se*. But many researchers who study intelligence have also come to the conclusion that human intelligence is richer and more complex than Spearman's concept of "g" suggests. One idea that stands in sharp contrast to Spearman's "g" is Gardner's (1993) theory of **multiple intelligences**. Notice that it's a theory of *intelligences*, plural. Gardner argues that there are many different ways to be smart – and that almost everyone naturally excels at something. Figure 20.3 summarizes Gardner's basic idea. His work with both kids and adults suggests that the eight unique forms of intelligence he has identified are pretty distinct from one another. Further, Gardner argues that whether a person excels in any given performance domain should have more to do with the person's talent in that specific domain than it does with the person's *general* intelligence.

Let's examine a few of the forms of intelligence summarized in Figure 20.3. Gardner (1993) argues that a person is much more likely to become an elite athlete if she excels in "body smarts" than if she excels in "logic smarts." People high in "body smarts" presumably have brains and bodies that are naturally suited to staying balanced and stringing together rapid, graceful, coordinated movements. Likewise, Gardner argues that some people are naturally skilled at music – whereas others are born with a knack for verbal self-expression – making them "word smart." We should add that the biggest proponent of research on expertise, K. Anders Ericsson, might disagree with Gardner's assumption that we are all *born with* varying degrees of each of these eight distinct forms of intelligence. One possible resolution to this debate is that if there are genes for being "body smart," "people smart," or "logic smart," they are genes that make people *keenly interested in* the kinds of activities that connect to these specific forms of intelligence. From this perspective, artists become artists because they love drawing, sculpting or painting, and they simply can't get enough of it. This often leads to *deliberate practice*, of course. That certainly describes artistic savants such as Richard Wawro and Alonzo Clemons. No one ever had to encourage them to draw or sculpt. Instead, they had to be torn away from it.

Critics of Gardner's theory argue that very few studies have put the theory to systematic tests. In contrast, they argue, there are hundreds of studies attesting to the validity of the standard IQ test (e.g., see Waterhouse, 2006). Some critics further argue that

Figure 20.3 Gardner's theory of multiple intelligences. To see if you understand it, match the name of each of the following people with one of Gardner's eight specific forms of intelligence. Photographer Ansel Adams, NBA star Lebron James, Mozart, poet Pablo Neruda, Albert Einstein, Charles Darwin, the late business leader Steve Jobs, and finally our mutual friend Anne, who always seems to know exactly what she wants and why it is good for her.

many educators have accepted the theory of multiple intelligences on faith and have used it to guide their teaching when it may simply be incorrect. Although the avid empiricist in each of us sees merit in such concerns, it would be premature to abandon this alternate view of intelligence. In our opinion, hundreds of studies already suggest that intelligence is not merely one thing. For instance, in research on strengths in the workplace (that place where high IQs are supposed to help you get things done), there is plenty of evidence that there are many distinct human strengths. Over the past few decades, the Gallup Corporation has developed the **Clifton Strengths Finder**^{TM} to identify which of 34 unique strengths people excel in most. That's right. Those who have developed the Strengths Finder argue that there are at least *34* unique strengths that allow people to become engaged and competent workers. We'll examine just a few of these 34 strengths. People for whom "Analytical" is a strength care deeply about data and reasoning. To those whose strengths include "Analytical," math and logic are old friends. Contrast "Analyticals" with "Includers." According to the Strengths Finder, "Includers" possess a powerful interpersonal talent. They naturally consider ways to make sure everyone in a group feels accepted. They avoid cliques. They make sure that people whose old friends are math and logic feel accepted by everyone – including

Table 20.1 The 34 Workplace Strengths in the Clifton Strengths Finder

Achievers are strongly driven to succeed.	**Activators** can't wait to get going.
Adaptability is living flexibly in the moment.	**Analytical** people adeptly use logic and data.
Arrangers are organized conductors.	**Belief** is a strength of ethics and values.
Command means you take charge of things.	**Communication** is about expression and storytelling.
Competition means you strive to win.	**Connectedness** is about building relationships.
Consistency is all about fairness.	**Context** means fully appreciating history.
Deliberative people carefully avoid danger.	**Developers** coach and improve others.
Discipline(d) people are good time managers.	**Empathy** means caring deeply for others.
Focus means keeping your eyes on the prize.	**Futuristic** people see the road ahead.
Harmony means always seeking peace.	**Ideation** means you're an "ideas" person.
Includers always try to widen the group circle.	**Individualization** means seeing uniqueness in others.
Input means absorbing all that is new.	**Intellection** means you are a deep thinker.
Learners enjoy constant skill development.	**Maximizers** focus on shining brightly.
Positivity means seeing life as glorious.	**Relators** create deep, stable relationships.
Responsibility: the buck stops with you.	**Restorative** people love to fix things.
Self-assurance is confidence in all that you do.	**Significance**: wanting to matter to others.
Strategic people are problem-solvers.	**Woo** means being good at "winning others over."

people who consider math and logic the enemy. By the way, "Empathy" is a separate strength in this 34-factor approach. We hope you can see how a person high in *both* empathy and inclusion would be very pleasant to work with. Table 20.1 contains a complete list of the 34 Strengths Finder strengths as well as a very short summary of each (paraphrased from Rath, 2007).

One of the strengths of the Strengths Finder approach is that it's based on data from millions of real employees – which has allowed researchers at Gallup to study how combinations of different strengths make us the unique people that we are. An arguable weakness, by the way, is that the Strengths Finder was developed (however painstakingly) as a business tool. Gallup uses it to make money, and it has not been subjected to the kind of scientific peer review process that one would ideally like it to survive. This also means the Strengths Finder test is not free. On the other hand, modern IQ and aptitude tests – such as the WAIS and the SAT – are not free either. Putting all this together, the commercial success of the Strengths Finder suggests that – whether you call something a strength or a form of intelligence – there are many unique skills and abilities that can bear a lot of fruit in the workplace and beyond.

The Popular Appeal of Learning Styles

If people have a particular set of strengths, does that also mean that they will learn better when the learning process is tailored to their areas of strength? A few decades ago, researchers interested in ensuring that all students could reach their maximum potential promoted the appreciation of learning styles. The basic idea behind **learning styles** is that different people learn differently. According to one popular theory of learning styles (Fleming, 2005), there are four kinds of learners: (a) visual, (b) auditory, (c) reading/writing, and (d) kinesthetic. Visual learners presumably learn best by seeing graphs and complex images. Auditory learners presumably learn best by listening.

Readers, then, learn best by being given reading materials, and kinesthetic leaners need to get their hands onto things. The idea of learning styles is *extremely* popular – both among laypeople and among teachers. Howard-Jones (2014) surveyed teachers in China, Greece, the Netherlands, Turkey, and the United Kingdom. Averaging across countries, more than 90% of teachers said they believed in learning styles. It seems likely that most American teachers – and their students – would agree (Willingham, Hughes, & Dobolyi, 2015).

But there is a big problem with learning styles. They don't seem to work. To be sure, some people *do* prefer reading while others prefer looking, listening, or doing. But numerous studies have now shown that these clear preferences don't seem to have any impact on how well people learn. If there is any merit to learning styles, visual learners should learn best when presented with visual information (such as graphs, charts, and Venn diagrams). Auditory learners should learn best when given lectures or audio recordings that cover the same material. But here's how Willingham and colleagues (2015, p. 267) summarized numerous reviews of studies testing such predictions:

> Several reviews that span decades have evaluated the literature on learning styles ... and each has drawn the conclusion that there is no viable evidence to support the theory. Even a recent review intended to be friendly to theories of learning styles ... failed to claim that this prediction of the theory has empirical support.

Willingham and colleagues are not the only experts to come to this conclusion. In their review of learning styles, Pashler and colleagues (2009) argued that very few methodologically rigorous studies of learning styles had ever been carried out. Worse yet, they argued, the small number of rigorous studies that have put learning styles to a careful test have yielded virtually no evidence that there are benefits to tailoring material to match a student's preferred style of learning. So, if you are a visual learner, there is nothing wrong with making graphs when you study. You'll probably enjoy so doing. Just don't expect this graphing process to help you learn any more quickly than usual.

Fluid vs. Crystallized Intelligence

In this module we have merely sketched out a few hills and trees in the sprawling landscape of research on human intelligence. We'd like to conclude this module by rounding out that picture a little. Let's take a quick peek at just one other perspective on human intelligence. A couple of decades after IQ tests were invented, the personality psychologist James Cattell became very interested in intelligence. Cattell added an important twist to conventional views of intelligence. He argued that there are two distinct forms of general intelligence. The first is known as **fluid intelligence**, and it refers to the ability to think quickly on one's feet when faced with unfamiliar problems.

Fluid intelligence often makes demands on short-term memory. After all, if something is unfamiliar, you cannot rely on your stored knowledge about it. Fluid intelligence involves thinking quickly ("on the fly"). But this does not mean it's sloppy. People who score high in fluid intelligence use their skills in logic and pattern recognition as well as both inductive and deductive reasoning. **Induction**, as we noted in earlier modules, refers to reasoning from the general to the specific. ("Robins have feathers, ostriches have feathers, and hummingbirds have feathers. Thus, all birds seem to have feathers.") In contrast, **deduction** refers to reasoning from a general rule to generate a specific prediction or answer a specific question. All glorks travel windward on the first day of Caldoon. Roz is a glork. It's the first day of Caldoon. Is Roz traveling windward? Deduction says so. In this example, using deduction is a form of fluid intelligence because it requires you to think about unfamiliar things, like Caldoon. The top half of Table 20.2 contains some more examples of fluid intelligence.

In contrast to fluid intelligence, **crystallized intelligence** is a form of intelligence that is built up by means of practice and learning. It is a close cousin of *expertise*, and thus it relies heavily on long-term memory. If your cousin Athena has a PhD in particle physics, she should have a *lot* of crystallized intelligence that helps her solve physics problems very easily. Likewise, if your two authors did not have a great deal of crystallized knowledge of psychology, they would not have been able to write this book. The bottom half of Table 20.2 contains a few additional examples of crystallized intelligence. As we hope you can see from these examples, crystallized intelligence maps very well onto the kind of expertise K. Anders Ericsson studied – which is quite distinct from fluid intelligence. This leaves us with many interesting questions about intelligence. For example, even if there is no immediate transfer of expertise in one area of thinking and reasoning to a different area, is it possible there would be savings? For example, would a great baseball hitter learn to become a great softball hitter more quickly than would a great tennis player? Perhaps time will tell. In the meantime, the idea that intelligence consists of both fluid and crystallized intelligence is yet another example of the basic idea that human intelligence is far from simple.

Table 20.2 Some Concrete Examples of Fluid vs. Crystallized Intelligence

---

Examples of Fluid Intelligence

1. Playing a card game you've never played before – but quickly realizing that you can play the game better if you remember which cards have and have not been played yet.
2. You are a novice slot car racer. However, before you begin your first race you notice that other novice racers wipe out their cars a lot on the curves of the large slot car track. You make it a point to reduce your own car's speed right before it hits each of the curves and thus reduce your own crash rate in your first race.
3. Identifying the pattern in pairs of numbers (e.g., 3,1   6,16   9,49   15,169   10,___)

Examples of Crystallized Intelligence

1. Crystal has worked for two years as a carpenter. On a new job, Crystal's boss tells her to cut him 100 2-foot-long blocks from a stack of 25 8-foot-long 2 x 4s. Crystal quickly asks, "Is it OK if I cut them all 23 and 7/8 inches?" Crystal asks this because she can see that the saw blade she'll be using will take 1/8 of an inch out of the wood with every cut – and make it impossible to get four 24-inch boards (but possible to get four 23 7/8-inch boards) out of each eight-foot-long board.
2. Barry is making pizza dough. When mixing water with his yeast (prior to adding the mixture to his flour), Barry uses a thermometer to make sure he first heats the water to the ideal temperature of 107° F. Much hotter, he knows, and the water will kill some of the yeast before it can do its job. Much colder and the yeast will not dissolve properly in the water.
3. Levon is a sculptor who uses the "ram's head" technique as a good way of working clay before he begins making anything out of it. When Levon makes taralli (a type of Italian pretzel) in huge quantities, he uses the same efficient ram's head technique to work the dough before shaping it into taralli. It works very well.

Group Discussion Activity for Module 20: Functional Fixedness and Creative Thinking

1. **Two Peas in a Pod?** Two high school seniors who looked like sisters were applying to the same job at the same time. After looking at the two applications, the interviewer said, "I can see that you two have the same address and same parents, go to the same high school, and have the same date of birth. You look a *lot* alike. You must be twins." The two women replied, in unison, "Actually we're not twins." How is this possible?

2. **Crazy like a Fox?** An old story (from the pre-smart phone era) states that a man was driving past a mental hospital that served patients with serious clinical disorders such as schizophrenia. The car had a flat, and the driver pulled over to the shoulder – within earshot of the fenced area where some patients were getting some fresh air. As the man was about to put the spare tire on, he looked around and saw that his lug nuts were all missing. He began cursing, knowing that he would miss a very important appointment. A patient apparently saw what was happening. "Sir, I can get you back on the road again." The driver knew that he was talking to a patient with a serious mental illness. "How the hell are you going to do that?" the driver asked. The patient did get the driver back on the road again, by just offering some advice. What advice?

3. **Scared Straight?** When your first author, Brett, was a starving student, he had a head-on motorcycle accident that seriously bent the front forks of his motorcycle. In fact, they were so bent that he could not turn the bike without having the front tire scrape the engine (see the image below). Brett asked a motorcycle shop what it would cost to replace the front forks and learned that it would be roughly the value of the bike. Brett found a way to fix the forks – and make sure they were perfectly straight, for about $30. How did he do so? *If you want a clue*, consider uses for the objects or devices depicted to the right of the image of the damaged motorcycle.

Figure 20.4

4. **Stuck on You.** The driver of an 18-wheeler was driving while using his cell phone and failed to notice a sign that stated the height of a tunnel. The tunnel was just one inch shorter than the height of the truck, and the truck was doing about 35 miles per hour when the driver carelessly tried to enter the tunnel. A horrible scraping noise ensued, and the driver discovered he was stuck. In fact, the big truck was wedged so tight that not even an oversized tow truck could budge it. Of course, the truck was blocking traffic. A kid who was watching the whole thing listened

carefully as the grownups debated what to do, which included some ridiculous ideas like jack-hammering away the part of the tunnel that held the truck's cab firmly in place, or cutting the top of the truck cab. After a while, the kid walked up to the adults who were puzzling over the problem and told them exactly how to get the truck out for free. What was the kid's solution?

Note. These questions do not assess IQ. But they probably do assess *functional fixedness* – which is the tendency to use an object only for the purpose for which it was designed when it readily serves another function (i.e., when it can do something else you need done). Functional fixedness, then, is essentially the opposite of solving a problem creatively. It's thinking "inside the box."

Multiple-Choice Questions for Module 20

1. World class chess players do *not* have higher IQs or better memories than other equally well-educated people, and their memories are perfectly average when it comes to tasks that have nothing to do with chess. This finding is highly consistent with the:

   A) difficulty of measuring IQ and general memory ability
   B) insularity of genius
   C) finding that chess has much more to do with spatial ability than memory or IQ

2. Raffi is a world class poker player. At your invitation she begins to play bridge (a different card game) weekly with you and some of your friends. How should you expect Raffi to do?

   A) because of her card-specific memory and reasoning skills, Raffi should be very good at bridge
   B) because of her high IQ, Raffi should be very good at bridge
   C) because the rules of bridge have little to do with the rules of poker, Raffi should be an average player
   D) because of skill-specific interference, Raffi will start slowly but quickly become very good at bridge

3. The existence of "prodigious savants" such as crayon artist Richard Wawro and sculptor Alonso Clemons suggests that:

   A) it is possible to recover fully from serious brain damage.
   B) some people with profound intellectual disabilities are capable of performing at a genius level.
   C) artistic genius is different than other forms of genius because it relies so much on spatial abilities.
   D) people who show early signs of genius in a specific area have a big advantage over other people.

4. Lisa Adolph studied infants who eventually learned not to crawl over a scary "visual cliff." Once the infants began to walk a few months later they:

   A) were even more cautious about *walking* off a visual cliff.
   B) reacted with fear on a familiar visual cliff but showed no fear if the cliff was painted a different color.
   C) walked off the same visual cliff, suggesting they had not generalized what they learned.

5. Both Jan and Marta have spent 5,000 hours practicing the piano. How might you be able to predict which of these two pianists is more skillful and accomplished?

   A) by watching a typical practice and seeing who engages in more deliberate practice
   B) by watching a typical practice and seeing who seems to enjoy herself more
   C) by finding out how well each girl performed in her very first piano practice session

6. According to Anders Ericsson, what is the key to becoming a true expert at something?

   A) deeply enjoying the activity
   B) having an inspiring role model, whom you try to emulate
   C) engaging in practices in which you push yourself hard even when it means frequently failing.
   D) using Ericsson's "scaffolding" technique in the early stages of training

7. A person with an average IQ who performs extremely well in one specific area (e.g. art, math, basketball) is referred to as a:

   A) mastermind
   B) genius
   C) savant
   D) prodigy

8. The argument that boys are inherently better than girls at math is undermined by data showing that:

   A) the gender difference disappears among professional mathematicians.
   B) the gender difference reverses in nations where people tend to associate women with math.
   C) there are nations where more women than men receive PhDs in math.
   D) math ability develops early in life before sex-specific hormones could have shaped people's brains.

9. Many people do not like to engage in deliberate practice because it requires them to:

   A) experience a lot of failure
   B) hire an expensive coach or trainer
   C) make use of high-tech equipment to which few people have access
   D) begin at a very young age

10. Which modern theory of intelligence suggests that Spearman's concept of "g" is seriously flawed?

    A) Gardner's theory of multiple intelligences
    B) Johnson's anti-g theory
    C) dichotomy theory

References

Adolph, K. E. (2000). Specificity of learning: Why infants fall over a veritable cliff. *Psychological Science*, *11*, 290–295.

Chase, W. G., & Simon, H. A. (1973). Perception in chess. *Cognitive Psychology*, *4*, 55–81.

Deutsch, D. (2013). Absolute pitch. In D. Deutsch (Ed.), *The psychology of music, 3rd edition* (pp. 141–182). San Diego: Elsevier.

Ericsson, A., & Pool, R. (2016). *Peak: Secrets from the new science of expertise*. New York: Houghton Mifflin.

Fleming, N.D. (2005). VARK: a guide to learning styles. Retrieved from http://www.vark-learn. com/english/index.asp

Gardner, H. (1993). *Multiple intelligences: The theory in practice*. New York: Basic Books.

Gladwell, M. (2008). *Outliers: The story of success.*. New York: Little, Brown & Company.

Guerlac, O. (1908). The separation of church and state in France. *Political Science Quarterly*, *23*(2), 259–296.

Howard-Jones, P. (2014). Neuroscience and education: myths and messages. *Nature Reviews, Neuroscience*, **15**, 817–824. https://doi.org/10.1038/nrn3817

McCoy, S. P., & Aamodt, M. G. (2010). A comparison of law enforcement divorce rates with those of other occupations. *Journal of Police and Criminal Psychology*, *25*, 1–16.

McFarland, D.J. (2013). Modeling individual subtests of the WAIS IV with multiple latent factors. *PLOSone*. Retrieved June, 2019 at https://doi.org/10.1371/journal.pone.0074980

Nosek, B. A., Smyth, F. L., Sriram, N., Lindner, N. M., Devos, T., Ayala, A., ... Greenwald, A. G. (2009). National differences in gender-science stereotypes predict national sex differences in science and math achievement. *Proceeding of the National Academy of Sciences*, *106*, 10593–10597.

Pashler, H., McDaniel, M., Rohrer, D., & Bjork, R. (2009). Learning Styles: Concepts and Evidence. *Psychological Science in the Public Interest*, *9*(3), 105–119. doi:10.1111/j.1539-6053.2009.01038.x

Pelham, B. W. (2013). *Intermediate statistics: A conceptual course*. Thousand Oaks: SAGE Publishing.

Rath, T. (2007). *Strengths Finder 2.0*. New York: Gallup Press.

Sakakibara, A. (2014). A longitudinal study of the process of acquiring absolute pitch. A practical report of training with the "chord identification method." *Psychology of Music*, *42*(1), 86–111.

Schacter, D. L. (1996). *Searching for memory: The brain, the mind, and the past*. New York: Basic Books.

Scheiber, D. (2011). Joan Joyce: The best Ted Williams ever faced. ESPN W. August 5, 2011. Retrieved at www.espn.com/espnw/news/article/6833700/best-ted-williams-ever-faced

Shapiro, A. (2017). Maybe you, too, could become a super memorizer. Retrieved Sept. 21, 2017 from: www.npr.org/templates/transcript/transcript.php?storyId=518815297

Waterhouse, L. (2006). Multiple Intelligences, the Mozart effect, and emotional intelligence: A critical review. *Educational Psychologist*, *41*(4), 207–225. doi:10.1207/s15326985ep4104_1

Willingham, D. T., Hughes, E. M., & Dobolyi, D. G. (2015). The scientific status of learning styles theories. *Teaching of Psychology*, *42*(3), 266–271.

Yocom, G. (2010, August 12). My shot: Sam Snead. *Golf Digest* retrieved October 5, 2017 from: www.golfdigest.com/story/myshot_gd0204

VIII
Lifespan Human Development

Module 21
Human Prenatal Development and Birth

This module focuses mainly on the biological investments human mothers make in their offspring – in the nine-month window that precedes a typical human birth. Because human mothers face unique birth challenges, and because many modern cultures have transformed birth from a natural to an unnatural process, we conclude this module with an analysis of the challenges faced by human mothers and infants who live in places where birth has become highly artificial. Before jumping in to the details of prenatal development, though, let's revisit why sexual reproduction is so prevalent. As E.O. Wilson (1978, p. 124) put it, sexual reproduction is a genetic insurance program. It's a way of hedging one's genetic bets in a changing world:

> When the two gametes unite in fertilization they create an instant mixture of genes surrounded by the durable housing of the egg. By cooperating to create zygotes, the female and male make it more likely that at least some of their offspring will survive in the event of a changing environment. A fertilized egg differs from an asexually reproducing cell in one fundamental respect: it contains a newly assembled admixture of genes.

So sexual reproduction yields novel combinations of genes. Sexual reproduction apparently works so well that few modern animals get by without it. From an evolutionary perspective, if sex goes well, it leads to the physical development of the fertilized egg that E.O. Wilson found so intriguing. With this in mind, let's examine human prenatal development. And let's focus on two of the most fascinating things about human prenatal development. First, what happens when it goes right? Second, what happens when it goes wrong.

What happens when it goes right? Almost 200 years ago, the embryologist Karl Ernst von Baer (1828) suggested that the embryonic development of a specific organism mirrors the ancient history of that organism. About 40 years later, shortly after Darwin proposed his theory of evolution, another guy named Ernst – Ernst Heinrich Philipp August Haeckel – made an even bolder proclamation: "**ontogeny recapitulates phylogeny.**" If those multi-syllabic words just made your eyes glaze over, you're in good company. So, let's break this down.

Haeckel's Time Machine

Haeckel meant that the development of an embryo over the course of days (ontogeny) repeats (recapitulates) what had happened over the ancient evolutionary

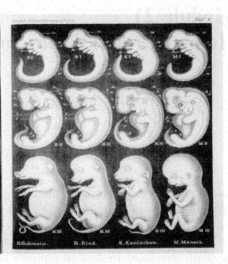

Figure 21.1 Haeckel's original (1874) drawings of eight different animals at three different stages of prenatal (or pre-hatching) development. The eight different animals look very much alike early in their early development. In fact, even at stage 2, it is still hard to tell the four mammals apart.

history of that organism (phylogeny). It's easy to see why Haeckel got excited when he compared the embryos of different animals. As shown in Figure 21.1, borrowed from Haeckel's (1874) *Anthropogenie*, animals as different as fish, turtles, and people look surprisingly similar when they first begin to develop. Then they dramatically diverge. In fact, early in our own embryological development we have gill pouches (Gould, 1977). The same pouches that become gills in fish become part of our necks and heads. In fact, one human adult in ten still retains a tiny, vestigial gill hole (Shubin, 2008). In Arnett's (2012, p. 60) description of the human embryo, he noted that at four weeks post-conception "even an expert embryologist would have trouble ... judging whether the embryo was to become a bird, a fish, or a mammal."

If you examine the top and middle images in the far-right column of Figure 21.1, you'll see that when we first begin to develop, we have a tail. In fact, we've retained a tiny tailbone inside our bodies. Some people are even born with short *external* tails. Having said this, Haeckel was accused of overstating his point. His famous proclamation proved to be an oversimplification. Many decades of embryological research have revealed that embryonic development is not quite the faithful evolutionary time machine in which Haeckel had believed. For example, Kalinka and Tomancak (2012) argued that the middle period of embryonic development tells us much more about an organism's phylogenetic history than does its beginning period. Presumably, the reason is that the middle period is when the details of an animal's body structures are really beginning to take shape.

In short, ontogeny *sort of* recapitulates phylogeny. On the other hand, as suggested by paleobiologists such as Neil Shubin, there's one aspect of Haeckel's view that has held up well. This is the idea that there's a lot of *conservation* in embryonic development. Out of all the millions of possible ways to build a goat from a zygote, nature has recycled a few basic ways across millions of species. According to Kalinka and Tomancak (2012), you always begin with fertilization, which gives us E. O. Wilson's genetically-admixtured zygote. This is followed by the development of two of the physical axes of the body (front-to-back and lateral to medial). The developing zygote for an organism like us must have an orientation before it can begin to take shape. A few steps and a great deal of cell division later, and we've made it from zygote to early embryo. Now we have the nearly universal arrangement of the three cell layers that reliably become certain parts of all animals that are bilaterally symmetrical.

In all bilaterally symmetrical animals, from crickets to cricket players, the **ectoderm** becomes the nervous system, and the **mesoderm** becomes the muscles. In mammals, the mesoderm will also become the skeleton whereas the ectoderm will become the skin. The **endoderm** will become some of the internal organs such as the lungs and the digestive tract. Of course, insects don't have bones or flexible skin, and so the parallels between human and insect development are fewer than those between people and other mammals. But the basic strategy of beginning with the three layers (endoderm, ectoderm, and mesoderm) exists in millions of animal species – and is used over and over in all vertebrates (Keller, Davidson, & Shook, 2003). Again, it is a great example of *conservation*. Moving from this general point to something more detailed, Table 21.1 – which we borrowed almost verbatim from Arnett's (2012, p. 59) edifying Table 2.2 – provides a timeline of the major events of human prenatal developmental.

Figure 21.2
Leonardo Davinci's famous Vitruvian Man illustrates bilateral symmetry. Like dogs, butterflies, robins, and turtles, we have a top and a bottom as well as a left and a right. If you divide us laterally (head to toe), our left and right halves are mirror images of one another.

A Step by Step Look at Human Prenatal Development

The pace at which prenatal development happens is dizzying. For example, before the fourth week of prenatal development, the neural tube mentioned in the second row of Table 21.1 is producing more than 4,000 neurons (4,000 brains cells) every *second*. Six months later, during the third trimester of pregnancy, the fetal

Table 21.1 Milestones of Prenatal Development

Trimester	Period	Weeks*	Milestones
First	Germinal	1–2	Zygote divides to form **blastocyst**, which implants in uterus and begins forming amnion, placenta, and umbilical cord
	Embryonic	3–4	Ectoderm, endoderm, and mesoderm form; neural tube begins to create neurons; heart begins to beat, ribs, muscles and digestive tract form
		5–8	Arms and legs form, then fingers and toes; placenta and umbilical cord function; digestive system develops; liver makes blood cells, embryo responds to touch
	Fetal	9–12	Genitals form and release sex hormones; fingernails, toenails and taste buds develop; heartbeat audible with stethoscope
Second		13–24	Mother feels fetal movement, fetus kicks, turns, hiccups, sucks thumb, breathes amniotic fluid, responds to sounds, especially familiar voices; protective vernix and lanugo develop on skin
Third		25–38	Lungs develop fully, over two-thirds of birth weight is gained (from 1 kg to about 3.4 kg); brain development greatly accelerates; sleep-wake cycles begin to resemble those of a newborn

*Note. Weeks refers to weeks post-conception.

brain is now sprouting new brain cells at a rate of more than 8,000 per second. Because we have such enormous brains, even when we are newborns, brain development picks up steam as prenatal development progresses. In fact, it looks like the newborn human brain reached its maximal size – unless there is to be a future revision in the human birth canal – about 200,000 years ago. This is when anatomically-modern human beings first walked the Earth (DeSilva, 2011). If our brains were meaningfully bigger, safe natural births would be physically impossible. But how do we make the transition from a zygote slightly wider than a human hair to the typical seven-pound cherub known as a human neonate? Let's take a whirlwind tour and see.

Step 1. For conception to take place in the typical fashion, a single sperm cell that was released during sexual intercourse must travel from the vagina of a woman who is about to ovulate (or who recently ovulated) to meet up with a mature egg in the woman's fallopian tubes. Women only ovulate once every four weeks or so, and sperm can only live in a woman's body for about two days. This means that where conception is concerned, timing is everything. After a typical ejaculation, as many as 500 million sperm begin the arduous trip from the vagina to the fallopian tubes. But very, very few sperm make it to the part of the fallopian tube where a fertile egg awaits. Notice that we said fallopian *tube* rather than tubes. Typically, women have two fallopian tubes, but an ovulating woman usually releases just one mature egg into one of her two fallopian tubes each month. If all continues to progress in ways that are to produce a pregnancy, a single, microscopic sperm penetrates the surface of the healthy egg – which is many thousands of times larger than the sperm (Sadler, 2012). The moment a sperm cell penetrates the egg, the egg undergoes chemical changes that make it impossible for any other sperm to enter.

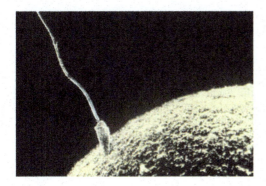

Figure 21.3
This image of a human sperm about to pene-
trate a human egg (ovum) reveals the enormous
size of the egg cell relative to the sperm. Once
a sperm penetrates an egg, no other sperm will
be allowed entry. The fact that the egg is so
huge allows cell division to happen many times
inside the egg in the absence of any nutrition.
Only the head of the sperm, which contains all
the genes the sperm carries, will make its way
into the egg. The tail will fall away.

Now the final stage of meiosis (cell division in which half of the chromosomes come
from each parent) begins to create the unique combination of mom's and dad's
genes that makes most people different from everyone else on the planet.

Step 2. Once meiosis is done, the egg is now a **zygote**. Unlike a sperm cell or an
egg, the zygote contains all the unique genetic information that may someday
become a newborn baby. But things aren't always this simple. In about one pregnancy in 60, a woman releases two eggs at once, and they *both* become fertilized –
each by a different sperm, of course. This is how fraternal or **dizygotic twins** come
to be. Fraternal twins share no more genes than siblings who are the product of
different pregnancies. Thus, about half of all fraternal twins are opposite-sex twins.
As Arnett (2012) notes, rates of fraternal twinning vary widely across the globe. In
Japan only about one in 700 births are to fraternal twins. In Nigeria that value is
one in 25. Another way in which twinning can occur happens shortly after the fertilization of one egg. As zygotes begin to divide and grow, a single zygote sometimes
splits into two genetically identical zygotes, which develop separately. Twins formed
this way are identical or **monozygotic** ("one zygote") **twins**. Only about one birth in
300 is a monozygotic twin. And as Arnett (2012) also notes, rates of monozygotic
twinning do *not* seem to vary meaningfully across the globe. Further, monozygotic
twinning does not seem to depend on any of the other factors that predict dizygotic
twinning. For example, monozygotic twinning does not seem to have a genetic component, and it does not vary with maternal age.

If you add up the two rates of twinning listed here, this yields a rate of about
one twin in 50 births. In fact, records of millions of U.S. births reveal that in 1980,
one U.S. birth in 53 was a twin. But in 2009, this value had increased to about one
birth in 30 (Martin, Hamilton, & Osterman, 2012). Part of this increase is
a consequence of rising maternal ages over the past few decades (older moms produce more fraternal twins). But the biggest part of the increase in rates of twin
births is technological rather than cultural. In the past few decades, there has been
a dramatic increase in the proportion of mothers giving birth after receiving fertility
treatments such as **in vitro fertilization**, more commonly known as **IVF**. An IVF
baby is a "test tube baby" in the sense that he or she was fertilized outside the
womb – often in a procedure in which doctors harvested multiple eggs from

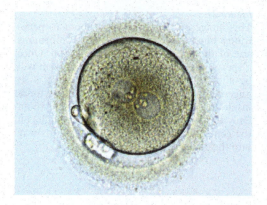

Figure 21.4
A fertilized egg or zygote contains all the genetic information it takes to make a unique person. Before the zygote implants in the uterus, it is no larger than the egg from which it came because the zygote has no source of nutrition other than the cytoplasm that was part of the egg (recall that the tiny sperm cell contributes nothing but genetic information). Like an egg, then, a zygote is about the width of a human hair, which makes it visible to the naked eye – though barely so.

a mother, fertilized several of the healthiest eggs, and then implanted the fertilized eggs directly in the woman's uterus. When medical professionals fertilize multiple eggs at once (hoping that at least one will develop normally), this can easily lead to multiple eggs that develop normally. Fertility treatments such as IVF produce high rates of multiple births.

From a developmental perspective, whether a baby shares the womb with others is very important. Birth complications and infant mortality rates are much higher for twins than for singletons – and higher still for triplets or quadruplets than for twins (Imaizumi, 2001). It's partly for this reason that most fertility clinics have become more cautious than they were in past decades about harvesting and implanting large numbers of eggs from mothers-to-be. In fact, over the past two decades or so, there has been a decrease in the percentage of U.S. births to mothers of quadruplets, quintuplets, or beyond. According to data from the Centers for Disease Control and Prevention (CDC), U.S. mothers gave birth to four or more babies at once (quadruplets or higher) 589 times in 1997. This declined to 242 such births in 2017 (see also Kulkarni, Jamie-son, & Jones, 2013).

Step 3. About 30 hours after conception, cells in the zygote begin to divide. By about a week post-conception, the zygote has become a ball of about 100 cells known as the **blastocyst** (see Table 21.1). As shown in Figure 21.5, it is during this **germinal period** of development (weeks 1–2) that the blastocyst usually attaches itself to the **uterus** – which is the organ from which the developing baby will get all its nutrients.

Step 4. During the **embryonic period**, covering weeks 3–4, there are a dizzying number of radical changes. First, this is when the three layers known as the endoderm, ectoderm, and mesoderm begin to develop. Second, some of the major organs begin to develop. This is when the heart first begins to beat. This is also a very dangerous time for parents hoping to have a baby because slightly more than half of all blastocysts or very young embryos fail to attach to the uterus – and then they stop growing. The undeveloped blastocyst then becomes part of a heavier than usual menstrual period. The first few weeks post-conception come with many risks.

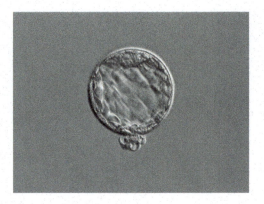

FROM OVULATION TO IMPLANTATION

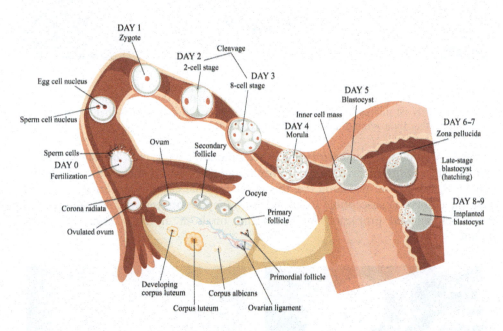

Figure 21.5 The top image is a micrograph of a human blastocyst, which is just a zygote after cells have divided for a few days. In the lower right-hand portion of the bottom image, you can see a blastocyst that has just implanted in the uterus, where it may develop into an embryo and then a fetus.

Blastocyst image credit: Vladimir Staykov/Shutterstock.com Uterus image credit: logika600/Shutterstock.com

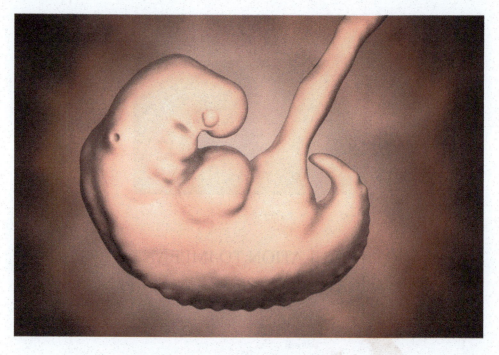

Figure 21.6 A human embryo at about four-weeks post-conception. At this point, you can see why both Haeckel (1874) and Arnett (2012) noted that the early human embryo could easily be mistaken for a duck or a frog embryo. But the genes that make us human rather than avian or amphibian will express themselves soon enough.

Step 5. Assuming the **embryo** is still developing after week four, **organogenesis** – the window when many major organs are beginning to form – comes into full bloom in weeks 5–8. But as you will soon see, this portion of the embryonic period is a window when the embryo is susceptible to harm from many **teratogens** – which can create serious developmental problems. We'll elaborate on both of these terms later in this module.

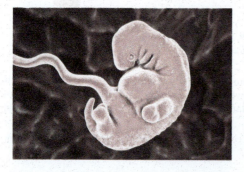
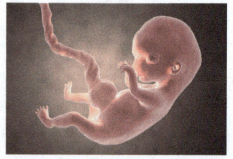

Figure 21.7 As you can see by comparing the 4-to-5-week-old embryo on the left with the 8-week-old embryo on the right, a great deal of development happens between weeks four and eight post-conception.

Steps 6–8. It is during the last 84% of a full-term pregnancy (weeks 9–38) that the embryo becomes a **fetus**. During the fetal period, the former embryo comes to look and act increasingly human. Tiny fingernails and toenails form, the heartbeat becomes easily detectable, the sex organs develop, and brain development skyrockets. During the second trimester, before the fetus is even viable, it begins to respond to sounds, starts to kick its feet, and may suck its thumb.

Human development during the fetal period is much more of a two-way street than most people would imagine. For example, recent research suggests that **fetuses kick for good reason**. Animal models suggest that when a fetus moves in the womb, it is building crucial neural circuits that promote both the physical development of limbs and the neural wiring that allows us to sense and control those limbs. Based on their experiments with late-term rat fetuses, Robinson, Kleven, and Brumley (2008) concluded that

> Experience that accrues from ongoing motor activity before birth ... may play a significant role in motor development during the last few days of gestation in the rat fetus, and by inference, during the last two trimesters of gestation in the human fetus.

Further, recent work with premature human infants suggests that the same kind of crucial feedback mechanisms that facilitate rat prenatal development also facilitate human prenatal development (Whitehead, Meek, & Fabrizi, 2018). Research suggests that if fetuses were not allowed to kick in the womb, they would never develop normal, working legs!

Prior to birth, fetuses also seem to be learning voice preferences. Newborns whose moms had read *The Cat in the Hat* to them twice a day during weeks 32–38 of gestation showed a clear preference for hearing this story over a similar story shortly after birth. Newborns whose moms had *not* read *The Cat in the Hat* showed no such preference (DeCasper & Spence, 1986). If you're wondering how in the heck we know what newborns prefer, the answer is surprisingly simple. As applied to this study, the answer is that newborns will suck on a pacifier more readily if it allows them to hear something they prefer over something they do not. We can only assume that there are developmentally important reasons why fetuses not only kick their feet but also move their arms, suck their thumbs, and come to recognize their mother's voices.

What Can Go Wrong Sometimes Does

So far, you've mainly heard about what happens when all goes well during prenatal development. Human development is predictable. But it's also fragile. The window of about 15–60 days post-conception is known as **organogenesis**. It is so named ("organo" and "genesis") because this is when all the major organs begin to develop. As suggested earlier, this makes it a crucial window for a pregnant woman to be concerned about teratogens.

To paraphrase Kimmel (2001) a **teratogen** is anything to which a mother and developing baby are exposed that causes abnormal development. A teratogen, then, is any disturbance to the mother during pregnancy that leads to an injury to the developing embryo. Teratogens range from nicotine and alcohol, both of which cross the placenta when a mother-to-be smokes or drinks, to psychological stress, which creates a strong risk of low birth weight (Lobel, Dunkel-Schetter, & Scrimshaw, 1992).

Perhaps the most dramatic example of a teratogen is the drug thalidomide, which pregnant women took to prevent morning sickness in Germany and other parts of Europe beginning in the late 1950s (LaBarba, 1981). **Morning sickness** is the nausea and vomiting that many women experience when pregnant. Unfortunately, thalidomide also prevents the embryo's arms and legs – and some internal organs – from developing normally. Until the medical community realized the potent teratogenic effects of thalidomide, thousands of European babies were born suffering from very serious deformities. About half of them did not survive to adulthood. As a more recent example, mothers who do not get enough **folic acid** (aka folate, B9 or B12) in their diets are at increased risk to give birth to babies with serious spinal cord problems such as spina bifida (Oakley, 2009). In most wealthy nations, women who wish to become pregnant are advised to take folic acid supplements – because deficiencies in this vitamin cause harm during the first month of pregnancy, when most women do not realize they are pregnant.

It is obviously very important for pregnant women to avoid teratogens, especially during the first trimester of a pregnancy. It is no accident, then, that morning sickness is most common during the first trimester of a woman's pregnancy. In fact, Flaxman and Sherman (2000) argued that morning sickness is the price many mothers-to-be pay to protect their developing embryos. Flaxman and Sherman summarized four pieces of evidence suggesting that **morning sickness protects developing embryos**. First, as already noted, morning sickness is most likely to occur at precisely the window of pregnancy when teratogens pose the greatest risk to the embryo. Second, women who have morning sickness are less likely to have miscarriages than are women who do not. Third, studies show that vomiting – not nausea – is the key symptom that protects the developing embryo. This is informative because there is no known benefit to the embryo to having mom feel nauseated but plenty of benefit to having her puke her poor guts out – to be sure the developing embryo isn't exposed to any teratogens. Finally, during their first trimester, many pregnant women develop distastes for specific foods and drugs, such as meats, caffeine, and alcohol – all of which pose a risk to the developing embryo. Bitter foods such as broccoli often become intolerable. This is probably no accident; many teratogens and poisons are naturally bitter.

If you're thinking that it can't be good for an embryo when its mother is puking her guts out for many weeks, remember that women who suffer from morning sickness do not starve; they are almost always able to keep some food down (usually bland stuff like saltines or oatmeal). Further, remember that during the first trimester of pregnancy the embryo is still teeny and does not yet require much nutrition to develop normally. On top of that, part of the reason eggs are 2,000 times larger than sperm is that they contain nutrients that feed the developing zygote for the first two-weeks post-conception. With all this in mind, remember that this process evolved. It is not the goal of evolution to keep moms-to-be as comfortable as possible. Evolution favors things, however unhappy, that favor successful reproduction.

We don't want to overstate the point that the first few months of pregnancy are the most worrisome window for exposure to teratogens. In fact, some teratogens – such as smoking, chronic maternal stress, malnutrition, drug use, or heavy alcohol consumption – are problematic at almost any stage of pregnancy. Research also suggests that maternal infection by the mosquito-borne **Zika virus** can lead to serious teratogenic effects at any period between 6–35 weeks of gestation (Petersen et al., 2016). Presumably, the window for damage to the brain is very wide because the brain begins to develop at three weeks post-conception and continues to develop until birth. So, moms-to-be would be well-advised to avoid any known teratogens for the entire duration of their pregnancies. Of course, if mom is living in a place without proper nutrition, pre-natal care, or mosquito nets, this is much easier said than done.

The Medicalization of Modern Birth

OK. Suppose mom and baby have been lucky enough to survive the harrowing nine-month journey known as a full-term pregnancy. This means that baby has a precious layer of fat reserves, has fully-developed lungs, and has a fully-developed brain. What happens next? We are sorry to say that in many wealthy nations, full-term babies who are being carried by healthy moms face yet another serious obstacle. This is the obs-tacle of modern, unnecessarily medicalized birth (see the 2015 WHO Statement on cesarean rates across the globe). As we use the term here, **medicalized birth** refers to a host of modern medical norms and procedures that make it hard for women to give birth naturally, from the routine use of the artificial hormone Pitocin to the induction of labor or the pervasive attitude that women need to be rescued from birth.

Despite the controversial nature of this issue, we are not going to shy away from it. This is because the way births happen is a crucial aspect of human development. Let's begin with few indisputable facts about modern births in wealthy nations, especially the United States. First, in the United States of the early 1900s, human birth was viewed as a natural process, and it almost always took place at home – under the supervision of midwives. But today almost all U.S. births take place in hospitals – supervised by sur-geons (doctors that specialize is obstetrics and gynecology are also trained to perform surgery). But in many other wealthy nations (e.g., Japan and much of Western Europe), modern births are still supervised by midwives. In such nations, the outcomes for both mothers and babies are substantially better than the outcomes in the United States. In fact, U.S. infant mortality rates are among the highest in the developed world. One reason for this is that the United States has an exceptionally high rate of birth by major surgery. CDC data covering millions of recent U.S. births show that about one third of all U.S. births have taken place by means of **cesarean section**. That's right. About one U.S. birth in three takes place when doctors cut through the mother's abdomen and uterus to extract the baby by major surgery. As recently as 1970, the rate of U.S. birth by cesarean section was 5.5% (for example, see www.cdc.gov/mmwr/preview/mmwrhtml/00036845.htm). In less than four decades, then, the U.S. rate of birth by major surgery increased six-fold. By contrast, in modern-day Finland and Norway, where midwives usu-ally assist with births, rates of birth by cesarean section are about 7%. In both nations, infant mortality and maternal mortality rates are half to one third what they are in the U.S. Using data from both the CDC and the OECD (the Organization for Economic Cooperation and Development) Pelham (2018) calculated that if the U.S. had the same infant mortality rate as either Finland or Norway, roughly 125,000 U.S. infants who died in the past decade would now be alive.

To see how artificial and medicalized U.S. birth has become in the past few decades, we need merely look at the daily patterning of U.S. births. We hope it's obvious that full-term babies do not know what day it is. Likewise, mother's bodies should not prefer to give birth on some days of the week more often than others. But for economic reasons, it is much better for hospitals if most births happen on weekdays. As you can see in Figure 21.8, that's precisely what happens today in U.S. hospitals. In fact, an

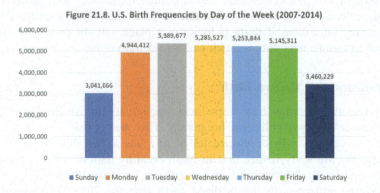

Figure 21.8 U.S. birth frequencies by day of the week (2007–2014).

analysis of more than 36 million recent U.S. births (Pelham, 2018) showed that mothers in the U.S. today are 77% more likely to give birth on a Tuesday than on a Sunday. This means that many modern U.S. births are being scheduled artificially.

Why does this happen? The short answer is that in the United States today there are huge financial and legal incentives that strongly favor highly medicalized births. When low-risk mothers-to-be are routinely given the artificial hormone Pitocin, for example, this dramatically speeds up labor and delivery – thus opening up hospital beds at a faster pace than would happen if birth proceeded naturally. But routinely giving low-risk mothers-to-be Pitocin creates unnecessary risks for mothers as well as babies (Hidalgo-Lopezosa, Hidalgo-Maestre, & Rodríguez-Borrego, 2016).

Likewise, giving mothers-to-be epidural anesthesia – especially if it is given very early in labor – is associated with increased risk for birth by cesarean section (Klein, 2006). Another example of an incentive that strongly promotes medicalized births is the fact that hospitals charge about twice as much for births by cesarean as they do for natural births (after all, major surgery is costly). In fact, in nations where there are little or no financial advantages to doctors for performing cesarean sections, rates of birth by cesarean section are much, much lower than in the United States. Within the United States, rates of birth by cesarean section are also higher at for-profit hospitals than at not-for-profit hospitals (Braveman, Egerter, Edmonston, & Verdon, 1995). And speaking of profits, costs associated with giving birth in the United States are higher than any other nation on Earth. Ironically, despite paying more for births than mothers pay in other wealthy nations, American mothers receive highly inferior birth outcomes – for both themselves and their babies (Kassebaum, Steiner, Murray, Lopez, & Lozano, 2016).

Interestingly, one of the best predictors of the medicalization of birth across U.S. states is state by state differences in people's attitudes about women. In states where people have more traditional attitudes about women, and where women have fewer political and economic opportunities relative to men, rates of birth medicalization are much higher than the national average. Conversely, in states where people have more progressive attitudes about gender, the level of medicalization of birth is much lower. At least part of the specific reason behind such differences may be **benevolent sexism** – the idea that women are pure but fragile and thus must be protected and put on a pedestal by men (Pelham, 2018).

But is medicalization really such a bad thing? Is it possible that American doctors really are protecting American mothers from the trauma of birth? Cross-national comparisons of millions of birth records suggest not. U.S. birth outcomes are vastly inferior relative to those in other highly-developed nations (OECD Health at a Glance, 2017). Further, U.S. birth outcomes – for both moms and babies – are worse in states with higher rates of birth medicalization than they are in states with lower rates of birth medicalization. Why is this the case? One likely reason is that highly medicalized birth practices often lead to unnecessary cesarean sections. There are many negative health consequences of birth by cesarean section. In addition to creating risks such as accidental cutting and post-surgical infection (Lydon-Rochelle, Holt, Martin, & Easterling, 2000), cesarean births are associated with problems with breastfeeding, infant breathing difficulties, and a variety of infant immunological problems (Sandall, et al., 2013). Research also shows that when infants are delivered vaginally they are exposed to biomes that promote the development of healthy infant immune systems. Birth by cesarean section denies babies this important natural health benefit (Dominguez-Bello et al., 2010). Finally, adding an ethnic insult to all this injury, research reveals a distressing trend in the patterns of medicalized birth in the United States. In comparison with extremely low-risk White mothers (e.g., mothers of singletons who are highly educated, got prenatal care, and who do not suffer from diabetes, high blood pressure, or eclampsia) matched groups of extremely low-risk mothers of color are more likely to give birth by cesarean section. In fact, when Pelham (2018) matched millions of White and Black mothers on 11 key risk factors for birth by cesarean section (from the age, education, and health of mothers to baby's weight or gestation length), *Black mothers were almost 50% more likely to give birth by cesarean section.* This research suggests that **medicalized birth is subject to ethnic biases**.

Although this research using CDC birth records cannot reveal exactly how and why this ethnic bias happens, survey research with mothers who have recently given birth offer insights into how U.S. birth has become so medicalized – and how some mothers are targeted more than others. In a nationally-representative survey, Jou et al. (2000) found that 21.5% of women reported feeling pressure from health care professionals to have either a C-section, a labor-induction technique, or both. Jou et al.'s (2000) findings also suggest that some women receive more pressure than others to accept medicalized births. Specifically, younger mothers (aged 18–24) were more than twice as likely as older mothers (aged 35+) to report having felt pressure to have an invasive procedure. This is surprising because, actuarially speaking, younger mothers are probably less likely to *need* cesarean sections. Women who had never given birth before were also about twice as likely as women who *had* given birth before to say they experienced pressure to have an invasive procedure. Such findings suggest that women with less power and less knowledge about birth are more likely to be pressured to accept invasive birth practices. In fact, we have known for decades that people who are high in power often exercise subtle but powerful influence over those who are low in power (French & Raven, 1959). Perhaps the most important finding from this survey was that when women reported feeling pressured by medical professionals to have invasive procedures, they were much more likely to report having *received* these procedures.

What's an expectant mother to do? In our view, the first thing is to educate herself about the risks of a medicalized birth and the benefits of a natural birth. When your first author's wife gave birth to their daughter, his wife was 42 and she had educated herself well about natural birth and midwifery. She even enlisted the help of a **doula** (a birth coach) as well as a highly trained **nurse-midwife**. This team worked together with Brett to assist his wife's birth in a mid-wife friendly hospital. However, even with a firm plan in place for a natural birth, and with Brett and two other natural birth advocates at her side, Brett's wife faced serious pressure from other hospital staff members to medicalize her birth. For example, within moments of her arrival at her room, she had to deal with a highly persistent nurse who wanted to give her an IV "to hydrate her and get her ready in case any medication became necessary." The nurse did not give up until Brett's wife very loudly instructed her to put the IV away. (Brett won't report the exact F-bomb count, but it wasn't zero.) Institutional policies that support the status quo can be hard to overcome – even with plenty of support at your side. On the other hand, if advocates of natural birth can get their message across and educate mothers-to-be about the merits of a natural birth – from mother-infant bonding to boosting infant immune systems – then there is hope that the United States can become more like Finland and Norway – and look forward to a future where more babies come into the world as healthy as they can possibly be.

Critical Thinking Questions for Module 21

Some of our physical traits are set for life in the womb. But not all these traits depend on genetic factors. Some depend on the *intrauterine environment* – that is, the hormonal environment inside mother's uterus while she is carrying an embryo or fetus. More specifically, hormone levels in the *amniotic fluid* (the liquid in which the fetus floats in the placenta) influence prenatal development. Consider testosterone. There are wide variations across mothers (and across different pregnancies for the *same* mothers) in exactly how much testosterone is in the amniotic fluid during prenatal developmental. For example, in mothers-to-be who have given birth several times in the past, testosterone levels in the placenta are usually lower than in first time mothers. As a different example, mothers who report being depressed during their pregnancies tend to have higher amniotic testosterone levels. Women carrying boys also have higher amniotic testosterone levels than women carrying girls. But independent of a fetus's sex, psychological and environmental variables also influence testosterone levels in the intrauterine environment.

This is important because what happens in the womb does *not* always stay in the womb. For example, testosterone levels in the womb influence finger development. A well-studied example of this is the 2D:4D digit ratio (where 2D means second digit or *pointer finger*, and 4D means fourth digit or *ring finger*). For both male and female babies, the relative length of the pointer finger (2D) and the ring finger (4D) vary with prenatal testosterone levels. Specifically, when there is a lot of testosterone in the womb, babies tend to develop ring fingers (4D) that are much longer than pointer fingers (2D). When there is less testosterone ring fingers may still be a little longer than pointer fingers, but the discrepancy is not so large. This finger comparison trait is known as the **2D:4D ratio**. Figure 21.9 gives you an idea of how it can be measured. To make this easier to see, notice that in the lower right-hand corner of each photo, there is an enlarged view of the ruler and the tip of each finger (D2 and D4). This man has a pointer finger (D2) that is 7.15 cm long. In comparison, his ring finger is 7.8 cm long. What matters for digit ratio is not the absolute length of any one finger but the *ratio* of the two. This man's digit ratio (for his left hand, at least) is 0.92. That's 2D/4D – which is 7.15/7.8 (rounded to the nearest two decimal places). Assuming you can gain access to a ruler like the one you see in Figure 21.9, you can calculate your own digit ratios.

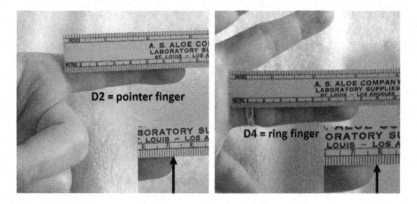

Figure 21.9 Assessing digit ratios (relative finger lengths).

But measuring digit ratios is not quite as simple as we have made it appear here. When the first author took a repeat set of measurements on the same man's hand, he got slightly different values. So digit measurement may not be quite as objective as you might think. If you are lucky, your instructor might have a pair of *Vernier calipers*, which reduce some guesswork and human error in measuring small objects, fingers included. But regardless of what tools you use to measure 2D:4D ratios, we'd like you to think about what you can do to make these measurements as reliable (repeatable) and valid (accurate) as possible.

1   Working in groups of at least three people each, come up with a highly specific, concrete proposal for your instructor that tells your instructor *exactly* how you'll obtain a reliable set of measurements of the D2:D4 ratio for every member of your group. Questions to consider include (a) how many raters per "participant," (b) how many hands (one or both) per participant, and (c) how many measurements made per judge of the same finger or fingers. Finally, exactly what constitutes the beginning and end of a finger?

2   If you do this group activity in a class that includes at least six or eight women and at least six or eight men, it might be worth comparing the final D2:D4 ratio score for each man (the mean score for men) with the final D2:D4 ratio score for each woman (again, the mean). Did you observe an apparent gender difference? To see if the difference you may have observed is consistent with what has been observed in large samples, check out Manning, Stewart, Bundred, and Trivers (2004) or Hönekopp and Watson (2010) – or perhaps save yourself some time by asking your instructor.

3   D2:D4 scores appear to predict many important psychological traits and outcomes (Jeevanandam & Muthu, 2016; Kociuba, Kozieł, & Chakraborty, 2016; Manning et al., 2004). These range from personality and aggression to handedness, hand strength, obesity, sperm counts (among men, of course), and even sexual orientation (though in this last case, only for men: Lippa, 2003).

There seem to be ethnic differences in D2:D4 ratios. Manning et al. (2004) found that Jamaicans had lower D2:D4 rations than Whites or Asians. But because environmental factors influence D2:D4 ratios, it is unclear whether ethnic difference are genetic or environmental. For example, it's well-known that stress increases cortisol levels. And high cortisol levels go hand in hand with high prenatal testosterone levels. Recall that prenatal testosterone leads to lower D2:D4 ratios.

4a   Going back to Module 4, what's the methodological word for a "third variable" that might be the true cause of an outcome – rather than some other variable that is correlated with the outcome? 4b. Fill in the label for the missing oval in the causal diagram (Figure 21.10) to show you understand.

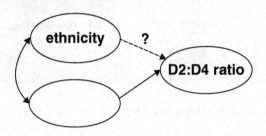

Figure 21.10

Multiple-Choice Questions for Module 21

1. Human embryos look a great deal like duck, rabbit, or turtle embryos. This observation led the German embryologist Ernst Haeckel to argue in the late 1800s that ontogeny:

   A) recapitulates phylogeny
   B) hides future development
   C) approximates redundancy

2. Which period of human pregnancy lasts the longest?

   A) the trigeminal period
   B) the embryological period
   C) the fetal period

3. After the cells in a zygote have divided enough to create a ball of about 100 cells, this is known as what?

   A) an ovum
   B) a blastocyst
   C) an embryo

4. Like exposure to certain infections or toxic chemicals during pregnancy, serious undernourishment during pregnancy is considered a _____.

   A) teratogen
   B) pollutant
   C) toxicity

5. The period in pregnancy when most of the major organs are forming is known as:

   A) the trigeminal period
   B) organogenesis
   C) organic divide

6. What appears to be the significance of kicking in the womb?

   A) it is a sign of sleep-wake cycles
   B) it promotes the ossification of the embryonic leg bones
   C) it plays a crucial role in the sensory and motor development of the legs

7. What have evolutionary psychologists proposed about morning sickness?

   A) it is a sign that a mother-to-be is probably carrying a male baby

   B) it is most common in the second trimester of pregnancy
   C) it is an adaptation that reduces embryonic exposure to teratogens

8. What's the main reason why rates of multiple births have increased in the U.S. in the past few decades?

   A) because more women are able to carry twins or triplets to a full-term birth
   B) because of the growth in the popularity of fertility treatments such as IVF
   C) because of reductions in the rates of spontaneous abortions

9. If two twins are the same sex and look almost exactly alike, there is a very good chance they are _____ twins.

   A) zygotic
   B) monozygotic
   C) bizygotic

10. Can a fetus learn while in the womb?

    A) no, because the brain is so poorly developed
    B) yes; as suggested by the *Cat in the Hat* study
    C) no: because it is impossible to reward a fetus

11. What is one of the most obvious signs that birth in the United States has become highly medicalized in the past few decades?

    A) increases in the duration of labor and delivery
    B) increased rates of diseases such as Down's syndrome
    C) many more births now take place on Tuesday than on Sunday

12. According to the text, modern birth has become highly medicalized mainly because of an exaggerated focus on _____ at most hospitals.

    A) profits
    B) the timing of birth
    C) technology

Answer Key: 1A, 2C, 3B, 4A, 5B, 6C, 7C, 8B, 9B, 10B, 11C, 12A

"Well you're in labor, Brittney. So we have a tough decision here. We *could* just let nature take its course, and you'd almost certainly have a safe and uneventful delivery. But we could *also* pump you full of a lot of drugs that will dramatically accelerate your labor. Then, once this artificial process puts the baby's life at risk, we can cut the baby out of you. It's really up to you."

Figure 21.11

References

Arnett, J. (2012). *Human development: A cultural approach*. Saddle River, NJ: Pearson.

Braveman, P., Egerter, S., Edmonston, F., & Verdon, M. (1995). Racial/ethnic differences in the likelihood of cesarean delivery, California. *American Journal of Public Health*, *85*, 625–630. doi:10.2105/AJPH.85.5.625

DeCasper, A. J., & Spence, M. J. (1986). Prenatal maternal speech influences newborns' perception of speech sounds. *Infant Behavior and Development*, *9*, 133–150.

DeSilva, J. M. (2011). A shift toward birthing relatively large infants early in human evolution. *Proceedings of the National Academy of Sciences*, *108*(3), 1022–1027. doi:10.1073/pnas.1003865108

Dominguez-Bello, M.G., Costello, E.K., Contreras, M., Magris, M, Hidalgo, G., Fierere, N., & Knight, R. (2010). Delivery mode shapes the acquisition and structure of the initial microbiota across multiple body habitats in newborns. *Proceedings of the National Academy of Sciences*, *107*, 11971–11975.

Flaxman, S.M., & Sherman, P.W. (2000). Morning sickness: A mechanism for protecting mother and embryo. *Quarterly Review of Biology*, *75*, 1–36.

French, J. R. P., Jr., & Raven, B. (1959). The bases of social power. In D. Cartwright (Ed.), *Studies in social power* (p. 150–167). Univer: Michigan.

Gould, S.J. (1977). *Ontogeny and phylogeny*. Cambridge: Harvard University Press.

Haeckel, E. (1874). *Anthropogenie* (4th edition). Leipzig: Verlag von Wilhelm Engelmann.

Hidalgo-Lopezosa, P., Hidalgo-Maestre, M., & Rodríguez-Borrego, M. A. (2016). Labor stimulation with oxytocin: Effects on obstetrical and neonatal outcomes. *Revista latino-americana de enfermagem*, *24*, e2744.

Hönekopp, J., & Watson, S. (2010). Meta-analysis of digit ratio 2D:4D shows greater sex difference in the right hand. *American Journal of Human Biology*, *22*, 619–630. doi: 10.1002/ajhb.21054

Imaizumi, Y. (2001). Infant mortality rates in single, twin and triplet births, and influencing factors in Japan, 1995-98. *Paediatric Perinatology and Epidemiology*, *15*(4), 346–351.

Jeevanandam, S., & Muthu, P. K. (2016). 2D:4D ratio and its implications in medicine. *Journal of Clinical and Diagnostic Research*, *10*(12), CM01–CM03.

Jou, J., Kozhimannil, K.B., Johnson, P.J., & Sakala, C. (2000). Patient-perceived pressure from clinicians for labor induction and cesarean delivery: A population-based survey of U.S. women. *Health Services Research*, *50*, 961–981.

Kalinka, A. T., & Tomancak, P. (2012). The evolution of early animal embryos: Conservation or divergence? *Trends in Ecology and Evolution*, *27*, 385–393.

Kassebaum, N. J., Steiner, C., Murray, C. J. L., Lopez, A. D., & Lozano, R. (2016). Global, regional, and national levels of maternal mortality, 1990–2015: A systematic analysis for the Global Burden of Disease Study 2015. *Lancet, 388*, 1775–1812.

Keller, R., Davidson, L.A., & Shook, D.R. (2003). How we are shaped: The biomechanics of gastrulation. *Differentiation, 71*, 171–205.

Kimmel, C.A. (2001). Overview of teratology. *Current Protocols in Toxicology, 13*, Unit 13.1.

Klein, M. C. (2006). Does epidural analgesia increase rate of cesarean section? *Canadian Family Physician (Medecin De Famille Canadien), 52*(4), 419–421, 426–428.

Kociuba, M., Kozieł, S., & Chakraborty, R. (2016). Sex differences in digit ratio (2D:4D) among military and civil cohorts at a military academy in Wroclaw, Poland. *Journal of Biosocial Science, 48*(5), 658–671.

Kulkarni, A.D., Jamieson, D.J., & Jones, H.W. Jr. (2013). Fertility treatments and multiple births in the United States. *New England Journal of Medicine, 369*(23): 2218–2225. doi:10.1056/NEJMoa1301467

LaBarba, R.C. (1981). *Foundations of developmental psychology.* New York, NY: Academic Press.

Lobel, M., Dunkel-Schetter, C., & Scrimshaw, S.C. (1992). Prenatal maternal stress and prematurity: A prospective study of socioeconomically disadvantaged women. *Health Psychology, 11*, 32–40.

Lippa, A. R. (2003). Are 2D:4D finger-length ratios related to sexual orientation? Yes for men, no for women. *Journal of Personality and Social Psychology, 85*(1), 179–188.

Lydon-Rochelle, M., Holt, V.L., Martin, D.P., & Easterling, T.R. (2000). Association between method of delivery and maternal rehospitalization. *The Journal of the American Medical Association, 283*, 2411–2416.

Manning, J. T., Stewart, A., Bundred, P. E., & Trivers, R. L. (2004). Sex and ethnic differences in 2nd to 4th digit ratio of children. *Early Human Development, 80*(2), 161–168.

Martin, J. A., Hamilton, B. E., & Osterman, M. J. K. (2012, January). Three decades of twin births in the United States, 1980–2009. NCHS Data Brief No. 80. Retrieved from www.cdc.gov/nchs/products/databriefs/db80.htm

Oakley, G. P. (2009). The scientific basis for eliminating folic acid–preventable spina bifida: A modern miracle from epidemiology. *Annals of Epidemiology, 19*(4), 226–230.

OECD. (2017). *Health at a glance 2017: OECD Indicators.* Paris: Author. doi:10.1787/health_-glance-2017-en.

Pelham, B. W. (2018). Ethnicity, culture, and rates of birth by unnecessary cesarean section in the United States. Under revision.

Petersen, L.R., Jamieson, D.J., Powers, A.M., & Honein, M.A. (2016). Zika virus. *New England Journal of Medicine, 374*, 1552–1563.

Robinson, S. R., Kleven, G. A., & Brumley, M. R. (2008). Prenatal development of interlimb motor learning in the rat fetus. *Infancy: The Official Journal of the International Society on Infant Studies, 13*(3), 204–228.

Sadler, T. W. (2012). *Langman's medical embryology.* Baltimore, MD: Lippincott Williams & Wilkins.

Sandall, J., Soltani, H., Gates, S., Shennan, A., & Devane, D. (2013). Midwife-led continuity models versus other models of care for childbearing women. *The Cochrane Library, 8*, 1–107.

Shubin, N. (2008). *Your inner fish: A journey into the 3.5-billion-year history of the human body.* New York: Pantheon Books.

von Baer, K. E. (1828). *On the developmental history of animals: Observation and reflection [original in German].* Königsberg: Bornträger.

Whitehead, K., Meek, J., & Fabrizi, L. (2018). Developmental trajectory of movement-related cortical oscillations during active sleep in a cross-sectional cohort of pre-term and full-term human infants, Scientific reports 8, 17516. Retrieved from www.nature.com/articles/s41598-018-35850-1

WHO statement on cesarean section rates. (2015, April). WHO/RHR/15.02.

Wilson, E.O. (1978). *On human nature.* Cambridge, MA: Harvard University Press.

Module 22
Critical and Sensitive Periods in Human Development

Human development is all about timing, and one of the most interesting topics in human development deals with the specificity of this timing. Are we equally able to learn or develop at all phases of life? Or are their certain crucial windows of opportunity for specific kinds of learning and development – after which the doors close forever? Even if a specific developmental door never closes forever, are there periods after which specific doors become much more difficult to open? Developmental psychologists refer to specific periods (i.e., specific age ranges) that are the *only* opportunities for something to develop normally as **critical periods**.

The evolutionary perspective known as **life history theory** predicts that there are indeed critical periods in both human and animal development (Stearns, 1992). Life history theory is all about biological tradeoffs that promote the survival of ones' genes. For the purposes of this chapter, the aspect of life history theory that is most relevant is the idea that *early in the life of many animals, they take developmental paths that can vary enormously with the environment in which they mature*. This means that in many animals, there are important aspects of development that can only happen normally at certain periods of life. Perhaps the most dramatic example of this principle is to be found in mammalian prenatal development (development in the womb). In people, the window of pregnancy when all the major organs are beginning to develop (roughly four to 12 weeks post-fertilization) is undoubtedly a critical developmental period. As we discussed in Module 21, if women consume a lot of alcohol, get bitten by a mosquito carrying the Zika virus, or take certain drugs, they may give birth to babies with serious deformities or disabilities. Ingested substances or negative experiences that lead to serious birth defects when mothers experience them during pregnancy are known as **teratogens**.

In most animals, critical periods of life are usually early periods. In fact, we know of no critical periods in people that happen in adulthood. In some animals, critical periods determine not only how they behave but how their bodies develop. Juvenile water fleas who develop in the presence of chemical clues indicating that predators abound become armored. They develop a large helmet and/or a sharp spine on their tails. They fail to develop this protective armor, though, if the chemical composition of their liquid neighborhood yields few signs of lurking predators (Weiss, Laforsch, & Tollrian, 2012). If lots of predators move in after water fleas have reached adulthood, they are out of luck. The critical period for triggering the development of armor has passed. Further, if these tiny critters were to produce armor when it was unnecessary, they would be wasting a lot of biological resources. Armor must be built and then maintained. Life history theory addresses the ways in which developing animals balance costs and benefits. And critical periods often determine which of two or more developmental routes an organism takes – based on the likely costs suggested by early life conditions.

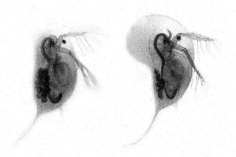

Figure 22.1
There is a critical period for the development of prickly defensive armor in water fleas. Whether water fleas develop a tiny suit of armor (like the one on the right) depends on the chemical composition of the water in which they develop as juveniles.

Credit: Dr Linda Weiss

The embryologist Charles Stockard seems to have been the first person to use terms like "critical moment" and "sensitive period." Stockard studied the crucial importance of timing in *prenatal* development, and he knew that different human organs and tissues develop at different times. As Stockard (1921, p. 139) put it,

> when an important organ is entering its initial stage of rapid proliferation or budding, a serious interruption of the developmental progress often causes decided injuries to this particular organ, while only slight or no ill effects may be suffered by the embryo in general.

We now know that many teratogens have terrible consequences for specific organs, including the brain, precisely because they mess things up at the very moment when that organ is first beginning to develop. As we saw in Module 21, during the unimaginably rapid period of growth and development known as pregnancy, there seem to be *lots* of critical periods.

The idea of critical periods gained momentum many years after Stockard's work – based on studies of critical periods in precocious birds such as ducks and geese – who can walk and swim shortly after hatching. Lorenz (1952) showed that shortly after hatching, geese enter a critical period for **imprinting**. During their first hour out of the shell, goslings become *very* strongly attached to any large moving object that happens to be nearby. This bonding – like the incredibly cute following process it produces – is very rigid. Lorenz demonstrated, for example, that when *he* was the only large moving object that was around when a group of goslings hatched, they imprinted on *him* – and followed him everywhere, as if they had joined a marching band. Further, once goslings had imprinted on him, it was impossible to retrain them to follow anything else. Following *him* was *imprinted* into their brains. This must surely have made for some adorable presentations by Lorenz at international conferences. I just hope Lorenz was careful to clean up after the poopy little fuzzballs afterwards. This rigid imprinting process makes evolutionary sense, by the way, because in the evolutionary history of ducks and geese, as well as the life history of any specific duck or goose, the large, moving object that was most likely to be handy shortly after hatching was almost always mom (Lorenz, 1952; Wilson, 1975). And mother ducklings and geese, like most other mother birds, are great caregivers (Fox, 1973).

Figure 22.2 This mother duck need not worry about her ducklings wandering away. Each of them imprinted on her very shortly after hatching.

Are there any critical periods in human *postnatal* development? It's hard to say this with great certainty for at least two reasons. First, it would be highly unethical to conduct the kind of rigorous experiments that would be necessary to settle important questions about critical periods in people. Second, many people have trouble settling the question of exactly what a critical period is in the first place. Let's address the simpler but more ethically sensitive question first. Why is it so hard to study critical periods in people?

It's Hard to Study Critical Periods in People

We know a great deal about critical periods in animals because it's possible to conduct highly informative but ethically sensitive experiments with animals. Until ethologists like Lorenz manipulated the specific objects on which goslings could become imprinted – and the precise window in which these objects first appeared to goslings – we didn't know for sure whether there was a critical period for imprinting. Consider an even more ethically-sensitive experiment by Wiesel and Hubel (1963). They wanted to know if there is a critical period for the development of vision in cats. To find out, they had to deprive some kittens of the normal visual experiences necessary for the development of vision. Sadly, they did so by sewing one eyelid of some kittens shut during certain early windows of kittenhood. Their harsh but carefully controlled experimental manipulation allowed them to see, for example, if it mattered exactly how long kittens were deprived of visual stimulation, and at exactly what age the deprivation began. Their experiment suggested that there is, in fact, a critical period for the development of certain aspects of normal vision in cats. The clear evidence of this, however, was some originally healthy kittens who ended up with messed up visual systems. These were the unlucky kittens who – by the flip of a coin – had been deprived of all visual stimulation in one eye during the critical period. After their eyelids were opened, they failed to develop normal vision. By today's standards, this research is ethically questionable, at best, because of the irreversible harm it caused to the kittens. If you tried sewing the eyelids of some *human* infants shut during certain key windows to see if there is a critical period for human visual development, you'd end up in prison. To the dismay of some animal rights activists, the ethical bar for research on people has always been much higher than the bar for research on animals. This means that human beings are hard to study.

So true experiments that make some people blind in one eye are out of the question. But some natural experiments with people loosely approximate true experiments. Consider a natural experiment that focused not on visual development but on cognitive and social development. The horrific conditions of some **Romanian orphanages** in the 1980s provided the conditions necessary for a series of natural experiments on how people think and connect to others. Infants in these orphanages got plenty of visual stimulation, but they were deprived of anything that even vaguely resembled normal interactions with caregivers. Many of these orphans suffered from abuse as well as neglect. They were kept isolated in cribs for their entire childhoods. Heartbreakingly, the only human contact they received was the minimal amount that kept them alive. When the news of this horrific maltreatment came to light worldwide in the early 1990s, many of the orphans were quickly adopted to comfortable and loving homes in Canada and the United Kingdom (Beckett, Maughan, Rutter, Castle, & Colvert, 2006).

How well the orphans fared in their new homes depended on the exact age at which they happen to have been adopted. In a study of the orphans' intellectual development, Beckett and colleagues (2006) followed a large group of the orphans until they were 11 years old. Infants lucky enough to have been adopted before the age of six months did very well. Those who had to endure the terrible conditions beyond the age of six months fared much worse. At age 11, the average IQ score of the infants who were adopted before the age of six months was a healthy 101. As a group, the infants were perfectly average. In contrast, the infants who had been in the same orphanages but had languished there between six and 24 months of life before the abuse was discovered had an average IQ of 87, which is well below average. Other studies from the same research team revealed major social as well as cognitive deficits – but mainly for the kids who were stuck in the orphanage during (or during and beyond) the sensitive period beginning at about the age of six months. Nine or ten years in a loving and stimulating home was not enough to compensate for a terrible early environment – unless kids were rescued from that terrible environment before a sensitive period of cognitive and social development.

Is Being Sensitive Better than Being Critical?

Did you notice we just used the phrase "sensitive period" rather than "critical period"? Most researchers who have studied the Romanian orphans have been careful to use this more cautious developmental term – because there is some room for debate about exactly how to interpret studies of these orphans. Because studies of people must often be less rigorous than studies of geese or cats, and because people seem to be a bit less susceptible to developmental *rigidity* than animals are, many developmental psychologists prefer the more cautious language of **sensitive periods** – somewhat narrow (but not rigidly narrow) periods in which we develop specific traits or abilities more easily than at other times.

Even if we accept this more cautious definition, however, there is still room for developmental debates. Consider the unfortunate Romanian orphans who fared poorly after late adoptions. Did these later-adopted kids suffer from serious cognitive deficits because they were starving for nurturance (social interaction) during a sensitive period? Or did they suffer these deficits merely because they had spent too much time starving? In this study, it's hard to separate nurturance from nutrition. Experimental research on rhesus monkeys reveals that depriving infant monkeys of routine social interaction with a nurturing caregiver produces huge developmental deficits that are independent of any possible effects of nutrition. We know this because experiments with monkeys have focused on monkeys who were reared without social contact but who were fed generously (by a mechanical device). These well-fed monkeys still suffered from major social and cognitive deficits (Harlow, Dodsworth, & Harlow, 1965). In fact, much like the researchers who studied Romanian orphans, Harlow and colleagues found that if infant rhesus monkeys were rescued from social isolation at a young enough age, they recovered well from the otherwise devastating effects of isolation. Likewise, if Harlow and colleagues waited until rhesus monkeys matured and *then* isolated them for a very long time, the monkeys suffered no permanent social or cognitive deficits. There appears to be a critical period for social and cognitive development in rhesus monkeys. But those who wish to understand *human* development must often draw their conclusions based on multiple sources, including some distressing animal studies. In light of all the data, it seems pretty safe to say that there is a sensitive, if not critical, period for human social and cognitive development. But the data that best inform what we know about people come from studies that – as clever as they are – can never be as rigorous as experiments conducted on our primate cousins.

The human evidence is a little clearer in some other areas of development. Consider language development. In keeping with the idea of sensitive (if not critical) periods, toddlers acquire the highly abstract thinking skill known as spoken language quickly and effortlessly. In contrast, the little tykes struggle tremendously with almost any other kind of abstract thinking. Thus, even the most well-spoken two-year-old kids are clueless when it comes to using the simplest possible map or model. Further, researchers have shown that it is precisely the inability of two-year old toddlers to think abstractly (rather than memory problems, for example) that make younger toddlers such poor map users (DeLoache, Miller, & Rosengren, 1997). In contrast to toddlers who soak up a first language effortlessly, adults who have mastered many other forms of abstract thinking usually have great difficulty acquiring a *second* language. Studies of grammatical proficiency or the ability to speak without an accent also reveal large advantages for those who acquire languages early rather than later in life. Most experts argue that there is a sensitive, if not critical, period for learning to talk (e.g., see Mayberry, Lock, & Kazmi, 2002).

Some of the strongest evidence that people learn language much more easily during early childhood than later in life comes from studies of learners of **American Sign Language** (**ASL**). Many deaf children who learn ASL often have no exposure to *any* language at all until they reach early to middle childhood. This is an ideal research situation because once people have already acquired a first language this could either facilitate or interfere with their ability to acquire a second. So, the exact age at which people first begin learning ASL is a natural manipulation of when people acquire a *first* language. Studies that take advantage of this natural manipulation show that those who first learn ASL at a very young age are, on average, much more proficient in communicating with ASL than are those who learn it later (Mayberry & Kluender, 2018). The ideal period for learning language is not as rigid and narrow as the one-hour period in which many water birds imprint on their mothers. But the best time to learn any language is when you are a kid. Studies of people who speak two or more languages, while not quite as elegant as studies of users of ASL, suggest very strongly that childhood is the ideal time to acquire a language. For example, children who are exposed to a second language before about the age of 15 (better yet before the age of five) are more skillful at grammar and syntax compared with those who acquire a second language as an adult (Patkowski, 1980). As we noted in Module 19, most people who acquire a second language as children also speak that language with little or no accent. In contrast, it is very rare for adults who acquire a second language to speak it accent-free (Patkowski, 1990).

Critical Periods in Humans

So, is there anything at all in human development that is as extreme as imprinting in water birds? Are there any truly critical periods in people after birth? Perhaps the clearest example of a critical period in people comes from research on sweating. Most everyone knows that sweating is the body's way of staying cool in the heat. But as Jared Diamond (1991, p. 4) noted in his review of the natural history of sweat, sweating doesn't just vary within people, based on current temperature. It also varies greatly *across* people, based on a critical period for the development of sweat glands:

> The hotter the conditions under which we grow up, the greater the number of our sweat glands that get programmed to function. By age two or three, the programming is as complete as it ever will be. If we grow up in a hot climate, most of our glands become activated, and for the rest of our lives we'll be able to stay comfortable in hot weather by sweating profusely. If we grow up in a cold climate, our body soon decides that that's what it will be like until we die, and barely more than half our glands become programmed.

In the jargon of modern biology, sweat gland function is fixed irreversibly by critical-period programming – that is, by conditions prevailing at a certain critical age,

Figure 22.3
Why do some people sweat much more than others when it is hot – and when exerting the same amount of physical effort? It depends heavily on the average temperature people experience in the first few years of life. In this critical period for the development of active sweat glands, our brains and bodies decide whether we need to sweat a lot. Because your first author spent his very early childhood in Georgia, without any air conditioning, he sweats a lot when it's hot. And there's nothing he can do now to change that.

usually early in life. The difference Diamond identified is not small. People who grow up in the tropics have about twice as many functioning sweat glands as people who grow up in cool climates. Studies also show that it's not where your ancestors grew up that determines how much you can sweat as an adult; it's where *you* grew up, the first two to three years of your life. After age two or three, the number of sweat glands you have is set for life. Moving from Philadelphia to the Philippines will certainly affect how much time you spend sweating, but it will not have any influence on your *capacity* to sweat.

Another candidate for a critical period in human beings also happens during the first two to three years of life. This is the window when some researchers think that an infant's **attachment style** develops. An infant's (or older child's) attachment style refers to his or her "working model" of whether primary caregivers (often parents) can be trusted or not. It is the child's conscious and unconscious theory about how to handle and interact with primary caregivers. To simplify a complex topic, it looks like infants and toddlers whose primary caregivers are highly nurturing and responsive between the ages of about six and 24 months develop **secure** attachment styles (Ainsworth & Bell, 1970). In contrast, when one's early caregivers are unavailable and/or unreliable, infants and toddlers are more likely to develop **insecure** attachment styles. This includes both an **avoidant** ("I can take care of myself.") and an **anxious-ambivalent** ("Oh my God, please don't abandon me!") attachment style. Although there can be no doubt that distinct infant and toddler attachment styles exist, they are not quite as strongly linked to caregiver treatment as one might expect. Further, they may change meaningfully over time. Thus, unlike the rigidly fixed development of sweat glands during the first two to three years of early childhood, the development of infant attachment style is not cast in stone. Thus, it seems safest to say that there is probably a sensitive period rather than a critical period for the development of infant attachment style. Table 22.1 summarizes some examples of studies that indicate critical or sensitive periods in human development, including a few not discussed in the body of this module.

It is also worth noting that people sometimes claim that there is strong evidence for critical periods – or even sensitive periods – without fully considering the strict definition of critical or sensitive periods. For example, people often note, correctly, that most extremely high-performing athletes or musicians began their serious athletic or musical

Table 22.1 Some Additional Developmental Outcomes for Which There are Likely Critical or Sensitive Periods

1. Under ideal conditions, we reach a genetically programmed adult height. But if we receive very little nutrition as children our growth will be stunted. A high calorie adult diet will not reverse this (Ramli et al., 2009).
2. If we grow up in the same household as other children, we will not be sexually attracted to them as adults – even if they are biologically unrelated to us (Shepher, 1971).
3. Exposure to an extremely enriched intellectual environment during early childhood may lead to superior personal, intellectual, and work outcomes in early adulthood (Sylva, 1997).
4. Infant and toddler nutrition (e.g., access to adequate calories and micro-nutrients, being breastfed) seems to influence later intellectual development (Nyaradi et al., 2013).
5. All infants are born being responsive to virtually any phoneme (any small bit of speech) that human beings can produce. But in the first year of life, infants "tune in" to the phonemes that occur frequently in their environment and "tune out" phonemes they rarely or never hear (Polka & Werker, 1994).

training at a very young age. However, those who make such claims are failing to consider the sheer amount of time people have been working hard to become great at something. Remember deliberate practice from Module 20? If you began learning the violin at age three and your twin sister didn't begin learning violin until age 17, you had a 14-year head start on her in becoming a virtuoso. Critical periods have to do with the age at which you first *begin* learning a skill (e.g., learning to speak a language) – or the only time of life in which a physical or psychological trait can develop at all (e.g., the development of more vs. fewer functional sweat glands). Evidence for a critical period is evidence that there is a very narrow window that shuts completely when the window is done. Evidence for a sensitive period is similar except that there is more wriggle room about the width of the window and some limited ability to develop something even once the sensitive period is done.

As we have seen in this module, there appear to be only a few truly critical periods of human postnatal development, but there are probably many sensitive periods. On the other hand, the line between critical and sensitive periods is sometimes fuzzy and gray (e.g., see Badcock, 2000). To cite an area where there is plenty of room for debate, consider research on the development of vision. Careful experiments with animals, including monkeys as well as kittens, suggested that there is a critical period for the development of most aspects of normal vision. Remember the poor one-eyed kittens? As Brown (1965) astutely noted long ago, studies of people who grew up blind but had been surgically granted sight in adulthood supported the idea of a critical period for the development of vision in people. As Brown further noted, one aspect of vision that usually develops effortlessly is **size constancy**. This is the ability to know the approximate size of an object by considering both its *apparent size* (how big an image it casts on your retina) and its *distance*. Even infants seem to know that things do not magically grow larger as we move toward them (or smaller as we move away). But in contrast to this observation, Brown described a previously blind woman who gained her sight as an adult. She was shown unfamiliar cards of various sizes and at different distances. "She thought the nearest of the cards the largest. It was in fact the smallest but was so near as to cast a larger retinal image than any of the others." (p. 215). Brown provided another example of a patient who gained his sight as an adult. This patient (1) judged a nearby candle's flame to be about the size of his arm and (2) judged the sun to be about the size of his hat! Either this newly sighted guy had a fantastically humungous head, or he failed to acquire size constancy. This is something toddlers do effortlessly.

But in contrast to observations suggesting a critical period, Ostrovsky and colleagues (2009) studied a woman who had been born virtually blind but gained vision in both eyes at age 12. The woman could see well enough 20 years later to walk without a cane and work as a maid, though she continued to suffer a few subtle deficits. To muddy the waters further, Huber and colleagues (2015) studied a man who lost his vision at age three, but had it restored at age 46. The man suffered from *major* visual deficits. More than a decade after his eye surgery, the man had great difficulty recognizing faces and three-dimensional shapes. It's thus hard to know exactly where we stand. Fans of the idea that there is a critical period for vision might argue that it's hard to know *for sure* just how visually impaired the woman had been for years when she had her eye surgery at age 12. It could also be crucial that the woman got corrective surgery in both eyes whereas the man got corrective surgery in only one. Given how slowly human vision develops, and how plastic the brains of children are, it's also likely that it's a lot better to get your corrective eye surgery at age 12 than at age 46. On the whole, it looks like there's a highly sensitive if not critical period for the development of vision in people. But whether research on vision in people supports a critical period depends on how critical we are of some of the clever research suggesting that this is true.

Critical Thinking about Critical Periods in a Developing Nation

In October of 2012, an initially uplifting National Public Radio (NPR) story about "The Peanut Butter Cure" became a bit of a downer. (Google "NPR Peanut Butter Cure" to find the story.) The story chronicled the efforts of researchers who wished to reduce rates of stunted growth in Haiti – the poorest nation in the Western hemisphere. As the NPR story noted, as many as 20% of Haitian children suffer from **stunted growth** – which refers to failing to reach the adult height one would have otherwise reached because of childhood malnutrition. In addition to stunting, children in poor nations may also suffer cognitive deficits if they fail to get adequate nutrition, especially micronutrients, when they transition from infancy to toddlerhood.

The NPR story that addressed this developmental crisis in Haiti began by noting that past research had shown that a "peanut butter cure" had previously saved the lives of many starving children in drought-stricken parts of Africa. This life-saving cure was a foil-wrapped packet of peanut butter. But this was not *just* peanut butter. A single foil packet of the stuff was fortified (additional nutrients were added) to contain as much protein as half a chicken breast and as much calcium as three cups of milk. And these "peanut butter cures" were loaded with micronutrients such as folic acid and vitamins A, C, and E. The point of the study was to get these foil packets to young toddlers and to prevent or reduce stunted growth. After all, the research team argued, these toddlers were entering a sensitive period for growth and brain development. The way the study worked was that the mothers of these young toddlers received 30 free packets of the peanut butter cure at the beginning of every month – and were instructed to give their toddlers exactly one packet per day. The monthly visits these moms made to the research site allowed the researchers to weigh and measure the toddlers. This dietary intervention was particularly important, the researchers argued, because these toddlers were being weaned, meaning they were about to stop receiving the nutritional benefits of breast milk.

The problem with this potentially important study was that the intervention did not seem to be working. The NPR story was a little fuzzy on methodological details, but a scientific expert who evaluated the results of the trials implied that they were not working at all – meaning that the kids who were randomly assigned to get 30 of these peanut butter packets every month (for many months, we assume) were *not* growing any bigger than a control group of kids who were getting no dietary supplements. These packets contained 500 calories of some highly nutritious peanut butter, by the way. The typical toddler needs something like 1,200 calories per day, and thus 500 extra calories per day could go a long way toward getting kids there.

Let's assume that the intervention was having no average effect *at all* on toddler growth. As you think about this, keep in mind that – for practical reasons – the researchers running this study did *not* go home with every mother every day to be sure she was following their careful instructions. Instead they sent moms home on the first of every month with 30 nutritious peanut butter packets. To make this question as clear as possible, let's assume that every last mother was loving and thoughtful but poor.

1. How might a mother's love in a collectivistic culture such as Haiti throw a monkey wrench into the design of the nutritional intervention?
2. How might the researchers fix this methodological (and arguably ethical) problem – to give the peanut butter cure a chance to do its intended job?

Multiple-Choice Questions for Module 22

1. Poison oak and poison ivy are genetically-identical. If a seed grows near a tree or a tall rock, it develops as poison ivy (a vine). If a seed grows where there is nothing to cling to, it becomes a standing poison oak plant (a bush). What's the term for "either-or" process that determines the way an organism develops?

   A) invariable period
   B) critical period
   C) sensitive period

2. Studies of deaf infants who begin to learn American Sign Language at different ages show that the younger a kid is when first exposed to sign language, the more proficient the kid will be at signing as an adult. This and other studies suggest that there is a(n) _____ period for the development of language.

   A) invariable
   B) judicious
   C) sensitive

3. What evolutionary theory suggests that organisms develop in very different ways in different environments – and often in ways that are highly sensitive to the age at which environments differ?

   A) life history theory
   B) the life-clock theory
   C) age-constraint theory

4. Like smoking, heavy drinking, and many infections that happen during pregnancy, being stressed out can also have harmful physical and psychological consequences for the developing baby. These harmful things are all known as:

   A) diatheses
   B) teratogens
   C) pathogens

5. According to your text, how much a person _____ is determined by the climate the person lives in during infancy and toddlerhood.

   A) craves potassium and other electrolytes
   B) needs to drink water, even in cool weather
   C) sweats in hot and humid conditions

6. During the first 24–48 hours after hatching, water birds such as ducks and geese become strongly attached to their moms (which makes them follow mom everywhere). This process of bonding to mom during a very narrow window is known as what?

   A) favoritism
   B) imprinting
   C) partiality

7. When all things go very well between mom and baby during infancy and toddlerhood, we'd expect a toddler to develop what kind of infant/toddler attachment style?

   A) favorable
   B) secure
   C) stable

8. Kira is a clingy and needy 9-month-old who responds with extreme distress every time her mother has to leave her. Further, when Kira's mom leaves Kira for a while and then returns, Kira is extremely difficult to soothe. Kira probably has what kind of infant attachment style?

   A) distressed
   B) worrisome
   C) anxious-ambivalent

9. To what does the term size constancy refer?

   A) the understanding that an object's apparent size varies dramatically with its distance from the viewer
   B) the fact that children's height and weight compared with their age-matched peers is pretty stable over time
   C) the fact that parts of the brain that are equally important are almost always the same physical size

10. Tobi is a ten-month-old who acts as if she could care less when her mom passes her off to others. Further, Tobi behaves as if she doesn't need her mom emotionally. What is Tobi's most likely infant attachment style?

    A) avoidant
    B) protective
    C) independent

Answer Key: 1B, 2C, 3A, 4B, 5C, 6B, 7B, 8C, 9A, 10A

References

Ainsworth, M. D., & Bell, S. M. (1970). Attachment, exploration, and separation: Illustrated by the behavior of one- year-olds in a strange situation. *Child Development, 41*, 49–67.

Badcock, C. R. (2000). *Evolutionary psychology: A critical Introduction*. Cambridge: Polity Press.

Beckett, C., Maughan, B., Rutter, M., Castle, J., Colvert, E., Groothues, C., ... & Sonuga-Barke, E. J. (2006). Do the effects of early severe deprivation on cognition persist into early adolescence? Findings from the English and Romanian adoptees study. *Child Development, 77*(3), 696–711.

Brown, R. (1965). *Social psychology*. New York, NY: Free Press.

DeLoache, J. S., Miller, K. F., & Rosengren, K. S. (1997). The credible shrinking room: Very young children's performance with symbolic and nonsymbolic relations. *Psychological Science, 8*, 308–313.

Diamond, J. (1991). Pearl Harbor and the emperor's physiologists. *Natural History, 100*, 2–5.

Fox, M. W. (Ed.). (1973). *Readings in ethology and comparative psychology*. Monterey, CA: Brooks/Cole/Wadsworth.

Harlow, H. F., Dodsworth, R. O., & Harlow, M. K. (1965). Total social isolation in monkeys. *Proceedings of the National Academy of Sciences of the United States of America, 54*(1), 90–97.

Huber, E., Webster, J. M., Brewer, A. A., MacLeod, D. I. A., Wandell, B. A., Boynton, G. M., ... Fine, I. (2015). A lack of experience-dependent plasticity after more than a decade of recovered sight. *Psychological Science, 26*, 393–401.

Lorenz, K. (1952). *King Solomon's ring; new light on animal ways*. New York, NY: Crowell.

Mayberry, R., & Kluender, R. (2018). Rethinking the critical period for language: New insights into an old question from American Sign Language. *Bilingualism: Language and Cognition, 21*(5), 886–905. doi:10.1017/S1366728917000724

Mayberry, R. I., Lock, E., & Kazmi, H. (2002). Linguistic ability and early language exposure. *Nature, 417*, 38.

Nyaradi, A., Li, J., Hickling, S., Foster, J., & Oddy, W. H. (2013). The role of nutrition in children's neurocognitive development, from pregnancy through childhood. *Frontiers in Human Neuroscience, 7*, 97. doi:10.3389/fnhum.2013.00097

Ostrovsky, Y., Meyers, E., Ganesh, S., Mathur, U., & Sinha, P. (2009). Visual parsing after recovery from blindness. *Psychological Science, 20*, 1484–1491.

Patkowski, M. (1980). The sensitive period for the acquisition of syntax in a second language. *Language Learning, 30*, 449–472.

Patkowski, M. S. (1990). Age and accent in a second language: A reply to James Emil Flege. *Applied Linguistics, 11*(1), 73–89.

Polka, L., & Werker, J. F. (1994). Developmental changes in perception of nonnative vowel contrasts. *Journal of Experimental Psychology: Human Perception and Performance, 20*, 421–435.

Ramli, K. E.A., Inder, K. J., Bowe, S. J., Jacobs, J., & Dibley, M. J. (2009). Prevalence and risk factors for stunting and severe stunting among under-fives in North Maluku province of Indonesia. *BMC Pediatrics, 9*, 64. doi:10.1186/1471-2431-9-64

Shepher, J. (1971). Mate selection among second generation kibbutz adolescents and adults: Incest avoidance and negative imprinting. *Archives of Sexual Behavior, 1*, 293–307.

Stearns, S. (1992). *The evolution of life histories*. New York, NY: Oxford University Press.

Stockard, C. R. (1921). Developmental rate and structural expression. *American Journal of Anatomy, 28*(2), 115–127.

Sylva, K. (1997). Critical periods in childhood learning. *British Medical Bulletin, 53*(1), 185–197.

Weiss, L., Laforsch, C., & Tollrian, R. (2012). The taste of predation and the defences of prey. In C. Bronmark & L.-A. Hansson (Eds.), *Chemical ecology in aquatic systems* (pp. 111–126). Oxford, England: Oxford University Press.

Wiesel, T. N., & Hubel, D. H. (1963). Single cell responses in striate cortex of kittens deprived of vision in one eye. *Journal of Neurophysiology, 26*, 1003–1017.

Wilson, E. O. (1975). *Sociobiology: The new synthesis.* Cambridge, MA: Harvard University Press.

Module 23
Cognitive Development
Going from the Concrete to the Abstract

In 1906, a ten-year-old Swiss boy named Jean became obsessed with biology. A year later, after much research, he began submitting biology papers to scientific journals. By the time Jean was a teenager, he had published several papers on mollusks. This boy was Jean Piaget, and it is lucky for psychology that Piaget eventually became more interested in kids than squids (Jean Piaget Biography, 2019). When Piaget died in 1980, he had become one of the most influential psychologists of all time – and the undisputed architect of modern developmental psychology (Haggbloom et al., 2002). Piaget's main contribution to psychology was his stage theory of cognitive development.

Like other **stage theorists**, Piaget argued that we undergo dramatic transformations at different ages, and in a predictable order. Because Piaget's theory focuses on *cognitive* development, it predicts that kids who have not yet reached certain stages will be unable to engage in certain kinds of reasoning. Conversely, kids who *have* made it to a specific stage should need no special training to perform the cognitive tasks that emerge during that stage. A likely reason why Piaget's theory has so strongly shaped the study of human development is that it makes clear and consistent predictions about how we think at different ages. Another reason is that Piaget and others developed many clever ways to test his theory. This module summarizes Piaget's theory. It examines how human thinking and perception evolve from the very basic to the highly complex.

Piaget's Stages of Cognitive Development

The Sensorimotor Stage

Piaget's first developmental stage is the aptly-named **sensorimotor stage** – which covers birth to about age two. During this stage, children learn to perceive the world (thus the prefix *sensori-*) and to control their bodies (thus the root word *-motor*). Of course, children also develop a very limited ability to think and reason during this stage, but this is called the *sensorimotor* stage for good reason. Infants and younger toddlers spend much of their energy, for example, merely learning to see, move around, and grab things. In so doing, they also begin to learn how the world works. If it strikes you as odd that people must develop the ability to see, let us remind you that your eyes are the only part of your sensory system where complex neural communication happens. Further, let us inform you that we are the planet's most **altricial** species. Unlike **precocial** organisms, which can perceive and move around in the world shortly after they enter it, altricial organisms enter the world clueless and helpless. All mammals are at least somewhat altricial. Many are born blind, and we know of no mammal that can find food right after birth. Human beings, however, are altricial even by mammalian standards. It takes us about a year to be able to walk, and we do not fully mature neurologically until about age 25. And let's not forget that we often live with our parents until at least the age of 18. Yep, we humans are born helpless, and we spend a very long time developing.

In contrast to mammals, most reptiles are highly precocial. They can thus hunt for their own food shortly after hatching. Their parents often ignore them altogether. Birds fall somewhere between these two extremes. Water birds such as ducks and swans are precocial whereas most song birds are more altricial; they're helpless when they first hatch. Getting back to people, one of the many ways in which we earn the title of the world's most altricial species has to do with vision. Human newborns have only one fiftieth (yes, 1/50th) the sensitivity to light that adults have. Further, human infants have very limited color vision, they can barely track moving objects, and they have horrible visual acuity. At the age of one week, infants can only see about 1/13th as well as human adults. In fact, our vision isn't fully developed until the age of five years. You can probably see better than your three-year-old niece can.

Figure 23.1 Babies should not be left in charge of UPC codes. The image on the left represents the limits of the visual acuity of a week-old infant. Make the stripes any narrower and a week-old baby can't see them at all. The image in the middle shows what a typical eight-month old can barely see. The image on the far right is the adult standard. Images were adapted from research by Brown and Yamamoto (1986) and Leat, Yadav, and Irving (2009).

Because those who study infants know how poor infant vision is, they make allowances. For example, those studying infant cognition use colorful, high-contrast objects – which they show to infants at close range. Consider research on object permanence, an important milestone of the sensorimotor stage. **Object permanence** is the awareness that objects continue to exist when we can no longer see them. The most popular approach to studying object permanence is what we call the **BOPP** – the **basic object permanence paradigm**. Here's how it works: Show an infant a novel colorful object (e.g., a small green squeaky frog) and then place the object under a small blanket that is well within reach of the child. Infants less than six months old usually behave as if they think the object no longer exists (meaning they do not try to retrieve the frog). Further, these same infants typically react with surprise and delight when the experimenter pulls the object back from under the little blanket. This suggests a *lack* of object permanence. An even more interesting result happens when the experimenter pulls away the blanket to show infants that the coveted green squeaky frog was, in fact, right under the blanket. If you repeat the procedure again, the lovable but goofy tykes still fall for the blanket trick. Piaget argued that five-month-old human brains just aren't capable of grasping object permanence. That's why peekaboo is such a fun game for infants. When you hide, the infant really thinks you're gone. So, when you reappear, the infant is truly delighted that you've reappeared out of nowhere.

Although Piaget was a stage theorist, he recognized that sometimes kids have gained only partial mastery of a cognitive ability. Babies don't wake up one day and suddenly have full-blown object permanence. Evidence of partial mastery of object permanence comes from kids who are about nine months of age. If you give these infants the basic BOPP test, they'll usually pass it with flying colors, meaning their little fingers will fly to the blanket and then pull it away – to reveal the colorful toy. They'll then grab the toy, and there's a good chance they'll taste it. I mean, what's yummier than a bright green frog? But suppose you make the task trickier and put out two little blankets. And suppose you do the activity a few times, always placing the toy under *Blanket A*. No problem. Most nine-month-olds consistently pull away *Blanket A*. But what happens when you put the toy under *Blanket A* several times and then allow older infants to see you place the toy under Blanket B. If kids truly understand object permanence, they should pull away Blanket B. But most nine-month-olds **perseverate** (they stick with what has worked recently) and pull away *Blanket A* again. This is known as the **A-not-B error**, and Piaget took it as evidence that most nine-month-olds have not fully mastered object permanence (Smith & Thelen, 2003). By the age of 12 months, very few kids still commit the A-not-B error, suggesting that kids this age have mastered object permanence (and, sadly, the game of peekaboo loses a bit of its magic).

By the way, you've just seen Piaget's typical approach to the study of cognitive development. It is this: First, identify a cognitive ability and determine the age at which kids ought to master it. Piaget often did this by observing his own children (Arnett, 2012). Second, develop a simple test kids should pass if and only if they possess the cognitive ability in question. Third, round up two groups of kids: (a) those who are presumably too young to possess the ability and (b) those who are old enough to possess the ability. Fourth, give the test to both groups – and see if the older kids outperform the younger kids. We call this approach the **Piagetian paradigm**, and it is a model example of rigorous developmental research methods. Let's see how Piaget and others have used this paradigm to study human cognitive development. Doing so will also allow us to identify the three remaining stages of Piaget's theory.

The Preoperational Stage

Piaget studied the development of *abstract thinking*, which he often referred to as mental *operations*. Piaget called his second stage the **preoperational stage**, and it applies to kids who are about two to six years old. Kids enter this second stage as extremely egocentric thinkers with little abstract thinking ability. For example, they can't fully appreciate other minds, and they don't realize that things can change their appearance but retain their essential nature. But despite what the prefix *pre-* in *preoperational* implies, Piaget argued that kids in this second stage can engage in *some* abstract mental operations. For instance, an important milestone of the preoperational stage is the acquisition of language. Language requires abstract (symbolic) thinking. Further, by the *end* of this stage, most kids are beginning to master some substantial mental feats. Let's see how we know this.

Piaget argued that human cognitive development involves going from concrete (sensory-driven) to abstract thinking. A classic test of this idea comes from work on toddlers who try to use maps or models. Maps and models are abstract *representations* of physical things. You can walk around in a zoo, but you can't walk around in a map of a zoo. Most 2.5-year-olds struggle to use even the simplest maps. For example, check out the small room whose floor plan is shown in Figure 23.2. Imagine that an experimenter showed you that she was hiding a troll ("Big Terry") inside the piece of furniture we've marked with four arrows. Now imagine that the experimenter took you to a *toy model* of this room (see the tiny portion of Figure 23.2). The experimenter tells you she hid a tiny troll ("*Little* Terry") in the same spot in the *toy* room where she hid Big Terry in the *real* room. Your job is simple: find Little Terry. Now imagine searching in the little room as if you had no clue whatsoever where Little Terry is. That's weird, right? But it's exactly what most 2.5-year-olds do. They don't seem to understand that one thing (a toy room) can *represent* something else (a real room). Only about one in five 2.5-year-olds who've been given this kind of test show that they can use such a model. But just six months later, by the age of three years, about four in five toddlers easily find Little Terry in the model room.

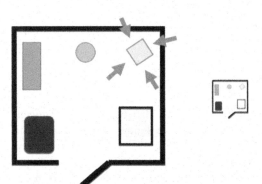

Figure 23.2
A floor plan for the real room (left) in which experimenters hid *Big* Terry and the toy room (right) in which they hid *Little* Terry (adapted from DeLoache, Miller, & Rosengren, 1997).

The traditional explanation of this striking age difference is that older toddlers can think *abstractly* in ways younger toddlers cannot. But a problem with this explanation is that older and younger toddlers differ in more than just one way. Older toddlers may have better *memories* – or longer attention spans – than younger toddlers. Thus, there are three competing reasons to expect three-year-olds to outperform 2.5-year-olds in this model room test: abstract thinking, memory, and attention span.

Is there any way to see which explanation is correct? There is. We adapted the floor plans you saw in Figure 23.2 from DeLoache, Miller, and Rosengren (1997), who found that very few 2.5-year-olds but most three-year-olds passed the model test. To see if this age difference reflected a difference in *abstract thinking per se*, DeLoache et al. tricked some toddlers. They arranged it so that *some* kids did *not* have to think abstractly to find Little Terry. Figure 23.3 suggests how. That's right. They gave one group of 2.5-year-olds the usual version of this task, but they convinced a second group of 2.5-year-olds that they possessed a *shrinking machine*. They first used the machine to shrink a troll doll (parents played along). In plain sight of the toddlers, they then hid Big Terry and set the machine to *shrink the room*. Everyone evacuated. Minutes later, the kids returned to see that, sure enough, the once-big room was now tiny. Because these kids believed the model room *was* the real room, they didn't have to think abstractly to find Little Terry. Under these conditions, about 80% of the 2.5-year-olds found Little Terry. This suggests that the memories and attention spans of these 2.5-year-olds were working just fine. In fact, they performed as well as three-year-olds. It wasn't memory they were lacking; it was the abstract thinking skills that emerge between ages 2.5 and 3.0.

Figure 23.3
The apparent work of the shrinking machine DeLoache et al. (1997) used to convince some toddlers that they could shrink a troll doll (or an entire room). Photo used by permission of DeLoache.

Kids who've reached the end of the preoperational stage also become less **egocentric**. **Egocentrism** (literally *self-centeredness*) refers to the tendency to view the world from one's own personal vantage point – failing to realize that others might view things differently. To study egocentrism, Piaget and Inhelder (1956) developed the **three mountains task**. A modern variation on this task requires kids to look at a table-top model of three mountains from opposite seats. First, kids tell an adult what they themselves can see from where they are currently seated (suppose it is currently what's in the right half of Figure 23.4). Kids then switch seats with the adult and describe what they (the kids) can see *now* (suppose it's currently what's in the *left* half of Figure 23.4). Finally, without moving anyone, the adult asks kids to describe what the kids think *he or she* can see – while seated exactly where the kids themselves were just seated. In most variations on this task, younger kids are much more egocentric than older kids. They think the adult sees what *they* see! For example, kids who are seeing the image on the left half of Figure 23.4 would report that the adult sitting across from them could see a small lake and a little house. Kids don't typically engage in adult-like levels of physical perspective-taking until they're about seven or eight. To see for yourself exactly how a modern version of the three mountains task works, complete with a very cute three-year-old, go to www.youtube.com/watch?v=OinqFgsIbh0. If this link does not cooperate, just try Googling, "Piaget three mountains video".

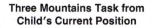

**Three Mountains Task from
Child's Current Position**

**Three Mountains Task from
Opposite Side of Table**

Figure 23.4 Preschoolers who saw a toy model of three mountains from the perspective on the left would almost certainly report that the person sitting directly across from the mountains could see a lake and a little house. In contrast, most kids who've graduated from the preoperational stage have no trouble with this perspective-taking task. They realize that another person doesn't see what they see.

The Concrete Operational Stage

Seven-year-olds who are *not* very egocentric take us to Piaget's third developmental stage. Kids aged six to 11 are usually in Piaget's **concrete operational stage**. At this stage, kids can engage in some impressive forms of abstract thinking. But they'll often struggle with complex logical problems, and they'll do much better with basic conceptual *operations* (to use Piaget's preferred term) when they can see or handle any physical objects that they must judge or mentally manipulate. Consider conservation, an important milestone reached during the concrete operational stage. **Conservation** is the awareness that objects often change their appearance without changing their essential nature. Because conservation is central to Piaget's theory, it has been studied many ways.

One very popular way to see if kids appreciate conservation is to see if they appreciate the law of *conservation* of matter. Let's consider two ways of doing this. First, take two identical balls of clay. Ask four-year-old Javi to confirm that the two balls of clay "have the same amount" of clay. Now, right in front of Javi, divide one of the balls into two balls of clay and ask Javi if the divided clay balls have more, less, or the same amount of clay the undivided ball has. If Javi is like most of his four-year-old peers, he'll believe that the divided clay now has "more clay." It's also easy to devise tests of conservation using water. As shown in Figure 23.5, just fill two identical glasses of water to the same level and then pour one of the glasses into a shallow, wide bowl (or a taller, much thinner glass). Unless Javi is a budding hydro-engineer, he'll probably report that the container whose water level is higher contains more water than the other. Kids who've reached the concrete operational stage will rarely fall for this kind of trick. They understand that matter is conserved – it doesn't increase or decrease just because of changes in appearance. If you'd like to see a highly engaged little learner take five very different conservation tests, Google "child on Piaget's conservation tasks" or go straight to www.youtube.com/watch?v=gnArvcWaH6I

Figure 23.5 Pouring water from a small glass to a flat and shallow bowl does *not* change the amount of water that was in the second glass. But you'll have a hard time explaining that to most kids aged five and younger – who have not yet reached Piaget's concrete operational stage. They have not yet mastered conservation.

Kids in the concrete operational stage usually have no trouble with seriation either. **Seriation** refers to ranking a set of many objects on any of several physical or psychological dimensions. For example, your first author has ranked the nine objects from his kitchen that you see in Figure 23.6 based on height (left image). But one could also rank them based on weight, which changes the rankings slightly (right image). And if you ranked them from your most to least favorite, this would probably lead to a very different set of rankings. Kids in the concrete operational stage usually have no trouble with seriation – while younger kids have trouble getting their heads around it.

Figure 23.6 Seriation. Kids in the concrete operational stage should have no trouble rank-ordering these nine objects from your first author's kitchen from tallest to shortest (left) – and then reordering them from heaviest to lightest (right). Younger kids would struggle, and they'd likely have trouble mentally separating height and weight.

If you noticed that kids in the concrete operational stage can do a lot of things adults can do, you might wonder what – if anything – comes next in Piaget's theory of cognitive development. Piaget's final stage describes people from puberty onward. Before we examine Piaget's final stage of cognitive development, let us remind you that Piaget was strictly interested in people's ability to *think abstractly*. Piaget surely recognized that most teenagers are not as knowledgeable or emotionally mature as fully-grown adults. But his theory suggests that when it comes to the raw ability to learn calculus, appreciate supply and demand, or infer causality based on the results of an experiment, adolescents are no different than adults.

The Formal Operational Stage

Piaget's **formal operational stage** begins in puberty. In most wealthy nations, puberty begins for most girls between ten and 14 years of age. For boys it's usually a bit later. But for both girls and boys, there is a lot of variation in puberty, which can make it trickier to test Piaget's model in teens than in toddlers. Furthermore, the age of puberty, especially for girls, has long been dropping in wealthy nations (Biro, 2005; Grumbach & Styne, 2003). As kids reach puberty at younger and younger ages, are they blossoming intellectually at younger and younger ages – *because of* earlier puberty? This is a tough question. For our purposes, we'll just say that Piaget's fourth stage begins with puberty – and that most older teenagers can engage in sophisticated, abstract thinking just as well as adults can.

But what, exactly, can mature adults do? The main difference between the cognitive capabilities of a typical nine-year-old and a teenager has to do with the ability to think in highly complex, purely abstract ways, which is the central milestone of the formal operational stage. For example, as you know, both nine-year-olds and teenagers can easily handle seriation. But only teenagers can usually handle the more sophisticated cousin of seriation known as transitive inferences. Making **transitive inferences** means drawing logical conclusions about the serial positions (rankings) of things based on purely abstract information about them. If I tell you that Emily is taller than Jason and that Jason is taller than Hart, you should only need to pause briefly to tell me who is the shortest and tallest in this three-person group. But without seeing the actual people – or a drawing thereof – many pre-adolescents would have trouble with this task. Of course, the capacity to make transitive inferences is not the only cognitive ability to emerge in adolescence. There are many other forms of higher-order reasoning. As far as we can tell, these many forms of complex thinking can be summarized by the acronym **ACID**. This may help you remember the details of Piaget's fourth stage because it is only during this fourth stage that most people can pass any of the acid-tests of fully complex adult thinking.

ACID stands for abstraction, creativity, induction, and deduction. **Abstraction** is a recurrent theme in Piaget's model. In each successive Piagetian stage, we learn to think more abstractly. **Creativity** refers to producing something (often something abstract) that has never been created before (e.g., writing a song, building a new kind of bridge). Creativity has not been studied nearly as often as abstraction, but the title of one of Piaget's last books was "To understand is to invent." In this book, Piaget (1972, p. 20) argued that fully mature thinking involves "production and creativity and not simply repetition." If you recall the two basic forms of logic that are at the root of many kinds of sophisticated reasoning, you know that **induction** refers to reasoning from many specific observations to come to a general conclusion (often called bottom-up processing). In contrast, you may recall that **deduction** refers to reasoning from general principles to generate specific, novel ideas, theories, or hypotheses (often called top-down processing). A great deal of scientific inquiry involves the form of deduction known as theory-testing (Copi, 1978).

Critiques of Piaget

Piaget was ingenious. But being ingenious is not the same as being omniscient. In the four decades since Piaget passed away, there have been many criticisms and refinements of his work. One common criticism is that how sophisticated children appear to be depends partly on the sophistication of one's measurements. The specific way we test Piaget's model matters a lot. Recall that many early studies of object permanence suggested that young infants do not appreciate object permanence. But Baillargeon (1994) found that, if we study object permanence in new ways, we gain new insights into the cognitive sophistication of infants. For example, studies suggest that infants look longer than usual at interesting or surprising events. Building on this idea, Baillargeon found that infants as young as 2.5 months *look longer than usual* at a live scene in which a toy car seems to have driven through a solid object. Baillargeon (1994, p. 133) summarized much of her work – using looking time as an indicator of surprise – as follows:

> even very young infants possess many of the same fundamental beliefs about objects as adults do ... For example, infants aged 2.5 to 3.5 months are aware that objects continue to exist when masked by other objects ... and that objects cannot move through the space occupied by other objects.

The ink on much of Piaget's seminal work was barely dry when Roger Brown offered a clever analysis of Piaget's work of *conservation*. Most kids can't pass a typical conservation task until age six or seven. But as Brown (1965) observed, even infants engage in *some* forms of conservation. Specifically, infants excel at correcting the *apparent size* of an object for the object's physical distance. To navigate the physical world, infants must learn that the size of a retinal image (how big an image something casts on the back of the eye) depends not only on the size of an object but also on the object's distance. It's possible to set up tests of *size-constancy* in ways that closely parallel traditional Piagetian conservation tasks. When experimenters have done so, they've found that the same tiny tots who fail woefully at traditional conservation tasks succeed wonderfully at size constancy. Infants seem to have gotten a decent handle on size-constancy by age six months (Cruikshank, 1941).

Another common critique of Piaget is that he may have stopped his stage theory prematurely. In the past three decades, researchers have argued that cognitive development continues after adolescence. In fact, some have argued that emerging adults (those aged 18–25) think differently than adolescents. For example, adults may be more inclined than adolescents to engage in **pragmatism** – which involves recognizing that logic alone cannot provide solutions to some of life's tricky problems (Basseches, 1989; Labouvie-Vief & Diehl, 2000). It might be logical to leave a spouse who is harsh, selfish, and critical. However, if this means you will rarely see your children again, it is less clear that the logical solution to an unhappy relationship is breaking the relationship off altogether.

Some have also argued that we get wiser as we get older. Grossmann and colleagues (2010) presented people in three age groups with difficult social conflicts and dilemmas – and recorded them while they commented on what was likely to happen because of the conflicts – and why. Blind raters later coded the responses for six different kinds of wisdom (e.g., flexibility, perspective-taking, and compromise). Middle-aged people scored higher than young people on a few of the measures. But seniors excelled relative to both young and middle-aged people on all six measures. But there may be a serious problem with this study, and it relates to what the authors describe as "blind" coders. Although the coders of these audio recordings were never *told* anyone's age, it is possible that raters could easily tell the voice of an 80-year-old from that of a 20-year old. Does wisdom come with age? Or is this just a stereotype that affected the ratings of the coders? Other highly-cited studies of age differences in wisdom (e.g., Smith & Baltes, 1990) seem to suffer from the same methodological problem (see Mickler & Staudinger, 2008, for a critical analysis).

On the other hand, studies that avoid any kind of perceptual bias do suggest that adolescents are not as cognitively sophisticated as adults. For example, studies using a variety of methods have shown that adolescents are more egocentric than older adults (Elkind, 1967; Frankenberger, 2000). Recent research using brain imaging technology also shows that the adolescent brain is not fully developed. This is particularly true when it comes to reward areas and areas known to be associated with emotional self-regulation and risk-taking (Arain et al., 2013; Foulkes & Blakemore, 2016).

Finally, there has long been debate about whether human development really happens in discrete stages – or whether it happens gradually and continuously. A prescient proponent of gradualism was the Russian psychologist Lev Vygotsky (1930–1934/1978), who argued – well before Piaget became well-known – that kids often possess hidden abilities that they can only express with some **scaffolding** (suggestions and support) by parents, teachers, or older children. Our spin on this idea is that Piaget's clever work makes development look a bit more stage-like than it is because most Piagetian tasks are dichotomous: you either pass or fail them. But many tasks in daily life are continuous (e.g., how many of 50 words you spelled correctly). Many tasks are also composed of subtasks. Consider the question of when a child learns to ride a bike. If Azar couldn't quite ride a bike yesterday, but she did so successfully today, few psychologists would take this as evidence that there is a pre-bicyclist and a post-bicyclist stage. Instead, they'd argue that Azar had probably mastered *most* of the skills needed to ride a bike yesterday (e.g., balancing, braking, pedaling, steering) but finally put them all together today. Although human development may ultimately be more gradual than the discrete stages that Piaget originally posited, there can be little doubt that Piaget's elegant simplification has greatly advanced our knowledge of human cognitive development.

Questions for Critical Thinking and Discussion for Module 23

There are other thoughtful criticisms of Piaget that we did not mention in this module. For example, Piaget (1995, p. 291) argued that "the structures of the newborn's behavior will be the same whether he is nursed by a robot or by a human being. As time goes on, however, these initial structures are more and more transformed through interactions with the surroundings." It's not clear that Piaget meant this *literally*, but assuming he did, was he correct?

1. Recall that Romanian orphans who were neglected during the first couple of years of life had serious intellectual deficits ten years later. Likewise, well-fed monkeys reared by "robots" develop social and cognitive deficits from which they never recover. What does this say about Piaget's implicit assumption that cognitive development is distinct from social development?

Piaget also seems to have accepted the idea that those who develop the ability to think logically can apply their domain-independent expertise to a wide range of problems. If you "get" conservation, you should be able to engage in any specific form of conservation. But kids who pass a test of conservation in one area (e.g., with water) will often fail a test of conservation in another area (e.g., with divided or flattened pieces of clay).

2. Do arguments about the specificity of human intelligence (including the specificity of genius, and the existence of savants and prodigies) raise any red flags about the basic assumptions Piaget seems to have made about human intellectual functioning? Was Piaget a fan of Spearman's "g"?

If Piaget identified universal developmental stages in people, then his results should hold up well across cultures.

3. What would it say about Piaget's model if people who never attended high school performed poorly on many of the intellectual tasks he often gave to teens and adults?

Finally, what – if anything – does it say about Piaget's model that people the world over engage in some kinds of logical reasoning much more readily than others? You may recall from Module 19 that the same people who fail the abstract card-turning task that Wason originally used to identify the positive test bias usually perform beautifully if you give them a *logically identical* version of the task that requires them to see if someone has *cheated*. Consider the cards in figure 23.7. The rule to be tested is this: "*If a person took a soda, he or she must put a dollar in the soda payment box.*" You'd like to know for sure if anyone broke this rule. You need to turn over exactly two of the cards to test the hypothesis properly. Which two cards should you flip over?

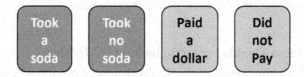

Figure 23.7

4. Even in cultures where no one attends school or drinks soda, few would have trouble answering this "cheater detection" version of Wason's card task (Tooby & Cosmides, 1988). Likewise, preadolescent kids usually have little trouble with "cheater detection" versions of the card task. Is this "card content" effect any kind of problem for Piaget's model?

Multiple-Choice Questions for Module 23

1. What is Piaget's first developmental stage?

   A) the stage of trust vs. isolation
   B) the conventional stage
   C) the sensorimotor stage

2. Kay understands economic concepts such as expected utility and supply-and-demand as well as evolutionary concepts such as adaptation and survival of the fittest. Kay is functioning at what Piagetian stage?

   A) the post operational
   B) the syllogistic
   C) the formal operational

3. Researchers who study human cognitive development use the **three mountains task** to measure what failure or limitation of human thinking?

   A) seriation
   B) egocentrism
   C) conservation

4. To what does the "Piagetian paradigm" refer?

   A) repeatedly looking at age group differences in lab performance on tests of specific cognitive abilities
   B) the basic idea that human cognitive development occurs in discrete, non-overlapping stages
   C) the use of longitudinal research designs to increase confidence in claims about what causes what

5. If eight-year-old Alejandra is doing fine in school but cannot reliably engage in any the four kinds of thinking summarized by ACID, what is your best guess about Alejandra's (Piagetian) level of cognitive development?

   A) preoperational
   B) concrete operational
   C) informal operational

6. What abstract thinking ability is the fancy, abstract version of the simpler process known as seriation?

   A) transitive inferences
   B) statistical reasoning
   C) analogical reasoning

7. Any kid who has made it to the beginning of this Piagetian stage should be able to succeed at conservation.

   A) sensorimotor
   B) concrete operational
   C) quasi-operational

8. Piaget argued that an eight-month-old who commits the A-not-B error has not quite achieved a complete appreciation of:

   A) object permanence
   B) perseverance
   C) attentional allocation

9. A specific form of reasoning that seems to be more advanced than what is typical in Piaget's fourth stage is:

   A) pragmatism
   B) dissection
   C) the process of elimination

10. Kids develop a sense of object permanence during what stage of cognitive development?

    A) sensorimotor
    B) pre-motoric
    C) oculomotor

Answer Key: 1C, 2C, 3B, 4A, 5B, 6A, 7B, 8A, 9A, 10A

References

Arain, M., Haque, M., Johal, L., Mathur, P., Nel, W., Rais, A., ... Sharma, S. (2013). Maturation of the adolescent brain. *Neuropsychiatric Disease and Treatment, 9*, 449–461.

Arnett, J.J. (2012). *Human development: A cultural approach.* Upper Saddle River, NJ: Pearson.

Baillargeon, R. (1994). How do infants learn about the physical world? *Current Directions in Psychological Science, 3*(5), 133–140. doi:10.1111/1467-8721.ep10770614

Basseches, M. (1989). Dialectical thinking as an organized whole: comments on Irwin and Kramer. In M. L. Commons, J. D. Sinnott, F. Richards & C. Armon (Eds.). *Adult development: Vol. I: Comparisons and applications of adolescent and adult development models* (pp. 161–178). Westport: Praeger.

Biro, F.M. (2005). Secular trends in menarche. *Journal of Pediatrics, 147*, 725–726.

Brown, R. (1965). *Social psychology.* New York, NY: The Free Press.

Brown, A.M., & Yamamoto, M. (1986). Visual acuity in newborn and preterm infants measured with grating acuity cards. *American Journal of Opthalmology, 102*, 245–253.

Copi, I. M. (1978). *Introduction to logic* (5th ed.). New York: Macmillan.

Cruikshank, R. M. (1941). The development of visual size constancy in early infancy. *The Pedagogical Seminary and Journal of Genetic Psychology, 58*, 327–335.

DeLoache, J.S., Miller, K.F., & Rosengren, K.S. (1997). The credible shrinking room: Very young children's performance with symbolic and nonsymbolic relations, *Psychological Science, 8*, 308–313.

Elkind, D. (1967). Egocentrism in adolescence. *Child Development, 38*(4), 1025–1034. doi:10.2307/1127100

Foulkes, L., & Blakemore, S. J. (2016). Is there heightened sensitivity to social reward in adolescence? *Current Opinion in Neurobiology, 40*, 81–85. doi:10.1016/j.conb.2016.06.016

Frankenberger, K. D. (2000). Adolescent egocentrism: A comparison among adolescents and adults. *Journal of Adolescence, 23*(3), 343–354. doi:10.1006/jado.2000.0319

Grossmann, I., Na, J., Varnum, M. E. W., Park, D. C., Kitayama, S., & Nisbett, R. E. (2010). Reasoning about social conflicts improves into old age. *Proceedings of the National Academy of Sciences, 107*(16), 7246–7250. doi:10.1073/pnas.1001715107

Grumbach, M.M. & Styne, D.M. (2003).Puberty: Ontogeny, neuroendocrinology, physiology, and disorders. In P.R. Larsen, H.M. Kronenberg, S. Melmed, & K.S. Polonsky, eds. *Williams textbook of endocrinology* (pp. 1115–1286). Philadelphia, PA: W. B. Saunders.

Haggbloom, S. J., Warnick, R., Warnick, J. E., Jones, V. K., Yarbrough, G. L., Russell, T. M., ... Monte, E. (2002). The 100 most eminent psychologists of the 20th century. *Review of General Psychology, 6*(2), 139–152. doi:10.1037//1089-2680.6.2.139

Labouvie-Vief, G., & Diehl, M. (2000). Cognitive complexity and cognitive-affective integration: Related or separate domains of adult development? *Psychology and Aging, 15*, 490–504.

Leat, S.J., Yadav, N.K., & Irving, E.L. (2009). Development of visual acuity and contrast sensitivity in children. *Journal of Optometry, 2*, 19–26.

Mickler, C., & Staudinger, U. M. (2008). Personal wisdom: Validation and age-related differences of a performance measure. *Psychology and Aging, 23*(4), 787–799.

Piaget, J. (1972). *To understand is to invent.* New York, NY: The Viking Press, Inc.

Piaget, L., (1995). In I. Smith, *Sociological studies* (2nd ed.). (Smith, et al., Trans.) London: Routledge (Originally published in 1977).

Piaget J., Inhelder B. (1956). *The Child's Conception of Space*, Trans. Langdon F. J., Lunzer J. L. London: Routledge.

Smith, J., & Baltes, P. B. (1990). Wisdom-related knowledge: Age/cohort differences in response to life-planning problems. *Developmental Psychology, 26*(3), 494–505. doi:10.1037/0012-1649.26.3.494

Smith, L. B., & Thelen, E. (2003). Development as a dynamic system. *Trends in Cognitive Sciences, 7*(8), 343–348.

Tooby, J. & Cosmides, L. (1988). The evolution of war and its cognitive foundations. *Institute for Evolutionary Studies Technical Report*, 88–1.

Vygotsky, L. S. (1930–1934/1978). *Mind in society: The development of higher psychological processes.* (M. Cole, V. John-Steiner, S. Scribner, & E. Souberman, Eds.). Cambridge, MA: Harvard University Press.

Module 24
Psychosocial Development
Navigating Challenges across the Lifespan

Much more than any other school of psychology, developmental psychology has been shaped in dramatic ways by just two or three intellectual giants. If you read the prior module on cognitive development, you know that one such giant in the developmental landscape was the precocious and self-confident Jean Piaget – who began publishing scientific papers in biology when he was barely a teenager. A second developmental giant could not have been more different than Piaget. Erik Erikson was born out of wedlock to a mother who reared him under what were initially very difficult circumstances. Erikson's biological father had been Danish, and Erikson looked very "Nordic." But his mother and his adoptive father reared him in the Jewish faith. According to Erikson's 1994 *New York Times* obituary, he felt out of place as a child because "his anti-Semitic schoolmates taunted him, while at the synagogue his Jewish friends rejected him because of his Nordic features." Erikson himself noted that for this and other reasons he "developed 'a morbid sensitivity' and often escaped into a fantasy world." Unlike the self-confident Piaget, then, Erikson admitted feeling deeply inadequate. But Erikson's personal struggles seem to have made him a great psychotherapist – as well as a great observer of the human condition.

By the time Erikson died in 1994, he had become one of the most influential psychologists ever – both within and outside developmental psychology. Erikson's interests were highly eclectic. He wrote award-winning biographies, stayed active as a psychotherapist, and conducted careful studies of two tribes of American Indians. But without a doubt, it was Erikson's work on lifespan human development that left his biggest mark on psychology. Having trained with Freud as a young man, Erikson seems to have considered himself a lifelong psychoanalyst. Yet, Freud's psychosexual theory focused heavily on sex, and Freud proposed that human development was done by the end of adolescence. In contrast, Erikson developed a **psychosocial theory** that had eight rather than five stages – with the sixth through eighth stages describing life transitions in early, middle, and late adulthood. Erikson's theory was psychosocial because he focused on how people deal with challenges that are grounded in social rather than sexual contexts. But like Freud, for example, Erikson argued that life is full of struggles and crises. This module summarizes Erikson's eight-stage psychosocial theory of lifespan development and grounds it in modern work on identity, personality, and motivation.

In our view, the best way to understand Erikson's psychosocial theory is to emphasize that Erikson was keenly aware of two profoundly important psychological needs. We can summarize these needs most succinctly with a quote from the social worker Dale Hardin (1994) who argued that "All kids need two things – love and structure." Beginning with love, our need for love and acceptance goes by many different names, and it has been studied in many different psychological traditions. Recall that the school of psychological thought known as humanism is based on our search for both social affirmation and self-acceptance. The name Maslow should come to mind. Remember his need for love and belonging? More recently, Baumeister and Leary's (1995) theory of the *need to belong*, which is grounded in social and evolutionary psychology rather than in humanism, made a similar point. All human beings are born with a basic need for connectedness, and when we cannot fill this need we suffer painful physical and psychological consequences. As you will see in a later module of this text, adults who are socially isolated or have very little social support are at increased risk of death in middle age (House et al., 1988). As you may also recall from Harlow's classic work with juvenile rhesus monkeys, all young primates seem to have a powerful need for "contact comfort." To state all this in the form of a principle, Erikson seems to have known that people possess a basic desire for **connectedness** – a desire to be loved and accepted by others. When we are infants, this means we cry out when we are cold, hungry, or unhappy. As teenagers, we often strive to be popular – and we may do crazy things to impress our peers. As young adults, the need for connectedness presumably drives us to seek out friends and romantic partners. And, at any age, the need for connectedness means we wish to be included in important social groups whether this means a family, a church, a synagogue, a mosque, a youth group, a musical band, a book club, or a ragtag intramural basketball team.

But human beings have another basic psychological need. This one relates to Dale Hardin's concept of structure. If you don't know what is true and what is false, if you don't know what is allowed and what is not allowed, if you don't know what is safe and what is dangerous, and if you cannot read or write, you are probably going to have a difficult life, even if everyone loves you. In addition to the need for connectedness, we all have a basic need for what we'll call mastery. As we define it here, the need for **mastery** is the desire to develop skills that allow you to *control* what happens to you. This includes the desire to make things, do things, learn, create structure, and explore. Incidentally, there is some debate among experts about whether the need for mastery is distinct from the need for *predictability and control*. Our answer is that both mastery and predictability are *ultimately* about control. If animals, human or otherwise, have no control over their worlds, they will usually perish – because they will approach carnivores as readily as they approach carnivals. They will drink polluted water as often as they drink spring water. If you have no control at all over your life, you're unable to feed yourself and stay out of harm's way. Even plants, for example, take some control over their worlds. They engage in *phototropism*, for example, moving toward rather than away from light sources (Have you ever noticed that plants in a room will gradually end up leaning toward the window?). Further, many plants send out roots in patterns that maximize their competitive advantage over their neighbors. Some plants even recognize genetic relatives and compete less fiercely than usual with the roots of plants with which they share genes (Depuydt, 2014). But getting back to people, we use the broad term mastery rather than the even broader phrase predictability and control because mastery is more intuitive and easier to spot and measure. This brings us back to Erikson because he also wrote in a language that is very easy to convert into terms like mastery and competence and a bit trickier to convert into the language of predictability and control.

A good way to think about Erikson's psychosocial stage model is that he recognized that at every stage of life we fill these two important needs in different ways. Infants cannot make themselves breakfast, and so they cry out when hungry. Ninety-year-olds may be less interested in learning a third language than are most 19-year-olds, but both groups will become frustrated if they can't communicate with those they love, or if they lose their driver's license. And precisely because 90-year-olds can't master some things as well as they could when they were 19, many 90-year-olds will experience an increased desire for connectedness. In our view, then, one implicit message of Erikson's stage theory is that everyone needs both connectedness and mastery. But for good reason, Erikson's theory also addresses how the relative balance of these two basic needs varies over the course of the lengthy human lifespan. Let's examine Erikson's psychosocial theory through the primary lenses of mastery and connectedness. We're going to see that both these basic psychological needs always matter – but that the relative importance of the two is different at different ages.

Erikson's Eight Stages of Psychosocial Development

Trust vs. mistrust (infancy = age 0–1). We hope the phrase *trust versus mistrust* tells you that Erikson's first stage focuses heavily on the need for *connectedness*. You probably recall that human infants are incredibly *altricial* – which means that they are largely helpless and rely heavily on the extensive care they typically get from their primary caregivers, most often their mothers (Dunsworth, Warrener, Deacon, Ellison, & Pontzer, 2012; Hawkes, O'Connell, & Blurton-Jones, 1997). Infants spend much of the first year of their lives trying to answer questions of security and connectedness: Can I trust those who surround me? Is my social world a safe place? Will my basic needs be consistently met? When I cry does someone usually pick me up? Of course, infants don't *consciously* ask themselves questions such as these because infants have not yet mastered language. But according to attachment theorists, a crucial psychosocial problem all infants face has to do with whether they can trust their caregivers. Infants develop implicit (unconscious) *working models* of their relationships with their primary caregivers. When caregivers are responsive and reliable, the very large majority of infants develop a **secure attachment style** (Ainsworth & Bowlby, 1965). They behave as if they know they can trust their caregivers.

Figure 24.1 Being highly responsive to the need of infants yields physical as well as psychological benefits, much as Erik Erikson would have expected. Recent evidence suggests that a lack of routine physical contact between infants and their primary caregivers may delay infants' physical development – even at the cellular and genetic level (Moore et al., 2017).

One of the main ways in which we know about infant (and toddler) attachment style comes from studies using Ainsworth's **strange situation**. In this paradigm, a primary caregiver and baby arrive at an unfamiliar room full of toys and distractions. Because primary caregivers are usually moms, we hope you'll forgive us if, in the next few examples, we use "mom" in place of the more accurate but much wordier "primary caregiver." In this "strange situation," there are usually many interesting objects for babies to explore. But precisely because the situation is unfamiliar, most babies like to keep mom close at hand. There are many variations on the strange situation, but in the simplest variation, mom hangs out with baby without anyone else present. But when mom receives a signal from the researcher, she quickly exits the room. Most babies cry. It's hard to blame them. Recall that they're just getting a decent handle on object permanence. From their perspective, when mom departs, she may be gone forever. On the other hand, if mom has always been there for them in the past, and if they are securely attached to her, they should be forgiving and easy to soothe as soon as mom comes back. And mom does always come back, of course. Attachment researchers may make quite a few babies cry, but they aren't monsters. Arguably, the most important part of the strange situation has to do with how babies respond when mom returns. We're happy to say that most babies calm down quickly when mom returns. Some are even joyful. They may keep slightly closer tabs on mom for a while, but they quickly get back to playing and exploring while using mom as a **secure base**. A secure base is a sort of emotional "home base" from which to explore. If mom acts as a secure base for you when she returns in the strange situation, then you're securely attached – that is, you have a secure attachment style.

But **insecurely attached** infants respond in sad, and sometimes ironic ways, when mom returns. Some babies are simply inconsolable. Even though mom picks them up and tries to reassure them, they continue to cry long after her return. In fact, they may even push her away as she tries to calm them. This specific type of insecure attachment style is known as an **anxious-ambivalent** attachment style because the same baby that was so sad when mom disappeared can't quite accept her return and is very hard to soothe. Attachment theorists assume that this ambivalent behavior (I want you, but I don't want you; I'm scared, but you can't console me) reflects the infant's precarious sense of trust in mom – and trust is at the heart of Erikson's first stage. By the way, in case you find yourself blaming poor mom for this unhappy infant attachment style, we should note that some infants seem to be born with a genetic predisposition toward an anxious attachment style. Major medical problems, both in infants and in moms, can also contribute to an insecure infant attachment style. When your first author's daughter was an infant, she suffered from extreme acid reflux that proved to be very resistant to treatment. So even though her parents tag teamed many a sleepless night, walking and rocking her for many hours, they were sure that she wondered – as much as infants can do so – why no one ever soothed her terrible pain.

There's another kind of insecure infant and toddler attachment style. Instead of becoming needy and hard to soothe, **anxious-avoidant** infants cope with separation from mom by behaving as if they don't need much mothering. When mom disappears in the first place, they're unlikely to follow her or cry. When mom returns, they often act as if they barely noticed. Further, they're less likely than most other infants to use mom as a secure base for exploration. Anxious-avoidant infants behave as if they've learned that they cannot trust their primary caregivers. Their avoidance is taken as evidence that they can't take any emotional risks in a world where caregivers can't be trusted. At the risk of being highly redundant, let us add that there are multiple reasons why an infant might develop an anxious-avoidant attachment style. From a child's genetic predisposition to the death of a caregiver, conditions that are sometimes out of a parent's control can make it hard for infants to develop trust in their primary caregivers. Your first author's dad was the child of a single, working mother who had five kids. It would be a miracle if he and his siblings had all developed secure infant attachment styles. Sometimes, the energy and resources it takes merely to feed kids and give them shelter can make it impossible for a single parent to be there whenever kids are in need.

Figure 24.2 Erikson would probably like the hurdle race metaphor of lifespan human development. Hitting a hurdle early in the race of life makes it more likely that we'll crash into a hurdle later – or finish poorly. Erikson seems to have believed that social life is a series of hurdles. After clearing each hurdle cleanly, we are better prepared for the next.

If Erikson were around today, he'd presumably be happy to see that we've focused disproportionately on his first developmental stage. Part of the legacy of Erikson's Freudian training was his belief that when things go badly early in life, unresolved issues make it harder to cope successfully with later developmental challenges. In our view a **hurdle race metaphor** illustrates well how Erikson conceptualized lifespan human development (see Figure 24.2). From this viewpoint, life is like a hurdle race. After clearing each hurdle successfully, you're better prepared for the next hurdle. However, each hurdle that gives you trouble early in the race puts you at risk of hitting other hurdles *later* in the race. At the very best, hitting a hurdle slows you down a lot. Erikson seems to have agreed with Freud that very early experiences are of paramount importance in human development. Whether we frame this idea in terms of critical periods, attachment theory, or the explosions in brain development that happen in infancy and toddlerhood, Erikson was probably right to argue that the first major life dilemma we face sets the stage for the seven that follow. Along these lines, longitudinal studies show that there is at least a modest connection between infant or toddler attachment to primary caregivers and adult attachment to romantic partners (McConnell & Moss, 2011). Securely attached toddlers are somewhat more likely than average to become securely attached to their spouses, for example.

Let us conclude this section on trust versus mistrust by noting that infants have plenty of things to keep them busy that are separate from trust versus mistrust. They learn to hear and produce some sounds (phonemes) rather than others. They must learn to crawl, see, and work their arms, each of which allows them to develop a basic sense of mastery. But according to Erikson, at least, infancy is a period when the need for connectedness trumps even the very powerful need for mastery.

Figure 24.3 Toddlers are *super* curious. They love exploring new things.

Autonomy vs. shame & doubt (toddlerhood = age 1–3). In infancy, connectedness trumps everything else. But not for long. Toddlerhood represents a dramatic shift in what little tykes care about. Younger toddlers may barely be able to walk, but they *can* walk, and their vocabularies explode at a dizzying rate. This linguistic explosion in vocabulary still describes toddlers well even when you ignore the four words they use more often than any others. These words, of course, are "no," "not," "me," and "mine." Toddlers are all about autonomy. They are little experimenters who are constantly testing the world to see how it works. More important, perhaps, they are seeing not just how gravity works but also what *they* can do to push back against gravity – and against anything or anyone else that might set limits on their curious behavior. Erikson argued that when caregivers gives toddlers freedom but not too much freedom, toddlers develop a sense of autonomy. This means keeping toddlers safe by curtailing inappropriate behavior but otherwise allow them to experiment and explore. When this happens, toddlers develop a clear sense of autonomy and self-determination. Conversely when parents are overprotective, toddlers may not be able to develop a basic sense of autonomy. Worse yet, if parents are highly punitive or overcontrolling, toddlers may develop a sense of shame and doubt rather than autonomy. And of course, if toddlers never develop a basic sense of autonomy (if they fail to clear this hurdle), this will make things difficult for them when early childhood arrives. On the other hand, if they successfully develop a sense of trust and autonomy, then they will be better equipped to clear the next hurdle.

Initiative vs. guilt (early childhood = age 3–6). In early childhood, autonomy morphs into what Erikson called initiative. In this third Eriksonian stage, kids continue to try to master and control their worlds. But now that kids can speak well and think clearly about the past and future, they set more elaborate goals and make highly specific plans and requests. In early childhood, kids try to take initiative. If this fails, they may develop a sense of self-focused guilt. When your first author Brett's son Lincoln was two, for example, he would often ask to go to the zoo. But by the time he was four, he would make very specific requests about exactly where we should go and when. He was particularly fond of predators, primates, and elephants, and his ideal trip involved lots of time viewing them. Further, once he was four, telling him that the elephants were "feeling very shy today" was not enough to deter him from insisting that they pay them a visit. Because Brett is an animal lover himself, there are worse things than getting convinced by a four-year-old that he must spend a lot of time visiting elephants. Besides, Brett admired his son's initiative.

Imaginative play becomes particularly important in early childhood, and kids may explore their sense of initiative by requesting time with specific playmates. In our view, parents must walk a tightrope between allowing kids a reasonable degree of decision-making without letting them make bad decisions – or play with kids who will set bad examples for them. Along somewhat similar lines, research by Carol Dweck and colleagues shows that parents should work hard to communicate to kids that it's their *efforts* that matter most and not just whether or not they succeed or fail. Dweck's research has demonstrated that when kids, teachers, and parents believe that success is the product of hard work – including lots of hard work that leads to failure – kids not only develop a healthy sense of competence but also keep going in the face of setbacks. In one experiment, Dweck and her colleagues gave kids a nonverbal IQ test. Half the kids were initially praised for their performance and their intelligence. The other half were praised for their *effort*. Although we suspect that the kids who were praised for initial performance felt good about being praised, this led to serious problems down the road. For example, when asked what they'd like to work on next, the kids who'd been praised for their performance chose to do a task that they thought would make them look smart over a task they believed would give them a chance to learn something new. These kids who had been praised for performing well (but not for working hard) also gave up on a subsequent task when it became difficult. Worse yet, these kids lied about their performance when they had a chance to communicate with other kids about how they had done. In contrast, kids who had been praised for their *effort* rather than their performance chose a future task that would allow them to learn more rather than look good. And they persisted on a future task when it got difficult. In fact, they outperformed the kids who had been the recipients of a lot of praise when both groups worked on a routine task that followed a very difficult task.

Based on studies such as these, Dweck (2019) concludes that parents, coaches, and teachers should reward kids of all ages for their efforts rather than their performances – and strongly encourage kids to adopt an orientation that recognizes that through effort and learning one can always improve. Or as the old adage says, "If at first you don't succeed, try, try again." If Erikson were around today, we have little doubt that he would agree.

Industry vs. inferiority (middle childhood = ages 6–12). As kids move on from pre-school to elementary school in wealthy nations, their parents and teachers require them to learn a lot. Of course, if kids grow up in the rainforest rather than a concrete jungle, the specific lessons they learn will be different. But during the middle childhood years that precede adolescence, the things kids learn become increasingly complex and demanding. Moreover, kids are expected to focus and pay attention for long periods rather than relying completely on parents or teachers to point the way. At our houses, this was the window when our kids first expressed a serious interest in cooking, including the kind that involves ovens, grills, and sharp knives. This period is also a window when kids' social circles may widen dramatically. Middle childhood is a period when most kids become much more heavily influenced by peers than they once were. But as the term industry suggests, this is the third developmental stage in a row in which Erikson felt that kids focus a lot on *mastery*.

Erikson suggested that this stage is distinct from initiative versus guilt in that older children dramatically widen their social circle and begin to think about how they stack up against a wide range of others. Kids in this age group begin to engage in serious social comparisons, and some kids become extremely competitive about their performance in school or sports. The mushrooming ability of kids to think abstractly at this age is both a blessing and a curse. Consider an example. Sheskin, Bloom, and Wynn (2014) gave kids aged 5–10 a series of choices – about receiving game tokens. The kids had to choose between different sets of tokens some of which would go to them and some of which would presumably go to an unnamed child who would show up later that day. The tokens were valuable. Kids knew that they could later be exchanged for toys and prizes. Figure 24.4 shows a five-year-old making one of her choices. As you can see, she is taking the option that gives her a slightly inferior outcome (seven rather than eight tokens) but gives the other unknown player a *dramatically* inferior outcome (zero versus eight tokens).

Like hundreds of other studies in social and developmental psychology, this study supports Festinger's (1954) **social comparison theory**, which suggests that we often figure out where we stand by comparing our own outcomes or performances with those of similar others. Because we each happen to be parents of two children, and because we have collectively spent many years working with kids of many different ages, we can both tell you that middle childhood is a period when most kids are heavily fixated on feeling competent and industrious. Of course, if things go very badly at home or at school, kids may come through this developmental stage feeling incompetent and inferior. Perhaps even worse, they may come through it feeling like it is OK to lie, cheat, or shortchange others to maintain their fragile sense of superiority. Of course, parents, teachers, and coaches who are aware of Dweck's work on mindsets can continue to reinforce effort and persistence without making a huge deal about stellar performance. This approach to socialization should allow kids to develop a sense of industry without being thrown for a loop every time they fail.

Figure 24.4
Kids can be competitive. This five-year-old girl has a choice. She can take *seven* tokens for herself and give zero (none) to a future participant (the choice she is making), or she can take *eight* for herself while also giving eight to the other child. In line with social comparison theory, and in contrast to simple self-interest, most kids preferred the competitive (spiteful) option – which maximized their outcomes relative to those of a stranger. In middle childhood, kids like to win. Perhaps this is true because they've learned that winning makes for a very high place in the social hierarchy. Line drawing adapted from images and description by Sheskin et al. (2014).

Identity vs. role confusion (adolescence = age 12–18). Like Piaget, Erikson realized that once kids reach adolescence, they can engage in highly sophisticated ways of thinking. They may push away from parents and try to figure out exactly who they are. Recall that Erikson himself spent a lot of time in his adolescence trying to find an identity that felt right to him. He almost became an artist, and then an art teacher, before settling on psychology. He also spent a lot of time trying to figure out his national and religious identities. We will discuss the self-concept and identity much further in a separate module of this text. For now, we'd just like to make two points. First, identity is complicated. We all have *many* identities, some of which support and validate other identities, and some of which conflict with other identities. Further, these identities vary greatly in their importance. It is extremely important to your first author, for example, to be a good father, only moderately important to him to be athletic, and not very important at all that he is about 20% Norwegian. But if he had spent much of his childhood in Norway, or if he had moved to Norway as an adult, he might feel different about this. The second point we'd like to add about identities is that identities may be grounded in *either* mastery *or* connectedness. Identities based on skill and performance (such as being a sprinter or a concert violinist) are based very much on mastery of specific skills. In contrast, being Latina, being a Muslim, or being a mom usually have more to do with connectedness than with mastery. In our view, then, adolescence is the first stage in life when people can take the route of mastery, the route of connectedness, or the route of both to make it to where Erikson says we should be.

Because we will spend the entirety of the next module on adult human development, we're going to offer somewhat briefer summaries of Erikson's three adult stages than we did of his five childhood stages. Nonetheless, if you want to appreciate Erikson's lifespan model, you need to know that he felt strongly that human development continues throughout the life span. With that in mind, let's leave the painful days of adolescence behind and consider young adulthood.

Intimacy vs. isolation (early adulthood = age 18–39). A simple way to express Erikson's view of young adulthood is this: He felt that young adults know who they are but not *with whom* they want to be. Thus, most young adults try to build meaningful friendships, work relationships, and especially romantic relationships. This means that the chances that a 20-year-old college student will meet a stranger at a party this weekend are much, much higher than the chances that a middle-aged textbook author will do so. We personally don't *mind* meeting new people, by the way, but we never build our weekends around doing so. Likewise, we don't ever swipe right or left because (we hope) our swiping days are over (swiping didn't exist when we were your age, of course). But most young adults are justifiably concerned with making friends and finding romantic partners. Of course, these two routes to connectedness are very different, and we use very different language to reflect that. Did you notice that we said young adults are concerned with "*making* friends" and "*finding* romantic partners"? Presumably, this linguistic convention reflects our assumption that there is one perfect romantic partner out there for each of us – whom we must *find* – the way you *find* your way to Kansas City, or *find* a lost smartphone.

By contrast, we seem to assume that we can "make" friends the way we make lunch or make mistakes. Especially for young people, friends come and go. Romantic partners can come and go, too, of course. But as most people find themselves in the latter half of this stage (their 30s), they often become interested in finding just one romantic partner. As you may recall from our discussion of Erikson's first stage, finding a partner with whom you can truly become intimate – not just sexually but psychologically – can prove to be a daunting task for people who have an insecure adult attachment style. Early experiences do pave the way for later experiences.

Generativity vs. self-absorption (middle adulthood = age 40–59). Middle-aged adults ask if they're changing the world in ways that will leave their kids, friends, patients, fellow worshippers, or students in a better place. Generativity is partly about unselfish connectedness and partly about "leaving one's mark" to signal very high levels of mastery. Having a college building named after you, setting up a college savings fund for your granddaughter, or publishing a college textbook book may help you achieve what Erikson called generativity. Being inducted into the NBA Hall of Fame is a very different, even more masterful, way to do the same thing. Moving on from mastery to connectedness, knowing that your grandchildren love you, or receiving an award for your years of service to the homeless may also help you achieve generativity. At this stage, making a difference matters, and we can make a difference through what we achieve and/or through the relationships we cultivate. In the same sense that young adults may develop a sense of identity by means of either mastery or connectedness, middle-aged adults may achieve a sense of generativity either by being connected to others or by demonstrating high levels of mastery. It is worth noting that not everyone achieves generativity. Further, some people who firmly believe they've achieved generativity may not have truly done so. If you'd like to see a very humorous example of someone who is highly self-absorbed rather than highly generative, check out Steve Martin's classic Christmas monologue *One Wish* at: www.youtube.com/watch? v=T_88eTrUPHI

Ego integrity vs. despair (late adulthood = age 60+). Erikson proposed that older adults realize that their lives are coming to an end. It probably won't be tomorrow, but it will almost certainly be in the next few decades. Older adults thus begin to ask themselves whether life has been good – or whether the major decisions they have made have been good ones. In late adulthood, then, we begin to think about how we have spent our lives and ask ourselves whether we lived with honor or whether our life was a waste. Making it over this last hurdle brings feelings of accomplishment and satisfaction. In contrast, failing to clear the hurdle brings feelings of regret and despair. Of course, no one is perfect. Thus, feeling that we have lived with integrity may have as much to do with what we have done to compensate for our personal flaws and mistakes as it does with living life well in the first place. We certainly hope that at the end of Erik Erikson's life, he looked back on everything he had done to advance psychology – and to help others – and felt that it was all worth it. We thus hope that Erikson's attitude about death was similar to that expressed by Mark Twain. Twain said that "The fear of death follows from the fear of life. A man [or woman] who lives fully is prepared to die at any time." As you will see in the module on adult development, modern research on socioemotional selectivity theory suggests that people who are lucky enough to make it to late adulthood very often feel like life has been good – and like they should enjoy what little time is left. This means that, compared with younger or middle-aged adults, most seniors don't worry very much about death – or about almost anything else for that matter (Newport & Pelham, 2009). That's right. A young whippersnapper like *yourself* probably worries about death a lot more than your grandparents do. We hope you're now worrying a little less – now that you know it won't bother you so much in the future.

Figure 24.5
This 81-year-old great, great grandmother took great joy in being with her extended family, especially her youngest descendants. That's consistent with both Erik Erikson's lifespan theory of human development and recent research on socioemotional selectivity theory – which you'll learn more about in the next module.

Thinking Critically about Erikson's Psychosocial Model of Human Development

We hope this module makes it clear that we are fans of Erikson's psychosocial model of lifespan development. Nonetheless, like any other psychological theory, Erikson's theory has its limits. One limit is that the theory has not been put to critical empirical tests at every stage of life. As Arnett (2012) reports, most tests of Erikson's model have focused on either identity issues in very young adults or questions about generativity and identity certainty in middle aged adults. That leaves six of eight stages that have not really been put to many direct empirical tests. Another critique of Erikson is grounded in research on cross-cultural psychology. As you'll see in an upcoming module, cross-cultural researchers argue that a great deal of psychological research may fail to describe most of the Earth's population. These cross-cultural researchers use the acronym WEIRD to remind us that most psychological research focuses on people living in Western, Educated, Industrialized, Rich, and Democratic (WEIRD) countries (Henrich, Heine, & Norenzayan, 2010). To what degree is Erikson's model biased by his limited experiences living in WEIRD cultures (such as Canada, Germany, and the United States)? Advocates of the WEIRD critique have suggested that many of the rules of human thoughts, feelings, and behavior may be different in WEIRD and non-WEIRD countries. Although we'll admit to being less worried about some of the WEIRD critiques than many other cross-cultural psychologists, we do believe the WEIRD critique raises some very important questions. Further, if we wish to be critical of Erikson's model, we think concerns about cultural biases are a great place to start. In fact, many of our own critiques of Erikson's model are based on the idea that he seems to have assumed that his model was culturally universal. Is it?

1. Let's begin with infancy. Perhaps Erikson's focus on trust vs. mistrust was an arti-fact of his experiences living in the West. In many non-WEIRD countries – for example, in many poor nations – infants are rarely away from their mothers. They are often carried everywhere mom goes, and they almost always sleep with their moms, which means mom is always there to meet their physical and emotional needs. Do Western worries about trust versus mistrust melt away in nations where infants are never away from their mothers? Or do infants in poor nations face more serious challenges when it comes to trust versus mistrust because their worlds are so unpredictable and uncontrollable?

2. There is empirical evidence that in countries where life is rough, parents often take a more punitive approach to childrearing. For example, in nations with high disease loads and high infant mortality rates, parents are more likely to say that it is OK for parents to beat their kids to be sure they are obedient. What are the likely consequences of highly punitive parenting for children in early to middle childhood? Is it possible such punitive parenting practices actually benefit kids by helping them stay out of trouble and master their worlds? Or do punitive prac-tices squelch a sense of autonomy, initiative, and industry? Finally, is it possible that the very idea that autonomy, initiative, and industry are good things is a biased Western idea?

3. Erikson can be taken to have suggested that in adolescence, we strive to develop unique identities – that is, identities that clearly distinguish us from other people. Is it possible that in non-WEIRD cultures, it is so important to be *like* others – rather than different from others – that identity issues operate very differently. For example, is it possible that in most non-WEIRD countries, the identities that are most important usually connect us to others (e.g., "I am a good daughter.") rather than documenting a high level of mastery (e.g., "I graduated at the top of my class.")? Or is it possible that mastery matters but that our successes say more

about our families and social groups than they do about us? Do Ethiopian Olympians run for the glory of their nation, or their families, rather than for their own personal glory?

4. Erikson seems to have assumed that in both middle age and old age we ask ourselves whether we have made the world a better place – or whether our lives have been meaningful. Across the globe, non-WEIRD cultures are *much* more religious than WEIRD cultures. Does living in a culture in which almost everyone is deeply religious mean that concerns about meaning or purpose become a moot point? Why or why not?

Multiple Choice Questions for Module 24

1. What are the two main ways in which Erikson's approach to lifespan human development was different than Freud's approach?

   A) Erikson's theory had eight rather than five stages and emphasized social rather than sexual processes
   B) Erikson conducted experiments rather than case studies, and Erikson was more optimistic than Freud
   C) Erikson explicitly addressed both culture and gender, both of which Freud's model largely ignored

2. Your textbook suggests that a good motivational lens for understanding Erikson's model of lifespan human development is the lens:

   A) offered by Maslow's motivational pyramid
   B) of mastery versus connectedness
   C) of cultural variation and diversity

3. What does Dweck's research suggest about the difference between praising kids for effort vs. praising kids for performance?

   A) kids who are praised for performance do better under difficult circumstances
   B) kids who are praised for effort do better under difficult circumstances
   C) which type of praise works better depends heavily on the culture in which one lives

4. What theory of the self and identity suggests that kids figure out who they are and what they are like by seeing how they fare relative to other kids?

   A) social hierarchy theory
   B) relative standing theory
   C) social comparison theory

5. Which of the following sets of three positive outcomes in Erikson's model is listed in the correct chronological order (youngest to oldest).

   A) autonomy, initiative, industry
   B) integrity, intimacy, generativity
   C) intimacy, identity, integrity

6. According to Erikson, at about what age are people heavily concerned with achieving generativity?

   A) older adulthood
   B) middle adulthood
   C) young adulthood

7. The hurdle metaphor of human development is:

   A) a competing model that suggests that life is more like a race than a series of social interactions
   B) a perspective on Erikson's model that suggests that mastery usually trumps connectedness
   C) a way to understand Erikson's view that early problems in life often lead to later problems

8. The strange situation paradigm is a technique for assessing or figuring out what?

   A) the attachment styles of infants and toddlers
   B) how much teenagers care about fitting in socially
   C) how adolescents cope with being rejected or stigmatized by peers

9. If we accept Erikson's model of lifespan development, during what two stages of life are most people most concerned about connectedness?

   A) early and middle childhood
   B) infancy and early adulthood
   C) infancy and toddlerhood

10. What are the two kinds of insecure human attachment styles?

    A) anxious-ambivalent and anxious-avoidant
    B) fearful and worrisome
    C) fragile and inflexible

11. Olivia just set up a savings account for her two young granddaughters that will help pay for a great deal of these children's college educations. According to Erikson's psychosocial model of development, this caring act should contribute to Olivia's sense of:

    A) nurturance
    B) integrity
    C) generativity

Answer Key: 1A, 2B, 3B, 4C, 5A, 6B, 7C, 8A, 9B, 10A, 11C

References

Ainsworth, M., & Bowlby, J. (1965). *Child care and the growth of love.* London: Penguin Books.

Arnett, J. J. (2012). *Human development: A cultural approach.* Upper Saddle River, NJ: Pearson.

Baumeister, R. F., & Leary, M. (1995). The need to belong: Desire for interpersonal attachments as a fundamental human motivation. *Psychological Bulletin, 117,* 497–529.

Depuydt, S. (2014).Arguments for and against self and non-self root recognition in plants. *Frontiers in Plant Science, 5.*Published online 2014, November 6.

Dunsworth, H. M., Warrener, A. G., Deacon, T., Ellison, P. T., & Pontzer, H. (2012). Metabolic hypothesis for human altriciality. *Proceedings of the National Academy of Sciences of the United States of America, 109*(38), 15212–15216. doi:10.1073/pnas.1205282109

Dweck, C. (2019). The mindset of a champion. GoStanford.com college news sit Retrieved March 20, 2019 from https://gostanford.com/sports/2014/5/2/209487946.aspx

Festinger, L. (1954). A theory of social comparison processes. *Human Relations, 7,* 117–140.

Hardin, D. (1994). *Personal communication – As transmitted by Hardin's son.* Curtis D. Hardin.

Hawkes, K., O'Connell, J. F., & Blurton-Jones, N. G. (1997). Hadza women's time allocation, offspring provisioning, and the evolution of long postmenopausal life spans. *Current Anthropology, 38,* 551–577.

Henrich, J., Heine, S. J., & Norenzayan, A. (2010). The weirdest people in the world? *Behavioral and Brain Sciences, 33,* 61–135.

House, J. S., Landis, K. R., & Umberson, D. (1988). Social relationships and health. *Science, 241,* 540–545.

McConnell, M., & Moss, E. (2011). Attachment across the life span: Factors that contribute to stability and change. *Australian Journal of Educational & Developmental Psychology, 11,* 60–77.

Moore, S., McEwen, L., Quirt, J., Morin, A., Mah, S., Barr, R., & Kobor, M. (2017). Epigenetic correlates of neonatal contact in humans. *Development and Psychopathology, 29*(5), 1517–1538.

Newport, F., & Pelham, B. (2009). Don't worry, be 80: Worry and stress decline with age. Gallup. Retrieved March 19, 2019 from https://news.gallup.com/poll/124655/dont-worry-be-80-worry-stress-decline-age.aspx

New York Times. (1994, May 13). *Erik Erikson, 91, psychoanalyst who reshaped views of human growth, dies* Retrieved March 19, 2019.

Sheskin, M., Bloom, P., & Wynn, K. (2014). Anti-equality: Social comparison in young children. *Cognition, 130*(2), 152–156.

Module 25
Adult Development
Getting There – and then Hanging in There

If you consider who you are now and who you were just a few years ago, you'll probably agree that you have not stopped developing – even if you have long been an adult. Human development is a lifelong process. This module explores that idea. We first discuss the gray stage that immediately precedes true adulthood in most wealthy nations. We then move on to early, middle, and late adulthood. We'll see that many physical and psychological changes take place in the typical human adult, many of them wonderful, a few of them the opposite of wonderful. We'll begin with a recently-recognized window of human development that has its fair share of the wonderful, along with some occasional examples of the confusing and even the tragic.

Emerging Adulthood

In most modern, wealthy nations, people who just became legal adults enter a stage of development that was first identified right after the turn of the 21st century. Arnett (2000) identified **emerging adulthood** as a developmental stage covering the ages of about 18 and 25. In this stage, people occupy a transitional zone between adolescence and true adulthood. This new stage came about largely because of dramatic cultural changes in most wealthy nations in the second half of the 20th century. In only a few decades, the cultural norms of the past 1,000 years – getting married and choosing a career shortly after becoming a legal adult – had been replaced by new norms that encourage young adults to get an advanced education and try out different roles and relationships. These cultural shifts pushed marriage down the road and created a significant transitional period. Arnett (2000) identifies several ways in which emerging adulthood is distinct from both adolescence and early adulthood. But a key feature of emerging adulthood is "**feeling in between**" (Arnett, 2012). Arnett asked people aged 18–25 if they felt like they had "reached adulthood." Fewer than 5% of people aged 18–25 said they had not. But only 40% said they *had*. That leaves more than half this age group who answered, "yes and no" (Arnett, 2000, Figure 2, p. 472). Arnett calls people aged 18–25 "emerging" adults because they feel and behave like adults in *some* ways but not in others. For example, almost all emerging adults can vote, but some cannot yet purchase alcohol, and many do not pay their own rent or tuition. A verbatim list of Arnett's (2012, p. 403) five features of emerging adulthood appears in Table 25.1.

As you can see in line 2 of Table 25.1, another defining feature of emerging adulthood is **instability**. As you already knew, emerging adults often move away to college. They may also date multiple people at once, and they may cohabit with romantic partners who prove to be temporary. Emerging adults who attend college may change

Table 25.1 Arnett's (2012) Five Features of Emerging Adulthood

1. the age of identity explorations
2. the age of instability
3. the self-focused age
4. the age of feeling in-between
5. the age of possibilities

their majors and career aspirations as often as they change roommates or hairstyles. Even emerging adults who jump right into the full-time work force sometimes reinvent themselves – as they find meaning in work, discover new social identities or political causes, change their diets, or bounce back and forth between different peer groups. As Arnett (2012) notes, there is also no period of life in which people change residences more often than emerging adulthood. Emerging adults are often in a state of flux.

Moving on from instabilities to **possibilities**, most emerging adults see the future through rose-colored lenses. This is a window of great optimism about the future. For most emerging adults, the future is a very happy place. When your first author was employed at Gallup – not long after Arnett made his pronouncement about early adulthood – he examined a representative sample of almost a million American adults and compared how people of all ages (from 18 to 90+) said their *current* lives were and how good they said they thought their lives would be in five years. The group that was most upbeat about their futures was the emerging adults. Let's all agree not to tell them about climate change, asteroids, deadly pandemics, or our growing resistance to once life-saving antibiotics.

As shown in line 1 of Table 25.1, Arnett (2012) also notes that emerging adulthood is a time of **identity exploration** – that is, a time when people begin to ponder and try on different adult identities (e.g., what does it mean to be a Latina engineer?). You may recall that Erikson proposed that *adolescence* was the life stage in which people figure out their identities. Arnett's idea is that Erikson was correct half a century ago. But in most modern, wealthy cultures – where many people put off parenting and launching a career until they are well into their 20s – the window in which people ponder their identities greatly expands. Some researchers have noted that emerging adulthood is a window when many people graduate from harmless optimism to self-absorbed narcissism. People who score high in the personality trait of **narcissism** are so **self-focused** and self-aggrandizing that they spend much of their time bragging and showing off, and they are prone to criticize and exploit others (Raskin & Terry, 1988; Twenge et al., 2008). Arnett (2012) argues that it's normal for emerging adults to be more self-focused than older adults. Thus, unlike those who bemoan the high levels of self-absorption and narcissism among today's emerging adults, Arnett counters that it's fine to be a *little* self-absorbed during emerging adulthood. After all, when emerging adulthood ends, most people face many decades of family commitments. If you'd like to see why there is room for debate about exactly how to interpret growing levels of narcissism in college students, just consult Table 25.2, which contains a sample of questions from the Narcissistic Personality Inventory (NPI). It shows that narcissism is a multi-faceted trait. Being highly self-confident or showing off, for example, is different than being willing to manipulate or prey on others. If you'd like to take the full-blown NPI measure yourself, just go to: https://openpsychometrics.org/tests/NPI/

Table 25.2 Sample Questions from Raskin and Terry's (1988) Narcissistic Personality Inventory

- o I have a natural talent for influencing people.
- o I am not good at influencing people.

- o Modesty doesn't become me.
- o I am essentially a modest person.

- o I would do almost anything on a dare.
- o I tend to be a fairly cautious person.

- o When people compliment me I sometimes get embarrassed.
- o I know that I am good because everybody keeps telling me so.

- o I find it easy to manipulate people.
- o I don't like it when I find myself manipulating people.

- o I prefer to blend in with the crowd
- o I like to the center of attention.

Note. The NPI is a forced-choice measure. This means respondents must choose the item from each pair that describes them better. Researchers then add up the number of times a person chose the more narcissistic of the two options.

In his more recent work, Arnett (2012) has identified other aspects of emerging adulthood. For example, he refers to emerging adulthood as the **"age of strength and beauty."** We think this has something to do with the fact that emerging adults are usually stronger and more beautiful than the rest of us. Of course, beauty is in the eye of the beholder. But most of Brad Pitt's fans would probably admit that he was even handsomer when he was 22 than he is now. Likewise, Usain Bolt held the title of "world's faster human" for almost a decade before he retired from track and field. But he set a personal best (and world record, of course) in the 100 meters, just before his 22nd birthday. In many years of intense training as an early adult, Bolt never matched the sheer speed he exhibited in emerging adulthood. Sadly, Arnett also describes emerging adulthood as the **"age of tragic risk taking."** Emerging adulthood is a time, for example, when many people abuse alcohol and drugs, crash their cars, engage in unsafe sex, and ignore the usual rules about sleep and nutrition. Of course, adolescents probably have at least as much attraction to tragic risk taking as do emerging adults. But luckily for most adolescents, they usually have many fewer *opportunities* to get into trouble in comparison with emerging adults. Most parents engage in a lot more oversight of 15-year-olds than of 22-year-olds.

Early Adulthood

If you're the kind of realist who wonders why emerging adults are so optimistic and self-focused, we think you may be on to something. That something is the next stage of life, and it's known as **early adulthood**. Early adulthood, which covers roughly the ages of 26–39, is the first period in a person's life when the brain is completely mature. For example, some of the extreme risk-taking behavior that characterizes both adolescence and emerging adulthood can be attributed to the fact that a crucial part of the human brain that helps people regulate their emotions – and balance risks and benefits – does not fully mature until about the age of 25 (Casey, Jones, & Hare,

2008). As you may recall, this part of the brain is the *prefrontal cortex*. It's a cortical region that sits just behind the forehead. In fact, we know from studies of adults who sustain serious damage to the prefrontal cortex that this higher-brain region helps us recognize the difference between rare opportunities and reckless gambles. People with serious damage to the prefrontal cortex often get themselves into trouble – by taking personal, physical, and financial risks that most people would recognize as ill-advised. Remember Phineas Gage?

Early adulthood, then, is a time when many people stop feeling so bullet-proof. With their degrees – and perhaps their lifelong romantic partners – in hand, many adults aged 26–39 begin the business of settling into careers and deciding where to live. Early adulthood is also a time when many people decide to start a family. You may recall that Erikson said people face the developmental tension between *intimacy* and *isolation* as soon as they emerge from adolescence. Based on what you now know about emerging adulthood, though, we hope it's clear that Erikson was correct about human development in the past. But in wealthy cultures today, many people put off serious concerns about intimacy until early adulthood, which begins at about age 26. In fact, according to the United States Census Bureau, the median age of first marriage for American women in 2018 was 27.8. For American men, that value was 29.8. As recently as 1970, these respective values for women and men were 20.8 and 23.2. That's a delay of about seven years in the age of first marriage in less than five decades (see www.census.gov/data/tables/time-series/demo/families/marital.html). At this rate, neither of us may ever see any grandchildren.

As the age of first marriage has increased over the past few decades, the proportion of single parents has also increased. Nonetheless, it is still the case that most Westerners continue to wait until marriage to begin to have children. This is noteworthy because for most Westerners, the event that best marks the transition to feelings of true adulthood is becoming a parent (Arnett, 2000). Early adulthood is surely a demanding period of life. But most young adults seem to be up to the many challenges that typically come with early adulthood. Both physically and mentally, early adults are usually at or near their peaks. In fact, some researchers have argued that both emerging adults and young adults have moved beyond Piaget's fourth stage of formal operations – and have begun to engage in post-formal thinking. In other words, research is beginning to suggest that Piaget may have been premature to argue that human cognitive development is done by the end of adolescence. **Post-formal thinking** refers to increased understanding of self and others, the ability to balance and process thoughts and emotions in complex ways, and the development of expertise. Perhaps the most obvious form of post-formal thinking is pragmatism (Labouvie-Vief, 1990). **Pragmatism** refers to a practical approach to thinking and problem-solving that incorporates social, financial, and emotional factors into what might otherwise seem like purely logical questions. Should a woman divorce her verbally abusive husband if he steadfastly refuses to get help for his drinking problem? Maybe. But what if he is a "functional alcoholic" who manages to hold down a steady job? And what if she has no family or friends who can offer her a place to live if she leaves him? What are the likely emotional consequences of divorce for her toddlers? The "post" in postformal thinking is meant to indicate that real life problems are emotional as well as logical – and that most people cannot live, and do not wish to live, by logic alone. It is also worth adding that although early adults may not be quite as physically fit or speedy as emerging adults, they often make up for their slight physical losses by being savvier and more knowledgeable. All else being equal, a 34-year-old pianist has had ten more years to experience and memorize great works of music than has her 24-year-old sister.

Middle Adulthood

After early adulthood comes middle adulthood. If we may wax a little cynical, recall that wonderful thing called experience to which we just alluded? Middle adulthood, which covers roughly the ages of 40–59, is when we have traded a great deal of energy and enthusiasm for all that experience. Erikson was at least partly correct that in middle age we finally begin to know exactly who we are (Zucker, Ostrove, & Stewart, 2002) But by middle age, who we are is often gray, wrinkled, and pudgy. When we feel this way, we remind ourselves of what a luxury middle adulthood is. After all, what we view today as *middle* adulthood was very late adulthood throughout most of human history. In ancient times, people very rarely lived beyond the age of 50. Both middle age and old age are modern luxuries, especially in the context of the roughly 200,000-year history of fully-modern human beings.

And like every other age, middle age is full of quirks. One such quirk is living long enough to see your grandchildren begin to grow up. That practically never happened 100,000 years ago. Another quirk of middle age in people that is virtually unknown in other animals is the existence of menopause in the only sex that can produce offspring. In fact, we're one of only a handful of mammals – and we're the *only* species of primate – whose females experience menopause. **Menopause** is the complete cessation of ovulation that happens in most women around the age of 50. Menopause might seem like a big evolutionary mistake. If evolution is all about producing lots of surviving offspring, why should women stop reproducing completely once they've gotten some wisdom under their belts? This is a hard question to answer, but that hasn't stopped folks from trying.

Austad (1994) suggested two clever ways to think about menopause. First, consistent with what we just mentioned about recent changes in human lifespan, menopause may be a quirk of the fact that we currently live much, much longer than we did in the past. Many millennia ago, women had no reason to conceive past the age of 50 because women rarely *lived* past the age of 50. Austad's second idea is even more interesting. Menopause may be a useful evolutionary adaptation; its benefits may outweigh its costs. Jared Diamond (1992) expressed this second idea by noting that in ancient groups of human hunter-gatherers, the costs of continuing to give birth throughout the lifespan would have been substantial. As you know if you read the module that covered human birth, one highly unusual human adaptation is our humungous heads. But our big heads create big difficulties for human mothers giving birth. Mother grizzly bears that weigh well over half a ton give birth to bear cubs that weigh *ounces*. Even chimps, who have huge brains compared with most other primates, have a relatively easy time giving birth. Our huge brains simply make it hard, and risky, for human mothers to give birth. When you consider the risks childbirth poses to mothers, especially older mothers, and when you add to this the fact that we're so altricial, menopause makes a lot of sense. Given how long it takes us to mature, it would *not* be a great idea for women in any era of human existence to give birth at age 70. Diamond goes further to note that the post-menopausal woman who doesn't risk death in childbirth at age 50 hangs around to help care for her existing children and grandchildren. She also hangs around to make substantial contributions to the collective labor and decision-making of her family or clan. This might include things like knowing where to get water after an unusually long drought – just like your mom taught you 40 years ago. Grandmothers are an invaluable human resource. And in ancient human history, menopause probably increased the length of time that many women got to be grandmothers (Diamond, 1992).

If you're wondering why there is no male equivalent of menopause in people, let us remind you that as most men age, they *do* slow down both physically and sexually (Singh, 2013). But unlike menopause, which happens very abruptly around the age of 50, **andropause** in men usually refers to a more gradual and linear reduction in things like testosterone levels and sperm count. Consider the debate about gender, age, and reproduction in the classic romantic comedy, *When Harry Met Sally*:

SALLY: [in tears] And I'm going to be 40!
HARRY: When?
SALLY: Someday!
HARRY: In eight years!
SALLY: But it's there! It's like a big dead end! And it's not the same for men – Charlie Chaplin had kids in his 70's!
HARRY: Yeah, but he was too old to pick them up.

So yes, in principle, men could produce offspring well in their 70s or 80s. But in practice, very few men do so. In middle age, then, both men and women feel the first painful stings of aging. This is probably why, as Erik Erikson argued, middle-aged adults begin to think about how they can "make their mark" or leave the world a better place than they found it. This is what Erikson called *generativity*. But of course, not everyone finds peace of mind though generativity. In fact, Carl Jung (1930) argued long ago that it is typical for middle-aged men to begin to question whether their lives truly have meaning, and to undergo a period of extreme distress in middle age. Jung argued that this distress includes depression, anxiety, fears of death, and sometimes an uptick in risk-taking behavior. Modern stereotypes of the "**mid-life crisis**" suggest that lots of middle aged-people, especially men, do engage in behaviors that suggest they are going through a crisis. But are they?

The Midlife Crisis: Fact or Fiction?

There are many reasons to expect middle-aged people to sit up and take notice of the fact that they're falling apart. By the age of 60, people have lost about half the photoreceptors that allow them to see. Several parts of the brain have shrunk, and other parts have become demyelinated which slows down neural communication. Episodic memory (which tells us both what we had for breakfast and where we just put our car keys) has long been declining. In most people, muscle mass has decreased as dramatically as wrinkles have increased. We have a mutual friend – who will go unnamed – who at the age of 30 weighed 175 pounds and could bench press about twice his body weight. Now that this friend is in 50s, he has exchanged a lot of his muscle for fat, and he is happy when his arthritis allows him to do ten pushups. Like most other middle-aged men – ourselves included – he also finds that his energy levels are on the decline. Such declines will only get worse as he ages (Arnett, 2012). It's not a pretty picture, is it, Jason? Wait, did we say we weren't going to out our friend? We blame our fading memories.

Speaking of fading memories, middle adulthood is also the beginning of some cognitive declines. And most middle-aged people know that there are even more dramatic cognitive declines on the horizon. Consider the findings in Figure 25.1, which we adapted from McCabe and Hartman (2008). They compared emerging adults (mean age 21.6) with older adults (mean age 69.3) on several different indicators of intellectual functioning. To facilitate comparisons across four very different intellectual tasks, we converted scores on all the tasks to scales that all have a grand mean of 100. (We did not, however, equalize the standard deviations.)

When it came to vocabulary, the older adults had a substantial *advantage* over the younger adults. Because vocabulary involves long-term memory for facts and definitions, the older adults had an unfair advantage. They'd had several additional decades to learn what a cubit is, or what attenuation means. But on all the other cognitive indicators, the younger adults far outperformed the seniors. Relative to the older adults, the younger adults had superior working memories, and they were better at a novel test of logical thinking. Younger adults also scored much better on a measure of perceptual speed. By the way, perceptual speed is measured in time rather than number of correct answers, and so the scores you see for perceptual speed mean that the younger adults were much faster than the older adults. In fact, a perceptual judgment task that took the average younger adult about two seconds took the average older adult more than three seconds. McCabe and Hartman (2008) did not study any *middle-aged* adults. But based on other studies, it's safe to assume that middle-aged adults would prove to be slower than the emerging adults but faster than the seniors (Willis & Schaie, 1999). On working memory, the middle-aged adults might have already fallen behind the emerging adults, though they'd probably surpass them a bit in vocabulary. In middle age, most forms of cognitive decline are usually subtle. One exception to this rule, as we noted earlier, is episodic memory, which begins a steady decline around the tender age of 18. It would be highly unusual indeed for a middle-aged adult to have a better episodic memory than a teenager.

Because many middle-aged people see middle age as the "beginning of the end," it wouldn't be too surprising if many middle-aged people experienced a reduction in well-being relative to their youth – and perhaps even relative to their senior years. Of course, this is exactly what Jung (1930) proposed long ago. He argued that during middle adulthood, many people (especially men), experience a mid-life crisis. But many contemporary developmental psychologists argue that the mid-life crisis is a myth. For example, in his insightful and popular lifespan human development textbook, Arnett (2012) argued that there is simply no good evidence for a midlife crisis (see also

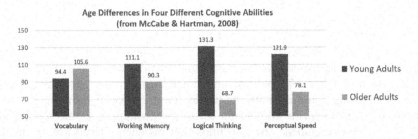

Figure 25.1 With the exception that older adults have larger vocabularies than emerging adults, older adults cannot usually match the cognitive functioning of younger adults. (All measures are coded so that higher scores are better).

Wethington (2000). On the other hand, Daniel Levenson (1977) conducted small scale interviews about 40 years ago with middle-aged men. Levenson claimed that 30 of his 40 interviewees showed evidence of a mid-life crisis. Taking a very different approach, Weiss and colleagues (2012) argued that (a) there is, in fact, a midlife dip in well-being for both women and men. In fact, arguing from an evolutionary perspective, Weiss et al. (2012, p. 19950) argue that in human evolutionary history, "there may have been selection for individuals who have higher well-being in youth and old adulthood." This argument gets tricky because, as you now know, "old adulthood" back in the Pleistocene was often age 40 or 50. Though we agree with Weiss and colleagues that the mid-life crisis is genuine, we take a slightly different view. We agree that it makes evolutionary sense for there to be selection pressures favoring happiness and optimism in young adulthood. Who the heck would have children, traipse across the Bering Strait, or go hunting for wooly rhinos if they *weren't* highly optimistic? But to argue that modern seniors benefit from high levels of well-being relative to middle-aged adults, we think we must take a cultural perspective. It has only been in the past century or so of human existence – and only in wealthy nations – that meaningful numbers of people have lived to be 70 or 80. It thus seems unlikely that we evolved specifically to be happy when we are 80. In human evolutionary history, almost no one ever made it to 80.

But before we delve further into the midlife crisis in people, we should note that there is some surprising evidence for a mid-life crisis in some of our primate cousins. Weiss et al. (2012) observed a **mid-life dip in well-being in chimps and orangutans**. This was no small study. Weiss et al. were able to locate a total of 508 great apes for this study. Of course, the researchers had to rely on human judges who could rate the well-being of these great apes. This introduces the possibility of bias (e.g., projection from human observers). But conceding this pragmatic necessity, Weiss et al. found that the observer ratings revealed a clear dip in well-being among the middle-aged great apes – followed by levels of well-being in late adulthood in these great apes that were almost as high as those observed for the young adults. There may be hormonal or biological influences on the mid-life crisis. After all, it seems unlikely that these middle-aged chimps and orangutans recognized that their days on Earth were numbered – or asked themselves how meaningful their lives were. On the other hand, the midlife dip in well-being is only one indicator of a possible mid-life crisis. Jung conceptualized the mid-life crisis as just that – a *crisis* – rather than a mere dip in well-being. A true crisis includes not only unhappiness but also dangerous and perhaps even suicidal behavior.

So is there any hard evidence for a true midlife crisis in people? Your first author recently examined several very large data sets (Pelham, 2019). Specifically, he examined five different indicators of risk-taking or crisis. The five indicators for which he was able to obtain either national or nationally-representative data for people by age included: (a) divorce or separation rates in the past year, (b) suicide rates, (c) motor-cycle ownership, (d) sports car ownership, and (e) reports of currently being "way below average" in life satisfaction. As you can see in Figure 25.2, which standardizes and averages the findings across all five indicators, there was a clear bump upward in these indicators of risk-taking and distress in middle adulthood. This was true for women as well as for men. In fact, in sharp contrast to the stereotype of the mid-life crisis – which is that it mainly applies to men – these data show that the midlife crisis is a bit *more* pronounced in women than in men.

By the way, we suspect that one of the reasons past studies have failed to detect the mid-life crisis is that they often involved very small samples of people who were all happy and

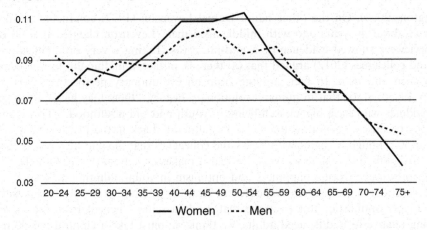

Figure 25.2 Average Score on Five Indicators of Crisis by Age Group. There appears to be a real midlife crisis for both American women and men. For most people. the crisis seems to hit its peak around the age of 50.

healthy enough to take part in surveys. Another reason past studies may have yielded few results is human variability. By studying very large samples – if not populations – and by including public health records of suicide rates as well as self-reports of things like motorcycle ownership, this study offered dramatic increases in statistical power relative to past studies. It's harder for individual variation over time to hide in a very large study that covers a wide range of ages. The problem of variation is much more pronounced, by the way, when studying adults than when studying infants, toddlers, or even adolescents. Almost all infants begin to toddle between about ten and 16 months of age. But unlike walking, speaking, or even shaving, which usually emerge in narrow temporal windows, a midlife crisis could emerge at age 40 or it could emerge at age 55. People are different. But many people between the ages of 40 and 60 do seem to experience a midlife crisis.

Late Adulthood and Socioemotional Selectivity Theory

Laura Carstensen and her colleagues argue that in response to the recent and unprecedented changes in human longevity, seniors in wealthy nations have responded to their dramatically increased lifespans by (a) valuing close, established relationships and (b) seeking positive emotional experiences much more than younger adults do. These two relative motivational tendencies are at the heart of **socioemotional selectivity theory.** The logic of this theory is that "I don't have much time left. I better enjoy myself." Carstensen and colleagues have conducted a great deal of research showing that seniors process and remember information in ways that "accentuate the positive" (Carstensen, Isaacowitz, & Charles, 1999). Research on socioemotional selectivity theory has also shown, for example, that you can make young people think like seniors by asking them to imagine that they're about to make a permanent move to the planet Mars (Chung & Baldwin, 2015). When people believe that time is short, even young people strongly prefer to spend their time with people they already know and love – rather than wanting to get to know new people.

"Can you hear me, honey? It's Irene. What do you say we just hang
a little – and get to know this nice boy I met in the cafeteria?"

Figure 25.3 If Irene's husband is like most other people whose days are numbered, he'd much rather
visit with his friends, siblings, or great grandchildren than meet an interesting stranger.

Many other studies support socioemotional selectivity theory. For example, if you show both happy and unhappy images to both younger and older adults, older adults have greater difficulty than younger adults remembering the negative as opposed to positive images (Charles, Mather, & Carstensen, 2003). Likewise, if you ask people about their memories for their own personal experiences, older people have weaker memories for things that made them angry than do their younger counterparts (Uzer & Gulgoz, 2015). But in our view the studies that most firmly support socioemotional selectivity theory focus on people's motivations rather than their memories. Most older adults are strongly motivated to spend what little time they have left with those they love. In comparison, younger adults are more interested in experiences that will fill their needs for mastery (e.g., learning or traveling to new places). Of course, younger adults also have a need for connectedness and belonging. But compared with older adults, younger adults are much more interested in forging *new* relationships. For good reason, then, all people value both mastery and connectedness. On average, though, young people value mastery more than older people do – while older people value connectedness more than younger people do. As a result, older adults usually say their daily lives are happier and less stressful than the lives of younger adults.

Of course, it is paradoxical for people to be so happy when death is on the horizon. Intuitively, one might expect people to experience a colossal crisis when they know death is just around the corner. But in the mid-life crisis data we reviewed earlier, as in much of Carstensen's data, the age group who is doing the best psychologically is often the oldest age group. Likewise, in a large and highly representative telephone survey of American adults of all ages, Newport and Pelham (2009) strongly confirmed a prediction of socioemotional selectivity theory. They found that relative to both younger and middle-aged adults, American seniors were a lot less likely to report having felt either worried or stressed on the day prior to being interviewed. Old age may come with its aches and pains, but many seniors seem to have learned to "go with the flow" and to enjoy a life relatively free of worry. Exceptions to the rule of greater happiness and well-being among seniors are just as informative as the main trends. For example, one exception to the rule that older Americans report less worry and stress than younger Americans comes from very old Americans who are still employed full-time. Newport and Pelham's (2009) huge sample allowed them to identify 2,877 interviewees aged 91 and older. A good number of these Ultra-seniors said they still worked full-time. Working adults in their 90s were twice as likely as working adults in their 70s or early 80s to say that they had experienced a lot of worry or stress yesterday. That settles it for us. If we live to be 90, we're going to consider retiring. On a more serious note, socioemotional selectivity theory notwithstanding, one apparent reason why most seniors are happier than the rest of us is that for most seniors – namely, the retired ones – every day is the weekend. Long live weekends.

Thought Questions for Module 25

Module 25 could be taken to suggest that middle age is a very rough time of life. Especially when it comes to sheer physical performance (e.g., running speed, strength, perceptual processing speed, memory for recent events) most middle-aged adults fare poorly in comparison with either emerging or young adults. Making matters worse, the midlife crisis that we once thought was a myth appears to be real. Middle-aged people are quite a bit more likely than seniors, for example, to become divorced or separated in a given year.

But as you recall there are exceptions to the rule of middle-aged decline. In middle-age most people have improved their vocabulary. And many people do develop a clearer sense of who they are in middle age. Perhaps more important, middle age is a time when people in many careers – especially intellectually challenging careers – reach their peak level of performance (Arnett, 2012). If you recall the module on the insularity of genius you know that what appears to be natural genius is more often the product of many years, perhaps even decades of deliberate practice. No one ever picks up a cello and becomes a world class player over the weekend. Even in physically-demanding professional sports such as basketball, players in their 30s seem to be able to compensate for losses in raw speed by increasing their "basketball IQ." A good way to summarize observations such as this is that in almost any area of intellectual activity or performance, there are two very different kinds of intelligence. (If you recall these forms of intelligence from Module 20, you can skip the review that follows.) Fluid intelligence refers to your ability to think quickly in a novel situation, that is to "think on your feet." Fluid intelligence requires flexibility, processing speed, and working memory. In contrast, crystallized intelligence is intelligence built up over months or years of intensive, deliberate practice. It relies heavily on stored knowledge and thus is only possible when a person has committed a great deal of information to long-term memory. So even though middle-aged people cannot usually keep up with youngsters when it comes to fluid intelligence, they often outshine them when it comes to crystallized intelligence. In this brief activity, we'd like you to categorize each of a set of 12 tasks, problems, or intellectual activities. Four of them mostly require crystallized intelligence, four mostly require fluid intelligence, and four would require people to use a combination of fluid and crystallized intelligence. Your answer options for the blanks for these 12 descriptions are thus "C" for crystallized, "F" for fluid, and "CF" for both. If you're allowed to work in groups, try answering all 12 questions yourself and then comparing notes with one or more classmates.

C = crystallized   F = fluid   CF = both

____ 1. Brook played the rapid-fire card game "Spot It" for the first time, and she quickly decided which is the only *matching* cartoon image on the two "Spot It" cards shown in Figure 25.4. In other words, Brook spotted which image is the only one to appear on *both* cards.

Figure 25.4

___ 2. Because KJ lived in Buffalo, New York, for ten years, she knows how to drive safely in the snow.

___ 3. Surya was an extremely accomplished child gymnast. When she began figure skating at age nine, she solved some novel problems involving jumps and spins by applying what she already knew about gymnastics.

___ 4. Justice was playing charades. He communicated the difficult word "cowgirl" to his teammates by pretending to lasso an invisible steer and then pretending to put on some lipstick.

___ 5. Kiran used a "code sheet" to decode a five-word message in which each letter of the alphabet is replaced by an arbitrary symbol (e.g., A = ¥ B = ♥ C = ••).

___ 6. Abe decoded a lengthy encrypted message by using his knowledge of the relative frequencies of the 26 letters of the English alphabet.

___ 7. Kayla converted a chi-square value (χ^2) to a phi coefficient (φ) to solve a stats problem – because she knows that this is much easier than using a more complex formula to do the calculations.

___ 8. Although Maricela speaks no Italian, she was usually able to figure out the meaning of road signs during a visit to Italy – because she speaks both Spanish and Portuguese.

___ 9. Stacy learned to play the specific form of poker known as Texas holdem very quickly because he had played several other kinds of poker many times.

___ 10. Juanita raised a big bet in a Texas holdem poker game because she knew that it was impossible for any other player to have a hand that was better than her own.

___ 11. Eight-year-old Joey spoke Pig-Latin to a friend after hearing the friend speak it for the first time just a few minutes ago.

___ 12. Rafaela knew that the answer to this question is CF because she kept a running count of the three answer types, and she knew that CF was the only answer option to have been used just three times in questions 1–11.

Superman, Age 25.

Superman, Age 52.

Figure 25.5

Multiple Choice Questions for Module 25

1. What term did Jeffery Arnett coin in 2000 to describe people between the ages of 18 and 25?

   A) post-adolescents
   B) Gen X
   C) emerging adults

2. What is Arnett's term for the finding that people aged 18–25 often view their futures very favorably?

   A) narcissism
   B) possibilities
   C) self-confidence

3. What big cultural shift in the past 50 years or so helped to set the stage for the emergence of a developmental stage that straddles adolescence and early adulthood?

   A) increases in the average age of first marriage
   B) dramatic increases in divorce rates and remarriages
   C) smaller family sizes

4. Younger adults often perform better on intellectual tests than do much older adults. What is a clear exception to this developmental rule?

   A) fluid intelligence
   B) vocabulary size
   C) episodic memory

5. According to the text, at what age are Americans most likely to change residences?

   A) emerging adulthood, because of educational and employment changes
   B) middle adulthood, because of career changes and job opportunities
   C) the beginning of late adulthood, because of retirement

6. According to your text, many past studies of the midlife crisis yielded little evidence for it because:

   A) researchers failed to control for the powerful effects of gender
   B) the studies employed small samples and didn't cover many age groups
   C) the midlife crisis is a stereotype that has very little basis in reality

7. Which theory of adult human development suggests that older Americans are usually much happier than most people assume?

   A) personal growth theory
   B) self-determination theory
   C) socioemotional selectivity theory

8. In a recent study that seems to have yielded evidence of a midlife crisis, were there any gender effects?

   A) yes, as Jung predicted only men showed clear evidence of a midlife crisis
   B) no; both men and women showed modest evidence of a midlife crisis
   C) yes; and women showed stronger evidence of the midlife crisis than men did

9. A team of evolutionary psychologists headed by Weiss et al., (2012) observed a midlife dip in well-being in a sample of more than 500:

   A) hunter-gatherers
   B) chimps and orangutans
   C) famous artists

10. Which is more gradual, andropause or menopause?

   A) andropause is more gradual
   B) menopause is more gradual
   C) neither is more gradual; they unfold in very similar ways

Answer Key: 1C, 2B, 3A, 4B, 5A, 6B, 7C, 8C, 9B, 10A

References

Arnett, J. J. (2000). Emerging adulthood: A theory of development from the late teens through the twenties. *American Psychologist, 55*(5), 469–480.

Arnett, J. J. (2012). *Human development: A cultural approach.* Upper Saddle River, NJ: Pearson.

Austad, S. N. (1994). Menopause: An evolutionary perspective. *Experimental Gerontology, 29,* 255–263.

Carstensen, L. L., Isaacowitz, D. M., & Charles, S. T. (1999). Taking time seriously: A theory of socioemotional selectivity. *American Psychologist, 54,* 165–181.

Casey, B. J., Jones, R. M., & Hare, T. A. (2008). The adolescent brain. *Annals of the New York Academy of Sciences, 1124,* 111–126.

Charles, S. T., Mather, M., & Carstensen, L. L. (2003). Aging and emotional memory: The forgettable nature of negative images for older adults. *Journal of Experimental Psychology. General, 132*(2), 310–324.

Chung, C., & Baldwin, A.J., (2015). The effect of christian belief in eternal life on age-related social partner choice. *The Internet Journal of Geriatrics and Gerontology, 9*(1), 1–7.

Diamond, J. (1992). *The third chimpanzee: The evolution and future of the human animal.* New York, NY: Harper Collins.

Jung, C.G. (1930). *Modern man in search of a soul.* New York: Harvest Books.

Labouvie-Vief, G. (1990). Modes of knowledge and the organization of development. In M. L. Commons, C. Armon, L. Kohlberg, F. A. Richards, T. A. Grotzer, & J. D. Sinnott (Eds.), *Adult development, Vol. 2. Models and methods in the study of adolescent and adult thought* (pp. 43–62). Praeger Publishers.

Levinson, D. J. (1977). The mid-life transition: A period in adult psychosocial development. *Psychiatry: Journal for the Study of Interpersonal Processes, 40*(2), 99–112.

McCabe, J., & Hartman, M. (2008). An analysis of age differences in perceptual speed. *Memory & Cognition, 36*(8), 1495–1508. doi:10.3758/MC.36.8.1495

Newport, F., & Pelham, B. (2009, December 14). Don't worry, be 80: Worry and stress decline with age. *Gallup News.* Retrieved June 27, 2019 from https://news.gallup.com/poll/124655/dont-worry-be-80-worry-stress-decline-age.aspx

Pelham, B. (2019). The realities of the midlife crisis. Evidence from national and highly representative data sets. In preparation.

Raskin, R., & Terry, H. (1988). A principal-components analysis of the Narcissistic Personality Inventory and further evidence of its construct validity. *Journal of Personality and Social Psychology, 54*(5), 890–902.

Singh, P. (2013). Andropause: Current concepts. *Indian Journal of Endocrinology and Metabolism, 17*(Suppl. 3), S621–S629.

Twenge, J.M., Konrath, S., Foster, J.D., Campbell, W.K., & Bushman, B.J. (2008). Egos inflating over time: A cross-temporal meta-analysis of the Narcissistic Personality Inventory. *Journal of Personality, 76*(4), 875–901.

Uzer, T., & Gulgoz, S. (2015). Socioemotional selectivity in older adults: Evidence from the subjective experience of angry memories. *Memory, 23*(6), 888–900. doi:10.1080/09658211.2014.936877

Wethington, E. (2000). Expecting stress: Americans and the "midlife crisis". *Motivation and Emotion 24,* 85–103. doi:10.1023/A:1005611230993

Weiss, A., King, J. E., Inoue-Murayamad, M., Matsuzawae, T., & Oswald, A. J. (2012). Evidence for a midlife crisis in great apes consistent with the U-shape in human wellbeing. *Proceedings of the National Academy of Sciences, 109,* 19949–19952.

Willis, S. L., & Schaie, K. W. (1999). *Intellectual functioning in midlife.* In S. L. Willis & J. D. Reid (Eds.), *Life in the middle: Psychological and social development in middle age* (pp. 233–247). Ne York: Academic Press. doi:10.1016/B978-012757230-7/50031-6

Zucker, A.N., Ostrove, J.M., & Stewart, A.J. (2002). College-educated women's personality development in adulthood: perceptions and age differences. *Psychology and Aging, 17*(2), 236–244.

IX
Social, Personality, and Cultural Psychology

IX

Social, Personality, and
Cultural Psychology

Module 26
Social Psychology

The Power of the Situation

Long ago, in a lab far away, Bob Rosenthal and Kermit Fode (1963) asked 12 bright college students to serve as experimenters in what must have seemed like a very mundane study. The experimenters would be finding out if rats who had been specially bred to be great maze learners learned T-mazes *faster* than rats specially bred to be poor maze learners. That's right; the experimenters would find out if "maze-bright" rats were, in fact, "maze-brighter" than "maze-dull" rats. Rosenthal and Fode trained the experimenters carefully, setting up clear rules for running the rats in T-mazes for five days. For example, the experimenters deprived all the rats of food for exactly 23 hours before each learning session. Thus, maze-dull and maze-bright rats were equally motivated to learn to get food. Further, none of the rats had ever seen a maze before. Thus, the maze-bright rats had no *learned* advantages prior to the study. Successful performance on this maze-learning task meant entering the darker of two arms in a T-maze (see Figure 26.1). But it wasn't quite that simple. To be sure the rats weren't just learning to go right or go left, the experimenters randomly varied whether the right or left arm on any given trial was the dark one. Only the dark arm ever contained the food reward.

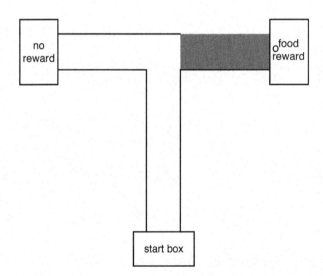

Figure 26.1 A T-maze much like the one used by Rosenthal and Fode (1963). Half the time the *left* arm was dark. Only the dark arm contained the reward.

As shown in Figure 26.2i, the maze-bright rats learned this maze much better than did the maze-dull rats. This is very interesting because the two groups of rats were *identical* prior to the experiment. That's right. The student experimenters working with the rats were intentionally misled. The part about the rats being specially bred to be good or bad maze learners was made up. Rosenthal and Fode simply got a bunch of maze-average rats and *randomly* split them into two groups. But the bright, motivated experimenters *thought* some of the rats were brighter than others. Rats labeled as geniuses performed like geniuses because the experimenters *treated* them like geniuses. When asked how *bright, clean, tame,* and *pleasant* they felt the rats were, the experimenters assigned to the "maze-bright" rats rated them more favorably. They also reported being more *relaxed, gentle* and *quiet* themselves with the presumably maze-bright rats. The maze-bright rats became teachers' pets. This – rather than how the rats were bred – was why they learned so fast.

Incidentally, these experimenters were *not* trying to cheat. Their biases were presumably unconscious. The unconscious tendency for experimenters to create (or see) what they expect to see is known as **experimenter bias**. Once we move from observing rats to observing people, things like experimenter bias can get even worse. This is because human expectations often have a powerful impact on human behavior. Research on **self-fulfilling prophecies** shows that when we expect something to happen to us, this expectation itself may cause us to confirm it (Merton, 1948). It's so hard to avoid experimenter bias in research on people that researchers often keep themselves and their human participants blind to their experimental conditions – by using *double blind* studies.

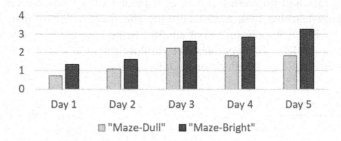

Figure 26.2i Average Number of Correct Maze Responses per Day among what Students Thought Were "Maze-Dull" and "Maze-Bright" Rats.

"'Maze-dull', 'a little slow', 'maze-impaired.'
It all starts to get to a guy after a while."

Figure 26.2ii

If you're thinking rats can't tell us much about human behavior, think again. Rosenthal and Jacobson (1966) showed that teachers and students are a lot like experimenters and rats. They conducted a classic study of **teacher expectancies** in elementary schools. For ethical reasons, they avoided creating any negative expectancies. But they did plant some *positive* expectations. First, they administered a real IQ test throughout a large elementary school. Then they selected a handful of kids from each classroom – *at random*. They informed the teachers, falsely of course, that the test results identified a few students in each class who would "bloom" over the course of the year. Bloom they did. The results for first graders appear in Figure 26.3. As you can see, kids who'd randomly been labeled "bloomers" showed more than twice the usual increase in IQ over the course of the year. Teacher expectancies can be powerful.

Perhaps you're wondering if Robert Rosenthal is a learning theorist or an educational psychologist. He is neither. Instead, he is a *social psychologist*, and the theme of this module – that situations are very powerful – is pulled from the pages of social psychological research. But what is social psychology? As Allport (1954, p. 3) put it, **social psychology** is "an attempt to understand and explain how the thought, feeling, and behavior of individuals are influenced by the actual, imagined, or implied presence of others." This module will build on Allport's classic definition by demonstrating that the "influence of others" is both powerful and ubiquitous. If there is a central theme in social psychology it's the **power of the situation**: what we think, feel, and do is strongly shaped by immediate social forces – by the places and contexts in which we find ourselves (Gilbert & Malone, 1995; Smith & Mackie, 2015).

The Power of the Situation and Social Facilitation

One of the first published research papers in social psychology dealt with the power of situations to affect athletic performance. This paper had to do with **social facilitation** – which you learned about in Module 13. Recall that, when tasks are very simple, people

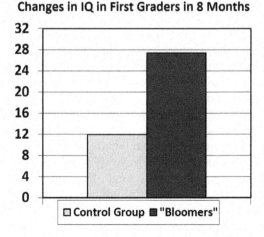

Changes in IQ in First Graders in 8 Months

Figure 26.3 In their classic study of teacher expectancies, Rosenthal and Jacobson (1966) found that first grade children falsely identified as intellectual "bloomers" – showed much larger increases in IQ over the course of a school year relative to their identical peers. This illustrates the *power of the situation* to shape human behavior.

usually perform much better when they are performing in the presence of audiences or co-actors than when performing alone. The first researcher to study this was Triplett (1898). Triplett believed that competitive cyclists produce better times when racing against other cyclists than when racing against the clock. To see if this was true, Triplett compared race times for cyclists who had raced against other competitors and those who had raced against the clock. Cyclists did, in fact, race faster in the presence of other competitors – and this did not seem to be a simple matter of physics (e.g., drafting). To put his findings to another test, Triplett ran a lab study, with both kids and adults as participants. Triplett asked participants to pull a small flag as quickly as possible around a 4-meter course. They did so by reeling in a long silk string that was attached to a fishing reel. Triplett observed the same finding among those reeling in flags that he had seen in athletes trying to reel in trophies. The presence of competitors usually facilitated performance.

Notice that we said *usually*. Triplett was careful enough to note that competition occasionally caused some people, especially very young children, to become "over-stimulated," leading to *decreases* in performance. Triplett described the participants who disconfirmed his original expectations just as carefully as he described those who confirmed them. He noted that whereas virtually everyone in his experiment *tried harder* to do well when they were competing against another person, some people's efforts did not pay off. We now know that when a task is highly complex or poorly learned (which reeling in a flag apparently was for some very young children) an "intense desire to win" often leads to what Triplett called "over-stimulation." This is because arousal brought about by the presence of others increases *dominant* (i.e., highly accessible, well-learned) responses on a given task. This means that the presence of others facilitates performance for highly skilled performers (where the dominant response is highly skillful) but disrupts performance for less skilled performers (where the dominant response is less skillful – and more likely to lead to failure).

The Power of the Situation and Conformity

The year after Norman Triplett passed away, another early social psychologist Muzafer Sherif (1935) published a clever study of the subtle but powerful form of social influence known as conformity. **Conformity** refers to changing one's beliefs or behavior to be consistent with the beliefs or behavior of others – even when no one asks you to do so. When you wear jeans rather than a kilt or try the kelp because Jean tried it, you are – perhaps without giving it much thought – engaging in conformity. Have you ever parked far from a sports stadium or concert arena without knowing exactly how to get where you wish to go? If you have, perhaps you chose to follow others who seemed to know where they were going. If you did so, you were engaging in conformity. And good for you. It worked, didn't it? Likewise, have you ever been to a fancy dinner and found that there were three forks (yes, three) near to your plate? When this has happened to us, we have typically begun eating our salad with whatever fork other people seemed to be using. That, too, is conformity, and it usually works. Sherif wanted to know how powerful conformity would be when people were thrown together with total strangers that they knew they'd never see again. He conducted a study that presumably focused on visual perception. In various phases of the study, participants estimated how far a stationary dot of light had moved in an otherwise dark room. Because of a visual illusion called the **autokinetic effect**, most people who viewed the stationary light felt that it moved. It never budged. But the participants in Sherif's experiment did lots of budging – almost always by conforming to the opinions of others.

In phase one of the study people took part alone and simply reported how far they felt that the light moved (in inches). The next day, though, people judged the movement of the light while sitting with two other naïve participants. So now people were exposed to the answers provided by two strangers. Sherif was careful *not* to tell people that they needed to arrive at any agreement or group answer. They were simply making the same judgments in the presence of others that they had originally made alone. In every group Sherif studied, though, people seem to have felt great pressure to conform to the judgments of the other goofballs who happened to be in the room with them. By the final group session, a nearly perfect consensus always emerged regarding exactly how far the light moved. There was substantial variation across the groups in their estimates of how far the light moved, but the norm *within* a given group seemed to become a subjective reality. The responses of a typical three-person group of Sherif's participants appears in Figure 26.4. Even when people came back to the lab alone, as much as a year later, most people stuck close to their group's original judgment. In a follow-up study, Sherif planted stooges in the groups and instructed them to give very high movement estimates. The confidently-expressed judgments of a stooge usually had a large effect on everyone else's answers. Further, these inflated group norms were readily passed along to new groups of complete strangers, across multiple generations of participants. We remind you that participants were never asked to follow the leads of the strangers around them. Yet, they did. They conformed – by moving their judgments in the directions of those offered by others. By the time of the third judgment made in the group setting, people agreed almost perfectly about how much the light moved.

Some of the most famous studies in social psychology were originally conceived in an effort to show the limits of Sherif's conformity findings. Solomon Asch felt that Sherif may have tipped the scales in favor of conformity by asking people to make a very difficult judgment. In a completely dark room, it is awfully hard to say for sure how far a tiny dot of light moved. When fumbling in the darkness, doesn't it make sense to seek the advice of others? Two decades after the publication of Sherif's work, Asch (1955, 1956) wanted to see what would happen to people's judgments when they heard a stranger report

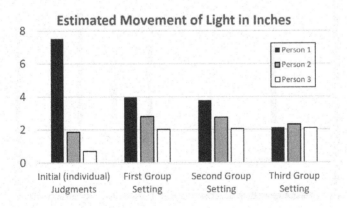

Figure 26.4 In Sherif's (1935) conformity study, participants who made independent (solo) judgments varied widely in how much they thought a stationary dot of light moved. But when they repeated their judgments three times in the presence of two other naïve participants, a group consensus emerged. In this group you can see that everyone eventually agreed that the light moved about two inches.

a judgment that they themselves absolutely knew to be wrong. Asch originally predicted that, when it was obvious what answers were correct, people would not be swayed by the publicly-reported (and patently wrong) answers of a bunch of complete strangers.

To identify the limits of conformity, Asch brought participants to his laboratory for what appeared to be a mundane perceptual study. In **Asch's conformity studies**, participants had a very simple job: report some judgments about the lengths of some lines. After taking a seat at a table with six other people who appeared to be co-participants, the real participants patiently waited their turns to announce which of three lines printed on a card was equal in length to a standard line. A reproduction of one of the stimulus sets used by Asch appears in Figure 26.5. The first couple of trials of this experiment passed uneventfully as the real participants watched their peers announce the obvious answers to Asch's questions. However, on several crucial trials, most participants found themselves rubbing their eyes in disbelief. One by one, each of the first five participants calmly and confidently provided *patently incorrect* answers to the questions. In a predesignated trial involving the stimulus set depicted in Figure 26.5, for instance, the trained confederates all calmly announced, one at a time, that line B (that's right, B) was identical to the standard.

This placed the real research participants in a big dilemma. Would they shoot straight from the hip and deviate from the unanimous judgments of the other five group members? Or would they ignore what their eyes were telling them and cave in to the subtle but potent pressure of the group? Most participants (75%) caved in and conformed on at least *some* of the crucial trials. If the facial expressions of Asch's participants were any indication of their state of mind during the experiment, they were perplexed and confused when five separate strangers gave patently wrong answers to some of these very simple questions. Yet the real participants often parroted these incorrect judgments to the experimenter as if they were their own true opinions. In a series of follow-up studies using this same line-judging procedure, Asch found that he could easily push around rates of conformity. For example, when Asch planted a single dissenter in the otherwise unanimous majority, conformity was

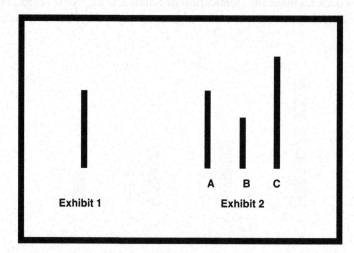

Figure 26.5 One of the crucial stimulus sets used by Asch (1955) to see if participants would conform to the patently incorrect judgments offered by five other participants in what they believed to be a perceptual study. Most of Asch's participants (75%) conformed to group answers that were clearly wrong on at least one of several crucial trials when the group gave an obviously wrong answer.

reduced to about 20% of the original levels. Social situations have great power to influence conformity. The presence of even one other person who was willing to disagree with the group greatly reduced conformity.

OK, so people are wimps. But why? What are the motivations that lead us to conform? Perhaps it's because, as Lou Penner (1984) put it, "Nobody likes to look like a schmuck." That's right, we behave the way others behave to avoid sticking out like a sore thumb, or maybe it's to be sure no one gives us the finger. Either way, almost no one enjoys being the oddball in a group. We prefer to fit in and be accepted by those around us. This is *normative social influence*, by the way. It happens when we conform because of the desire to fit in and be accepted. In contrast, sometimes we conform because we think other people may know something that we don't! This includes knowing whether to take the fork in the road to the concert and whether to begin with the fork farthest from the plate at the fancy dinner. This is *informational social influence*. It happens when we conform because we think others provide us with useful information. Regardless of why we conform, conformity can sometimes have grave consequences. Consider kids who take drugs because they are trying to fit in with their peers.

The Milgram Obedience Studies

But the grave consequences of conformity among kids who abuse drugs pales in comparison with the atrocities that were commonplace in World War II. In the early 1960s, social psychologist Stanley Milgram wanted to see if the power of the situation could make ordinary people behave in extraordinary ways that could sometimes prove deadly. After wrestling with distressing questions about the holocaust for years, Milgram decided to address his troubling questions empirically. In the clever and controversial **Milgram obedience studies**, Milgram (1963) examined the limits of human **obedience** to authority. Obedience differs from conformity. Whereas conformity includes no explicit request to engage in a behavior, obedience is a form of social influence in which a higher-status person tells a lower status person what to do. Children who clean their rooms at the behest of their parents, like people who put their hands up at a police officer's instructions, are engaging in obedience – not conformity. Milgram's obedience studies shed a bright but unsettling light on the social forces that drove many distressing events in the holocaust. Powerful social situations can turn lovable, kindhearted people like us into callous people who are willing to hurt innocent strangers.

Milgram recruited American men from all walks of life to take part in "a study of memory" at Yale University. A portion of one of Milgram's advertisements for his famous study appears in Figure 26.6. When recruitment began in 1961, the total payment of four dollars (plus carfare) was a decent reward for an hour of interesting work. When participants arrived at the lab, they met a pleasant co-participant (who was actually in cahoots with the experimenter). Because of a clever ruse, real participants felt that they lucked out and would get to play the role of "teacher." It would thus be their job to teach the other participant – "the learner" – a series of word pairs. They did so by reading the learner all the pairs (e.g., "fat–neck," "slow–train") from a list. After the training, the learner was supposed to repeat the second word in each word-pair after the teachers read only the first word – and then offered the learner four answer options. Of course, one way in which people learn in real life is by getting punished when they make mistakes. Milgram's "teachers" must have thought little of it when they learned that they would have to deliver a brief electric shock to the learner every time he made a mistake.

Public Announcement

WE WILL PAY YOU $4.00 FOR
ONE HOUR OF YOUR TIME

Persons Needed for a Study of Memory

*We will pay five hundred New Haven men to help us complete a scientific study of memory and learning. The study is being done at Yale University.

*Each person who participates will be paid $4.00 (plus 50c carfare) for approximately 1 hour's time. We need you for only one hour: there are no further obligations. You may choose the time you would like to come (evenings, weekdays, or weekends).

*No special training, education, or experience is needed. We want:

Factory workers	Businessmen	Construction workers
City employees	Clerks	Salespeople
Laborers	Professional people	White-collar workers
Barbers	Telephone workers	Others

All persons must be between the ages of 20 and 50. High school and college students cannot be used.

*If you meet these qualifications, fill out the coupon below and mail it now to Professor Stanley Milgram, Department of Psychology, Yale University, New Haven. You will be notified later of the specific time and place of the study. We reserve the right to decline any application.

*You will be paid $4.00 (plus 50c carfare) as soon as you arrive at the laboratory.

Figure 26.6 As you can see here, participants in Stanley Milgram's obedience studies *thought* they were signing up for a study of memory and learning. Most of them would learn something very uncomfortable about how willing they were to obey an authority figure. Because of a few simple cues of status, people in positions of authority often wield great power over others.

But this study of "teaching" was an elaborate ruse that thrust the participants (the "teachers") into a very powerful situation. First, the learner was seated in a separate room by himself. Milgram was slyly putting some physical and psychological distance between teachers and learners. Second, the learner was strapped firmly into a sturdy chair "to avoid excessive movement." This process was sanitized and made very technical. For example, the teachers looked on as the experimenter applied electrode paste to the learners' skin "to avoid blisters and burns" from the electrical leads. Third, the teacher learned – *after* agreeing to play the role of teacher – that he would have to give *increasingly large* shocks to the learner each time the learner made a mistake. The first shock would be a "slight" punishment of 15 volts. The second would be 30 volts. With each new mistake, the teacher would have to deliver a little more shock. As you can see in Figure 26.7, the punishment for a wrong answer increased in 15 volt increments to a maximum of 450 volts. Toward the end of this scale, the highest two groups of shock switches were labeled "DANGER SEVERE SHOCK" followed by a label of "XXX" for the last three switches.

The experiment began innocently enough, but the learner did not seem to be learning much. He gave about three wrong answers for every correct answer. For a long time, he seemed willing to accept the increasingly painful shocks. If participants delivered the 300-volt shock, however, they heard the apparently distraught learner kick on the wall and ask to be released. The learner said he refused to continue and kicked the wall again at 315 volts. But after that point the learner went silent – offering no further answers. Invariably participants asked the experimenter how they should repond to this. He calmly told them that the absence of an answer was considered a wrong answer.

If participants asked to stop the study at this or any other point, the experimenter calmly and firmly said things like "Please continue" and "The experiment requires that you continue." In some versions of the study the learner specifically complained about the pain.

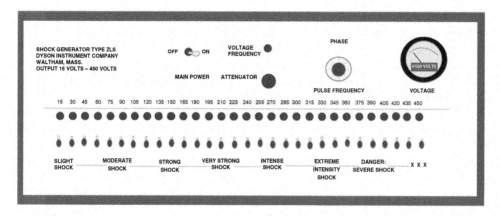

Figure 26.7 A drawing of Milgram's shock delivery machine. The machine began at only 15 volts but increased 15 volts at a time to a maximum of 450 volts. Beginning at about 360 volts a label clearly stated "DANGER SEVERE SHOCK." The last couple of switches were ominously labeled "X X X." Just how far would the nicest, most compassionate person *you* know go in this situation of serving as a "teacher" to a hapless learner?

If participants expressed concerns about this, the experimenter stated, "Although the shocks may be painful, there is no permanent tissue damage; so please go on." It would be hard to overstate how uncomfortable most of the teachers seem to have felt. The teachers were clearly very concerned about the learner. But in the end, 65% of Milgram's original group of 40 participants kept giving shocks all the way up to the maximum level. As Jerry and Elaine once commiserated in a classic *Seinfeld* episode, "I will *never* understand people." "They're the *worst!*" Virtually everyone who first learns about the Milgram study is shocked to learn that 65% of the participants gave the poor confederate the most extreme levels of shock possible even when the distraught learner had cried out in pain, demanded to be released, and then stopped responding altogether. Most participants seem to have checked their morality at the door to Milgram's laboratory.

Just how far would *you* go in this uncomfortable situation? We can't really answer that question, but we can use Milgram's original data to answer an even more important question: Just how far did *everybdy* go? You already know that in Milgram's original (1963) study, 35% of the men disobeyed the experimenter at some point (100% – 65% = 35%). But where, exactly, did the *most* disobedient (and presumably most compassionate) person draw the line? It's worth noting that, before the study began, teachers received a 45-volt "sample shock." Suffering this real shock was no piece of cake. Did any participant refuse to give more shock than the 45 volts he himself had experienced? Did at least one principled person refuse to deliver any shocks at all? In short, exactly how much shock did everyone deliver? If *everyone* delivered 120 volts, for example, it should be pretty hard to argue that you are sure you – or your great aunt Vivian – would have stopped at 45 volts.

So how much shock did everyone deliver in the original Milgram study? The answer is 300 volts. Yes, 300 volts. *Everyone* who took part in the version of Milgram's study described here gave the learner what they thought was a 300-volt shock. It wasn't until the learner began kicking the wall in protest that a brave five out of 40 participants courageously insisted they could no longer deliver the shocks. So even if you feel you are as brave and principled as the five in 40 people who disobeyed the experimenter at this point, we'd like to reiterate that *everyone* – including these five heroes – gave the learner what they thought was a 300-volt shock. It's hard for us to believe we would have done differently. Further, in case you're wondering whether people thought these shocks were painful, they did. At the study's end, teachers were all asked "How painful to the learner were the last few shocks that you administered to him?" The answer scale ranged from 1 (*not at all painful*) to 14 (*extremely painful*). The most common response was 14. The mean was 13.4. Ouch! If you're thinking that people today are not nearly as obedient as people more than five decades ago, you'd be wrong. In a replication that avoided the difficult ethical issues raised by Milgram's original study, Burger (2009) showed that modern rates of obedience – at least at the low to moderate levels of shock studied by Milgram – are virtually identical to those observed in Milgram's day.

Why are we so ridiculously obedient? Because in a hyper-social species like ours, social situations matter greatly. Everything about this potent social situation – except for the victim's plight – suggested that the thing to do was to obey an authority figure. Human beings, because we are such social creatures, are keenly attuned to power, authority, social status, and social contracts. A police officer's uniform, a doctor's white lab coat, a person's height, the letters that follow a person's name (PhD, MD) are all factors that Milgram recognized as drivers of obedience to authority.

It was no accident, then, that the experimenter in Milgram's original study was wearing a white lab coat. In follow-up studies, Milgram directly manipulated this simple status cue. Taking away the white lab coat greatly reduced obedience. Along similar lines, obedience to the experimenter's orders dropped a great deal when teachers had to touch the learner to deliver the shock. It's easier to harm a physically or psychologically distant victim. The principle of distance also applied to teachers and the experimenter. When the experimenter gave his orders and instructions by telephone, teachers were much more willing than usual to disobey. All of these findings suggest that situations (e.g., physical distance, simple status cues) have an extremely powerful influence on our thoughts, feelings, and behavior.

Incidental Similarity, Helping, and Attraction

As yet another example of the power of the situation, let's examine how the power of the situation can influence helping and attraction rather than hurting. It has long been known that people like – and help – those who are meaningfully similar to themselves. Highly educated people tend to befriend and marry other highly educated people. Catholics are more likely to hang out with and marry fellow Catholics. Lovers of both Trump and trumpets associate with others who are like-minded. There is, in fact, some truth to the aphorism that "birds of a feather flock together."

But research also suggest that even arbitrary similarities between the self and others can increase helping or attraction. Burger, Messian, Patel, del Prado, and Anderson (2004) found that participants who believed they shared a birthday (Study 1), a first name (Study 2), or even fingerprint similarities (Study 3) with a confederate were more likely than usual to comply with the confederate's request for a favor. In Burger et al.'s Study 2, participants were even given the impression that the person with whom they shared a name was unaware of this coincidental resemblance. Thus, it is unlikely that these participants expected the confederates to reciprocate their liking. Nonetheless, those who thought they shared a first name with a person who was asking for a favor were much more likely than those who did not share a name to agree to perform the favor. Social situations are powerful.

The list of social psychological studies that show that social situations are powerful is a very long one indeed. Contextual factors such as whether it is hot outside, whether people are in a hurry, and whether people are alone or in the presence of others are big predictors of when and whether we help or hurt others (as you will see in modules 28 and 29 of this text). Finally, research on processes as diverse as tipping at restaurants (Guéguen & Jacob, 2005), cooperation and group conflict (Sherif, 1958), performance on standardized tests (Steele & Aronson, 1995), and voter turnout (Gerber, Green, & Larimer, 2008) all converge to suggest that social situations are powerful drivers of what we think, feel, and do over the course of our lives. Making matters worse, most people grossly underestimate the power of the situation. You will get a brief taste of this to follow, and we'll discuss it even further in the next module on social perception.

Cognitive Dissonance: The Power of the Situation, Attitudes, and Persuasion

As a final example of the power of the situation, let's consider research on one of the most heavily studied topics in social psychology. This topic is attitudes. To paraphrase Bill McGuire (1985), **attitudes** are the thoughts and feelings we have about things that presumably influence how we behave toward those things. Do you like the Marvel Cinematic Universe? Or do you consider it ridiculous? That's an attitude. Do you believe in God? Would you consider a job in sales? Do you love cinnamon rolls? Those, too, are attitudes. The list of things about which you have attitudes is endless. Further, everyone from advertisers to zookeepers is in the business of trying to change people's attitudes. If your physician could get you to exercise more often, you might live longer. Politicians want to persuade you that they have your best interests at heart – so that you'll vote for them. Our attitudes influence what we do. However, because of the power of the situation – and our powerful assumptions that attitudes influence what we do – *what we do also influences our attitudes*. This means that one of the most powerful ways to change people's attitudes does not rely on facts or arguments. It relies on getting people to engage in a behavior that suggests a certain attitude.

Because most people strongly believe that attitudes drive behavior, and because it is easier than most people think to get people to behave as you wish them to, you can often change a person's attitudes by getting them to do something **counter-attitudinal** (something that is at odds with their original attitudes). Suppose you use the power of the situation to get Rosa to eat a live grasshopper or write an essay in favor of a tuition increase. If Rosa fails to appreciate how powerful situations are, she might conclude that her unusual behavior reflects a more "pro-grasshopper" or "pro-tuition hike" attitude than she would have previously said she possesses. In fact, many decades ago, Leon Festinger developed a theory known as cognitive dissonance theory that explains just this kind of attitude change. The gist of **cognitive dissonance theory** is that people become very uncomfortable when they believe their attitudes and their behavior are logically inconsistent with one another. This uncomfortable state is known as **cognitive dissonance**, and people are strongly motivated to *reduce* it. To reduce their dissonance, Festinger argued, people who have no good explanation for their recent behavior will change their attitudes to be as consistent as possible with that behavior.

In a classic study of cognitive dissonance, Festinger and Carlsmith (1959) asked participants to spend an hour doing an extremely boring peg-turning task. The experimenter then convinced participants that they would be doing him a big favor if they would tell an unsuspecting person (who was about to do the same task) that the boring task was interesting. Although the experimenter made people feel that he really needed their help, he was careful not to make his influence attempts too obvious. In fact, he made people feel personally responsible for their behavior by letting them know that, as much as he needed their help, participants had a choice not to help him. Yet, in a sense, participants didn't *really* have a choice about helping the experimenter. This is because the sense of obligation to help in this situation is very powerful. Virtually all the thousands of participants who've been placed in this situation have agreed to help the experimenter – by telling the white lie (by saying the task was interesting) to the unsuspecting new participant.

To manipulate how much dissonance people experienced about the fib, the experimenter manipulated whether people had a good (non-attitudinal) excuse for telling it. In one condition, the experimenter offered participants the small reward of only one dollar to fib to the future peg-turners. In a second condition, he offered participants $20 to tell the same fib. Presumably, $20 was enough to prevent people from experiencing a great deal of dissonance about telling the lie. People will often say things they don't believe if the price is right. However, one dollar was not a good justification for telling the fib (it was not a sufficient reward). How could the dissonance-riddled one dollar participants reduce their dissonance? The only obvious way would be to decide that the task was more enjoyable than they had originally thought. This is exactly what the poorly paid participants did. They justified their fib by *changing their attitudes* to be more consistent with their behavior. In comparison with the well-paid participants (or a third group of participants who were not asked to tell the fib at all), the one dollar participants reported that they felt the experimental task was interesting. Our lack of appreciation of the power of the situation makes us highly susceptible to a common form of persuasion – cognitive dissonance reduction. Literally thousands of studies have shown that dissonance reduction is a powerful source of persuasion, on a wide range of topics (see McGrath, 2017). So, if we haven't yet convinced you that situations are really powerful, please do us the small favor of telling a couple of people you know and like that situations are very powerful. We're not saying you *have* to tell them, by the way, but you'd be doing us a big favor.

Questions for Critical Thinking and Group Discussion for Module 26

In a classic study of social judgment, Jones and Harris (1967) discovered what has become known as the correspondence bias. To paraphrase Gilbert and Jones (1986) the *correspondence bias* is the tendency to make dispositional judgments for a person's behavior (e.g., "Boy, is she fast!") when a better explanation for the behavior would be something about the situation ("But she was running with the benefit of a very strong tailwind."). Another way to say this is that the correspondence bias means that many of our explanations for the behavior of other people are based too much on traits and attitudes and not enough on situations. Jones and Harris (1967) asked judges to estimate the *personal attitudes* of essayists who praised or denounced Cuban leader Fidel Castro. Some judges learned that the essayists had been free to endorse any view of Castro they wished. Others learned that all essayists had been arbitrarily assigned a position on Castro by a debate coach. Not surprisingly, judges who thought they were reading freely written essays assumed that essayists said what they meant and meant what they said. That's logical. But even when judges thought essayists had *no choice* at all about whether to praise or denounce Castro (because they were *assigned* the pro-Castro or anti-Castro essay), they still concluded that the essayists meant what they had said *to some*

degree. This apparently happened because these judges *automatically* drew dispositional inferences about the essayists ("That essayist is one *crazy* Castro lover.") and then failed to adjust
their dispositional judgments completely for information about the situation ("I wonder what
he would have said if he had been free to write anything? ... Well, anyway, I bet he's a *sort of
crazy* Castro lover;" see Gilbert, Krull, & Pelham, 1988).

The correspondence bias has been observed for many judgments, including judgments of
personality as well as attitudes. Snyder and Frankel (1976) showed participants a silent
video of a woman behaving somewhat anxiously. Some participants were told that the
woman was discussing *sex* (which ought to make anyone a bit anxious). Others were told
the woman was discussing *politics*. Those told that the woman was discussing sex judged
her to be *more* of an anxious person – not less so – than did those told that she was discussing politics. That's illogical. People should have concluded that the woman who was discussing sex behaved nervously because of the stressful (you might even say powerful)
situation. In Western cultures, at least, the correspondence bias is very robust.

1.   What does the correspondence bias suggest about how easy it will usually be to get
     people to appreciate the power of the situation? Will this pervasive judgmental bias
     nudge people toward appreciating the power of the situation, or will it make it
     harder for people to appreciate the power of the situation? Why?
2.   A judgmental cousin of the correspondence bias is the actor-observer bias. To see
     how the actor-observer bias works, please answer the following eight questions. For
     each trait dimension, circle one of the three options – first for yourself and then for
     your best guess about Michelle Obama.

I AM:			*MICHELLE IS:*		
outgoing	shy	it depends	outgoing	shy	it depends
creative	uncreative	it depends	creative	uncreative	it depends
hardworking	lazy	it depends	hardworking	lazy	it depends
traditional	nontraditional	it depends	traditional	nontraditional	it depends

When you're done with your ratings, compare the number of times you chose "it
depends" for yourself and the number of times you chose "it depends" for Michelle. Most
people choose the "it depends" answer more often for themselves than for others. Is that
what you did? Your instructor may tabulate data from this activity for everyone in your
class. Even if this does not happen, consider the logic of how your judgments of yourself
and Michelle could reveal an actor-observer bias. According to Jones and Nisbett (1971)
the *actor-observer bias* is the tendency for people to make more dispositional judgments
for the behavior of others than they make for their own behavior.

3.   Explain why the actor-observer bias predicts that people will circle "it depends"
     more often when judging the self than when judging others. If this bias is common,
     do we better understand the power of situations to affect us personally or the
     power of the situation to affect others? Along related lines, if the actor-observer
     bias is true, are we more likely to commit the correspondence bias when judging
     the self – or when judging others?

Short Answer and Multiple-Choice Questions for Module 26

1. In about two to three sentences per topic in the list that follows, summarize how research on each topic supports the power of the situation. If you work in small groups, each person should select one or two topics, prepare an answer for that topic or topics, and present an answer to the group. The group will then debate, critique, and improve each offered explanation – to come up with a group consensus that would make Sherif proud.

   I) teacher expectancies
   II) conformity
   III) obedience
   IV) social facilitation
   V) incidental similarity and helping/attraction
   VI) persuasion that results from dissonance reduction

2. Talia recently visited a new synagogue. She noticed that she was the only young adult wearing dress clothes. The next Saturday, she attended the same synagogue, but she dressed casually. What social influence process best describes this?

   A) agreement
   B) orthodoxy
   C) conformity

3. During a Seder on the Jewish holiday of Passover, Talia's grandmother tells her to read aloud in Hebrew. Talia hates being the center of attention, but she does the reading because her grandmother insists. What social influence process best describes Talia's behavior?

   A) respect
   B) obedience
   C) compliance

4. In his classic studies of conformity, Sherif capitalized on a visual illusion. What illusion?

   A) the autokinetic effect
   B) the phi phenomenon
   C) the point-light illusion

5. In the original version of Milgram's obedience studies, what percentage of "teachers" administered at least 300 volts of shock to a suffering "learner"?

   A) 33%
   B) 65%
   C) 100%

6. Which research topic covered in the module on the power of the situation is similar to the concept of teacher expectancies?

   A) the correspondence bias

B) experimenter bias
C) self-defeating tendencies

7. Asch observed high rates of conformity in his studies in which five or six confederates gave patently wrong answers to some simple questions. In some follow-up studies, Asch changed the procedure in a way that greatly reduced conformity. What was this change to the original procedure?

   A) reassure participants that it is not at all necessary for everyone to agree about their judgments
   B) make the real participant the group "foreman" and tell them they have the final word on all answers
   C) have one confederate offer an answer that is different than the answer of all the other confederates

8. When Burger (2009) replicated the Milgram obedience studies, he changed a few details of the original study. For example, he stopped the experiment when "teachers" agreed to deliver 150 volts. He also made sure that none of his participants had any history of clinical disorders (e.g., clinical depression). What is the main reason why Burger deviated from Milgram's exact procedures?

   A) to reduce ethical concerns
   B) to increase internal validity
   C) to increase external validity

9. In Rosenthal and Jacobsen's original research on teacher expectancy effects, they began the study by doing something that increased the likelihood that each teacher in the school would believe that a handful of their own students would be "bloomers." What time-consuming procedure did they use to set the stage for their manipulation?

   A) they showed teachers fake report cards for the bloomers
   B) they administered a real IQ test to every child in the school
   C) they had a panel of experts interview each child individually

10. Research on attitude change suggests that people fail to appreciate the power of the situation. After all, if people fully appreciated how powerful situations are, they would not experience any _____ when they made a counter-attitudinal statement at the request of an experimenter.

    A) self-blame
    B) cognitive dissonance
    C) confusion

Answer Key: 1 N/A, 2C, 3B, 4A, 5C, 6B, 7C, 8A, 9B, 10B

References

Allport, G. (1954). *The nature of prejudice.* Reading, MA: Addison-Wesley.

Asch, S. E. (1955). Opinions and social pressure. *Scientific American, 193,* 31–35.

Asch, S. E. (1956). Studies of independence and conformity I: A minority of one against a unanimous majority. *Psychological Monographs, 70,* 1–70.

Burger, J. M. (2009). Replicating Milgram: Would people still obey today? *American Psychologist, 64,* 1–11.

Burger, J. M., Messian, N., Patel, S., del Prado, A., & Anderson, C. (2004). What a coincidence! The effects of incidental similarity on compliance. *Personality and Social Psychology Bulletin, 30,* 35–43.

Festinger, L., & Carlsmith, J. M. (1959). Cognitive consequences of forced compliance. *Journal of Abnormal and Social Psychology, 58,* 203–210.

Gerber, A. S., Green, D. P., & Larimer, C. W. (2008). Social pressure and voter turnout: Evidence from a large-scale field experiment. *American Political Science Review, 102*(1), 33–48. doi:10.1017/S000305540808009X

Gilbert, D. T., & Jones, E. E. (1986). Perceiver-induced constraint: Interpretations of self-generated reality. *Journal of Personality and Social Psychology, 50,* 269–280.

Gilbert, D. T., Krull, D. S., & Pelham, B. W. (1988). Of thoughts unspoken: Social inference and the self-regulation of behavior. *Journal of Personality and Social Psychology, 55,* 685–694.

Gilbert, D. T., & Malone, P. (1995). The correspondence bias. *Psychological Bulletin, 117,* 21–38.

Guéguen, N., & Jacob, C. (2005). The effect of touch on tipping: An evaluation in a French bar. *International Journal of Hospitality Management, 24,* 295–299.

Jones, E. E., & Harris, V. A. (1967). The attribution of attitudes. *Journal of Experimental Social Psychology, 3,* 1–24.

Jones, E. E., & Nisbett, R. E. (1971). The actor and the observer: Divergent perceptions of the causes of behavior. In E. E. Jones, D. E. Kanouse, H. H. Kelley, R. E. Nisbett, S. Valins, & B. Weiner (Eds.), *Attribution: Perceiving the causes of behavior* (pp. 79–94). Morristown, NJ: General Learning Press.

McGrath, A. (2017). Dealing with dissonance: A review of cognitive dissonance reduction. *Social and Personality Psychology Compass, 11*(12), e12362.

McGuire, W.J. (1985) Attitudes and Attitude Change: G. Lindzey & E. Aronson, Eds., *Handbook of Social Psychology, 3rd Edition, Vol. 2* (pp. 233–346). New York: Random House.

Merton, R. K. (1948). The self-fulfilling prophecy. *The Antioch Review, 8,* 193–210.

Milgram, S. (1963). Behavioral study of obedience. *Journal of Abnormal and Social Psychology, 67,* 371–378.

Penner, L. (1984). Personal communicatin.

Rosenthal, R., & Fode, K. (1963). The effect of experimenter bias on the performance of the albino rat. *Behavioral Science, 8,* 183–189.

Rosenthal, R., & Jacobson, L. (1966). Teachers' expectancies: Determinants of pupils' IQ gains. *Psychological Reports, 19,* 115–118.

Sherif, M. (1935). A study of some social factors in perception: Chapter 2. *Archives of Psychology, 27,* 17–22.

Sherif, M. (1958). Superordinate goals in the reduction of intergroup conflict. *American Journal of Sociology, 63,* 349–356.

Smith, E. R., & Mackie, D. M. (2015). *Social psychology* (4th ed.). New York, NY: Psychology Press.

Snyder, M.L., & Frankel, A. (1976). Observer bias: A stringent test of behavior engulfing the field. *Journal of Personality and Social Psychology, 34*(5), 857–864. doi:10.1037/0022-3514.34.5.857

Steele, C. M., & Aronson, J. (1995). Stereotype threat and the intellectual test performance of African Americans. *Journal of Personality and Social Psychology, 69*(5), 797–811.

Triplett, N. (1898). The dynamogenic factors in pacemaking and competition. *American Journal of Psychology, 9,* 507–533.

Module 27
Stereotypes and Social Perception

Because we are highly social creatures, we are constantly trying to figure out other people. After all, much of what *we* think, feel, and do depends on what we think *other people* think, feel, and do. If you think your joke about your sister's painting will hurt her feelings, you'd better keep the joke to yourself. If you believe your mechanic shafted you on the repairs to your drive shaft, you'd better look for a new mechanic. Further, because you can find a new mechanic much more easily than you can find a new sister, you should judge your sister more generously than you judge your mechanic.

This module is about judging other people. This includes snap judgments based on things like heuristics (taking mental shortcuts) and stereotypes, and more thoughtful judgments based on logic and careful observation. This includes things like what a person just did, what she has done in the past, and what others have done in similar situations. Social psychologists refer to the many ways in which we try to figure out others using the single phrase social perception. But **social perception** includes everything from blatantly stereotyping others to thinking hard about why there are more male than female engineering majors in U.S. colleges. Social perception often boils down to judging why people do what they do. This means that a lot of research on social perception involves the study of **attributions**, which are causal judgments about another person's behavior. The cause might be a stable personality trait ("she's a neat freak."). Alternately, the cause might be a powerful situation ("her mom demanded that she clean her room"). Further, social motivations can bias social perception, sometimes for the better and sometimes for the worse. For example, the *need to belong* influences how we view others. Merely knowing that we're about to interact with another person causes us to view this person more favorably than we otherwise would (Darley & Berscheid, 1967). Likewise, Carvallo and Pelham (2006) found that female college students interpreted a man's sexist comments about their own work more favorably than usual when they wanted the man to like them. Social motivations can shape attributions.

Moving from the social to the cognitive, we'll argue in this module that the principle of *automatic vs. controlled information processing* can help explain a great deal of research in stereotyping and social perception. More specifically, we'll emphasize that social perception is often a multi-staged process that has both automatic (i.e., quick, effortless) and controlled (i.e., slow, effortful) components. But before delving into the details of automatic and controlled social perception, let's begin by admitting that social perceivers often judge others by relying on things like stereotypes and pre-existing expectations. Many social judgments are influenced by our pre-existing expectations. Recall from Module 10 that *constructivism* means that perceivers *create* much of what they perceive in the world around them. Put simply, *what we expect influences what we perceive*. The writer Anaïs Nin seems to have been aware of this when she argued "We don't see the world as it is, we see it as we are." Of course, stereotypes are expectations, but there are other kinds of expectations as well. Let's begin with the close cousin of stereotypes known as scripts.

Scripts and Stereotypes: Expectations that Drive Our Perceptions

Scripts

Please carefully read the story that follows. It's adapted from Abelson (1981). As soon as you've done so, we'll ask you to perform a brief activity:

> Old professor Snorkwerth was feeling very hungry as he entered the restaurant. He settled himself at a table and noticed that the waiter was nearby. Unfortunately, however, he realized that he had forgotten his reading glasses. When the waiter came by to take his order, Professor Snorkwerth felt embarrassed and asked for the "daily special." Fifteen minutes later, he realized that he should have asked what the daily special *was*. Now he had to eat a plate full of snails on an empty stomach.

If you think old Professor Snorkwerth is *absent-minded*, there could be two good reasons. First, the story specifically says that Snorkwerth forgot his reading glasses. Second, absentmindedness is a *stereotype* of both old people and college professors. According to Gordon Allport's (1954) classic definition, a **stereotype** is "a false or overgeneralized and typically negative belief about the members of a social group." Let us repeat that it is a well-known stereotype of both old people and college professors that they are absentminded. If we'd replaced "Old professor Snorkwerth" with "The actor Chris Hemsworth," it's possible you would not have jumped so quickly to the conclusion that this guy is absent-minded. But let's forget about absent-mindedness and move on to a more memorable activity. Consider the following list of six words. Now – *without looking back at the story* – see if you can remember which words appeared in the story. Be sure to write down only the words that *did* appear.

1. waiter 2. grown 3. settled 4. kiss 5. menu 6. window

Almost everyone remembers reading the word "waiter." But many people miss the less important word "settled." Most people also remember reading the word "menu." However, if you read the story again, you'll see that the word "menu" did *not* appear in the story. How is it that, shortly after reading a story, most people misremember reading a common word? One answer is that perception involves *constructivism*.

But a more specific explanation for this memory bias is that we often make sense of familiar event sequences by relying on scripts (Abelson, 1981; Schank & Abelson, 1977). **Scripts** are learned expectations about how familiar social events typically unfold. They're prototypical event sequences. From this perspective, many people falsely remember reading the word "menu" because a menu is part of the *script* for going to a restaurant. Most people have scripts for all kinds of events, from visits to the dentist to bank robberies. In the case of a visit to the dentist, a script might involve checking in with a receptionist, reading a dated issue of a popular magazine while you wait, being seated in a reclining chair, being reminded that you haven't been flossing, and trying to make polite conversation while someone probes your mouth with sharp objects. Scripts are useful because they allow us to fill in missing pieces of incomplete stories. But scripts can be problematic because they can bias what we perceive or remember ("Yes, officer, the robber was definitely carrying a gun. And he was also carrying a menu").

In addition to constructing social judgments based on scripts, we construct them based on many other preexisting ideas. These include ideas about how different physical characteristics are associated with different personality traits, ideas about which kinds of traits go hand in hand, and ideas about what group memberships tell us about people's personalities. All three of these can be understood as examples of stereotypes. Let's briefly examine each of these ways in which stereotypes influence person perception.

Stereotypes Based on Physical Characteristics

If you recall the module on genetics, you know that physical traits such as attractiveness, height, and skin tone have a big impact on how we are viewed by others. Most people are content to "judge a book by its cover." For example, you may recall that most people assume that tall people are good leaders. Whereas the average height of American men is about 5'10," the average height of U.S. (male) Senators is between 6'1" and 6'2" (Boller, 1984). U.S. Presidents also tend to be taller than average. Furthermore, U.S. Presidents that people generally consider "great" were much taller than those people generally consider "failures" (Young & French, 1996, 1998). If you wonder which Presidents most people consider great, just consider which Presidents have their own monuments or memorials in Washington, DC.

People also judge others based on facial characteristics such as attractiveness and facial babyishness. In fact, the effects of a person's physical attractiveness on the way a person is judged are so well documented that some refer to this as the **physical attractiveness stereotype**. This refers to the assumption that physically attractive people possess a wide range of mostly favorably personality characteristics (Dion, Berscheid, & Walster, 1972; Eagly, Ashmore, Makhijani, & Longo, 1991). The traits that people associate most strongly with physical attractiveness are interpersonal traits such as being outgoing, having good social skills, being emotionally mature, and being honest. The physical attractiveness stereotype applies to male and female targets, to targets of all ages (including babies), and to targets from virtually all cultures and ethnic groups (Eagly et al., 1991; Langlois, Ritter, Casey, & Sawin, 1995). This stereotype can also create self-fulfilling prophesies (covered in Module 26). Attractive people sometimes behave more sociably than unattractive people because they are treated in ways that strongly encourage them to be sociable (Snyder, Tanke, & Berscheid, 1977).

Figure 27.1 Scripts are theories about prototypical *event sequences*. In bank robberies, people steal money, of course. In weddings, people have usually stolen hearts. In baseball, people steal bases.

There are also stereotypes about people with baby faces. Research on **facial babyishness** suggests that people treat others with baby faces as if they possess some of the psychological characteristics of babies. For good reason, we think babies have qualities such as innocence and naivete. However, Berry and colleagues have found that people overgeneralize from babies to adults with baby faces (e.g., people with big eyes, tall, round foreheads, and small chins). Thus, we judge baby-faced *adults* as more honest, naïve, and trusting than other adults of the same age. People with baby faces do seem to have *some* of the personality traits people ascribe to them (Berry & Brownlow, 1989; Berry & Landry, 1997). However, it also looks like human judges are much too willing to rely on this facial babyishness as a cue for traits such as innocence. Cunningham (1986) found that men who were shown photographs of baby-faced vs. more mature-looking women reported that they would be more willing to risk their lives to save the lives of the women with baby-faces.

Stereotypes Based on Implicit Personality Theory

Most people also seem to make strong assumptions about how different traits fit together. **Implicit personality theory** refers to people's unstated assumptions about which physical and personality traits tend to go together – and which do not (Schneider, 1973; Schneider & Blankmeyer, 1983). For example, if you learn that Myron is "shy" and "uncoordinated," you are much more likely to assume that he is "intelligent" than to assume that he is "competitive." Likewise, if you learn that Mary is "courteous" and "helpful," you're likely to assume that she is also "honest" rather than "manipulative." Implicit personality theory is tightly linked to stereotypes because many common stereotypes include assumptions about how different traits fit together. For example, people draw many conclusions about the psychological traits people possess based on physical traits such as skin tone, height, weight, and age-related physical features.

Our assumptions about which personality traits go together appear to allow us to process certain kinds of information more readily than others. Harris and Hampson (1980) found that when people thought that someone was "friendly," they took very little time to decide whether that person was "generous" but took much longer to decide whether the person was "careful." In the early 1990s, a humorous example of implicit personality theory was provided by a running sketch on the TV show "Saturday Night Live." The premise of the sketch was that two men with their own call-in talk show had formed the "Gay, Communist Gun Lovers' Club." As the two members of the club often had to remind those who wished to join their club, there were three strict membership requirements – to join the club a person had to be openly gay, devoutly communist, *and* an avid gun lover. The fact that the club only had two members confirmed most viewers' implicit theories that these three traits *don't* usually go together.

Stereotypes Based on Group Memberships

When most people think about stereotypes, they think about beliefs about others based on their group memberships. You may recall that Allport's classic definition of stereotypes involves false or exaggerated beliefs about the members of social groups. To complement Allport's classic definition, Hardin's (2018) modern definition is that **stereotypes** are "socially shared beliefs about the members of a group" (e.g., women, Germans, truck drivers, dentists, tennis players, etc.). Notice that Hardin's definition is neutral with respect to whether these beliefs are spot on or woefully inaccurate. According to Hardin

(2018) stereotypes can still be dangerous even if they are factually supported. This is because socially shared beliefs may feel right even if they are morally wrong, and because socially shared beliefs are very hard to change. For example, it is factually correct that men work as truck drivers much more often than women do. But if this gender stereotype makes it harder for women than for men to get jobs as truck drivers, this is still a social problem.

Although stereotypes creep into our social judgments in many ways, two of the most common ways are that they (a) direct our attention and (b) bias our memories. Remember the knife that changed hands from a White to a Black character in the classic Allport and Postman (1947) study? Although a detailed analysis of the nuts and bolts of stereotypes is beyond the scope of this text, we must acknowledge that stereotypes play a powerful role in person perception. Further, Allport and Hardin would surely agree that stereotypes are also very difficult to change because they serve at least three important psychological functions, all of which are relevant to perceiving and understanding people (including ourselves). Let's briefly explore each of these three functions of stereotypes.

First, stereotypes **simplify**. This is why Allport described them as "overgeneralized." Stereotypes seem to fill the human needs for order, predictability, and control by taking a complex world and making it much easier to handle. Simply placing people into categories is much easier than thinking deeply about them as individuals. If we believe that women rarely work in STEM fields because we endorse the stereotype that women are not cut out to do math and science, we have a very simple answer to why there are so few female engineers. In contrast, if we recognize that women are often discouraged in invisible ways from taking part in STEM fields, the world is much more complex. Likewise, if we stereotype Black people as both poor and lazy, the world is much simpler for us than it would be if we had to think hard about the legacy of slavery, Jim Crow, racial profiling, unjust housing policies, and public schools that spend much more money on rich kids than on poor kids. In fact, Gunn (2019) reports that in the presumably progressive states of California and New York, poor non-White school districts spent $4,000 less per student per year on education than poor White school districts. Stereotypes help us avoid wrestling with complexities by allowing us to put people into very simple categories.

Second, stereotypes **justify**. They allow us to excuse and defend norms and laws that put certain groups of people at a decided disadvantage. If we have a stereotype that Muslims are terrorists, and a stereotype that women are irrational and "hormonal," this justifies taking away rights from Muslims and women. Along these lines, a large body of research on **system justification theory** suggests that the desire to live in a world that is fair is so powerful that we often justify unfair norms and rules by concluding that these norms and rules are fair and equitable – even when they are grossly unfair. System justification processes are so powerful that people will often justify the very rules that single out their *own* disadvantaged groups. For example, after Congress finally recognized women's right to vote in 1919 (by passing the 19th Amendment), many American women still refused to vote because they believed they did not truly deserve this basic human right. In fact, it was not until 1980 that American women finally began to vote at the same rate as men. Likewise, Jost and colleagues (2003) found that sometimes the very people who suffer most under "system justifying" belief systems are the most likely to accept and endorse the rules behind those systems. For example, they showed that Black Americans living in the South were more likely than both White Americans and Black Americans living in the North to endorse the idea that in America working hard *guarantees* that people will become financially successful. Worse yet, the poorer Southern Blacks were, the more likely they were to accept this system-justifying attitude. Stereotypes justify.

Finally, a third function of stereotypes is that they **identify** (they help define our identities). They tell us who we are and who we are not. The groups to which we belong are our **ingroups**, and groups to which we do not belong are our **outgroups**. Identifying who we are through our ingroups can be very satisfying and empowering. For example, Latinos, Lebanese, and lesbians who strongly identify with their own social groups have a sense of purpose and meaning that they would not have if they gave little thought to their identities (Lutanen & Crocker, 1992; Roberts, et al., 1999). We often benefit from propping up our ingroup ("College professors work hard to help their students learn") and putting down the outgroup ("Students don't do the readings and don't come to office hours. Then they complain about doing poorly on the exams"). On the other hand, research also shows that the desire to know who we are – and even the sense of belonging we get from being a member of a social group – can make us accept some of the negative stereotypes that are strongly associated with our groups. It is probably because stereotypes help us identify with other members of our social groups that we give people special permission to derogate or joke about a social group if they are a *member* of the group. Because your first author grew up in rural Georgia, he is much more comfortable than your second author would ever be making jokes about rednecks. Likewise, as a Jew who lived in Israel for seven years, your second author has some social permission to take an occasional poke at his fellow Jews.

All three of these functions of stereotypes play a role in social judgment. For example, Bodenhausen (1990) found that we are more prone to stereotype others at times of days when we're likely to be tired. Simplification is more irresistible than usual when we are tired. Likewise, Sherman et al. (1998) showed that because stereotypes are well-learned simplifications, they can sometimes free people up to think deeply about more than one thing at a time. Plenty of studies of social judgment also show that when we learn that something terrible has happened to a person, our belief in a *just world* sometimes demands that we

Figure 27.2 This U.S. cartoon from the 1880s relied to some degree on all three functions of stereotypes. The cartoon implied that the inventor of the "Missouri Steam Washer" would help rid America of a foreign threat (foreign workers taking "our" jobs). In what ways does the cartoon simplify Chinese Americans? How could it help justify discrimination against them? How does it suggest that only non-Chinese people should identify as true Americans?

blame the victim. More specifically, research on Lerner's **just world hypothesis** shows that when something bad happens to a person (even when the bad event is outside the person's control), many social judges conclude that the person must have done something to deserve the bad outcome (Lerner & Simmons, 1966). For example, the desire to believe that the world is fair is associated with blaming people who live in poor nations for their own suffering (Harper, Wagstaff, Newton, & Harrison, 1990). Likewise, simply observing a person receive painful electric shocks in the lab can lead people to blame the victim and conclude that people "reap what they sow" (Lerner & Miller, 1978). Finally, the desire to identify with other members of our own groups may be so powerful that we sometimes "self-stereotype" and apply stereotypes of our own social groups to ourselves (Sinclair, Hardin, & Lowery, 2006). One way to acknowledge the power of stereotypes is to recognize that stereotypes are part of a dangerous triad. Our negative beliefs (**stereotypes**) are connected to our **prejudices** (our negative feelings about people based on their group memberships). Further, both stereotypes and prejudice are connected to **discrimination** – which refers to negative behavior directed at the members of a specific social group.

The Role of Attribution Theory in Social Perception

Scripts and stereotypes notwithstanding, social perceivers sometimes make highly sophisticated judgments. As noted earlier, *attribution theories* explain how people assess the causes of another person's behavior. One kind of *attribution* is a causal judgment about exactly why someone did something (Heider, 1958) – and there are two fundamentally different causes of human behavior. Almost any behavior can be explained in terms of either **situational** or **dispositional** causes. Situational attributions are explanations that identify *external* or contextual causes of behavior. Sometimes physical or social forces determine what a person does. Situational explanations for a behavior may be as subtle as a polite request or as blatant as the barrel of a gun. In contrast, dispositional attributions focus on *internal* causes – such as attitudes or personality traits (Gilbert & Malone, 1995).

Discounting and Augmenting

Kelley (1967, 1973) suggested two logical rules for sorting out dispositional vs. situational attributions. These rules are *discounting* and *augmenting*. **Discounting** means making a *less* dispositional attribution than you otherwise would when situational factors *promote* the performance of the behavior. If situational influences can fully account for a person's behavior, you should *not* assume anything about the person's dispositions. If a toddler is crying, but you learn that she was just stung by a hornet, you should not conclude that the toddler is chronically unhappy. When it has been shown in court that a defendant committed an aggressive act, defense attorneys may try to get jurors to engage in discounting by pointing out situational forces that contributed to the aggressive action (e.g., "Ms. Goode, didn't Mr. Killingsworth leap at you with a knife in his hand?" "And hadn't he just threatened to kill you?"). The degree to which the jury accepts these arguments about discounting can mean the difference between a murder conviction and an acquittal. As another example, there are many athletes who've been denied personal credit for world record performances because they used performance-enhancing drugs. Taking away their personal credit is a form of discounting.

Kelley's second principle for separating situations and dispositions is **augmenting**. Augmenting is the reverse of discounting. It refers to making a *more* dispositional attribution than you otherwise would have when situational factors *inhibit* (i.e., get in the way of) the performance of the behavior. To the degree that a situational influence makes it harder than usual for a person to engage in a behavior, we should give the person more personal credit (or more blame) than usual for performing the behavior. If a teenage girl refuses to smoke a cigarette even though her friends all pressure her to do so, we should give her some extra credit for resisting temptation. That's augmenting. Athletic competitions are great grounds for both discounting and augmenting.

Consider track and field. In April of 2019, Matthew Boling posted the fastest 100-meter dash time ever by a U.S. high schooler (9.98 s). But Boling did not set the official U.S. high school record for that performance because he had a favorable tailwind that was a bit above the allowable limit. A fast tailwind pushes runners along a little in the direction of the finish line, and so there are limits to just how fast a tailwind can be if a runner is to receive credit for a record performance. When an athlete performs well despite facing challenges, on the other hand, judges should engage in augmenting rather than discounting. If a sprinter breaks a record despite running into a head wind, or pitches a great game while injured, augmenting is in order. An example of augmenting from college wrestling happened in March of 2011, when Arizona State wrestler Anthony Robles went undefeated and became an NCAA champion in the 125-pound weight class. He did so despite having only one leg. Many wrestling fans gave Robles extra athletic credit for winning despite his disability. Again, that's *augmenting*.

The Correspondence Bias

Another early attribution theory was Jones and Davis's (1965) **theory of correspondent inferences.** Like Kelley's theory, this theory focused on how social perceivers disentangle situational vs. dispositional explanations for a person's behavior. Many of the predictions of correspondent inferences theory boil down to this: Perceivers shouldn't make dispositional attributions for a person's behavior if a *situation* (e.g., the demands of a job or social role) easily explains the behavior. For example, social perceivers shouldn't make dispositional attributions about why Zeke owns a sports car if Zeke didn't *freely choose* the sports car. We should discount the behavior of people who have no choice about what they do. One of the first tests of correspondent inferences theory focused on this prediction. Incidentally, if you read the supplemental section at the end of Module 26, you received a very brief summary of this classic study. In this module, we'd like to take a closer look at it.

Jones and Harris (1967; Study 2) specifically looked at the role of choice in the attributions people made about the attitudes of some essayists. They did so by asking participants to read an essay that had presumably been written by a fellow Duke University student. The essay either praised or condemned a (then) young Cuban leader named Fidel Castro. Regardless of which essay participants read, half the participants thought the essayists had all expressed their own opinions of Fidel Castro. The other half of the participants thought the essayists had been told exactly what position to take in the essay – because they wrote the essay for a debate coach. In this case, the student's opinions had nothing to do with the position they adopted in the essay that they wrote. As you can see in the left half of Figure 27.3, participants in the free choice condition decided that the essay writer they evaluated said what he meant and meant what he said. They freely drew dispositional inferences from what they thought were freely written essays. In the no-choice condition, however, the results were more surprising – and less consistent with a careful attributional analysis. These results are summarized in the right half of Figure 27.3. Even though the essayist presumably had no choice about which position he supported, participants decided that he meant at least *part* of what he said. Judges did not completely discount the essayists' completely dictated behavior. To be clear, participants were not oblivious to the fact that the essayists had no choice about what position he favored. Judges discounted. They just didn't discount completely.

This bias to take make overly dispositional judgments has proven to be very robust. Many other studies confirmed what Ross (1977) called the **fundamental attribution error** and what Gilbert and Jones (1986) later called the **correspondence bias** (Gilbert & Malone, 1995; Ross, Amabile, & Steinmetz, 1977). For our purposes, these two terms can be treated as synonymous. Each refers to the tendency for people to *provide dispositional explanations for behavior that is more logically explained in terms of situations.* The correspondence bias can help explain a lot of important social beliefs. For example, it can explain the formation of many stereotypes. Just as people may fail to appreciate the potency of a debate coach's instructions, they may fail to appreciate the debilitating effects of years of poverty or a lack of educational opportunities. People do not usually appreciate the power of situational influences.

Why the Bias?

By the mid- to late-1980s, it was well established that the correspondence bias was robust. However, it wasn't very clear *why* people fall prey to this bias. So why *do* they? The broadest answer is grounded in the principles of *automatic* and *controlled* information-processing. Consistent with the theme of *automatic* (rapid, unconscious, easy) and *controlled* (slow, conscious, cognitively demanding) information processing emphasized elsewhere in this text, researchers suggested that assigning causes (making attributions) consists of multiple stages (Gilbert, 1989). To simplify things a bit, the early stages of

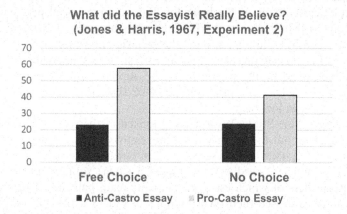

Figure 27.3 A classic study of the perceived attitudes of four essayists. Participants thought the essayists on the left had free choice to say whether they felt Fidel Castro was a good or bad leader. But they felt the essayists on the right were *assigned* a specific position on Castro by debate coaches. If the essayists on the right had no choice about what position they took, why did judges decide they believed what the essayists wrote – to at least a modest degree? That's the correspondence bias.

person perception are highly automatic. Social perceivers who see a person engage in a behavior that suggests aggression, kindness, nervousness, or intelligence engage in an automatic process known as **characterization**. They leap quickly to the judgment that behavior reflects whatever disposition would normally promote the behavior (e.g., "What a nervous guy!"). If and only if social perceivers have plenty of cognitive resources, they then engage in what Gilbert (1989) calls **correction**. They consider the possible influence of situational factors that might facilitate or inhibit the behavior, and they try to adjust for these situational influences. Unlike the characterization process, the correction stage requires *controlled* processing. It's highly effortful. For this reason, correction is easily disrupted. Anything that competes for a perceiver's attention or cognitive capacity may cause the perceiver to be left with an uncorrected *characterization* (aka an *overly dispositional* judgment about a target – which is the essence of the correspondence bias; Gilbert, Pelham, & Krull, 1988). One of the most important implications of the correspondence bias is that this robust bias plays a role in many common stereotypes. Uncorrected characterizations often promote stereotypes. In contrast, correcting for a lack of opportunity is likely to raise doubts about the validity of a stereotype.

So the main reason why people fall prey to the correspondence bias is that characterization is easy and automatic (and thus irresistible) whereas making corrections to our characterizations is hard (and thus easily disrupted). Gilbert (1989) also noted that the inherently social nature of person perception means that we will frequently be cognitively preoccupied when we are trying to figure out other people's personalities. The demanding nature of real-world person perception may increase the chances that we will fall prey to the correspondence bias. It also seems likely that people who are immersed in cognitively demanding social interactions will engage in other automatic social judgment processes without being able to correct them. It's likely, that is, that preoccupied social judges (which is most of us) may show a stronger than usual preference for tall leaders, express a stronger than usual willingness to save a baby-faced stranger, or jump to the conclusion that women are highly nurturing. Automatic social information processing makes us more susceptible than usual to both the correspondence bias and widely-shared stereotypes.

Moderators of the Correspondence Bias

Although the correspondence bias appears to be very potent, many factors can increase or decrease the likelihood that people will commit the correspondence bias. Here we'll briefly review just two – each of which is consistent with Gilbert's multi-stage model. First, most people seem to have a lot more practice thinking about *some* specific situations than they do thinking about others. Most people realize that when Larry offers a glowing appraisal of his boss's new tie, Larry's appraisal probably says more about Larry's desire to win the boss's favor than it does about Larry's taste in ties. In line with this reasoning about ulterior motives, Fein, Hilton, and Miller (1990) showed that when judges had reason to be *suspicious* about the behavior of the person they were judging, they usually did a great job of adjusting fully for the power of the situation that aroused their suspicion. Notice that this is a case in which a social motivation probably increases the accuracy of social perception.

It's also possible that some forms of attributional correction are so well-practiced that people may habitually *over*-apply them. Consider the *overjustification effect* you may recall from the module on motivation. Lepper, Greene, and Nisbett (1973) gave some children a promised reward for engaging in a behavior the children had originally found highly pleasurable (coloring with magic markers). Other children engaged in the same fun marking behavior but received no reward. A week or two later, the children were given the chance to play with the markers during some free time. Those who had been rewarded were only about half as likely to play with the markers as were those who had not been rewarded. They seem to have concluded that there was a *situational* reason (the rewards) why they had played with the markers. These children were clearly sensitive to the power of external rewards to control their behavior. This suggests that when a specific situational constraint is highly familiar (to the point of being automatic), even young children are capable of high levels of attributional correction.

Conclusions

Many of our social judgments are influenced by our pre-existing ideas about the social world. Many of these pre-existing ideas have a close connection to stereotypes, and most of them seem to operate unconsciously. Moreover, despite some possible exceptions for highly familiar judgments, many of our social judgments seem to be biased by a preference for person-centered rather than situation-centered explanations. Taken together, the various cousins of stereotypes and the correspondence bias suggest that many of our social judgments are overly simplistic. That is, they suggest that we perceive our social worlds to be populated not by the complex and flexible social creatures of reality but by stereotypic and predictable caricatures of these people. Our perceptions of other people do not seem to do justice to the power of the situation emphasized in Module 26 (Gilbert & Malone, 1995). But a more positive spin on the research summarized here is that if we truly wish to understand another person well, we do not *have* to rely solely on stereotypes or initial impressions. By spending the time and energy it takes to piece together all the facts about a person, we may be able to move beyond first impressions to develop a richer appreciation for the complex people who inhabit our social worlds.

Hands-On Activity and Thought Questions for Module 27

One of the take-away points of Module 27 is that unless people think very carefully about other people, they may be prone to biases based on automatic judgmental processes such as judging people based on their appearance, using familiar scripts, and relying on stereotypes. Although this is true, there is also research on person perception and social cognition that suggests that there are good reasons why social judges use most of the rules that they use. You may recall, for example, that when it comes to assessing the six basic emotions, most people can usually tell very quickly and accurately what basic emotions a total stranger is expressing. Of course, emotions are fleeting. If you read the module on judgmental heuristics, you may also recall that the same heuristics that can sometimes get us into big trouble prove to be very useful on a daily basis. Is there any evidence that our quick (and presumably automatic) judgments of the personalities of total strangers have any validity? One answer to this question is that it depends on which specific personality traits we are judging. One of the personality traits that most people are able to judge pretty well based on very limited information is extraversion, that is sociability and outgoingness. Dave Kenny and colleagues (1992) refer to this as *"consensus at zero acquaintance."* By that, they mean that most people can look at a photo of a complete stranger and come to pretty high levels of agreement with others (come to a consensus, that is) about whether the person is an introvert or an extrovert.

Not too long ago, your first author put Kenny et al.'s idea to an independent test. He directly measured extraversion by giving a group of about 150 students a popular measure of extraversion. In fact, he gave it to them twice, during the beginning and middle of a semester, and he averaged their two scores. As you can see in Figure 27.4, the measure asked students to report the degree to which they were "extraverted," "energetic," "talkative," and "bold," for example. Figure 27.4 shows you the exact seven-item measure.

After scoring everyone on this measure, the first author randomly selected four male and four female students who scored in either the top (extraverted) or bottom (introverted) quarter of the trait of extraversion. He was careful to select two male and two female introverts and two male and two female extraverts. Because he had taken photos of all the students in this class as part of a different research project, he had photos of all eight students. These photos appear in Figure 27.5. See if you can go at least six for eight in identifying the four introverts and the four extraverts. When your first author has asked groups of ten to 30 students to vote on the introverts and extroverts, the group votes have always proven to yield all eight correct answers. But how well can you do? Remember that the selection of eight students includes (a) two male and two female extraverts and (b) two male and two female introverts.

Notice that the eight students are numbered. Simply number a blank page 1–8 and write *EX* (for extravert) or *IN* (for introvert) next to each number. Then circle the number of the one male student and the one female student that you are most certain is an extravert (an outgoing "people person"). Before you see how you did, we must remind you that if you only got four answers correct, this reflects chance levels of guessing. Do you see why? But we're guessing you got at least six out of eight questions correct on this test of "consensus at zero acquaintance." But in this case, maybe we should call it "*accuracy* at zero acquaintance."

I determined a person's level of extraversion based on What you see below.

PERSONALITY MEASURE

The next measure assesses five core personality dimensions...

Please rate Yourself on each specific dimension or personality trait.

Introversion-Extraversion

introverted	1	2	3	4	5	6	7	8	9 extraverted
unenergetic	1	2	3	4	5	6	7	8	9 energetic
silent	1	2	3	4	5	6	7	8	9 talkative
timid	1	2	3	4	5	6	7	8	9 bold
inactive	1	2	3	4	5	6	7	8	9 active
unassertive	1	2	3	4	5	6	7	8	9 assertive
unadventurous	1	2	3	4	5	6	7	8	9 adventurous

Figure 27.4

Figure 27.5

Thought Questions

1. Some researchers have argued that women are better than men at both expressing and decoding emotions? How could you use the given stimuli to test the idea that women are better (or worse) than men at expressing and decoding *extraversion*? Be specific.

2. We did not post the correct answers to this quiz. Only your instructor has the answers. But if consensus is, in fact, highly correlated with accuracy, and if past students who have taken the test have proven to be very good at guessing the answers to this test, how could you and your classmates figure out with a high degree of certainty what the answers are to this test of social perception?

3. Does a high degree of accuracy on this test invalidate Hardin's definition of stereotypes (offered in this module)? Whether it does so or not, does the existence of accuracy at zero acquaintance make it OK to stereotype others? Why or why not?

Multiple-Choice Questions for Module 27

1. According to the text, what is the relation between person perception and attribution.

   A) Attributions are one specific route via which people engage in person perception.
   B) Attributions are mostly cognitive processes whereas person perception is mostly social
   C) The two terms are interchangeable; they mean the same thing.

2. "The audience sings the National Anthem, someone famous throws out the first pitch, the pitcher for the home team faces the start of the visitor's lineup, a batter argues with the umpire about a called strike." A social psychologist would say that these events are parts of a _____ for a baseball game.

   A) plot
   B) storyline
   C) script

3. Pat is tall, hairy, loves sports, and has poor personal hygiene. If you jumped to the conclusion that Pat is also male and also likes beer, you probably did so based on what judgmental process?

   A) attribution
   B) characterization
   C) implicit personality theory

4. In what sense does the physical attractiveness stereotype fit the textbook definition of a stereotype?

   A) like most other stereotypes, the physical attractiveness stereotype involves mostly negative beliefs
   B) the physical attractiveness stereotype is applied to some social groups but not others
   C) it is a socially shared belief that attractive people possess certain personality traits

5. Scripts and stereotypes, including stereotypes based on height or facial babyishness, are probably difficult to avoid because they are all:

   A) controlled
   B) automatic
   C) cross-culturally invariant

6. When a guy in a red Camry cuts Brad off on the freeway, Brad jumps to the conclusion that this guy is a terrible driver – and perhaps a terrible person. In fact, the Camry driver's three-year-old daughter caused the problem when she threw a drink in his lap (all the way from the back seat). Brad seems to have fallen prey to what judgmental error or bias?

   A) the actor-observer effect
   B) the ultimate attributional error
   C) the correspondence bias

7. Despite running in the rain and running into a strong headwind, Jerome set a school record in the 110-meter high hurdles. Concluding that Jerome is even more talented than his very good time would suggest is an example of judgment based on what attributional principle?

   A) augmenting
   B) discounting
   C) exaltation

8. If you were the defense attorney for a client who had admitted to killing someone who had physically abused her for many years, what *attributional process* would you try to get the judge or jury to engage in – to reduce how much they blamed your client for her violent actions?

   A) I'd want them to engage in discounting
   B) I'd want them to engage in augmenting
   C) I'd want them to engage in exaltation

9. The three major functions of stereotypes include the ideas that stereotypes simplify, justify, and:

   A) clarify
   B) identify
   C) verify

10. According to Gilbert's multi-stage model of attribution, which of the following is an automatic step in making an attribution about another person's behavior?

    A) characterization
    B) assimilation
    C) attention

11. Which attributional process is the most cognitively demanding?

    A) correction
    B) dissection
    C) neither; it depends on whether a person is judging a stranger or a well-known other

Answer key: 1A 2C 3C 4C 5B 6C 7A 8A 9B 10A 11A

408 *Social, Personality, and Cultural Psychology*

References

Abelson, R. P. (1981). The psychological status of the script concept. *American Psychologist, 36,* 715–729.

Allport, G. W., & Postman, L. (1947). *The psychology of rumor.* New York: Henry Holt.

Berry, D. S., & Brownlow, S. (1989). Were the physiognomists right? Personality correlates of facial babyishness. *Personality and Social Psychology Bulletin, 15,* 266–279.

Berry, D. S., & Landry, J. C. (1997). Facial maturity and daily social interaction. *Journal of Personality and Social Psychology, 72,* 570–580.

Bodenhausen, G. V. (1990). Stereotypes as judgmental heuristics: Evidence of circadian variations in discrimination. *Psychological Science, 1*(5), 319–322. doi:10.1111/j.1467-9280.1990.tb00226.x

Boller, P. F., Jr. (1984). *Presidential campaigns.* Oxford: Oxford University Press.

Carvallo, M., & Pelham, B. W. (2006). When fiends become friends: The need to belong and perceptions of personal and group discrimination. *Journal of Personality and Social Psychology, 90,* 94–108.

Cunningham, M. R. (1986). Measuring the physical in physical attractiveness: Quasi-experiments on the sociobiology of female facial beauty. *Journal of Personality and Social Psychology, 50,* 925–935.

Darley, J. M., & Berscheid, E. (1967). Increased liking as a result of the anticipation of personal contact. *Human Relations, 20,* 29–40.

Dion, K., Berscheid, E., & Walster, E. (1972). What is beautiful is good. *Journal of Personality and Social Psychology, 24,* 285–290.

Eagly, A. H., Ashmore, R. D., Makhijani, M. G., & Longo, L. C. (1991). What is beautiful is good, but...: A meta-analytic review of research on the physical attractiveness stereotype. *Psychological Bulletin, 110,* 109–128.

Fein, S., Hilton, J. L., & Miller, D. T. (1990). Suspicion of ulterior motivation and the correspondence bias. *Journal of Personality and Social Psychology, 58,* 753–764.

Gilbert, D. T. (1989). Thinking lightly about others: Automatic components of the social inference process. In J. S. Uleman & J. A. Bargh (Eds.), *Unintended thought* (pp. 189–211). New York, NY: Guilford Press.

Gilbert, D. T., & Malone, P. (1995). The correspondence bias. *Psychological Bulletin, 117,* 21–38.

Gilbert, D. T., & Jones, E. E. (1986). Perceiver-induced constraint: Interpretations of self-generated reality. *Journal of Personality and Social Psychology, 50,* 269–280.

Gilbert, D. T., Pelham, B. W., & Krull, D. S. (1988). On cognitive busyness: When person perceivers meet persons perceived. *Journal of Personality and Social Psychology, 54,* 733–740.

Gunn, D. (2019, February 26). None-White school districts get $23 billion less funding than White ones. Pacific Standard. Retrieved from https://psmag.com/education

Hardin, C.D. (2018). Personal communication.

Harper, D. J., Wagstaff, G. F., Newton, J. T., & Harrison, K. R. (1990). Lay causal perceptions of third world poverty and the just world theory. *Social Behavior and Personality: An International Journal, 18*(2), 235–238.

Harris, P. L., & Hampson, S. E. (1980). Processing information within implicit personality theory. *British Journal of Social and Clinical Psychology, 19,* 235–242.

Heider, F. (1958). *The psychology of interpersonal relations.* New York, NY: Wiley.

Jones, E. E., & Davis, K. E. (1965). From acts to dispositions: The attribution process in person perception. In L. Berkowitz (Ed.), *Advances in experimental social psychology* (Vol. 2, pp. 219–266). San Diego, CA: Academic Press.

Jones, E. E., & Harris, V. A. (1967). The attribution of attitudes. *Journal of Experimental Social Psychology, 3,* 1–24.

Jost, J. T., Pelham, B. W., Sheldon, O., & Sullivan, B. N. (2003). Social inequality and the reduction of ideological dissonance on behalf of the system: Evidence of enhanced system justification among the disadvantaged. *European Journal of Social Psychology, 33,* 13–36.

Kelley, H. H. (1967). Attribution theory in social psychology. *Nebraska Symposium on Motivation, 15,* 192–238.

Kelley, H. H. (1973). The processes of causal attribution. *American Psychologist, 28*, 107–128.

Kenny, D. A., Horner, C., Kashy, D. A., & Chu, L. (1992). Consensus at zero acquaintance: Replication, behavioral cues, and stability. *Journal of Personality and Social Psychology, 62*, 88–97.

Langlois, J. H., Ritter, J. M., Casey, R. J., & Sawin, D. B. (1995). Infant attractiveness predicts maternal behaviors and attitudes. *Developmental Psychology, 31*, 464–472.

Lepper, M. R., Greene, D., & Nisbett, R. E. (1973). Undermining children's intrinsic interest with extrinsic reward: A test of the "overjustification" hypothesis. *Journal of Personality and Social Psychology, 28*, 129–137.

Lerner, M. J., & Miller, D. T. (1978). Just world research and the attribution process: Looking back and ahead. *Psychological Bulletin, 85*(5), 1030–1051. doi:10.1037/0033-2909.85.5.1030

Lerner, M., & Simmons, C. H. (1966). Observer's reaction to the 'innocent victim': Compassion or rejection?" *Journal of Personality and Social Psychology, 4*(2), 203–210.

Roberts, R. E., Phinney, J. S., Masse, L. C., Chen, Y. R., Roberts, C. R., & Romero, A. (1999). The Structure of Ethnic Identity of Young Adolescents from Diverse Ethnocultural Groups. *The Journal of Early Adolescence, 19*(3), 301–322.

Ross, L. (1977). The intuitive psychologist and his shortcomings. In L. Berkowitz (Ed.), *Advances in experimental social psychology* (Vol. 10, pp. 173–220). San Diego, CA: Academic Press.

Ross, L. D., Amabile, T. M., & Steinmetz, J. L. (1977). Social roles, social control, and biases in social-perception processes. *Journal of Personality and Social Psychology, 35*(7), 485–494. doi:10.1037/0022-3514.35.7.485

Schank, R. C., & Abelson, R. P. (1977). *Scripts, plans, goals and understanding: An inquiry into human knowledge structures*. Hillsdale, NJ: Erlbaum.

Schneider, D. J. (1973). Implicit personality theory: A review. *Psychological Bulletin, 79*, 294–309.

Schneider, D. J., & Blankmeyer, B. L. (1983). Prototype salience and implicit personality theories. *Journal of Personality and Social Psychology, 44*(4), 712–722.

Sherman, J. W., Lee, A. Y., Bessenoff, G. R., & Frost, L. A. (1998). Stereotype efficiency reconsidered: Encoding flexibility under cognitive load. *Journal of Personality and Social Psychology, 75*(3), 589–606. doi:10.1037/0022-3514.75.3.589

Sinclair, S., Hardin, C. D., & Lowery, B. S. (2006). Self-stereotyping in the context of multiple social identities. *Journal of Personality and Social Psychology, 90*(4), 529–542. doi:10.1037/0022-3514.90.4.529

Snyder, M., Tanke, E., & Berscheid, E. (1977). Social perception and interpersonal behavior: On the self- fulfilling nature of social stereotypes. *Journal of Personality and Social Psychology, 35*, 656–666.

Young, T. J., & French, L. A. (1996). Height and perceived competence of U.S. presidents. *Perceptual and Motor Skills, 82*, 1002.

Young, T. J., & French, L. A. (1998). Heights of U.S. presidents: A trend analysis for 1948-1996. *Perceptual and Motor Skills, 87*, 321–322.

Module 28
Six Lenses on Human Aggression

This module introduces readers to three forms of human aggression: physical aggression, relational aggression, and verbal aggression. It also examines aggression fueled by two different motives, namely angry vs. instrumental aggression. The module then examines six influential perspectives on aggression, including an evolutionary perspective, the frustration-aggression hypothesis, the link between heat and aggression, the role of reciprocity in aggression, the social learning perspective, and the idea that economic inequality fuels aggression. The module concludes by noting that, despite all the media attention acts of aggression routinely receive, we're living in an era of unprecedented civility; aggression is on the decline.

Types of Aggression

If you've ever played a sport, watched a political debate, or observed preschoolers, you are familiar with aggression. Aggression is everywhere. But what, exactly, is **aggression**? To paraphrase Berkowitz (1981), aggression is anything a person does to try to harm another living being. Aggression includes **physical aggression** (e.g., punching or biting), **verbal aggression** (e.g., speaking ill of a person, or sending someone an insulting text), and **relational aggression** (e.g., falsely telling Leah she cannot trust Rachel). These are important distinctions. For example, they help us understand gender and aggression. Many people think that boys and men are simply more aggressive than girls and women. Of course, boys and men are usually more physically aggressive than girls and women. But gender differences in verbal aggression are tiny by comparison. When it comes to *relational aggression* (hurting a person by harming a relationship) girls and women appear to be slightly more aggressive than boys and men (Ostrov, Kamper, Hart, Godleski, & Blakely-McClure, 2014). Don't tell anyone we said that, by the way, or we won't be your friend. We hope that reminds you that even nuns and nurses are capable of relational aggression. Aggression comes in many shapes and sizes.

Aggression varies not only in its form but also in its motivational origins. Psychologists have argued that two basic motivations fuel aggression. It is impossible to understand aggression without understanding the two basic reasons why people engage in it.

Angry aggression (also termed *hostile aggression*) is motivated by anger and the accompanying desire to hurt someone *for the sake of hurting them* (e.g., punching your brother during a heated argument). Many cases of assault and homicide qualify as angry aggression. People often do things in anger they would never do if they calculated the costs and benefits. Especially in honor cultures, many murders seem to happen because a homicide victim did something to belittle the killer. Historically, **honor cultures** are often places where people had to make a living in a high-risk world. As a result, cultural norms developed that emphasized treating people honorably within a hierarchy. This meant responding with aggression when someone threatened your honor (e.g., by taking your property, having an affair with your spouse, or by insulting you). Historically, cattle and sheep herders had to be constantly on the lookout for rustlers. These are high-risk environments in the sense that if a person steals all of a herder's cattle, sheep, or goats the herder has lost everything. Farmers, in contrast, rarely had to worry that someone would ever rustle away a wheat field (Nisbett & Cohen, 1996). Malcom Gladwell (2008, p. 254) summarized research on the culture of honor and violence in the U.S. as follows. In the South, he argued, "violence wasn't for economic gain. It was *personal*. You fought over your honor." We'll return to honor cultures later in this module.

Sometimes it is *not* personal. **Instrumental aggression** is aggression performed in the service of a goal. In this case, the aggressor's true goal is to earn some reward, no matter what the cost to others. Robbing a bank and cheating in a sporting event are good examples. Tripping a close competitor in a marathon so you can beat them in the race is an example. Many examples of corporate greed are also examples. In 2015, Turing Pharmaceuticals came under attack after they increased the price of a life-saving drug from $13.50 to $750.00 per pill (yes, price gouging is aggression because it hurts people). In the spring of 2016, Volkswagen got caught designing their cars' computerized exhaust systems to cheat on emissions tests. This made the cars look much more environmentally friendly than they really were. If you're wondering where the harm was in this, just ask someone who paid thousands of extra dollars for an environmentally friendly, fuel-efficient car they never really got. These examples qualify as instrumental aggression in our book (that'd be this one) because the goal of both Turing and Volkswagen was to make money any way they could – *not* to hurt people out of anger.

Notice that aggression – committing an act *meant to* harm someone – involves intention. U.S. Navy SEALS meant to kill Osama Bin Laden. VW meant to steal from consumers. Some things that look aggressive on the surface (punishing

Figure 28.1 Aggression can be humorous (left) or tragic (right). Some of the most distressing examples of aggression constitute instrumental (not angry) aggression. The sniper who shot and killed Harambe the gorilla on May 28, 2016 at the Cincinnati Zoo (after a child got into his pen) engaged in instrumental aggression to save the child.

a child who disobeys) are ambiguous with respect to aggression. Parents who punish a child know this will make the child unhappy. But if the parent's goal was to help the child become better behaved, there is room for debate about what parents meant to do most. As a more obvious example, 19th century doctors sometimes sawed off their patients' limbs (without the benefit of anesthetics) because they hoped to save their patients' lives. In fact, people once referred to doctors (especially surgeons) as "sawbones." Although we're sure that having a limb sawed off was very painful, the intent of the doctor in this case was to do good rather than to harm.

Getting back to true aggression, aggression occurs for many specific reasons. Let's examine six of these reasons. That is, let's examine six popular theories of aggression.

The Origins of Aggression

Evolution

People are not the only creatures to behave aggressively. An evolutionary view of aggression suggests that aggression often happens because it gets organisms what they want or need – and it follows a set of cruel but rational rules. Predators kill prey not out of meanness but because they are programmed to hunt and kill when hungry. Richard Dawkins (1976) argued that "proto-carnivores" have been around since the very early history of life on Earth. Presumably, such creatures were favored with mutations that allowed them to "break up molecules of rival varieties" and use the chemicals for their own survival (Dawkins, 1976, p. 20). The phrase "**selfish gene**" summarizes Dawkins's argument that genes *have* to be selfish – even aggressive – to survive. Any gene that does not promote specific traits and behaviors that increase the odds of survival or reproduction of the organism that happens to carry it around will eventually be booted out of the proverbial "gene pool." For example, in a world in which rams butt heads for the right to mate, genes that make skulls better able to absorb shocks will be more likely to survive and be passed on to future generations. The same logic applies to pounding a tree with your beak to extract delicious insects. Ask any woodpecker.

Evolutionary scientists have argued that just as some genes make predators kill appropriate prey, and fight members of their own species over scarce resources, other genes inhibit aggression against organisms that are good at fighting back. Lions are quick to attack antelopes but slow to attack elephants – whose sheer size and strength make them more dangerous to lions than lions are to them. When lions do hunt large animals such as water buffalo, they cooperate with each other and hunt in groups – which minimizes their risk of death or injury. Notice that **cooperation** among lions can often be in the service of aggression against their prey.

It is no accident that rates of deadly aggression are almost always higher *between* species than within a species. Most evolutionary scientists would say that this does *not* mean that organisms are doing anything "for the good of the species." Instead, it means that the costs of aggressing within your own species are often greater than the costs of aggressing against an organism with whom you share very few genes (Pelham, 2017). Social organisms such as people, lions, and zebras often control aggression within groups by means of clear **hierarchies** (i.e., "pecking orders," rules about each member's relative standing in the group). If we know who the boss is, this eliminates constant fighting. Putting all this together, one useful perspective on why we behave aggressively emphasizes the fact that aggressive behavior often promotes survival or reproduction. From this **cost-benefit perspective**, animals (people included) will usually behave aggressively when the benefits of so doing outweigh the costs.

Frustration

One of the oldest theories of aggression is the **frustration aggression hypothesis** (Dollard, Doob, Miller, Mowrer, & Sears, 1939). The original version of this idea assumed that frustration *always* leads to aggression. That has not proven to be true. Berkowitz (1989, 1990) developed a more sophisticated version of the hypothesis that suggests that frustration often leads to **anger**, which often leads to aggression. Research suggests that frustration *can* lead to aggression, especially if people blame someone in particular for their unhappy state of affairs. Dill and Anderson (1995) tested the frustration-aggression hypothesis by motivating participants to learn to make an origami (paper) sculpture. The experimenter served as the origami instructor, and he either (a) took his time so that anyone could follow his instructions or (b) worked and talked so quickly that it was impossible for participants to succeed at the origami task. In one highly frustrating condition of the experiment, a (fake) fellow participant politely asked the experimenter to slow down, and the experimenter responded that "I would like to hurry and get this over with. My girlfriend is coming soon to pick me up and I don't want to make her wait."

When the frustrated participants had a chance to make critical ratings of their origami instructor (which they knew would be seen by his supervisor) they seem to have been pretty bent out of shape. Compared with a group who had not been frustrated by the teacher, they gave him more negative ability ratings and assigned him a much lower grade for his teaching skills. Further, analyses showed that across all conditions of the experiment, the more frustrated people said they felt, the more harshly they graded the experimenter ($r = .40$). Despite the appeal of the frustration aggression hypothesis, it does not have quite as much empirical support as you might expect. One reason for this seems to be that frustration does not always lead to the anger that seems to be more directly linked to aggression (as Berkowitz argued). On the other hand, *lots* of research, on both people and animals, shows that directly causing people pain, anger, or discomfort does usually make people more aggressive than usual. For example, Azrin, Rubin, and Hutchinson (1968) found that animals who receive a painful electric shock often attack anything that is handy – whether it is another animal or even a rubber or wooden object that is nearby.

Heat

One painful experience that makes people aggressive is heat. The phrase "hot under the collar" may be more than just a metaphor. In a classic field study, Kenrick and Mac-Farlane (1986) found that on hotter days, drivers in Arizona were especially likely to honk their horn at another driver who was taking too long to get going at a green light. This effect was particularly large for drivers who had their windows rolled down (and who presumably were not enjoying the benefits of air conditioning). Plenty of lab experiments, too, have shown that hot temperatures increase both aggression and the aggressive thoughts and feelings that often precede it.

Some of the best evidence that heat causes aggression comes from baseball. Reifman, Larrick, and Fein (1991) analyzed 862 major leagues baseball games. On hotter days, pitchers were more likely to hit opposing batters with "bean balls." But does heat makes pitchers more aggressive, or just make them less accurate? The answer is clear. On hotter days pitchers walked batters a little *less* often than on cooler days, and they threw slightly *fewer* wild pitches. Heat doesn't destroy a pitcher's aim. But it may make him want to destroy his opponent. More recently, Larrick, Timmerman, Carton, and Abrevaya (2010) analyzed an impressive 57,293 major league baseball games. They found, again, that pitchers hit batters more often when it was hotter. This was particularly true when it was hot *and* when it was "payback time" – that is, when a pitcher from the opposing team had hit one of their own teammates in the same game. Heat becomes more dangerous than usual when the norm of **reciprocity** gives it an extra nudge. Incidentally, temperature increases angry but *not* instrumental aggression. In hotter weather, rates of assault go up, but bank robberies don't (Anderson, 1987). "Yeah, Richie, I know I promised to rob First National with you today, but it's awfully hot out? Can I give you a rain check?"

Reciprocity

Unfortunately, both your authors grew up fighting older and stronger brothers. Thus, a phrase we both spoke to our mothers on many occasions when we were kids was "He started it!" (Another very common phrase was, "Help!") Violence truly begets violence. Israelis and Palestinians have been fighting for a long time, and each side has often argued that they are retaliating for the aggressive actions of the other group. According to Dallas Chief of Police David Brown, the killer who took the lives of five Dallas police officers on July 7, 2016 seems to have been engaging in "payback" for the actions of officers in highly publicized killings of young Black men at the hands of the police. Anderson and Bushman (2002, p. 37) argued that "Perhaps the most important single cause of human aggression is interpersonal provocation … Provocations include insults, slights, other forms of verbal aggression, physical aggression, interference with one's attempts to attain an important goal, and so on." In principle, most of us probably agree that "an eye for an eye makes the whole world blind." But in the heat of the moment, many people want revenge. Breaking cycles of violence between people who have traded injuries with one another in the past is one of the biggest challenges of psychology.

The principle of reciprocity appears to apply much more strongly in some cultures than in others. As we noted earlier in this module, **honor cultures** are particularly fertile ground for reciprocity. In honor cultures, powerful norms dictate that threats to one's status or worth must be readily answered. If someone insults you or one of your family members in an honor culture, that person has invited a conflict – perhaps a violent one. Thus, if someone fails to stand up to a rival – especially a bullying rival – in an honor culture, this person will often be seen as dishonorable or even pitiful. Threats must be answered, and insults and injuries must be met with "payback." Nisbett and Cohen (1996) found that men who grew up in an honor culture (the Southeastern U.S.) were more likely than men who grew up elsewhere to get angry, and to behave aggressively, when they were insulted by a stranger. The large-scale study of major league pitchers conducted by Larrick and colleagues also revealed an effect of the culture of honor. The tendency for pitchers to payback one bean ball with another was stronger than usual for pitchers who had grown up in the Southeast. This was true regardless of where the pitcher's current team happened to be located. The culture of honor is apparently learned during childhood, and then carried around for life.

Modeling

Speaking of learning, one of the *least* controversial theories of aggression is the idea that we often learn to copy aggressive behavior when we have observed other people engage in it. In fact, the only controversy is about what we should call it. The idea of copycat aggression has been dubbed modeling, social learning, emulative violence, and vicarious learning. Because Albert Bandura is the best-known advocate of this theory, and because he usually calls copycat violence **modeling**, we will use that term here. Please note, however, that modeling applies to all kinds of behavior rather than just aggressive behavior. One of the best ways to *reduce* aggressive behavior, then is to model prosocial behavior (i.e., being nice) especially as a response to provocation.

Figure 28.2

You may recall that in Module 12, we discussed a classic study of children who modeled aggressive behavior. In a variation on the study you heard about previously, Bandura, Ross, and Ross (1961) ensured that *all* the kids being studied were frustrated. They did so by showing the kids some very cool toys and then telling the kids that they could not play with them. Bandura knew that frustration could set the stage for aggression. But he also felt that whether frustrated kids behaved aggressively might be heavily influenced by what kind of behavior they had just observed in an adult model. In a control condition, kids who'd just been frustrated observed an adult who did not model any kind of aggressive behavior. In an aggressive model condition, however, the frustrated kids watched a video of an adult woman smacking down an inflatable pop-up Bobo doll (much like the one you can see in Figure 28.2). In addition to pummeling poor Bobo with a hammer, the woman threw him up in the air, kicked him forcefully, and yelled things like "Sock him in the nose!" By clicking on the link that follows, you can see a video segment of a boy who not only copied the exact behaviors of the aggressive model but also generated his own creative ways to beat up Bobo: www.youtube.com/watch?v=dmBqwWlJg8U

The boy was not alone. In Bandura's classic experiment, frustrated kids who observed the *aggressive model* were much more likely than frustrated kids who had *not* observed an aggressive model to engage in a wide range of aggressive behavior. Studies of real-world violence, including serious acts such as suicide and homicide, also reveal human tendencies to copy the aggressive behavior of others (Phillips & Carstensen, 1986). There is a sense, then, in which both suicide and homicide are socially contagious. The phrase "monkey see-monkey do," applies to a wide range of acts, both harmful and harmless. And it applies just as well to people as it does to monkeys.

Economic Inequality

In his book, *Killing the Competition*, Martin Daly (2016) argues that a powerful and frequently overlooked source of aggression – especially homicide – is **economic inequality**. Economic inequality exists in a culture or social group when some members of the group possess much more wealth than others do. This is not just about poverty. Instead, it's about the *difference* in income between the rich and the poor. It's a **wealth gap**. From a global perspective, both Denmark and the U.S. are very wealthy. But the percentage of people living below the poverty line is much higher in the United States than in Denmark. This is particularly true for childhood poverty rates. According to a 2018 policy briefing by the Organization for Economic Cooperation and Development (OECD), children in the United States are almost seven times as likely to live in poverty as are children in Denmark. Further, America's rich are much richer than Denmark's rich, and America's poor are much poorer than Denmark's poor. About 10% of Americans have no health insurance. Everyone in Denmark is guaranteed health insurance. But what does all this have to do with aggression? Here's how Daly (2016, p. 17) put it. He argued that:

> Income inequality is the single best predictor of the variability in homicide rates both between and within nations, and the reason why is evidently that greater inequality implies more intense social competition, especially among young men. However, the relationship between inequality and lethal violence is not widely appreciated, partly but not solely because the proposition that income inequality has destructive effects of *any* sort is fiercely opposed by inequality's beneficiaries.

Daly goes on to show that most murders in most nations are committed by young men – and are perpetrated disproportionately against *other* young men. And one by one, he picks apart common criticisms of the idea that inequality contributes to violence. For example, he shows that a popular indicator of income inequality (the GINI coefficient for you economists) is a much better predictor of state by state differences in homicide rates than is state by state median income. Simple poverty may matter a little, but income inequality matters a lot more. The same observation applies to nation by nation analyses of poverty vs. economic inequality. It is nations with big wealth gaps – rather than merely poor nations – that have high murder rates. In short, when there is a great deal of inequality in a culture, young men who find themselves at the bottom of the economic ladder, and who are striving for status, often compete lethally with others who are in the same unhappy boat that they are in.

But wait. If social inequality causes aggression, does that mean frustration and modeling does not? Absolutely not. Like many other social problems, aggression has many separate causes. So none of the theories of aggression we have summarized here should be seen as competing theories. Further, it's likely that some of the six factors discussed here work together to influence aggression. For example, it is possible that frustration has a larger than usual effect on aggression in honor cultures, or when economic inequality is high. Having said that, each of the forces we have identified here is powerful enough that it and it alone can be enough to fuel serious acts of aggression. If your honor has been severely challenged, you're likely to strike back even on the coolest day of the year. That, of course, is why aggression is so common. But is it more common today than it was yesterday? Most people certainly think so.

Trends in Aggressive Behavior

Aggression Is Declining

After noting many reasons why we hurt one another, we'd like to offer you some good news. We're living a less violent world than at any other time in human history. Pinker (2010) recently argued that people today are much less aggressive than people of yesteryear. As Pinker noted, all you need to do to see how aggressive people used to be is to read the fairy tales parents used to tell their children. In one old version of Rumpelstiltskin, Rumpelstiltskin becomes so angry when the queen learns his name, and prevents him from taking her child, that he physically rips himself in half. In old versions of both Little Red Riding Hood and Goldilocks, the price children pay for not following the rules is being eaten by wolves or bears.

In addition to offering many very compelling anecdotes, Pinker presents an ocean of objective evidence that violence has declined. We live in a modern world with levels of violence that are much, much lower than they used to be. This is true whether one defines violence in terms of homicide rates, forms of punishment for criminal violations, the frequency of punitive parenting practices, rates of harming animals while making motion pictures, killing others in warfare, or abortion. Pick your poison, and you'll see that the world has been getting less poisonous. Further, this is true whether you compare us with those who lived 100,000 years ago, 1,000 years ago or 100 years ago. In fact, the further back we go in human history, the more violent we used to be. The good old days would be more aptly named the gory old days.

Are We *Really* Getting Nicer

In an era of widely publicized murders and mass shootings, you may be wondering if Pinker's provocative book should be revised a little. Maybe Pinker was right when he made his point back in 2010 but dead wrong today. Roughly a decade after Pinker made his point, are things *still* getting better? They sure are. People often think violent crime is getting worse because of the availability heuristic. When violent crime does happen, it gets a *lot* of media attention. And violent events are memorable events.

This leads many people to conclude that the world is going to hell in a handbasket even when – on average – things are becoming a bit more heavenly. Consider a few findings summarized by John Gramlich (2019) of the Pew Research Center. Between 1993 and 2017, both violent crime rates and property crime rates in the U.S. dropped by about 50%. In

1993, there were 747 violent crimes per 100,000 people living in the United States. By 2017, this value had dropped to 383. Likewise, in this same period, the number of property crimes (e.g., vandalism) dropped from 4,740 to 2,363 per 100,000 people. But as Gramlich (2019) also noted, Americans consistently report that crime is getting worse and worse. In 1993, a Gallup poll showed that 83% of Americans believed that "there is more crime in the U.S. than a year ago." By 2017, this figure had dropped a bit, but 67% of Americans still believed that national crime rates were on the increase. If you still don't believe that violence is on the decline, stop watching so much TV, or cut back on your use of social media. One of the reasons so many people falsely believe the world is getting more violent is that news of murder and mayhem gets a ton of attention in all kinds of media outlets – from broadcast TV news to Twitter feeds.

Why Are We Getting Nicer?

Pinker identifies five reasons why "the better angels of our nature" have largely won out over our more aggressive impulses in modern times. The first is that in most modern cultures, violence is less often rewarded than it used to be. Now that most nations have well-developed police forces, for example, it's simply much harder than it used to be to get away with murder. From fingerprint evidence to DNA analysis and the ubiquity of smart phone videos, it's a lot harder than it used to be to hurt another person without detection.

Pinker also argues that technological developments such as dramatically increased ease of travel and internet access are shrinking the once narrow definition of "we." It would have been almost unheard of 400 years ago for anyone to conceptualize him- or herself as an Asian or Asian American. Back in the 1600s, your identity would have been something more like the "eldest son of the Kim family who lives by the three great oaks." If we both are dog lovers, or fellow members of the European Union, rather than Northern and Southern Irishmen, then we are a lot less likely to fight. As the world shrinks and people cooperate more across ancient group boundaries, we become less interested in harming each other. Pinker cites several other important reasons why we hurt each other a lot less often than we once did. Perhaps the most interesting is that feminization (i.e., the growth of female voices in daily life) has led to a cultural sea change as more and more women have gained social and political power. When only men could vote, for example, you can be sure that the voices of women – who lobby for peace and cooperation more often than men do – were heard only faintly if at all. We trust that this trend of reduced violence will continue in the future so that our grandchildren's grandchildren will find routine violence to be a rare human quirk rather than a mundane fact of life.

Questions for Critical Thinking and Discussion for Module 28

Unfortunately, there are many reasons why people behave aggressively. This chapter reviewed just six of them. Even if you have not recently observed aggression, if you are not at all frustrated, and if no one has recently harmed you, you might behave aggressively just because it is hot outside. To at least some degree, human beings surely evolved to be aggressive. On the other hand, almost all researchers who study aggression do so because they assume that if we can better understand the causes of aggression, we can more easily create a world in which aggression is minimized. In fact, as noted in this chapter, the evolutionary psychologist Steven Pinker (2010) argued that human beings have become less violent over the course of human history. This has been particularly true, Pinker argued, in the past century or so. In fact, some of the reasons Pinker identifies for why we've become less aggressive recently are consistent with the six principles examined here. Consider three questions inspired by Pinker's thesis.

According to Pinker one reason why we're becoming less violent is that violence is much less likely to be *rewarded* these days than it was in the past.

1. What two perspectives discussed in this chapter (one in the introductory section and one in the section on evolution) are highly consistent with the idea that we become less likely to behave aggressively when the *rewards* for aggression are reduced? How so? Thinking about modern vs. ancient human cultures, what roles do you think well-trained police forces and formal legal systems have played in this process? What about things like fingerprint analysis and DNA testing? What about laws that require penalties for creating an unsafe work place? Finally, what role might routine video surveillance play? Can smart phones reduce violence?

Pinker also argues that "feminization" has played a big role in modern reductions in violence. In short, he argues that the growth of female voices in modern daily life has led to a cultural sea change in attitudes about physical aggression.

2. In the U.S. in 1900, only men could vote. How was this political fact likely to have shaped decisions about declaring war, creating programs designed to reduce violence, or the passage of capital punishment laws?

Pinker also notes that we're living in an "age of reason" that has radically changed the ways in which the average person thinks. Settlers in the American prairie in the 1800s didn't read the *New Yorker*, take sociology courses, or watch documentaries about the American Civil Rights Movement. If we take the long view, at least, the value people place in reason vs. superstition has increased over time.

3. Is Pinker completely correct that reason reduces aggression? Or is the age of reason also the age of atheism? Studies consistently show that, in wealthy nations at least, people have become a lot less religious over the past few decades. Should we worry that this so-called *secular trend* will lead to increases in human violence in the coming decades? Why or why not? Looking across the globe are crimes rates higher or lower in countries where fewer people are religious? What are some limitations to using naturalistic studies to see if being more religious makes people less likely to harm others? Would it be possible to fix such methodological problems by manipulating religiosity in the lab, and then assessing the subsequent likelihood of aggressive behavior?

Multiple Choice Questions for Module 28

1. After getting a flat tire on her bicycle, and being late for work, Juneau was fired from her job as a bouncer. Juneau walked the bike home and then smashed it up with a baseball bat. According to Berkowitz's famous definition, does this bicycle-smashing behavior qualify as aggression?

    A) yes, because Juneau acted out of anger
    B) yes, because Juneau damaged an expensive piece of property
    C) no, because Juneau did not appear to harm another living being

2. In honor cultures, people often react violently to others who threaten their:

    A) status in a social hierarchy
    B) customs and attitudes
    C) religious beliefs

3. What form of aggression is common in people but unheard of in other animals?

    A) cultural aggression
    B) verbal aggression
    C) systemic aggression

4. Which of the following statements best describes gender differences in relational aggression?

    A) girls and women are much less likely than boys and men to engage in relational aggression
    B) girls and women are much more likely than boys and men to engage in relational aggression
    C) girls and women are slightly more likely than boys and men to engage in relational aggression

5. Compared with human adults, human toddlers engage in more _____ aggression.

    A) interpersonal
    B) relational
    C) physical

6. In some American cities, police officers ticket drivers for minor offenses such as broken tail lights. Those so charged are required to show up in court during the workday to defend themselves. Many poor drivers are unable to do this. When they don't show up in court, a warrant is issued for their arrest. They are eventually arrested, go to jail, and must pay large fines to get out. Cities often defend such practices by saying that they rely on them to raise much needed money. This a clear example of what kind of aggression?

    A) instrumental
    B) structural
    C) economic

7. High temperatures appear to increase rates of:

    A) angry aggression
    B) instrumental aggression
    C) structural aggression

8. According to the frustration-aggression hypothesis, if you block a person's goals, this is likely to lead the frustrated person to engage in:

    A) instrumental aggression
    B) symbolic aggression
    C) angry aggression

9. Which societal and environmental factor seems to be the best predictor of rates of violence in a particular region?

    A) poverty
    B) economic inequality
    C) unemployment

10. The modern version of the frustration-aggression hypothesis states that:

    A) frustration often activates "fight or flight," which can lead to aggression
    B) frustration usually leads to anger, which often leads to aggression
    C) frustration promotes physical but not verbal aggression

11. Research suggests that hot temperatures:

    A) increase both angry and instrumental aggression
    B) increase instrumental aggression but not angry aggression
    C) increase angry aggression but not instrumental aggression

12. According to evolutionary psychologist Steven Pinker, author of "*The Better Angels of Our Nature*:"

    A) violence in human beings has declined radically over the centuries, and especially so in recent decades
    B) day to day violence has declined but extreme acts of violence (e.g., terrorism) have become more common
    C) here has been no decline in violence, despite many efforts to reduce it (because violence is in our genes)

Answer Key: 1C, 2A, 3B, 4C, 5C, 6A, 7A, 8C, 9B, 10B, 11C, 12A

References

Anderson, C. A. (1987). Temperature and aggression: Effects on quarterly, yearly, and city rates of violent and nonviolent crime. *Journal of Personality and Social Psychology, 52*(6), 1161–1173.

Anderson, C.A., & Bushman, B.J. (2002). Human aggression. *Annual Review of Psychology, 53,* 27–51.

Azrin, N. H., Rubin, H. B., & Hutchinson, R. R. (1968). Biting attack by rats in response to aversive shock. *Journal of the Experimental Analysis of Behavior, 11,* 633–639. doi:10.1901/jeab.1968.11-633

Bandura, A., Ross, D., & Ross, S. A. (1961). Transmission of aggression through imitation of aggressive models. *Journal of Abnormal and Social Psychology, 63,* 575–582.

Berkowitz, L. (1981). The concept of aggression. In P. E. Brain & D. Benton (Eds.), *Multidisciplinary approaches to aggression research* (pp. 3–15). Amsterdam and New York: Elsevier and North-Holland.

Berkowitz, L. (1989). Frustration-aggression hypothesis: Examination and reformulation. *Psychological Bulletin, 106,* 59–73.

Berkowitz, L. (1990). On the formation and regulation of anger and aggression: A cognitive neo-associationistic analysis. *American Psychologist, 45,* 494–503.

Daly, M. (2016). *Killing the competition: Economic inequality and homicide.* New Brunswick, NJ: Transaction Publishers.

Dawkins, R. (1976). *The selfish gene.* Oxford: Oxford University Press.

Dill, J., & Anderson, C. A. (1995). Effects of justified and unjustified frustration on aggression. *Aggressive Behavior, 21,* 359–369.

Dollard, J., Doob, L. W., Miller, N. E., Mowrer, O. H., & Sears, R. R. (1939). *Frustration and aggression.* New Haven, CT: Yale University Freer.

Gladwell, M. (2008). *Outliers: The story of success.* New York: Little, Brown and Company.

Gramlich, J. (2019). 5 facts about crime in the U.S. Retrieved July 2019 from the Pew Research Center website at www.pewresearch.org/fact-tank

Kenrick, D. T., & MacFarlane, S. W. (1986). Ambient temperature and horn honking: A field study of the heat/aggression relationship. *Environment and Behavior, 18,* 179–191.

Larrick, R. P., Timmerman, T. A., Carton, A. M., & Abrevaya, J. (2014). Temper, temperature, and temptation: Heat- related retaliation in baseball. *Psychological Science, 22,* 423–428.

Nisbett, R. E., & Cohen, D. (1996). *Culture of honor: The psychology of violence in the South.* Boulder, CO: Westview Press.

Ostrov, J. M., Kamper, K. E., Hart, E. J., Godleski, S. A., & Blakely-McClure, S. J. (2014). A gender-balanced approach to the study of peer victimization and aggression subtypes in early childhood. *Development and Psychopathology, 26,* 575–587.

Pelham, B. W. (2017). *Evolutionary psychology: Genes, environments, and time.* London: Palgrave-MacMillan.

Phillips, D. P., & Carstensen, L. L. (1986). Clustering of teenage suicides after television news stories about suicide. *New England Journal of Medicine, 315,* 685–689.

Pinker, S. (2010). *Better angels of our nature: Why violence has declined.* Westminster, London, UK: Penguin Books.

Reifman, A. S., Larrick, R. P., & Fein, S. (1991). Temper and temperature on the diamond: The heat-aggression relationship in Major League Baseball. *Personality and Social Psychology Bulletin, 17,* 580–585.

Module 29
Is There an "I" in Altruism?
Human Prosocial Behavior

About 25 years ago, your first author, Brett, received a free five-day vacation to Hawaii. Well, s*ort of.* Brett's boss Will required him to work in Hawaii for two of the five days, but in addition to paying Brett well for the work, Will paid all his expenses for all five days. This included the cost of bringing Brett's dear friend Joanne. ("Dear friend Joanne" sounds a lot better than "his wife at the time," doesn't it? Yeah, let's go with that.) It was a sweet deal – especially for Joanne. On the days when Brett was working, she hung out on a gorgeous beach – slowly sipping mai tais. On the days when Brett *wasn't* working, she hung out on a gorgeous beach – slowly sipping mai tais. On his days off, Brett, too, had his share of mai tais in the evenings. But he spent his mornings hiking and kayaking, both of which were Joanne's idea of torture rather than of paradise.

Brett came to agree with Joanne about the kayaking part. On his second kayaking trip, he had only been out a few minutes when a wave the size of Kansas City took him out. The huge wave was followed by several others, and he was positive he was going to drown. He had lost his kayak after that first hit, and although he frantically searched for it whenever he came up for air, he was unable to find it. Did we mention that Brett is a *really* horrible swimmer?

To make matters worse, he'd been pulled into a sharp coral reef, which roughed him up a lot until he escaped that additional danger. He couldn't have been more than a few hundred meters off shore, but he was unsure of whether he could swim back given the conditions. At one point, he saw a couple on a jet ski – who'd obviously been spared by the giant waves. He wasn't shy about asking for help. "I'm drowning!" he yelled. He wasn't *sure* he was drowning *at that moment*, but he wasn't taking any chances. "He's got a life jacket. He'll be OK," Brett heard the jet ski driver say. They sped away, presumably anxious to get back to their jobs serving mai tais to Brett's dear friend Joanne.

Eventually, a teenage girl on a kayak made her way to him. She said she had seen part of what happened and had come out as soon as she felt it was safe. She had towed an empty kayak behind her, and she offered it to him. Brett gladly accepted it, and awkwardly boarded it in the rough water. He then paddled back to shore. He'd never been so glad to be on dry land.

Both Will's decision to send Brett to Hawaii and this teenager's rescue mission qualify as examples of prosocial behavior. If the teenager had gone further and had sacrificed her own life to save Brett's life, this puzzling behavior, too, would have qualified as pro-social behavior. **Prosocial behavior** is simply behavior that benefits another person, period. But within that broad category of good deeds, researchers make some very important distinctions. The most interesting distinction is called altruism. Altruism refers to the noblest category of good deeds. To paraphrase experts such as Daniel Batson (2008), **altruism** is prosocial behavior that is *also* voluntary, costly to the doer, and performed without expecting any reward. Whereas Will's generous offer to pay for Brett's trip was prosocial behavior, he also turned a profit from Brett's work. In contrast, we believe the young kayaker's behavior qualified as true altruism. No one forced her to help Brett, there was a serious risk to her of so doing, and she seems to have expected nothing at all in return for her good deed. We hope you see the difference. Prosocial behaviors happen constantly. They're a dime a dozen. Don't get us wrong, prosocial behaviors are wonderful. They make the world a better place, and they deserve a heartfelt thank you. Altruism, however, is the crown jewel of helping. It deserves something more like a purple heart (that's a medal received for being shot in the line of military duty).

There are many examples of altruism that are more dramatic than the unselfish behavior of the kayaker. People dive into freezing bodies of water or dash into burning buildings hoping to save others, and some would-be heroes never make it out alive (Marsh, 2017). This module focuses on prosocial behavior and altruism, with an emphasis on how altruism could be possible at all if evolution always favors genes that promote survival. But before we address the question of whether any form of altruism is possible, we'll need to discriminate the most and least controversial forms of altruism. As we hope you'll see, these varieties of altruism have different motivational origins, and they operate by means of different mechanisms. So just as aggression has many causes, prosocial behavior and altruism have many causes.

Types of Altruism

Kin Selection

In his classic book, *The Selfish Gene* (1976), Richard Dawkins argued that the strictest form of altruism is evolutionarily implausible. Dawkins argued that the "selfish gene" is the primary unit of evolution. Individual organisms never survive for very long in the grand scheme of things, but genes that strongly promote survival can be practically immortal. Dawkins conceded that certain kinds of altruism make perfect sense. For example, kin selection is an evolutionarily sensible form of altruism. **Kin selection** refers to costly helping behavior directed at one of your genetic relatives (Hamilton, 1964a, 1964b; Trivers, 1971). The more closely related you are, the more it is the case that helping the relative is practically like helping yourself. So if a gene or set of genes nudges us toward helping a close relative, *with whom we share many genes*, that gene has a good chance of surviving. Kin selection is not controversial. As Dawkins (1976) put it:

> The truth is that all examples of child protection and parental care, and all associated bodily organs, milk secreting glands, kangaroo pouches, and so on, are examples of the working in nature of the kin-selection principle.

Reciprocal Altruism

In addition to kin selection, there's a second evolutionarily plausible way in which a weak form of altruism can happen. There are quite a few species of social mammals who seem to borrow from – and then later repay – their neighbors. This give-and-take process is known as **reciprocal altruism**, which means helping another animal who then *repays the favor* in the future. The part about the future is important. Trading favors in the immediate present ("scratching my back *while* I scratch yours") is known as **mutualism** (Brosnan & de Waal, 2002), and it's not as impressive as reciprocal altruism. Mutualism doesn't require any kind of mental scorekeeping, and it usually poses little or no risk to either party. Reciprocal altruism has been documented in several mammals, including mammals that you probably do not consider very cute and cuddly. A study of vampire bats by DeNault and McFarlane (1995) showed that vampire bats often share food with one another, by regurgitating a portion of a night's blood meal to a cave-mate who had the misfortune of finding no blood that night. Because vampire bats can only go two to three days without food before starving, genes that promote reciprocal altruism in vampire bats are not just advantageous; they might be a necessity. Furthermore, a large longitudinal study of vampire bats by Carter and Wilkinson (2013) showed that over the course of many months, the best predictor of whether a potential bat donor shared blood with a hungry potential bat recipient was *not* genetic-relatedness. Genetic-relatedness did matter, by the way, but the strongest predictor of sharing blood with a hungry cave-mate was how often that bat had shared blood with you in the past. Bats also "traded" grooming for blood. If a bat had groomed another bat repeatedly in the past, she was more likely to receive a repayment of blood in the future. So if a vampire bat ever asks you for a loan, please help her out. She's good for it.

As primatologist Frans de Waal (1997) has documented, many primates readily engage in reciprocal altruism. In a study of captive chimpanzees, de Waal kept careful track in the morning of how much time one chimp, say Maxine, spontaneously spent grooming another, say Audrey. In case we haven't clarified this yet, primates *love* to be groomed. It feels good, and it keeps ticks and other annoying parasites out of your hair. Later in the day, de Waal gave all the Audreys (the chimps who had or had not received a lot of grooming from the Maxines), a delicious bundle of leaves, sometimes with a nice 2011 Napa Valley merlot. The more time Maxine had spent grooming Audrey that morning, the more of the leaves Audrey usually shared with Maxine that afternoon. Furthermore, this generosity wasn't just based on being in a good mood. Well-groomed chimps didn't share more than usual with just any chimp – only with the ones that had done the grooming.

Reciprocal Altruism in People

Reciprocal altruism is also extremely common in people. We are good at keeping track of who has helped us in the past, and we often feel compelled to pay back past favors. In fact, both the sociologist George Homans (1958) and the social psychologists John Thibaut and Harold Kelley (1959) developed elaborate and influential **social exchange theories**. These theories share the assumption that we keep track of what others have done for us and carefully compare this with what we have done for them. Paying back favors is both powerful and mundane. Let's consider just one concrete example. Willer, Sharkey, and Frey (2012) wanted to see if reciprocity would influence people's behavior in a "highly structured group environment ... in which reciprocity does not clearly serve individual or group interests." The environment they chose is NBA basketball, and one routine way in which players do favors for one another on the court is referred to as an **assist** – passing the ball to a teammate so he or she can take a high percentage shot. There is nothing irrational about assists. They help teams win championships. But logically speaking, the fact that I gave you an assist earlier in the game should *not* make you more likely than usual to give me an assist later in the same game. Offensive players should always try to get the ball to the person who happens to be in the best position to take a high percentage shot. But Willer et al. (2012) found that NBA players *did* pay back assists. Further, they paid them back specifically to the teammate(s) who had given them assists earlier in the game (rather than just "paying it forward" by becoming a more frequent assist-giver). Finally, this tendency to pay back assists was strongest shortly after a player had just received an assist. Like the tendency to pay back other kinds of favors, the payback of an assist faded with increased time since the last assist was received.

Unscrupulous salespeople, con artists, and parents often realize the power of reciprocity, and they've learned to use it to their own advantage (Cialdini, 1993). Consider sales. Many salespeople know that one of the best ways to get potential customers to buy things they don't need is to do the potential customers a small favor. This compliance technique comes in many flavors. One is the free sample technique, which involves giving a consumer a "free" sample of a food, material good, or service – with the goal of getting the person to purchase the real thing. The smiling woman at the mall who offers you a free piece of chicken on a toothpick knows that if you accept the free sample, you'll feel at least a small compulsion to purchase a whole meal – even if your free sample of Genera Tso's chicken was only so-so. Along the same lines, consider the real reason the Mazda salesman offered you a bottle of Coke and a hot dog while you were waiting for Lenny to pull the new car around for a test drive. It was *not* that he was worried about you dying of thirst or hunger before you decided to buy a new car. Instead, he was doing you a favor. Unless you were thoughtful enough to bring a Sprite and a hot dog as a gift for the salesman, you were going to feel some pressure to *pay this favor back*. As any sales expert could tell you, that payback involves Mustangs or pickups more often than it involves mustard or ketchup. We'd never fall for such transparent tricks if we weren't powerfully programmed to feel that we should always pay back favors. Reciprocal altruism is real. And salespeople know how to exploit it.

Empathy and True Altruism

Empathy Promotes True Altruism

We're drifting ever closer to the altruistic kayaker, but we're not there yet. There appears to be another route to altruism, and this is the kind that evolutionary psychologists have had a harder time accepting. In our view, the most extreme forms of altruism, involve a uniquely social, culturally universal *emotion* called **empathy**. When we experience true empathy for another person, including a person we just met, we often treat the person as if he or she were a member of the family – who had recently done us many favors! Before we delve too deeply into the relation between empathy and altruism, we should briefly note that different researchers have used the word "empathy" somewhat differently. When we use the term **empathy** in this module, we're referring to what is more technically known as empathic concern (Marsh, 2017). When you have **empathic concern** for another person, you can feel that person's pain – but you aren't so freaked out by the pain that you fall apart. The fabled Good Samaritan, who rescued a robbery victim that others overlooked and ignored, presumably experienced empathic concern for the beaten-up stranger he came across on his travels. The person who has done the most to help us understand empathic concern is social psychologist Daniel Batson.

Figure 29.1
Altruism. What you see here is surely heroic – but it doesn't necessarily qualify as altruistic. This is because even very *costly* forms of helping only qualify as altruism if they are also *voluntary* and if those who do the good deeds also do so without anticipating any kind of *reward*. In other words, the bar for altruism is so high that sometimes you can't even clear it with a helicopter.

Photo by Neil Thomas.

In a classic experiment by Batson, Duncan, Ackerman, Buckley, and Birch (1981), participants learned that they'd be playing the role of observer while another participant, Elaine, performed a task requiring her to endure ten mild electric shocks. Before any of the shocking happened, though, the experimenters manipulated how much the participants felt empathy for Elaine. They did so by informing participants that Elaine was very much like them (which is known to promote empathy) or that Elaine was very different from them (which is known to reduce empathy). This empathy manipulation proved to be very telling.

As you've probably guessed by now, Elaine was an actress playing the part rather than a real participant – so no Elaines were harmed in the making of this research paper. In fact, very often, Elaines were helped. Here's how. After receiving a couple of electric shocks, Elaine asked for a break and explained to the experimenter that the shocks were very hard for her to take. As it turns out, Elaine had been badly shocked – by an electric fence – as a child, giving her a bit of a shock phobia. But Elaine was a trooper. She asked for a glass of water, and she said she was willing to see if she could make it through the eight remaining electric shocks.

The experimenter was reluctant to put poor Elaine through this, but he didn't want to have to cancel the experiment. After puzzling over the dilemma, the experimenter happened on an idea. If by any chance the observer participant could trade places with Elaine, she could play the role of observer, and the experiment wouldn't be ruined. Of course, this was a lot to ask, and so the experimenter made it clear that this decision to help was totally up to the real participant. But there was a little more to the experiment than this. First, some participants learned that if they couldn't trade places the experimenter would cancel the study, and they would be free to go, earning full credit for their partial participation. Woo hoo! Everyone loves free credit. Other participants learned, however, that if they couldn't trade places, they would have to stay and continue to watch poor Elaine suffer. Assuming that none of these participants would have enjoyed watching Elaine suffer, these participants faced a big cost of not helping. Notice that the free credit option offered to some participants made it very easy for them to escape the obligation of helping. For participants who were informed that Elaine was very different from them – and thus were less likely to empathize with her – this manipulation of cost had a big effect. More than 60% of those told they'd have to watch Elaine suffer agreed to take her place. In contrast, when easy escape was an option, only 20% of participants offered to take her place. In fact, we suspect that many of them just sped off on their jet skis.

People can be so selfish. But they can also be so helpful. Remember that this study was about empathy and helping. Recall that the researchers also informed some participants that they had a lot in common with Elaine. This simple empathy manipulation had a huge effect. People who felt empathy for Elaine almost always helped her. In fact, among those led to feel empathy for Elaine, 90% offered to take the shocks, even when it would have been very easy for them to walk away with full credit. The option to be selfish isn't as big a temptation when you can feel a victim's pain. Findings such as these support Daniel Batson's once controversial **empathy-altruism model**. In a nutshell, this model says that experiencing true empathy for another person, putting yourself in his or her emotional shoes, often promotes true altruism, even for a complete stranger.

It's no secret that some people are more empathic than others, and there is now strong evidence supporting another prediction of Batson's empathy-altruism model. People who are chronically more empathic should be chronically more altruistic. Marsh and colleagues (2014) conducted a nice test of this idea. Taking advantage of the modern neuroimaging method known as *fMRI*, they compared the brains of 19 people who had donated a kidney with the brains of a matched set of 20 controls (non-donors). We mentioned fMRIs much earlier in this text. So, in case the term fMRI (that's functional magnetic resonance imaging) is not ringing any bells, let us assure you that no altruists were harmed in the making of this brain research. This technology allows researchers to see what's happening in a living person's brain based on indirect, high-tech (and very safe) measurements of blood flow to different regions of the brain. The only risk of getting an fMRI is a little claustrophobia from laying inside a large tube. It's worth noting, by the way, that Marsh and colleagues knew where to look. They already knew, that is, that the right amygdala plays a crucial role in feeling negative emotions, especially fear and sadness. Compared with the rest of us, the kidney donors had larger right amygdalae. Marsh and colleagues also found that the right amygdalae of the kidney donors became especially active when these altruists were asked to view fearful expressions in strangers. These findings suggest that true altruism in human beings may be as plain as the nose on your face. It's just that it's sitting an inch or so behind it, and a little to your right.

Clever studies such as these may never completely resolve the heated debate about whether people ever engage in true altruism (see Maner et al., 2002, for a dissenting opinion). But in combination with many other laboratory and field studies, the weight of the recent neuroscientific evidence has begun to suggest that true altruism isn't nearly as evolutionarily puzzling as many once believed. And people do not appear to be the only species to engage in unselfish helping. Nobuya Sato and colleagues (2015) found that rats quickly come to the aid of a cage-mate who appears to be at risk for drowning. What's more, some of the potential rat rescuers in Sato et al.'s main study had recently been dropped themselves into the same "drowning pool" in which their cage-mate was trapped. These rats were even quicker than rats who had never been threatened with drowning to offer help to a cage-mate. Rats seem to be more likely than usual to help a cage-mate when they have walked a mile (or is it, swum?) in that other rat's moccasins.

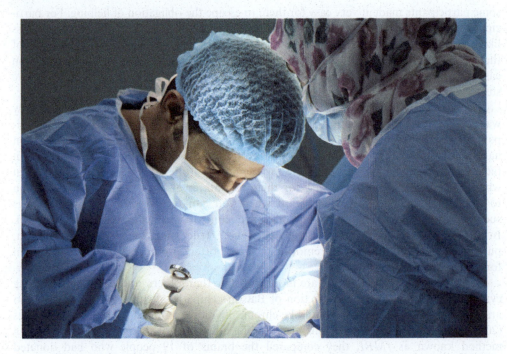

Figure 29.2 Have you ever been to the hospital to have a major organ removed – even though you were perfectly heathy? We're guessing you have *not* – unless you happen to be a living kidney donor. Abigail Marsh and colleagues (2014) studied the brains of living kidney donors – people who had one of their kidneys removed so it could be given to a complete stranger who was in need of a kidney transplant. The brains of the kidney donors were measurably different than the brains of a group of closely matched non-donors. The kidney donors had larger than usual right amygdalae. Further, a brain imaging study showed that their right amygdalae were also highly responsive to fearful human faces.

Photo courtesy of Jafar Ahmed.

A Little Help Here, Little Guys

A very different line of evidence for true altruism comes from research by Warneken and colleagues. They argue that if we evolved to be altruistic, even toddlers who can barely speak – who are unlikely to have been socialized to put the needs of others ahead of their own – might help others. One trick, though, might be making sure toddlers *understand* that help is really needed (recall that toddlers are very concrete thinkers who respond to their immediate physical worlds). A second trick is making sure toddlers are able to do something to help in the first place. One implication of Warneken's (in press) research (see also Warneken & Tomasello, 2006) is that researchers in technologically advanced countries may have underestimated children's natural desire to help simply because it's so unusual for kids to be *able* to help in a modern world. We know that we rarely ask toddlers for their help when we have problems with Microsoft Word or advanced statistical software (which we use often in our jobs). In contrast, Warneken argues that in tribal cultures and traditional farming cultures, virtually all children routinely help the adults in their small social groups, especially their extended families. Twenty thousand years ago, six-year-olds could not track a mastodon or start a fire, but they could easily stick close to their caregivers and offer to throw a few sticks on the fire. Any amount of help children could offer, however small, would certainly promote their own survival. Fetching firewood, delivering a simple message, or babysitting one's much younger siblings, for example, could free up one's adult caregivers to do the heavy lifting or skilled labor for which children themselves were not yet well suited.

In keeping with the idea that children may be naturally predisposed to help – even in the absence of any rewards – Warneken (in press) showed that toddlers spontaneously helped an adult stranger as long as the need for help was clear (see also Svetlova, Nichols, & Brownell, 2010). Just as telling, toddlers did *not* help an adult stranger when it was clear that help was unnecessary (e.g., when the adult *discarded* an item rather than accidentally dropping it). Warneken and Tomasello (2006) looked at several specific forms of toddler helping (e.g., helping an adult deal with a physical obstacle, helping the adult retrieve a dropped object). They found that toddlers were especially likely to help an adult stranger when the stranger had dropped a useful object and was actively trying to reach it. Warneken concluded that we are a naturally helpful species. In further support of this view, Lara Aknin, Elizabeth Dunn, and colleagues have shown that being helpful makes us feel happy. More specifically, they've found that both adults and toddlers seem to experience true happiness after giving something to another person (Aknin, Hamlin, & Dunn, 2012; Dunn, Aknin, & Norton, 2008). For example, blind raters reported that toddlers looked more delighted after giving one of their own treats (a coveted Goldfish cracker) to a puppet than they did after receiving eight of these delicious treats themselves.

Helping Others is Intrinsically Rewarding

This leads us to what may be the strongest evidence that people are inherently helpful – at least under the right conditions. This hypothesis does not yet seem to have a name, by the way, and so we'll call it the **helping-is-rewarding hypothesis.** Neuroscientists such as Naomi Eisenberger and Matt Lieberman are fans of this hypothesis. They've carefully studied the neurological basis of both pain and pleasure. In study after study, they've found that human beings (a) truly crave the acceptance of others, (b) experience pleasure when they see good things happen to deserving others, and (c) experience pleasure when they help others, even when it is at their own expense. They had people (whose brains were being scanned via fMRI) play *Cyberball* with two other players (Eisenberger, Lieberman, & Williams, 2003). *Cyberball* is a simple virtual ball-passing game. You just pass the ball to the avatar of one of two other people – who are both playing the game with you on-line. The person controlling that avatar either passes the ball back to you or passes it to the third player. That's it. It's worth adding, though, that participants who played *Cyberball* in this study did *not* think they were taking part in a study of social rejection. Instead, they thought they were helping these neuroscientists understand "how brains coordinate with one another to perform even simple tasks like ball tossing" (Lieberman, 2013).

In fact, there were no other on-line *Cyberball* players, just the one real participant and a computer program that made sure two fake virtual players always threw the ball to the real person at first but eventually iced the person out – by exclusively throwing the ball back and forth to each other. Even in this *really* simple on-line game – that people thought they were playing with complete strangers – people still reported being hurt by rejection. Eisenberger and colleagues have the brain scans to prove this social pain was real. While participants were being rejected, their brain scans showed a distinctive pattern of activation (in the dorsal anterior cingulate cortex) that is a known signature of *physical* pain. In a follow-up study, Eisenberger, Lieberman, and their colleagues repeated the *Cyberball* experiment but had some participants take Tylenol every day for three weeks prior to taking part in it. Other participants took a placebo that they only thought was Tylenol. The result: Tylenol eradicated the social pain that normally stems from rejection in much the same way that it eradicates physical pain. We are wired to desire social acceptance.

Of course, feeling pain in the wake of social rejection is not the same as being inherently *helpful*. But in his provocative book *Social*, Lieberman (2013) argues that it is precisely because we are such hyper-social creatures that we have been wired by evolution to feel pleasure when we see good things happen to needy or deserving others. This can even be the case when others benefit at our own expense, and it can motivate us to be truly altruistic. For example, Tricomi and colleagues (2010) scanned the brains of participants who played a game of chance with another participant. Early in the game participants got very lucky and won 50 dollars. The other participant got very *un*lucky and won absolutely nothing. Unsurprisingly, winning 50 dollars produced activity in areas of participants' brains known to be associated with reward. Surprisingly, there was even *more* activity in these reward regions on later trials of the game, when the *other player* finally won some money, even though it was always at people's own expense.

Another example of how helping can be inherently rewarding comes from a brain imaging study by Jorge Moll and colleagues (2006). These researchers measured activity in the reward regions of the brain (a) while people had the chance to accept some cash or (b) while they had a chance to donate some of their cash to charities. When people were simply asked if they wished to receive five dollars with no consequences for any charity, people were happy to accept the gift. Sure enough, the fMRI scanner showed that getting paid reliably lit up the brain's reward regions. But these same reward regions lit up even *more* brightly when participants had the chance to accept some money while also giving some of their money to a charity. For example, giving up two dollars so that a charity would receive five dollars led to stronger signals of reward than simply receiving five dollars. Lieberman (2013) reviews many other studies like this one – which all use brain imaging techniques to see what is happening in the brain's reward regions when people help others. People truly feel reward, for example, when they are able to soothe loved ones who are in pain (by touching their arms). Teenagers feel reward when they are able to give some of their winnings in an experimental game to other members of their own families (knowing these family members will not be allowed to give it back, by the way). Lieberman (2013, p. 90) summarized neuroscientific studies such as these very succinctly, "Our supposedly selfish reward system seems to like giving more than receiving." These modern neuroimaging studies – in combination with both classic and modern laboratory research on extreme generosity – strongly suggest that the hyper-social species known as human beings is capable of true altruism. The secret to a happier human future may be finding clever ways to nurture and harness the natural human tendency to do good.

Back to the Good Samaritan

In contrast to all this modern evidence that people are inherently helpful, there is a lot of classic evidence that might seem to suggest that most people heartlessly ignore the suffering of strangers. The Good Samaritan was clearly heroic. But why were there no

"Good Samaritans" in Queens, New York, in 1964? This is when Kitty Genovese returned home at 3 a.m. In the courtyard by her apartment, Kitty was brutally attacked by a guy with a knife. She screamed loudly, waking many of her neighbors (at least 38 of them). In fact, she screamed for help repeatedly for half an hour. No one did anything to stop the attack. There is some controversy about whether the police were called, but there is no debate that Kitty Genovese fought for her life while many people did nothing. Her attacker eventually killed her. The media took a very negative view of this tragedy. As you can see in Figure 29.3, reporters wrote headlines such as "Screams for Help Ignored" (Myers, 2013). Even many social scientists argued that Kitty Genovese's story uncovered the callousness of human nature.

But John Darley and Bibb Latané begged to differ. These two social psychologists began a program of research that showed that people often fail to help others not because people are inherently callous but because *powerful situations* often get in the way of helping in an emergency. Darley and Latané conducted numerous studies of the barriers to helping those in distress. In the interest of space, we'll focus mainly on just one of their findings – one they refer to as bystander intervention. **Bystander intervention** refers specifically to helping a stranger during an emergency. The Good Samaritan certainly engaged in bystander intervention. Why didn't any of Kitty Genovese's neighbors do so?

Darley and Latané did *not* argue that everyone is a hero. But they noted people in serious trouble may sometimes be better off if only one person – rather than many – observes their plight. To paraphrase Darley and Latané, the **bystander effect** is the finding that people are less likely to help, and slower to help, when *other people* are present. Thus, Kitty Genovese might have been better off if only one person had witnessed her screams. But can five bystanders really be less helpful than one? Darley and Latané (1968) showed that the answer is yes. For example, in an experiment that was ostensibly designed to study communication, participants were asked to take part in a group discussion. To protect people's privacy (so participants were told) each person in the communication study would talk to all of the others (who were in different booths) via an intercom. People took part in groups that they thought included two, three, or six people. In a group of two members, then, each participant communicated with just one stranger. In a group of six, participants thought they were communicating with five strangers. And they further believed that everyone in the group could hear everything that anyone said. Before any of the conversations began, participants were told that it was very important that they stay in their booths. After all, leaving the booth would interrupt the conversation. It might also compromise everyone's anonymity.

Figure 29.3
After the brutal murder of Kitty Genovese in Queens, New York in 1964, many people, including some social scientists, argued that human beings are inherently callous and selfish. But John Darley and Bibb Latané concluded, instead, that we need to better understand the conditions and social motivations that promote or inhibit helping strangers who are in serious trouble. They dubbed helping in such situations bystander intervention.

So this all began as a mundane study of communication. But after some introductions and some mundane chatting, one of the fake participants (the victim) seemed to have a seizure. Through the intercom, each real participant heard a scary and convincing recording: "I-er-um-I think I–I need-er-if-if could-er-er-somebody er-er-er-er-er-er-er give me a little-er give me a little *help* here because-er-I-er-I'm-er-er-h-h-having a-a-a real problem ..." By the way, the victim had mentioned during the introductions that he suffered from seizures. Nobody thought this was a prank. It's also important to note that participants believed that the *experimenter* could not hear the conversation. This was in keeping with the cover story that everyone's privacy was being carefully guarded. So, did participants ruin the study by leaving their booths to seek out help for the seizure victim? It depended on the bystander effect. As you can see in Figure 29.4, 85% of the participants who thought they were the only bystander left their booths very quickly to seek help for the victim. But even the presence of one other bystander dropped helping to a rate of 62%. And when participants thought there were four other bystanders who all heard what they heard, rates of helping dropped further to just 31%. This bystander effect appears to be robust in all kinds of emergencies. In fact, even when people *themselves* seem to be at risk of being harmed (when fake smoke is pouring into the room in which participants themselves are seated), the presence of other bystanders inhibits people from taking action to deal with the emergency.

Why the bystander effect? There are several reasons Two of the more important ones are (a) diffusion of responsibility and (b) evaluation apprehension. **Diffusion of responsibility** refers to the fact that if you are the only person observing an emergency, the blame for any failure to act falls solely on your shoulders. Conversely, if other observers are also present, your portion of any blame for inaction now becomes fractional rather than complete. If you and nine others *all* did nothing, you bear only 10% of the blame. At least that's how most people seem to think about it. Another important reason behind the bystander effect is evaluation apprehension. **Evaluation apprehension** refers to the fear of embarrassing ourselves in front of other people if we act. After all, if no one else is acting, perhaps it means action is inappropriate. If you start giving CPR to a stranger who was taking a nap rather than lying unconscious, that's unlikely to end well. Darley and Latané suggest that many emergencies are highly ambiguous. It's not always clear if help is truly needed – or whether you are the best person to jump in and start helping

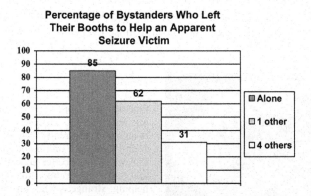

Figure 29.4 The Bystander Effect: People were much less likely to get out of their seats to help a person who seemed to be having a seizure when they believed that other people (other bystanders) who could have conceivably helped were present during the emergency. The presence of other bystanders leads a lot of people to just, well, *stand by* and do nothing.

(Darley, Teger, & Lewis, 1973). Ironically then, one of the main reasons why we fail to help others during emergencies is because we are such highly social creatures that we care deeply about what total strangers think about us. We hope it's clear that a failure to help in emergencies does not necessarily reflect callousness. In fact, people often want to help but are paralyzed by uncertainty. The cure for that, then, may be clarity. Consider the classic study of Elaine. Research on the bystander effect suggests that empathy may have received a little nudge in this classic experiment by *concentrating* responsibility rather than diffusing it. Participants who watched Elaine suffer knew very well that they and they alone were the only ones who could trade places with her. So, if you ever become the victim in a serious emergency, please *don't* yell "Somebody please help me!" Instead, yell something more like, "*You*, the guy in the Chicago Cubs cap, please help me!" (Wegner & Schaefer, 1978). It would help even more, of course, if you happen to be wearing a Chicago Cubs cap yourself.

Critical Thinking and Group Discussion Activity for Module 29

A recent example of research on prosocial behavior builds on the idea of the collective self-concept. Consider the following measure based on research on the self, close relationships, and groups.

In the image you see in Figure 29.5, replace "Group" with "The Other Students at My College." Now choose the image in this figure that best describes your feelings about your fellow students (if you've been to more than one college, pick your favorite). OK, we hope that was easy. Now we have a much tougher question. This question is a variation on the classic philosophical problem known as the *trolley problem* (Foot, 1967). Here's *our* version of the problem: A maniac has tied five randomly chosen students at your college to a trolley track. Let's assume you do *not* personally know any of these five students. Unfortunately, the engineer who is driving the trolley has no idea that the trolley is headed toward the five students. You can stop the trolley from running over and killing five of your fellow students by jumping in front of the trolley yourself (about 30 meters before it would get to those students). Here's the tough question. Would you jump in front of the trolley, or would you allow five of your fellow students to die? Please answer this question quickly, without giving it too much thought. After all, this is a split-second (or maybe we should say *splat*-second) decision.

Research on *identity fusion* ("a visceral sense of oneness with the group") has asked the members of many different groups to answer both the identity fusion (circles) question and the trolley question (always directed at the appropriate group in question, of course). Studies show that people who report very high levels of identity fusion for a specific group are more likely than people who report low levels of identity fusion for that group to say they'd give up their own lives to save five members of the group. For

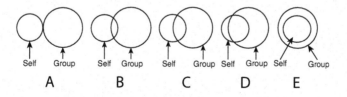

Figure 29.5 Swann, Gómez, Seyle, Morales, and Huici's (2009) identity fusion scale is designed to measure how deeply connected people feel to specific groups.

example, Swann et al. (2014) asked Spaniards to report their level of identity fusion for their fellow Spaniards. That's a group of 47 million people, by the way. Those who reported being highly fused to their fellow Spaniards were much more likely than those who said they were *not* so strongly fused to say they'd jump in front of the trolley.

1. Did you say you'd take a dive in front of the trolley for your fellow college students? Why or why not? What are some of the advantages and disadvantages of this research strategy? For example, how easy would it be to get these data from 100 students at your school? How hard would it be to know for sure if students would really do in daily life what they said they'd do in this hypothetical scenario?
2. If we replaced "My Parents and Siblings" with the word "Group," would this change your answer? Do any differences in your answers to the college question and the family question support research on identity fusion? Or do they conflict with it?

Multiple Choice Questions for Module 29: Prosocial Behavior and Altruism

1. In addition to being voluntary and costly to the helper, helping behavior that qualifies as *altruism* must also have what feature?

   A) it must be considered desirable by the members of one's culture
   B) it must be done without any expectation of reward
   C) it must put the life of the helping person at risk

2. Which happens more often, prosocial behavior or altruism?

   A) altruism happens more often
   B) prosocial behavior happens more often
   C) they happen with equal frequency because they mean the same thing

3. Bubba often helps his sister Rose (a genetic relative) without giving it any thought. But he's very reluctant to help equally needy strangers. What evolutionary theory does this pattern support?

   A) family survival theory
   B) kin selection
   C) reciprocal altruism

4. LaDonna loaned José her car this week because she recalled that José brought her dinner many times last month, when she was very sick. What evolutionary theory of helping does this support?

   A) reciprocal altruism
   B) mutualism
   C) personal exchange theory

5. The free sample technique for getting others to do you favors seems to work because of the powerful human tendency to obey the rule(s) of:

   A) maximizing personal gain
   B) economic maximization
   C) social exchange theories

6. Which emotional state seems to be a big driver of truly exceptional forms of helping, such as taking on the pain of another person – or risking one's own safety to help another person?

   A) love
   B) empathy
   C) inspiration

7. Daniel Batson's classic study of Elaine showed that some people helped poor Elaine avoid some painful shocks even when they could have very easily done what?

   A) walked away from the difficult situation
   B) chosen a person they did not know to take Elaine's place
   C) allowed her to receive a punishment that she herself admitted was fair

8. What modern research technique did Abbigail Marsh use to show how kidney donors are different than non-donors (regular people)?

   A) magnetic resonance imaging
   B) electroencephalography
   C) the computerized IAT

9. Recent research examining what activates different areas of the brain suggests that helping others:

   A) can happen even when doing so disables reward areas
   B) is independent of reward – and is driven by higher-order moral reasoning
   C) can be inherently rewarding

10. Cyberball studies have been used extensively to study the impact of what?

    A) feeling capable – which plays a role in heroic forms of helping
    B) feeling ostracized or rejected by others
    C) exposure to video games and proneness to violence

Answer Key: 1B, 2B, 3B, 4A, 5C, 6B, 7A, 8A, 9C, 10B

References

Aknin, L. B., Hamlin, J. K., & Dunn, E. W. (2012). Giving leads to happiness in young children. *PLoS One, 7*, e39211.

Batson, C. D. (2008, March) Empathy-induced altruistic motivation. Invited address at the Inaugural Herzliya Symposium on "Prosocial Motives, Emotions, and Behavior."

Batson, C. D., Duncan, B., Ackerman, P., Buckley, T., & Birch, K. (1981). Is empathic emotion a source of altruistic motivation? *Journal of Personality and Social Psychology, 40*, 290–302.

Brosnan, S. F., & de Waal, F. B. M. (2002). A proximate perspective on reciprocal altruism. *Human Nature, 13*, 129–152.

Carter, G. G., & Wilkinson, G. S. (2013). Food sharing in vampire bats: Reciprocal help predicts donations more than relatedness or harassment. *Proceedings of the Royal Society B, 280*, 20122573.

Cialdini, R. B. (1993). *Influence: Science and practice* (3rd ed.). New York, NY: Harper Collins.

Darley, J. M., & Latané, B. (1968). Bystander intervention in emergencies: Diffusion of responsibility. *Journal of Personality and Social Psychology, 8*, 377–383.

Darley, J. M., Teger, A. I., & Lewis, L. D. (1973). Do groups always inhibit individuals' responses to potential emergencies? *Journal of Personality and Social Psychology, 26*(3), 395–399.

Dawkins, R. (1976). *The selfish gene.* Oxford: Oxford University Press.

de Waal, F. B. M. (1997). The chimpanzee's service economy: Food for grooming. *Evolution and Human Behavior, 18*, 375–386.

DeNault, L. K., & McFarlane, D. A. (1995). Reciprocal altruism between male vampire bats, *Desmohs votundus. Animal Behavior, 49*, 855–856.

Dunn, E. W., Aknin, L. B., & Norton, M. I. (2008). Spending money on others promotes happiness. *Science, 319*, 1687–1688.

Eisenberger, N. I., Lieberman, M. D., & Williams, K. D. (2003). Does rejection hurt? An fMRI study of social exclusion. *Science, 302*(5643), 290–292.

Foot, P. (1967). The problem of abortion and the doctrine of the double effect. *Oxford Review, 5*, 5–15.

Hamilton, W. D. (1964a). The genetical evolution of social behavior I. *Journal of Theoretical Biology, 7*, 1–16.

Hamilton, W. D. (1964b). The genetical evolution of social behavior II. *Journal of Theoretical Biology, 7*, 17–52.

Homans, G. C. (1958). Social behavior as exchange. *American Journal of Sociology, 63*, 597–606.

Lieberman, M. D. (2013). *Social: Why our brains are wired to connect.* New York, NY: Broadway Books.

Maner, J. K., Luce, C. L., Neuberg, S. L., Cialdini, R. B., Brown, S., & Sagarin, B. J. (2002). The effects of perspective taking on helping: Still no evidence for altruism. *Personality and Social Psychology Bulletin, 28*, 1601–1610.

Marsh, A. (2017). *The fear factor: How one emotion connects altruists, psychopaths, and everyone in between.* New York, NY: Basic Books.

Marsh, A. A., Stoycos, S., Brethel-Haurwitz, K., Robinson, P., VanMeter, J., & Cardinale, E. (2014). Neural and cognitive characteristics of extraordinary altruists. *Proceedings of the National Academy of Sciences, 111*(42), 15306–15314.

Moll, J., Krueger, F., Zahn, R., Pardini, M., de Oliveira-Souza, R., & Grafman, J. (2006). Human fronto-mesolimbic networks guide decisions about charitable donation. *Proceedings of the National Academy of Sciences, 103*(42), 15623–15628.

Myers, D. G. (2013). *Social psychology* (11th edition). New York, NY: McGraw-Hill.

Sato, N., Tan, L., Tate, K., & Okada, M. (2015). Rats demonstrate helping behavior toward a soaked conspecific. *Animal Cognition, 18*(5), 1039–1047.

Svetlova, M., Nichols, S. R., & Brownell, C. A. (2010). Toddlers' prosocial behavior: From instrumental to empathic to altruistic helping. *Child Development, 81*, 1814–1827.

Swann, W.B., Jr., Gómez, Á., Buhrmester, M.D., López-Rodríguez, L., Jiménez, J., & Vázquez, A. (2014). Contemplating the ultimate sacrifice: Identity fusion channels pro-group affect, cognition, and moral decision making. *Journal of Personality and Social Psychology, 106*, 713–727.

Tricomi, E., Rangel, A., Camerer, C. F., & O'Doherty, J.P. (2010). Neural evidence for inequality-averse social preferences. *Nature, 463*(7284), 1089–1091.

Thibaut, J. W., & Kelley, H. H. (1959). *The social psychology of groups.* New York, NY: Wiley.

Trivers, R. L. (1971). The evolution of reciprocal altruism. *Quarterly Review of Biology, 46*, 35–57.

Warneken, F. (2015). Precocious prosociality: Why do children help? *Child Development, 9*(1), 1–6.

Warneken, F., & Tomasello, M. (2006). Altruistic helping in human infants and young chimpanzees. *Science, 311*, 1301–1303.

Wegner, D. M., & Schaefer, D. (1978). The concentration of responsibility: An objective self-awareness analysis of group size effects in helping situations. *Journal of Personality and Social Psychology, 36*(2), 147–155.

Willer, R., Sharkey, A., & Frey, S. (2012). Reciprocity on the hardwood: Passing patterns among professional basketball players. *PLoS One, 7*(12), e49807.

Module 30
Personality
Our Uniqueness and Why It Matters

Almost anyone who has ever reared more than one child will tell you that kids are – in the words of Lady Gaga – "born that way." Despite the best efforts of your first author to rear his son and daughter in very similar ways, Lincoln has always expressed much greater interest in sports than his sister Brooklyn. Moving from sports to the arts, Brooklyn has always taken a much stronger interest than Lincoln in all things artistic. This is true across the board, from drawing and sculpting to theater, puppetry, and dance. And whereas Brooklyn excels in her empathy and compassion for others, Lincoln excels at honesty. This includes telling others what no one else will tell them – which is occasionally uncomfortable – and keeping his promises, which is always comforting. He's much like his namesake, Honest Abe. When Lincoln was a third grader, your first author packed him a special lunch that included a six-pack of his favorite cookies. We won't name the brand, but it rhymes with algoreo. Your first author told Lincoln that he was to save the cookies for last – that he could eat them only *after* he finished his carrots, his apple, and his sandwich. After Lincoln had returned home that day, his lunchbox proved to be empty except for an unopened package of chocolate cookies. When asked why he hadn't opened the cookies, Lincoln said, quite dejectedly, "I didn't have time to finish my sandwich." That is one honest kid.

The differences between Brooklyn and Lincoln reveal a basic psychological truth: People are different. In this module, we'll explore one of the major ways in which this is true: People have different personalities. Are you conscientious, or are you disorganized? Outgoing or shy? As you'll soon see, those are examples of the important personality traits known respectively as conscientiousness and extraversion. Do you eat your broccoli and salad first – and then enjoy your steak? Or do you eat the steak first and then suffer through your greens? That's related to delay of gratification. Do you enjoy bungee jumping, or are you horrified by the very thought of it? That's the personality trait of risk-taking. All of these things taken together – along with many, many other traits – give you your own unique personality.

But what, exactly, is personality? According to Pervin, Cervone, and John (2005, p. 6), personality refers to "those characteristics of the person that account for consistent patterns of feelings, thinking, and behaving." To paraphrase this definition, your **personality** is all the stable aspects of who you are that consistently influence what you think, feel, and do. Your personality makes you reliably different from others. It's your own private psychology. This broad definition might seem to include everything about you. For example, your physical height has a consistent effect on your ability to reach high shelves without a step ladder. Your skin tone has a consistent effect on how easily you get sunburned. But for better or worse, personality psychologists rarely study the physical aspects of who we are (though social psychologists certainly study them; see

Eberhardt et al., 2006; Olivola & Todorov, 2010). Most personality psychologists tend to focus on specific personality traits. **Personality traits** refer to broad preferences and ways of behaving that affect what you do in a wide range of settings. This is still a *lot*. For example, people differ from one another in how intensely they feel emotions, how aware they are of the possibility of being stigmatized, how optimistic they are about the future, and how willing they are to try unusual things. These many characteristics combine to create a mosaic of who you are that is as unique as your fingerprints.

In fact, many decades ago Gordon Allport (1961) identified more than 13,000 personality trait terms in an unabridged English dictionary. Although some of these trait terms are pretty obscure (How avaricious are you? How obsequious?), Allport made his count to make the point that there wouldn't be so many traits terms in the dictionary if people weren't keenly interested in personality.

The Structure and Organization of Personality Traits

Allport's Trait Theory

Allport believed that some traits are more trait-like than others. According to Allport, **cardinal traits** are central, self-defining traits that shape most everything we do. At the other extreme, **secondary traits** are traits that, while real and measurable, readily fall to the wayside in powerful situations. For many college professors, curiosity is a cardinal trait. For people (professors or otherwise) for whom curiosity is a cardinal trait, curiosity colors almost everything they do. Consider Athena. When she isn't studying how moisture gets to the leaves atop very tall trees, she is steering a casual conversation about weddings toward the cultural question of why people exchange wedding bands. Further, she shows up for book club having actually *read* the appropriate chapters of this week's book on behavioral economics. But for Stacy, for whom extraversion (outgoingness) is a cardinal trait, it would be the promise of lively conversation that drove her to show up for book club. And for Bella, the person for whom seeking pleasure is a cardinal trait, the main reason to come to book club would be Mauricio's Chilean wines and Brook's triple fudge brownies. If you've ever heard the comedian Jim Gaffigan, you know that, for him, life is all about the wine and brownies. Gaffigan firmly believes human beings were put here on Earth to enjoy delicious food and drink – and to steer clear of green vegetables. For Gaffigan, experiencing deliciousness seems to be a *cardinal* trait.

We're sorry to say Allport's idea of categorizing traits based on their potency or centrality never fully caught on among empirically-inclined psychologists. This seems to have been true, in large part, because of how difficult it is to measure whether a particular personality trait is cardinal or secondary. An arguable exception to this rule is that some self-concept researchers have capitalized on Allport's idea to study differences in people's specific self-views (Pelham, 1991, 1993). For example, Pelham (1991) showed that specific self-views of which people are more certain, and specific self-views that people consider more important, are more stable over time.

Attachment Style as a Personality Trait

So Allport didn't popularize his precise view of personality. But he did generate a lot of scientific interest in personality. In fact, new measures of personality traits are created every year. Further, many social, clinical, developmental, and cognitive psychologists integrate research on personality into their basic research. For example, many experts on adult close relationships study **adult romantic attachment style.** This personality trait refers to the ways in which people typically think of themselves and others in romantic relationships. As you may recall, people who have no trouble getting close to their romantic partners and who feel they can trust others to be there for them when needed have **secure attachment styles.** People who do *not* feel others can be trusted fall into one of several categories of **insecure attachment style.** One specific way to be *in*secure is to be avoidant. People with **avoidant attachment styles** report that they do not really need others and that they do not like to depend on others. Finally, people who desperately wish to get close to others and really want to depend on others – but who think others are likely to let them down in times of crisis – are said to have **anxious attachment styles.** You may recall that it's possible to assess attachment style (with one's primary caregivers) in human infants and toddlers. Personality theorists argue that what happens early in life with one's parents sets the stage for what happens later in life with one's romantic partners.

Researchers who study close relationships have found that adult romantic attachment styles influence our behavior in close relationships. To show this, Simpson, Rholes, and Nelligan (1992) gave some Texas women quite a scare in the laboratory. The women, students at Texas A&M University, took part in the study with their boyfriends. But the women and their boyfriends were quickly separated. With the boyfriends safely out of the way, the experimenters gave the women the impression that they could be badly shocked by some faulty equipment during some electrophysiological measurements. Of course, none of the women ever received any electric shocks. But by raising the specter of a dangerous shock and secretly recording the women's facial expressions during this part of the experiment, Simpson and colleagues could tell how afraid the women had felt during this stressful event. When the women were reunited with their boyfriends, the securely attached women sought out more social support from their boyfriends when their faces suggested that they had been more afraid. "Well, duh!" you might be thinking. "That's what romantic partners are for. They're the ones you confide in when you've just been through something terrible." But not if you have an avoidant adult romantic attachment style. For women with an avoidant attachment style, the more afraid they had looked while hooked up to the ominous electrical machinery the *less* likely they were to turn to their partners later for social support. These results appear in Figure 30.1.

So that's the sad dilemma of romantic life if you have an avoidant adult romantic attachment style. The more you need to open up to someone you love, the less able you are to do so. In the classic rock song "Slip Slidin' Away," singer-songwriter Paul Simon seems to have come to this conclusion without threatening anyone with electric shock. As Simon soulfully put it:

> And I know a father who had a son
> He longed to tell him all the reasons for the things he'd done
> He came a long way, just to explain
> He kissed his boy as he lay sleeping
> Then he turned around and headed home again.

Sometimes a thirsty horse makes a long trip to the water on its own – but can't bring itself to take a drink.

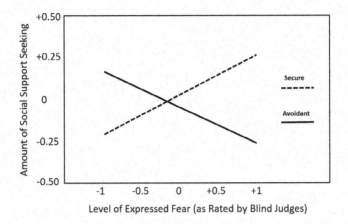

Figure 30.1 For securely attached women, fear led them to seek social support from their romantic partners. For women with an avoidant attachment style, more fear led to *less* support seeking (adapted from Simpson et al., 1992).

In the past few decades, many empirical studies have shown that adult romantic attachment style is an important aspect of human personality (e.g., see Carvallo & Gabriel, 2006; Collins & Read, 1990; Kane et al., 2007). For example, Carvallo and Gabriel (2006) found that although people with a dismissive avoidant attachment style claim not to need others, they are happier than people with a secure attachment style when they are told that the future of their close relationships is very bright. People with avoidant attachment styles need others just as much as the rest of us. They've just learned to be guarded and self-protective.

If you believe you have an anxious or avoidant attachment style, and you worry that you are doomed to a life devoid of love or social support, there is plenty of reason for hope. First, avoidant people do not usually avoid close relationships *altogether*; they just avoid making themselves emotionally vulnerable in close relationships. Second, in a longitudinal study of newlyweds, Davila, Karney, and Bradbury (1999) found that, for both brides and grooms, being more satisfied with one's marriage for the first two years seems to have caused newlyweds to become less concerned about abandonment and more comfortable with closeness. In other words, attachment style can change somewhat, even in adulthood. To quote Lloyd from the classic comedy *Dumb and Dumber*, "So you're telling me there's a chance!" Hope springs eternal. Adult romantic attachment processes seem to be no exception to this rule.

The Big Five

Recall that attachment theory is just one of many possible examples of research on personality and behavior. Thousands of studies of human personality have uncovered hundreds of specific personality traits. In our view, however, the most satisfying thing about research in personality is not the growing list of personality traits. Instead, it's a large and still growing body of research suggesting that almost all of the thousands of specific personality traits that Allport identified boil down to just five basic traits. These five traits are known as the "**Big Five**" because these five traits may encompass every human personality trait ever measured (Goldberg, 1990; McCrae & Costa, 1987). In short, Big Five researchers argue that there are only five core aspects of human personality.

What are the Big Five traits? We like to remember them using the acronym **OCEAN**. They begin with **Openness** – which is an interest in *learning* and experiencing new things. You shouldn't be too surprised to learn that some people call this trait "Intellect." People high in openness are very interested in expanding their minds. The second Big Five trait is **Conscientiousness** – which refers to a tendency to be punctual, tidy, organized, and disciplined. The fact that your second author had to add a few headings, a few missing references, and correct some of your first author's typos in this text tells you that David is more conscientious than Brett (and yet, just as fun). The third Big Five trait is **Extraversion** – which refers to an interest in talking to and connecting to others. Extraversion also includes enjoying the spotlight in social situations and being willing to take both physical and psychological risks. Extraverts treat everyone like their long-lost neighbor, and sometimes it can be hard to get them to stop talking. The fourth Big Five trait is **Agreeableness**. Agreeable people are slow to anger and quick to compliment or agree with you. They are rarely fussy, domineering, or pushy. They've always been our favorite kind of people. Finally, the fifth Big Five trait is **Neuroticism**. Neurotic people are worrisome, insecure, pessimistic, and emotionally volatile. They see the world as a dangerous place, where harm lurks around every corner. Filmmaker Woody Allen loves to make fun of himself for being so neurotic. We won't disagree. If you're a fan of the Marvel Cinematic Universe, you also know that Peter Parker is pretty neurotic. He's always worrying, for example, about whether he is really worthy of membership in the Avengers. Table 30.1 offers a concise summary of the Big Five. The first example is typical of a person scoring low on the trait in question, and the second is more typical of a person scoring high on the same trait.

If you have ever seen the classic Pixar film *Finding Nemo*, you can probably think of characters for whom each Big Five (ahem ... OCEAN) trait is a very obvious trait. Beginning with **openness**, Gill is not content to live in the tiny world of a dentist's aquarium. He is constantly plotting ways to escape – so that he can experience everything the big blue ocean has to offer. One of Gill's aquarium mates, Jacque, is the perfect example of **conscientiousness**. Jacque keeps everything tidy, clean, and well-organized. We're tempted to say that Dory is the perfect example of **extraversion**, but we're going to make Nemo himself

Table 30.1 The Big Five Personality Traits and Examples that Illustrate the Low and High End of Each Trait

	Low on Trait	*High on Trait*
Openness	Unwilling to try novel foods	Enjoys documentary films
	Likes staying put	Likes to learn about other cultures
Conscientiousness	Is often late	Keeps spices organized in kitchen
	Wears wrinkled clothing	Uses an electronic organizer or calendar
Extraversion	Is quiet and cautious	Strikes up conversations with strangers
	Enjoys solitude	Tells jokes loudly in groups
Agreeableness	Refuses to help sick classmate	Compliments others on their work
	Uses sarcasm to win arguments	Has trouble saying no to others
Neuroticism	Doesn't worry much about death	Assumes headache means brain cancer
	Assumes the best in others	Is paranoid and gloomy

the poster fish for this trait. Nemo meets other creatures easily. He is also an energetic risk-taker who has a level of self-confidence you'd never expect from a little guy who's had such a painful childhood. That gets us to **agreeableness,** and we hope you'll agree that Dory is even more agreeable than she is extraverted. Dory is always willing to lend a helping hand – even to a complete stranger. She truly loves making others happy. The first thing she ever says to Marlin after he crashes into her is, "Sir, are you OK? ... There, there. It's alright. It'll be OK." Having said all that, let us add that when anyone traverses the entire Pacific Ocean with a neurotic downer like Marlin, they're bound to lose their temper now and then. Dory is no exception. That gets us to the fifth Big Five trait, **neuroticism.** Nemo's dad, Marlin, is the prototypical neurotic. He worries about everything, and he is the master of finding drops of despair in an ocean of hope. Of course, it's hard to blame the guy. He did lose a wife and hundreds of kids to a *disagreeable* barracuda. That's just the kind of self-defining life experience that many personality theorists think is so important to personality development.

If you're wondering if the Big Five system captures the personalities of real people as well as it captures those of fictional characters, the answer is yes. In fact, Gosling and John (1999; see also Gosling, 2008) have shown that the Big Five scheme works pretty well with animals as well as with people. Especially when it comes to extraversion, neuroticism, and agreeableness, many different animals can be reliably rated by those who observe them regularly as having obvious personalities. Table 30.2 is adapted from Gosling and John (1999). It shows that whereas the Big Five applies extremely well to chimps, only a Big Four seems to apply to gorillas. When it comes to guppies and octopi, there is apparently only a Big Two rather than a Big Five. But by showing that some semblance of the Big Five applies to many non-human animals as well as to people, Gosling and John suggest that the Big Five traits may all exist because they have important implications for survival in different environments. For example, some degree of neuroticism may prove useful in a world full of hidden dangers.

Table 30.2 The Apparent Existence of the Big Five Personality Factors in Some Non-Human Animals

	Big Five Trait				
Species	*Neuroticism*	*Agreeableness*	*Extraversion*	*Openness*	*Conscientiousness*
Chimp	x	x	x	x	x
Gorilla	x	x	x		
Rhesus monkey	x	x	x	x	
Vervet monkey		x	x		
Hyena	x	x		x	
Dog	x	x	x	x	
Cat	x	x	x	x	
Donkey		x			
Pig		x	x	x	
Rat	x	x			
Guppy	x		x	x	x
Octopus	x		x		

Note. Based on Gosling and John (1999). An x means that dimension exists of that species. An x placed *between two columns* means a dimension appeared for that species that had characteristics of both traits.

Gosling and colleagues have also shown that, knowingly or not, people give off cues that reliably tell others where they stand on at least three of the Big Five personality traits. Gosling and colleagues (2002) had observers examine photos of people's office space in one study and of people's bedrooms in another. For three of the five Big Five traits, there was strong evidence that traits showed up in photos of people's living spaces. In both studies, observers of the rooms agreed well with one another, and with participants themselves, about the participants' levels of (a) openness, (b) conscientiousness, and (c) extraversion. You may recall from the hands-on activity at the end of the module on person perception that people can also judge a stranger's level of extraversion by merely looking at a photo of the person. This is known as *consensus at zero-acquaintance*, and it's another example of the fact that human judges are keen to understand the personality and preferences of those with whom they're likely to interact. Although some social psychologists would dispute this interpretation, evidence that we can judge a person's personality from a photo or two may also be a testament to the power of personality.

The Big Five model also applies well to both women and men and to people from different ethnic groups. Big Five traits also vary predictably with age. Perhaps you can guess whether older adults or younger adults are more conscientious. Focusing on how people perceive the personalities of others, there is also plenty of evidence that the Big Five traits apply to people across the globe. McCrae, Terracciano and colleagues (2005) asked college students in 50 nations to select men and women they knew and rate their personalities using translations of a popular 240-item measure of the Big Five traits. Collectively, the participants in this global study rated the personalities of almost 12,000 people they knew well. This included ratings of an equal number of male and female targets and an equal number of younger and older adults. The personality patterns McCrae and Costa had observed in Western samples held up well across the globe. First, the tendency for the personality traits to cluster into the five distinct Big Five groups held up very well. Second, the same age and gender differences that had been observed in research in Western samples showed up in the global sample. Averaging across the 50 nations, women scored higher than men on all five of the Big Five factors. For example, relative to male targets, female targets were rated as more extraverted, more conscientious, and more open to experience. Further, in 45 of the 50 nations, noteworthy gender differences appeared on at least one of the Big Five traits – and very often on four or five of them. Likewise, in all 50 nations, judges rated older adults as at least slightly more conscientious than younger adults. The age differences observed on the Big Five in Western cultures seem to hold up pretty well across the globe. In sum, there is good evidence that the Big Five is a very good way to think about the puzzle of human personality.

As useful as the Big Five model has proven to be, it cannot cover everything. Many people consider intelligence and specific abilities (e.g., athletic ability) to be part of personality. Likewise, self-esteem and the self-concept arguably fit under the big umbrella of personality. But with the exception of neuroticism, none of the Big Five traits are linked in any obvious way to self-esteem and identity. Finally, if you recall Freud's (1923) view of personality (summarized in Module 2), you know that Freud considered human personality to be a balancing act involving (a) the selfish *id*, (b) the strict and reverent *superego*, and (c) the *ego* – which strives to find a balance between these two opposing aspects of personality. Freud thought that one of the most telling aspects of human personality is whether the id or the superego usually wins the internal psychological battles that make up daily life. Freud (1923) argued, for example, that the id dominates infancy and early childhood. But through the socializing efforts of parents, coaches, teachers, and religious leaders, the superego presumably grows stronger as we mature. But Freud argued that just as some people have overdeveloped ids, which run the show, other people have overdeveloped superegos – which keep the show from getting very interesting. Needless to say, the person whose personality is dominated by the id gets in lots of trouble in life. The person who has an overdeveloped superego stays safely out of trouble but rarely has any fun. But things don't always have to be out of balance. Freud argued that people high in *ego strength* usually find healthy ways to balance what the selfish id craves and what the strict superego condemns. We don't have to steal dessert to enjoy it, and we don't always have to forego dessert altogether.

Personality and Behavior

The Marshmallow Test

But does a person's personality actually predict his or her daily behavior? Or does the work of Gosling and colleagues merely attest to the power of widely shared stereotypes? Advocates of the power of personality have argued that personality traits shape much of what we do every day (Funder, 1995). Let's critically analyze this idea by examining a classic study that seems to attest to the power of personality to determine important life outcomes. In 1990, Shoda, Mischel, and Peake published the results of a clever and intriguing longitudinal study. The paper built on Mischel's classic work on delay of gratification in preschool children. Mischel used a test of the ability to delay gratification now known as the "**marshmallow test.**" In this test, four-year-old kids at a Stanford University nursery school were seated in a chair at an empty table populated by nothing but a single delicious marshmallow. Children were told by an experimenter that they were free to eat the marshmallow. However, before they could pop the marshmallow in their mouths, kids were also told that the experimenter had to run a quick errand. If kids could sit tight for several minutes *without* eating the marshmallow, they learned, the experimenter would return with a bonus marshmallow. So, if you can wait a while, you'll get two marshmallows. If you can't wait, just dive right in.

We hope you can see that these studies involved **delay of gratification**. That's the ability to refrain from doing something you'd like to do right now with the promise that you'll get a bigger reward at some point in the future. The beauty of Shoda et al.'s study is a testament to their hard work. About ten to 12 years after Mischel's many lab studies of the marshmallow test were completed, Shoda, Mischel and Peake tracked down a large group of kids who had taken part in the marshmallow test as little kids and checked back in on almost 200 of them. For most of these teenagers, Shoda et al. got both high school teachers and parents to report (a) how much self-control the kids had and (b) how good the kids were at planning ahead and dealing with stress. For a smaller number of these teenagers, Shoda et al. also got access to the kids' scores on the SAT (Scholastic Aptitude Test). Shoda and colleagues report many findings, but the most crucial findings are that the longer these kids waited in the lab (in minutes and seconds) before caving in and eating the beloved marshmallow, the better they were doing – on all three important measures – in high school. These were not small effects. This suggests that the personality trait known as delay of gratification – whether measured using marshmallows or mathematics performance – is both powerful and highly stable across time. For good reason, this study got a great deal of attention. Despite our emphasis on the power of the situation in Module 26, this study suggests that personality may often be quite powerful as well.

But one elegant study is rarely the final word on anything. Watts, Duncan, and Quan (2018) noted that as impressive as the Shoda et al. study was, it focused on a pretty elite sample of kids, almost of whom were White and almost none of whom were poor. This is particularly important, they noted, because in the wake of the Shoda et al. study, many researchers had designed interventions for struggling school children based on this single study. If we could just teach preschoolers to delay gratification, maybe they'd all get into Stanford, where they might even be able to take a course from one of the authors of this classic paper. But as Watts et al. respectfully noted, very few kids in the Stanford preschool (where kids took the original marshmallow test) were struggling in any dramatic way. To put this a little differently, if you remember the OOPS! Heuristic, you should be asking yourself what would happen if someone conducted a replication of the marshmallow study on a more diverse and representative sample of kids. Likewise, if you remember the GAGES confounds, you should be asking yourself what variables might be *confounded* with delay of gratification at age four and with social and academic outcomes later in life. How much of the apparent effect of the ability to delay gratification is really an effect of home environment, poverty, or the intellectual skills kids already possessed at age four? **Watts and colleagues (2018)** measured these confounding variables – and then some – in a large-scale replication of the marshmallow study. Watts et al. began with much more diverse and representative samples of 4.5-year-olds than Shoda et al. had been able to study. They then gave these kids the marshmallow test, along with many other psychological measures, and then waited dutifully for these kids to make it to high school. At this point, Watts et al. (2018) assessed the same kind of academic and social outcomes that Shoda, Mischel, and Peake (1990) had assessed.

In this much larger and more representative study, Watts et al. replicated the basic finding that kids who waited longer for a highly desirable treat to double did better academically more than a decade later. But Watts et al. also found that in their own original laboratory setting, kids from poorer and less educated families had substantially less ability to delay gratification than kids from richer and more highly educated families. If you're familiar with life history theory, this finding makes a lot of sense. As an anonymous social observer put it, "Life is uncertain. Eat dessert first." Watts et al. also found that in their larger and more representative sample, the academic effects they observed were much smaller than those observed by Shoda and colleagues. In other words, kids who waited for a marshmallow (or other equally delicious treat) did do a bit better on the SAT a dozen years later. But this effect was much smaller than the one Shoda et al. observed in their smaller sample of more financially-comfortable kids. If you recall that the measured genetic component of IQ is much bigger in rich neighborhoods than in poor neighborhoods, this difference between the two studies shouldn't come as a surprise. Early indicators of personality, like genes, may matter more than usual in safe, comfortable, and highly predictable worlds. Watts et al. also found that the effects of delay of gratification became quite a bit smaller when they put delay of gratification in a statistical footrace against some of the confounding variables they assessed. In other words, little kids who scored high on the marshmallow test did well on the SAT in high school, in part, because they already had excellent intellectual skills as preschoolers. There is sure to be some debate about the best way to integrate the findings of Watts et al. (2018) with the original findings of Shoda et al. (1990). But in our view, all the findings taken together suggest that personality traits such as delay of gratification have a modest but impressive ability to predict how kids will be doing in high school more than a decade after such traits are measured in preschool.

We'd like to offer one more critical look at research using the marshmallow test by directly examining the power of the situation to influence delay of gratification. **Kidd and colleagues (2013)** conducted a "marshmallow-test" study that suggests that kids' recent experiences with the person who is supposed to deliver the coveted bonus marshmallow can have a big impact on how long kids are able to wait. Prior to taking part in the standard version of the marshmallow test, kids interacted with a friendly female experimenter who told them they'd be doing an art project. Kids further learned that if they wouldn't mind waiting a bit to start their art projects, the experimenter would step out and return with a set of art materials that was much better than the small set of heavily-used crayons the kids could see sealed in a glass jar. All of the kids agreed to wait for the much better set of art supplies. Here's where the experimental manipulation comes in. For half of these kids, the experimenter returned after a couple of minutes – bringing with her the awesome set of art supplies. For the less fortunate kids, the experimenter returned with a sincere apology rather than a sweet set of art supplies. She explained that she had made a mistake and that the awesome art supplies were not available. She cheerfully reminded the kids in this "unreliable" condition that they could still use the pitiful crayons she had shown them a few minutes ago (though she didn't say they were "pitiful").

Once the kids had finished their art projects, the experimenter returned and gave them all the same basic version of Mischel's marshmallow test. The kids who had recently experienced a reliable state of affairs waited four times as long (about 12 minutes) for the bonus marshmallow as did the kids who had experienced an unreliable state of affairs (about 3 minutes). Thus, the ability of these kids to delay gratification was dramatically influenced by the particular situation in which they found themselves (something they were told would happen actually did happen – or it did not). Life history theorists and personality psychologists would presumably argue that this powerful experiment did a great job of approximating a social world in which things were reliable or unreliable. Even big fans of the power of the situation would probably have to agree that if a person spent his or her entire childhood in an unreliable world, it might make sense to go through the rest of one's life adopting a fast ("I'll take the good stuff *now*") strategy. If life really is uncertain, that is, maybe it's not a bad idea to go through life eating dessert first.

Hands-On Activities for Module 30

Part 1. Recall that some personality psychologists believe that virtually every personality trait that exists boils down to one of five universal personality traits. To give you some practice thinking about the Big Five, this hands-on activity asks you to do two things. First, as a warm up, consult Table 30.1 and see if you can list the one Big Five trait that best describes five of the most famous Muppets from the educational TV show *Sesame Street*. Try to use each Big Five trait exactly once and see if you agree with our opinions about which character best exemplifies each Big Five trait. In case you haven't watched *Sesame Street* in a while, let us remind you that Kermit works as a reporter and is very curious about the world in which he lives. Ernie doesn't work much at all, but he is fun-loving and popular, and he connects immediately to everyone he meets. Bert is a negative worry wart who is very easily frazzled. The Count is obsessed with counting and seems to use it to make his world orderly. Finally, Big Bird is a gentle giant who wouldn't hurt a fly.

Table 30.3 The Big Five Personality Traits on Sesame Street. Copy the traits and names to a worksheet and match each Muppet to the Big Five trait that describes that Muppet best.

Traits	Muppets	Cardinal or Secondary (by Muppet)
Openness	Bert	C S
Conscientiousness	Big Bird	C S
Extraversion	Ernie	C S
Agreeableness	Kermit	C S
Neuroticism	The Count	C S

Because your instructor may ask you to do this Big Five activity in small groups and come up with a group answer, we are not providing an answer key for this activity. When you are done with this matching process, you should also make an argument for each Muppet about whether the trait that best describes him is truly a *cardinal trait* (meaning it is truly central to who this character is) or is more like a *secondary trait*.

Part 2. To take your knowledge of the Big Five to the next level, let's see how well you can use your intuitions and your analytical skills to put each of 25 specific personality traits into one of the Big Five trait categories. We've created this activity by simply beginning with an abbreviated version of a popular Big Five personality measure developed by Goldberg (1990). We then listed the 25 bipolar (opposing) trait pairs that are used in this measure in alphabetical order (beginning each pair of terms with the term that indicates a *lack* of a specific Big Five trait). Next to each bipolar pair of traits, use a letter from the acronym OCEAN to indicate which specific Big Five (OCEAN) factor each specific trait term matches. For example, if you felt a specific trait-pair were an indicator of Extraversion, you'd put an "E" in the blank next to that trait-pair. You should use each letter of OCEAN exactly five times, because each Big Five trait has five specific indicators in this abbreviated measure of the Big Five.

Note. Focus on the trait term to the *right* in each pair of opposites, recognizing that more of this trait (e.g., more nervousness for item 01) should indicate more of one of the *Big Five* traits. A trait that gives many people trouble is "practical" (number 8). It might thus be practical to save that OCEAN judgment for last.

____	01.	at ease	nervous
____	02.	calm	angry
____	03.	careless	thorough
____	04.	cold	warm
____	05.	disagreeable	agreeable
____	06.	disorganized	organized
____	07.	distrustful	trustful
____	08.	impractical	practical
____	09.	inactive	active
____	10.	irresponsible	responsible
____	11.	lazy	hardworking

___ 12.	not curious	curious
___ 13.	not envious	envious
___ 14.	quiet	talkative
___ 15.	relaxed	tense
___ 16.	selfish	unselfish
___ 17.	silent	talkative
___ 18.	stable	unstable
___ 19.	unadventurous	adventurous
___ 21.	uncreative	creative
___ 21.	unenergetic	energetic
___ 22.	unimaginative	imaginative
___ 23.	unintelligent	intelligent
___ 24.	unkind	kind
___ 25.	unsophisticated	sophisticated

Note. Because this activity, too, works well as a group activity, we have not posted an answer key.

Multiple-Choice Questions for Module 30

1. What's the connection between a person's personality and any specific personality trait (such as friendliness or fearfulness)?

    A) a person's personality includes wishes and aspirations as well as personality traits.
    B) a person's personality is the total combination of all of the person's specific personality traits.
    C) a person's true personality reflects nature whereas specific personality traits reflect nurture.

2. What are the two most common *insecure* adult romantic attachment styles?

    A) timid and self-doubting
    B) dismissive and permissive
    C) anxious and avoidant

3. Both attachment theorists and personality theorists believe that the origins of adult romantic attachment can be found where?

    A) in infant and toddler attachment to primary caregivers
    B) in early childhood crushes and close friendships
    C) in adolescent crushes and sexual fantasies

4. Mr. Stevens is madly in love with Ms. Kenton, but he cannot bring himself to tell her how he feels about her. In fact, on the rare occasions when Mrs. Kenton flirts with him, Mr. Stevens either pulls away from her or scolds and belittles her. What kind of attachment style does Mr. Stevens appear to have?

    A) avoidant
    B) hostile
    C) self-protective

5. Which of the following is one of the key findings from Simpson et al.'s (1992) classic study of attachment style in college student couples at Texas A&M?

    A) the more afraid avoidant women felt, the less likely they were to ask their boyfriends for support
    B) the more afraid anxious women felt, the more likely they were to ask their boyfriends for support
    C) women who felt secure in their close relationships faced a scary situation with less fear and worry

6. On a self-report personality measure, Robi reports being extraverted. But in reality, she doesn't usually give much thought to being a "people person." Robi can also be very quiet if the situation seems to call for it. Allport would say that, for Robi, extraversion seems to be a _____ trait.

    A) primary
    B) secondary
    C) ordinal

7. The gist of Allport's idea of the idiographic personality is that for any given person, some specific personality traits:

    A) are expressed only with certain people and in certain social or work contexts
    B) are central, important, and self-defining
    C) remain latent (hidden) until early adulthood

8. In the Big Five acronym OCEAN, what does the C stand for?

    A) carelessness
    B) creativity
    C) conscientiousness

9. In the Big Five acronym OCEAN, what does the E stand for?

    A) egalitarianism
    B) extraversion
    C) enthusiasm

10. What is the "marshmallow test" designed to measure?

    A) whether a person has a "sweet tooth"
    B) a person's level of physical fitness
    C) a child's ability to delay gratification

11. Shoda et al. (1990) conducted a famous study that showed that a kid's behavior in the lab at about the age of four predicted what?

    A) whether the kid would prove to be a good reader in elementary school
    B) how happy and healthy the kid proved to be at home
    C) the kid's high school SAT scores

12. Kidd et al. (2013) conducted a lab experiment to investigate the nature of a kid's ability to delay gratification. They found that:

    A) by the time kids are about five or six, their level of delay of gratification is hard to change
    B) it's possible to measure delay of gratification even in infants and toddlers
    C) it's easy to change a kid's ability to delay gratification by changing the kid's environment

Answer Key: 1B 2C 3A 4A 5A 6B 7B 8C 9B 10C 11C 12C

References

Allport, G. W. (1961). *Pattern and growth in personality.* Holt, Reinhart & Winston.

Carvallo, M., & Gabriel, S. (2006). No man is an island: The need to belong and dismissing avoidant attachment style. *Personality and Social Psychology Bulletin, 32*(5), 697–709.

Collins, N. L., & Read, S. J. (1990). Adult attachment, working models, and relationship quality in dating couples. *Journal of Personality and Social Psychology, 58*(4), 644–663.

Davila, J., Karney, B. R., & Bradbury, T. N. (1999). Attachment change processes in the early years of marriage. *Journal of Personality and Social Psychology, 76*, 783–802.

Eberhardt, J.L., Davies, P.G., Purdie-Vaughns, V.J., & Johnson, S.J. (2006). Looking deathworthy: Perceived stereotypicality of Black defendants predicts capital-sentencing outcomes. *Psychological Science, 17*, 383–386.

Freud, S. (1923). The ego and the id. In J. Strachey et al. (Trans.), *The standard edition of the complete psychological works of Sigmund Freud, Volume XIX.* London: Hogarth Press.

Goldberg, L. R. (1990). An alternative "description of personality": The Big-Five factor structure. *Journal of Personality and Social Psychology., 59*, 1216–1229.

Gosling, S. D. (2008). Personality in non-human animals. *Social and Personality Psychology Compass, 2*(2), 985–1001. doi:10.1111/j.1751-9004.2008.00087.x

Gosling, S. D., & John, O. P. (1999). Personality dimensions in non-human animals: A cross-species review. *Current Directions in Psychological Science, 8*, 69–75.

Kane, H. S., Jaremka, L. M., Guichard, A. M. C., Ford, M. B., Collins, N. L., & Feeney, B. C. (2007). Feeling supported and feeling satisfied: How one partner's attachment style predicts the other partner's relationship experiences. *Journal of Social and Personal Relationships, 24*(4), 535–555.

Funder, D. C. (1995). On the accuracy of personality judgment: A realistic approach. *Psychological Review, 102*(4), 652–670. doi:10.1037/0033-295X.102.4.652

Gosling, S. D., Ko, S. J., Mannarelli, T., & Morris, M. E. (2002). A room with a cue: Personality judgments based on offices and bedrooms. *Journal of Personality and Social Psychology, 82*(3), 379–398. doi:10.1037/0022-3514.82.3.379

Kidd, C., Palmeri, H., & Aslin, R. B. (2013). Rational snacking: Young children's decision-making on the marshmallow task is moderated by beliefs about environmental reliability. *Cognition, 126* (1), 109–114.

McCrae, R. R., & Costa, P. T., Jr. (1987). Validation of the five-factor model of personality across instruments and observers. *Journal of Personality and Social Psychology, 52*, 81–90.

McCrae, R. R., Terracciano, A., & 78 Members of the Personality Profiles of Cultures Project. (2005). Universal features of personality traits from the observer's perspective: Data from 50 cultures. *Journal of Personality and Social Psychology, 88*(3), 547–561.

Olivola, C.Y. & Todorov, A. (2010) Fooled by first impressions? Reexamining the diagnostic value of appearance-based inferences. *Journal of Experimental Social Psychology, 46*, 315–324.

Pelham, B. W. (1991). On confidence and consequence: The certainty and importance of self-knowledge. *Journal of Personality and Social Psychology, 60*, 518–530.

Pelham, B. W. (1993). The idiographic nature of human personality: Examples of the idiographic self-concept. *Journal of Personality and Social Psychology, 64*, 665–677.

Pervin, L.A., Cervone, D., & John, O.P. (2005). *Personality: Theory and research.* Hoboken, NJ: Wiley.

Shoda, Y., Mischel, W., & Peake, P. K. (1990). Predicting adolescent cognitive and self-regulatory competencies from preschool delay of gratification: Identifying diagnostic conditions. *Developmental Psychology, 26*(6), 978–986.

Simpson, J. A., Rholes, W. S., & Nelligan, J. S. (1992). Support seeking and support giving within couples in an anxiety-provoking situation: The role of attachment styles. *Journal of Personality and Social Psychology, 62*(3), 434–446.

Watts, T. W., Duncan, G. J., & Quan, H. (2018). Revisiting the marshmallow test: A conceptual replication investigating links between early delay of gratification and later outcomes. *Psychological Science, 29*(7), 1159–1177.

Module 31
Culture
How Psychology Varies with Geography

Human culture is incredibly diverse. According to Anderson of the Linguistic Society of America (no date), human beings speak almost 7,000 languages. Specific religious beliefs, beliefs about kinship (who is related to whom), levels of aggression, and dietary rules also vary radically across the globe (Cohen, Nisbett, Bowdle, & Schwarz, 1996). For example, in many cultures, it is considered taboo to marry your cousin. In others, it is considered a great idea. There is virtually no aspect of human experience that it is not touched by culture. As we'll use the term in this module, **culture** refers to a group's shared beliefs, feelings, customs, and social norms, including the way people communicate, sustain themselves, care for children, work, worship, and exist in groups. The groups to which we refer in this definition may be as broad as states or nations or as narrow as companies or small towns. In this module, however, we will focus mainly on the broad end of this spectrum.

To see how music varies across the globe, consider the four musical instruments shown in the top row of Figure 31.1. We hope you'll agree that these four very different musical instruments are as different as are the five languages depicted in the middle of Figure 31.1. And they are as varied as the three unusual food sources shown in the bottom row of Figure 31.1. Consider the food that is arguably the craziest in this short list: **cow's milk**. In many parts of the world, including where you most likely live, people routinely consume this mammary secretion from cows as if it's totally normal and without risk. This is true despite the fact that cow's milk is very hard for most human adults to digest. To paraphrase anthropologist Greg Downey (interviewed in Noone, 2016), the only kind of milk we evolved to consume is milk from human mothers, and only during the first couple of years of life. To be sure, most people whose ancestors herded cows can drink milk with fewer problems than can people whose ancestors did not herd cows. But, biologically speaking, cow's milk is a weird food (Slade & Schwartz, 1987). As medical researcher Deepa Verma (2017) argued, cow's milk messes up your metabolism, is bad for your bones, can increase your risk of allergies and breathing problems, and is bad for your kidneys! Very often milk also contains bad things such as bovine growth hormone and antibiotics, as well as fat and cholesterol.

In contrast to all the adults on Earth who are lactose intolerant, very few people seem to be either tarantula-intolerant or grub-intolerant. But if you grew up in a culture that considers spiders and grubs disgusting rather than delicious, it's unlikely we've convinced you to consider serving fried spiders or roasted grubs at your next dinner party. The point of this assault on your beliefs about milk is not to stop you from drinking it. It is merely to clarify that culture is very powerful. The same cultural socialization forces that make many Western Europeans love milk make people in other parts of Earth consume dog meat,

Left to right: The ocarina, the mbira, the Veena, and the harmonica.

te amo   nakupenda   أحبك   我愛你   Я люблю тебя

Left to right: "I love you" in Spanish, Swahili, Arabic, Mandarin, and Russian.

Left to right: fried tarantulas, grilled grubs, and the mammary secretions of ... eww gross, cows.

Figure 31.1 There is tremendous cross-cultural variation in almost everything people do.

whale blubber, grasshoppers, or raw oysters. Moving from what we put in our bodies to what we put on them, consider the tremendous cross-cultural variation in how we adorn ourselves. Of course, some of this is practical. People living in polar regions must cover their bodies much more heavily than people living in the tropics. But a great deal of cultural variation in how we dress goes well beyond the practical.

OK. You've probably known for a long time that cultures vary. But you may not have known that there are also many **human cultural universals**. Culture may not be quite as arbitrary and capricious as it seems at first blush. In fact, Murdock (1949) argued long ago that all human cultures do many of the same things. For example, there can be no doubt that the specific rules about sex vary dramatically across cultures. But at the same time, all cultures have rules about sex. You may also recall from the module on language and thought that there are no known cultures where people do not use language. Murdock's list of cultural universals is surprisingly long. To list just a few of them, there has never been

Figure 31.2 The specific ways in which we adorn ourselves vary widely across the globe.

a recorded human culture in which people did not use personal names, did not make jokes, did not dance, or did not possess cosmological beliefs (ideas about how the world came to exist). Table 31.1 contains Murdock's complete list of 66 presumed human cultural universals. As you can see, human cultures are not completely arbitrary. Some things show up over and over again. It's just the specific details of these things that vary.

Agriculture and the Early Evolution of Power and Wealth

One way to see how cultures can vary so widely while also adhering to cultural universals is to recognize that the specific details of culture (e.g., exactly how marriage works, what kind of housing people build) develop in direct response to specific environmental factors – to which we have all evolved to respond. In other words, we evolved to be a certain kind of animal – with many specific needs and abilities. But the precise way in which we fill those needs and use those abilities will vary greatly depending on where we happen to live (Gangestad, Haselton, & Buss, 2006). Evolutionarily-inclined thinkers have argued that this general rule applies to almost all aspects of culture, from who decides whom we marry to how we speak, and whether we live for the moment or save a lot for retirement (Diamond, 1997; Wilson, 1975). Remember life history theory? We seem to be programmed to develop and behave very differently in different environments (Gellatly, 2009; Legare & Nielsen, 2015; Starkweather & Hames, 2012; Stearns, 1992). Much like the weather, then, human cultures vary. But at least some of this variation is predictable. One of the best examples of this idea is Jared Diamond's (1997) ingenious analysis of how European and Asian cultures came to dominate the Earth – politically, militarily, and economically.

The Cultural Evolution of Guns and Butter

According to Diamond's **"Guns, Germs, and Steel" hypothesis**, it all goes back to **agriculture**. After all, before the invention of agriculture (about 10,000 years ago), people lived pretty much the same lifestyle all across the Earth. They hunted and gathered. Of course, Eskimos hunted seals whereas Navaho hunted bison. Samoans fished whereas desert-dwellers extracted water from cacti. But for the first 190,000 years of human existence, all human beings lived in small cooperative groups in which they spent a lot of their time finding food. Of course, Murdock's list of universals means that ancient human beings found plenty of time for other things, from joking and playing games to creating hairstyles and making tools. But no one in any hunter-gatherer culture ever

Table 31.1 Murdock's (1949) List of 66 Apparent Human Cultural Universals

age-grading, community organisation, cooking, cooperative labour, cosmology, courtship, dancing, decorative art, divination, division of labour, dream interpretation, education, eschatology, ethics, ethno-botany, etiquette, faith healing, family feasting, fire-making, folklore, food taboos, funeral rites, games, gestures, gift-giving, government, greetings, hair styles, hospitality, housing, hygiene, incest taboos, inheritance rules, joking, kin groups, kinship nomenclature, language, law, luck superstitions, magic, marriage, mealtimes, medicine, obstetrics, penal sanctions, personal names, population policy, postnatal care, pregnancy usages, property rights, propitiation of supernatural beings, puberty customs, religious ritual, prescience rules, sexual restrictions, soul concepts, status differentiation, surgery, tool-making, trade, visiting, weather control, and weaving invented guns, tamed horses, collected taxes, or held elections. All these modern inventions depended on the invention of agriculture. This is because it was only once people began growing and storing crops that they began living in **cities** and doing a great deal of trading. And it wasn't until people began trading things in large quantities that someone invented **written language** to keep track of economic transactions. And when people began using written language and living in cities, this transformed human culture in ways no hunter-gatherer could have ever imagined. Living in cities allows for **specialization**. You become great at making shoes, and I become great at making plows. Your first cousin tames ducks and horses, and your second cousin learns to make saddles. His duck saddle business fails miserably, but his horse saddle business makes him a fortune. Through a combination of synergy and tinkering around, cultures that got agriculture long ago got things like guns and steel as part of the extreme task specialization that could develop in such cultures. Because Europeans and Asians got things like guns and steel well before native Africans, native Australians, or native Americans did, they used their power to take over the globe. And the social psychologist in each of us will remind you that once one group of people conquers another group of people, the conquerors develop a wide range of culturally-shared beliefs that justify and maintain their unfair treatment of the conquered (Jost & Hunyady, 2002).

To summarize 10,000 years of recent human history, then, the synergistic coming-together of dozens of high-tech inventions, from alphabets to atomic bombs, all depended on agriculture. And Diamond (1997) showed that some particular locations on Earth made it much, much easier than other locations for people to invent agriculture. More specifically, Diamond showed that the specific wild plants and animals that lent themselves well to the invention of farming happened to exist 11,000 years ago in only a few highly unusual places on the planet. Two such places were the two **fertile crescents** – one in the Middle East (not too far from Europe) and another in east central Asia. These were places with climates just right for farming and naturally-existing plants that are easy to grow, easy to store, and easy to eat. They're also places where lots of species of wild animal didn't fight back too hard when people tried to domesticate them. Consider the six animals in Figure 31.3. The animals in the top row are all naturally more peaceful and cooperative than their cousins in the bottom row. And most of the cooperative animals on Earth happened to live in Eurasia. So once Europeans and Asians got a huge head start on people elsewhere on Earth by inventing agriculture, they were able to gain control of a disproportionate share of the Earth's natural and economic resources.

In fact, 10,000 years after the invention of agriculture, a small number of very wealthy nations have control over the vast majority of the world's wealth. When we last checked in 2015, CIA Factbook data showed that in the 16 poorest countries in the world (e.g., Afghanistan, Liberia, Somalia), the average person lives on one to three dollars per day. That's a couple of dollars a day for *everything*, from food and clothing to shelter and health care. In contrast, these same data showed that in the 40 richest countries on Earth (e.g., Australia, Japan, Norway, Qatar), the average person lived on 100 to 300 dollars per day! That's a factor of 100. Figure 31.4 summarizes this state of affairs using a map of how well-lit different parts of Earth are at night. Notice that most of the electric light (indicating wealth) is located in Northern Asia, Europe, and the giant land masses that European colonists have taken over in the past couple of centuries (e.g., Australia, the United States). All of this from some wheat and goats? Yes. That's the intriguing agricultural story of cultural evolution.

Figure 31.3 Long ago, Eurasia happened to be home to a lot of wild animals that proved to be pretty easy to domesticate (top row). This was not the case in other parts of the Earth (bottom row).

Figure 31.4 If you wonder where all the wealth is on planet Earth, just take a look at this 2016 NASA image of the Earth at night. Like access to electricity, which makes light, average per capita income across the world varies dramatically with region. And it all started with agriculture.

Source: "2012 Black Marble," The Earth Observatory. https://earthobservatory.nasa.gov/features/NightLights

Cultural Evolution and Human Behavior

Diamond is not the only person to point out that cultural variation is often predictable. Research in the rapidly growing field of **cultural evolution** (the study of how cultures change over time – how they come to be the way they are) has now shown repeatedly that things that were once considered arbitrary aspects of culture have been powerfully shaped by specific environmental conditions (Varnum & Grossmann, 2017). For example, people reach puberty at an earlier age in places where food is plentiful and there is little disease than in places where food is scarce and there is lots of disease (Stearns, 1992). Along these lines, Herman-Giddens (2007) showed that over the past 170 years or so, the average age at which girls in wealthy nations reach menarche (their first menstrual period) has decreased from about the age of 17 to about the age of 11 or 12. Likewise, in wealthy nations such as the United Kingdom, the average human lifespan has increased from about 48 in the early 1840s to about 81 at the turn of the 21st century. That kind of radical change, and all the changes in cultural practices that go along with it (e.g., retirement plans, social safety nets for seniors) is unprecedented in human history.

Moving from old age to birth, women seem to give birth to fewer male babies in difficult environments than in safer and more comfortable environments (Dama, 2011; Gellatly, 2009). Even some details of human language seem to vary with the environment. In a study of more than 3,700 languages, Everett, Blasi, and Roberts (2015) found that tonal languages (those that rely heavily on subtle aspects of pitch to communicate meaning) have rarely developed in places where the air is very dry. Apparently, this is the case because dry air is not good for one's vocal cords. Specifically, dry air makes it hard for people to produce the subtle vocal movements that using tonal languages requires. That's presumably why singers take a drink of water or spray that fancy mist into their mouths right before they begin to sing. If dry air were good for precise vocal control, singers would presumably carry around saltines and blow dryers to dry out their vocal cords while warming up. Please don't try this unpleasant experiment at home.

Moving from what comes out of our mouths to what goes in them, the culture of food is also somewhat predictable. Cultural variation in whether people cook with hot spices depends on environmental factors that promote a food's shelf life. In their study of 4,578 recipes in 36 nations, Billing and Sherman (1998) found that whether people in a given culture prepare spicy vs. bland meat dishes depends on both the average local temperature and the abundance of microbes that would spoil any poorly-preserved meat dishes. In hot places, where more micro-organisms exist that could spoil your food, ancient cooks learned to use a wide range of strong spices – such as curry and chili powder – that keep food from going bad quickly. If this description is making you crave either Indian or Mexican food, you now know that it is partly the sweltering heat of Mexico and India that prompted cooks centuries ago to experiment with very strong spices. Of course, modern refrigeration makes those chemical solutions outdated in wealthy nations, but once you develop a fondness for spicy food, you're unlikely ever to give it up.

Environmental Origins of Collectivism, Openness, and Extraversion

If you know anything at all about culture, you've probably heard that cultures vary widely on the dimension of individualism vs. collectivism. An **individualistic** cultural orientation emphasizes the stable properties, rights, and personal desires of the single person. In contrast, a **collectivistic** orientation emphasizes the way people exist in relation to important social groups. Whereas individualistic cultures are all about "I" and "me," collectivistic cultures are all about "us" and "we." People living in individualistic cultures typically emphasize the ways in which they are different from others, and they often claim highly stable traits and identities (Markus & Kitayama, 1991; Triandis, 1989). In contrast, people living in collectivistic cultures are much more likely to emphasize their connectedness to the members of important social groups, meaning they usually place great emphasis on family, work, community-based groups, and religious memberships. A typical individualistic self-view is "I graduated third in my class of 300." A typical collectivistic self-view is "We are good Baptists."

Levels of individualism vs. collectivism vary widely across the globe, and research in cultural evolution shows that a big reason why is historical disease levels. In countries where **pathogen loads** (infectious disease rates) have long been very high, a collectivistic cultural orientation has usually been the norm. Presumably, banning together in tightly-knit groups – and following strict rules about unnecessary contact with outsiders – is a highly adaptive way to cope with a world where people are dropping like flies. In contrast, when disease levels are low, and the risks of death and devastation are thus low as well, people can afford the luxury of focusing on the individual self – and trying new things. Along these lines, Schaller and Murray (2011) showed that in countries with higher rates of communicable disease there are fewer extraverts, more conformists, and fewer people who are open to trying new things. In other worlds, when the going gets tough, people don't just stick together with anybody. They stick together with those they know and trust, but they become cautious and suspicious around strangers. We hope you noticed that Schaller and Murray's findings call to mind several of the Big Five personality traits we reviewed in Module 30. Cultures have personalities, and those personalities are influenced by environmental factors such as pathogen load, death rates, and scarcity of basic resources (Varnum & Grossmann, 2017).

Pathogen loads also seem to influence other aspects of behavior within a culture. For example, in keeping with *life history theory*, places where there is a lot of contagious illnesses typically become home to people who adopt a "fast" life strategy. This means people take frequent risks (*within the group* at least) and seize almost any opportunity to reproduce or increase their chances of survival. In contrast, in friendlier worlds where major disease and death are not so commonplace, people more often adopt a "slow" strategy that involves making safer, long-term bets in life (Dunkel, Mathes, & Beaver, 2013). And of course, when lots of people adopt a strategy, the norms and rules that promote that strategy ("Strike while the iron is hot.") become woven into the culture. We can be almost positive that in ancient human history, most people adopted what modern, wealthy people would consider a fast strategy. As an obvious example, waiting two decades after puberty to bear children 100,000 years ago would have usually been a recipe for disaster, when many people were dead by age 45. But in modern, wealthy cultures, many mothers defer childbirth until they are sure they can provide well for a small number of children – who are all very likely to survive to adulthood. That's a slow life history strategy. In today's complex world, there are both fast and slow cultures. Across the globe today, historical pathogen loads in a country are a strong predictor not only of how many kids people have but also of when they first begin having them (see also Störmer & Lummaa, 2014). Cross-national differences in pathogen loads also predict how parents expect kids to behave once they get here. In cultures where disease abounds, most parents very strongly value child obedience (Pelham, 2019). We hope you can see that in a world where one wrong turn can get a kid killed, obedience to one's parents takes on special importance (Quinlan, 2007).

Culture and Marriage: Polygamy and Polyandry

As we noted earlier, marriage is one of Murdock's cultural universals. However, the norms and rules of marriage differ *dramatically* across the globe. From the ideal age of marriage and whether divorce is ever permitted to whether you have any voice in whom you marry, the rules of marriage are as different as France and Fiji. In the interest of time and space, we're going to have to choose just one example of how marriage varies cross-culturally. You've probably heard that the Earth still contains quite a few cultures where people practice **polygamy**. This is the practice of taking more than one spouse at the same time. But there are two distinct forms of polygamy. When a man takes two or more wives, this is known as **polygyny**. Polygyny is very rare in wealthy nations, but it still exists in many parts of Africa, the Middle East, and Southeast Asia. You may have already known this. But unless you have taken a course in cultural anthropology, you probably did not know that there are plenty of cultures where people practice **polyandry**. Polyandry is the practice of having multiple husbands (though they do not all have to be named Andy). For a long time, social scientists thought polyandry was very rare. But recent research has shown that it is much more common than we once thought. In fact, it exists in a wide variety of forms, and it exists in some form or another all over the globe. Starkweather and Hames (2012) identified 53 cultures worldwide that practice some form of true polyandry.

Suffice it to say that there is a lot of debate about the nature of polyandry. Because polyandry is virtually unheard of in non-human animals, many evolutionary experts consider polyandry a puzzle. But Starkweather and Hames (2012) argue not only that polyandry exists all over the globe but also that it exists in quite a few cultures resembling those in which we evolved (such as hunter-gatherer cultures). Furthermore, there seem to be some reliable cross-cultural predictors of polyandry. For example, polyandry is more common than usual in cultures where there are many more marriageable men than women. When there are more men than women to go around, some simple math suggests that some women might want to hedge their bets and take more than one husband. Polyandry is also more likely to exist in cultures in which male mortality rates are high, because of war or social conflict. A second husband, we suppose, is a pretty

Figure 31.5 This is just the kind of hilly, rugged Himalayan farmland that makes a woman wish she had several husbands, to help her run the farm – and keep it in the family for generations to come.

good life insurance policy against the first. Polyandry also seems to be at least somewhat more likely in cultures in which there's a great deal of male "absenteeism." This might happen, for example, because of frequent male hunting trips, as is true in native Canadian Inuit cultures. In farming cultures, polyandry is also much more common in specific places – such as the Himalayan regions of Tibet, Nepal, and India – where there is very little land – and where the rugged land that does exist is difficult to farm. In such places, polyandry seems to control population growth while also allowing two or more men to work together to run farms that no one man could easily run by himself. It's probably no accident that in these "land-starved" cultures, people care deeply about keeping their plots of land in their own families. We sure wouldn't want to be a real estate agent in such places. From a purely selfish perspective, we hope it's obvious that it could be nice to have two husbands. Your chances of having someone agree to do the dishes or laundry could practically double. But Starkweather and Hames (2012, p. 152) also make a clever argument for what may be in it for some of the men who become "junior husbands." As they put it, sometimes:

> it may be in the interest of a male with low competitive abilities to make the best of a bad situation by becoming a junior husband and having some chance of reproduction. Through time the marriage market may improve, and by working hard the junior husband may be able to demonstrate his attractiveness as a mate to another female and marry her.

All of this, with his wife's permission, we assume.

Culture and the Validity of Psychological Research: The WEIRD Problem

We hope that if you have absorbed nothing else in this module, you now know that the world is an incredibly diverse place – where the rules for almost anything people do vary a great deal from place to place. It is precisely because the world is so diverse that cross-cultural psychologists go to great lengths to see if the principles of psychology we've uncovered in places like the United States and Western Europe hold up well in the rest of the globe. Some cross-cultural psychologists have argued that many of the psychological principles that dictate our thoughts, feelings, and behavior in places like the United States do not seem to hold up in other nations. More specifically, Henrich, Heine, and Norenzayan (2010) argued that, despite the growth in cross-cultural psychology in recent decades, most psychological research continues to overlook the tremendous cultural diversity of the planet. As they put it, most research in psychology involves WEIRD people – people from societies that are "**W**estern, **E**ducated, **I**ndustrialized, **R**ich, and **D**emocratic." Henrich et al. further argue that psychological findings in areas as diverse as visual illusions, human development, social cognition, group processes, self-evaluation, and moral reasoning vary dramatically in WEIRD and non-WEIRD nations. In fact, as they put it, WEIRD nations are often global psychological outliers – the exceptions, not the rule.

For example, Henrich et al. cite a classic study by Segall et al. (1966) that examined the well-known *Müller-Lyer illusion* – which is depicted in Figure 31.6. As you might guess from experiencing this visual illusion yourself, people from all walks of life in the United States experience this illusion. When shown the two images, they perceive the image on the right to contain a longer center horizontal line than the image on the left.

Figure 31.6 The Müller-Lyer illusion. If you perceive the horizontal line on the right to be longer than the one on the left (even when you know it's an illusion), it's likely because you grew up in a world full of right-angled carpentry.

But as Segall et al. (1966) showed, a group of foragers from Africa's Kalahari Desert showed little or no evidence of this visual illusion. Henrich et al. (2010) provide many other examples of how people from WEIRD nations think, reason, and relate to others in ways that are different than people elsewhere in the world. For example, they note that the highly favorable self-views reported by most Westerners stand in sharp contrast to the modest self-views reported by many Easterners. Likewise, studies of conformity that have compared people across cultures reveal that Americans and Western Europeans engage in less conformity than people in most other parts of the world.

We think Henrich et al.'s findings need to be interpreted with caution. For example, the fact that one of hundreds of specific visual illusions disappears in cultures where most people see very few right angles does not mean that the basic principles of visual perception (e.g., size constancy, the power law, simultaneous contrast) differ radically across cultures. Likewise, average levels of conformity surely vary across cultures, but the function and purpose of conformity is arguably very similar across the globe. In fact, one can predict the precise level of conformity in a culture pretty well by knowing about the environmental conditions of that culture (Schaller & Murray, 2011). As we noted earlier, in places where pathogen loads are high, and it is easy to get sick, conformity levels are usually higher than the global average. This makes sense if part of the function of conformity is to keep people from doing things that will get them in trouble. Likewise, the ability to detect cheaters in social transactions seem to be quite robust across the globe (Cosmides & Tooby, 1997). You may also recall from the module on human sexuality that, in 48 nations across the globe, men expressed a more relaxed attitude about causal sex than did women (Schmitt, 2005). There was plenty of cross-cultural variation in how comfortable people were with casual sex. But in every nation Schmitt studied, he found that men were always more interested in casual sex than were women.

Although we think Henrich et al.'s findings should be interpreted with caution, we'd like to add that we feel it was high time that Henrich et al. asked a very important question. To what degree do the rules and principles of psychology differ across the globe? In our view, the answer to this question probably depends on how deeply one digs. Whereas there can be little doubt that the surface details of human behavior vary radically across the globe, we believe that cross-cultural research will eventually reveal that many basic psychological principles – such as the need to belong discussed in the module on motivation – are cross-cultural universals.

To make this point about depth of analysis more concrete, consider research on self-enhancement. A great deal of research in cross-cultural psychology seems to show that Americans are very *self-enhancing* relative to Easterners (Markus & Kitayama, 1991). **Self-enhancement** refers to a desire to view the self favorably – and it seems to come hand in hand with unrealistically positive views of the self (Taylor & Brown, 1988). This often translates into things like tooting your own horn and bragging about the individual self. In the United States, this tendency toward self-adoration is so overlearned that words like "I" and "me" strongly prime positive words such as "good," "gift," and "wonderful." So, if we briefly expose most Americans to the word "me," this makes it easier than usual for them to identify the word "good" – and harder than usual for them to identify the word "bad." In contrast, for most Americans, exposure to words such as "they," "she," or "he" doesn't have this kind of positive priming effect. However, Hetts, Sakuma, and Pelham (1999) showed that this pattern of positive associations to the self does not disappear in Eastern cultures. It is just expressed in a very different way. Whereas Westerners have more positive associations to words like "I" and "me," Easterners have more positive association to words like "we" and "us." In other words, whereas Americans feel very good about the *individual* self, Easterners feel very good about the *social* self. Thus, at a deeper level, it seems clear that across the globe, people self-enhance. Yet, on the surface, the precise path taken toward self-enhancement (via the individual self or the group) just happens to differ in different nations.

Having said all this, we do not wish to minimize the tremendous importance of cross-cultural research. People who live in different cultures do, in fact, live by very different rules. This matters a great deal. What is undeniable about Henrich et al.'s (2010) highly influential point about culture is that psychologists have focused almost all of their past research attention on a very limited number of mostly WEIRD nations. Whether extending the net of psychological research to include many other nations validates what

Figure 31.7 Do you think these family members live in a collectivistic or an individualistic culture? Here are some hints: The child lives with his mother, father, grandmother, and six siblings. The family is also deeply religious, and they all focus a lot on "we" and not so much on "me." Painting by Rhonda Lynn Keith, photo by Brooklyn Pelham.

we already thought we knew about psychology or turns much of it on its head, we will be in a better position to understand human nature if we heed Henrich et al.'s advice – by studying people in cultures that aren't so WEIRD.

Allow us to conclude with an example that supports the WEIRD critique – while also acknowledging an apparent cultural universal. Cross-cultural research suggests that anger is a universal human emotion (Ekman, 1992). However, the exact way in which anger is expressed and interpreted differs greatly from culture to culture. This means that if you make someone angry in a non-honor culture, this person may let you know about this, and this may lead to a very unpleasant conversation. But if you make someone angry in an honor culture, that person is much more likely to hit you with a brick than with a witty barb. Along much the same lines, recall from the module on aggression that regional differences in economic inequality are a very powerful predictor of regional differences in homicide rates. This is true both within and across nations. And it's true despite the fact violence is a part of human nature. Sadly, there is simply no place on Earth where the concept of murder is an unknown. But if we wish to create a future where homicide rates are on the decline, we must carefully study the tremendous cultural variation in how often people kill each other. Understanding how we are different can deepen our appreciation of the complexity of human nature. And it can also help us create worlds where we are nicer to one another – both within and across cultures.

Critical Thinking Questions for Module 31

One of the most frequently studied cultural variables is individualism vs. collectivism. As we hope you recall, most people living in individualistic cultures value the individual person. Individualistic cultures are "I and me cultures." In contrast, most people living in collectivistic cultures are expected to put the needs and wishes of the group ahead of their own personal needs. Collectivistic cultures are "us and we" cultures. Given what you know about these different cultural orientations, see if you can guess which kind of culture – an individualistic one (I) or a collectivistic one (C) – scores higher on each important variable listed. Be sure to defend your answer. The first one is done for you.

_C_ 1. percentage of workforce employed in agriculture. This should be higher in collectivistic cultures because farmers must often work together in groups to earn their living. In the past, at least, farmers traditionally had large families to help with all the labor required to run a farm.

___ 2. rates of regular attendance at religious services

___ 3. infant mortality (the rate at which kids die in the first year of life).

___ 4. total fertility (the average number of children the average woman will bear in her lifetime)

___ 5. economic innovation, inventions, and patents.

___ 6. harsh parenting practices such as frequent and/or severe physical punishment

___ 7. languages that make it easy to express status and/or affection (e.g., *Usted* vs. *tu* in Spanish)

___ 8. personal rights and freedoms (such as the right to vote, peacefully protest, and own property)

___ 9. greater gender equality (e.g., equal access to education for boys and girls)

__ 10. suicide rates

__ 11. alcohol abuse and alcoholism

__ 12. popularity of birthday cards and birthday wishes (physical or virtual)

__ 13. percentage of people living alone

__ 14. percentage of people who own a personal motor vehicle

Did you notice that both collectivistic and individualistic cultural orientations have their pros and cons?

Answer Key (without justifications): 1C 2C 3C 4C 5I 6C 7C 8I 9I 10I 11I 12 C*, 13I 14I

*Note. Although one could argue for the opposite pattern, birthday cards and memes that send birthday wishes are empirically more popular in collectivistic cultures.

Multiple-Choice Questions for Module 31

1. Jory studies regional differences in how people worship, work, and rear children. Is Jory likely to be a cultural psychologist?

   A) no; because she doesn't seem to study social norms or language
   B) maybe; I'd need to know what theory she is testing
   C) yes; she fits the basic definition of cultural psychologist very well

2. The fact that there are many human cultural universals suggests that:

   A) many aspects of culture reflect evolved tendencies
   B) cultures today vary less than cultures of long ago
   C) the universals were arbitrary features of a very ancient culture that all people once shared

3. In his book *Guns, Germs, and Steel*, Jared Diamond argues that Europeans and Asians have long dominated the Earth (both militarily and economically) because:

   A) their cold climates made them have to plan ahead for long, cold winters
   B) they are the only places on Earth where iron and other metals were available for easy surface mining
   C) agriculture was invented first in these regions because there were lots of easily-domesticated plants and animals there

4. What very important invention seems to have put human beings on the road to developing city-states and complex technology?

   A) governments
   B) written language
   C) the wheel

5. The fertile crescent refers to:

   A) a system of lunar seasons used by ancient farmers
   B) areas of the Earth where it was easy to invent farming

   C) areas of the Earth where people could hunt and gather food without needing to farm

6. The study of how cultures have gotten to be the way there are is known as:

   A) cultural evolution
   B) cultural anthropology
   C) cultural psychology

7. As any cultural psychologist could tell you, the wealthy nations in Western Europe (e.g., Germany, England, Sweden) are highly:

   A) eccentric
   B) individualistic
   C) self-sufficient

8. Nations in which people focus heavily on family, religion, and responsibilities to one's groups are known as:

   A) allocentric
   B) communal
   C) collectivistic

9. Polygyny and polyandry are both specific forms of:

   A) arranged marriages
   B) family inheritance and kinship
   C) polygamy

10. In cross-cultural psychology, what does the "W" in the acronym WEIRD refers to?

    A) "World"
    B) "Western"
    C) "Wealthy"

11. Research in cross-cultural psychology suggests that the Muller-Lyer illusions involving the apparent length of lines exists in:

    A) every culture in which it has been studied.
    B) cultures where carpentry is highly developed.
    C) cultures in which people walk, drive, or bike a lot on straight roads and paths.

Answer Key: 1C 2A 3C 4B 5B 6A 7B 8C 9C 10B 11B

References

Anderson, S. R. (no date). How many languages are there in the world? Linguistic Society of America. Retrieved July 2019 from www.linguisticsociety.org/content/how-many-languages-are-there-world

Billing, J., & Sherman, P. W. (1998). Antimicrobial functions of spices: Why some like it hot. *The Quarterly Review of Biology, 73*, 3–49.

Cohen, D., Nisbett, R. E., Bowdle, B. F., & Schwarz, N. (1996). Insult, aggression, and the southern culture of honor: An "experimental ethnography." *Journal of Personality and Social Psychology, 70*(5), 945–960.

Cosmides, L., & Tooby, J. (1997). *Evolutionary psychology: A primer.* Available at http://www.cep.ucsb.edu/primer.html

Dama, M. S. (2011). Sex ratio at birth and mortality rates are negatively related in humans. *Plos One, 6*(8), e23792.

Diamond, J. (1997). *Guns, germs, and steel: The fates of human societies.* New York, NY: W.W. Norton & Company.

Dunkel, C. S., Mathes, E., & Beaver, K. M. (2013). Life history theory and the general theory of crime: Life expectancy effects on low self-control and criminal intent. *Journal of Social, Evolutionary, and Cultural Psychology, 7*(1), 12–23.

Ekman, P. (1992). Are there basic emotions? *Psychological Review, 99*(3), 550–553.

Everett, C., Blasi, D. E., & Roberts, S. G. (2015). Climate, vocal folds, and tonal languages: Connecting the physiological and geographic dots. *PNAS, 112*, 1322–1327.

Gangestad, S. W., Haselton, M. G., & Buss, D. M. (2006). Evolutionary foundations of cultural variation: Evoked culture and mate preferences. *Psychological Inquiry, 17*, 75–95.

Gellatly, C. (2009). Trends in population sex ratios may be explained by changes in the frequencies of polymorphic alleles of a sex ratio gene. *Evolutionary Biology, 36*(2), 190–200. doi:10.1007/s11692-008-9046-3

Henrich, J., Heine, S. J., & Norenzayan, A. (2010). The weirdest people in the world? *Behavioral and Brain Sciences, 33*, 61–135.

Herman-Giddens, M.E. (2007). The decline in the age of menarche in the United States: Should we be concerned? *Journal of Adolescent Health, 40*, 201–203.

Hetts, J. J., Sakuma, M., & Pelham, B. W. (1999). Two-roads to positive regard: Implicit and explicit self-evaluation and culture. *Journal of Experimental Social Psychology, 35*, 512–559.

Jost, J., & Hunyady, O. (2002). The psychology of system justification and the palliative function of ideology. *European Review of Social Psychology, 13*. doi:10.1080/10463280240000046

Legare, C. H., & Nielsen, M. (2015). Imitation and innovation: The dual engines of cultural learning. *Trends in Cognitive Science, 19*(11), 688–699. doi:10.1016/j.tics.2015.08.005

Markus, H. R., & Kitayama, S. (1991). Culture and the self: Implications for cognition, emotion, and motivation. *Psychological Review, 98*, 224–253. doi:10.1037/0033-295X.98.2.224

Murdock, G. P. (1949). *Social structure.* New York, NY: The MacMillan Company.

Noone, Y. (2016, June 6). Can't stomach milk? Blame your ancestors. Retrieved July 2019 from www.sbs.com.au/topics/life/health/article/2016/06/06/cant-stomach-milk-blame-your-ancestors

Pelham, B. (2019). Life history and the cultural evolution of parenting: Pathogens, mortality, and birth across the globe. *Evolutionary Behavioral Sciences.* Advance online publication. doi:10.1037/ebs0000185

Quinlan, R. J. (2007). Human parental effort and environmental risk. *Proceedings of the Royal Society Series B, 274*, 121–125. doi:10.1098/rspb.2006.3690

Schaller, M., & Murray, D. R. (2011). Infectious disease and the creation of culture. In M. Gelfand, C.-y. Chiu, & Y.-y. Hong (Eds.), *Advances in culture and psychology* (pp. 99–152). New York, NY: Oxford University Press.

Schmitt, D. P. (2005). Sociosexuality from Argentina to Zimbabwe: A 48-nation study of sex, culture, and strategies of human mating. *Behavioral and Brain Sciences, 28*, 247–275.

Segall, M., Campbell, D. and Herskovits, MJ. 1966. *The influence of culture on visual perception.* New York: Bobbs-Merrill.

Slade, H. B., & Schwartz, S. A. (1987). Mucosal immunity: The immunology of breast milk. *Journal of Allergy & Clinical Immunology, 3*, 348–358.

Starkweather, K. E., & Hames, R. (2012). A survey of non-classical polyandry. *Human Nature, 23*, 149–172.

Stearns, S. (1992). The evolution of life histories. New York, NY: Oxford University Press.

Störmer, C., & Lummaa, V. (2014). Increased mortality exposure within the family rather than individual mortality experiences triggers faster life-history strategies in historic human populations. *PLoS One, 9*(1), e83633. doi:10.1371/journal.pone.0083633

Taylor, S. E., & Brown, J. D. (1988). Illusion and well-being: A social psychological perspective on mental health. *Psychological Bulletin, 103*(2), 193–210. doi:10.1037/0033-2909.103.2.193

Triandis, H. C. (1989). The self and social behavior in differing cultural contexts. *Psychological Review, 96*, 506–520.

Varnum, M. E., & Grossmann, I. (2017). Cultural change: The how and the why. *Perspectives on Psychological Science, 12*(6), 956–972.

Verma, D. (2017). Is drinking milk healthy for humans? Retrieved July 2019 from https://milk.procon.org

Wilson, E. O. (1975). *Sociobiology: The new synthesis.* Cambridge, MA: Harvard University Press.

X
Clinical Psychology

Module 32

Everybody Hurts

Understanding Psychological Disorders

In the spring of 2019, your first author received a distressing voicemail from a young relative. To protect the identity of the person who left the message, we have changed almost all of the proper names (including numbers and place names), but all of the other details of the voicemail included here are transcribed verbatim:

HEY BRETT: I'm getting recommended to commit suicide *live*, through third sting harassment. From 6242 Tennessee Drive, the same people that killed Dorothy Pelham, your mother and my ancestor, gave Melissa Porter a pacemaker and f**d over Benny Johnson and his son Geronimo. Ummm ... it's 6242 Tennessee Drive, Jennifer Carver, I'm pretty sure Rudy's involved ... with Ken Clark & Rocky Seaford, AKA Kenny Clark, AKA Steve Craig .COM and from ... I Pilates ... meant fresh out of jail, vandalizing the Navy Career Center.

Psychological disorders touch the lives of many people. The particular disorder that this young man seems to be experiencing is schizophrenia, and we will offer more information about this troubling disorder later in this module. For now, however, this voicemail raises a broad question that is relevant to all psychological disorders. How do we separate *psychological disorders* from quirky opinions or rare (statistically unusual) behavior? For example, the day before writing this paragraph, your first author was waiting in line at the post office, and he observed a postal clerk who was picking her nose in public. This created some discomfort when a customer loudly called her out on this behavior – and asked to be served by a different clerk. But we do not conclude from this incident that this unusual postal clerk – who was clearly violating American social norms about nose care – suffered from a psychological disorder. What makes one thing a psychological disorder and another thing a bad habit?

Defining Disorder

As it turns out, the official definitions for the psychological disorders treated by clinical psychologists actually come from **psychiatrists** (medical doctors who specialize in diagnosing and treating mental illness) rather than psychologists. Every decade or two, the American *Psychiatric* Association (not to be confused with that *other* APA – the American *Psychological* Association) produces a giant book called the **DSM** (Diagnostic and Statistical Manual of Mental Disorders). The DSM lays out all the details for diagnosing all known psychological disorders. The most recent version of the DSM, the DSM-5, came out in 2013 – after about a dozen years of expert debate and discussion.

You will notice that the DSM uses the term "mental disorder" in its title whereas we use the term "psychological disorder." These terms are often used interchangeably. We will use the term "psychological disorder" going forward because it has more neutral connotations than "mental disorder." In our view, "psychological disorder" also better reflects the complex nature of the many disorders covered by the DSM. As you will soon see, psychological disorders are disturbances that involve the way we think, feel, and behave; they are not merely "mental."

The Three Key Features of Psychological Disorders

So what, exactly, is a psychological disorder? First, according to all recent versions of the DSM (the DSM-5 included), all psychological disorders involve **disturbances** in thought, feeling and behavior. Did you notice that by highlighting thought, feeling, and behavior, this definition maps very closely onto our definition of psychology? Psychological disorders are psychological disturbances. But we are often disturbed. You were probably disturbed when you were cut off on the highway yesterday, and you were probably disturbed at age seven when your favorite pet died. So, disturbance is only part of the picture. Second, the person must be experiencing symptoms that impair daily functioning. Psychological disorders involve **impairment**. As we examine some specific psychological disorders in this module, you will notice that the symptoms of these disorders persist over time and get in the way of (impair) key aspects of our lives – our work, sleep, diet, or interpersonal relationships. Third, psychological disorders are **internal dysfunctions**. This means that they are presumed to have a meaningful psychological and/or physical basis. For example, clinical depression has been associated with feelings of helplessness and with imbalances in levels of the neurotransmitter serotonin. This suggests that depression has both a psychological and physiological basis. The requirement that psychological disorders are internal dysfunctions also means that extremely inappropriate or antisocial behavior that is fueled by external forces may not qualify as a symptom of a psychological disorder. This means that if a person gets caught up in a violent protest and sets a car on fire, this is not sufficient, *in and of itself*, to establish that the person has a psychological disorder. To summarize, the **three key features of psychological disorders** are *disturbance, impairment*, and *internal dysfunction* (Schacter, Gilbert, & Wegner, 2011).

Having asserted that psychological disorders are defined by these three basic properties, we'd like to make it clear that *all* our thoughts, feelings, and behaviors fall on a broad continuum ranging from normal (non-disordered, if you like) on one end of the continuum to abnormal (disordered) on the other end. At one time in your life, you have probably experienced a wave of panic during an exam, felt extreme fear, or experienced grief as a result of loss. We have all experienced these emotions. Each of these normal reactions shares key characteristics with the symptoms of at least one clinical disorder. This is what we mean by falling on the same continuum – from normal to abnormal. The reason why our ordinary fear, anxiety, and sadness fall on the non-disorder end of the continuum is because experiencing these emotions does not impair our ability to carry on with our lives. When our disturbances are more extreme, impair our daily activities, and are linked with internal dysfunction, then the disturbances fall on the disorder end of the continuum. Understanding this continuum is important because it underscores that people with disorders are not that different than people without disorders. As REM lead singer Michael Stipe put it, "Everybody hurts!"

This continuum also provides a framework for understanding the goal of psychotherapy (which we will cover in the next module): A good way to think about psychotherapy is that it is designed to move the client along the continuum toward the normal, less impaired end of the continuum. The idea of a continuum also highlights one of the reasons clinical diagnosis can be so challenging. Where on the continuum does one draw the line to separate that which needs to be treated from that which does not? Exactly when is an emotional, social, or behavioral problem a disorder, and when is it, well, just a problem? By specifying the nature and severity of the symptoms associated with a disorder, the DSM tries to help clinicians address this challenge. But it's not easy. To understand the extent of the challenge, consider Table 32.1 which contains the 22 broad categories of psychological disorders that are included in the DSM-5 (influenced heavily by Schacter et al.'s 2011, summary of the older DSM-IV). As you can see, clinical disorders come in many shapes and sizes. In fact, a critique of the DSM-5 is that the modern list of clinical disorders has ballooned to such an extent that there is a risk of "pathologizing" many normal behaviors. We will briefly address that issue in Module 33. For now, we hope you can see that being a "worry wart" – even if you have been one your whole life – is very different than having a full-blown anxiety disorder. Likewise, being sad and sorely missing a friend who just moved far away is very different from being diagnosed with clinical depression. Psychological disorders involve extreme disturbances that impair normal functioning. Of course, they also represent internal dysfunctions.

Table 32.1 Twenty-Two Categories of Mental Disorder according to the DSM-5.

1. **Neurodevelopmental Disorders.** Examples are autism spectrum disorder and learning and communication disorders.
2. **Schizophrenia Spectrum and Other Psychotic Disorders.** These disorders involve major disturbances in language, thought, emotions, and behavior. Schizophrenic spectrum disorder will be covered briefly in this module.
3. **Bipolar and Related Disorders.** This includes a family of disorders that involve extreme mood swings that vary cyclically over long periods. Both bipolar 1 disorder and bipolar 2 disorder, for example, involve periods of extreme agitation and positive mood followed by periods of clinical depression. Cyclothymia, for example, is a less extreme version of these extreme mood swings.
4. **Depressive Disorders.** Once categorized as a "mood disorder," depression now has its own category. This includes long periods of "sad, empty, or irritable mood" and the physical or cognitive deficits that often come with this. We cover major depressive disorder in this module.
5. **Anxiety Disorders.** This includes disorders such as Generalized Anxiety Disorder (GAD) and specific phobias (both to be covered in this module) as well as panic disorder. Agoraphobia (fear of certain outdoor or public situations) gets its own subcategory.
6. **Obsessive-Compulsive and Related Disorders.** This group includes obsessive-compulsive disorder (OCD) itself (once considered an anxiety disorder) as well as disorders such as excoriation disorder (skin picking) and hoarding disorder.
7. **Trauma- and Stressor-Related Disorders.** This includes posttraumatic stress disorder (PTSD) as well as acute stress disorder – which is much like PTSD except that it immediately follows a traumatic event and may prove to be short-lived.

(Continued)

Table 32.1 (Cont.)

8. **Dissociative Disorders.** These are disorders in which normally integrated memories and identities are split. An example is dissociative identity disorder (to be covered in this module). Long ago, this was referred to as "multiple personality disorder."

9. **Somatic Symptom Disorder and Related Disorders.** This includes disorders grounded in one's preoccupation with one's physical health. The symptoms often have no obvious physical basis, but it is more central to the definition of this disorder that the person has a persistent, extreme, and troubling focus on the symptoms.

10. **Feeding and Eating Disorders.** This broad group of disorders involves dangerous or dysfunctional problems with food – such as anorexia nervosa and bulimia nervosa (both of which are covered in this module).

11. **Elimination Disorders.** This is a group of disorders that often begin in childhood. The two most common disorders are enuresis (urinating in one's clothing) and encopresis (defecating in one's clothing). This may be voluntary or involuntary.

12. **Sleep-wake Disorders.** This includes such serious sleep problems as insomnia, sleep terrors, and nightmare disorder.

13. **Sexual Dysfunctions.** This includes sexual activity problems such as erectile dysfunction or premature ejaculation in men and female orgasmic disorder (lifetime lack of orgasm).

14. **Gender Dysphoria.** This controversial category refers to "the distress that may accompany the incongruence between one's experienced or expressed gender and one's assigned gender." In previous versions of the DSM this was referred to as "gender identity disorder." This category is controversial for many reasons, one of which is that, until 1974, homosexuality was tragically categorized as an official psychological disorder. Many transgender rights activists worry that this category is grounded in some of the same gender-traditional views that plagued psychiatry prior to 1974.

15. **Disruptive, Impulse-Control, and Conduct Disorders.** Kleptomania (uncontrollable stealing), pyromania (fire setting), and conduct disorder are examples of these disorders. These disorders almost always emerge in childhood or adolescence.

16. **Substance-Related and Addictive Disorders.** Obvious examples are dependence on alcohol, cocaine, tobacco and any other psychoactive drug. But even "Caffeine Intoxication" is on this list – as is "Gambling Disorder" (problematic gambling).

17. **Neurocognitive Disorders.** This includes problems with memory, movement, and thinking. It thus covers problems such as Parkinson's disease, Alzheimer's disease, and cognitive problems that can be caused by head trauma or HIV infection.

18. **Personality Disorders.** As the name suggests, this refers to unhealthy lifelong behavior patterns such as self-centeredness, (e.g., narcissistic personality disorder) and overdependence. Such traits obviously fall on a continuum. They become disorders when they chronically and seriously disrupt a person's life.

19. **Paraphilic Disorders.** This category refers to sexual behavior that is considered socially inappropriate. However, to qualify as a psychological disorder this unusual behavior must either lead to personal distress or create "harm, or risk of harm, to others." Voyeuristic disorder (sexual spying) and exhibitionistic disorder (getting aroused from showing one's genitals to unsuspecting people) are examples.

20. **Other Mental Disorders.** This refers to disorders that do not fall neatly into any other categories, but which nonetheless involve disturbance, impairment, and internal dysfunction.

21. **Medication-Induced Movement Disorders and Other Adverse Effects of Medication.** This refers to long-term problems that may emerge as a consequence of long-term use of medication. An example is the tardive dyskinesia (involuntary motor movements) that often results from the long-term use of anti-psychotic drugs used to treat schizophrenic spectrum.

22. **Other Conditions That May Be a Focus of Clinical Attention.** This includes serious problems grounded in abuse, relationship problems, and occupational problems.

In our view, clinical disorders are often tied to two other ideas with which you should be familiar (from prior modules). First, clinical disorders often involve *automatic thinking*. Remember FUME (fast, unconscious, mandatory, and efficient)? As you will soon see, for example, the debilitating fears that are symptoms of Generalized Anxiety Disorder often prove impossible for people to control when they have this disorder. In people with GAD, the worrisome thoughts that most other people easily shake off become the first (fast) thoughts that come to mind – and they become unstoppable (i.e., mandatory). Second, most psychological disorders have an emotional component, and that means that many psychological disorders follow the rule that emotions often dominate cognition. Remember the milk in a condom? To some degree, all of us are ruled by our emotions. In the case of many clinical disorders, though, our emotions dominate cognition in ways that seriously compromise our long-term health and well-being. Further, many forms of psychotherapy for psychological disorders involve helping clients develop new skills for managing their emotions (Ehrenreich, Fairholme, Buzzella, Ellard, & Barlow, 2007).

The Pervasiveness of Psychological Disorders

In this short module, we will only be able to explore the details of eight psychological disorders. This is one of the reasons why we included Table 32.1 in this module – to give you a basic sense of just how many psychological disorders there are. The precise number of clinical disorders that appear in the DSM-5 depends heavily on exactly what one counts as a separate disorder. But almost everyone agrees that there are at least 150 official disorders, and some experts put the figure as high as 265 (Ghaemi, 2013). Further, careful studies that have looked at the likelihood that a person will suffer from at least one official psychological disorder in his or her lifetime put the figure just below 50% (46% to be precise; Kessler et al., 2005). At some point in life, about half of all people will experience a psychological disorder. Thus, whereas the incidence of some specific disorders is very low, the total incidence rate for psychological disorders of any kind is very high. If you apply this logic to families or groups of people rather than individual people, the odds that a psychological disorder has touched your life go up dramatically. If we ignore the fact that many psychological disorders run in families, the likelihood that none of your four biological grandparents ever experienced a psychological disorder is less than one in 12. Psychological disorders are important not just because they influence lives but also because they are pervasive. If you are curious to know how we know just how pervasive psychological disorders are in the first place, check out the details of the Epidemiologic Catchment Area study (Regier & Burke, 1987). It took an enormous effort to estimate the population incidence rates for a wide range of psychological disorders.

Psychological Disorders Have Multiple Roots

Before we dig into the details of the disorders covered in this module, we also want to touch on the origins of psychological disorders. The roots of psychological disorders are complex, and they vary from disorder to disorder. There is virtually *no* psychological disorder that has a single, simple cause. Experts agree, then, that most psychological disorders have multiple roots. There are three broad categories of the causes of psychological disorders. They include (1) biological causes – including chemical imbalances, variations in brain structure, and genetic influences, (2) psychological causes – including perceived stress, feelings of helplessness, and cognitive distortions, and (3) social and environmental causes – including social learning, normative, and sociocultural influences. These three categories of causes are often lumped under an umbrella term, which is the **biopsychosocial model** of the origins of clinical disorders. (Notice that this fancy term breaks down into (1) bio, (2) psycho, and (3) social.) For any given disorder, the relative influence of these causes varies, and this variation in origins is part of the reason why it's easier to treat some psychological disorders than others. For example, schizophrenia appears to have a strong genetic component whereas specific phobias appear to have a strong learning component. Thus, it is often possible to get at the root cause of specific phobias in only a handful of treatment sessions (using behavioral approaches such as exposure therapy). In contrast, it is much more difficult to treat the genetic root causes of schizophrenia. Instead, as you will see in Module 33, the best forms of treatment for schizophrenia are typically anti-psychotic medication – which can only reduce the symptoms. In sum, there are many disorders, many differences in where they come, and thus many differences in how they are best treated.

In the remainder of this module, you'll learn the basic definitions of eight clinical disorders. We'll also try to touch very briefly on the likely origins and/or consequences of these eight disorders. Then, after this module is done, you may wish to try your hand at the hands-on activity that asks you to diagnosis some fictional patients – many of whom, we assumed in the exercise, are experiencing a psychological disorder. Doctoral students in clinical and counseling psychology programs spend many years training to diagnose clinical disorders. Thus, we don't want to give you the impression that clinical diagnosis is easy. It is not. Clinical interviews are typically *much* more extensive than the brief quotations we'll provide. But the specific quotations we chose are a vehicle for challenging you to discriminate between a handful of different disorders. One of the best ways to begin to understand psychological disorders is to see how they are officially defined and to apply those definitions when making diagnoses. With this in mind, let's see what the DSM-5 has to say about eight clinical disorders. The very large majority of the descriptions in this module come directly from the DSM-5. In most of the specific descriptions of eight clinical disorders, we simply paraphrased the official DSM-5 statements, always with the goal of making the clinical language more accessible.

Depressive Disorders and Bipolar Disorders

Clinical Depression

The "common cold" of clinical disorders is **clinical depression** (aka, major depressive disorder), so called because depression is the most common of all clinical disorders. To be diagnosed with clinical depression, a person must have been experiencing *five or more* of the following symptoms for at least *two weeks*. Further, at least one of the five-plus symptoms must be either symptom 1 or 2 on this list.

1. Depressed mood most of the day.
2. Greatly reduced interest in (or reduced pleasure taken from) almost all normal activities.

3. Notable weight loss when not dieting, weight gain, or decrease or increase in appetite.
4. Insomnia (not sleeping enough) or sleeping excessively
5. Agitation or greatly slowed thinking and reduced physical activity (as seen by others).
6. Feeling tired or having a lack of energy.
7. Feeling worthless or experiencing great amounts of inappropriate guilt.
8. Difficulty thinking, concentrating, or making simple decisions.
9. Repeated thoughts of death or suicide, a plan to commit suicide, or an attempted suicide.

We hope you can see that there's a big difference between experiencing clinical depression and feeling "down in the dumps" now and then. People who are experiencing clinical depression are often at serious risk for suicide, and they may have great difficulty just getting out of bed in the morning (impairment is high). Singer Paul Simon probably was *not* clinically depressed when he wrote, "It's been a long, long day." In contrast, singer Todd Snider *may* have depressed when he wrote, "it's been a long, long *year*." Biographies of Abe Lincoln strongly suggest that Lincoln often suffered from depression. A history of early loss is a risk factor for depression, and Lincoln's mother died when he was young. Here is a sample of how Shenk (2005) described Lincoln:

As a young man he talked more than once of suicide, and as he grew older he said he saw the world as hard and grim, full of misery, made that way by fate and the forces of God. "No element of Mr. Lincoln's character," declared his colleague Henry Whitney, "was so marked, obvious and ingrained as his mysterious and profound melancholy." His law partner William Herndon said, "His melancholy dripped from him as he walked."

Figure 32.1 Like the woman depicted in this 1892 lithograph (left), U.S. President Abe Lincoln (right) seems to have battled clinical depression. In Lincoln's case, this seems to have happened on more than one occasion.

Bipolar Disorder

There are three bipolar disorders that all fall within the Bipolar and Related Disorders category. We'll examine only one of the three members of this family – what is known as **bipolar I disorder**. According to the DSM-5, this disorder involves "dramatic mood swings." This means people alternate (often over long windows) between extreme elation and risk-taking (feeling "on top of the world") and experiencing episodes of clinical depression. This disorder was once called "manic depression" because people cycle between mania ("being on top of the world – though not in control of it") and being clinically depressed. Note that people who suffer from this disorder never experience the two opposing sets of symptoms at the same time. Thus, a therapist or doctor must rely on reports of a person's past behavior (perhaps over several years) rather than just considering what has been happening in the past few weeks or months.

If you love the voice of the genie from Disney's animated version of *Aladdin*, you may be familiar with at least one famous person who struggled with bipolar disorder. The lovable actor and comedian Robin Williams apparently spent much of his life coping with the extreme mood swings that are characteristic of this disorder. It is crucial to understand that bipolar disorder is *not* just moodiness or emotionality. This is one of the more dangerous clinical disorders because people with this disorder often put themselves in harm's way during both the peaks and the valleys of this disorder. During periods of mania, people may take extreme risks, empty their bank accounts, and run their bodies into the ground by going days or even weeks with little or no sleep. At the other extreme, during periods of depression, people with bipolar disorder are at elevated risk for suicide and accidental forms of self-harm such as overdosing on alcohol and narcotics. The tragic stories of Robin Williams, singer Amy Winehouse, and actor Phillip Seymour Hoffman all seem to be connected by the common thread of bipolar disorder (Ghaemi, 2014).

Anxiety Disorders

Generalized Anxiety Disorder (GAD)

If you have ever been around a person who is manic, you know that the person loses all sense of what is dangerous – and thus can get badly hurt. Those who suffer from **Generalized Anxiety Disorder** (GAD) are much the opposite. They *chronically worry* about many, many things, and their level of worry can become psychologically paralyzing. According to the DSM-5 this disorder applies to people who experience extreme worry or anxiety "more days than not for at least 6 months." The chronic worries must apply to more than one kind of activity (e.g. both family *and* school). It must also be difficult or impossible for such people to control their worries. On top of all this, the chronic worries that are part of GAD must be accompanied by at least three of the following six symptoms (happening more days than not for six months or more):

1. restlessness, feeling "on edge"	4. irritability
2. fatigue, getting tired easily	5. muscle tension
3. difficulty concentrating	6. sleep disturbance (e.g., insomnia)

Furthermore, all these symptoms (e.g., the anxiety, the irritability) must get in the way of the person's life – by harming relationships, by making it hard or impossible to work, etc. Notice the repeated references to disturbances and impairment. This, again, is what distinguishes GAD symptoms from normal, day to day worries. The DSM also specifies that a GAD diagnosis is only possible if these symptoms cannot be easily explained by medical conditions such as thyroid disease or by more specific clinical disorders such as panic attacks, social phobia, or schizophrenia. Thus, one must rule a lot of problems *out* before ruling GAD in.

Figure 32.2
Anxiety disorders go way beyond the day to day fears and worries that are an inescapable fact of life. Unlike a little performance anxiety or stage fright, for example, anxiety disorders are debilitating.

Your first author is all too familiar with this specific psychological disorder. His maternal grandmother Catherine suffered from this disorder much of her adult life. Her worry seems to have begun when her husband, J.L., became a tank driver in World War II. But for reasons that seem to defy explanation, Catherine's worry about J.L.'s safety as a solider seems to have metastasized into worries about tiny things that no one else found worrisome. Logically speaking, most of the things Catherine worried about were not very big risks. They were things like her own health, her dog's whereabouts, or whether her husband was in danger (long after he survived his time in World War II). But no amount of reassurance could help her shed her fears. She was not irritable – at least not to her grandchildren. But she slept poorly and was always tired. There were periods of several years when she absolutely refused to leave her home. As you will see in the next module, we have little difficulty accepting the research that suggests that there is a genetic component to this disorder. Both one of Catherine's daughters and one of her granddaughters also experienced this clinical disorder. If you noticed that all three of these people are female, you won't be too surprised to learn that this disorder is about twice as common in women as it is in men (McLean, Asnaani, Litz, & Hofmann, 2011).

Phobias

Like GAD, specific phobias also qualify as examples of anxiety disorders. But phobias are different than GAD. Unlike people with GAD, who worry about many, many things, people with a specific **phobia** just worry a great deal about one specific thing. An extreme fear of heights is known as acrophobia, and an extreme fear of spiders is known as **arachnophobia**. An extreme fear of the number 13 (yes, it exists) is known as **triskaidekaphobia**. An extreme fear of people who are pointing shotguns at you is known as common sense. As the shotgun example suggests, being extremely afraid of specific things (shotguns pointed at you, bears charging at you) is *not* the same as having a phobia. Being diagnosed with a specific phobia means six unusual things must be true.

1. The fear must be "unreasonable" and "excessive." Dislike or discomfort doesn't count.
2. The fear response must be rapid and unreasonable in response to the feared stimulus.
3. The person must take extreme actions to avoid the stimulus or must be impaired if forced to be around the stimulus.
4. The fear must get in the way of the person's life by interfering with school, work, etc.
5. This all must have been going on for at least six months.
6. This can't be another kind of anxiety problem in disguise (e.g., panic disorder or GAD)

Phobias are common enough that we would be surprised if you do not know someone well who has a *bona fide* phobia. Your first author's daughter may have a bona fide spider phobia. Brooklyn will not enter a room if she knows that a dead spider is in the room. We hope you notice that being unable to enter a room is an impairment that could cause a significant disruption. Her brother Lincoln loves to tease her about her fear of spiders, but he grows quiet when reminded that his extreme fear of bees is almost as powerful as his sister's powerful fear of spiders. If there is any good news about phobias, it is that they are easier to treat than most other clinical disorders. Forms of exposure therapy, such as *systematic desensitization*, can cure people of phobias, sometimes in only a few therapy sessions. We will discuss psychotherapy for phobias in some detail in Module 33.

Feeding and Eating Disorders

Anorexia nervosa gets enough popular attention that you have probably heard of it, and you probably knew that this clinical disorder affects women much more often than men. But you probably did *not* know that this disease has the highest death rate of any of the many disorders covered by the DSM-5. To be diagnosed with this specific eating disorder, a person must experience three serious problems.

1. The person must restrict his or her food intake to the point of being unreasonably thin, meaning having a weight that is "less than minimally normal" or "less than minimally expected." Past versions of the DSM used a standard of weighing less than 85% of a normal body weight, but this has been replaced by a grading scale for exactly how thin a person is.

On top of this, the candidate for this eating disorder must also experience:

2. extreme worry or fear about gaining weight – despite already being underweight.

And finally, it must also be true that the person in question:

3. has a highly distorted perception of his or her body (thinking you're fat when you're dangerously thin) and bases his or her self-worth in an extreme way on being thin.

In short, for those who have this disorder, being thin becomes so important and self-consuming that the person may starve and/or exercise him- or herself to death. If you wonder why people with this disorder don't just get really hungry and eat, one answer is that their brains seem to stop responding to hunger signals. Blood levels of the so-called "hunger hormone" (ghrelin) are extremely high in people with anorexia. Something must be happening, then, that causes the brain to suppress the otherwise powerful motivational signal that it is time to eat (Méquinion et al., 2013). Although there's healthy debate about the exact causes of anorexia, it seems clear that both biology and culture play a role in the development of this serious disorder. On the cultural front, rates of anorexia nervosa are higher in cultures where food is plentiful than in cultures where food is scarce (Makino, Tsuboi, & Dennerstein, 2004). Further, within wealthy nations such as the United States and much of Western Europe, psychological risk factors for anorexia seem to include perfectionism and negative self-evaluations (Fairburn, Shafran, & Cooper, 1999). Given the images of extremely thin women that dominate popular magazines and entertainment channels in wealthy nations, it is no wonder that so many American women wish they could be thinner (Rozin, Bauer, & Catanese, 2003). Cultural norms can be extraordinarily powerful. Not surprisingly, anorexia nervosa became more common in many wealthy nations in the latter part of the 1900s as the norm of thinness was becoming more pervasive. But it seems to have leveled out in the past couple of decades. Despite its somewhat low incidence rate relative to disorders such as depression and GAD, anorexia nervosa still poses a serious public health risk. This is because – as we hope you recall – it has the highest mortality rate of any psychological disorder (Arcelus, Mitchell, Wales, & Nielsen, 2011).

Bulimia Nervosa

Along with anorexia nervosa, **bulimia nervosa** is an eating disorder. However, in contrast to people with anorexia nervosa, people with bulimia nervosa do *not* become dangerously thin. In fact, people who experience bulimia nervosa can be average in weight or heavier than average. However, for people with this clinical disorder, concerns about food are still self-defining. To be diagnosed with bulimia nervosa, a person must experience four serious problems. According to the DSM-5, the person must:

1. engage in binge eating. This means *both* (a) eating a very large amount of food in a small amount of time (considering the circumstances) and (b) feeling a lack of control over such eating episodes.
2. engage in extreme behavior intended to make up for the episode of extreme eating. This may include making oneself vomit, using laxatives, fasting, taking part in extreme exercise, or any other unusual "compensatory" behavior intended to prevent weight gain.
3. engage in both binge eating and inappropriate compensatory behaviors (1 and 2), on average, at least once a week for three months.
4. base his or her self-evaluation heavily on body shape and weight.

On top of all this, this "binge and purge" process cannot occur exclusively while the person is suffering from anorexia. Like anorexia nervosa, bulimia nervosa surely has a cultural component. As you can see from point number four, people with bulimia nervosa, like people with anorexia nervosa, base their self-evaluations heavily on their weight and body shape. The same popular messages and unrealistic media images that contribute to other eating disorders surely contribute to bulimia nervosa. Further, although death rates from bulimia nervosa pale in comparison with death rates from anorexia nervosa, there is a long list of undesirable health consequences of bulimia nervosa, most of which are side effects of self-induced vomiting and/or laxative abuse. For example, self-induced vomiting can seriously damage a person's teeth and throat, and abuse of laxatives can cause serious gastrointestinal problems (Mehler & Rylander, 2015).

Schizophrenia Spectrum

One of the most puzzling and distressing clinical disorders is also one of the most difficult to treat. Schizophrenia – renamed the **schizophrenia spectrum** in DSM-5 – refers to a set of disorders involving highly unusual, disorganized, and inappropriate thought and behavior. According to the DSM-5, a diagnosis of schizophrenia requires that a person experience at least two of the following five symptoms – with the qualification that at least one of the two or more symptoms must be one of the first three symptoms in the list. These symptoms are:

1. delusions (e.g., thinking you can read minds or time travel)
2. hallucinations (hearing, seeing, feeling, or tasting things that are not real)
3. disorganized speech (e.g., using "word salad" such as "He said the why of the ghost fume is never the one you can't trust ... like Jesus three did.")
4. disorganized or catatonic behavior (e.g., freezing up for no reason)
5. negative symptoms such as social withdrawal or extreme apathy

It is worth adding that students who first learn about schizophrenia often assume that "**negative symptoms**" involve negative attitudes or emotions. In the case of schizophrenia spectrum, though, a "negative" symptom refers to something normal that is curiously *missing*. The negative symptom of social withdrawal refers to the *absence* of the usual human desire for contact. Likewise, the negative symptom of "extreme apathy" refers to the *absence* of the intense negative emotions that one would normally expect people to express when they sincerely believed that someone was plotting to kill them. One of the most obvious clinical signs of schizophrenia is the *calmness* with which patients who experience this disorder describe some very scary stuff.

There are still many unanswered questions about the origins of schizophrenia spectrum, but we have long known that this disorder often emerges during adolescence and very early adulthood. And most experts agree that it has a substantial genetic component. It now looks like schizophrenia may develop when synaptic pruning (brain "fine tuning") goes seriously wrong. This may help explain why schizophrenia is so difficult to treat. As we noted previously, therapy cannot treat the root cause of schizophrenia – the way therapy can sometimes treat specific phobias. In fact, a major problem faced by the loved ones of

Figure 32.3 Many people imagine that those with schizophrenia are in extreme distress all the time. Wouldn't you be if you thought a loved one was trying to kill you? There is some truth to this, but the *negative symptoms* of schizophrenia – such as social withdrawal and blunted emotions – are also defining features.

patients with schizophrenia spectrum is the fact that patients who are benefitting greatly from anti-psychotic medication often stop taking it. A review of multiple studies revealed that there are many reasons why the problem of non-compliance with medication is more pronounced with schizophrenia than it is with many other clinical disorders. A big part of the problem is that the very symptoms of schizophrenic spectrum itself often get in the way of compliance with medical instructions. The same paranoia, disordered thinking, hallucinations, and delusional beliefs that are defining features of this disorder often foster beliefs that get in the way of taking much-needed medication. And the list of beliefs and risk factors that get in the way of medical compliance with anti-psychotic medication is a long one. In their review of 37 recent studies of schizophrenia, Higashi et al. (2013) identified more than a dozen social or psychological predictors of whether patients with schizophrenia reliably took their medication. These included "lack of insight," false or negative beliefs about medication, and substance abuse. Further, patients whose schizophrenia spectrum symptoms were more severe in the first place were at greater risk for failing to take their medication. This is important because among patients with this disorder, one of the many risks of failing to stay medicated is hospitalization.

Dissociative Identity Disorder (DID)

If you thought schizophrenia was puzzling, you'll be even more stupefied by what the DSM-5 refers to as **Dissociative Identity Disorder (DID)**. People with this disorder possess two or more very different identities. Further, each identity is often wholly unaware of all the other identities. To an observer, it *looks like* multiple people inhabit one physical body. It is for this reason that this disorder was once called "multiple personality disorder." This disorder – and dissociative disorders in general – are characterized by a distinct disconnect between aspects of ourselves and our memories that are normally seamlessly integrated. The fact that one identity usually has little or no memory of anything said or done by a different identity could be considered a form of amnesia. But by definition, the unique form of amnesia that is often part of this disorder is not attributable to any of the usual sources of amnesia (e.g., alcoholic blackouts, injuries to the hippocampus). A person with DID might truly seem to *be* Ria, Sara, Jimmy, or Raj on different days. The DSM-5 also specifies that the amnesia includes even the most routine events, rather than just traumatic events. It is also necessary here (as with all clinical disorders) that the disorder causes serious impairments in the person's daily life.

More than is the case with other disorders, DID is often met with skepticism. There has been some substantial scientific debate about whether this disorder is real. Although the DSM-5 treats this disorder as an official clinical disorder, critics argue that this rare and highly unusual disorder might be something people often fake. Why? To avoid taking responsibility for one's inappropriate or illegal behavior. In recent years, experts have begun to use techniques such as fMRI and implicit measures to assess the reality of DID. Both of these approaches have provided evidence of the reality of DID. To cite just one example, Eich and colleagues (1997) studied nine patients diagnosed with DID and tested their memories when they were exposed to information while in one personality state but were then tested on that information either (a) while in that same identity state or (b) in a different identity state. For example, suppose Sara (P1) studied the memory words "APPLE," "CAMEL," & "SPRUCE." Later, Jenn (P2) would be asked to complete some word fragments with the first word to come to mind:

APP_____   CAM_____   SPR_____

Recall that research on implicit memory suggests that even incidental exposure to words should prime the production of the words on this kind of implicit word-completion task. But Eich et al. only observed semantic (word) priming among people who *didn't* change their identities between exposure and testing. They argued that different identities in patients with DID do not necessarily share "language use." One could quibble with some of the details of this study, but it is just one example of carefully collected evidence suggesting that – whereas DID is very rare – it is also very real. At a minimum, research on DID had to survive some critical scientific scrutiny to make it into the DSM-5.

Comorbidity

As we close out this module on psychological disorders, we want to note that psychological disorders do not occur in isolation. Just because a person has one psychological disorder does not mean that they cannot also be experiencing another disorder at the same time. When two disorders co-occur (are experienced at the same time), they are considered comorbid with each other. This is more common than you might think. In fact, the authors of the DSM-5 explicitly acknowledge *comorbidity* as early as page 5 of the DSM. **Comorbidity** happens when people possess two or more psychological disorders at the same time. For example, clinical depression is often *comorbid with* anorexia nervosa. Clinical depression is also often comorbid with many of the anxiety disorders. If you know someone who has ever been clinically depressed, that person is also at elevated risk for GAD, for example. The frequency of comorbidity between specific psychological disorders varies greatly, but comorbidity is particularly high between many personality disorders and some of the common disorders we have reviewed here.

For example, borderline personality disorder refers to a chronic tendency toward emotional instability and relationship problems. You can probably see how people with borderline personality disorder might become depressed or experience high levels of anxiety relative to people without borderline personality disorder. As you can imagine, psychological treatment for multiple disorders is more challenging than psychological treatment for just one neat and simple disorder. This is yet another way in which the day to day realities of experiencing psychological disorders is more complex than one might assume after reading the well-specified lists of symptoms that define specific psychological disorders. You already knew that most psychological disorders have many roots. Now you know that those roots – and the disorders they feed into – are sometimes entangled with one another in complex ways.

Hands-On Activity for Module 32: Identifying Clinical Disorders

Identify the psychological disorder at work – *if any* – in each description or conversation that follows:

_____ 1. "Well, the CIA is in on it with the Russians. They know none too well … hooks and wires, my almighty powers are too transcendent. They'll kill you, too."

_____ 2. "Here's the problem with your advice. I can't change any of it, and it's going to ruin things worse than they are now. I mean, why even wake up in the morning?"

_____ 3. "I just can't stop worrying. I wish I could. It's my fibromyalgia. It's the money. It's mom's diabetes. It's my grades. It's just overwhelming."

_____ 4. "I know you say – and the doctors say – I'm starving. But I know what I look like in the mirror, and I just hate how fat I am. I hate myself."

_____ 5. "Oh my God. That's a spider. Stop this car, Dwayne! I'm getting out of here right now! I don't care … Right now, Dwayne; I'm serious!!!!"

_____ 6. "No, I don't think I'm fat, but I don't want to *get* fat. And just be clear, I don't *choose* to do this vomiting thing. It's like some force is making me do it."

_____ 7. "It's been a week since my divorce went through, and I've just felt numb ever since I signed the papers. I just want to go to sleep and never wake up."

_____ 8. "How the hell did it get cold? And how am I *fired*?! The last thing I remember we were at the beach house about to head home. And now it's *January*?!"

_____ 9. Ren to therapist: "Look, I'm not going to tell you if I have a plan to hurt myself – because I know if I say I've even thought about it, you'll have me committed."

_____ 10. Jo to therapist: "Look, I'm not going to tell you if I have a plan to hurt myself – because I can't re-stanzify yet if you're in on it. I'll know when the device is ready."

_____ 11. "I know you say I'll flame out, but I just know I can do this. And I *am* thinking clearly, probably for the first time ever. Since when is it mania to start a business? And the more I invest now, the richer I'll get. You'll be visiting me on my yacht in a few weeks."

_____ 12. A patient who had a stroke last year can barely move the right-hand side of her body. Her typical speech includes things like "With the them over there … and the them … and boats, boats people … sure enough already."

_____ 13. Gloria is of average build, but she worried constantly about her weight. About twice per week, she eats an enormous amount of food and then either makes herself vomit or spends the next day or two fasting and/or exercising.

Note: The answer key appears after the references.

References

American Psychiatric Association. (2013). *Diagnostic and statistical manual of mental disorders* (5th ed.). Arlington, VA: Author.

Arcelus, J., Mitchell, A. J., Wales, J., & Nielsen, S. (2011). Mortality rates in patients with anorexia nervosa and other eating disorders. *Archives of General Psychiatry, 68*(7), 724–731.

Ehrenreich, J. T., Fairholme, C. P., Buzzella, B. A., Ellard, K. K., & Barlow, D. H. (2007). The role of emotion in psychological therapy. *Clinical Psychology: A Publication of the Division of Clinical Psychology of the American Psychological Association, 14*(4), 422–428. doi:10.1111/j.1468-2850.2007.00102.x

Eich, E., Macaulay, D., Loewenstein, R. J., & Dihle, P. H. (1997). Memory, amnesia, and dissociative identity disorder. *Psychological Science, 8*(6), 417–422. doi:10.1111/j.1467-9280.1997.tb00454.x

Fairburn, C.G., Shafran, R., & Cooper Z. (1999). A cognitive behavioural theory of anorexia nervosa. *Behavior Research and Therapy, 37*(1), 1–13. doi:10.1016/s0005-7967(98)00102-8

Ghaemi, S.N. (2013, October 4). Taking disease seriously in DSM. *World Psychiatry.* doi:10.1002/wps.20082

Ghaemi, N. (2014). Not "depression": Manic-depression and Robin Williams. Retrieved July 2019 from www.psychologytoday.com

Higashi, K., Medic, G., Littlewood, K. J., Diez, T., Granström, O., & De Hert, M. (2013). Medication adherence in schizophrenia: Factors influencing adherence and consequences of nonadherence, a systematic literature review. *Therapeutic Advances in Psychopharmacology, 3*(4), 200–218. doi:10.1177/2045125312474019

Kessler, R. C., Berglund, P., Demler, O., Jin, R., Merikangas, K. R., & Walters, E. E. (2005). Lifetime prevalence and age- of-onset distributions of DSM-IV disorders in the National Comorbidity Survey Replication. *Archives of General Psychiatry, 62*(6), 593–602.

Makino, M., Tsuboi, K., & Dennerstein, L. (2004). Prevalence of eating disorders: A comparison of Western and non-Western countries. *Medscape General Medicine, 6*(3), 49.

McLean, C. P., Asnaani, A., Litz, B. T., & Hofmann, S. G. (2011). Gender differences in anxiety disorders: Prevalence, course of illness, comorbidity and burden of illness. *Journal of Psychiatric Research, 45*(8), 1027–1035. doi:10.1016/j.jpsychires.2011.03.006

Mehler, P. S., & Rylander, M. (2015). Bulimia nervosa – Medical complications. *Journal of Eating Disorders, 3*, 12.

Méquinion, M., Langlet, F., Zgheib, S., Dickson, S., Dehouck, B., Chauveau, C., & Viltart, O. (2013). Ghrelin: Central and peripheral implications in anorexia nervosa. *Frontiers in Endocrinology, 4*, 15. doi:10.3389/fendo.2013.00015

Regier, D. A., & Burke, J. D. (1987). Psychiatric disorders in the community: The epidemiologic catchment area study. In R. E. Hales & A. J. Frances (Eds.), *American psychiatric association annual review* (Vol. 6, pp. 610–624). Washington, DC: American Psychiatric Press.

Rozin, P., Bauer, R., & Catanese, D. (2003). Food and life, pleasure and worry, among American college students: Gender differences and regional similarities. *Journal of Personality and Social Psychology, 85*(1), 132–141. doi:10.1037/0022-3514.85.1.132

Schacter, D.L., Gilbert, D.T.,& Wegner, D.M. (2011) *Psychology* (2nd Edition). New York: Worth.

Shenk, J.W. (2005, October). Lincoln's great depression. *The Atlantic.* Retrieved November 2019 from https://www.theatlantic.com/magazine/archive/2005/10/lincolns-great-depression/304247/

Answer Key: 1. schizophrenia spectrum 2. clinical depression 3. GAD 4. anorexia nervosa 5. spider phobia 6. bulimia nervosa 7. Clinical depression 8. DID 9. clinical depression 10. schizophrenia spectrum 11. bipolar disorder 12. Wernicke's aphasia (NOT schizophrenia spectrum) 13. Bulimia nervosa

Module 33
Getting Well
Treatment of Psychological Disorders

In December of 2017, your first author's sister Melanie died at the age of 52. Melanie's autopsy states that she died of complications due to diabetes. But it wasn't really diabetes that killed her. Melanie's diabetes would have been quickly brought under control at any hospital. Unfortunately, Melanie suffered not only from diabetes but also from Generalized Anxiety Disorder (GAD). Melanie died because she was petrified of medical care. On more than one occasion, Melanie's older sister called an ambulance to Melanie's house because of Melanie's deteriorating physical health. But Melanie was afraid to get in the ambulance. Apparently, ambulance drivers in Georgia cannot forcibly take a conscious adult to a hospital if the adult refuses to go. It was always clear that Melanie had GAD rather than a specific phobia because she worried about many, many things. She was too anxious to attend the wedding of her beloved niece, even though the wedding was held only a few miles from her home. She worried about her physical appearance, her dogs, her home, her sons, and even her religious beliefs. Melanie's sad story is a drop in the sea of damage done daily to millions of people worldwide who experience psychological disorders.

Help does exist, of course. When people experience psychological disorders, there are, broadly speaking, two different paths to treatment that may be taken (and sometimes both are taken). First, if a patient is experiencing dysfunction or is in a great deal of distress, he or she might be prescribed a chemical intervention. **Chemical interventions** are drugs that can reduce or eliminate the symptoms of a psychological disorder. Drugs used to treat psychological disorders are called **psychotropic drugs**. Second, a patient might receive some kind of psychotherapy. **Psychotherapy** refers to professional interactions between a patient and a person formally trained to help people reduce or eliminate their clinical symptoms. Fittingly, the experts who offer psychotherapy are known as **psychotherapists**. One kind of psychotherapist is a licensed **clinical psychologist**. But there are other kinds of psychotherapists. Licensed clinical social workers (LCSWs) and people with master's degrees in marriage, family and child counseling (MFCCs or MFTs) also do lots of psychotherapy. In fact, those with master's degrees in psychotherapy outnumber licensed clinical psychologists (with doctoral degrees) about four to one (Hamp, Stamm, Christidis, & Nigrinis, 2014).

In this module, we will examine each of these two approaches to treating psychological disorders. We'll begin with chemical interventions and move on to psychotherapy. We'll then summarize a few developments for treating psychological disorders using new technologies (e.g., deep brain stimulation). It is important to note that we will be highly selective in what we present in this module. We'll provide you with examples of just a few chemical interventions for just a few specific psychological disorders. And we'll discuss just a few basic approaches to psychotherapy, without delving very deeply into any of the details of any one approach. We offer information about only a selective sample of chemical interventions for psychological disorders because the list of drugs used to treat psychological disorders is even longer than the DSM-5's list of some 250 psychological disorders. According to the Royal College of Physicians (2019), there are about *30 chemical interventions for clinical depression alone*. If you wish to see a more detailed discussion of chemical interventions for common psychological disorders, consult an expert source such as Shaywitz and Marder (2011). In the case of psychotherapy, we'll keep things brief by summarizing the key features of just a handful of the most common kinds of psychotherapy.

Treatment through Chemical Interventions

The Medical Model

The idea of giving people drugs to combat clinical symptoms is built on the medical model. The **medical model** of psychological illness refers to the idea that, like diabetes and tuberculosis, depression and schizophrenic spectrum are *diseases*. These and other psychological disorders are presumed to have a physiological basis in the body and the brain that can be treated with medicine – aka chemical interventions, aka drugs. So, the medical model views a psychological disorder as an illness to be treated rather than as a sign of weakness in the person experiencing the disorder. Your first author, Brett, knows something about this from personal experience because of his sister's losing battle with GAD. In fact, Brett's family has a long history of coping with psychological disorders. One of his close relatives suffers from schizophrenia. Both of his grandmothers had anxiety disorders. For these people and others experiencing psychological disorders, the medical model is important because it removes the blame from the patient. Prior to the medical model, and for much of human history, people who experienced psychological illness were highly stigmatized. Even today, the widely-shared attitude that psychological illness is a sign of personal weakness is probably one of the reasons why men seek out treatment for psychological disorders less often than women do (Noone & Stephens, 2008; Valenstein-Mah et al., 2019).

While the medical model has important strengths, it does raise some tough practical and ethical questions. For example, is being a poorly behaved, angry, and disobedient child a psychological disorder to be treated with drugs? That might seem an odd question. But the DSM-5 includes *oppositional defiant disorder* as an official psychological disorder for children. According to the DSM-5, this disorder is characterized by:

> A pattern of angry/irritable mood, argumentative/defiant behavior, or vindictiveness lasting at least 6 months as evidenced by at least four symptoms from any of the following categories, and exhibited during interaction with at least one individual who is not a sibling.

Some of the details of oppositional defiant disorder include (a) anger problems or irritable mood, (b) being defiant, and (c) having been hateful (spiteful or vindictive) to an adult or non-sibling at least twice in the past six months. Nick Haslam might raise questions about the DSM-5's inclusion of this disorder. Haslam (2016) has argued that in the past several decades, our efforts to understand human problems have caused psychologists to engage in "**concept creep**." To paraphrase Haslam, concept creep is a process by which definitions of harmful behaviors are expanded so that criteria for labeling social problems or diagnosing psychological disorders become looser. Ponder this definition as you consider the given description of oppositional defiant disorder – which includes characteristics of bullying. In the past, definitions of bullying were narrower, and behaviors that people now define as bullying were considered normal childhood experiences. But Haslam suggests that concept creep has created both beneficial and harmful consequences. For example, it is certainly good to be aware of and reduce bullying. But it is also possible to broaden the definition of bullying so much that the concept loses much of its original meaning. If almost any negative behavior qualifies as bullying, cases of highly abusive bullying may be lumped together with good-natured teasing. In keeping with this idea, Haslam argued that although concept creep "is inevitable and often well motivated," it also "runs the risk of pathologizing everyday experience."

Along similar lines, the clinical psychologist Ofer Zur has been critical of the DSM as a guide to clinical diagnosis. As Zur has put it, the DSM, while useful, "is a document that has been developed to some extent in service to the psychopharmacological and psychiatric industries. It pathologizes many normal behaviors so that medications can be prescribed." The distinction between clinical depression and normal grieving after the loss of a loved one is a compelling example. It underscores the concerns raised by Zur. Whereas the prior DSM had an explicit exclusion highlighting the differences between normal grieving and clinical depression, the DSM-5 *removed* that exclusion. This opened the door for diagnosing normal grieving as depression and then treating it with drugs. Although the American Psychiatric Association attempted to explain the reasons for the removal of the exclusion, we find their explanations lacking. The distinctions between normal grief and a major depressive episode are many, as are the dangers of labelling someone's normal grieving as clinical depression. Though we cannot speak for these authors, we believe the concerns raised by both Zur and Haslam raise a lot of tough questions. Whereas the DSM is still a helpful diagnostic tool, therapists and psychological health providers that use it must exercise caution. Normal behavior should not be turned into a disease to be treated with chemical interventions (Thieleman & Cacciatore, 2013). Those interventions must be reserved for the treatment of clearly diagnosed psychological disorders – a topic to which we now turn.

Chemical Interventions for Psychological Disorders

Chemical interventions can, if used judiciously, greatly improve the quality of life for many who experience psychological disorders. Patients diagnosed with an anxiety disorder such as GAD (General Anxiety Disorder) might be given a prescription for an **anxiolytic** (an anxiety-reducing drug) such as alprazolam (trade name *Xanax*) or diazepam (trade name *Valium*). Likewise, people suffering from *clinical depression* might be prescribed a **new generation anti-depressant** such as fluoxetine (trade name *Prozac*). As you already know, about 30 different drugs can reduce symptoms of clinical depression. But in the past few decades, the most commonly prescribed category of new generation anti-depressants has been **selective serotonin uptake inhibitors** (SSRIs) so named because they prevent the normal reuptake of serotonin that happens in the synaptic gaps between neurons.

The original explanation for why SSRIs work is that they keep the neurotransmitter serotonin out there longer than usual in the tiny synaptic gap between sending and receiving neurons. This, it was long assumed, gave serotonin more time to do its neuro-chemical job and make people feel better. However, if this were the main reason why SSRIs work, they should go to work very quickly. They don't. It usually takes several weeks for SSRIs to reduce the symptoms of depression. Contrast this with the 30 minutes it might take for an aspirin or an anxiolytic (anxiety reducer) to kick in. Recent research suggests that SSRIs take several weeks to work because they actually rewire the brain a bit. Specifically, they seem to increase the *long-term potentiation* in the synaptic gaps of neurons that respond to serotonin (Dale et al., 2015). You may recall that long-term potentiation is the microbiological route through which at least some forms of learning occur. Synapses that once were not very responsive to serotonin become much more so. In a sense, then, SSRIs help your brain learn to become more responsive to serotonin and, in turn, more energetic and upbeat.

People Are Different, Darn It

One serious challenge involved in prescribing chemical interventions for many psychological disorders (especially depression and schizophrenia) is that there is a lot of variation in which drugs work for which patients. For reasons that are poorly understood, a drug that might work wonders for one patient might have little effect on a patient who has the same diagnosis – and who has very much the same set of specific symptoms. For lack of a better term, we refer to this as the **matchmaker problem**. Lots of suffering patients have difficulty finding their biochemical soulmates. Take clinical depression as an example. Zeke and Zach might both suffer from a lack of energy, a loss of appetite, difficulty thinking clearly, and suicidal thoughts – while reporting none of the other specific symptoms of depression. Limiting our choice of treatments to popular SSRIs, fluoxetine might work well for Zeke but yield no relief at all for Zach. In contrast, Zach might benefit from sertraline (trade name *Zoloft*) but learn that he also suffered badly from its side effects. Eventually, Zach and his therapist might learn that citalopram (trade name *Celexa*) is the drug that helps Zach the most while yielding the fewest side effects.

Within a broad category of drugs such as anti-depressants, finding the one drug that works best for a specific patient can be a matter of a lengthy trial-and-error process. Recall that, in the case of depression, it often takes about a month to see if a specific drug works at all. Worse yet, there are some patients who do not seem to benefit from *any* of the commonly-used chemical interventions that have an average positive effect. A similar story applies to schizophrenia spectrum. A drug that greatly reduces hallucinations, delusions, and disordered thoughts in one patient might do little or nothing to help a different patient who suffers from the same set of symptoms. Like anti-depressants, chemical treatments for schizophrenia also take a while to show their full effects. While the benefits of chemical interventions are often life-changing, finding the right drug for a specific patent can take a lot of time. If only there were speed dating for chemical soulmates.

Finally, as noted in Zach's example, most drugs have side-effects. **Side effects** are unintended physical or psychological consequences of using a drug. For example, a common side effect of the SSRIs that are used to treat clinical depression is a loss of sexual desire. This is one of several reasons why responsible modern psychotherapists are beginning to pay attention to how to wean their patients off drugs. Patients who use a drug for more than a year or two may also find that they can never stop taking the drug without a relapse of clinical symptoms (Bagshaw, 2019). Further, just as there

are differences across patients in which specific drugs work well, there are also differences in whether and how powerfully patients experience specific side effects. Of course,
there are also big differences across patients in how much any particular side-effect represents a personal problem. The loss of sexual interest that comes with most SSRIS
may not be a big problem for someone who has taken a lifelong vow of celibacy. But it
could be very distressing for a sexually-active 30-year-old.

Some Side Effects Are Falling by the Wayside

As bothersome as side effects can be, they are less of a problem today than they were a few
decades ago. SSRIs are known as *"new generation" anti-depressants* to distinguish them
from older drugs such as tricyclics or *mono-amine oxidase inhibitors* (*MOAIs*). These older
drugs for depression were about as effective at reducing the symptoms of depression as are
modern drugs (such as SSRIs). But on average these older interventions were more likely
to cause side effects than are the newer drugs. In fact, the side effects of the older ant-
depressants known as MOAIs can be lethal if you consume them with either alcohol or
certain rare kinds of *cheese* (yes, cheese; Kramer, 1993). "Sorry, honey, we're going to have
to cancel that trip to Wisconsin. I'm back on the MOAIs." Needless to say, any drug that
can become lethal when you take it with wine or rare cheeses should be prescribed cautiously. Like MOAIs, tricyclics were once a popular chemical intervention for depression.
But tricyclics have many side effects. The list includes constipation, dry mouth, vision problems, weight gain, weight loss, and heart and blood pressure problems. And then there are
rashes, hives, and seizures (Kramer, 1993). Of course, no one patient would be likely to
suffer from all of these side effects. But none of these side-effects are a piece of cake –
though we suppose eating many pieces of cake could contribute to the side effect of weight
gain. It's for this reason – a reduction in side effects – that new generation anti-depressants
are now more popular than the older treatments. That being said, MOAIs and tricyclics
have not disappeared completely from the market because each has proven to be the only
chemical intervention that works well for some specific patients.

Along similar lines, newer chemical treatments for schizophrenia are referred to
as **second generation anti-psychotics**. This is true mainly because they represent a big
step forward in reducing side effects. The term "anti-psychotic" in that long label refers
to the fact that **anti-psychotic drugs** reduce the disordered thoughts and feelings that
are a hallmark of disorders such as schizophrenia. Second generation anti-psychotics
(abbreviated **SGAs**) typically have fewer and less serious side effects than the chemical
interventions that were available 50 years ago (abbreviated **FGAs** for **first generation
anti-psychotics**). Like most of the older chemical interventions for schizophrenia, newer
antipsychotic medications for schizophrenia often influence the neurotransmitter dopamine – but with a reduced risk of side effects. A common side effect of many older
drugs for schizophrenia is **tardive dyskinesia** – which is involuntary motor movements
of the face, trunk, and hands. Although patients who suffer from schizophrenia sometimes develop tardive dyskinesia even in the absence of any chemical intervention, older
drugs greatly increased the likelihood of this problem. Newer drugs (SGAs) also pose
an increased risk of tardive dyskinesia, but the risk is greatly reduced relative to the
older FGAs (Carbon, Kane, Leucht, & Correll, 2018). Concerns about side effects are
particularly important when it comes to schizophrenia because schizophrenia usually
requires chronic, life-long medication. In contrast, many patients recover fully from
clinical depression or anxiety disorders and never suffer from them again.

"I wouldn't worry, honey. They say there's always
a crackpot just before the spawning grounds.

Figure 33.1 Anti-psychotic medications reduce the disordered thoughts that can lead people to believe
and do highly unusual and socially unacceptable things (unless the end really is near).

So why can't we just make drugs that work without side effects? The short answer is
that the human brain is too complex for our current level of technology. Side effects
exist because drugs that are used to treat psychological disorders often target specific
neurotransmitters. But most specific neurotransmitters play multiple roles in the brain.
Dopamine, for example, plays a role in both the experience of pleasure and the initiation of voluntary motor movements. Because most neurotransmitters have many jobs,
a drug that influences a given neurotransmitter will thus influence *more than one aspect
of brain activity*. Because SSRIs affect *serotonin*, they can influence what happens to
and with serotonin in areas of the brain that have nothing to do with depression. For
example, serotonin plays a role in the experience of sexual pleasure. In men, serotonin
is released in the anterior lateral hypothalamus (an ancient part of the brain that helps
regulate sex) during an ejaculation (Hull, Muschamp, & Sato, 2004). Along these lines,
one theory about why SSRIs can reduce people's interest in sex is that SSRIs may convince your brain that you recently had an orgasm (Kramer, 1993).

Tolerance and the Risk of Abuse or Overdose

If concerns about side effects weren't enough to worry about, many chemical interventions – especially anxiolytics (anxiety-reducing drugs) – can become drugs of abuse, and
they can also lead to overdose. In 2014, the beloved actor Philip Seymour Hoffman
died of an overdose of a cocktail of drugs that included benzodiazepine – which is
a common treatment for many forms of anxiety. A major problem with benzodiazepine
is the same problem posed by many other anxiolytics. It can lead to abuse and addic-
tion. This is true, in large part, because as patients continue to use benzodiazepine over
time, they begin to experience **tolerance** (a reduction in the usual psychological effects
of the drug). A common response is to increase the dosage, mix the drug with other
drugs, or both. As Hoffman's troubling story reminds us, this can be fatal. Of course,
not all drugs used to treat psychological disorders are addictive or dangerous. But even
drugs that cannot easily kill a person can lead to withdrawal symptoms once patients
stop taking them. Fluoxetine (*Prozac*) is a good example. This anti-depressant does not
produce the high feeling that many anxiolytics create, and it is very difficult to overdose

on it (but see Suchard, 2008). Nonetheless, patients who have been using fluoxetine for a while will need to taper their way down from their usual dosage over many days rather than quitting it "cold turkey." Failing to do so can lead to any of several withdrawal symptoms ranging from a return of depressive symptoms to headaches, flu-like symptoms, dizziness, and even the sensation of electric shock.

By the way, in most U.S. states only medical doctors can prescribe drugs, and that includes drugs for psychological disorders. This means that psychotherapists who may have PhDs or PsyDs in psychology but no degree in medicine must either consult with or refer their patients to a psychiatrist (a medical doctor with a specialty in psychological illness) who will prescribe the patient's medication. In the ideal case, a psychiatrist will work closely with a clinical psychologist or other psychotherapist – who is much more likely than a psychiatrist to be conducting psychotherapy with a patient. According to the American Psychological Association's Center for Workforce Studies (2014), psychiatrists make up only about 9% of all "behavior health providers." Clinical psychologists, licensed clinical social workers, and other kinds of psychotherapists without medical degrees make up the other 91% (Hamp et al., 2014). This 91% must work collaboratively with medical doctors for their patients who need medication.

Psychotherapy for Psychological Disorders

Because psychiatrists are medical doctors who have specialized knowledge of the brain and psychological disorders and because it is often the business of doctors to treat people with medicine, you shouldn't be too surprised to learn that psychiatrists often view psychological disorders as medical problems that require, well, medication. In contrast to this approach, most psychotherapists who do not have an MD place more confidence in what Freud called the "talking cure" or what is more generally known as psychotherapy. The intent of psychotherapy is to nurture, support, and educate clients about the psychological basis of their disorder – with the goal of reducing the symptoms associated with the disorder and improving the client's quality of life. Recall from the prior module that when our thoughts, feelings, and behaviors fall on the far end of a wide continuum – the abnormal end – then psychological disorder is the result. In this framework, the goal of psychotherapy is to bring clients' thoughts, feelings, and behaviors closer to the more normal end of the continuum. This is the common purpose of all psychotherapy. We can see this goal embedded in the origins of the word "psychotherapy" itself. The word comes from the ancient Greek "psyche" which meant *soul*, and "therapeuo," which meant *heal*. Psychotherapy: Heal the soul. But because there are many different schools of thought in psychology, there are many different forms of psychotherapy – each shaped by a different window on human nature. The following section briefly summarizes a few common forms of psychotherapy.

Psychoanalysis

Freud was the first psychoanalyst, and he adopted an unusual approach to psychotherapy that focused on the important influence of unconscious conflicts, particularly those grounded in unfortunate childhood experiences. Given what a powerful personality Freud seems to have had, perhaps the most surprising part of Freud's "talking cure" is that Freud let his patients do most of the talking. Freud hoped to help his patients develop insight by asking them questions – questions whose answers would help make them aware of unconscious influences that had led them to become distressed. In Freud's day, this meant meeting with his patients for psychotherapy almost every day of the week, and often for many years (Schacter, Gilbert, & Wegner, 2011). Freud got to know his patients very well. We hope they had good health insurance.

But Freud wasn't so happy to learn that his patients often wanted to get to know *him* very well. Freud coined the term "transference" to refer to the fact that his patients often bonded to him emotionally as if he were a parent, or even a romantic partner. Freud called this **transference** because he felt his patients were transferring their old feelings for those they loved, admired, or hated as children to the person who was trying to help them uncover how their childhoods had gone awry. As you may recall from the module on schools of thought in psychology, transference seems to be a very real phenomenon, both in and out of psychotherapy. We often treat people who subtly remind us of others as if they *were* those others (Miranda & Andersen, 2007). Another of Freud's compelling insights about psychotherapy was what he termed **resistance**. Resistance refers to pushing back against a therapist's suggested ideas about why something is going wrong for the patient. For example, if Freud suggested to Karl that Karl might be projecting his own anger onto others – or treating a coworker as if she were his mother – Karl might strongly insist that he did not have any anger problems, or that his behavior toward his coworker had nothing to do with Karl's mother and everything to do with his co-worker.

If your image of Freud conducting psychoanalysis resembles the image you see in Figure 33.2, you're not too far off the mark. Freud did, in fact, ask his patients to lie in a reclining position and he did not typically face them during psychotherapy. If you notice that the cartoon suggests that our problems often have their roots in our earliest experiences, you have also put your finger on a key idea behind psychoanalytic theory. Freud believed that our problems with our primary caregivers in early childhood manifested themselves in our adult lives. It's for this reason that Freud often relied on highly indirect ways of trying to understand his patient's unconscious conflicts and problems. This included asking patients to do **free associations**. To Freud, this meant getting patients to report absolutely anything that pops to mind – without worrying about how petty, vulgar, selfish, or oversexed it made them seem. Of course, Freud had to establish a lot of trust in his patients to get them to become comfortable doing this.

Freud also relied heavily on the **interpretation of dreams**. In this case, Freud would often ask his patients for their own interpretations of their dreams in a way that was highly collaborative. Freud's main goal in almost everything he did during

"In your case, Jeff. we're going to have to go back a little farther. Tell me about your great, great grandmother."

Figure 33.2 Just how far do Jeff's psychological problems go back? Freud felt it all began at birth.

psychotherapy was to help patients become aware of the unconscious desires and conflicts that they had presumably repressed long ago (notice that Freud made several assumptions here). Given the centrality of the unconscious in Freud's approach, there is probably no concept in psychoanalysis that is more important than **repression**. Repression refers to the process by which the ego or the superego banishes thoughts that are too uncomfortable to the unconscious (Freud, 1962/1923). According to Freud, then, most defense mechanisms operate mainly at an unconscious level, and his many defense mechanisms are just highly specific ways that we cope with psychological pain. This means that we often express such thoughts and wishes indirectly (e.g., by dreaming about the issue, by projecting our wishes, fears, and flaws onto others, or by overcompensating for a felt insecurity).

A more modern version of psychoanalysis is **psychodynamic therapy**. Modern psychodynamic therapists typically sit facing their clients (as opposed to having clients lay on a couch and sitting behind them) and these therapists certainly do not accept everything Freud said as the unimpeachable truth. But they do accept Freud's most basic assumptions – such as his idea that the unconscious is very powerful, and his idea that the events of early childhood years play a disproportionate role in our psychological landscapes. Another not-too-distant – and younger – cousin of psychoanalysis is **interpersonal psychotherapy**. Schacter et al. (2011) have suggested that interpersonal psychotherapy took the idea that early relationships are of paramount importance and really ran with it. As practiced today, most forms of interpersonal therapy focus mainly on helping people identify and repair problems in their existing adult relationships. Thus, interpersonal therapy is more present-focused and more pragmatic than traditional psychoanalysis. It is also much more personal and face-to-face. Interpersonal therapists also downplay the role of sexual motivations – relative to Freud at least – while underscoring the role of social motivations. Finally, as noted by Schacter et al. (2011) two other differences between interpersonal therapy and traditional psychoanalysis are that many patients only see their interpersonal therapists once a week and that during therapy interpersonal psychotherapists are much freer with support and advice. How can you expect your patients to develop better relationships with others if you don't show them that you can connect to them?

Behavioral Therapy

If you remember anything at all about behaviorism, we hope it is that behaviorism is very far removed indeed from psychoanalysis. Whereas psychoanalysts focus on the unconscious (and unobservable), behaviorists focus on what we can observe with great certainty. Behaviorists thus placed great faith in observable learning processes such as classical and operant conditioning. You may recall a well-known example of classical conditioning from Module 11, in which an 11-month old baby named Little Albert was conditioned to have a phobia of white rats. In fact, Albert's phobia seemed to *generalize* to other objects that only resembled the white rat (e.g., a rabbit, a white beard). Many behaviorists concluded from studies such as this one that many phobias are a matter of classical conditioning.

Behaviorists further reasoned that if we apply what we know about *extinction* to the treatment of phobias we can pretty easily cure people of them. This became the basis for Wolpe's (1958) classic work on systematic desensitization – and many studies that have since followed it. The idea behind **systematic desensitization** is that when people are repeatedly exposed to a phobic object or situation and they learn that nothing bad becomes of them, their conditioned fear response will extinguish. However, one problem with this idea is that the phobic object itself makes people extremely uncomfortable and the fear created by the feared object itself keeps the phobia going. Wolpe and those who followed in his footsteps got around this problem by getting people to practice physical relaxation techniques (such as slow deep breathing and guided imagery) in the presence of a very mild version of the object or situation that would normally freak them out. Once people became comfortable with the watered-down version of the feared object or situation, Wolpe exposed his patients to something a little worse. Of course, this made his patients very uncomfortable, but Wolpe got them to use physical relaxation techniques to calm themselves down. This process is repeated in a step-by-step fashion in which, with each successive step, the patient gets more and more comfortable with the feared object. Over the course of a handful of exposure sessions such as this, many patients are able to shed their phobia – and then fly on a plane, touch a non-venomous snake, take swimming lessons, or give a well-rehearsed speech (Choy, Fyer, & Lipsitz, 2007; Menzies & Clarke, 1993). Table 33.1 contains a graduated list of stimuli to which people might be exposed if they suffered from a fear of heights.

Table 33.1 Systematic Desensitization. A Hypothetical Series of Exposures that Might Be Used to Help a Person Overcome Acrophobia (a Major Fear of Heights).

1.	Stand on a sturdy wooden box that is 4 inches tall. Use relaxation techniques until you no longer feel afraid.
2.	Now do the same thing with a sturdy 8-inch-high box. Use your relaxation techniques.
3.	Stand up on the second step of a stepladder while holding the hand of a person you trust. Relax as usual.
4.	Repeat but let go of the hand of the person you trust. Relax. This may take a while. That's OK.
5.	Move up to the third step on a taller, sturdier stepladder. Relax.
6 & 7.	Move up to the fourth and then the fifth step of the big stepladder. Relax.
8.	From that fifth step on the tall stepladder, change a lightbulb in a 12-foot ceiling. Relax.
9.	Wearing sneakers, use a ten-foot roofing ladder to climb up onto the 8-foot tall roof of your back porch. Relax.
10.	Walk around a bit while you're up there, staying away from the edges. Relax.
11.	Climb slowly to the highest point on your roof and sit down, far away from any edges. Relax.
12.	Get comfortable enough being on a tall ladder or a roof that you can now clean your own gutters. Relax.
13.	Save a lot of money on gutter cleaning and roof work.

Cognitive and Cognitive Behavioral Therapies

Although behavioral therapy is a highly effective way of helping people deal with irrational fears, behavioral therapy is not nearly as effective for Generalized Anxiety Disorder (GAD) as it is for specific phobias. Systematic desensitization, for example, is topic-specific. Helping Daniela overcome her phobia of snakes will not rid her of her fear of spiders, heights, or Visigoths. When a person worries unduly about a long list of unlikely catastrophes, cognitive therapy is often more effective than behavioral therapy. Unlike behavioral therapy, which is very visceral ("Take 10 slow and deep breaths."), cognitive therapy is very cerebral. **Cognitive therapists** focus on getting patients to identify, challenge, and replace maladaptive beliefs with more adaptive beliefs. Cognitive therapists also offer their patients insights into the physical, social, or emotional cues that can trigger maladaptive thoughts, feelings, and behavior. For example, here is what a cognitive therapist might say to a client: "I noticed that you and CJ often get into big arguments when you are packing for a trip to visit your mother." "Now that you're aware of this, what steps can you take to make such arguments less likely in the future?"

Perhaps the best way to summarize cognitive therapies is that they try to offer patients a way to *think their way* into a better life. This means they try to help patients replace automatic, and often negative, ideas about themselves and the world with ideas that are less self-blaming, more constructive, and more hopeful. Finally, cognitive therapists often encourage **mindfulness. Mindful** people are attentive both to their own surroundings and their own thoughts and feelings. Like good drivers, mindful people live fully in the moment without drifting off into the mindlessness state you read about in the module on consciousness. Further, like good drivers, mindful people keep their hands on the wheel – and they're ready to make quick adjustments and corrections when signs of danger appear on the horizon. And just as rookie drivers can benefit from practicing in driving simulators, patients in cognitive therapy may engage in *roleplaying* with a therapist – to practice new coping skills in a safe situation. Alternately, another safe technique is to keep a journal in which patients write about their experiences – including writing about how they will practice replacing maladaptive thoughts with more constructive thoughts.

If you have a basic idea of how behavioral therapies and cognitive therapies work, you are now in a good position to understand how cognitive behavioral therapy works. **Cognitive behavioral therapy** (CBT) combines an application of the basic learning principles of purely behavioral therapy with the cognitive and emotional benefits of purely cognitive therapies. Cognitive behavioral therapists acknowledge that the conscious mind cannot always take the wheel when highly overlearned schemas, habits, and irrational fears kick in. But they also teach their patients to recognize the power of belief to shape new habits – which can come to compete with older, less adaptive habits. To put this a little differently, cognitive behavioral therapists freely move back and forth between purely behavioral techniques and more cognitive techniques depending on both (a) the patient and (b) the specific disorder with which the patient is struggling. For example, a therapist using CBT might use systematic desensitization with an adult patient who wants to overcome a fear of dogs. As another example, when coaching parents or teachers to help a child sit still in the classroom, a therapist might teach the adults to set up a **token economy**. This is a system in which clients receive tokens (stars, buttons, colored-in boxes on a goal-chart) in exchange for engaging in desirable behaviors. Eventually, accumulated tokens can be traded for positive reinforcers (for rewards). Both systematic desensitization and token economies are behavioral approaches. In contrast, when helping an adult cope with clinical depression, the same therapist may switch to cognitive techniques such as helping the patient identify negative self-blaming explanations for negative events and replacing them with more balanced or upbeat beliefs. Instead of concluding that "I failed, I will fail again in the future, and it will ruin my life," a patient would be encouraged to re-think and replace this negative conclusion with something a bit rosier. "I did fail. But I don't have to fail next time, and a VisV- in Visigoth Studies is not going to ruin my entire life."

Therapeutic Odds and Ends

Allow us to conclude this selective review of psychotherapy by noting that we did *not* cover all the bases. For example, we did not yet discuss **group therapy**. This is therapy in which multiple people with similar problems or disorders meet in a group – often supported and assisted by a trained psychotherapist. Group therapy may take many forms, depending on the philosophy of the group leader, the kind of clinical disorder that is tackled in the therapy, and so forth. Recent research suggests that, all else being equal, carefully conducted group therapy is just as effective as carefully conducted individual psychotherapy (Burlingame et al., 2016). Two big advantages of group therapy, by the way, are reduced cost to individual patients and direct opportunities to build and improve upon relationships. On the other hand, two disadvantages are the potential loss of confidentiality and the conflict that may emerge between group members. Needless to say, trained therapists are very good at keeping their patient's secrets, and they rarely pick fights in therapy. We cannot say the same for all of those who participate in group therapy.

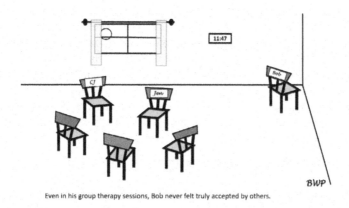

Even in his group therapy sessions, Bob never felt truly accepted by others.

Figure 33.3 One of the most important jobs of a leader in group therapy is to make sure group members never feel like Bob.

Getting back to individual psychotherapy, we also overlooked humanistic psychotherapy in this module. Humanistic therapy focuses on reducing mismatches between our ideal and real selves. Humanistic therapies rely on building mutual trust, care, and respect between therapists and their clients. It is also important to note that many modern psychotherapists consider themselves eclectic therapists (Norcross & Beutler 2000). **Eclectic therapists** are so called because they borrow ideas and techniques from multiple schools of thought. If we assume that each major school of psychological thought offers us some unique insights into psychological disorders, perhaps this is a very wise route. If different patients who present in very similar ways require different chemical interventions, it would not be too surprising to see that patients who suffer from different psychological disorders might benefit from very different kinds of psychotherapy. This is exactly what eclectic psychotherapists believe. Accordingly, they use different techniques for different patients and for different psychological disorders. We also have not addressed the complex ethical and methodological question of how we know that therapy really works in the first place. Like drugs, psychotherapy does not

"I get it, Jeremy. You're in distress. But until we identify the root
cause of that distress, I'm not sure I see things getting any better."

Figure 33.4 Most real psychotherapists are *much* more insightful than this fictional one – we promise.

always work. But, on average, most forms of psychotherapy have a positive effect that is meaningfully better than just waiting for people to get better on their own (see Schacter et al., 2011, for a highly accessible summary). The unhappy story of Brett's sister is a powerful reminder that those who cannot or do not get help in the battle against psychological disorders often face a dire fate. Psychotherapy, on the other hand, offers real hope of moving people back along the continuum to more functional thoughts, feelings, and behavior. Ideally, psychotherapy allows us to see that, even with all its imperfections, life is beautiful. Well, at least it doesn't suck as badly as we once thought.

Supplemental Section and Thought Questions for Module 33

Promising New Directions in the Treatment of Psychological Disorders

In the past decade or so, there have been some remarkable developments that promise to make it easier to treat psychological disorders. We'll examine three examples. One promising high-tech intervention for both depression and anorexia nervosa is deep-brain stimulation. *Deep-brain stimulation* or *DBS* refers to a recently developed surgical procedure that has been performed on "treatment resistant" patients who have found no relief from either drugs or psychotherapy. The logic behind deep brain stimulation for depression is to deliver a tiny, precisely-calibrated electrical boost to an area of the brain that is crucial to healthy mood-regulation. At the time of this writing, in 2020, this experimental surgical procedure had only been given to patients who had long suffered from clinical depression that was resistant to both drugs and psychotherapy.

In an interview with Peter Tarr (2018), cutting-edge researcher Helen Mayberg summarized more than a decade of research on DBS. Mayberg reported that DBS led to meaningful reductions in depression for 40–80% of the previously hopeless patients who had received it. Mayberg's current research is focusing on how this new technique can be improved. For example, it's possible that patients who showed little or no benefit from this new treatment simply had the bad luck of imperfectly-positioned implants. Even with the benefit of modern brain-imaging techniques, finding a precise destination in the human brain is no easy matter. We can imagine a future in which we not only know more about the brain's role in depression but also benefit from nanotechnological brain implants that resemble a net more than a needle.

The preliminary success doctors have had with DBS for depression is matched by equally promising data from patients with anorexia nervosa. In a study of 18 treatment-resistant patients who were at serious risk of dying from anorexia, Lipsman and colleagues (2017) followed the women for 12 months after a surgical DBS intervention. On average, the women showed improvements in self-reported depression, anxiety, and affective regulation. Perhaps more important, the 12-month follow-up revealed that the women increased their body mass index ("heaviness") scores from a mean of 13.8 to a mean of 17.3. This is roughly the equivalent of going from looking like a victim of starvation to being slightly heavier than the average female model. Presumably, this technique, like DBS for clinical depression, will be fine-tuned and improved in the future.

One of the reasons DBS is currently a method of last resort is that it requires brain surgery. Such surgery always brings the risk of surgical complications or post-surgical infection – especially in patients who may already have heavily compromised immune systems. With this in mind, the most promising new interventions for treating psychological disorders may be *transcranial magnetic stimulation (TMS)*. According to Machado and colleagues (2013, p. 192) transcranial magnetic stimulation is "a non-invasive procedure whereby a pulsed magnetic field stimulates electrical activity in the brain." This stimulation comes from a magnetic field that begins on the scalp – which is what makes it noninvasive. At the time of Machado et al.'s (2013) review of research using TMS to treat psychological disorders, the most powerful magnets could stimulate or suppress brain function in regions almost an inch below the skull – without any significant discomfort and without any serious side effects.

Machado et al. (2013) report positive effects of repeated TMS treatments for psychological disorders as varied as depression, schizophrenia, post-traumatic stress disorder, and panic disorder. Further, all the studies they reviewed made use of a sham-TMS (fake TMS) control group to be sure any observed effects were not due to a placebo effect. In other words, patients who received the repeated TMS treatments showed greater improvements in clinical symptoms than did patients who thought they were receiving TMS treatments but were receiving nothing. As Machado et al. explain, this preliminary work is promising because TMS is quick, painless, and noninvasive. However, they also note that the effects of TMS on psychological disorders appear to be pretty short-lived. Unless treatment protocols can be discovered that produce long-lasting benefits, it is not clear if TMS will ever become the go-to treatment for any psychological disorders. Right now, it is simply not practical for patients to go in twice weekly for their TMS "booster shots." Right now, TMS treatment using current technology is also prohibitively expensive. But that's what people said about cell phones 25 years ago.

A third high-tech solution to treating some psychological disorders has been up and running for more than two decades – and it's *not* prohibitively expensive. In fact, it's a big money-saver. Increasingly, clinical psychologists who treat patients with specific phobias are using the same virtual reality systems many kids have in their game rooms. They're using virtual reality systems to create highly realistic simulations of exposure therapy, such as systematic desensitization. In case, you've never used a *virtual reality system*, a typical system includes a helmet that projects realistic images onto one's visual field and a set of gloves that allow users to interact with and manipulate objects in the virtual world. An advantage of using a virtual reality system to conduct exposure therapy is that rather than keeping a ladder, a cage full of spiders, and an airplane in one's office, psychotherapists can keep highly realistic virtual realities in their office. When patients arrive, the therapist can select a starting point for the exposure therapy and guide their patients through a customized set of experiences that get them ready to try the real thing. The fact that patients themselves are in full control of the virtual world that provides them with exposure to the things they fear is also a plus in virtual reality therapy. Therapists have now been using virtual reality to treat psychological disorders for more than two decades, and it looks like the future is bright for this method of blending modern technology and well-established psychotherapy (Kampmann et al., 2016).

Thought Questions

1. Drugs affect brain activity, and as we know most drugs have serious side effects. DBS and TMS also affect brain activity but neither technique seems to have any very serious side effects. Why not?
2. An amazing fact about DBS therapy for depression is that when it works it eliminates virtually all of the symptoms of depression. That is, it does not merely eliminate suicidal ideation, improve sleep quality, or boost positive mood and enjoyment of daily activities, it does all of them. Does this suggest that depression is one single thing or that it is a set of separate, unhappy symptoms that have been arbitrarily bundled together?
3. Assuming that most virtual reality users experience it as inherently fun and interesting, is this aspect of virtual reality therapy for phobias likely to be an asset, an impediment, or a mere distraction when it comes to creating the ideal experience that facilitates the extinction of a learned phobia?
4. Suppose that in a couple of decades, some completely healthy people begin to use what we might call designer DBS (or designer TMS) to increase happiness, facilitate concentration, or improve sexual performance. Is this an ethical and acceptable use of neuroscientific technology.? If a decent college basketball player can increase her stamina and coordination enough using TMS that she becomes a WNBA-caliber player, should she be allowed to use this technology – or is this the magnetic and electrical equivalent of performance enhancing drugs?

Multiple Choice Questions for Module 33

1. The two most common interventions for psychological disorders include psychotherapy and what?

   A) self-improvement
   B) social support
   C) drugs

2. SSRIs are a category of what?

   A) second generation anti-psychotics
   B) new generation anti-depressants
   C) anxiolytics

3. What category of therapeutic drugs usually take about a month to reduce clinical symptoms?

   A) anti-depressants such as fluoxetine (Prozac)
   B) anxiolytics such as diazepam (Valium)
   C) NSAIDs such as ibuprofen

4. What worrisome side effect of anti-psychotic medications was discussed in this module on treating psychological disorders?

   A) tardive dyskinesia
   B) loss of sexual appetite
   C) weight gain

5. Which category of drugs is usually a better choice for treating schizophrenia spectrum: FGAs or SGAs?

   A) FGAs because they are the FIRST choice for treatment
   B) SGAs because they are the SAFEST choice for treatment
   C) FGAs because they have a lower risk of side effects
   D) SGAs because they have a lower risk of side effects

6. Can licensed clinical psychologists usually prescribe drugs for depression or anxiety disorders?

   A) Yes; that's part of what it means to be licensed
   B) Maybe; you have to have a PhD and be licensed in clinical neuroscience
   C) No; in most U.S. states, only medical doctors can prescribe any kind of drug

7. What kind of psychotherapy is very strongly associated with the theories and clinical practices of Sigmund Freud?

   A) family therapy
   B) neobehavioral therapy
   C) psychoanalytic therapy

8. What kind of psychotherapist is most likely to be a fan of token economies?

   A) a behavioral therapist
   B) an economic psychologist
   C) a cognitive behavioral therapist

9. What is a major potential advantage of eclectic psychotherapy?

   A) the ability to apply different techniques to different clinical problems
   B) membership in a close-knit group of therapists who all have different clinical skill sets
   C) a deep knowledge of both Eastern and Western philosophies of clinical practice

10. Nora's therapist asks Nora to begin a psychotherapy session by looking at a book full of photos of spiders. Whenever Nora shows signs of anxiety, her therapist reminds her to use a deep breathing technique that Nora finds highly relaxing. From what kind of *psychological disorder* is Nora's likely to be suffering?

    A) a phobia
    B) Generalized Anxiety Disorder
    C) obsessive-compulsive disorder

11. Nora's therapist asks Nora to begin a psychotherapy session by looking at a book full of photos of spiders. Whenever Nora shows signs of anxiety, her therapist reminds her to use a deep breathing technique that Nora finds highly relaxing. What *behavioral technique* does Nora's therapist seem to be using?

    A) spontaneous recovery
    B) systematic desensitization
    C) discrimination learning

Answer Key: 1C, 2B, 3A, 4A, 5D, 6C, 7C, 8A, 9A, 10A, 11B

References

Bagshaw, J. (2019). Personal communication.

Burlingame, G. M., Seebeck, J. D., Janis, R. A., Whitcomb, K. E., Barkowski, S., Rosendahl, J., & Strauss, B. (2016). Outcome differences between individual and group formats when identical and nonidentical treatments, patients, and doses are compared: A 25-year meta-analytic perspective. *Psychotherapy, 53*(4), 446–461.

Carbon, M., Kane, J. M., Leucht, S., & Correll, C. U. (2018). Tardive dyskinesia risk with first- and second-generation antipsychotics in comparative randomized controlled trials: A meta-analysis. *World Psychiatry: Official Journal of the World Psychiatric Association (WPA), 17*(3), 330–340. doi:10.1002/wps.20579

Choy, Y., Fyer, A. J., & Lipsitz, J. D. (2007). Treatment of specific phobia in adults. *Clinical Psychology Review, 27*(3), 266–286. doi:10.1016/j.cpr.2006.10.002

Dale, E., Pehrson, A. L., Jeyarajah, T., Li, Y., Leiser, S. C., Smagin, G., ... Sanchez, C. (2015). Effects of serotonin in the hippocampus: How SSRIs and multimodal antidepressants might regulate pyramidal cell function. *CNS Spectrums, 21*(2), 143–161. doi:10.1017/S1092852915000425

Freud, S. (1962/1923). *The ego and the id* (translated by J. Riviere, revised and edited by J. Strachey). New York: Norton & Company.

Hamp, A., Stamm, K., Christidis, P., & Nigrinis, A. (2014). What proportion of the nation's behavioral health providers are psychologists? Retrieved from www.apa.org/monitor/2014/09/datapoint

Haslam, N. (2016). Concept creep: Psychology's expanding concepts of harm and pathology. *Psychological Inquiry, 27*, 1–17.

Hull, E. M., Muschamp, J. W., & Sato, S. (2004). Dopamine and serotonin: Influences on male sexual behavior. *Physiology and Behavior, 83*(2), 291–307.

Kampmann, I. L., Emmelkamp, P. M. G., Hartanto, D., Brinkman, W. P., Zijlstra, B. J. H., & Morina, N. (2016). Exposure to virtual social interactions in the treatment of social anxiety disorder: A randomized controlled trial. *Behaviour Research and Therapy, 77*, 147–156. doi:10.1016/j.brat.2015.12.016

Kramer, P.D. (1993). Listening to Prozac. New York: Penguin Books.

Lipsman, N., Lam, E., Volpini, M., Sutandar, K., Twose, R., Giacobbe, P., ... Lozano, A. M. (2017). Deep brain stimulation of the subcallosal cingulate for treatment-refractory anorexia nervosa: 1 year follow-up of an open-label trial. *The Lancet Psychiatry.* doi:10.1016/S2215-0366(17)30076-7

Machado, S., Arias-Carrión, O., Paes, F., Vieira, R. T., Caixeta, L., Novaes, F., Marinho, T., Almada, L. F., Silva, A. C., & Nardi, A. E. (2013). Repetitive transcranial magnetic stimulation for clinical applications in neurological and psychiatric disorders: an overview. *The Eurasian Journal of Medicine, 45*(3), 191–206. doi:10.5152/eajm.2013.39

Menzies, R. G., & Clarke, J. C. (1993). A comparison of in vivo and vicarious exposure in the treatment of childhood water phobia. *Behavior Research and Therapy, 31*(1), 9–15.

Miranda, R., & Andersen, S. M. (2007). The therapeutic relationship: Implications from social cognition and transference. In P. Gilbert & R. L. Leahy (Eds.), *The therapeutic relationship in the cognitive behavioral psychotherapies* (pp. 63–89). Routledge/Taylor & Francis Group.

Noone, J. H., & Stephens, C. (2008). Men, masculine identities, and health care utilisation. *Sociology of Health & Illness, 30*, 711–725.

Royal College of Physicians. (2019). Interventions for prevention and treatment. Retrieved July, 2020, from: https://www.rcplondon.ac.uk/projects/outputs/interventions-prevention-and-treatment

Schacter, S., Gilbert, D. T., & Wegner, D. (2011). *Introduction to psychology* (2nd ed.). New York, NY: Worth.

Shaywitz, J., & Marder, S. (2011). Medication treatment for anxiety, depression, schizophrenia, and bipolar disorder in the community setting. In G. Thornicroft, G. Szmukler, K. T. Mueser, &

R. E. Drake (Eds.), *Oxford textbook of community psychological health*. Oxford, UK: Oxford Univeristy Press.

Suchard, J. R. (2008). Fluoxetine overdose-induced seizure. *The Western Journal of Emergency Medicine, 9*(3), 154–156.

Tarr, P. (2018). "A cloud has been lifted": What deep-brain stimulation tells us about depression and depression treatments. *Brain & Behavior*. Retrieved May 5, 2019 from www.bbrfoundation. org/content

Thieleman, K., & Cacciatore, J. (2013). The DSM-5 and the bereavement exclusion: A call for critical evaluation. *Social Work, 58*, 277–280. doi:10.1093/sw/swt021

Valenstein-Mah, H., Kehle-Forbes, S., Nelson, D., Danan, E. R., Vogt, D., & Spoont, M. (2019). Gender differences in rates and predictors of individual psychotherapy initiation and completion among Veterans Health Administration users recently diagnosed with PTSD. In *Psychological trauma: Theory, research, practice, and policy*. Advance online publication.

Wolpe, J. (1958). *Psychotherapy by reciprocal inhibition*. Stanford, CA: Stanford University Press.

XI
Applied Psychology

Module 34
Health Psychology
How the Psychological Becomes the Physical

In the 1930s, Hans Selye (1956) began exposing some unfortunate laboratory rats to a wide range of "nocuous agents." If you know that *in*nocuous means harmless, you may have guessed that Selye was no friend to these poor rats. He abused them, over-exercised them, and injected them with all sorts of drugs and chemicals, from morphine to formaldehyde. Selye was no sadist. Instead, he strove to understand the basic mammalian response to major **stressors** – obnoxious chemical or physical events that your body justifiably treats as an attack. Today we know that stressors can come from a much wider swath of experiences, including both positive and negative experiences. Running into a bear on a hiking trail is an example of a negative stressor. Walking down the aisle in a wedding, on the other hand, is an example of a mostly positive stressor (we hope). But as anyone who's married can tell you, weddings are fraught with stress as well as joy. **Stress** is the experience of a perceived threat (real or imagined) to one's well-being. Stress is the physical and psychological *response* to stressors in our environment. Bears and weddings are stressors, and our experience in response to those events can be stress. We hope you're familiar enough with the idea of constructivism to know that stress is mainly – though not exclusively – a matter of interpretation. Just as there are people for whom weddings barely feel stressful at all, there are surely people for whom coming across a bear is purely delightful. Nature photographers and bear hunters both come to mind.

Selye's GAS Model: Alarm, Resistance, Exhaustion

Perhaps you've heard people say, "That which does not kill me makes me stronger." Hans Selye would have surely disagreed. After a lot of laboratory rats had suffered through a great many stressors, Selye concluded that stressors lead to the **General Adaptation Syndrome (GAS)**. The essence of this three-stage model is "That which does not kill me right now will eventually get around to it." The GAS is the body's response to physical, viral, chemical, or psychological assaults. If those assaults (the stressful stuff) keep happening to an organism over a long period, the outcome of that accumulated extreme stress will be significant harm – and potentially even death.

Stage one of the GAS is **alarm**. People who've just been exposed to a stressor become highly vigilant as their *sympathetic nervous system* kicks in. This enables the "fight or flight" response discovered by Cannon (1914). The sympathetic nervous system instantly mobilizes the body in response to a perceived threat. This mobilization is characterized by things like increases in heart rate and blood pressure, increases in blood-glucose levels, and pupil dilation. But that's not the whole story. While the sympathetic nervous system is gearing us up for action, it's also slowing our digestion and putting our immune system on pause. This reflects a highly adaptive process that channels energy away from areas that are not immediately needed to areas that are in dire need of energy. You won't die if you don't immediately digest that latest burger – or if you can't immediately ward off that cold – but you might die if you don't quickly respond to that charging bear. The alarm stage is no laughing matter. It's your body getting ready to do physiological battle.

Stage 2 of the GAS is **resistance**. In this second stage (which typically begins 24–48 hours after exposure to a stressor), the organism begins to fight back. If the assault is a virus, your body will begin to produce antibodies that stop the virus from replicating. This general process is known as the **immune response**. A good way to understand it in the case of an attacking virus is to think of the **lymphocytes** (white blood cells) that fight off infections as the soldiers of your immune system. In fact, just as soldiers who've faced an enemy before will remember that enemy, some of the white blood cells that helped you fight off a particular virus many years ago will "remember" that particular virus and will quickly shut the virus down if you're exposed to it years later. This is one reason why you may catch some specific colds while easily fighting off others. To be clear, resistance extends well beyond contagious diseases to apply to any kind of stressor. In fact, one of Selye's biggest insights is that our bodies respond to physical and psychological threats in much the same way that they respond to viral infections. But let's stick with viral attacks for now. Just as soldiers cannot fight forever, resistance does not last forever.

If you are exposed to a stressor long enough, Stage 3 of the GAS will begin. This third stage is **exhaustion**. During exhaustion, your body is no longer able to resist the stressor. In this unhappy stage, you could easily die without some medical intervention. Selye noted (1956) that for many of the low-level stressors he studied, exhaustion often began after a couple of months. But he also noted that if a stressor is powerful enough, exhaustion could begin very quickly. Severe burn victims sometimes die within hours of being badly burned because serious damage to the skin creates all kinds of havoc, ranging from severe dehydration to a loss of the potassium that regulates many crucial physiological functions (Herndon & Tompkins, 2004). As another example, consider a soldier in a war zone. When the first bullets fly, that soldier's physiological activity will spike instantaneously as the soldier mobilizes to fight. This is the alarm stage. As the battle continues, the soldier will enter the resistance stage, literally and figuratively fighting back. During this second stage, the body's physiological activity will drop off slightly from the initial spike of the alarm stage, but the soldier remains vigilant and continues to channel energy away from non-vital activities and into the vital activity of fighting back. And there's the rub: You can only last so long in a constant state of vigilance (redirecting your energies and pausing other critical systems). If the battle wages on, the soldier will enter the exhaustion stage and will be unable to continue the fight. This is why military leaders always try to rotate their troops in and out of war zones – to minimize the chances that soldiers will enter the exhaustion stage.

Selye's work on GAS and our response to threat has touched anyone who has ever heard the word "stress" in a medical or psychological context. Prior to Selye's work, the word "stress" had only a physical meaning. Physicists and engineers studied the mechanical stresses that could lead to the failure of physical systems, like collapsed bridges or snapped guitar strings. But Selye extended the use of the term **stress** to refer to our psychological response to physical, chemical, and psychological assaults. So when your aunt Sella says she was stressed out when planning your cousin's wedding, Sella is unknowingly paying tribute to Selye. Selye appears to have been the first human being to spell out the details of how psychological events can affect our physical health. Our psychology and our physiology are intimately intertwined.

Figure 34.1 In November of 1940, strong, persistent winds created stresses in the recently built Tacoma Narrows Bridge. The stresses eventually accumulated until the bridge collapsed. Hans Selye adapted the metaphor of physical stresses on building materials from engineering – and thus began the use of the term "stress" in psychology.

Figure 34.2 These screen captures of some November 1940 video footage show what it looked like to be *on* the Tacoma Narrows Bridge seconds before it collapsed. *Stressful*, huh?

The Bad News: Stress Causes Illness

That makes Selye the first health psychologist because **health psychology** is the scientific study of how psychological events are related to physical health. This broad definition includes a lot. If you study why people fail to exercise, eat well, or take their prescribed medication, you are a health psychologist. If you study whether optimists live longer than pessimists, how people sometimes select their dates of death, or why there are large ethnic gaps in health and longevity, you, too, are a health psychologist. In this module on health psychology, we'll examine just a few key questions studied by health psychologists. The question we'll examine most carefully is whether positive and negative psychological events influence physical health.

Do psychological events truly influence physical health? If so, how? Selye believed that stress can make you sick, but he could not ethically conduct the kind of well-controlled experiments on people that he conducted on rats. Would you volunteer to receive a sublethal dose of formaldehyde – or to have your spine crushed – so that researchers could study how your body responded to these stressors? For ethical reasons, most early health psychologists who studied *people* relied on (a) cross-sectional and (b) passive observational designs. This meant that early studies (a) did not follow people over time, and (b) did not use experimental methods. Such studies showed, for example, that people who were suffering from colds reported being more stressed out than people who were not suffering from colds. It is no secret why many health psychologists, even today, rely on cross-sectional survey studies (e.g., see Abdulghani, AlKanhal, Mahmoud, Ponnamperuma, & Alfaris, 2011). Such studies yield a lot of information about important associations between stress and illness, and they are much, much easier to carry out than prospective studies – which may require many years to complete.

But as you'll recall from Module 3, cross-sectional studies (without any experimental manipulations) do not usually offer solid information about causality. If being highly stressed is associated with greater levels of physical illness, did stress make people get sick? Or did getting sick make people feel stressed out (e.g., because they were worried about falling behind in work or school)? Or did a third variable – such as having a chronically compromised immune system – create *both* stress and susceptibility to the common cold? Cross-sectional studies cannot usually answer such important questions.

Stress and the Common Cold

Despite these challenges, there has been a lot of prospective and quasi-experimental research in the past few decades showing that psychological factors cause illness. Many such studies focus on the common cold because it is one of the few illnesses that is easy to study without doing people any serious harm. For example, what we'll call the **Cohen, Tyrrell, and Smith (1991) cold study** quarantined 394 healthy British adults for nine days in large apartments. Participants had to be very healthy to begin the study, and on each day of the study, they were examined carefully by medical professionals – to see if they had caught a cold. At the beginning of the study, participants filled out three different measures of how much stress they had been under lately. The researchers pooled these measures to determine each participant's pre-existing stress level. Cohen and colleagues didn't have weeks to wait around and see who happened to catch a cold. Instead, on day two of the nine-day study, they dropped one of five live cold viruses directly into people's noses! That's right; they intentionally exposed people to live cold viruses. Of course, everyone knew this was coming when they signed up for this study. So this study was ethical. It was also highly informative. In a group of 26 lucky control participants who got saline drops instead of cold virus drops, *no one* caught a cold. In contrast, 38% of those who got one of the viruses caught a cold. More important, for each of the five cold viruses examined, those who reported having been stressed out prior to taking part in the study were more likely to catch a cold than were those who reported little or no stress. Figure 34.3 summarizes these findings.

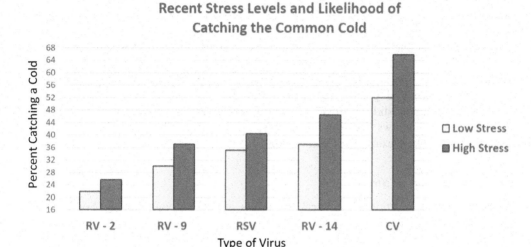

Figure 34.3 Psychological stress and likelihood of catching a cold after exposure to one of five live cold viruses (from Cohen et al., 1991).

Research has also shown that being stressed out reduces our ability to fight off upper respiratory illnesses. Cohen and colleagues (1995) found that people who experienced a lot of negative emotions and later caught a cold or the flu produced more mucous (yes, more snot) during their illnesses than did participants who had reported very few negative emotions. So psychological events sometimes influence the severity of one's illness in addition to predicting who will become ill in the first place. Field studies that have looked at who succumbs to the flu during flu season have likewise shown that, all else being equal, families who are stressed out get the flu more often than do families who are not (Clover, Abell, Becker, Crawford, & Ramsey, 1989). Finally, Cohen and colleagues (1998) found that it is chronic (long-lasting) stressors rather than short-term stressors that are most likely to compromise a person's immune system in the face of an upper respiratory attack. Can you say *exhaustion*? Can you say COVID-19?

From the Common Cold to an Unpopular War

Critics of research on upper respiratory infections might argue that the size of the stress-cold association is not that large. Not everyone who is stressed out succumbs to a cold. Likewise, not everyone who is chillaxed always fights off a cold. Nonetheless, for an illness that is familiar to virtually everyone on Earth, stress does matter. More severe stress probably matters even more. In fact, another classic study in health psychology looked at the long-term consequences of exposure to an *extremely* stressful event – being drafted to serve in the Vietnam War. Hearst, Newman, and Hulley (1986) took advantage of the fact that Vietnam War draft boards used *random assignment* to decide who would become soldiers. By randomly choosing men with different birthday numbers, draft boards guaranteed that the millions of men who were told to go fight were exactly like the millions of men who were excused from fighting. Hearst et al.

(1986) looked at the thousands of draft-eligible men who died in California or Pennsylvania between 1974 and 1983. This natural experiment showed that the draft-eligible men were more likely than the draft-exempt men to commit suicide in the ten-year window following the war. The men who were draft-eligible also had higher rates of dying in motor vehicle accidents in this same window. Exactly how big this effect was depended on how the researchers sliced the data. But in the analyses that we consider most sophisticated and precise, the men who served as soldiers were almost twice as likely as the men who did not do so to commit suicide in the ten-year window after the war. This research shows that long-term stress can sometimes have lethal consequences. That is another likely example of exhaustion.

More Bad News about Stress

There's plenty of additional evidence that stress is bad for your health. Some of the most impressive studies of stress and health measure what happens in the immune systems of people who have recently experienced specific highly stressful situations. Smyth and colleagues (1998) tracked adults by randomly beeping them six to 12 times per day. When beeped, participants reported their stress levels and their current mood. Six times daily, participants also provided saliva samples. The researchers tested these samples for a stress hormone known as **cortisol**. Smyth and colleagues wanted to see if levels of cortisol increase after stressful events. That's exactly what they found. Cortisol levels reliably increased after (or just before) stressful events. As you can see in Figure 34.4, Smyth et al. further observed that having recently experienced two or three stressful events was associated with greater increases in cortisol than having experienced just one such event. Finally, when Smyth et al. focused on single events, they found that the more stressful participants said a specific event had felt to them, the more their cortisol levels shot up. Caring for a sick mother might lead to modest increases in cortisol levels. Being told that your mother only has a few days to live would almost certainly lead to larger increases.

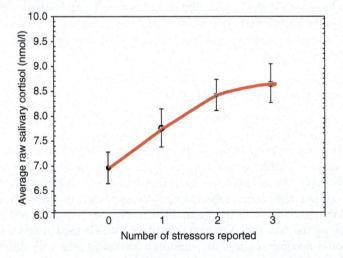

Figure 34.4 Smyth et al. (1998) found that the more stressful events people had experienced within the past couple of hours, the more their cortisol ("stress hormone") levels increased.

Researchers have now examined the association between chronic stress and a great many diseases. As Slavich (2016, p. 346) put it,

> stress is involved in the development, maintenance, or exacerbation of several mental and physical health conditions, including asthma, rheumatoid arthritis, anxiety disorders, depression, cardiovascular disease, chronic pain, human immunodeficiency virus/AIDS, stroke, and certain types of cancer. Stress has also been implicated in accelerated biological aging and premature mortality.

Studies of pregnancy add the risk of low-birth weight to that list (Lobel & Dunkel Schetter, 2016). We're guessing COVID-19 could go there, too.

The Good News: Positive Influences on Health

Optimism, Marriage, and Health

If you're getting the feeling that health psychologists are all about doom and gloom, cheer up. Rather than merely documenting the negative effects of stress, health psychologists have also shown that interventions that help people manage or reduce their stress often have positive health consequences (Mohr et al., 2012). Health psychologists have also documented the mental and physical benefits of regular aerobic exercise. In fact, even if you hate aerobic exercise and wouldn't be caught dead doing yoga, this is no reason to give up hope. Variables such as hope and optimism also play an important role in physical health. For example, Scheier and colleagues (1989) found that seeing the proverbial glass as half full (or agreeing that "every cloud has a silver lining") has positive health consequences. In one study, Scheier and colleagues assessed dispositional optimism in a group of patients who were about to undergo coronary bypass surgery. Even after controlling for a host of other important variables, they found that optimists recovered more quickly from the surgery. If all this has you bummed out because you are a life-long pessimist, there may be hope even for you. Just find another life-long pessimist and marry them. King and Reis (2012) studied more than 200 patients who underwent coronary bypass surgery in the late 1980s. At the time of their surgeries, patients reported their marital status. A year later, they reported their marital satisfaction. King and Reis then patiently waited for 15 years to see who was still alive and kicking. Those who were married (rather than single or divorced) at the time of their surgeries, especially those who proved to be *happily* married, were much more likely to be alive 15 years post-surgery. But there were still measurable increases in survival rates even for those who were *not* very happily married. Maybe even the most difficult spouses still remind people to take their heart medication.

If you recall the famous "nuns study" from the module on external validity, you are familiar with another example of how positive attitudes about the world can promote longevity. Recall that Danner, Snowdon, and Friesen (2001) studied a large group of nuns from Baltimore and Milwaukee. When these women became nuns, in about 1930, they had to write brief autobiographies – which the church held onto for many decades. In the late 1990s, Danner and colleagues got permission to analyze these autobiographies. Recall that a very strong predictor of how long these nuns lived was the number of positive emotion words they had used in their life stories – written at the beginning of their careers as nuns. In fact, the nuns who were in the top quartile (top 25%) for the use of positive emotion words in their life stories were more than three times as likely to live to be 93 as were the nuns whose stories placed them in the bottom quartile for the use of positive emotion words. A positive attitude about life seems to give people a longer life to be positive about.

Social Support and Health

King and Reis interpret their findings about marriage as a specific example of a robust finding in health psychology: Social support is good for you (Cohen & Hoberman, 1983). **Social support** refers to having other people in your life on whom you can depend in times of emotional, physical, or financial distress. If Kayla always "has your back," then she probably qualifies as a source of social support for you. Brothers Click and Clack of NPR's *Car Talk* also had a good way of expressing the essence of social support. They argued that: "A friend will help you move. A *good* friend will help you move a body." We're happy to say that we've never had to move a body. But we're even happier to say that if we do ever need to do so, we have a few social support agents we could count on to help us do it.

Getting back to why social support matters, people who have strong social support networks tend to live longer than those who do not. The House, Landis, and Umberson (1988) **social support study** summarized the results of five sophisticated longitudinal studies of social support. The samples studied included adults of all ages from California, Michigan, and Georgia as well as Swedish and Finnish samples. The researchers were careful to control for worrisome confounds such as age when the study began, cholesterol levels, and smoking status. On average people with little social support were more likely than those with lots of social support to die over the course of the ten-year follow up windows. To frame this positively, social support promoted survival. These results are summarized separately for women and men in Figure 34.5. As you can see, the beneficial effects of social support are a bit larger for men than for women, but the survival effect is robust for both genders.

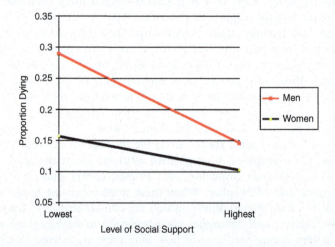

Figure 34.5 Both men and women who had lots of social support were less likely to die over the course of about a decade (adapted from House et al., 1988).

Helping and Health

Although there is a great deal of evidence linking social support and health, there may sometimes be a down side to receiving love, emotional support, or even money. Although receiving social support may make you feel loved, it could also make you feel indebted or helpless, especially if you never get to pay the social support back. Brown and colleagues (2003) argued that, for this reason, people who *give* social support might benefit even more than those who receive it. Is it really good for your health to help others? It sure looks like it. Brown and colleagues followed more than 800 seniors (aged 65+) for five years – to see who survived. Those most likely to survive were those who initially reported offering the most emotional and physical help to others. This sounds impressive. But it's possible that something other than helping *per se* was the real reason some of these seniors lived longer than others. Consider an obvious confound: Women help other people more than men do. Women also live longer than men do. All else being equal, older seniors probably help other people less than younger seniors. And older seniors, almost by definition, are less likely than younger seniors to be alive and kicking in five years. These are but two of several possible confounds that might be the real reasons why seniors who help others a lot might be more likely to be alive five years down the road. In addition to gender and age, are there any other confounds to worry about?

Brown and colleagues thought so. Accordingly, they controlled statistically for a very long list of things that might be confounded with how much older people helped others. This list of confounds included age, gender, education, income, exercise level, smoking status, alcohol consumption, subjective well-being, health satisfaction, self-rated functional health, interviewer rated health, the five basic human personality traits, marital satisfaction, perceived marital equity, receipt of social support, psychological dependence on one's spouse, and the kitchen sink. OK, you're right. They didn't really throw in the kitchen sink, but they threw in just about everything else. The result? Those who reported giving more help to others still lived longer. No matter what the exact mechanism is behind this effect, it is clear that good deeds are often rewarded (see also Poulain, 2012). One of those rewards seems to be superior health. In case you're still not convinced that helping others is good for your health, consider an experiment by Nelson-Coffey and colleagues (2017). This research team *randomly assigned* some participants to engage in prosocial acts to specific others for four weeks – while randomly assigning other participants to engage in a variety of control activities. Those who helped others showed improvements in a physical marker of healthy immune system function (leukocyte gene expression profiles). Or to paraphrase these authors, kindness makes its way into your blood. By the way, our good deed for the week is promising our students that the exact term "leukocyte gene expression profiles" *won't* be on the exam (though the point made by this clever experiment might be). But please check with your own instructor to see if the same deal holds for you.

In this module, we have only scratched the surface of the deep and rich connection between the psychological and the physical. Five decades ago, there was a lot of debate about whether the heart and mind can truly affect the body. Today, the only debates are about exactly when and how this happens. For example, today's health psychologists are working hard to understand exactly how and why stress compromises physical health. How much of it happens when stress undermines the normal operation of the immune system? How much of it happens when stress undermines our good judgment about smoking or drinking? Your own health and longevity (not to mention that of your aging authors) may well depend on the answers to such important questions.

Critical Thinking and Group Discussion Questions for Module 34
Health Psychology

Recall that a landmark study in modern healthy psychology was conducted by Sheldon Cohen and colleagues (1991) – who showed that people who reported having been under a lot of stress recently were more susceptible than usual to the common cold. Cohen's more recent work suggests that stress may get under people's skin in an even more unsettling way than his classic work suggested. At least some of the long-term effects of stress on health may be permanent. Stress may prematurely age us and weaken our immune systems. One way in which this happens is through damage to our telomeres.

Telomeres are the tiny biological caps that exist at the end of chromosomes. As we age, our telomeres naturally get shorter because of cell division. In fact, once telomeres become extremely short, our cells can no longer divide, and this can hasten our deaths. But telomeres gradually disappear at different rates in different people. Consider the chronic stress levels of people who live in extreme poverty, survive in war zones, or live with daily concerns about assault. People who live in such high-stress worlds experience accelerated damage to their telomeres. In fact, Epel and colleagues (2004), p. 17312) found that postmenopausal women who had lived very stressful lives had telomeres that were "shorter on average by the equivalent of at least one decade of additional aging compared to low stress women." This accelerated cellular aging process can be observed even in young people.

Building on the idea that telomere length is a biomarker of aging, Cohen and colleagues (2013) assessed whether telomere length was a marker for people's susceptibility to the common cold. It was. By at least one way of measuring telomere length, people with shorter telomeres were twice as likely as people with longer telomeres to catch a cold when Cohen and colleagues dropped a live cold virus in their noses. The connection between telomere length and susceptibility to catching cold was also stronger among people aged 30 and older than it was among college aged adults. Needless to say, studies such as these have created a lot of interest in telomeres in both health psychologists and medical practitioners.

Thought and Discussion Questions

It looks like inevitable telomere reduction puts a natural age limit on the human lifespan – so that no matter how well-behaved and healthy a person is, very few people naturally live beyond about 100 years of age (Steenstrup et al., 2017). It also looks like knowing a person's telomere lengths can tell you about how long that person has left to live (especially in older people). Let's assume that health psychologists eventually develop a simple and inexpensive blood test that can accurately predict exactly how long a person has to live.

1. Would you want to know your own (telomere-length-based) lifespan? Why or why not?
2. As the Black comedian George Wallace put it when he was in his 40s, "The average Black man in this country lives to be 63 years old. What in the hell am I paying social security for?" Wallace said this in jest, but how might knowing your own telomere length make it easier for you to plan for your retirement?
3. Researchers recently discovered a technique that can turn back the telomeric clock in cells living in a lab dish. If this technology ever becomes an extremely expensive anti-aging treatment (costing say, $250,000) what legal, practical and ethical questions will this raise. For example, if a wealthy woman purchases this treatment and adds 30 years to her life, will it be fair for American taxpayers to continue to pay her Social Security Benefits until she dies at the age of 120 (right now that would easily be a total payout of $750,000)?

Multiple Choice Questions for Module 34: Health Psychology

1. Kairee studies the role of self-esteem in risky behavior such as binge drinking, recreational drug use, and reckless driving. Kairee probably considers herself a(n):

   A) health psychologist
   B) behavioral health specialist
   C) clinical psychologist

2. The acronym "GAS" in Hans Selye's GAS model of coping with stress stands for:

   A) Glutamate Amine Synthesis
   B) General Adaptation Syndrome
   C) Generic Aphasic Shift

3. What is the second of the three phases in Selye's GAS model of coping with stress?

   A) Alarm
   B) Resistance
   C) Imbalance

4. The term "burnout" that is used often in work contexts is very similar to which of Selye's three phases of the human stress response?

   A) exhaustion
   B) frustration
   C) disengagement

5. The process in which your body fights back against stress, infection, or physical irritation is known as the:

   A) adaptive compensation
   B) homeostatic correction
   C) immune response

6. How did Sheldon Cohen and colleagues show that stress can *cause* the common cold – rather than merely being a *consequence* of having a cold?

   A) they quarantined people, measured their recent stress levels, and exposed them to live cold viruses
   B) they had people keep a dairy for 90 days, reporting both their daily health and their daily stress levels
   C) they identified people with highly stressful vs. less stressful occupations and followed them for a year to see which group got colds more often.

7. Do health psychologists ever study the consequences of major natural stressors – such as being drafted or not drafted to serve in a war?

   A) no; such a study of war service would be both ethically sensitive and overly expensive
   B) yes; this is what researchers did by looking at things like suicide rates following the Vietnam War
   C) no: researchers have proposed such work but have not been able to get research funding for it.

8. Which of the following is a commonly-studied stress hormone, meaning it increases right before and during stressful situations?

   A) melatonin
   B) testosterone
   C) cortisol

9. King and Reis did a study of marriage and health in which they followed people for 15 years after open-heart surgery. They found that:

   A) marriage promotes longevity; married people lived longer than single or divorced people
   B) happy marriages promote longevity, but unhappy marriages are associated with dying young
   C) marriage promotes health in men but is weakly associated with poorer health outcomes in women

10. One of the most powerful psychological variables that is associated with health and longevity is:

    A) extraversion ("outgoingness")
    B) social support
    C) realism

11. In Stephanie Brown's prospective study of a large group of seniors, she followed them for five years. She found that a surprising but robust predictor of health and longevity in seniors is the amount of:

    A) activation in the reward system people experience when they are with loved ones
    B) dopamine people have in their brains when in a stressful situation
    C) help people give to other people

Answer Key: 1A 2B 3B 4A 5C 6A 7B 8C 9A 10B 11C

References

Abdulghani, H. M., AlKanhal, A. A., Mahmoud, E. S., Ponnamperuma, G. G., & Alfaris, E. A. (2011). Stress and its effects on medical students: A cross-sectional study at a college of medicine in Saudi Arabia. *Journal of Health and Population Nutrition, 29*(5), 516–522.

Brown, S. L., Nesse, R. M., Vinokur, A. D., & Smith, D. M. (2003). Providing social support may be more beneficial than receiving it. Results from a prospective study of mortality. *Psychological Science, 14*, 320–327.

Cannon, W. B. (1914). The emergency function of the adrenal medulla in pain and the major emotions. *American Journal of Physiology, 33*, 356–372.

Clover, R. D., Abell, T., Becker, L. A., Crawford, S., & Ramsey, J. C. N. (1989). Family functioning and stress as predictors of influenza B infection. *Journal of Family Practice, 28*, 535–539.

Cohen, S., Tyrrell, D. A., & Smith, A. P. (1991). Psychological stress and susceptibility to the common cold. *The New England Journal of Medicine, 325*(9), 606–612. doi:10.1056/NEJM199108293250903

Cohen, S., Doyle, W. J., Skoner, D. P., Fireman, P., Gwaltney, J. M., Jr., & Newsom, J. T. (1995). State and trait negative affect as predictors of objective and subjective symptoms of respiratory viral infections. *Journal of Personality and Social Psychology, 68*, 159–169.

Cohen, S., Frank, E., Doyle, W. J., Skoner, D. P., Rabin, B. S., & Gwaltney, J. M., Jr. (1998). Types of stressors that increase susceptibility to the common cold in healthy adults. *Health Psychology, 17*, 214–223.

Cohen, S., & Hoberman, H. (1983). Positive events and social supports as buffers of life change stress. *Journal of Applied Social Psychology, 13*, 99–125.

Cohen, S., Janicki-Deverts, D., Turner, R. B., Casselbrant, M. L., Li-Korotky, H. S., Epel, E. S., & Doyle, W. J. (2013). Association between telomere length and experimentally induced upper respiratory viral infection in healthy adults. *JAMA, 309*(7), 699–705. doi:10.1001/jama.2013.613

Danner, D. D., Snowdon, D. A., & Friesen, W. V. (2001). Positive emotions in early life and longevity: Findings from the nun study. *Journal of Personality and Social Psychology, 80*(5), 804–813. doi:10.1037/0022-3514.80.5.804

Epel, E. S., Blackburn, E. H., Lin, J., Dhabhar, F. S., Adler, N. E., Morrow, J. D., & Cawthon, R. M. (2004). Accelerated telomere shortening in response to life stress. *Proceedings of the National Academy of Sciences of the United States of America, 101*(49), 17312–17315. doi:10.1073/pnas.0407162101

Hearst, N., Newman, T. B., & Hulley, S. B. (1986). Delayed effects of the military draft on mortality: A randomized natural experiment. *The New England Journal of Medicine, 314*(10), 620–624. doi:10.1056/NEJM198603063141005

Herndon, D. N., & Tompkins, R. G. (2004, June 5). Support of the metabolic response to burn injury. *Lancet, 363*(9424), 1895–1902.

House, J. S., Landis, K. R., & Umberson, D. (1988). Social relationships and health. *Science, 241*, 540–545.

King, K. B., & Reis, H. T. (2012). Marriage and long-term survival after coronary artery bypass grafting. *Health Psychology, 31*(1), 55–62. doi:10.1037/a0025061

Lobel, M., & Dunkel Schetter, C. (2016). Pregnancy and prenatal stress. In H. S. Friedman (Ed.), *Encyclopedia of mental health* (2nd ed., Vol. 3, pp. 318–329). Waltham, MA: Academic Press. doi:10.1016/B978-0-12-397045-9.00164-6

Mohr, D. C., Lovera, J., Brown, T., Cohen, B., Neylan, T., Henry, R., ... Pelletier, D. (2012). A randomized trial of stress management for the prevention of new brain lesions in MS. *Neurology, 79*(5), 412–419. doi:10.1212/WNL.0b013e3182616ff9

Nelson-Coffey, S. K., Fritz, M. M., Lyubomirsky, S., & Cole, S. W. (2017). Kindness in the blood: A randomized controlled trial of the gene regulatory impact of prosocial behavior. *Psychoneuroendocrinology, 81*, 8–13.

Poulain, M. (2012, May). The longevity of nuns and monks: A gender gap issue investigated with new Belgian data. Presented at the 2012 Annual Conference of the Population Association of America, San Francisco, CA.

Scheier, M. F., Matthews, K. A., Owens, J. F., Magovern, G. J., Lefebvre, R. C., Abbott, R. A., & Carver, C. S. (1989). Dispositional optimism and recovery from coronary artery bypass surgery: The beneficial effects on physical and psychological well-being. *Journal of Personality and Social Psychology, 57,* 1024–1040.

Selye, H. (1956). *The stress of life.* New York: McGraw-Hill.

Slavich G. M. (2016). Life Stress and Health: A Review of Conceptual Issues and Recent Findings. *Teaching of psychology (Columbia, Mo.), 43*(4), 346–355. doi:10.1177/0098628316662768

Smyth, J., Ockenfels, M. C., Porter, L., Kirschbaum, C., Hellhammer, D. H., & Stone, A. A. (1998). Stressors and mood measured on a momentary basis are associated with salivary cortisol secretion. *Psychoneuroendocrinology, 23,* 353–370.

Steenstrup, T., Kark, J. D., Verhulst, S., Thinggaard, M., Hjelmborg, J., Dalgård, C., ... Aviv, A. (2017). Telomeres and the natural lifespan limit in humans. *Aging, 9*(4), 1130–1142. doi:10.18632/aging.101216

Module 35
Mind Games, in a Good Way
Sport Psychology

If you recall the work of Anders Ericsson, on the specificity of genius, you know that it takes a long time to become highly skillful at any complex activity. No matter how smart you are, there's no way you're going to master particle physics – or become a world class gymnast – in only a year. But this does not mean that you can't quickly make important improvements at specific activities. Ask any sport psychologist. **Sport psychology** is the study of how psychology may be used to increase athletic engagement and performance, whether this means sticking with an aerobic exercise plan, increasing group cohesion ("team spirit") on a rugby team, or helping athletes make clutch free throws. This module is a quick tour of sport psychology. One of the first questions one might ask about sports is why people play them in the first place. The simple answer is that sports are fun. Remember Murdock's (1949) list of cultural universals? There is no known culture on Earth where people do not play some kind of athletic sports. But why do some people stick with a sport for decades whereas others quickly abandon the same sport? Tamara Scanlan and her colleagues (1993) have shown that one of the best predictors of sticking to a sport for a long time is not people's natural talent or skill level but rather how much they truly *enjoy* the sport in question, something Scanlan fittingly calls "**sport enjoyment**." When your first author was a high school track athlete, he was amazed to see that very fast runners seem to have dropped out of the sport about as often as those struggling to earn a varsity letter. Apparently, not everyone who can run fast truly enjoys doing so.

Research also shows that exercise is really good for people – and in some unexpected ways. One well-established way to prevent premature aging and increase **brain plasticity** (your brain's ability to adapt to changes by learning and rewiring itself) is regular **aerobic exercise** (Molteni, Zheng, Ying, Gómez-Pinilla, & Twiss, 2004; Tomporowski, 2003).

Aerobic exercise is called *aerobic* ("with oxygen"), in part, because it means that you use oxygen to burn energy. But a more intuitive definition of aerobic exercise is engaging in activities that tax your cardiovascular system – meaning they elevate your heart rate – for a meaningful period. Playing an hour of vigorous tennis or pick-up basketball, going for a jog, and going for a brisk 30-minute walk are all examples of aerobic exercise. This is because these activities will elevate your heart rate well above its resting level for more than just a few minutes. Running to catch the bus does not count as aerobic exercise – unless it takes you a mile or more to catch up with the bus. So, if you want to increase your chances of staying mentally keen your whole life, put away that video game and put on your running shoes. Likewise, if you want to add healthy years to your life, sport psychologists would be the first to tell you to "just keep swimming" – or biking, or jogging. Lifting weights may help you sculpt a more muscular body, by the way, but it does little to increase your cardiovascular fitness, and it will not help you live longer. Even if you didn't know about the connection between exercise and brain plasticity, you surely knew that aerobic exercise is good for you. The problem for most people is sticking to an aerobic exercise program.

Figure 35.1
You don't have to be an elite athlete to take part in aerobic exercise. Just keep your arms and legs moving.

Sport psychologists can help with that, too. Abby King and colleagues (2007) showed that simply giving middle-aged walkers an encouraging phone call about once per month roughly doubled how much they walked over the course of a year. An automated reminder from a computer rather than a live person was almost as effective at increasing the number of miles people walked. Having a live person who agrees to work out with you on a regular basis can be even more important. But there are subtler ways in which others can help. Carron and colleagues (1996) conducted a systematic review of many exercise intervention studies. They found that having family members who support your intention to keep exercising is strongly associated with sticking to an exercise plan.

As you may recall from Module 18 on judgment and decision-making, sport psychologists have also examined some popular beliefs about athletic performance. For example, Gilovich, Vallone, and Tversky (1985) examined the "hot hand" in basketball. Believers in the hot hand often refuse to abandon their belief that it is real. Players get hot, and when they do, they're practically unstoppable. Consider the following set of 30 shots taken by the Utah Jazz's Rudy Gobert in the 2016–2017 NBA season:

> made, missed, made, made, missed, made, missed, made, missed, missed, made, missed, made, made, missed,
>
> made, made, missed, **made, made, made, made, made, made, made**, missed, **made, made, made, made**.

Did you notice the streak of seven consecutive made shots, followed by a shorter streak of four made shots? Most Jazz fans certainly would. But let us correct ourselves. That sequence of shots *was not* 30 real shots. Instead, we generated this list of 30 shots by looking up Gobert's 2016–2017 season shooting statistics (413 field goals made in 625 attempts). Then we plugged these season figures into a *random number generator*. So streaks of six, seven, or eight consecutive shots will often happen by *chance* when someone, like Gobert, has a very high (66%) shooting percentage. If we had sampled 625 shots rather than a mere 30, there would surely have been some *much* longer "streaks." But these are not due to a hot hand. Instead, they're due to the natural but unappreciated "clumpiness" of chance events. As Gilovich and colleagues showed, the best predictor of whether a player will make any shot he or she is about to take is that player's season shooting percentage, *not* how many shots that player has made in the last few minutes. The *hot hand bias*, then, is the illusory belief in streak shooting in sports. Sport psychologists don't just study sports. They also study people's beliefs about sports.

Sport Psychology is Multi-faceted and Interdisciplinary

Have you noticed that this module has already covered a lot of different topics? We've meandered from brain plasticity and healthy aging to sports enjoyment and how to get people to stick to an exercise program. We then revisited the hot hand bias you first learned about in the module on judgmental heuristics. We've already cited an anthropologist (Murdock). This is no accident. As a group, sport psychologists have diverse interests. They wish to understand anything and everything that is connected to sports. This means that sport psychologists are happy to borrow and integrate theories and empirical findings not only from any subfield of psychology but also from any physical or social science. The only question is whether the insights provided by a field of study helps us better understand sports. This means sport psychologists are interested in everything from evolution and genetics to stereotyping and prejudice – so long as these topics help us better understand sports.

Consider a genetic example. In his provocative book, *The Sports Gene*, Epstein (2013) argues that in the modern world of elite sports – in which playing sports can sometimes become lucrative careers – there are powerful selection pressures that determine who does and does not become a world class athlete. This means that the bodies of different athletes vary in predictable ways, including quite a few ways you'd be unlikely to notice based on casual observation. For example, both boxers and basketball players have long wingspans for their heights. For the average person, wingspan (the distance from fingertip to fingertip if you spread your arms as wide as they can go) is just 1% greater than height. If you don't believe us, carefully measure your own wingspan. We predict that it will be within about an inch of your height (without shoes, of course). But professional boxers and basketball players are much more likely than the rest of us to have wingspans that greatly exceed their heights. The average NBA basketball player has a wingspan that is 4–5 inches greater than his height. Likewise, if you compare world class swimmers and world class distance runners, you'll see that runners have much longer legs – proportionally speaking – than swimmers. It's pretty obvious that longer legs are a big advantage to runners. It may not be so obvious that long arms and torsos are a big advantage to swimmers, but that is also the case. In light of these two facts you won't be too surprised to learn that 6'4" Michael Phelps has a wingspan of 6'8" – and the same inseam measurement (about 30 inches) as 5'9" Hicham El Guerrouj – the world-record-holding middle distance runner.

Figure 35.2
McDonald's All-American and UT Austin standout Mohamed Bamba was the sixth player to be selected in the 2018 NBA draft. Teams liked him because he is seven feet tall. They liked him even *more* because he has a 7'10" wingspan. For Bamba, dunking is slightly more difficult than giving someone a high five.

Image credit: Featureflash Photo Agency/Shutterstock.com

Yet, as K. Anders Ericsson would be quick to remind us, athletic performance is not *all* about genes. Long arms may be inherited, but what you do with those long arms depends heavily on *deliberate practice*. Many other factors also influence athletic performance. You already know that the personality factor of sports enjoyment influences how long people stick to an athletic activity. Another way to view this is that people who are intrinsically motivated ("soccer is fun; I love it") rather than extrinsically motivated ("how much money can one make playing soccer?") are more likely to stick with a sport. But in addition to genes, deliberate practice, and personality, there are many other drivers of athletic performance. A partial list of these additional factors includes emotional intelligence, basic rules of judgment and decision-making, leadership and group processes, culture, and immediate contextual forces (the power of the situation). The fact that many sports are group activities, for example, means that fields such as sociology, social psychology, and management have a lot to teach us about sports. In short, sport psychologists study sports from a broad range of perspectives because they realize that athletic performance is complicated – and has many roots. Let's examine just three research questions in sport psychology to get a more detailed look at what sport psychologist do – and what they can teach us about athletic performance.

The Home Field Advantage in Sports

Many people believe that there is a hot hand in basketball. But as you now know, this belief is at least partly an illusion. A lot of people also firmly believe that there is a home-field advantage in sports. This is why most fans of a team would prefer to see their team play a crucial game at home than on the road. As is the case with many firmly-held popular beliefs, this one is correct. That's right. The belief in the home field advantage is well justified. If not for sport psychology, however, we wouldn't know just how robust this advantage is – and we'd have almost no idea exactly why it exists. Let's begin with how real – and robust – the home field advantage is. In a meta-analysis of many large-scale studies, of the home field advantage, Jamieson (2010) showed that the home field advantage is very robust. For example, he showed that the advantage enjoyed by the home team has been around for a long time (it is robust across time, at least for the periods for which we have data). The absolute size of the home field advantage is also meaningful. Averaging across many sports and many years, Jamieson observed an overall home field advantage of 60.4%. Of course, if there were no home field advantage, we'd expect that figure to be 50%. That 60% figure means winning three games for every two games you lose. In many sports, this kind of final record gets you to the playoffs. Speaking of the playoffs, Jamieson also found that the home-field advantage was a bit larger in playoff games as compared with regular season games.

Many of the studies Jamieson summarized included studies of many, many games. So there can be little doubt that the home-field advantage is real. But Jamieson (2010) also found that there is substantial variation in the size of the home field advantage across sports. As shown in Table 35.1, the home field advantage was much larger for soccer, rugby, and basketball than it was for cricket, American football, or baseball.

So the home field advantage is real. But why does it happen? There are probably many reasons (Courneya & Carron, 1992), but we'll save the most interesting reason for last. One reason, which may be particularly true in professional sports, is that the physical and psychological toll of *travel* (e.g., jet lag, sleeping in an unfamiliar place) may put visiting teams at a disadvantage. The fact that the home field advantage still holds for teams that do very limited traveling (e.g., local high school competitions) suggests travel alone cannot be the only explanation for the home field advantage. On the other hand, as Jamieson (2010) duly notes, studies have shown that the home field advantage gets bigger as the absolute distance traveled by visiting teams gets bigger. Travel matters, but it's not everything. Player's attitudes may also matter. The fact that most players know about the home field advantage may simply put home-field athletes in a better state of mind than they'd be in if there were no such thing as a home field advantage.

Table 35.1 The Home-field Advantage in Ten Popular Sports

Sport	Percentage of Games Won by Home Team
Soccer	67
Rugby/Australian football	64
Basketball	63
Tennis	62
Boxing	61
Hockey	60
Golf	57
Cricket	57
American Football	57
Baseball	56

Note. Figures are rounded to the nearest whole percentage point. A value that exceeds 50 (50% wins) indicates a home-field advantage. Adapted from Jamieson (2010, p. 1836).

Simple *familiarity* with one's home field or court may also be part of the home field advantage. If you remember the *mere exposure effect*, you know that people prefer familiar over unfamiliar stimuli. Familiarity may thus translate into helpful psychological states such as comfort and a favorable mood. Above and beyond any effects of mere exposure, people also know more about what is familiar. For example, if your home field is grass, you may know very well what it's like to play on grass in the rain. If your opponent's home field is artificial turf, she may be less, well, *at home* in the wet grass than you are. Likewise, if you get a lot of snow in Buffalo, or a lot of 98-degree days in Miami, familiarity with these conditions may give your team an advantage over some visiting teams. So, as you can see, there are many reasons for the home field advantage. But this list is not complete. Perhaps the most interesting reason for the home field advantage is the referees. Before we go any further, let us say that in our view the two most unfairly maligned groups of people on Earth are referees and weather forecasters – who are both routinely blamed for not being omniscient. The next time you get mad at your local weather forecaster, try predicting whether you need to carry an umbrella tomorrow by merely consulting your intuitions. And the next time you get mad at a ref, remember that referees don't have access to the slow-motion, super-high-definition video footage that CBS showed you to reveal that the refs made a bad call.

So why are we blaming refs now? We're not really blaming them; we're *explaining* them. They are human beings who, like the rest of us, are subject to the *power of the situation* that was the focus of Module 26 on social psychology. Like the rest of us, refs also *construct* much of what they perceive. When you put all this together, it means that referees often respond to crowds of thousands of screaming home-crowd fans by making slightly more generous calls for the home team than they make for the visiting

Figure 35.3 If you're a ref and a player argues with you, you can charge him with a technical foul. But if 30,000 rabid home-team fans are screaming at you, the best you can usually do is to favor their home team a little. Research in sport psychology suggests that referees are not made of stone.

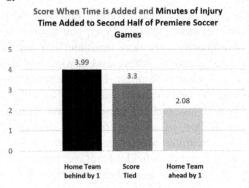

Score When Time is Added and **Minutes of Injury
Time Added to Second Half of Premiere Soccer
Games**

Figure 35.4 In Spanish professional soccer games, referees gave teams more injury make-up minutes when the home team was slightly behind than when the home team was slightly ahead. Adapted from Garicano et al. (2005).

team. Quite a few lines of evidence come together to support this conclusion. For example, the home field advantage is bigger in sports in which judges and referees have to score a performance or make a judgment call (e.g., figure skating, basketball) than for sports in which the outcomes are more objective (e.g., track and field; Jamieson, 2010). The home-field advantage also appears to be bigger in sports in which a single game matters more (e.g., soccer vs. baseball) and in sports in which the crowd is physically closer to the referees (Jamieson, 2010). The home field advantage in soccer is also larger in leagues in which the fans are known for being obnoxious and rowdy rather than well-behaved. Finally, a clever study of soccer – which is a sport for which the home field advantage is very large – revealed that where there is judgmental wiggle room, referees make calls that favor the home team (Garicano, Palacios-Huerta, & Prendergast, 2005). Soccer is a 90-minute game, and the clock runs continuously in two 45-minute halves. But anything from legitimate injuries to dawdling players and naked fans who storm the field can briefly stop play. To be sure players really play for the full 90 minutes, referees routinely add minutes to the end of each half of a soccer game. In what we'll call the Garicano et al. (2005) **soccer study**, this research team studied the length of these add-on periods in the premiere soccer league in Spain. Using data from two complete seasons, they found that, on average, referees added just under three minutes of injury time to the second half of a soccer match. When the score in the match was tied, the refs added slightly more time than average. But, as shown in Figure 35.4, when the home team was ahead by exactly one goal, the referees added only a bit more than two minutes. Finally, when the home team was *behind* by exactly one goal, the referees added an average of four minutes. Needless to say, getting extra playing time at the end of a game offers a team who is behind a greater chance to tie the game up. Taken together with the results of other studies that look at referee biases and the home field advantage (e.g., Nevill, Balmer, & Williams, 2002), these findings suggest that screaming crowds who are rooting for the home team give their home team an advantage by influencing referees.

Reciprocity: How Social Motivations Influence Athletic Behaviour

Referees are great, but they are only human. Of course, players, too, are only human. Even professional athletes sometimes take off their athletic caps and put on their reciprocity caps. Recall that the norm of reciprocity is essentially the norm of fairness. This norm says we should do unto others as they have done unto us. You may recall from Module 29 on helping behavior that most people feel compelled to pay back past favors. You may even recall that Willer, Sharkey, and Frey (2012) showed that NBA players paid back assists in basketball. When a teammate gave you an assist in a game, this increased the likelihood that you would later give that teammate an assist in the same game. This payback effect was specific to the player who had given you an assist earlier in the game. Players did not merely "pay it forward" by becoming a more frequent assist-giver to just any teammate. That's the nice side of reciprocity. On the nasty side, you may recall from Module 28 (on aggression) that professional baseball pitchers are more likely to hit a batter on the opposing team with a "bean ball" when the pitcher from the opposing team has hit one of the pitcher's teammates in that same game. From a purely rational perspective, neither paying back an assist nor paying back a bean ball make sense. Players who repay assists to LeBron may pass up the chance to get the ball to Kevin – who is a better shooter. Pitchers who hit batters with a bean ball risk a fist fight. Worse yet, perhaps, they can be ejected from a game. But sometimes athletes, like referees, are people first and players second.

The Quiet Eye

So social factors play an important role in sports, from how referees call a game to why we feel so compelled to pay back favors. Cognitive and motivational factors also play an important role in athletic performance. Our last example of sport psychology reveals how sport psychologists may take what we know about human perception, cognition, and motor movement to help athletes improve their "shooting skills." This includes things as varied as how to make a bank shot in billiards, how to shoot a bow and arrow accurately, and how to improve one's free throw percentage in basketball. To be clear, K. Anders Ericsson is surely correct that it takes thousands of hours to become a truly elite all-around basketball player. Expert players must seamlessly master and connect many different skills, from setting a pick to switching to a zone defense when a man-to-man defense isn't working. Your first author Brett didn't learn to play basketball until he was about 30, and it took him a few months merely to learn to dribble without looking at the ball. More than twenty-five years later, Brett still hasn't mastered the pick and roll. But he's a very good free throw shooter. The reason why is that a free throw is the simplest possible version of a "set shot," a shot where you have time to get your feet under you and take aim before you shoot. Brett used to be amazed to see skillful NBA players who never mastered this simple shot. But once he learned that expert athletic performance, like any other kind of genius, is domain-specific, it made more sense that a person could become extremely skilled at many specific aspects of playing basketball while failing to master free throw shooting. The good news for such players is known as the **quiet eye**. Before we take a close look at the quiet eye, let's take a closer look at the quirky problem of being a great basketball player but a poor free-throw shooter.

Everyone has seen skillful basketball players who shoot well from 18 feet with defensive players in their faces but have difficulty making a 15-foot free throw. In case you're not familiar with basketball, let us remind you that a free throw shot is taken right in front of one's goal, always from a distance of exactly 15 feet, with no one between the shooter and the basket. What could be easier? Ask NBA Hall of Famer Shaquille

O'Neal – who shot just under 53% from the free-throw line in his career. Or ask Andre Drummond, who makes Shaq look pretty good by comparison. In January of 2016, Drummond missed an NBA record 23 of 36 free throws in one game. The fact is, though, that anyone can be a good free-throw shooter. A pretty simple training program can turn most 55% shooters into 75% shooters. And shooters who are already good can improve, too. In fact, there are people who are so good at shooting free throws that they practically never miss. In 1993, a 71-year-old foot doctor named Tom Amberry broke the world record for consecutively made free throws. In about 12 hours, Amberry made 2,750 consecutive shots. No one had yet published a paper on the *quiet eye* technique, but Amberry was surely using it.

What are the keys to successful free throw shooting? Assuming that players already have solid shooting mechanics, there are just a couple of secrets to free-throw success. Before we cover the way to become a good free-throw shooter in painstaking detail, let us say that if you have no interest at all in sports, and if you just want us to cut right to the chase, you should simply know that sport psychologists can help people become much better free throw shooters by (a) teaching them what to do with their eyes and (b) making free throw practice more like what happens in a real basketball game.

The most important secret to almost any kind of skillful throwing or shooting is the **quiet eye**. It's a technique studied by sport psychologist Joan Vickers. If Harle and Vickers (2001) technical article were a little easier for non-scientists to decipher, we suspect that every basketball coach on the planet would be using the quiet eye. The last athlete your first author introduced to the quiet eye, Georgetown's Cynthia Petke, used it in a few months to improve her free throw shooting percentage from 55% to 77%. Harle and Vicker used the quiet eye on an elite women's basketball team to increase team free throw shooting from 54% to 77%. To be fair, most of this increase came in the second season of quiet eye training. But many individual players saw increases in their free throw shooting just weeks after learning the technique. So what, exactly, is the quiet eye?

The quiet eye is a way of training that helps athletes (a) rid themselves of all distractions and (b) focus their visual attention on the rim just before releasing a free throw. A result of this is that athletes become a lot more confident when shooting free throws. But quiet eye training isn't about confidence as much as it's about focus. In case you're a basketball player, here's a set of first-person instructions for how to use the quiet eye to become a good free throw shooter (paraphrased from Harle & Vickers, 2001).

Step 1. Start a ritual: Step up to the free throw line with your head up, looking at the basket. Bounce the ball three times and say to yourself "nothing but net." By the way, this is what Harle and Vickers said. Your first author's ritual was to bounce the ball twice and mentally say "I'm a 71-year- old man" (a 71-year-old man once held the world record for consecutive free throws). The key is to do the *same thing* every time – to clear your mind of all distractions.

Step 2. Stare at the rim: Hold the ball as if you're about to shoot and *stare* at the front, middle, or back of the *rim* for 1.5 seconds. Keep your gaze on the one chosen spot, and say to yourself "Sight. Focus." If you prefer, you may repeat your version of "nothing but net." It does *not* matter if you select the front or back of the rim, but you must pick a central spot and stick with it. **Do *not* choose anything else** as your focus spot. People who look at the backboard or the side of the rim, for example, increase their chances of *missing* the shot.

Step 3. Shoot: After 1.5 seconds of visual focus on the *rim* (while saying "Sight. Focus.") take a quick, fluid shot. It's OK that the ball will block your view of the rim as you shoot. Many players make an error during this step because they rush things. It's a natural response to want to be done with a free throw, especially for those who have had little previous success at the stripe (aka the free throw line). So relax and take your time. Stare at the rim for 1.5 seconds, and then take a quick shot.

That's the quiet eye technique. Players who master this visual focus technique show much better shooting improvements than players who do not. We know this because of Vickers's painstaking research using a computerized eye tracker that comes with a helmet and a video camera. Alternatively, shooters who can't afford an eye tracker can find out if they've gotten control of their eyes by relying on a training partner – who focuses on the shooters' eyes as they practice the quiet eye. A partner can often tell whether a shooter is about to make or miss a free-throw as the ball leaves the player's hands – by seeing if the shooter kept her eyes on the rim for 1.5 seconds before shooting. (By the way many experienced players don't need the full 1.5 seconds, but when learning the quiet eye, it's better to stare too long than to stare too briefly).

That's not quite the whole story, though. There's a basic principle in sport psychology that boosts good quiet eye training even further. Many players practice free throws by shooting 10, 20, even 100 free throws at a time. But one of the most important principles in psychology is a close cousin of Ericsson's **specificity principle**. We usually get good at things by practicing *exactly those things*. To build endurance you run long distances. To get stronger you gradually lift *heavier* and *heavier* weights. The same principle applies to free throws. Unless you're a total beginner, the best way to practice free throws is to practice them in sets of *two shots – not* in sets of ten or 20. Does this mean players have to stop what they are doing every six minutes in practice to shoot just two free throws? No. It's quite effective for players to shoot in spaced blocks of ten shots per sessions. But in doing so, players should step up to the free throw line and take two shots at a time, just as they would in a game. After two shots, players step out of the circle, pause, and step back in. In this way players take five sets of two shots at a time, making the situation as much like a real game as possible.

That's still not quite the whole story. There's one more important thing players can do. If practicing with a partner, players should have the partner stand under and to the right of the basket, just as referees do in a game. The mock referee should thus pass the player the ball for each free throw. This, too, simulates a realistic game situation. The most important thing a training partner can do, though, is to *watch the player's eyes carefully* while the player shoots. Human beings are very good at gaze assessment. Thus, an assistant might not know *exactly* where a player is looking for the 1.5 second window before releasing the ball, but the assistant will always be able to tell if the player focused on a single spot on the rim. If you don't believe us, stand under the basket, where the referee would be, have your friend stand at the stripe, and ask the friend to stare at the front of the rim. Then ask the friend to try to look away (even to the backboard or the side of the rim) *without* you detecting the eye movements. Unless you need glasses, you'll catch the subtle eye movements every time.

We should also add that quiet eye training is a very specific form of what Anders Ericsson called *deliberate practice*. It builds on the knowledge of experts, and it requires people to step out of their comfort zones and try something new. We hope you won't be surprised to learn that training with the quiet eye is much more efficient than simple *repetition*. Harle and Vickers's (2001) players trained with the quiet eye while shooting 100 practice free throws per week. A matched control team did not use the quiet eye at all, but they shot about 300 free throws per week! This worked pretty well – even without the quiet eye. But one third as many practice shots with the quiet eye (100 vs. 300 weekly shots) led to about twice the improvement in the quiet eye group (54% to 77% rather than 62% to 74%). A second control team that shot 100 free throws per week the usual way showed no improvement whatsoever.

Vickers and colleagues have shown that quiet eye training improves all kinds of skilled kicking, throwing, or shooting. The quiet eye works for darts, billiards, soccer, and volleyball, for example. But the quiet eye will not work for any sport unless players use it properly. Thus, without having a partner to check up on your visual focus during practice, players probably won't know if they're practicing the quiet eye technique effectively (eye movements are usually unconscious). Good free throw shooters naturally use some variation on the quiet eye, without realizing it. Quiet eye training, then, is learning to do self-consciously what free throw geniuses may do naturally. Finally, even if you're a couch potato who has no interest whatsoever in sports, you now know something about sports that most highly trained athletes do not. You might even consider sharing your new knowledge with a highly athletic friend. This way she will have you, the couch potato, to thank when she becomes a much better billiard player or free throw shooter.

Questions for Critical Thinking and Group Discussion for Module 35

Sport psychologists study every imaginable aspect of sports. Consider two unusual examples we have considered elsewhere in this text. You may recall from the essay on judgmental heuristics that the **representativeness heuristic** appears to influence referee's judgments of penalties in professional football and hockey. Frank and Gilovich (1988) found that NFL and NHL teams wearing black jerseys were penalized more often than teams wearing any other color jersey. You may also recall from the chapter on archival research methods that Gilovich and colleagues studied the emotional reactions of Olympians who won gold, silver, or bronze in the 1992 Olympics. Because of **counterfactual thinking**, bronze medalists seem to have been much happier than silver medalists. It should come as no surprise, then, that sport psychologists study some of the predictors of winning vs. losing an athletic competition in the first place. In this activity we'll explore just two of them.

1. The role of color in psychology is substantial. The American Express "Blue Card" is blue for a reason. People associate blue with peace, happiness, and relaxation. Along similar lines, "Red Bull" beat out options such as "Pink Bull" or "Blue Bull" as a name for an energy drink. People associate the color red with energy, speed, and perhaps danger. In keeping with this idea, Hill and Barton capitalized on a clever natural experiment that occurred in the 2004 Olympics. In boxing, judo, taekwondo, Greco-Roman wrestling, and free-style wrestling, Olympic organizers randomly assigned competitors to wear either red or blue outfits. Presumably they did so to help referees better see who did what in a match. Uniform color proved to be important. Across all four of these combat sports, competitors wearing one color of uniform won more fights than competitors wearing the other color. First,

the easy question: which color (red or blue) gave competitors an advantage? Second, would you expect these effects to be bigger when two competitors were very closely matched – or when one competitor was ranked much higher than the other? Third, what are some of the possible psychological mechanisms by which this may have happened? Try to come up with at least one *behavioral* mechanism and at least one *perceptual* mechanism. As a big clue, your respective answers should include the words "*priming*" and "*constructivism.*"

The health psychologist Jim Blascovich and his colleagues (see, for example, Blascovich, 2008) have shown that when people are put in a difficult situation (e.g., when people take a difficult exam or unexpectedly have to give a speech) some people conceptualize this tough situation as a "*challenge*" while others perceive exactly the same tough situation as a "*threat.*" Health psychologists can detect this challenge vs. threat mentality by looking at people's physiological reactions (e.g., total peripheral response) to the demanding situation. Moore and colleagues (2012) studied this "threat vs. challenge" response among novice golfers. In fact, they conducted an experiment in which they encouraged some of these novice golfers to consider a golfing task a *challenge*. They encouraged others to think of the same golfing task as a *threat* – a very difficult task that very few people were able to perform successfully. Notice that the task itself never changed. Moore and colleagues just manipulated whether people *perceived* it as a challenge vs. a threat. The threat manipulation worked. Following the experimental manipulation, participants showed the kind of physiological patterns known to be associated with threat vs. challenge. Moore et al. then made some careful, high tech measurements of how people performed on the golfing task. In fact, one of their many outcome measures was how well people engaged in the "*quiet eye*" – by looking exactly where they ought to be looking just before they began their putts. On all their indicators, from how golfers "pointed" or swung the putter to whether golfers had a "quiet eye," they found that the threat condition messed up athletic performance. Psychologist Jeff Stone – who studies stereotype threat in sports – would really like this study.

2. Jeff Stone and colleagues (1999) applied *stereotype threat* to athletic performance. Recall that stereotype threat happens when people believe that others expect them to perform poorly on a task because of their group membership. Whereas most research on stereotype threat examines academic stereotypes, Stone et al. (1999) examined athletic stereotypes. Their study also examined golfing (indoor putting), and they used a simple and elegant manipulation of stereotype threat. They told Black vs. White participants that their golfing task assessed "sports intelligence" or that it assessed "natural athletic ability." When people thought the task involved sports IQ, White participants outperformed Black participants. But when people thought the task involved natural athletic ability, Black participants outperformed White participants. Based on what you now know about stereotype threat and sport psychology, propose a novel experiment to assess the role of stereotype threat in athletic performance. Be sure to consider the OOPS! heuristic – to try to extend the external validity of Stone et al.'s findings. For example, exactly what *population* would you sample? How would you *operationalize* athletic performance?

Multiple Choice Questions for Module 35: Sport Psychology

1. According to your *text*, what is one of the biggest benefits of aerobic exercise?

   A) reduced risk of depression
   B) brain plasticity
   C) higher maximum heart rate

2. Which of the following qualifies as aerobic exercise?

   A) a one-hour hike in the mountains
   B) a 45-minute weight-lifting workout
   C) both A and B qualify as aerobic exercise

3. Sport psychologists often study drivers of top athletic performance. According to your text, sport psychologists also study:

   A) how to help people stick with a healthy exercise program
   B) age differences in people's interest in gambling
   C) stereotypes about athletes vs. non-athletes

4. Which is more interdisciplinary, sport psychology or social psychology?

   A) sport psychology
   B) social psychology
   C) because both of these fields are applied, they are both highly interdisciplinary

5. In his book *The Sports Gene*, Epstein argues that agents and coaches who wish to recruit great basketball players should pay more attention than they have in the past to what?

   A) vertical leaping ability
   B) 20-yard dash speed (while dribbling)
   C) wingspan

6. In what sport does the "home-field advantage" seem to be the largest?

   A) soccer
   B) American football
   C) baseball

7. The biggest reason for the home-field advantage in sports seems to be grounded in the fact that:

   A) players expect to win at home, and this become a self-fulfilling belief
   B) refs don't like to make home crowds angry, and they show biases favoring the home team
   C) compared with home teams, visiting teams usually bring fewer players to a game

8. The social psychological principle known as _____ can explain both "paying back" aggressive behavior and paying back helpful behavior in sports such as baseball and basketball.

   A) reciprocity
   B) benevolence
   C) conformity

9. A modern technique for improving the accuracy of one's shooting, throwing, or kicking (in many different sports) is the:

   A) muscle-memory technique
   B) goal-focus technique
   C) quiet eye technique

10. Becoming a great free-throw shooter does not merely require thousands of practice shots. It's important that shooters try a technique they have never tried before to improve their free-throw-shooting percentage. This general idea is consistent with K. Anders Ericsson's idea of:

    A) scaffolding
    B) optimal focus
    C) deliberate practice

Answer Key: 1B 2A 3A 4A 5C 6A 7B 8A 9C 10C

References

Blascovich, J. (2008). *Challenge and threat*. In A. J. Elliot (Ed.), *Handbook of approach and avoidance motivation* (pp. 431–445). Psychology Press.

Carron, A. V., Hausenblas, H. A., & Mack, D. (1996). Social influence and exercise: A meta-analysis. *Journal of Sport & Exercise Psychology, 18*, 1–16. doi:10.1123/jsep.18.1.1

Courneya, K.S. & Carron, A.V. (1992). The home advantage in sport competitions: A literature review. *Journal of Sport and Exercise Psychology, 14*, 28–39.

Epstein, D. (2013). *The sports gene: Inside the science of extraordinary athletic performance*. New York: Penguin Books.

Frank, M.C., & Gilovich, T. (1988). The dark side of self- and social perception: Black uniforms and aggression in professional sports. *Journal of Personality and Social. Psychology, 54*, 74–85.

Garicano, L., Palacios-Huerta, I., & Prendergast, C. (2005). Favoritism under social pressure. *The Review of Economics and Statistics, 87*(2), 208–216.

Gilovich, T., Vallone, R., & Tversky, A. (1985). The hot hand in basketball: On the misperception of random sequences. *Cognitive Psychology, 17*, 295–314. doi:10.1016/0010-0285(85)90010-6

Harle, S. K., & Vickers, J. N. (2001). Training quiet eye improves accuracy in the basketball free throw. *The Sports Psychologist, 15*, 289–305.

Jamieson, J. P. (2010). The home field advantage in athletics: A meta-analysis. *Journal of Applied Social Psychology, 40*(1819–1848). doi:10.1111/j.1559-1816.2010.00641.x

King, A. C., Friedman, R. M., Marcus, B. H., Castro, C., Napolitano, M., Ahn, D., & Baker, L. (2007). Ongoing physical activity advice by humans versus computers: The Community Health Advice by Telephone (CHAT) Trial. *Health Psychology, 26*, 718–727. doi:10.1037/0278-6133.26.6.718

Molteni, R., Zheng, J. Q., Ying, Z., Gómez-Pinilla, F., & Twiss, J. L. (2004). Voluntary exercise increases axonal regeneration from sensory neurons. *Proceedings of the National Academy of Sciences, 101*, 8473–8478. Epub 2004 May 24.

Moore, L. J., Vine, S. J., Wilson, M. R., & Freeman, P. (2012). The effect of challenge and threat states on performance: an examination of potential mechanisms. *Psychophysiology, 49*(10), 1417–1425. doi:10.1111/j.1469-8986.2012.01449.x

Murdock, G. P., (1949). *Social structure*. New York: The MacMillan Company.

Nevill, A. M., Balmer, N. J., & Williams, A. M. (2002). The influence of crowd noise and experience upon refereeing decisions in football. *Psychology of Sport and Exercise, 3*, 261–272.

Scanlan, T. K., Carpenter, P. J., Schmidt, G. W., Simons, J. P., & Keeler, B. (1993). An introduction to the Sport Commitment Model. *Journal of Sport and Exercise Psychology, 15*, 1–15.

Stone, J., Lynch, C. I., Sjomeling, M., & Darley, J. M. (1999). Stereotype threat effects on Black and White athletic performance. *Journal of Personality and Social Psychology, 77*(6), 1213–1227. doi:10.1037/0022-3514.77.6.1213

Tomporowski, P. D. (2003). Effects of acute bouts of exercise on cognition. *Acta Psychologica, 112*, 297–324.

Vickers, J. N. (2007). *Perception cognition, and vision training: The quiet eye in action*. Champaign, IL: Human Kinetics. [Quiet Eye™ is a trademark of Joan Vickers].

Willer, R., Sharkey, A., & Frey, S. (2012) Reciprocity on the hardwood: Passing patterns among professional basketball players. *PLoS ONE 7(12)*: e49807.

Module 36
Saving the Planet
Psychology and Climate Change

For much of the 200,000-year history of modern human beings on planet Earth, our population increased very gradually. Experts estimate that as recently as 7,000 years ago (when agriculture was taking root in Eurasia), there were only about five million human beings on the planet. This means it took about 4.5 billion years for humans to evolve and then make it to a global population smaller than the modern population of Barcelona (about 5.5 million people). As shown in Figure 36.1, for a very, very long time, the human population only increased bit by bit.

At the time of the birth of Jesus (0 A.D.), there were fewer people on the planet Earth than now live in Mexico or Brazil. Even in the year 1600, shortly before Cervantes published *Don Quijote*, there were fewer people on Earth than currently live in the European Union (a bit more than 500 million people). Then, not long after the Industrial Revolution, the Earth's population began to increase *dramatically*. By 1960, the beginning of the decade in which both of your authors were born, there were about 3 billion people on the planet. By 2019 there were more than 7.7 billion.

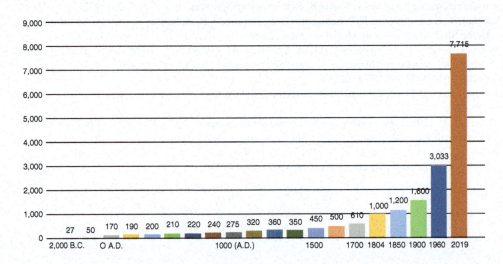

Figure 36.1 The Earth's population on selected dates over the past few thousand years.

Source: World Population Clock: www.worldometers.info/world-population/

For those who take delight in being the species that has taken over the entire planet, from the Arctic to the Antilles, this may seem like good news. But for our great grandchildren, this is almost certainly terrible news. The same fossil fuels that have long allowed us to get around quickly and keep warm in the winter are now straining the Earth's fragile ecosystem. Having had a great 250-year run with fossil fuels will be little consolation if the Earth is covered in water in 100 years – because of melted polar ice caps. Climate change due to human activity, especially greenhouse gas emissions, has the potential to make the earth *extremely* difficult to inhabit, even in the next century. In this module, we will discuss climate change through the lens of psychology. We'll discuss public opinion about climate change, and we'll discuss the psychological sources of that public opinion and its likely consequences for the planet.

If all people were well educated about the science of climate change, there would be widespread agreement that we must find a solution to this impending global disaster. Ask most Americans, however, and you'll hear that they do not expect climate change to become a serious threat during their lifetimes (Jones, 2014). Luckily, there are some nations where almost everyone recognizes the reality of climate change. In Japan, South Korea, and Costa Rica, roughly 90% of the population believes human activity has caused climate change (Pelham, 2009). Further, in countries in which more people believe human activity is responsible for climate change, people behave much more responsibly. In 2009, Costa Ricans were six times as likely as Uzbekistanis to say that climate change is caused by human activity. Costa Ricans also produced about 12 times as much per capita GDP as Uzbekistanis for every gallon of fossil fuel they burned (Pelham, 2009). GDP stands for gross domestic product, and it is a measure of all the goods and services produced in any given country. Put simply, then, Costa Ricans are producing more useful stuff for every unit of fuel they use.

In countries where more people believe in climate change, more people are getting things done in an Earth-friendly (lower greenhouse gas emissions) fashion. Of course, the causal arrow can run in either direction. People who burn fewer fossil fuels might justify their efforts by concluding that climate change is a very real problem. But it seems obvious that taking responsibility for climate change is one big step on the road to fighting it. It seems even more obvious that *denying* the reality of climate change, as many Americans do, is a huge stumbling block to fighting it. Why work hard to fight something that isn't real? This denial reached a new low in March of 2017 when Scott Pruitt, the newly appointed head of the U.S. Environmental Protection Agency (EPA) publicly affirmed his own skeptical position on climate change (Davenport, 2017). About a year later, Pruitt went so far as to suggest that warming temperatures might be good for the planet (Stone, 2018). In July of 2018, Pruitt resigned as head of the EPA. When Andrew Wheeler took Pruitt's place, environmental groups were quick to note that Wheeler held some equally troubling attitudes about pollution and greenhouse gas emissions. According to Keith Gaby (2018) of the Environmental Defense Fund, Wheeler spent much of his pre-EPA career lobbying for coal companies that were frequently fined for breaking pollution laws. Environmentalists believe that the fox is guarding the henhouse – except that it's not a mere henhouse, it's our planet.

"Is it getting hotter down here?
Or is it just me?"

Figure 36.2

Denial, Optimism, and Belief in Climate Change

Why don't most Americans take climate change more seriously? At least one big reason is probably the optimistic bias, which is a close cousin of more familiar terms such as denial and defensiveness. As self-help gurus love to put it, "Denial ain't just a river in Egypt." Tell William that we're endangering future life on the planet, and instead of recycling, car-pooling, or eating less meat, he'll simply discredit the scientists whose data show in dozens of different ways that climate change is caused by human activity. This natural tendency to deny a scary future doesn't just apply to climate change. Most people firmly believe that they are invulnerable to a long list of bad things that frequently happen to other people. For example, Weinstein's (1980) original work on the **optimistic bias** found that most college students believe they are less likely than the average student to get divorced or have a drinking problem in the future. Conversely, most students think they are more likely than the average student to live to be at least 80 or write a successful introductory psychology textbook. OK, we added the part about the intro psych textbook, but we did so to make the point that middle aged professors can also be overly optimistic. Further, nationally representative polling data from 142 nations showed that most people across the world, especially young people, think that their future lives will be brighter than their current lives (Gallagher, Lopez, & Pressman, 2013).

The scary implications of the optimistic bias are worsened by several other unfortunate aspects of the way we think. These include the facts that human beings tend to (a) think locally rather than globally, (b) respond to immediate rather than long-term rewards and dangers, and (c) deal with the concrete rather than the abstract (Center for Research on Environmental Decisions, 2009). As Seymour Epstein (1994) put it, we evolved to think **experientially** (i.e., intuitively, emotionally) more often than **rationally** (i.e., logically, analytically). Dry charts and abstract statistics will not be enough to convince us to take dramatic actions regarding a probabilistic event, no matter how dire the abstract consequences. Epstein suggests, for example, that if we want to change people's behavior, we will have to activate their emotional experiential systems, perhaps by using imagery and/or emotional arguments.

Heuristics and Belief in Climate Change

Many judgmental heuristics also get in the way of thinking clearly about the long-term risks of climate change. The concept of the Earth's average temperature increasing by "only a few degrees" is certainly not highly **representative** of a global disaster. In fact, it more strongly resembles most people's idea of a slightly hotter than usual summer picnic. Perhaps we should remind people, in a concrete way, that whether thousands of square miles of glaciers turn into trillions of gallons of very cold sea water is a matter of a degree or two of temperature change, and a few decades. Unfortunately, there's another judgmental heuristic that seems to contribute to skepticism about climate change, at least for people in cooler parts of the Earth. The **availability heuristic** also plays a big role in many people's skepticism about the reality of climate change, especially "global warming." In both an analysis of U.S. states and an analysis of 117 nations across the globe, Pelham (2018) found that in places where the *climate* is cool, fewer people believe in global warming. This was true in the U.S., for example, even after controlling statistically for median household income, education levels, and political party affiliation by state. Careful studies of how people respond to short-term variation in the local weather, and experiments in which people are primed to think about unseasonably hot or cold weather yield conceptually similar effects (Egan & Mullin, 2012; Joireman, Truelove, & Duell, 2010). Many people only seem to believe the planet Earth is getting warmer when their own *neighborhood* has been warm lately (or is chronically warm). These studies demonstrate the availability heuristic in action. That which is readily available in people's memory is biasing their judgments. So one reason the typical resident of Maine is less likely to believe in global warming than the typical resident of Maui is that Maine has a pretty low average temperature.

We once thought that a brief bit of unseasonably-cold weather only made people skeptical of global warming for a week or so, but Pelham's (2018) data suggest that both seasonal temperature trends and long-term average regional temperature also influence public opinion about climate change. Figure 36.3 illustrates monthly variation in public skepticism about global warming in the United States, Canada, and the United Kingdom. In all three nations, people engaged in Google searches expressing the greatest skepticism about global warming at the beginning of winter. Conversely people engaged in searches suggesting the least skepticism about global warming toward the end of summer. In short, rather than trusting scientists who study climate change, many people assess the realities of climate change the way they assess the weather in their own backyards. If he were still alive today,

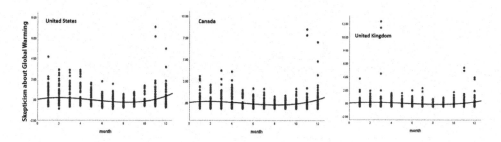

Figure 36.3 Monthly variation in skepticism about global warming based on variations in the national volume of Google searches for phrases such as "global warming hoax" in three English-speaking nations.

Adapted from Pelham (2018).

psychologist Jean Piaget would be quick to remind us that judging the planet based on how things are in your own back yard is a dramatic example of adult *egocentrism*.

Why Doesn't Your Friendly Neighborhood Meteorologist Believe in Climate Change?

Of course, there is one group of people who take climate change very seriously. Poll almost any climate scientist who has no financial ties to big business or politics, and he or she will tell you that long term climate change due to human activity is a certainty. But only a little more than half of the American public is persuaded by this chorus of scientific opinion. Most scientists who have no special training in climate modeling fall somewhere between public opinion and expert opinion. However, there is one group of scientifically-trained reporters who are collectively quite skeptical of climate change. According to a 2011 survey conducted by the George Mason University Center for Climate Change Communication, *only 19% of U.S. TV weather reporters reported that they believed in climate change!* That's right. That subset of weather experts known as meteorologists are collectively very skeptical of climate change (at least they were in 2011)! This is bad news for the planet. Many people consider their local weather forecasters a trustworthy source of information. But these forecasters did not appear to trust the climate change data.

Why didn't they? There are several reasons (Bagley, 2012). But the most interesting, by far, seems to be that meteorologists are very much like the professional baseball players or chess masters who have been asked to play a slightly different game. Remember the module on the insularity of genius? Meteorologists are specifically trained to model the extremely unpredictable world of *weather*, not climate. Meteorologists are in the business of reducing complete uncertainties to decent gambles on a *specific day*, and they find it intuitively implausible that anyone could use data vaguely resembling their own to predict anything with great precision years down the road. They need to be reminded that predicting climate change is more like predicting whether June will be warmer than May than predicting whether you should invite May and June to a picnic next Saturday. The science of predicting long-term climate change is quite different from the science of predicting next week's weather.

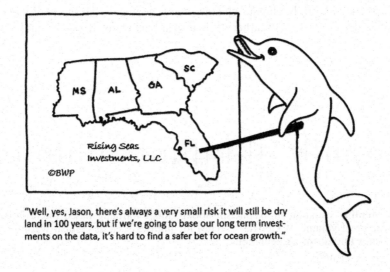

"Well, yes, Jason, there's always a very small risk it will still be dry land in 100 years, but if we're going to base our long term investments on the data, it's hard to find a safer bet for ocean growth."

Figure 36.4

Some Solutions: Default Effects

So human beings think in short-sighted ways that conspire to make us poor stewards of a planet we are choking with CO_2. Can psychologists offer any insights about what we can do to turn things around? We can. First, with a little help from informed local and national policy-makers, we can use something known as the status quo bias to promote green behaviors – especially when we combine our understanding of this bias with simple applications of learning theory (Thaler & Sunstein, 2008). The **status quo bias** is psychological inertia: it's the tendency to do what we and others have always done in the past – which is often what takes the least amount of effort in the present situation. In the U.S. we keep doing things like minting pennies (which cost much more to make and manage than they are worth) and electing U.S. Presidents using an outdated Electoral College system (which sometimes allows the person who comes in second in the popular vote to win the U.S. Presidency). After all, these are the default systems we have come to know. We do lots of wacky things because we always *have* done them. Sticking with a brand of bread, beer, or butter because you have long consumed it, preferring the familiar over the unfamiliar, and denying people the right to vote or marry whom they chose because your ancestors did so are all examples of the status quo bias. We human beings do a *lot* of weird and even harmful stuff simply because we have done it in the past. Of course, powerful emotions are often associated with things we have long done. The good feelings we have about traditions only magnify the status quo bias.

Back to Fixing Climate Change

But if we *know* about the status quo bias, we can use it to make good things happen. As suggested in a 2009 report by the Center for Research on Environmental Decisions (CRED), it's often possible to use **default effects** to promote and maintain green behavior. One example of this is to set the default on copy machines to produce double-sided copies. People can switch to single-sided copies if they like, but the very large majority of people will accept the double-sided default. The 2009 CRED report indicated that by switching to the double-sided default in all of their campus copiers and printers, Rutgers University saved more than a million sheets of paper the first year of the change. Many other schools and businesses have followed this example. Many auto makers are also setting new defaults to cut down on the use of fossil fuels. When your first author, Brett, purchased a Hyundai Accent in January of 2014, he was at first dismayed to see that it came without a spare tire.

Figure 36.5 This is Pederson Glacier, Alaska, in 1917 (left) and then in 2005 (right). You can see these before and after NASA images and many more in Dina Spector's (2016) *Business Insider* article on climate change. Each reveals a visceral, before and after view of what climate change is doing to the planet.

But carrying around all that weight in millions of cars across the country burns a lot of extra fossil fuel. Brett's first reaction to the change was that he felt vulnerable without a spare and would soon get one. It's been more than five years since he bought his car, and he hasn't gotten around to it. Besides, Hyundai makes up for this with free roadside assistance. Now, Brett wouldn't be caught dead driving a car in which he is constantly lugging around a heavy spare tire.

Removing even the smallest barriers to change and offering immediate rewards can also go a very long way to promoting green behavior. Many universities and businesses who noticed that people were not consistently recycling reduced a barrier to recycling by moving to "single-stream recycling" – so that people didn't have the perceived hassle of trying to figure out where to recycle what. If it all goes in one bin, there goes a very big barrier. Having recycling receptacles in every individual office and making recycling receptacles larger and more visible than the trash receptacles is another way to create a new status quo. As another example of removing barriers, many solar power companies in Maryland offer consumers a chance to switch to solar power without having to purchase the solar systems themselves. Some companies install solar panels on consumers' roofs for free, and some do so and charge them *less* for power than they had paid before going green. The growing opportunities for solar power are even brighter in sunny Arizona, which is the state your second author calls home. Once they finish this book, your authors both plan to add home solar-panel installation to their personal lists of green behaviors.

The U.S. government's **"Cash for Clunkers"** program that ended in 2009 also appears to have helped Americans remove about half a million gas guzzlers from U.S. roads. Moving from the carrot to the stick, however unpopular it has been, the Gas Guzzler tax that has existed in the U.S. since 1978 may have soured a few consumers on new cars that don't meet EPA guidelines for fuel economy. We strongly suspect, though, that programs that reward people for buying green cars will have a bigger long-term impact on consumer behavior than will taxes for misbehavior. Such programs do not always require congressional action. As the U.S. Environmental Protection Agency reported on their official website in 2015, Clemson and MIT offer either discounted or preferred parking to students who can document that they drive "SmartWay" vehicles. Several states (including Maryland and Arizona) also make their highway carpool lanes available to hybrid or electric cars as an incentive for drivers to go green. Many U. S. government agencies also provide partial reimbursements to employees who use public transportation rather than driving to work. As we hope you are beginning to see, if Americans are to follow the lead of many European and Latin American countries, who tend to be much greener than we are, we will have to combat climate change by taking many small actions – and sticking to them.

Speaking of sticking to things, there can be no doubt that one of the best ways to promote any positive (or negative) social behavior is to engineer a new set of *social norms* surrounding the behavior. People in your first author's suburban Maryland neighborhood take great pride in filling their recycling bins higher than their trash bins. In contrast, his siblings in rural Georgia seem to have never heard of recycling. Theories such as Hardin and Higgins's (1996) **shared reality theory** suggest that whenever change agents or policy-makers can get a large enough group of people to engage in any kind of behavior, powerful social norms to support the behavior will quickly follow. The same basic *need to belong* that propels infant monkeys to cling to their mothers can propel people to recycle or engage in prosocial behavior. Your first author can recall living in Texas back when it was as commonplace for people to throw trash on the highway. A very successful "Don't Mess with Texas" anti-littering campaign that began in the mid-1980s – and capitalized on people's pride in their social identities – seems to have forever changed norms about littering. Campaigns against smoking in public buildings have also had a great deal of success in cities all over the U.S.

Combating climate change will be no easy battle, and despite progress in a few areas, there is still plenty of cause for alarm. For example, the rules of self-regulation that help people save face can often make it harder to save the planet. This is true, at least in part, because most forms of self-regulation are geared toward either (a) protecting oneself from unpleasant information or (b) maintaining one's existing beliefs rather than (c) maximizing the accuracy of one's beliefs (see Swann, 1987; von Hippel & Trivers, 2011). For example, threatening people's self-concepts makes people more likely to stereotype others. It also makes people more likely to evaluate themselves and their fellow ingroup members favorably (Fein & Spencer, 1997; Jones et al., 2002). Unfortunately, self-regulation can also short-circuit green behavior. Getting people to take one pro-environmental action sometimes *reduces* people's felt need to engage in a *different* pro-environmental action. Purchasing energy-efficient light bulbs, for example, can make people feel it is more acceptable to leave lights on when the lights are not needed (Herring, 2006)! Further, those who are most likely to practice green behaviors such as recycling are also the most likely to take overseas vacations – replacing many small carbon footprints with one huge one (Barr & Prillwitz, 2011).

But there are still reasons for optimism. For example, it's possible to take advantage of what we know about human decision-making to craft pro-environmental arguments that are maximally effective. Consider *shared reality theory* again (Hardin & Higgins, 1996). Like a great deal of classic work in social influence, research on shared reality theory suggests that people are extremely sensitive to information about social consensus. Remember Sherif's work on the power of consensus and conformity? Learning that everyone (or virtually everyone) accepts a norm or judgment has a much more powerful effect on persuasion and compliance than learning that a decided majority accepts the same norm or judgment (see also Asch, 1955). There is something very powerful about consensus. It should thus come as no surprise that a very powerful way to convince people of the reality of climate change is to inform people that there is a great deal of scientific consensus on the reality of

"Sure, they look harmless enough. But they're an invasive species if ever there was one."

Figure 36.6

climate change (van der Linden, Leiserowitz, Feinberg, & Maibach, 2015). Likewise, capitalizing on the power of social consensus is a very good way to ameliorate a wide variety of other social problems, from stereotypes to public health risks (Sechrist & Stangor, 2001; van der Linden, Clarke, & Maibach, 2015). In short, getting the public to accept and act on the realities of climate change may require climate change educators and policy-makers to better understand the nature of human social cognition and motivation. If people are inherently egocentric and hyper-social creatures, we cannot easily change these natural neural and social realities. But we can certainly try to capitalize on them in our efforts to avert future global climatic disasters.

Questions for Critical Thinking and Group Discussion for Module 36

If this module on climate change is getting you down, we get it. There is good reason to be concerned. On the other hand, some experts on climate change argue that there is more reason to be optimistic about solving the problem of climate change than many people realize. For example, in her blog on reasons to be optimistic about climate change, social psychologist Shira Gabriel (2019) cites psychological research in five different areas that all suggest that things are not quite as bleak as some climate change experts have suggested. One of Gabriel's points is that public opinion may generally be headed in the right direction. Climate change deniers still exist, but as more and more scientific evidence accumulates about the reality of climate change, fewer people seem to be willing to deny climate change completely. You can see an example of this in Figure 36.4, which is based on the most recently available ten-year window of Google search data available to Pelham (2018). To be fair, not too many Americans were searching for things like "climate change hoax" and "against climate change" *prior* to 2007. But after three years of skeptical Google searches between 2007 and 2009, there was a sharp reduction in the number of people who conducted climate change denying searches.

Gabriel also argues that there are some good ways to get people to think about the long-term consequences of their behavior – which should make people more willing to do the right thing for the planet. These include rewarding people financially for green behavior

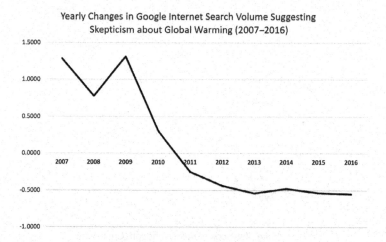

Figure 36.7 Average yearly U.S. Google search volume for three terms suggesting skepticism about the reality of global warming: "climate change myth," "climate change hoax," and "against climate change."

and providing people with information about things like their electricity consumption and their automobile emissions. As Gabriel also notes, once legislation forces people to behave in more responsible ways, their attitudes will often follow their greener behavior.

1.   Research discussed elsewhere in this text suggests that people become more open to hearing uncomfortable messages when they have recently been self-affirmed. Recall that *self-affirmation* refers to allowing people to spend time writing about things they deeply value (e.g., being deeply religious, being loved by family members). Consider people who say they deeply value family. Why might asking such people to write about why they deeply value *younger* family members have an especially big impact on their openness to adopting green behavior?

2a.   You may recall that research on *identity fusion* (a deep sense of emotional connectedness to the other members of one of your social groups) shows that people are more willing to make sacrifices for a group when they feel they are "identity fused" with the members of that group – whether it be Spaniards or fellow freedom fighters. How would you respond to each of the following measures of identity fusion? The top one assesses how fused you are with your future *grandkids* (or your actual ones if you have any). The middle one asks you to think about how fused you are with *environmentalists*. The bottom one asks you to think about how fused you are with our *entire planet*, including all the people and animals that live on it.

2b.   On which specific measure did you score highest? Which specific measure, if any, do you think would best predict people's willingness to make personal sacrifices to reduce climate change? Would the measure that works best vary depending on whether people grew up in a collectivistic culture (a "we" and "us" culture) or an individualistic culture (an "I" and "me" culture)?

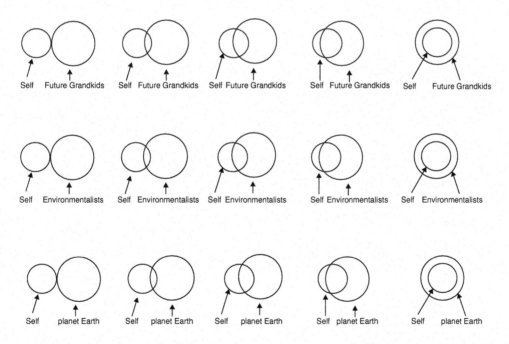

Figure 36.8

Multiple Choice Questions for Module 36: Psychology and Climate Change

1. What pattern best describes *human population growth* on planet Earth?

    A) it grew very slowly for thousands of years and exploded around the time of the industrial revolution
    B) it has been growing slowly but steadily for about 10,000 years, since the invention of agriculture
    C) it has been exploding since the invention of agriculture, about 3,000 years ago

2. What aspect of human activity causes climate change?

    A) large-scale greenhouse gas emissions (such as CO_2)
    B) the artificial heat production that happens when most fuels are burned
    C) the same kind of air pollution (tiny particles in the air) that causes smog and asthma

3. What implications does the **optimistic bias** have for public efforts to combat climate change?

    A) it means human beings will not give up hope until we have solved the problem of climate change
    B) it means many people will underestimate the negative future consequences of climate change
    C) it means happy people will be more willing to work to combat climate change than unhappy people

4. There is a great deal of scientific evidence suggesting that climate change is real and is already having real consequences for the planet (e.g., more severe hurricanes and tornadoes). But many people across the globe do not take climate change very seriously. Why?

    A) people evolved to think locally rather than globally
    B) people are more responsive to immediate than to long term threats
    C) people are more responsive to concrete than to abstract threats
    D) A-C are all correct

5. The availability heuristic seems to play a role in public skepticism about global warming (an aspect of climate change). For example, people who:

    A) know more about meteorology are much more likely to believe global warming is real
    B) live in cold climates are more skeptical of global warming than those who live in warm climates

    C) own and use a thermometer at home are more likely to believe in the reality of global warming

6. Do most weather forecasters believe in climate change?

    A) no, because they wrongly assume that it is hard to predict long-term climate patterns
    B) yes, because their training in weather forecasting involves a lot of statistical reasoning
    C) maybe, those with modern training usually believe in climate change; those without it usually do not

7. A few years ago, Rutgers University saved more than a million sheets of paper in the first year in which they enacted a new pro-environmental policy. This policy involved:

    A) making the default on all campus copy machines double-sided rather than single-sided printing
    B) using concrete thinking by telling people how many trees it takes to make 10,000 copies
    C) using concrete thinking by keeping a running tally of the total number of copies made daily at Rutgers

8. Selling new cars that have free roadside assistance service rather than having a spare tire to carry around is a way of promoting green behavior by means of a behavioral economic principle known as:

    A) cost-benefit analysis
    B) financial tradeoffs
    C) default effects

9. What was the goal of the **Cash for Clunkers** program that ended in the U.S. in 2009?

    A) to pay people to get them to take public transportation rather than driving fuel-inefficient cars
    B) to buy and destroy fuel-inefficient cars so that people find it easier to buy fuel-efficient cars
    C) to make free engine repairs to cars that do not pass state smog emissions tests

10. What theory suggests that a powerful way to change people's attitudes about climate change is to nudge people toward different norms – or to change laws that require large groups of people to change their daily behavior?

    A) consensual choice theory
    B) forewarning persuasion theory
    C) shared reality theory

Answer Key: 1A 2A 3B 4D 5B 6A 7A 8C 9B 10C

References

Asch, S. E. (1955). Opinions and social pressure. *Scientific American, 193*, 31–35.

Bagley, K. (2012). Why don't TV meteorologists believe in climate change? Retrieved from www. alternet.org/story/155571/why_don%27t_tv_meteorologists_believe_in_climate_change

Barr, S.,& Prillwitz, J., (2011). Green travelers? Exploring the spatial context of sustainable mobility styles. *Applied Geography. 32*, 798–809.

Center for Research on Environmental Decisions. (2009). *The psychology of climate change communication: A guide for scientists, journalists, educators, political aides, and the interested public.* New York, NY.

Davenport, C. (2017). E.P.A. head stacks agency with climate change skeptics. *The New York Times.* Retrieved March 17, 2017 from www.nytimes.com/2017/03/07/us/politics/scott-pruitt-environmental-protection-agency.html?_r=0

Egan, P. J., & Mullin, M. (2012). Turning personal experience into political attitudes: The effect of local weather on Americans' perceptions about global warming. *The Journal of Politics, 74*, 796–809.

Epstein, S. (1994). Integration of the cognitive and the psychodynamic unconscious. *American Psychologist, 49*, 709–724.

Fein, S., & Spencer, S. J. (1997). Prejudice as self-image maintenance: Affirming the self through derogating others. *Journal of Personality and Social Psychology, 73*, 31–44.

Gaby, K. (2018, July). This coal lobbyist is now running EPA. Retrieved July 31, 2019 from www. edf.org/blog

Gabriel, S. (2019, June 6). There may be reasons to be optimistic about the climate crisis. *Character and Context.* Retrieved july 18, 2020 from http://www.spsp.org/news-center/blog/gabriel-climate-optimism#gsc.tab=0

Gallagher, M. W., Lopez, S. J., & Pressman, S. D. (2013). Optimism is universal: Exploring the presence and benefits of optimism in a representative sample of the world. *Journal of Personality, 81*(5), 429–440.

Hardin, C. D., & Higgins, E. T. (1996). Shared reality: How social verification makes the subjective objective. In E. T. Higgins & R. M. Sorrentino (Eds.), *Handbook of motivation and cognition: The interpersonal context* (Vol. 3, pp. 28–84). New York, NY: Guilford Press.

Herring, H. (2006). Energy efficiency—a critical review. *Energy 31*, 10–20.

Joireman, J., Truelove, H. B., & Duell, B. (2010). Effect of outdoor temperature, heat primes and anchoring on belief in global warming. *Journal of Environmental Psychology, 30*, 358–367. doi:10.1016/J.Jenvp.2010.03.004

Jones, J. T., Pelham, B. W., Mirenberg, M. C., & Hetts, J. J. (2002). Name letter preferences are not merely mere exposure: Implicit egotism as self-regulation. *Journal of Experimental Social Psychology, 38*, 170–177.

Jones, J. M. (2014). In U.S., most do not see global warming as major threat. Retrieved from http://news.gallup.com/poll/167879/not-global-warming-serious-threat.aspx

Pelham, B. W. (2009). Views on global warming relate to energy efficiency. Retrieved from http://news.gallup.com/poll/117835/views-global-warming-relate-energy-efficiency.aspx

Pelham, B. W. (2018). Not in my back yard: Egocentrism and skepticism about climate change. *Environmental Science and Policy, 89*, 421–429.

Sechrist, G. B., & Stangor, C. (2001). Perceived consensus influences intergroup behavior and stereotype accessibility. *Journal of Personality and Social Psychology, 80*, 645–654.

Spector, D. (2016, November 9). Donald Trump doesn't believe in climate change — here are 16 irrefutable signs it's real. *Business Insider.* Retrieved July 18, 2020 from https://www.businessinsider.com/irrefutable-signs-climate-change-is-real-2016–11

Stone, M. (2018, February 7). Now Scott Pruitt thinks climate change could be good. *Earther.* Retrieved May 21, 2018 from https://earther.com

Swann, W. B., Jr. (1987). Identity negotiation: Where two roads meet. *Journal of Personality and Social Psychology, 53*, 1038–1051.

Thaler, R. H., & Sunstein, C. R. (2008). *Nudge: Improving decisions about health, wealth, and happiness.* New Haven, CT: Yale University Press.

van der Linden, S., Clarke, C., & Maibach, E. (2015). Highlighting consensus among medical scientists increases public support for vaccines. *BMC Public Health, 15*, 1207. doi:10.1186/s12889-015-2541-4

van der Linden, S., Leiserowitz, A., Feinberg, G., & Maibach, E. (2015). The scientific consensus on climate change as a gateway belief: Experimental evidence. *PLoS One.* doi:10.1371/journal.pone.0118489

von Hippel, W., & Trivers, R. (2011). The evolution and psychology of self-deception. *Behavioral and Brain Sciences, 34*(1), 1–56.

Weinstein, N. D. (1980). Unrealistic optimism about future life events. *Journal of Personality and Social Psychology, 39*, 806–820.

Glossary

2D: 4D ratio   the length of a person's s digit ("pointer finger") divided by the length of that person's fourth digit ("ringfinger"). This ratio is influenced by testosterone levels in the womb.

absolute pitch (aka *perfect pitch*)   the ability to hear a single musical note out of context and reliably identify it. This rare ability was once thought to be a genetic gift, but recent studies suggest that with **deliberate practice** almost anyone can develop it.

absolute threshold   the minimal amount or level of a stimulus that is required for people to be able to perceive it more than half the time under ideal conditions. So called "absolute" thresholds actually vary from person to person and with a person's motivational state. Nonetheless, see Table 9.1.

accessibility   the idea that things that have recently been experienced or recently retrieved from long-term memory either (a) can be retrieved more easily than usual or (b) will have an impact on judgment or behavior (a form of priming).

acetylcholine   a well-studied *neurotransmitter* ("chemical messenger") in the human brain. In people, acetylcholine plays a crucial role in the initiation of movement, and in sleep, attention, and learning.

ACID   an acronym that summarizes the four kinds of abstract thinking that define Piaget's fourth cognitive stage. This includes **abstraction, creativity, induction**, and **deduction**.

Acquired Immune Deficiency Syndrome (AIDS)   A sexually transmitted disease that seriously compromises people's immune systems. If left untreated, it leads to death.

action potential   the "all or nothing" electrical signal that is carried along an axon and causes the release of neurotransmitters (from one or more synaptic boutons) at the synaptic gap(s).

active genotype-environment effects   a situation in which the developing person selects environments (e.g., partners, activities) that facilitate the expression of phenotypes consistent with the person's genetic make-up. See the **PEA model**.

adaptation   the process by which organisms change over long periods in ways that promote reproductive success in specific environments. Adaptation is the way genes ends up sticking around inside one or more species.

adolescence   the psychological window of life when people are getting ready to take on adult roles. Views of adolescence vary radically across cultures.

adult romantic attachment style   one of three attachment styles in adults that closely parallel the three **infant attachment styles (secure, anxious, and avoidant)**. An adult with an anxious style, for example, frequently worries about being abandoned by his or her romantic partners.

aerobic exercise   exercise "with oxygen," meaning exercise in which you use oxygen as you go – to burn energy. This means elevating your heart rate for a meaningful period. Aerobic exercise promotes **brain plasticity**.

"age of strength and beauty"   a way of saying that emerging adults are usually stronger, healthier, more athletic, and more physically attractive than the rest of us.

"age of tragic risk taking"   a way of saying that relative to people of other ages, emerging adults take many risks – from abusing alcohol and drugs, to crashing vehicles, engaging in unsafe sex, and ignoring good advice sleep and nutrition.

aggression   According to Berkowitz, this is anything a person does to try to harm another living being. In animals it refers to actions that harm others, period (e.g., battling over a mate, predation).

agonists   chemicals that strengthen or promote the activity of a specific neurotransmitter. For example, dopamine agonists are often used to treat the movement disorder known as Parkinson's disease. Dopamine is involved in beginning motor movements.

agreeableness   the "Big Five" trait that refers to being slow to anger and quick to compliment or agree with others.

agriculture   farming, the invention of which radically altered human culture and destiny. See "**Guns, Germs, and Steel.**"

alarm   stage one of Selye's **General Adaptation Syndrome (GAS)** model. People who've just been exposed to a stressor become highly vigilant as their *sympathetic nervous system* kicks in. This enables the adaptive "fight or flight" response.

Alex could engage in categorization   a way of saying that Alex the parrot could perform sophisticated acts of reasoning – such as telling what material something was made of or whether two novel objects were made of the same or a different material.

all or none   a way of describing the fact that neurons either fire (send an electrical signal) or don't fire; they do *not* fire signals of various strengths (though they can and do fire many, few times, or not at all per second).

allele   a variation on a specific gene. For the genes in all cells except sex (sperm and eggs) cells people carry one allele from their dads and one allele from their moms.

altricial   a term describing organisms whose young are helpless and who thus depend on parental care to survive. Altricial species are also very slow to reach adulthood. Contrast with **precocial**.

altruism   **prosocial behavior** that is voluntary, costly to the doer, and performed without expecting any reward.

American Sign Language (ASL)   a language in which people use the hands, fingers, and body to communicate visually. Studies of deaf infants first exposed to ASL at different ages supports the idea that there is a sensitive period for learning a first language.

analogical reasoning   solving a problem by using what you know about the solution to a logically similar (analogous) problem.

anchoring and adjustment bias   the tendency to stick too close to an initial starting point, including an arbitrary starting point, when revising a judgment that you know to be incorrect.

andropause   the gradual and linear reduction in things like testosterone levels and sperm count that begins in middle age and is the rough male equivalent of **menopause** in women.

anger   a basic emotional reaction to threat or harm that occurs when the threatened person feels more powerful than the thing (often a person) that caused this emotion. In a fight or flight situation, anger promotes fight rather than flight.

angry aggression see **hostile aggression**.

animism the belief that natural phenomena or objects are alive – and thus have many of the same wishes and motives as people. Infants and toddlers have many animistic beliefs, as did ancient people. See also **intuition**.

anorexia nervosa an eating disorder in which a severely thin person nonetheless restricts his or her food intake, is chronically worried about gaining weight, has a highly distorted body image, and bases his or her feelings of worth heavily on being thin.

A-not-B error see **perseveration**.

anterograde amnesia a form of memory loss in which a person can recall things from his or her past (prior to the brain injury that caused the amnesia) but cannot form any new long-term memories. See **hippocampus**.

anti-psychotic drugs drugs that reduce the disordered thoughts and feelings that are characteristic of schizophrenia spectrum.

anxiety disorders a category of psychological disorders that includes Generalized Anxiety Disorder (GAD), specific phobias, panic disorder, and agoraphobia.

anxiolytic an anxiety-reducing drug. Examples are alprazolam (trade name *Xanax*) or diazepam (trade name *Valium*).

anxious-ambivalent an insecure infant attachment style characterized by chronic worry about abandonment, especially in scary or unfamiliar situations. It has a close analogue in adults.

anxious-avoidant an insecure attachment style in which, in response to separation or threat, an infant or toddler behaves in a dismissive or distant fashion with a primary caregiver.

anxious adult romantic attachment style an adult romantic attachment style that is characteristic of people who desperately wish to get close to others and really want to depend on others – but who think others are likely to let them down in times of crisis.

anxious infant attachment style an insecure infant attachment style characterized by chronic worry about abandonment, especially in scary or unfamiliar situations.

aphorism a popular saying about what many people think is true. It's a piece of "folk wisdom." "Birds of a feather flock together" is an example.

arachnophobia an extreme fear of spiders. If this is truly a phobia rather than a fear, it will lead to extreme distress and will sometimes interfere with a person's daily functioning.

arbitrariness in linguistics, the fact that the sounds of most words have no obvious connection to their meanings. According to linguists such as Hockett this is one of the unique and universal features of all human languages.

archival research research that uses public records (e.g., homicide records, marriage records) to test a research hypothesis.

Asch's conformity study a classic study in which people had to report judgments about the lengths of some lines after (sometimes) hearing a group of other judges report an obviously incorrect answer. About 75% of participants conformed to the erroneous group answers on at least some trials.

asexual reproduction reproduction that involves making exact copies of oneself. In some single-celled organisms, it happens by means of fission (splitting into exact copies of oneself). In complex animals, it happens in many other ways.

assimilation a perceptual principle that happens when an object is perceived to be more *similar* than it really is to something else. For example, if you know two women are sisters, you might perceive them as more physically similar than they really are.

assist   in basketball, passing the ball to a teammate so he or she can take a high percentage shot. Research on reciprocity and prosocial behavior shows that NBA players tend to give assists in a game to teammates who gave them assists earlier in the game.

assist   in basketball, passing the ball to an open teammate who immediately takes a shot and scores. The assist is awarded to the passer. A study of NBA players showed that they seem to engage in *reciprocity* by paying back recent assists.

association between income and happiness   in keeping with the **power law**, this association is not linear. Somewhat poor people are much happier than very poor people. But very rich people are only slightly happier than somewhat rich people.

attachment style   see **infant attachment style** or **adult romantic attachment style**.

attitudes   the thoughts and feelings we have about things that presumably influence how we behave toward those things.

attributions   causal judgments about a person's behavior (including one's own behavior).

augmenting   in attribution theory, this means making a *more* dispositional attribution than you otherwise would when situational factors *inhibit* or stand in the way of the performance of a behavior. See also **discounting**.

authority   one of four "ways of knowing." Authority refers to accepting the views and opinions of leaders, experts, or others high in status. Examples are believing something because it is in the U.S. Constitution or because your professor said it.

autokinetic effect   a visual illusion that makes a stationary dot of light in an otherwise dark room look like it is moving. Sherif capitalized on variation in this illusion to study conformity.

automatic processing   a term for very well-learned information-processing and/or behavioral patterning that is prototypically fast, unconscious, mandatory and efficient. See also **controlled processing**.

automatic social tuning   an unconscious tendency to adopt more favorable attitudes about the social group of a person with whom you are currently interacting. This finding supports *shared reality theory*.

autonomy vs. shame & doubt   the second stage in Erikson's psychosocial theory of development, which covers toddlerhood (ages 1–3). During this stage, toddlers try to develop a basic sense of control over their bodies and their lives. If they are stifled or overcontrolled, they will develop a sense of shame rather than self-sufficiency.

availability heuristic   a rule of thumb that involves judging the frequency or likelihood of an event based on how easily the event is called to mind. If examples are easy to generate, people conclude that the events in question happen frequently.

avoidant adult romantic attachment style   an adult romantic attachment style that is characteristic of people who report that they do not really need others and do not like to depend on others.

avoidant infant attachment style   an insecure **infant attachment style** characterized by psychological detachment from one's primary caregiver, even in unfamiliar situations. People can also have avoidant **adult romantic attachment styles**.

axon   the part of a neuron that transmits a message to another neuron. Virtually all neurons have just one axon.

backward conditioning   presenting a neutral stimulus *after* rather than *before* the presentation of an unconditional stimulus. Backward conditioning does *not* lead to classical conditioning – as explained by the **predictiveness hypothesis**.

Balcetis and Dunning (2007) studies studies that showed that wishes and desires can influence perception. When people hope to see a farm animal rather than a sea animal, they usually see an ambiguous seal/donkey figure as a donkey.

basic emotions the universal – or nearly universal – emotions that seem to exist in cultures all over the earth and are first expressed at a very young age. Paul Ekman says they include *happiness, sadness, fear, anger, disgust* and *surprise*.

basilar membrane the tiny portion of your inner ear that resembles a cinnamon roll and converts auditory information of different frequencies to perceived sounds of different pitches. The main spot in your ear where transduction happens.

behavioral neuroscience the school of thought in psychology that emphasizes the role of the nervous system (including the parts of your nervous system that exist outside your brain) in determining how we think, feel, and behave.

behavioral priming the finding that activating a concept without people being aware of it can influence people's behavior. For example, students who had recently been thinking about old people walked more slowly than usual to an elevator.

behavioral therapy an approach to psychotherapy that emphasizes and applies the principles of learning theory. **Exposure therapies** such as **systematic desensitization** and *flooding* are good examples.

behaviorism a school of thought in psychology that rejects the unobservable unconscious and emphasizes observable behaviors. Behaviorism also emphasizes the idea that our behavior follows the rules of *learning theory*. See also **Law of Effect**.

Ben Underwood a boy who became blind as a toddler and then taught himself to "see" using echolocation. His case highlights the flexibility of human development and the extreme specificity of genius.

benevolent sexism the idea that women are pure but fragile and thus must be protected and put on a pedestal by men. This may play a role in the medicalization of modern birth.

"Big Five" a set of five personality traits that seem to sum up a great deal of the hundreds of specific personality traits ever measured. The five traits appear to be **openness, conscientiousness, extraversion, agreeableness**, and **neuroticism**.

bilateral symmetry the fact that like many other animals, human beings have bodies whose left and right parts are mirror images of one another.

bilaterally symmetrical having two halves (hemispheres) that are mirror images of one another, a property of the vertebrate brain (people included).

binocular vision vision that integrates information from two eyes that point in the same general direction to produce depth perception.

bionic eyes artificial vision devices that may someday allow otherwise blind people to see – by performing transduction and sending visual signals directly to the brain.

biopsychosocial model the view that psychological disorders have three kinds of origins: (1) biological causes (e.g., genetic, neural), (2) psychological (e.g., perceived stress, biased thinking), and (3) social and environmental (e.g., cultural influences).

bipolar and related disorders a family of psychological disorders that involve extreme mood swings that vary cyclically over long periods.

bipolar 1 disorder a psychological disorder involving lengthy mood swings that impair daily functioning. The positive phases are known as mania and the negative phases are clinical depression.

black box the snarky term behaviorists used to refer to the human mind or brain. Their point was that because we can't observe what happens in the brain, we should focus on what we can observe, which is behavior. See also **behaviorism**.

blastocyst the ball of about 100 cells that a zygote becomes after roughly a week of cell division.

blind spot the small spot in the back of the retina where the optic nerve leaves the eye for the brain. There are no photoreceptors in this spot, which is why it is aptly named the blind spot.

BOPP – the basic object permanence paradigm a method for studying **object permanence**. It involves showing an infant a novel colorful object (e.g., a small green squeaky frog) and then placing the object under a small blanket that is well within reach of the infant. Infants who pull up the blanket and grab the toy presumably have a pretty good handle on object permanence.

brain plasticity the brain's ability to recover from damage or injuries or to adapt to radically new environments. Generally speaking, as brain injuries get larger, there is less of a chance of recovery of lost functions.

Broca's area the speech production area of the brain. In most people this area is in the left hemisphere, a bit forward of the left ear. See also **Wernicke's area**.

bulimia nervosa an eating disorder in which a person does *not* become dangerously thin but nonetheless has self-defining concerns about food along with three kinds of symptoms: (1) binge eating, (2) compensatory purging, and (3) basing one's feelings of worth on weight and body shape. These symptoms must also happen at least once per week for three months or longer.

bystander effect the finding that people are less likely to help needy or distressed others, and slower to help them, when *other people* are present. See also **diffusion of responsibility** and **evaluation apprehension**.

bystander intervention helping a stranger during an emergency.

Cannon-Bard theory of emotions the theory that our body's physiological and psychological reactions to emotion-inducing stimuli occur simultaneously and independently. Compare this with the **James-Lange theory**.

cardinal traits central, self-defining personality traits that shape most everything we do. Contrast with **secondary traits**.

"Cash for Clunkers" a U.S. government program that ended in 2009. By lowering barriers to getting a new car, it appears to have helped Americans remove about half a million gas guzzlers from U.S. roads.

cell body the central part of a *neuron* that contains the nucleus and performs calculations that determine whether the neuron will fire (and thus send a message to other neurons to which it is connected).

Cerebellum the "little brain" that sits at the lower rear portion of the brain. The cerebellum is involved in ballistic movements and in at least some aspects of language, emotions, and memory.

cerebral cortex the bumpy outer layer of the forebrain that's divided into four lobes (e.g., the frontal lobe). The cerebral cortex is everything in the forebrain but the deep (subcortical) structures. It plays a role in almost everything you perceive, think, feel, and do.

cesarean section a birth procedure in which doctors cut through the mother's abdomen and uterus to extract a baby surgically. CDC data show that almost one in three modern U.S. births is a birth by cesarean section.

chameleon effect   the finding that when a person subtly mimics our own nonverbal behavior – in ways that we do not consciously recognize – we come to like this "chameleon" more than we otherwise would.

change blindness   the finding that – after a very brief interruption – it's often possible to change an important aspect of a person's immediate environment without the person detecting the change.

characterization   the automatic attributional tendency to make dispositional (attitudinal or personality) judgments for many mundane behaviors.

cheater detection module   a presumably evolved, domain-specific rule for assessing cheating in what ought to be a fair social exchange.

chemical interventions (aka **psychotropic drugs**)   drugs used to reduce or eliminate the symptoms of a psychological disorder.

chimeric faces   "mixed" faces whose right and left halves look very different. Stimuli other than faces can also be chimeric, meaning that the right half of the image is different than the left. Such stimuli are very useful for studying *split-brain patients*.

chunking   a form of organizational encoding that helps people hold extra information in short term memory by putting individual bits of information into groups. For example, you might chunk 1 4 7 3 1 5 7 7 6 2 into "147," "315," and "7762."

Cinderella effect   the distressing but well documented tendency for stepparents to neglect, abuse, and even kill stepchildren at a much higher rate than biological parents of children do.

CIPA   See **congenital insensitivity to pain with anhidrosis**.

cities   densely populated areas, which only became possible in the wake of **agriculture**. See "**Guns, Germs, and Steel**."

Clark and Hatfield (1989; 2003) studies   two field studies that suggest that men are more sexually promiscuous than women. Average-looking strangers on the Florida State University campus made a proposition to strangers – which ended with "Would you go to bed with me tonight?" None of the women but 70% of the men so approached verbally accepted the offer.

classical conditioning   a form of learning that occurs when an organism forms an association between a previously neutral event and a naturally meaningful event that reliably follows the originally neutral event. In Pavlov's experiments, dogs came to know that when a buzzer rang, meat powder usually followed. They eventually began to drool to the sound of the buzzer.

Clifton Strengths Finder^{TM}   an aptitude tool developed by the Gallup Corporation that is built on the assumption that people have a wide range of specific workplace-relevant skills. These 34 workplace strengths are as diverse as adaptability, empathy, analytical skills, and "harmony" (being a peacemaker).

clinical depression (aka, **major depressive disorder**)   a psychological disorder characterized by a period of two or more weeks of symptoms such as negative mood, lost interest in normal activities, sleep and appetite disturbances, fatigue, and dulled thinking.

clinical psychologist   a psychologist who is trained in the diagnosis and treatment of clinical disorders. Clinical psychologists are one kind of **psychotherapist**.

closure   the **Gestalt** principle that states that we often interpret partial, imperfect, or corrupted versions of a complete object as the complete ("closed") thing. It is a perceptual form of "filling in the blanks."

cochlear implants artificial hearing devices that convert auditory information into signals that are sent to the brain. Unlike hearing aids, cochlear implants actually perform **transduction**.

cocktail party effect when people are asked to ignore the message played to one ear in a **dichotic listening task**, they seem to be able to shut one message out. But if a person's own first name is presented in the ear they're trying to ignore, this will almost always grab the person's attention.

codominance in contrast to dominant-recessive inheritance, a form of inheritance in which each of two differing alleles is expressed completely in organisms heterozygous for a specific trait (e.g., a homozygous red mom and a homozygous white dad might produce offspring with white and red patches).

cognitive behavioral therapy (CBT) an approach to psychotherapy that combines an application of the basic learning principles of purely behavioral therapies with the cognitive and emotional benefits of purely cognitive therapies.

cognitive dissonance theory the theory that people dislike it when there is disharmony in their attitudes. This may happen, for example, when people's recent behavior is inconsistent with their prior attitudes. This creates cognitive dissonance, which people try to reduce.

cognitive dissonance the discomfort people feel when there is a mismatch between their attitudes and behavior – or between their attitudes and the attitudes or behavior of meaningful others.

cognitive psychology a modern school of psychological thought that examines human attention, consciousness, perception, memory, reasoning, and judgment.

cognitive therapy an approach to psychotherapy in which patients are taught to identify, challenge, and replace maladaptive beliefs with more adaptive beliefs.

cognitive unconscious the idea that a great deal of human thought, feeling, and behavior becomes automatic (e.g., because it is so well-learned) and thus operates outside of awareness.

Cohen, Tyrell, and Smith (1991) cold study a rigorous study that showed that being stressed out increases people's chance of catching a cold. The researchers quarantined people, measured their recent stress levels, and exposed people to live cold viruses. A few days later, more stressed out people caught the colds at higher rates than less stressed out people.

collectivism a cultural orientation that emphasizes group wishes and social identities over individual wishes and personal identities. **Collectivistic** cultures are thus "we" cultures rather than "me" cultures. See also **individualism**.

Comorbidity the co-occurrence of clinical disorders (e.g., having both clinical depression and PTSD).

communication a process in which one organism transmits information to another. Many organisms engage in communication, but few – if any – other than people use abstract language. A frog's mating call is communication. A poem is **language**.

communicators one of the six key features of the human brain emphasized in this text (brains are communicators). This flows logically from the fact that brains are *compartmentalized* and are *computers*. Via axons and dendrites your brain constantly transmits information (e.g., including incoming sensory information, neuron to neuron communication).

compartmentalized one of the six key features of the human brain emphasized in this text. The brain is highly organized into regions and structures that do very different things. Parts of the brain responsible for vision, for example, are physically separate from the parts responsible for hearing.

complex   one of the six key features of the human brain emphasized in this text. Our brains are more complicated than that of any other known creature. This is grounded in the tremendous number of neurons in the brain (approaching 100 billion), the compartmentalization of the brain, and the trillions of synapses (nerve connections) in the brain.

computers   one of the six key features of the human brain emphasized in this text (brains are computers). The job of the brain is to calculate and integrate information (e.g., information coming in from different sensory systems) to keep us functioning.

"concept creep"   Nick Haslam's phrase for a recent tendency to expand definitions of harmful behaviors so that the criteria for labeling something a social problem, or an official psychological disorder, becomes wider. This is both good and bad.

concrete operational stage   Piaget's third stage of cognitive development, which covers ages 6–11 or so. Kids in this stage can engage in pretty complex reasoning – but only if you give them physical objects or models to manipulate. Kids at this stage should have mastered both **conservation** and **seriation**, for example.

conditional response (CR)   in classical conditioning, a learned response to a positive or negative stimulus that reliably occurs before the delivery of an event that an organism finds inherently desirable or undesirable. Drooling in reaction to a buzzer (when it has predicted the delivery meat powder) is an example.

conditional stimulus (CS)   in classical conditioning, a stimulus that was originally neutral, but which has been repeatedly paired with a stimulus that an organism naturally finds desirable or undesirable. Classical conditioning has happened with the organism begins to treat the conditional stimulus (e.g., a buzzer) as if it were the unconditional stimulus (e.g., meat powder).

cones   the photoreceptors that specialize in high-contrast, detailed, color vision. These are heavily concentrated in the pin-head sized portion of the **retina** known as the fovea. Contrast with **rods**.

conformity   changing one's beliefs or behavior to be consistent with the beliefs or behavior of others – even in the absence of any request to do so. Sherif documented this in his studies of the **autokinetic effect**.

confound   a third variable or "nuisance variable" that naturally co-occurs with a presumed cause – and thus may be the real reason for any changes in an outcome of interest.

confounded   the adjective form of confound. If a confound is at work in a study, a presumed cause is said to be confounded with the nuisance variable (aka the *confound*). In kids aged 5 to 15, vocabulary size is confounded with biological age.

congenital insensitivity to pain with anhidrosis   a chronic debilitating inability to feel any physical pain. Case studies of people with this rare disease reveal the importance and survival value of our sense of pain.

conjunction fallacy   mistakenly reporting that A *and* B can be more likely than A all by itself. People often fall prey to this logical mistake because they base probability judgments on **representativeness**. Remember Linda, the feminist?

connectedness   see **need for connectedness**.

conscientiousness   the "**Big Five**" trait that refers to a tendency to be punctual, tidy, organized, and disciplined.

conscious   one of the six key features of the human brain emphasized in this text. Because our brains are complex, and perhaps because we are such social creatures, we can become keenly aware of ourselves and our own thoughts.

consciousness   our subjective personal experience of the world, including both everything outside us and all of our own thoughts and feelings. Consciousness is closely associated with awareness.

conservation   the awareness that objects often change their appearance without changing their essential nature. This begins to emerge at the very end the preoperational period and should be solidified early in the concrete operational period.

conservative   one of the six key features of the human brain emphasized in this text. This is based on the evolutionary idea of conservation; evolution builds on existing structures and rarely begins from scratch. From neurons to hemispheres, our brains are much like those of other organisms.

constructivism   the idea that a great deal of what people perceive and remember is determined by their preexisting theories and expectations.

contact hypothesis   the well-supported hypothesis that a powerful way to reduce stereotyping, prejudice, and discrimination is to foster equal status contact among the members of groups who have historically disliked or misunderstood one another.

contrast   a basic perceptual principle that happens when an object is judged to be (a) smaller or less intense than usual when compared with something bigger or more intense or (b) bigger or more intense than usual when compared with something smaller or less intense. Contrast this with **assimilation**.

controlled processing   prototypically, this refers to thinking processes that are slow, conscious, optional, and cognitively taxing.

convenience sample   a research sample that proved to be handy to a researcher but which may not be at all representative of the population about which the researcer would like to draw conclusions.

cooperation   working together in a dyad or larger group to achieve a desirable group goal.

correction   the (usually) controlled attributional process of engaging in **discounting** or **augmenting**.

correspondence bias   (aka the **fundamental attribution error**): the tendency to make somewhat dispositional judgment for behavior even when the behavior is more logically explained by one or more powerful situational forces.

cortisol   the so-called "stress hormone," whose levels increases in response to actual or anticipated stressors.

cost-benefit perspective   a perspective on aggression that emphasizes that organisms usually behave aggressively only when the perceived benefits of so doing outweigh the perceived costs.

counterfactual thinking   a term for "what if" thinking – which may strongly influence people's reactions to events that could have worked out differently. Being glad you were not killed in an accident usually leads to a happier mood than thinking of how the accident could easily have been avoided.

counter-attitudinal   at odds with (in disagreement with) someone's original attitudes about something. Researchers often get people to write *counter-attitudinal* essays to create **cognitive dissonance**, which people often reduce by changing their attitudes.

covariation   the first of John Stuart Mill's three requirements for establishing that one variable causes another variable. Covariation means correlation. This requirement has been met when the level of one variable varies systematically with the level of the other variable. See also **temporal sequence** and **eliminating confounds**.

cow's milk   milk harvested from lactating cows. This is an example of how culture powerfully shapes what people find desirable as a food source because there are lots of drawbacks to drinking milk.

critical periods   specific periods that are the *only* opportunities for something to develop normally. **Imprinting** in geese happens in a brief critical period. Human sweat glands also develop in a critical period. See also **sensitive period**.

cross-sectional study   a kind of passive observational ("correlational") study in which everything was measured just once. A one-shot survey or interview is a good example.

crystallized intelligence   a form of intelligence that is built up by means of practice and learning. It is a close cousin of *expertise*, and thus it relies heavily on long-term memory. If you have a PhD, you have crystallized intelligence in at least one area.

cultural evolution   the study of how cultures change over time – how they come to be the way they are, especially as this process is influenced by local variables such as climate, geography, and **pathogen load** (disease load).

culture of honor   a culture, in which people are taught that their honor, like their possessions, must be constantly defended against threats or insults. This often leads to violence.

culture   a group's shared beliefs, feelings, customs, and social norms, including the way people communicate, sustain themselves, care for children, work, worship, and exist in groups. This also refers to the *region* where shared beliefs exist and the *people* who adopt them.

cuneiform   an ancient Sumerian writing system invented to keep track of economic transactions. This led to modern written language and mathematics.

Cyberball   a simple virtual ball-passing game. This game is often used to study the consequences of being ostracized or socially excluded by others.

cyborg   a person who is part machine. Technically, people with cochlear implants are cyborgs, as is artist Neil Harbisson, who uses a high-tech device to "hear" colors.

decussation   a quirky aspect of the wiring of the vertebrate brain that means that the right half of the brain is connected to the left half of the body while the left half of the brain is connected to the right half of the body.

deduction   reasoning from a general rule to generate a specific prediction or answer a specific question. All mammals nurse their young. Moles are mammals. Thus, moles nurse their young.

default effects   using the **status quo bias** to promote and maintain green (or prosocial) behavior. Examples of this include making defaults on all copy machines two-sided and not putting spare tires in new cars (to reduce fuel use).

defector argument   an argument against altruism. It states that if a gene *did* promote unselfish behavior, many other members of the animal's group would take advantage of the do-gooders – and the unselfish gene would die out.

defense mechanism   a psychological route for protecting oneself from uncomfortable or disturbing thoughts. Freud argued that there are dozens of such self-protective mechanisms, including denial, repression and reaction formation.

deindividuation   a state in which people don't feel personally identifiable, in which they lose their sense of self, and in which they thus behave more aggressively than usual.

delay classical conditioning a form of classical conditioning in which a novel training stimulus (such as a buzzer) is presented and then an unconditional stimulus is presented or applied a second or two later.

delay of gratification the ability to refrain from doing something you'd like to do right now with the promise that you'll get a bigger reward at some point in the future. See "**marshmallow test**."

deliberate practice a highly focused, and challenging, form of practice in which people constantly pushes themselves to pick up new skills and look for better ways to do things. Deliberate practice seems to be necessary if one is to become a genius.

dendrite the part of a neuron that transmits incoming information to the cell body.

dependent variable the variable that is measured in a true experiment after participants receive an experimental manipulation. In an experiment on pain relievers, levels of self-reported pain would be the dependent variable. See also **independent variable**.

depressive disorders a category of psychological disorders that share symptoms such as long periods of "sad, empty, or irritable mood" and the physical or cognitive deficits that often come with this.

deviation IQ score a way of calculating the IQ of a person of any age by seeing how the person's total score falls above or below the mean in what is known to be a normal distribution of scores. A person who scores exactly one standard deviation above the mean would receive an IQ score of 115, for example.

dichotic listening task an attentional task in which participants use headphones to listen to a *different* message in each ear. Participant are told to ignore the message in one ear, and they are often asked to *shadow* (repeat) what is being said in the attended ear. This sets the stage for the **cocktail party effect**.

diffusion of responsibility the fact that if you and many people are observing an emergency, the others share a lot of the blame for any failure to act. This is one of the reasons for the **bystander effect**.

discounting in attribution theory, this means making a *less* dispositional attribution than you otherwise would when situational factors *promote* the performance of a behavior. See also **augmenting**.

discrimination learning the conditioning process that allows an organism to engage in **discrimination**.

discrimination (1) learning *not* to respond to a stimulus that resembles a CS when the UCS continues to follow the CS but does *not* follow the stimulus that resembles the CS (learning not to engage in **generalization**). See also **discrimination learning**.

discrimination (2) negative behavior directed at the members of a specific social group.

displacement in linguistics, the fact that language allows us to describe things that are not in front of us right now. This allows us to communicate about the distant past or future. Hockett argued that this is a universal feature of human languages.

dispositional an attribution (explanation) for a person's behavior that emphasizes the stable and internal properties of the actor rather than contextual forces. "Jobi slipped because he is clumsy."

disruptive, impulse-control, and conduct disorders a category of psychological disorders that includes kleptomania (uncontrollable stealing), pyromania (fire setting), and conduct disorder. These almost always emerge in childhood.

dissociations observed disconnections between things that one might logically expect to be related. The many dissociations he observed led Fodor to his conclusions about **mental modularity** – which is much like the **insularity** of human genius.

dissociative disorders psychological disorders in which normally integrated memories and identities are split. An example is dissociative identity disorder (once called "multiple personality disorder").

Dissociative Identity Disorder (DID) a psychological disorder characterized by the possession of two or more very different identities, each of which is often wholly unaware of the other identities. To qualify as DID, this must cause serious impairments.

dizygotic twins "fraternal" twins; those who, like siblings from different births, share only half of their genes. See **monozygotic twins** and **twin studies**.

dizygotic fraternal or non-identical twins. Like other siblings, dizygotic twins share about half of their genes.

dominant eye the eye that is prioritized in visual perception. This means that the way you view the world is based mainly on the signal your brain gets from your dominant rather than your non-dominant eye. (See Figure 6.4.)

dominant in genetics, the term used to describe an allele for a specific gene that is fully expressed *phenotypically* when it appears along with a *recessive* allele for the same gene. In people, brown eyes are mostly dominant over blue eyes.

dominant-recessive inheritance a kind of genetic inheritance in which there is a dominant allele and a recessive allele for a given trait. When an organism has one dominant and one recessive allele, only the dominant allele is expressed phenotypically.

dopamine a neurotransmitter involved in motor movement, motivation, and the experience of pleasure or reward.

double-blind procedure a form of control often used in lab experiments. This means that neither the participants nor the experimenters know exactly what experimental treatment participants received. This prevents *experimenter bias*.

doula a birth coach who works with mothers-to-be to facilitate natural births.

Dreaming having a story-like experience, while one is sleeping, that usually feels real to the sleeping person.

drive excitement or arousal due to the strength of an unfulfilled need. A hungry rat experiences higher levels of drive than a rat that just ate.

DSM (the Diagnostic and Statistical Manual of Mental Disorders): A lengthy official book that lays out all the details for diagnosing all known psychological disorders. At the time of this writing, the most recent DSM was the DSM-5, which came out in 2013.

Dutton and Aron bridges study a study that supported two-factor theories of emotions. It did so by showing that men who had just crossed a scary bridge later expressed more interest in an attractive woman than did men who had just crossed a safe bridge.

early adulthood the ages of 26–39, which is the first window of life when people's brains are fully mature – and when people often begin settling into careers and serious relationships – and deciding where to live.

Ebbinghaus illusion a visual illusion in which a circle that is surrounded by much larger circles looks smaller than an identical circle that is surrounded by much smaller circles. This supports the perceptual principle of **contrast**.

eclectic therapists psychotherapists who borrow ideas and techniques from multiple schools of psychotherapeutic thought – depending on the perceived needs and abilities of the individual patient and the specific disorder with which the patient is dealing.

economic inequality a situation in which some members of a culture or group possess much more wealth than others do. This is a powerful predictor of rates of violence. Violence is more common in places where the rich have much more than the poor.

ectoderm the part of a developing embryo that will become the nervous system. In mammals the ectoderm will also become the skin.

Ego the part of the human psyche that, according to Freud, had to balance and resolve conflicts between the childish, selfish, violent id and the overly strict, guilt-ridden superego.

ego integrity vs. despair the eighth and final stage in Erikson's psychosocial theory of development, which covers late adulthood (age 60+). Erikson proposed that as we realize our lives are coming to an end, we ask ourselves whether our lives have been good and meaningful – or whether we have lived a life to be regretted.

ego the thoughtful "adult" portion of the psychoanalytic psyche (or personality). In psychoanalysis, the mostly-conscious ego tries to balance the needs of the selfish id and the overly restrictive superego.

egocentrism (adjective form **egocentric**) *self-centeredness*, the tendency to view the world from one's own personal vantage point – failing to realize that others may view things very differently. See the **three-mountains task**.

eliminating confounds the third of John Stuart's Mill's three requirements for establishing that one variable causes another variable. This means showing that no other variables that happen to be correlated with a presumed cause are the real reason why there is covariation (correlation) between a presumed cause and a presumed consequence. One of the best ways to eliminate all possible confounds is to conduct a **true experiment**. See also **covariation** and **temporal sequence**.

elimination disorders a group of psychological disorders that often begin in childhood. It includes enuresis (urinating in one's clothing) and encopresis (defecating in one's clothing).

embryo a developing offspring that is between about 2–8 weeks post-conception. See also **embryonic period**.

embryonic period the brief but important period of prenatal development covering weeks 3–4 post-conception. This is when the **endoderm**, **ectoderm**, and **mesoderm** begin to develop, and when **organogenesis** begins.

emerging adulthood a term coined by Jeffrey Arnett to characterize the extended period of adolescence (ages 18–25) that occurs today in most wealthy countries. Emerging adults are done with puberty, but they've not yet taken on fully adult roles.

emotions the affective states (feelings) we have in reaction to the good and bad events of everyday life. They are also the way we feel when we wish to approach or avoid something.

empathic concern feeling distress when we see others who are in distress. This can motivate us to help others even when it is very costly for us to do so – and even when the others are complete strangers.

empathy (more technically **empathic concern**) putting yourself in the emotional shoes of another person who is suffering. As predicted by the **empathy-altruism model**, this appears to promote true altruism.

empathy-altruism model a theory of helping that states that experiencing true **empathic concern** for another person (putting yourself in his or her emotional shoes) often promotes true altruism.

empiricism   the idea that the best way to figure out the nature of the world is to make careful, systematic observations.

emulative violence   the tendency to repeat aggressive actions after seeing others engage in them (aka "copycat violence") See **social learning**.

encoding   the stage in which information enters the memory system – and in which the person who will remember the information forms a mental record of it. Encoding means moving things from **short-term memory** to **long-term memory**. Encoding is the first of three basic stages of memory. See also **storage** and **retrieval**.

endoderm   the part of a developing embryo that will become the internal organs such as the lungs and the digestive tract.

endorphins   the body's natural painkillers. This is a category of neurotransmitters that both decrease pain and increase mood and feelings of wellness. Long bouts of exercise may cause the release of endorphins.

engram   the elusive location in the brain where a memory resides. The problem with engrams is that most specific memories don't have a single location. Instead, the engram is often distributed all throughout the brain.

episodic memory   memory for a past event or experience (e.g., the memory of eating a meal with a friend – or putting your keys on the kitchen table).

Eros   Freud's hypothesized "life-instinct" – which presumably drives people to avoid danger and death.

evaluation apprehension   the fear of embarrassing ourselves in front of other people. This is one of the reasons for the **bystander effect**.

evocative genotype-environment effects   a situation in which the developing person elicits ("evokes") responses from others in his or her world that facilitate the expression of phenotypes consistent with the child's genetic make-up. See the **PEA model**.

evolution   the process by which organisms have changed and diversified over the course of Earth's history. Evolution occurs when genes that promote reproductive success in a particular organism in a specific environment become more numerous than genes that provide no such advantage. See *adaptation* and *natural selection*.

evolutionary psychology   the interdisciplinary scientific study of how our thoughts, feelings, and behavior are influenced by evolutionary biological processes such as *adaptation* and natural selection.

excitation transfer theory   a popular and well-supported two factor theory of emotions. Research on this theory shows that if you artificially increase physiological arousal (e.g., by having people walk or jog on a treadmill) before they are exposed to something that creates anger, they will experience higher levels of anger than usual.

exhaustion   stage three of Selye's **General Adaptation Syndrome (GAS)** model. During exhaustion, you can no longer resist the stressor. Now you could easily die without some serious medical intervention.

exotic becomes erotic (EBE) theory   a theory of sexual attraction and sexual orientation. EBE theory states that during childhood people play with likeminded others. Girls who like rough and tumble play will thus hang out with boys, and they will feel that other girls are exotic. When puberty begins, the gender that was exotic during childhood presumably becomes erotic during adolescence and young adulthood.

experiential   Epstein's way of describing emotional or intuitive thinking. Contrast with **rational** thinking. Experiential thinking can lead to many myths and misunderstandings about climate change.

experiment   See true experiment.

experimenter bias   the unconscious tendency for experimenters (or others) to create or see what they expect to see.

expertise heuristic   a rule of thumb that means relying on a person's apparent level of status or knowledge as a short-cut to deciding whether to believe the person. The expertise heuristic says it is usually safe to trust an expert. It's a pretty good rule. Trust us. See also **authority**.

exposure therapy   a form of treatment for phobias and some anxiety disorders that involves presenting a patient with a fear-inducing stimulus or situation in ways that will lead to extinction of the fear response. See **systematic desensitization**.

external validity   a form of validity (accuracy, correctness) in research that refers to whether a finding is likely to hold up in the real world. This means holding up across different operationalizations of key variables, different occasions (different times), different populations, and different situations. See also **OOPS! heuristic**.

extinction   the reduction or disappearance of a classically conditioned response (a CR) after the CS is repeatedly presented *without* being followed by the UCS. See also **spontaneous recovery**.

extraversion   the "**Big Five**" trait that refers to an interest in talking to and connecting to others. Extraversion also includes enjoying the spotlight in social situations and being willing to take both physical and psychological risks.

extrinsic motivation   the desire to do something for reasons that are *not* connected to the activity itself (e.g., because you were paid to do something).

eye-bee-rose experiment   a classic experiment conducted on *split-brain patients. Split-brain patients* saw *chimeric stimuli* meaning that the left half of each stimulus was one thing (an eye, for example) whereas the right half was something different (a bee, for example). When asked to say what they saw, patients named the object that was processed in their verbal left hemispheres. But when asked to point to a (full) picture of what they had seen – using their left hands – patients usually pointed to the image that had been processed by their right nonverbal hemisphere. (Recall that the right hemisphere controls the left hand.)

face vs. vase   an ambiguous image in which either a central vase or two faces (one on the right and one on the left, each facing the other) can be perceived as the figure in a *Gestalt figure-ground* battle for attention.

face-in-the-crowd effect   the finding that people are quicker to recognize that a sea of otherwise similar faces contains an "oddball face" (a face expressing an emotion different than the emotion expressed in all the other faces) when the mismatching face expresses *anger* than when the mismatching face expresses non-threatening emotions such as happiness.

facial babyishness   a phrase used to describe adults who have "baby faces" (e.g., big eyes, small chins, and other cute features). Adults with baby faces are perceived as possessing childlike personality traits, such as naivety,

falsification   an approach to scientific discovery in which the researcher looks for evidence that could clearly disprove rather than confirm a theory or hypothesis of interest. Logical positivists like this idea.

false consensus effect   the tendency to believe that one's own attitudes, preferences, and behaviors are more common (held by more people) than is actually the case.

fast mapping   learning the meaning of a new word – and being able to use it properly yourself – after being exposed to the new word just once or twice. Toddlers do this very readily. Adults do not. This is a good example of **preparedness**.

fear a basic emotional reaction to threat or harm that occurs when the threatened person feels he or she is less powerful than the person or creature who caused harm or threat. In a fight or flight situation, fear promotes flight rather than fight.

feeding and eating disorders This broad group of disorders involves dangerous or dysfunctional problems with food – such as anorexia nervosa and bulimia nervosa (both of which are covered in this module).

"feeling in between" a key feature of **emerging adulthood**. This refers to the fact that in highly developed nations, a majority of people aged 18–25 say they no longer feel like kids and yet have not yet reached true adulthood.

feelings override thoughts the idea that when strong feelings (such as disgust) run counter to one's carefully reasoned thoughts, feelings will win out because they are grounded in powerful behavioral aversions (or desires) that have long been adaptive.

fertile crescents two highly unusual places on Earth (one in the modern Middle East, one in modern China) where a perfect storm of climate and easily domesticated plants (plus a few easily domesticated animals) allowed for the invention of **agriculture** about 11,000 years ago. See "**Guns, Germs, and Steel**."

fetus the developing offspring from about 9–38 weeks post-conception. It is during this lengthy fetal period of development that the former embryo becomes biologically male or female, gets fingernails, starts to move, and comes to look increasingly human.

fetuses kick for good reason a way of saying that when a fetus moves in the womb, it is building crucial neural circuits that promote both the limb development and motor wiring. If fetuses did not kick, they would not develop normal, working legs!

fight or flight a physiological response to threat that includes an increase in heart rate and a dramatic reduction in digestive activity. These two physiological changes ready an organism to either (a) attack or (b) escape from a source of danger.

figure In Gestalt psychology, this is the point of focus in a scene. It is "center stage," and it stands in contrast to the ground (the background or context).

figure-ground distinction The *Gestalt* idea that when viewing most scenes, we have to decide what is figural ("center stage") and what is background (context).

first-generation anti-psychotics the drugs first used more than 50 years ago to treat what is now called schizophrenia spectrum. They work pretty well but often have serious side effects. See **tardive dyskinesia**.

five key features of evolution (1) It's *slow*, occurring over thousands, millions, or billions of years. (2) It's *conservative*; adaptations that work well are rarely discarded. (3) It creates *baggage*; many useful adaptations come with drawbacks. (4) It implies *continuity*; people are a lot like other mammals. (5) It's *orderly*; genes program adaptive developmental patterns. Mammals aren't born with their adult teeth, for example.

fixed genes genes for which there is virtually no variation – for which only one *homozygous* version of an allele exists – in a particular species. Genes for walking with an upright gait are fixed in people.

fixed interval schedule a reinforcement schedule in which the organism is reinforced for making the first operant response after a specific amount of time has passed (with no variation around that time period). See **reinforcement schedules**.

fixed ratio schedule a reinforcement schedule in which the organism is reinforced for making the first operant response after a set (i.e., fixed, unvarying) number of previous operant responses. See **reinforcement schedules**.

fixed schedule   a reinforcement schedule in which a reinforcer *always* comes after a certain number of responses (which could be just one response or many) or after at least one response after a set amount of time. The key to being *fixed* is that the ratio rule or interval rule does not vary. Contrast with a **variable schedule.**

flashbulb memories   quickly formed, vivid, and long-lasting memories for dramatic, personally meaningful events. These memories are not necessarily more accurate than other memories, but they are both rapidly-formed and enduring.

fluid intelligence   the ability to think quickly on one's feet when faced with unfamiliar problems.

fMRI   see functional magnetic resonance imaging.

folic acid   Healthy levels of this vitamin (B9 or B12) are necessary for early prenatal development, especially spinal cord development.

forebrain   the newest and most complex of the three basic regions of the brain. Your forebrain consists of many subcortical (deep brain) structures as well as the wrinkly cerebral cortex that you probably picture when you think of a brain. See also **midbrain** and **hindbrain**.

forgetting curve   Ebbinghaus's discovery that after you're exposed to new information, forgetting happens very quickly at first, but then tapers off.

formal operational stage   Piaget's fourth and final stage of cognitive development, which begins in adolescence. Piaget felt that kids who have made it to this stage can reason in sophisticated and abstract ways, just as well as adults can. This includes making **transitive inferences** and passing what we summarized as the **ACID** test of abstract thinking.

fovea   the small spot in the back of the eyeball that is much more densely packed with photoreceptors than are any other parts of the retina.

free associations   a psychoanalytic technique that involves getting patients to report absolutely anything that pops to mind (no matter how inappropriate) in response to a therapist's prompts. Freud thought this might offer insights into the unconscious.

Freudian unconscious   the psychoanalytic idea that much of what we think, feel, and do is determined by invisible and largely inaccessible thoughts and desires. Freud's selfish id, for example, operates largely via unconscious processes.

frontal lobes   the large and well-named *front* portion of the forebrain. The frontal lobes (one in each hemisphere) play a crucial role in complex phenomena such as planning and emotional decision-making. The rear portion of the frontal lobes also contains the motor cortex that allows for voluntary muscle movement.

frustration aggression hypothesis   the idea (in its modern form) that frustration often leads to **anger**, which often fuels aggression.

functional magnetic resonance imaging   (fMRI, for short) a high-tech technique for determining what is happening in a living person's brain without any. FMRI works by using a very powerful magnet and radio waves to detect blood flow from one region of the brain to another.

functionalism   an early school of thought in psychology (popularized by William James). Functionalism builds on Darwin's concept of natural selection. Functionalists are still around today. They ask what adaptive functions are at the root of human experience.

fundamental attribution error   See the **correspondence bias**.

fungiform papillae   the little round bumps on your tongue that are visible to the naked eye. These are the sites that contain your *taste buds*, which convert things such as fats, acids, or sugars to perceptions such as rich, sour, or sweet.

"g" (general intelligence)   This is Spearman's idea that IQ has a stable general component that will show up across the board (for many different tasks). In our view, the data on separate intellectual skills have not supported this assumption.

GABA   see gamma-aminobutyric acid.

gamma-aminobutyric acid   an inhibitory neurotransmitter that tells neurons that receive it *not* to fire. The anti-anxiety drug Valium is a GABA *agonist*, which leads to greater inhibition of the neural systems that produce anxiety.

Garicano et al. (2005) soccer study   A study of Spanish professional soccer matches that showed that when a home team was down by one goal at the end of regulation play, referees added more "injury time" (more extra playing time) to the match than when the home team was ahead by one goal.

gender dysphoria   a controversial category of psychological disorders that refers to "the distress that may accompany the incongruence between one's experienced or expressed gender and one's assigned gender."

gender roles   culturally dictated rules and norms about what kind of behavior is appropriate for each gender. Gender roles prescribe how to be feminine or masculine, who should do what, and in what context (e.g., work vs. home).

gender stereotypes   thoughts and beliefs about others based solely on their male or female group membership (e.g., "men are aggressive," "women are nurturing.").

gender   a psychological self-classification based on how a person identifies (e.g., thinking of oneself as male, identifying as gender non-binary or transgender). See **sex**, **gender roles**, and **gender stereotypes**.

gender-nonconforming people   people who violate the written and unwritten stereotypical rules for how men and women ought to look and behave. This can happen because of dress, activity preference, sexual orientation, etc. See **LGBTQ**.

gene   the basic unit of inheritance, a small section of DNA that is located at a specific spot on a chromosome. Its function is to program protein synthesis, which leads to physical and psychological development.

General Adaptation Syndrome (GAS)   Hans Selye's three-stage model of how people respond to threats or stressors. Stage 1 is **alarm** (vigilance and readiness to fight or flee). Stage 2 is **resistance**, which is physical and immunological fighting back. Stage 3 is **exhaustion**, which happens when a stressor is so severe and long-lasting that we cannot match its challenges.

generalization   responding to a stimulus that resembles a CS as if it were that CS. The closer the resemblance between the two stimuli, the more likely generalization is. But see also **discrimination**.

Generalized Anxiety Disorder (GAD)   a psychological disorder that involves *chronic and severe worry* about multiple things for "more days than not for at least six months." The chronic worries must be accompanied by at least three other clinical symptoms, including restlessness, fatigue, difficulty concentrating, irritability, muscle tension, and sleep disturbance.

generativity vs. self-absorption   the seventh stage in Erikson's psychosocial theory of development, which covers middle adulthood (ages 40–59). Middle-aged adults ask if they're changing the world to leave their loved ones or fellow human beings in a better place. Generativity may involve either unselfish connectedness or "leaving one's mark" by means of mastery.

genetics   the scientific study of the biological transmission of physical and behavioral traits from parents to their offspring, including how environments can influence this transmission process.

genome   all of the possible genetic blueprints for a specific species, including every gene and all of its possible forms (alleles). The human genome consists of 46 chromosomes and about 20,000 specific genes.

genotype   all of the versions of all of the specific genes possessed by a specific organism (that organism's exact genetic make-up). Contrast with **phenotype**.

genotype-environment correlations   the idea that genotypes and environments often support one another – as is the case, for example, when genetic relatives of a child create environments that promote or magnify the simple effects of particular genes. Genotype-environment effects may be **passive**, **evocative**, or **active**.

germinal period   the period of human prenatal development that covers weeks 1–2 post-conception. This is when the blastocyst usually attaches itself to the **uterus**.

Gestalt perspective   a perspective on human perception that suggests that we're constantly seeking out form, structure, and meaning in what we perceive. Perceptual principles such as *closure* and *proximity*, for example, often help people make sense of ambiguous stimuli.

Gick and Holyoak's analogical reasoning study   A classic study in which students had to read a story about the solution to a difficult military attack problem and then were asked to solve a logically similar (analogous) problem involving a medical emergency. Very few participants made the connection that the two problems had the same kind of answer.

glial cells   helper cells in the brain that do everything from cleaning up dead cells to providing nutrition and speeding up nerve transmission (by insulating an axon). The brain has about as many glial cells as it does basic neurons.

grammar   an appreciation of the deep *rules* of language. This includes how to express future tense, how to convert singulars to plurals, and how to switch words around to change meaning. See **"wug test."**

ground   In *Gestalt* psychology, this is the surroundings or context (the background) for what is the focus of attention, which is known as the *figure*.

group therapy   a form of psychotherapy in which several people meet at the same time with a psychotherapist – who guides the group in therapeutic discussions.

"Guns, Germs, and Steel" hypothesis   the hypothesis that because it was much easier to invent and refine agriculture in Eurasia, Eurasians developed cities, and then written language and technology, well before the residents of other continents. This – rather than superior intelligence – allowed Eurasians to conquer and dominate the globe.

h^2   see *heritability coefficient*.

health psychology   the scientific study of how psychological events are related to physical health. This includes topics such as how to get people to exercise, why people fail to take needed medication, and how social support buffers people from illness.

hearing   what we experience when sound waves of different frequencies strike our eardrums and make their way to our **basilar membrane**, where **transduction** takes place.

heat   a contextual influence on aggression. Numerous field studies and lab experiments show that heat increases the likelihood of angry aggression.

helping-is-rewarding hypothesis   the hypothesis that because we are such highly social creatures, we are hard-wired to enjoy helping others – at least under the right circumstances. Modern fMRI studies show, for example, that the brain areas that are activated when we do pleasurable things are also activated when we help others.

hemispheres   like the globe, your brain is divided into two halves or hemispheres (in the case of the brain, a right and a left one). In most people each hemisphere is specialized (*lateralized*) to do somewhat different things.

heritability coefficient (also h^2)   the estimate of the degree to which a physical trait or behavior is genetically (rather than environmentally) determined. Score theoretically ranges from 0 (no genetic contribution) to 1.0 (completely genetic).

heritability   the genetic transmission of properties from parents to their offspring

Hess, Adams and Kleck (2004)   a study showing that when men and women pose the same facial expression known to indicate anger, women are perceived as angrier than men. This seems to happen because women who look angry are perceived to be more strongly in violation of gender norms.

heterosexist (noun form *heterosexism*)   an idea, assumption, or explanation that accepts heterosexuality as a normal default that requires no explanation.

heterozygous   a genotype in which the organism carries different alleles for a specific gene from its mother and its father. If dominant-recessive inheritance is at work the organism will only express the dominant gene.

heuristics   judgmental shortcuts or rules of thumb for making rapid judgments – including estimating the frequency, magnitude, or likelihood of events. See, for example, **availability** and **representativeness**,

hierarchies   status systems that place some organisms higher than others. Organisms at or near the top of the hierarchy ("alpha males" or "alpha females") normally enjoy more privileges than low status organisms.

hierarchy of needs   see Malsow's hierarchy of needs.

hierarchy   a "pecking order" or set of well understood rules about each member's relative status in a group.

hindbrain   the oldest and most primitive of the three basic regions of the brain. Your hindbrain sits just above our spinal cord and directs traffic coming in and out of the spinal cord. The cerebellum, which is a large portion of the hindbrain, helps controls complex motor movement and plays a role in emotions and language. See also **midbrain** and **forebrain**.

hippocampus   a seahorse shaped deep brain structure that plays a crucial role in our ability to form new long-term memories. When you learn about the hippocampus, this requires the use of your hippocampus.

homeostasis   the tendency for a system to remain within a set of optimal parameters. Loosely speaking, homeostasis is balance. Many theories of human motivation assume that human motivation follows homeostatic rules.

homology   the tendency for animals that share a common ancestor (and thus genes) to share physical and/or psychological traits. For example, all members of the cat family have very similar skeletons, and they are all meat-loving carnivores.

homozygous   a genotype in which the organism carries matching alleles for a specific gene from its mother and its father. If dominant-recessive inheritance is at work the organism will express a recessive gene only if homozygous for that allele.

honor cultures   cultures in which people emphasize status in a tenuous hierarchy. In honor cultures, threats to a person's status (his or her honor) are often met with violent resistance.

hostile aggression (aka *angry aggression*)   aggression motivated by anger and the accompanying desire to hurt someone *for the sake of hurting them* (e.g., punching a sibling during an argument). See **frustration-aggression hypothesis**.

"hot hand" (aka **"hot hand bias"**)   a term often used by sports fans to indicate that they believe success comes in streaks. Dozens of studies show that this is largely a myth.

hot vs. cold motivational states   states of high desire and need vs. states of satiation or passivity. People in cold states have trouble predicting how they'll behave in hot states. People who just ate fail to realize how much they will wish to eat in six hours.

House, Landis, and Umberson (1988) social support study   a summary of five sophisticated longitudinal studies that combined to show that both men and women with higher levels of social support are less likely to die in adulthood. The study also showed that social support matters more for men than for women.

human cultural universals   a long list of practices, rules, and behaviors that seem to exist in all (or virtually all) cultures across the globe. This suggests that culture is not *completely* arbitrary.

human immunodeficiency virus (HIV)   the sexually-transmittable virus that causes **AIDS**.

humanism   a school of psychological thought that emphasizes connectedness, self-acceptance, and the human potential for love and growth. Humanists disagree with Freud's idea that human beings are naturally selfish.

hurdle race metaphor   a way of thinking about Erikson's argument that when people have difficulties in an earlier stage of life, this makes it more difficult for them to develop successfully in future stages. In short, if people do not clear a developmental hurdle, this makes it harder to clear future hurdles without incident.

hypo-tasters   People with very few fungiform papillae on their tongues and thus a smaller than average number of taste buds. This makes hypo-tasters the roughly 25–30% of the population who do not experience tastes very strongly.

hypothalamus   the brain's master thermostat; a subcortical structure in the forebrain that is involved in many kinds of basic regulatory activities, including eating and drinking, sex, and fighting vs. fleeing when faced with threat.

hypothesis   a specific scientific prediction. Hypotheses are usually generated based on theories or past observations.

id   the selfish, greedy, oversexed, and aggressive part of the human psyche. The id is also childlike in that it cannot engage in sophisticated reasoning. See also **ego**, **superego**, and **pleasure principle**.

identify ("stereotypes identify")   a way of summarizing one of the three functions of stereotypes – one of which is that they help define people's social identities (e.g., mother, Latina).

identity explorations (the age of)   a key feature of emerging adulthood. This refers to the fact that emerging adults are pondering and exploring numerous adult identities – from careers to social and religious identities.

identity vs. role confusion   the fifth stage in Erikson's psychosocial theory of development, which covers adolescence (age 12–18). In this stage, kids try to figure out exactly who they are. The role of peers becomes crucial. If things go poorly, kids question who they are and may not identify with important social groups.

immune response   a key aspect of how your body responds to pathogens such as viruses or harmful bacteria. If you encounter a virus, your body should begin to produce antibodies that stop the virus from replicating.

implicit egotism   an unconscious preference for people, places and things that resemble the self. This is presumably why people named Carpenter gravitate toward working as carpenters.

implicit personality theory   people's unstated assumptions about which physical and personality traits tend to go hand in hand.

imprinting   the process by which many precocial birds attach to (and immediately follow) their mothers shortly after hatching. See **critical period**.

in vitro fertilization (IVF)   a modern fertility treatment in which some mature eggs are harvested from a woman and fertilized outside the womb. Some of the healthiest fertilized eggs are then implanted directly in the woman's uterus in the hopes that at least one will begin to develop normally. This can easily lead to multiple births.

incomplete dominance   in contrast to dominant-recessive inheritance, a form of inheritance in which each of two competing alleles is expressed to some degree in organisms heterozygous for a specific trait (e.g., a homozygous red mom and a homozygous white dad might produce pink offspring).

independent variable   the variable that is manipulated in a true experiment. In an experiment designed to see if a new pain reliever reduces headaches, the dose of the drug received is the independent variable. See also **dependent variable**.

individual differences   the fact that people vary. Individual differences make psychological research tricky because they are often a source of confounds. See also **confound**.

individualism   a cultural orientation that emphasizes individual wishes, desires, rights, and individual social identities, over group wishes, desires, etc. **Individualistic** cultures are thus "me" cultures rather than "we" cultures. See also **collectivism**.

induction   reasoning from the general to the specific. Finches have feathers, emus have feathers, and albatrosses have feathers. All birds seem to have feathers.

industry vs. inferiority   the fourth stage in Erikson's psychosocial theory of development, which covers middle childhood (ages 6–12). Kids develop knowledge of the world – and a basic sense of competence – that begins to rival what adults know. At this age, kids also begin to feel the powerful influence of peers. If things go poorly, kids conclude that they are inferior to others.

infant attachment style   an infant's (or a toddler's) characteristic way of relating and depending upon his or her principle caregiver. See **secure, anxious**, and **avoidant attachment styles**. Infant attachment styles presumably set the stage for **adult romantic attachment styles**.

informed consent   the permission researchers should get from research participants before potential participants take part in a study. Before participants offer their consent, they should be told about any known risks they may face by taking part.

ingroups   groups to which a person belongs.

initiative vs. guilt   the third stage in Erikson's psychosocial theory of development, which covers early childhood (ages 3–6). During this stage, autonomy morphs into initiative. Kids continue to try to master their worlds, but now they set more elaborate goals and make highly specific plans and requests. If things go poorly, kids develop a sense of guilt.

insecure attachment   one of a couple of infant styles of connecting to a primary care-giver – when things do not go well for the infant. Contrast with a **secure attachment** style.

instability   a key feature of emerging adulthood. This refers to changes and volatility that are typical of emerging adulthood. It includes moving residences, changing friends and romantic partners, and changing one's career plans.

instinct theory of motivation   an old perspective on motivation that suggests that we have numerous highly specific motivations to do particular things (e.g., a hunting instinct, a "life instinct"). Today, this approach is considered problematic because it is more **tautological** than informative.

Institutional Review Board (IRB)   a committee of experts who review research proposals (often at universities) to ensure that proposed studies do not cause physical or psychological harm to participants. IRB members follow principles such as the *risk-benefit rule* in deciding what procedures researchers must follow.

instrumental aggression   aggression in which the victim is harmed as a means to an end. Robbing a bank or taking a desirable toy from another child are examples. Contrast with **hostile aggression**.

insularity of genius   the idea that the human mind is *not* a good or bad general-purpose thinking machine. This means that people may be extremely good at some intellectual tasks and average or very poor at others. See **savants** and **prodigies**.

intelligence quotient (IQ)   according to the proponents of IQ tests, this is a person's overall intellectual capability. It includes such abilities as memory, attention span, judgment, reasoning, and problem solving. Spearman thought that "g" (general intelligence) common to all these abilities.

internal review boards (IRBs)   committees of experts who carefully evaluate whether it is ethical for a researcher to carry out a proposed study involving human participants.

internal validity   a form of validity (accuracy, correctness) in research that refers to whether we can be sure that one variable is truly a cause of another variable. True **experiments** are usually high in internal validity.

interpersonal psychotherapy   a modern descendant of Freud's original psychoanalytic therapy that focuses heavily on the idea that early relationships are of paramount importance in psychological well-being. Interpersonal therapists thus focus on helping people identify and repair problems in their close relationships.

interpretation of dreams   a psychoanalytic technique in which patients are asked to help the therapist interpret the patient's dreams. Freud felt that this could help patients understand their repressed (and thus unconscious) desires and conflicts.

interval schedule (of reinforcement)   a reinforcement schedule in which the organism gets rewarded based on whether it has produced a response after a certain amount of time has passed. Contrast this with **ratio schedule**.

intimacy vs. isolation   the sixth stage in Erikson's psychosocial theory of development, which covers early adulthood (ages 18–39). In this stage, adults are focused on close relationships. This is often when people get married. If things go poorly, people may feel chronically isolated or lonely, or they may get stuck in unfulfilling relationships.

intrinsic motivation   a desire to do an activity *for its own sake* – because you find the activity inherently challenging or joyful.

introspection   an early method for studying human thought and perception. Participants had to be trained in this. It might involve looking at a familiar object and describing its essential features (e.g., large, gray, long-nosed) *without* any labels (e.g., elephant).

intuition one of the four "ways of knowing." Intuition refers to a hunch, guess, or feeling about what is true that is based on things like casual observation, faint memories, or evolved preferences.

IRB see **internal review boards.**

James-Lange theory of emotions the theory that our quick physiological responses to stimuli lead to felt emotions such as happiness or fear – and that each emotion should thus have a unique physiological signature. Compare this with the **Canon-Bard theory of emotions.**

jelly bean lottery a study in which participants preferred ten chances out of 100 to select a red jelly bean over one chance in ten to select a red jelly bean. This result is consistent with the **numerosity heuristic**.

judgmental heuristics see heuristics.

just world hypothesis the popular belief that when something bad happens to a person, the person must have done something to deserve the bad outcome. This allows people to maintain the illusion that bad things are unlikely to happen to good people.

justify ("stereotypes justify") a way of summarizing one of the three functions of stereotypes – one of which is that stereotypes validate and support norms and laws that put certain groups of people at a disadvantage.

Kidd and colleagues (2013) a research team whose experiment showed that it's easy to create large differences in how long kids wait for a second marshmallow in the "marshmallow test." They did so by giving kids a recent experience that suggested that their present worlds were either highly predictable or highly unpredictable.

kin selection costly helping behavior offered to a genetic relative. This usually poses no problems for evolutionary theory because relatives share many of our genes.

kin selection costly helping behavior offered to a genetic relative. This poses no problems for evolutionary theory because relatives share many of our genes.

Koffka ring a ring that – depending on how one adjusts two adjacent geometric figures – yields evidence of either contrast or assimilation. See Figure 10.13.

language instinct according to experts such as Chomsky and Pinker, this is an evolved tendency to enjoy, use, and learn the complex, abstract form of human communication known as language.

language the use of abstract symbols – most often spoken or written words – to communicate with others.

latent learning learning in the absence of any obvious rewards. This might happen, for example, if you took a route on a bus several times and then were later able to drive the route in your car.

lateralization the noun form of *lateralized*. The state of being lateralized.

lateralized in reference to brains, this means specialized; consisting of two hemispheres, each of which performs somewhat different functions.

Law of Effect Thorndike's rule that behaviors that are followed by reinforcers (pleasant states of affairs) become more likely whereas behaviors that are followed by punishers (unpleasant states of affairs) become less likely.

learning styles the idea that different people learn differently and thus that we learn best when material is presented in our preferred learning mode (e.g., visual vs. auditory material). Unfortunately, a wide range of carefully conducted studies suggest that there is little or no validity to the idea that people learn best when a style of teaching matches their learning style.

Len Bias Law   a national law passed in 1986 that mandated very lengthy penalties for possessing even small amounts of drugs, especially crack cocaine. This has led to dramatic increases in incarceration rates in the U.S. since 1986.

life history theory   an evolutionary theory that makes two key predictions: (a) there are tradeoffs between different survival and reproduction strategies (e.g., having a lot of kids and offering them very little care vs. having fewer kids and offering them more care) and (b) that the same organism will develop very differently in different environments.

lobes   the four main divisions of the forebrain (each of which exists in both hemispheres). They include the **frontal**, **parietal**, **occipital** (rear), and **temporal** lobes, each of which has a host of very different jobs.

logic   one of the four "ways of knowing." Logic refers to the formal rules of reasoning and includes both **induction** (reasoning from specific examples to derive a rule) and **deduction** (reasoning from a rule to a specific example or prediction).

long-term memory   the relatively permanent form of memory that has a virtually unlimited capacity – but which must be retrieved ("called up") to be used in the moment. Long term memory includes **episodic**, **semantic**, and **procedural** memory. It may also include **priming** (the fourth kind of memory).

long-term potentiation   changes in the wiring of the brain that may be the primary route through which new memories are formed. Long-term potentiation is a strengthening of the connection between two neurons. It promotes *brain plasticity.*

lucid dreaming   dreaming while realizing that one is dreaming.

lymphocytes   the white blood cells that help you fight off infections. They are the soldiers of your immune system.

making and using tools   a sign of intelligence and logical reasoning that we once thought to be unique to people. We now know that many animals – including some fish and invertebrates – make and use tools.

marshmallow test   a test used to assess **delay gratification** in preschoolers. Kids are told that they can eat a single marshmallow now or wait for an experimenter to go and retrieve a bonus marshmallow. Little kids who wait longer have better academic and emotional outcomes as high schoolers.

Mary Whiton Calkins   the first female student of William James and the first female president of the American Psychological Association. Calkins's story illustrates the roadblocks women and ethnic minorities faced in the early days of psychology.

Maslow's hierarchy of needs   Maslow's theory that people must fill their basic physiological needs and then their needs for safety before they can fill higher-order psychological needs such as the need for love and belongingness, the need for esteem, and finally the need for **self-actualization**. See Figure 13.4.

mastery   see **need for mastery**.

matchmaker problem   one of the challenges of using chemical interventions to treat psychological disorders. It is that a drug that works very well for one patient might not work at all for a second patient with exactly the same clinical diagnosis.

McGurk effect   the finding that visual cues (the exact way in which a speaker's lips are moving) sometimes override auditory information in speech perception. For example, if people see a video of a person saying, "fa fa fa" and hear a carefully synched recording of a person saying "ba ba ba," they will hear "fa fa fa."

meaning (semantic encoding)   in the context of memory, this refers to the robust finding that things that matter to people – or things that people can understand well – are much easier to remember than things that have little or no meaning.

medical model   a model of psychological illness that treats psychological disorders as diseases – which are presumed to have a physiological basis in the body and the brain.

medicalized birth is subject to ethnic biases   the finding that, in the United States, healthy ethnic minority mothers are more likely than healthy White mothers to give birth by cesarean section.

medicalized birth   modern norms and medical procedures that make it hard for women to give birth naturally, from the routine use of epidurals and Pitocin to the induction of labor or the very high rates of birth by **cesarean section**.

medication-induced movement disorders and other adverse effects of medication   this category of psychological disorders refers to long-term problems that may emerge as a consequence of long-term use of medication.

memory consolidation   the active transfer and organization of information from short-term into long-term storage. This happens at a high rate during **sleep**.

memory   a mental record of an event, procedure, or fact. This includes the storage and retrieval of remembered information.

menarche   the appearance of a girl's first menstrual period. In the last 150 years, the age of menarche in wealthy countries has been getting younger and younger.

menopause   in people the point, at about age 50, when women stop ovulating and thus become infertile. Menopause occurs in only a few known species, all of which are long-lived and **altricial**.

mental modules   according to Fodor, these are highly distinct mental systems, each of which is geared toward solving a different problem (e.g., visual contrast, cheater detection).

mere exposure effect   the robust tendency to like things more when we have been exposed to them more often.

mere ownership effect   the tendency for people who have been given an object to evaluate that object more favorably than usual.

mesoderm   the part of a developing embryo that will become the muscles. In mammals, the mesoderm will also become the skeleton whereas the ectoderm will become the skin.

meta-analysis   a "study of studies;" an approach to research in which scientists mathematically combine the results of two or more (often very many) studies. In a meta-analysis, for example, a researcher tries to determine if an effect is bigger for women than for men.

meta-cognition   thinking about thinking. A higher form of reasoning that plays a role in consciousness and executive functioning (thoughtful analysis of one's own thoughts and decisions).

midbrain   the small region of the human brain that sits between the primitive **hindbrain** and the complex **forebrain**. The midbrain regulates movement, arousal, and attention to abrupt changes in the environment.

mid-life crisis   the presumed response to aging that involves a reduction in well-being and an increase in risky and self-focused, perhaps even self-destructive, behavior in middle age. Recent findings suggest that the timing of the midlife crisis is highly variable but that it is real and measurable.

mid-life dip in well-being in chimps and orangutans   the findings of a study of more than 500 great apes for this study. Judges rated middle-aged great apes to be lower in well-being than either younger or older great apes of the same species.

Milgram obedience studies   Milgram's studies of obedience, which showed that virtually everyone he studied was willing to inflict a great deal of pain on a fellow participant in a study of learning, merely because an authority figure told them to do so.

mindfulness (adjective form is mindful)   being chronically attentive to one's surroundings and to one's thoughts and feelings. Many cognitive and cognitive behavioral therapists think that becoming mindful is key to a patient's success in psychotherapy.

mirror test (aka **mirror self-recognition**)   a sign of a basic sense of **self-awareness**. Only about seven or eight animals on our planet seem to be able to learn that what they see in a mirror is the self.

mnemonic devices   memory tricks that often capitalize on meaning, organizational encoding, or both. Recall that COM-4, CON-2 is a mnemonic for remembering six key features of the human brain.

modeling   see **social learning**.

monozygotic twins   "identical" twins; those who share virtually all of their genes. In twin studies of the heritability of a trait, it's important to know whether twins share all (monozygotic) or only about half (dizygotic) of their genes.

monozygotic   identical twins (literally "one zygote"), who share virtually 100% of their genes.

Morganucadon   see **Morgie**.

Morgie   a primitive mammal (*Morganucadon*) about the size and shape of a chipmunk (see Figure 1.1). Morgie co-existed with the dinosaurs before they became extinct. Early mammals like Morgie eventually evolved into the incredibly diverse array of mammals alive today.

morning sickness protects developing embryos   there are four lines of evidence that this is the case. (1) morning sickness is most pronounced during organogenesis, (2) women with more serious morning sickness have fewer miscarriages, (3) it is vomiting, not nausea, that protects the embryo, (4) foods women find unpleasant during pregnancy are likely to be teratogens.

morning sickness   the nausea and vomiting that many women experience when pregnant. It's most common during the first trimester of a woman's pregnancy and seems to reduce the risk of birth defects based on ingested **teratogens**.

motivation   the desires and drives that fuel what we think, feel, and do. This includes everything that pushes us toward or pulls us away from things (e.g., curiosity, hopes, fears, and needs). Recall that motivation is closely linked to **emotions**.

motor cortex   the mostly vertical band of cortex at the very rear of the frontal lobe that allows you to control voluntary muscle movements in different parts of the body.

multiple intelligences   Howard Gardner's theory that there are at least eight basic kinds of intelligence, including talents such as "body smart" (bodily-kinesthetic intelligence), "music smart," "word smart," and "people smart" (interpersonal intelligence).

mutualism   a form of cooperation in which each member of a dyad does (or allows) something that is beneficial to both parties. Unlike **reciprocal altruism**, mutualism requires no accounting for past or future favors.

myth of race   the erroneous idea that there are dramatic psychological differences between the people who have historically inhabited different regions of the earth.

Genetic analyses show that we are all one race and that the differences between the so-called races are superficial, reflecting specific adaptations (e.g., dark skin) to local physical environments.

naive scientist Fritz Heider's term for laypeople, who think like scientists in the sense that they carefully try to figure out the *causes* of the behavior of other people.

narcissism a personality trait that is higher in emerging adulthood than in any other age except for adolescence. This refers to being proud, self-absorbed, vain, and entitled, and being willing to exploit others to get what one wants. See **self-focus (age of)**.

natural selection the process by which genes that promote reproductive success in a specific environment become more common in future organisms.

naturalistic fallacy the assumption that because a human tendency evolved (or because it promotes survival), this makes it morally reasonable or ethically acceptable. Many selfish and violent tendencies evolved, but that doesn't make them good.

need for mastery the desire to develop skills that allow you to *control* what happens to you. This includes the desire to make things, do things, learn, create structure, and explore. The relative needs for mastery and connectedness vary across the stages of Erikson's theory of psychosocial development.

need to belong (need for connectedness) the human motivation to be connected, both physically and psychologically, to other people. People suffer when they cannot fill this basic need, and it seems to influence much of what we do including prosocial behavior, and perhaps even altruism. See **Maslow's hierarchy of needs**.

needs states that drive us to achieve certain goals. Unlike instincts, needs are usually tied in obvious ways to survival. Further, needs can often be filled in a wide range of specific ways (e.g., hunger may be reduced by a cheeseburger or a bowl of berries). Needs obey the principle of **homoeostasis**.

negative punishment having something pleasant removed or taken away after engaging in an operant behavior. The Law of Effect says that this will make the behavior less likely to occur in the future. An example is losing dessert after hitting a sibling.

negative reinforcement experiencing relief from something undesirable after engaging in an operant behavior. The Law of Effect says that this will make the behavior more likely to occur in the future. An example is taking a pain reliever.

negative symptoms the symptoms of schizophrenia that involve the *absence* of the level of emotional distress one might expect to accompany this disorder. Social withdrawal is also a negative symptom in that it is an absence of social motivations.

negativity bias a bias (such as the face-in-the-crowd effect) to recognize and respond to negative emotions more readily than to positive ones. This bias is presumed to be evolutionarily adaptive because it keeps us alive.

neurocognitive disorders a category of psychological disorders that involve problems with memory, and/or movement, and/or thinking. It covers disoders such as Parkinson's disease and Alzheimer's disease, for example.

neurodevelopmental disorders psychological disorders such as autism spectrum disorder and learning disorders.

neurogenesis nerve growth, the making of new neurons. This is rare in the human brain, but even adult human brains can grow new neurons in small amounts in response to new challenges or brain injuries. This allows some degree of **brain plasticity**.

neuron a nerve cell; any of the highly specialized communication cells in the brain that are responsible for brain activity. Virtually all neurons contain *three basic parts*: a single **axon**, one or more **dendrites**, and a **soma** (cell body).

neurotransmitter   one of about 70 chemical messengers that allow for the electrochemical transmission of information to and from brain cells (neurons).

neuroticism   the "**Big Five**" trait that refers to worrying a lot, and being insecure, pessimistic, and emotionally volatile.

neurotransmitters   the "chemical messengers" of the brain. There are about 70 known neurotransmitters. All 70 are specific ways in which a neural signal bridges the gap between the sending part (axon) of one neuron and the receiving parts (dendrite or cell body) of another neuron. **Dopamine** is an example.

new generation anti-depressants   a family of modern drugs used to treat clinical depression, usually with fewer side effects compared with those of older drugs. The most commonly prescribed category is **selective serotonin uptake inhibitors**.

nonsense syllables   see **trigrams**.

normally distributed   a statistical term for a "bell-shaped" set of scores, which means, for example, that scores near the mean are very common.

numerosity heuristic   the judgmental bias of assessing magnitude by paying too much attention to frequency information and not enough attention to the absolute size of the individual pieces.

nurse-midwife   a licensed nurse who is highly trained in natural birth techniques and helps mothers-to-be give birth naturally.

obedience   a form of social influence in which a lower-status does what a higher-status tells them to do. See Milgram obedience studies.

object permanence   the awareness that objects continue to exist when we can no longer see them. This develops during Piaget's first sensorimotor stage and is studied using the **BOPP** – the **basic object permanence paradigm**.

observation   one of the four "ways of knowing." Observation refers to counting and/or measuring, with an eye toward precisions, transparency, and objectivity. Using a microscope and taking a public opinion poll are good examples.

observational learning   see social learning.

obsessive-compulsive and related disorders   a group of psychological disorders that includes obsessive-compulsive disorder (OCD) as well as disorders such as excoriation disorder (skin picking) and hoarding disorder.

occasions   the second dimension of the **OOPS! heuristic** for assessing **external validity**. This has do with whether a research finding holds up across different times, ranging from time of day to historical and even geological times.

occipital lobes   the rear and somewhat lower lobes (sections) of the forebrain. The occipital lobes (one in each hemisphere) play a crucial role in vision.

olfactory bulb   a brain region that is devoted to processing information about smell. Dogs have olfactory bulbs that take up a much greater percentage of their brains than do people's modest olfactory bulbs.

one-trial learning   a surprising form of classical conditioning that happens when the CS and UCS are paired only once. This happens because of **preparedness** and usually happens only with extremely unfavorable outcomes (e.g., getting very sick the first time you try a new food).

"ontogeny recapitulates phylogeny"   Haeckel's idea that that the embryonic development of a specific organism mirrors the ancient history of that organism – which has proven to be *somewhat* true.

OOPS! heuristic a heuristic for summarizing four issues researchers should consider when evaluating the *external validity* of a research finding. The four issues are **operationalizations, occasions, populations, and situations.**

openness the "**Big Five**" personality trait that refers to an interest in trying, learning about, and experiencing new things and ideas.

operant conditioning (aka, instrumental conditioning) a form of learning in which an organism learns that a reinforcer (e.g., food) or a punisher (e.g., electric shock) happens when the organism engages in a specific behavior. This is different than classical conditioning because the organism must now *do* something for the good or bad event to occur. See **Law of Effect.**

operational definition a way of making it possible to examine abstract theories and ideas empirically. An operational definition is a concrete physical procedure or activity for assessing something. An operational definition of helping might be the amount of time or money given to a person in need.

operationalizations One of the four aspects of the *OOPS! heuristic* for assessing the external validity of a specific study or program of research. "Operationalizations" refers to whether a research finding holds up across many different ways of converting an idea into a measurable procedure. See **operational definition.**

optimistic bias a cousin of overconfidence, the common belief that your future will be better and brighter than that of people very much like you (e.g., your fellow college students). This may contribute to the denial and minimalization of climate change.

organizational encoding a technique for improving learning, memory, and retention by mentally sorting, arranging, and/or classifying the to-be-learned information. See **mnemonic devices.**

organogenesis the window of prenatal development (from about 15–60 days) when all the major organs begin to develop.

other conditions that may be a focus of clinical attention a category of psychological disorders that includes serious problems grounded in abuse, relationship problems, and occupational problems.

other mental disorders a special category of DSM disorders that do not fall neatly into any other categories, but which nonetheless involve disturbance, impairment, and internal dysfunction. our modern knowledge of things like attachment theory, the cognitive unconscious, and the biopsychosocial model.

outgroups groups to which a person does not belong.

overconfidence the tendency to be more confident than correct. This includes providing overly narrow confidence intervals when asked to guess the answers to trivia questions, thinking you will get a job done before you actually do, and thinking you will be able to answer questions correctly at a higher rate than is actually the case.

overjustification effect the reduced interest people often show in an activity after they've been rewarded for doing it. It means you can reduce someone's intrinsic motivation by rewarding them for doing something they would have done for free.

overlearning a good way to increase long-term retention of things you learn. This memory tips means that once you think you have learned something perfectly, you should still study it a bit more – to reduce forgetting.

overregularization the tendency to apply the rules of grammar *too* stringently – by making irregular words regular (e.g., saying "gooses" instead of "geese"). Kids often do this, suggesting that they have a deep knowledge of **grammar.**

oxytocin   the "love hormone" that is involved in processes such as romantic bonding, giving birth, and nursing. Oxytocin is also a neurotransmitter, meaning it can act quickly in the brain.

paired-associate memory paradigm   an early technique for studying memory. People are presented with many pairs of words (e.g., canoe-green, apple-dark), and then later asked to remember the second word in each pair – with the first word in the pair serving as a memory cue. See Mary Whiton Calkins, who created this technique.

panty hose study   a classic study that raises doubt about whether people know why they do things. Shoppers were made to prefer a pair of panty hose by simply making it the last of four pairs shoppers examined. But when asked why they preferred this pair, the shoppers all fabricated plausible but incorrect explanations for their preferences.

paraphilic disorders   a category of psychological disorders that involves sexual behavior that is considered socially inappropriate. To qualify as a disorder this behavior must either lead to personal distress or create "harm, or risk of harm, to others." Voyeuristic disorder (sexual spying) is an example.

parental investment theory   the theory that if one sex makes greater biological and behavioral investments in its offspring, that sex will be sexually choosier and less promiscuous.

parietal lobes   the upper and somewhat rear portion (lobe) of the forebrain. The parietal lobes (one in each hemisphere) play a crucial role in your sense of touch.

partial reinforcement effect   the finding that rewarding an organism only some of the time during operant conditioning (rather than rewarding it all the time) makes the learned response less susceptible to **extinction**.

partial report technique   a procedure for studying the very short-lived form of visual memory known as **iconic memory**. Sperling developed this technique to show that people can hold a lot of visual information in memory for a very brief period, but that iconic memory decays so rapidly that we cannot usually report it all.

passive genotype-environment effects   a situation in which parents or other family members (who share genes with a child) create worlds that facilitate the expression of phenotypes that are consistent with a child's genetic make-up. Children are *passive* in that they "soak up" such environments. See the **PEA model**.

passive observational study   a study in which the researcher measures the variables of interest rather than manipulating any of the variables (in an experiment). Both cross-sectional surveys and prospective studies that follow people over time are passive observational studies (unless there is an experimental manipulation at work as well).

pathogen loads   infectious disease rates, which turn out to be important predictors of many aspects of culture, including collectivism, parenting practices, and fast vs. slow **life history** strategies.

penile plethysmograph   a device that measures changes in the volume of the penis. This was once a popular method used by sex researchers to supplement self-report measures of sexual arousal with something more objective. Now that **thermographic stress analysis** exists, this measure is rarely used (because it only works for men).

perceptions   our interpretations of sensations. Thus, like sensations, perceptions are subjective and internal. But perceptions are usually more complex and may be based on multiple sensations. "That's a funny joke." and "That's Juanita." are perceptions.

perseveration (verb form **perseverate**)   a tendency often seen in infants about nine months of age who are given a test of object permanence (see **BOPP**). Although such infants will usually pull up a blanket to uncover a toy, they will often keep pulling up *this blanket* (they'll repeat or *perseverate* their initial action) even after the researcher hides the toy under a different blanket. This mistake is known as the **A-not-B error**.

personality disorders a category of psychological disorders that involve lifelong behavior patterns such as self-centeredness, and overdependence (e.g., narcissistic personality disorder).

personality traits broad preferences and ways of behaving that affect what you do in a wide range of settings. See **Big Five**.

personality all the stable aspects of who you are that consistently influence what you think, feel, and do. See also **personality traits** and **Big Five**.

phenotype an organism's observable physical and psychological features or appearance – as contrasted with *genotype*, which is an organism's exact genetic makeup. Most organisms carry at least some genes that are not expressed phenotypically.

philosophy + physiology = psychology a brief way of noting that psychology became a science in 1879, when researchers began addressing questions philosophers had addressed logically by collecting data in much the same way that physical scientists do.

phobia a psychological disorder in which a long-lasting fear of one specific thing (e.g., snakes, flying) is unreasonable, severe, and uncontrollable and disrupts work or daily life. The fear must also be distinct from broader anxiety disorders such as GAD

phoneme restoration effect the finding that when a tiny part of a word is replaced by a cough or blast of noise, people fill in the missing "letter sound" (the missing phoneme) without realizing they are doing so. "It was found that the *EEL was on the table" will usually be heard as "It was found that the *meal* was on the table," for example.

photoreceptors the sensory neurons (*rods* and *cones*) that line much of the inside of your eyeball and thus allow you to see.

physical aggression aggression that involves physical harm to another person (e.g., by punching or poisoning the victim).

Piagetian paradigm Piaget's basic approach took to testing his stage theory of cognitive development. The key idea is identifying a cognitive ability that is presumed to develop at a certain age and then to see if kids who are, or are not, old enough to possess the ability in question pass a test of the ability.

pituitary gland a pea sized subcortical structure deep in the forebrain that is often called the "master gland." The pituitary gland works closely with the hypothalamus to control the body's hormonal systems. The pituitary also regulates physical growth.

placebo effects a psychological phenomenon that happens when people feel or perform differently than they would otherwise because they *expect* to do so. Inactive pills often reduce headaches.

placebo a pill, injection, or other fake treatment that has no active ingredients but looks and feels just like the real thing. Ironically enough, placebos allow researchers to correct for *placebo effects*.

pleasure principle Freud's idea about the driving force behind the selfish **id**; the pleasure principle states that the id wants that which feels good and steers away from all things painful.

polyandry the practice of having two or more husbands at the same time. See **polygamy**.

polydactyly the state of having more than five fingers or toes. This is not to be confused with *pteradactyly*, which is the state of having at least one pet pteradactyl.

polygamy   the practice of taking more than one spouse at the same time. This includes both **polygyny** and **polyandry**.

polygyny   the practice of having two or more wives at the same time. See **polygamy**.

populations   the third dimension of the **OOPS! heuristic** for assessing external validity. The degree to which a research finding holds up for a wide range of people (e.g., women as well as men, the poor as well as the wealthy, robins as well as rats).

positive punishment   experiencing something unpleasant after engaging in an operant behavior. The Law of Effect says that this will make the behavior less likely to occur in the future. An example is getting shocked when you grab a live wire.

positive reinforcement   receiving something desirable after engaging in an operant behavior. The Law of Effect says that this will make the behavior more likely to occur in the future. An example is getting an A on an exam when you study hard.

positive test bias   the tendency to test hypotheses by paying more attention to evidence that would support the hypotheses than to evidence that would invalidate or disconfirm the hypotheses. "What do you like most about jazz?"

possibilities   a key feature of emerging adulthood. This refers to the fact that most emerging adults see the future through rose-colored lenses. It's a window of great optimism about the future.

post-formal thinking   a form of adult thinking that goes beyond Piaget's fourth and presumably final stage. This refers to increased understanding of self and others, the ability to balance and process thoughts and emotions in complex ways, and the development of expertise. See **pragmatism**.

power law   in psychophysics, this is the idea that for most dimensions of perception and judgment, the relation between (a) objective stimulus magnitude (how much of something there is) and (b) how intense we perceive that something to be is curvilinear and concave downward.

power of the situation   a central premise of social psychology. It's the idea that much of what we think, feel, and do is strongly shaped by immediate social forces – by the places and contexts in which we find ourselves.

pragmatism   a practical approach to thinking and problem-solving that incorporates social, financial, and emotional factors into what might otherwise seem like purely logical questions. This is a form of **post-formal thinking**.

precarious manhood   the idea that, to a much greater degree than womanhood, manhood is easily threatened. Research on this topic shows that men whose masculinity has recently been threatened are, in fact, much more likely than women whose femininity has been threatened to behave in ways that assert or re-establish their gender identity.

precocial   a term describing organisms whose young can fend well for themselves at a very young age. Alligators, geese, and sea turtles are very precocial. Contrast with **altricial**.

predictiveness hypothesis   the idea – well supported by research – that classical conditioning only happens when a CS predicts that an UCS is usually coming. This explains why **backward conditioning** doesn't work.

prejudice   negative feelings about people based on their group memberships.

preoperational stage   Piaget second stage of cognitive development, which covers ages 2–6 years. During this stage kids become less **egocentric** and begin to develop some of the simplest abstract thinking skills (e.g., using very simple maps or models).

preparedness an innate readiness to learn some things easily. Examples: It is very easy for many mammals to learn to fear snakes, it is easy for human children to acquire language, and it is easy for most predators to learn to stalk and hunt.

prevarication lying, intentionally deceiving people or misrepresenting things. Hockett argues that this is one of the universal features of human language. But it's possible, at least in theory, that Hockett was lying.

primary emotional/motivational system According to Ross Buck, this is the single psychological system that drives us to try to get what we want, steers us away from that which we fear, and helps us maintain **homeostasis**.

priming being influenced by your previous exposure to information – usually without being aware of this influence. Quickly recognizing an ambiguous creature as a chimp after having recently been to the zoo is an example of priming.

principle of contagion the irrational assumption that the properties of good or bad "rub off" onto you if you touch those things and that things that merely look disgusting (e.g., chocolate shaped like poo) truly *are* disgusting.

problem content effects the robust finding that how well we reason about many logical problems depends heavily on the specific way in which we label the components of a problem. The difficult **Wason card task**, for example, becomes easy if we convert the problem to a logically-identical **cheater-detection** problem.

procedural memory memory for how to perform something; it's action memory for the rules of doing. Changing a tire on a car, playing the piano, knitting, and "bending it like Beckham" in soccer all require procedural memory.

prodigies people in the normal IQ range who have a specific area of genius. LeBron James is a basketball prodigy. Your cousin who taught herself calculus in 7th grade may be a math prodigy. The existence of prodigies supports the **insularity of genius**.

proliferation the very rapid production of *trillions* of synaptic connections between brain cells all over the brain that occurs during infancy and toddlerhood – and then again in adolescence.

proprioception an often-overlooked sense that is separate from the five you probably learned about as a kid. This refers to your ability to sense the position of your body, limbs, fingers, and toes in space (even with your eyes closed).

prosocial behavior behavior that benefits another person, period, regardless of what motivated the behavior.

prospective study (prospective design) a study or research design in which researchers measure all the variables of interest on at least two occasions. This makes it possible to address the requirement of temporal sequence.

proximity the **Gestalt** principle that we perceive objects that are physically near one another as related (as part of a group or as two or more parts of the same entity). Adding labels to grouped objects strengthens this impression.

psychiatrists medical doctors who specialize in diagnosing and treating mental illness. It is psychiatrists who developed the **DSM**.

psychoactive substances substances – such as alcohol and drugs – that change our states of consciousness.

psychoanalysis a school of thought in psychology developed by Freud. Psychoanalysis emphasizes the role of unconscious desires and motives in human experience. It also emphasizes what Freud assumed were basic drives (mainly sex and aggression).

psychodynamic therapy   in its modern form, this is a kind of psychoanalytic therapy that integrates Freud's original ideas with modern updates of Freud's ideas and/or modern forms of psychotherapy.

psychology   the scientific study of human thought, feelings, and behavior. It is the topic of this textbook and includes everything from how we see and hear to what happens when two people don't see eye to eye on an important issue.

psychophysics   the study of how our subjective sensory experiences (e.g., sweetness, loudness) change with objective changes in the physical stimuli we are judging (e.g., sugar concentrations, the changing energy levels of a sound).

psychosocial development, theory of   Erik Erikson's eight-stage theory of lifespan human development – which, in our view, focuses on the relative balance in the needs for connectedness and the need for mastery in different life stages.

psychosocial theory   Erik Erikson's eight-stage theory of human development – which emphasizes both mastery and social processes, such as connectedness.

psychotherapists   experts who offer **psychotherapy**. This includes licensed **clinical psychologists** as well as licensed clinical social workers (LCSWs) and people with master's degrees in marriage, family and child counseling (MFCCs or MFTs).

psychotherapy   professional interactions between a patient and a person formally trained to help people reduce or eliminate their clinical symptoms.

puberty   the biological changes associated with sexual maturation.

Punishment   experiencing something unpleasant after making a response. Normally, punishment reduces the future likelihood of the response. Example: Speeding tickets are punishments for fast driving.

Punnett square   typically, this is a 2 x 2 matrix in which the two alleles of one parent are listed in the columns, and the two alleles of the other parent are listed in the rows, allowing calculations of the likelihood of different offspring genotypes.

puzzle box   a device (a wooden trap) used by E.L. Thorndike to study trial and error escape learning in cats.

quantitative genetics   the (highly common) type of genetic transmission that occurs when many different genes all contribute (usually some more than others) to a phenotype. In people, for example, height is influenced to at least a small degree by about 700 hundred genes.

quiet eye   a well-studied technique for improving one's throwing or shooting performance in sports. It requires players to rid themselves of all distractions and then keep their eyes focused precisely on the exact spot where they hope to throw or shoot something (right before they release the ball or shot object). Developing the quiet eye requires **deliberate practice**.

random assignment   placing specific people in different conditions in an experiment based on nothing but chance (e.g., coin tosses). This means that every participant in an experiment has the same chance as every other participant of being assigned to any condition of the experiment. This is essential to conducting a true **experiment**.

ratio IQ   a way of calculating IQ in children. This is a child's *mental age* divided by the child's *chronological age* (all multiplied by 100). The ratio IQ score of a child aged 5.0 who could answer as many IQ questions correctly as the typical kid aged 6.0 years would be 120 (100 x 6.0/5.0).

ratio schedule (of reinforcement)   a reinforcement schedule in which the organism gets rewarded based on whether it has produced a response after a set number of previous responses – regardless of *when* the responses occurred. Contrast this with **interval schedule**.

rational Epstein's way of describing logical, rigorous, or empirically-based thinking. Contrast with **experiential** thinking. Rational thinking is a prerequisite for understandings the nature of climate change.

rationally (rational thinking) In Epstein's model of human thinking, this is the route to thinking that people take when they have lots of time, energy, and desire to answer a question.

reaction formation one of Freud's defense mechanisms. It refers to adopting a conscious attitude that reflects the opposite of what one really wants or believes (usually because of the id).

recall memory recollection; that is, unaided, open-ended memory. Contrast this with **recognition memory**.

receptor neurons see **sensory neurons**.

recessive in genetics the term used to describe an allele for a specific gene that is not expressed **phenotypically** when it appears along with a **dominant** allele for the same gene.

reciprocal altruism "trading favors," prosocial behavior directed at a genetically unrelated animal who has helped you in the past (or who you expect to help you in the future). Many social animals engage in reciprocal altruism.

reciprocal altruism helping another person (or animal) who has helped you in the past.

reciprocity the powerful social norm that we should pay back favors to those who have helped us in the past – and are allowed to pay back injuries to those who have harmed us. Reciprocity can fuel either helping behavior or aggression.

recognition memory memory for which of several currently or recently presented stimuli is correct. Answering questions on a multiple-choice exam is a good example.

redback spider a venomous species of Australian spider. Male redbacks often throw themselves into the mouths of the females with whom they are mating. Female redbacks often eat the males, but the male self-sacrifice helps male redbacks fertilize a greater number of eggs.

reflexes extremely specific, hardwired, and automatic responses to specific stimuli. Shivering when cold is an example.

Regier, Kay and Cook (2005) color-word study an impressive cross-cultural study of color words in cultures that used 110 different languages. The study revealed a lot of cross-cultural similarities in word use for basic color terms.

rehearsal mentally repeating material held in short-term memory – which can extend the life of the otherwise short-lived information until it can be recorded or committed to long-term memory.

reinforcement schedules the specific rules that determine when and if an organism receives rewards during **operant conditioning**. According to Skinner the two most important dimensions of reinforcements schedules have to do with *time* vs. *frequency* (interval vs. ratio schedules) and reliability (fixed vs. variable reinforcement schedules). Reinforcement schedules have a big impact on **extinction**. See also **partial reinforcement effect**. And see, for example, **fixed interval** and **variable ratio** schedule.

relational aggression harming someone psychologically by damaging a personal connection the person has to someone else. Both stealing a person's mate and spreading lies about a person qualify as relational aggression.

representativeness heuristic   a rule of thumb that involves judging the likelihood or magnitude of an event based on how much it resembles (is similar to) some other event. An example is judging people to be more aggressive if they wear black.

repression   one of Freud's **defense mechanisms**. Repression refers to banishing uncomfortable thoughts to the unconscious, so that we are not consciously distressed by them. But Freud thought that repressed thoughts still impact what we feel and do.

reproduction   in evolutionary thinking, this refers to passing on your genes successfully to future generations. This turns out to be even more important in natural selection than long-term survival. See, for example, **redback spider**.

resistance   Freud's observation that patients often push back against (resist) a therapist's suggestions about why something is going wrong for the patient. This is ironic because patients pay therapists to help them and then sometimes refuse this help.

resistance   stage 2 of Selye's **General Adaptation Syndrome (GAS)** model. In this stage (which typically begins 24–48 hours after exposure to a stressor), the organism begins to fight back. If the assault is a virus, for example, you'll begin to produce antibodies.

response generalization   in operant conditioning this is producing an operant response that resembles but is not identical to the originally reinforced response – which may or may not lead to reinforcement. Contrast with **stimulus generalization**.

responses   in the context of psychophysics, this is our subjective internal reactions to stimuli. Both sensations and perceptions are responses. In the context of learning theory, responses are observable reactions to stimuli.

retina   the lining of the inside portion of your eyeball, especially the back part. The retina is covered in millions of *photoreceptors* (**rods** and **cones**) that allow the eye and brain to convert light to perceptions such as color, shape, and brightness.

retrieval practice   strengthening memories by seeing if you can recall them. This is one reason why testing yourself on material is one of the best ways to commit the material to long-term memory.

retrieval   calling up stored information from memory, usually for immediate use. Loosely speaking, this is "remembering." See also **encoding** and **storage**.

reverse causality   a problem that can occur with passive observational research – when a researcher assumes that A causes B but B is actually the cause of A. Do negative attitudes cause poor health? Or does poor health cause negative attitudes?

risk-benefit rule   this ethical rule states that if there any meaningful risks at all to the participants who take part in research, there must be some potential benefits to society to offset those risks (e.g., a decrease in violence).

rods   the photoreceptors that specialize in black and white, low light vision. These are most common in a donut-shaped ring outside the fovea. In fact, there are no rods at all in the fovea.

Romanian orphanage studies   prospective studies of infants and toddlers who were rescued from terrible conditions in Romanian orphanages. Studies show that infants who were rescued before about six months of age suffered little or no negative consequences. Infants and toddlers rescued at older ages, however, later experienced serious social and intellectual deficits.

Sapir-Whorf linguistic relativity hypothesis   the long-lived but only scantily supported hypothesis that human thought depends heavily on language, which implies a great deal of cross-cultural variability in how people think.

satisficers   pragmatic judgmental realists. This is Herb Simon's term for human judges who balance the need for accuracy against the need to get very quick answers.

savants (aka **"prodigious savants"**)   people who suffer from profound mental disabilities – such as learning disorders or severe autism – and yet who perform at the genius level in art, memory, music, or other intellectual tasks. See **insularity of genius**.

savings   the advantages people have in learning material that they once knew but seem to have completely forgotten.

scaffolding   providing people who cannot quite succeed at a physical or cognitive task with just enough help or advice that they can complete the activity – and thus move a step closer to mastering the task.

schizophrenia spectrum and other psychotic disorders   psychological disorders that involve major disturbances in language, thought, emotions, and behavior.

schizophrenia spectrum   a set of psychological disorders involving disorganized and inappropriate thought and behavior. A formal diagnosis requires that a person experience delusions, hallucinations, or highly disorganized speech. Two other common symptoms include disorganized or catatonic ("freezing up") behavior as well as social withdrawal and/or extreme apathy.

scripts   learned expectations about how familiar social events typically unfold (prototypical event sequences). You have scripts, for example, about weddings, elections, and birthday parties.

secondary traits   personality traits that, while real and measurable, fall to the wayside in powerful situations.

second-generation anti-psychotics   a modern category of drugs used to treat schizophrenia spectrum. The "second generation" part of the term reflects the reduced side effects these drugs have compared with **first generation anti-psychotics**.

second-order conditioning   a complex form of classical conditioning in which – after learning that a CS predicts the delivery of the UCS – the organism learns that a different stimulus predicts the delivery of the previously learned CS. $CS_x \rightarrow CS_y \rightarrow$ UCS. If you consider a text message a CS (because text messages are not *inherently* reinforcing), then responding favorably to the sound your smartphone makes when you've gotten a text is an example of second-order conditioning.

secure attachment style   an adult romantic attachment style that is characteristic of people who have no trouble getting close to their romantic partners and who feel they can usually trust others to be there for them when needed.

secure base   a term for the fact that a primary caregiver should ideally serve as the "home base" from which a securely attached infant or toddlers can explore an unfamiliar environment.

secure   a positive, trusting **infant attachment style**. Infants develop this when their primary caregivers are available and highly responsive to infant's needs. There is also a secure **adult romantic attachment style**. See also **anxious** or **avoidant** styles.

selective fitness   the number of surviving offspring an organism produces in its lifetime (aka "reproductive success")

selective serotonin uptake inhibitors (SSRIs)   a category of **new generation antidepressants** that prevent (inhibit) the normal reuptake of serotonin that happens in the synaptic gaps between neurons. SSRIs also appear to promote **brain plasticity**. They are often used to treat **clinical depression**.

self-actualization   according to humanist Abe Maslow, this is the desire "to become everything that one is capable of becoming." Maslow put this at the top of his pyramid of basic human needs.

self-awareness   an appreciation of the fact that you exist as a physical entity with a body of your own. See **mirror test**.

self-enhancement   a desire to view the self favorably – and to possess highly positive views of the self. Some say this is a uniquely **WEIRD** phenomenon whereas others argue that it is just expressed differently in cultures that value and celebrate social groups.

"Self-esteem = Success/Pretension"   William James's idea that we get self-worth from achieving the specific goals that are important to us. James meant that being good at something won't do much for your self-esteem unless you value that thing.

selfish gene   the idea that evolution happens at the level of genes rather than organisms – and that any gene that does not increase the selective fitness of its host will fall by the evolutionary wayside.

self-focus (age of)   a key feature of emerging adulthood. This refers to being very concerned (perhaps overly so) with one's own plans, well-being, and activities. In extreme cases, this can mean **narcissism**.

self-fulfilling prophecy   a prediction or expectation that leads to biased judgment or behavior – which then makes the prediction or expectation come true.

self-medication   using nonprescribed drugs to reduce unpleasant states such a stress, sadness, or anxiety.

self-referent memory effect   the powerful and robust finding that one of the best ways to learn material quickly and to retain it better than usual is to relate the material in some way to *yourself*.

self-socialization   the process in which kids act like the "gender police" and enforce the gender-based rules of socially-acceptable behavior for boys and girls. See also **gender-nonconforming**.

semantic memory   memory for facts, concepts, and definitions. Semantic memory is abstract, which means it depends heavily on language. An example is knowing the capital of the Dominican Republic. Sí, Santo Domingo.

semi-restrictive nation   a nation whose rules and norms about sex place it about halfway between **sexually permissive** ("lax") nations and **sexually restrictive** ("strict") nations. The United States is a semi-restrictive nation. See also **STDs**.

sensations   our subjective internal reactions to stimuli – such as felt warmth, color, brightness, loudness, etc.

sensitive periods   somewhat narrow (but not rigidly narrow) periods in which we develop specific traits or abilities more easily than at other times. Contrast with **critical periods**. There seems to be a sensitive period for human language development.

sensorimotor stage   Piaget's first stage of cognitive development, which covers birth to age two. During this stage, children learn to perceive the world (*sensori-*) and to control their bodies (*-motor*) and have almost no ability to think abstractly.

sensory neurons   (also known as *receptor neurons*), nerve cells that are devoted to transduction, which allows us to experience sensations.

seriation   the ability to rank a set of many objects on any of several physical or psychological dimensions (e.g., weight, length, darkness, deliciousness). Kids can do this in Piaget's third, **concrete operational**, stage.

serotonin   a neurotransmitter that plays a role in mood regulation and many other processes from nausea, digestion, and arousal to sexual functioning and the maintenance of bone health. Low levels of serotonin are associated with **clinical depression**.

sex a biological classification of someone as male or female based on physical or chromosomal characteristics (such as having two X chromosomes). Contrast this with **gender**.

sexual dysfunctions a category of psychological disorders that includes erectile dysfunction or premature ejaculation in men and female orgasmic disorder (lifetime lack of orgasm) in women.

sexual reproduction reproduction that requires two parents, who both pass on half of their genetic information to offspring.

sexually permissive nation a nation (such as many Western European nations) in which most people have open attitudes about sex and consider premarital sex acceptable as long as it is safe. In such nations, parents have plenty of honest conversations with their teenage children about sex, and rates of **STDs** and teenage pregnancies are usually very low.

sexually restrictive nation a nation (such as much of Asia and the Middle East) in which most people have very strict attitudes about sex and consider premarital sex wholly unacceptable (even if it safe).

sexually transmitted diseases (STDs) communicable diseases (such as herpes, chlamydia, and HIV infection) that are spread by means of unprotected sexual contact.

shadow in the context of a dichotic listening task, verbally repeating back what one has just heard in one ear – to prove that one is paying attention to message played to that ear.

shaping an operant conditioning technique in which the trainer produces a very complex behavior by initially rewarding rough approximations of the desired behavior but becoming increasingly selective over time about exactly what gets reinforced.

shared reality theory a theory that suggests that we are strongly motivated to connect to and agree with important others. This theory can be used to promote green behavior (for example, by correctly informing people that 99% of scientists believe that climate change is a real and serious threat to future human well-being).

short-term memory (aka **working memory**) a temporary, limited-capacity memory for things one is currently experiencing or has just experienced. People can hold only six or seven things in short-term memory. See also **iconic** and **echoic** memory.

side effects unintended physical or psychological consequences of using a drug. For example, a common side effect of the SSRIs that are used to treat clinical depression is a loss of sexual desire.

similarity the Gestalt principle that means we assume that like goes with like. Thus, making two shapes green and making three shapes red causes us to assume that the shapes that are the same color belong together

simplify ("stereotypes simplify") a way of summarizing one of the three functions of stereotypes – one of which is that they make the world simpler and easier to understand. See also **justify** and **identify**.

Simpson, Rholes, and Nelligan (1992) attachment study a lab study of attachment style and coping with threat. Among securely attached women, those who looked most afraid in a stressful situation were most likely to seek support from their partners. Among women with an avoidant attachment style, those who looked most afraid were *least* likely to seek support.

situational an attribution (explanation) for a person's behavior that emphasizes context (environmental) causes. "Cayla slipped because the floor was wet."

situations   the fourth dimension of the **OOPS! heuristic** for assessing external validity. This one has to do with generalization across different situations (e.g., across formal vs. informal situations, at work vs. at play, or across cultures).

situation(s)   in the context of the OOPS! heuristic, the specific context in which a study was conducted (e.g., experimenter style of dress, neatness of room, loud vs. quiet setting).

size constancy   the ability to estimate the size of an object by considering both its *apparent size* (how big an image it casts on your retina) and its *distance*. Most infants are great at this, but most people who grow up blind and then get their sight restored surgically in adulthood have great difficulty with size constancy, suggesting a sensitive, if not critical, period for developing it.

sleep   in the context of memory, getting plenty of sleep is a tip for improving memory. This is based on the finding that during sleep, people mentally refine, organize, and finalize things like encoding. See **memory consolidation**.

sleep hygiene   getting adequate amounts of sleep on a regular basis, and at about the same time every day.

sleep-wake disorders   a category of psychological disorders that includes insomnia, sleep terrors, and nightmare disorder.

smell   olfaction, the sense that informs you about faint traces of chemicals in the air. It begins in your nose, of course.

social comparison theory   a social psychological theory that states that when we wish to know where we stand on any evaluative or attitudinal dimension, we compare ourselves with others. This produces a social form of **contrast**.

social exchange theories   theories that share the assumption that we keep track of what others have done for us and carefully compare this with what we have done for them.

social facilitation theory   a theory that predicts that knowing that one is being evaluated by others will facilitate performance if a performer is highly skilled at the activity in question but will disrupt performance if a performer is less skilled at the activity.

social inequality   a state of affairs in a culture or region in which poor people have dramatically less wealth than wealthy people. Social inequality appears to be a better predictor of rates of violent crime than is poverty.

social learning (aka, **modeling**)   a form of operant learning in which an organism learns by observing the behavior of another organism and (a) copying behaviors that are rewarded or (b) avoiding behaviors that are punished.

social norm of *reciprocity*   the norm that dictates that when someone does a favor for you, you should try to pay back the favor.

social norms   powerful but often unspoken rules about how we ought to behave in social situations. Eating pasta with a fork and refraining from playing with a stranger's hair are both social norms.

social perception   the process of trying to figure out the attitudes, traits, and behavior of other people.

social psychology   As Allport put it, this is "an attempt to understand and explain how the thought, feeling, and behavior of individuals are influenced by the actual, imagined, or implied presence of others."

social psychophysics   the application of psychophysics, especially the power law, to social judgments and perceptions. Studies of wealth and happiness or audience size and feelings of nervousness qualify as social psychophysics.

social support   having people in your life on whom you can depend in times of emotional, physical, or financial distress.

socioemotional selectivity theory   a theory of lifespan development that suggests that in cultures where longevity is high, seniors place (a) great value on experiencing positive emotions and spending time with loved ones while (b) placing less value than they once did on having novel experiences.

somatic symptom disorder and related disorders   a category of psychological disorders grounded in one's preoccupation with one's physical health and characterized by persistent, extreme, and troubling focus on one's physical health symptoms.

somatosensory cortex   the vertical strip of the parietal lobe that borders the frontal lobes and allows us to sense what is happening in our bodies. See also **somatosensory homunculus**.

somatosensory homunculus   the cartoonish human character that represents the percentages of the somatosensory cortex that are devoted to processing sensations from different parts of the body.

Specialization   focusing one's energies on a particular job or activity and thus becoming very good at it. This is a big cultural consequence of living in cities.

spacing effect (distributed learning)   a technique for improving learning and memory by distributing study or practice over many sessions separated by breaks or irrelevant activities (rather than studying or practicing in one long interrupted session).

specificity principle   in the context of sport psychology this refers to the fact that we usually get good at things by practicing *exactly those things*. To build endurance you run long distances. To get stronger you gradually lift *heavier* and *heavier* weights.

split-brain patients   patients who have had their *corpus callosa* (plural of **corpus callosum**) surgically severed. Without this network of nerve fibers that connect the two hemispheres of the brain, split brain patients possess two functionally independent brains. This can teach us about **lateralization**.

spontaneous recovery   the (post-**extinction**) return of a conditional response (CR) after a delay during which the CS was not presented at all. This "just in case" response is adaptive (in case the original rules that led to conditioning are active again).

sport enjoyment   how much a person truly *enjoys* (likes or adores) a sport. This has proven to be a strong predictor of how long people stick to a sport.

sport psychology   is the study how psychology may be used to increase athletic engagement, enjoyment, and performance.

SSRI   see selective serotonin uptake inhibitor.

stage theorists   developmental experts who believe that we undergo dramatic transformations at different ages, and in a predictable order. Piaget's four-step theory of cognitive development is a stage theory, for example.

status quo bias   psychological inertia. It's the tendency to do what we and others have always done in the past – which is often what takes the least amount of effort in the present. This is often problematic, but policy makers can capitalize in it to nudge people to behave in a greener fashion (e.g., by setting all copies machines to the default of making double-sided copies).

stereotype   According to Allport's classic definition, "a false or overgeneralized and typically negative belief about the members of a social group." Hardin's simpler and more modern definition is that a stereotype is a "socially shared belief about the members of a group."

stimulus generalization   the tendency to treat something that resembles a CS as if it were that CS. Example: feeling happy around someone who strongly resembles your best friend.

stimulus generalization   producing an operant response in reaction to a stimulus that resembles but is not identical to the originally reinforced response – which may or may not lead to reinforcement.

stimulus   an object or source of energy in the external world – to which a person's sensory system might respond. Stimuli are objective (e.g., the mass or temperature of a stone). Contrast this with *perceptions* and *sensations*. The plural form is *stimuli*.

stomach contraction study   a classic study of motivation in which a psychologist swallowed an inflatable device that directly measured stomach contractions. His stomach contractions very shortly preceded his self-reported hunger pangs.

storage   holding on to or maintaining long-term memories. This is what makes memory highly durable or long-lasting. Storage is the second of three basic stages of memory. See also **encoding** and **retrieval**.

strange situation   a research paradigm used to assess **infant attachment style** – by seeing how infants respond to a separation and then a reunion with their primary caregiver, usually in an unfamiliar setting.

stress   experiencing a felt threat (real or imagined) to one's well-being. Stress is the physical and psychological *response* to stressors. This is partly constructed because stress often depends on one's personal interpretation of an event.

stressors   potentially harmful chemical or physical events that your body justifiably treats as an attack. Both negative (getting fired) and positive (getting married) events can be stressors. See also **stress**.

Stroop interference effect   the difficulty people have naming letter colors when the letter colors spell color words that are different than the letter colors. This reveals the mandatory nature of **automatic processing**.

structuralism   an early school of psychological thought whose goal was to uncover the basic building blocks of human thought and perception. In Wundt's efforts to do this, he often asked people to engage in **introspection**.

stunted growth   failing to reach the adult height one would have otherwise reached because of childhood malnutrition.

subcortical structures   the deep parts of the forebrain that lie well *beneath* the bumpy cortical gyri and sulci ("wrinkles") that you can see if a brain is in a jar. They include the hypothalamus, the hippocampus, and the pituitary gland, just to name a few.

substance-related and addictive disorders   a category of psychological disorders that includes dependence on alcohol, cocaine, tobacco and any other psychoactive drug as well as "gambling disorder."

superego   the moral, rule-following, "hung up" portion of the mind in psychoanalysis, the superego acts as a check or counterbalance against the selfish and shortsighted **id**. See also **ego**.

supertasters   people with a great number of fungiform papillae on their tongues and thus a much greater than average number of taste buds. This makes supertasters the roughly 25–30% of the population who experience tastes very strongly.

surrogate mother   a substitute or replacement mother. In his classic studies of infant rhesus monkeys, Harlow offered the monkeys (a) a surrogate mom that fed them but was not physically soft and (b) a surrogate mom that never fed them but was covered in cuddly terrycloth. Infant monkeys strongly preferred the terrycloth mother.

synaptic bouton the part of the end of an axon (the "button") where neurotransmitters are released into the synaptic gap between two neurons.

synaptic gap the tiny space between the end of an axon (the synaptic bouton) and the part of another neuron whose cell body or dendrites receive a signal from the sending neuron. This is where neurotransmitters jump from one neuron to another.

systematic desensitization a form of exposure therapy that involves exposing patients with phobias to mildly threatening versions of the feared object (e.g., a photo of a spider), helping them relax in the presence of the feared object, and gradually moving up a hierarchy to more threatening stimuli or situations. If done, well this leads to **extinction** of the fear response.

tardive dyskinesia involuntary motor movements that are often experienced by patients with schizophrenia spectrum. Although these symptoms often develop even in unmedicated people with schizophrenic spectrum, they are hastened and worsened by the use of anti-psychotic medications, especially first-generation anti-psychotics.

tasters The 40–50% of the population who have an average number of fungiform papillae on their tongues and thus have an average number of taste buds.

tautology a statement or way of thinking that refers back to itself and thus is circular. See "*the wonderful thing about Tiggers.*"

teacher expectancies the educational version of **experimenter bias** or **self-fulfilling prophecies**. This happens when teachers expect kids to perform well (or poorly) and then unknowingly treat kids in ways that lead them to perform well (or poorly).

temporal lobes the lower, central-to-rear portion (lobe) of the forebrain. These paired lobes (one in each hemisphere) are devoted mainly to helping you understand the meaning of sounds (from speech to gunshots).

temporal sequence the second of John Stuart's Mill's three requirements for showing that one variable causes another variable. This means showing that changes in a presumed cause happened before changes in the presumed consequence. See also **covariation** and **eliminating confounds**.

teratogens harmful foods, drugs, or experiences (e.g., stress) that can easily harm a developing embryo or fetus. Most, but not all, teratogens have the most potential to do harm during the first couple of months of pregnancy, during **organogenesis**.

Thanatos Freud's hypothesized "death-instinct" – which presumably drives people to kill and murder others – or even commit suicide.

the home field advantage in sports a robust tendency for home teams to win more games, on average, than visiting teams. It holds up across many sports and exists for many reasons, ranging from player familiarity with a court or field to "pro-home team" biases in how referees judge ambiguous plays.

The Sports Gene Epstein's provocative (2013) book, in which he argues that in the world of high-paying elite sports, there are powerful selection pressures that mean you need different body types to play different elite sports. Both NBA players and world-class swimmers, for example, have arms that are very long, even for their heights.

theory of correspondent inferences a classic theory that states that judges should not make **dispositional** attributions for a person's behavior when it is easily explained by a powerful situation. Social judges are not usually quite this logical.

theory a general statement about the causal relation between two or more variables. Theories are strengthened when the specific hypotheses that flow from them are supported by research.

thermographic stress analysis (TSA)   a method of assessing sexual arousal in both men and women. This method quickly detects even small changes in genital temperature that occur with increased sexual arousal.

third-variable problem   see confound.

third variable problem   the problem of **confounds**. See also **eliminating confounds**.

three basic parts   a reference to the fact that all neurons (all nerve cells) contain (1) a single axon, (2) one or more dendrites, and (3) a soma or cell body.

three key features of psychological disorders   the summary idea that psychological disorders involve (a) **disturbances** in thought, feeling and behavior, (b) **impairment**, meaning disorders disrupt daily functioning, and (c) **internal dysfunctions**, meaning that disorders have a meaningful psychological and/or physical basis.

three mountains task   a test that requires kids to look at a model of three mountains from opposite seats. The test measures **egocentrism** by asking kids what they can currently see and asking them to report what a person sitting right across from them can see (from a spot where they just sat minutes ago). Preschoolers often fail to realize that the person sitting across from them cannot see what they see. Older kids are less egocentric.

triskaidekaphobia   an extreme fear of the number 13. If this is truly a phobia rather than a superstition, it will lead to extreme distress and will sometimes interfere with a person's daily functioning.

tip-of-the-tongue phenomenon   the frustrating feeling of *almost* being able to retrieve something that you are sure you know. If you have a word on the "tip of the tongue," you can often report what letter it starts with, and even how many syllables it has. But you can't quite produce the word.

token economy   a carefully designed reward system in which clients with psychological disorders routinely receive rewards if, and only if, they engage in desirable behaviors.

tolerance   a reduction in the usual psychological effects of a drug after long-term use of the drug. This is problematic, for example, when it comes to using anxiolytic drugs.

touch   the sense you experience when your skin comes into contact with stimuli that vary in texture, warmth, roughness, etc.

transduction   the physiological process by which physical stimuli become electrochemical signals that are sent to the brain for interpretation.

transference   Freud's term for how his patients often bonded to him as if he were a parent or romantic partner. Freud argued that his patients were *transferring* their feelings about someone else onto him (the therapist).

transitive inferences   a form of reasoning that involves transforming comparative statements about (or rankings of) different things. ("If Bo is older than Zee, and Zee is older than Iska . . .") The ability to do this well typically emerges in adolescence.

trauma- and stressor-related disorders   a category of psychological disorders that includes posttraumatic stress disorder (PTSD) as well as acute stress disorder.

trigrams (aka nonsense syllables)   the consonant-vowel-consonant fake words that Ebbinghaus had people study to reduce or eliminate the powerful effects of meaning on learning and memory. In English, trigrams are fake words such as KUJ and SEP.

true experiment   a research design in which participants are placed in one or more conditions based on random assignment. Participants in different conditions receive different levels of the independent variable, and then the researcher measures the **dependent variable**.

trust vs. mistrust   the first stage in Erikson's psychosocial theory of development, which covers infancy (ages 0–1). In this first stage, infants figure out if their primary caregivers can be trusted to meet their basic needs.

twin studies   studies that attempt to assess the **heritability** of traits by assessing the phenotypic correlations (e.g., between heights or IQ scores) of **monozygotic** or **dizygotic** twins who were separated at birth.

two-factor theories of emotions   theories that assume that emotions are often the combination of diffuse (vague, non-specific) physiological arousal (factor one) plus the way we label that arousal (factor two).

two-fold cost of sexual reproduction   a problem identified by John Maynard Smith. It's that compared with *asexually* reproducing organisms, sexually reproducing organisms produce only half as many organisms per parent and produce organisms who share only half their genes.

unconditional positive regard   love and acceptance independent of what we do. Rogers argued that children crave unconditional positive regard from their primary caregivers, and that good psychotherapists offer this to their clients during therapy.

unconditional response (UCR)   in classical conditioning, a natural response to a positive or negative stimulus. Drooling in the presence of meat powder or yelping in response to a shock are examples.

unconditional stimulus (UCS)   in classical conditioning, a stimulus that produces a natural response without requiring any learning. Meat powder and painful electric shocks are unconditional stimuli. Dogs don't have to be taught to love or hate them.

unconscious (cognitive)   see cognitive unconscious.

uterus   the organ from which the developing blastocyst, then embryo, then fetus get all their nutrients during pregnancy.

variable interval schedule   a reinforcement schedule in which the organism is reinforced for making the first operant response after an average amount of time has passed (but with some unpredictable variation around that average). See **reinforcement schedules**.

variable ratio schedule   a reinforcement schedule in which the organism is reinforced for making the first operant response after an average number of responses (but with some unpredictable variation around that average). See **reinforcement schedules**.

variable schedule   a reinforcement schedule in which a reinforcer comes after an unpredictable average of a certain number of responses or after making at least one response after an unpredictable average amount of time. The key to being *variable* is limited predictability around an average. Contrast with **fixed schedule.**

verbal aggression   aggression that involves using language to harm another person (e.g., spreading rumors about the person).

vision   what we sense and perceive (what we see) in response to some ranges of electromagnetic radiation.

Wason's card task   a judgment task in which participants have to decide which of four cards to turn over to test a rule (every vowel must have an even number on the other side). If the rule is unfamiliar and abstract, most people fail to test it properly.

Watts and colleagues (2018)   a team who conducted a large-scale longitudinal replication of the "marshmallow test." Watts and colleagues replicated the basic longitudinal findings on delay of gratification but with a few caveats (e.g., the basic effect is not nearly as big among poor kids as among rich kids).

ways of knowing   ways of gathering information about the world. As far as we know, there are only four of them: **intuition**, **authority**, **logic**, and **observation**.

wealth gap   one indicator of **economic inequality**, the difference in income or accumulated wealth between the top and bottom income groups in a culture or nation. In Denmark, for example, the wealth gap is much smaller than in the United States.

Weber-Fechner law   the idea that perception is *proportional*, not absolute. We can only detect a change in a stimulus, this rule says, if it is increased or decreased by a certain *percentage* of the original stimulus (rather than an absolute amount).

WEIRD critique   the cross-cultural criticism that too much research in psychology focuses on WEIRD people, meaning people from "**W**estern, **E**ducated, **I**ndustrialized, **R**ich, and **D**emocratic" cultures, who are likely to be very different than the majority of the world's inhabitants.

well-being   life satisfaction, how favorably we evaluate our lives. Studies of well-being are loosely consistent with the idea that people usually focus on filling Maslow's lower-order needs before they fill other needs. See **Maslow's hierarchy of needs**.

Wernicke's area   the part of the brain that is devoted to understanding the meaning of speech (which also allows you to produce grammatical and meaningful speech). See also **Broca's area**.

within-subjects design   a study design in which the same group of people experience two or more different experimental conditions – to see if people think, feel, or behave differently in these different "within-subject" treatment conditions.

working memory   see **short-term memory**.

written language   representing language via long-lasting visual symbols – which followed in the wake of **agriculture** and **cities**, and which led to the **specialization** and technological sophistication that allowed Eurasians to dominate the globe. See "**Guns, Germs, and Steel**."

"wug test"   a test Brown and Berko (1960) used to see if kids understand **grammar**. The test required kids to make plurals or change verb tenses for artificial words the kids had never before seen.

Yerkes-Dodson Law   The motivation rule that states that for difficult or challenging tasks, there is an optimal (medium) level of arousal that leads to superior performance. See Figure 13.3. And see **social facilitation theory**.

Zika virus   a mosquito-borne virus that has serious teratogenic effects, leading to major developmental problems such as microcephaly (insufficient brain development).

zygote   a recently fertilized egg.

Index

Page locators in *italics* and **bold** refer to figures and tables, respectively.

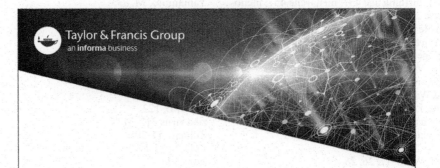

Taylor & Francis Group
an **informa** business

Taylor & Francis eBooks

www.taylorfrancis.com

A single destination for eBooks from Taylor & Francis
with increased functionality and an improved user
experience to meet the needs of our customers.

90,000+ eBooks of award-winning academic content in
Humanities, Social Science, Science, Technology, Engineering,
and Medical written by a global network of editors and authors.

TAYLOR & FRANCIS EBOOKS OFFERS:

A streamlined
experience for
our library
customers

A single point
of discovery
for all of our
eBook content

Improved
search and
discovery of
content at both
book and
chapter level

REQUEST A FREE TRIAL
support@taylorfrancis.com

 Routledge
Taylor & Francis Group

 CRC Press
Taylor & Francis Group